# NUMERICAL SIMULATION - FROM BRAIN IMAGING TO TURBULENT FLOWS

Edited by **Ricardo López-Ruiz**

## Numerical Simulation - From Brain Imaging to Turbulent Flows

http://dx.doi.org/10.5772/61500
Edited by Ricardo López-Ruiz

### Contributors

Stanford Shateyi, Fazle Mabood, Gerald T Marewo, Zikuan Chen, Laura Castro, Gustavo Urquiza, Paweł Ludowski, Jan Marian Taler, Dawid Taler, Sandile Motsa, Vusi Mpendulo Magagula, Sicelo Goqo, Ibukun Oyelakin, Precious Sibanda, Beata Jackowska-Zduniak, Juan M. Mejía, Amsini Sadiki, Farid Chejne, Alejandro Molina, Sabine Bauer, Tatsuo Kitajima, Zhonggang Feng, Azran Azhim Noor Azmi, Antonio Gameiro Lopes, Nasser Sweilam, Najeeb Khan, Amber Shaikh, Sidra Khan, Faqiha Sultan, Alexander Ivanovich Kartushinsky, Peep Lauk, Medhat Hussainov, Ulo Rudi, Igor Shcheglov, Sergei Tisler, Karl Erik Seegel, Andrei Polonscky, Oyoon Razzaq, Fatima Riaz, Asmat Ara, Alejandro Alonzo-García, José Alfredo Jiménez-Bernal, Claudia Del C. Gutierrez-Torres, Mohammad Javad Ketabdari

**CBS,** Edition **2018**

**Published by InTech**

Janeza Trdine 9, 51000 Rijeka, Croatia



**Publishing Process Manager** Iva Lipović

**Technical Editor** SPi Global

**Cover Designer** InTech Design Team

Additional hard copies can be obtained from orders@intechopen.com

Numerical Simulation - From Brain Imaging to Turbulent Flows, Edited by Ricardo López-Ruiz
p. cm.
Print ISBN 978-953-51-2564-8
Online ISBN 978-953-51-2565-5

INTECH

open science | open minds

# Contents

# Preface

Nowadays mathematical modeling and numerical simulations play an important role in life and natural science. Numerous researchers are working in developing different methods and techniques to help understand the behavior of very complex systems, from the brain activity with real importance in medicine to the turbulent flows with important applications in physics and engineering. This book presents an overview of some models, methods, and numerical computations that are useful for the applied research scientists and mathematicians, fluid tech engineers, and postgraduate students.

The first section of the book presents models and simulations for the analysis of the behavior of some parts of the human body. In Chapter 1, Chen and Calhoun discuss some imaging (fMRI) aspects of brain functional (BOLD) activity. In Chapter 2, Bauer and Paulus study the biomechanical behavior of a lumbar spine model that take the spinal structures with their specific material properties into account. In Chapter 3, Kitajima et al. investigate some aspects of computational neuroscience by using RC and RCL circuits to model the neurons and the cell membrane. The last chapter of this section, Chapter 4 by Jackowska-Zduniak, introduces a two-coupled van der Pol equation model to describe the heart action potential to recreate some pathological behavior, such as the most common (AVNRT) tachycardia.

The second section of the book presents some mathematical and numerical methods to integrate different types of differential equations. In Chapter 5, Khan et al. simulate fractional differential equations by using Chebyshev- and Legendre (ChSANN and LSANN)-simulated annealing neural networks. In Chapter 6, Sweilam and Assiri introduce and numerically study some real-life model problems that can be formulated as ordinary differential equations. In Chapter 7, Motsa et al. explore the application of a novel multi-domain spectral collocation method for solving general nonlinear Lane-Emden-type differential equations. Finally, in Chapter 8, Khan et al. provide a comprehensive discussion of systems of fuzzy fractional differential models in imprecise environment.

The third section of the book presents different problems of heat transfer where fluids are involved. In Chapter 9, Castro et al. analyze the convection heat transfer in an experimental heat exchanger using experimental and numerical simulation data. In Chapter 10, Ludowski et al. propose solving steady-state inverse heat transfer problems using Computational Fluid Dynamics (CFD) software. In Chapter 11, Lopes addresses the physical principles and numerical models implemented in the software package EasyCFD. In the last chapter of this section, Chapter 12, Shateyi et al. analyze the problem of magnetohydrodynamic (MHD) micro-polar fluid, heat and mass transfer over unsteady stretching sheet through a porous medium.

The final section of the book presents some models and techniques for turbulent flows. In Chapter 13, Alonzo-García et al. provide an overview of the technical, theoretical, and numerical applications of Computational Fluid Dynamics (CFD) using the finite volume technique, restricted to incompressible turbulent flows. In Chapter 14, Lauk et al. investigate a novel 3D model based on the Reynolds Turbulence Stress Model (RSTM) closure of equations of carrier and particulate phases for channel turbulent flows. In Chapter 15, Ketabdari discusses and evaluates different free surface simulation methods based on computational grid. Finally, in Chapter 16, Mejía et al. address the use of Large Eddy Simulation (LES) for analyzing transport and mixing of passive and reactive scalars at high Schmidt regimes.

As the editor of this book, I would like to thank all the authors who have contributed to this volume as well as the reviewers for their assessment. Also, I express my gratitude to the InTech editorial staff for their invitation to be editor of an initial book project that, with the particular help of Ms. Iva Lipovic, the publishing process manager (PPM), we have arrived to convert in this new InTech book. Finally, at this moment where my father recently passed away, I dedicate all this effort to his memory and to him, Ricardo López-Barasoain (1935–2015), from Villafranca, Navarra, Spain. Of course, the rest of my family and all my friends and advisors are not forgotten in this dedicatory final paragraph.

**Ricardo López-Ruiz**
University of Zaragoza
Spain

Section 1

# Models and Applications in Medicine

Chapter 1

# BOLD fMRI Simulation

Zikuan Chen and Vince Calhoun

Additional information is available at the end of the chapter

http://dx.doi.org/10.5772/63313

## Abstract

**Background:** Brain functional magnetic resonance imaging (fMRI) is sensitive to changes in blood oxygenation level dependent (BOLD) brain magnetic states. The fMRI scanner produces a complex-valued image, but the calculation of the original BOLD magnetic source is not a mathematically tractable problem. We conduct numeric simulations to understand the BOLD fMRI model.

**Methods:** A brain cortex volume of interest (VOI) is configured with vasculatures (vessels or beads). Brain activity results in a local vascular blood magnetic susceptibility change in VOI (denoted by $\chi(\mathbf{r},t)$), manifesting as a dynamic magnetic source for BOLD fMRI. The MRI scanner produces a timeseries of complex-valued images reflecting the dynamic source $\chi(\mathbf{r},t)$. A voxel BOLD fMRI signal is simulated by calculating the intravoxel spin precession dephasing signal, a 3D BOLD fMRI by a multivoxel image of voxel signals for a 3D $\chi$ source distribution, and a 4D BOLD fMRI by a timeseries of 3D multivoxel images. The simulation data are subject to pattern analysis and statistical parametric mapping.

**Results**: Both MR magnitude and phase signals (images) are different from a predefined $\chi$ source due to data transformations inherent in the MRI scanning process. The 3D BOLD fMRI simulation shows the spatial distortions between the $\chi$ source and the MR image. The 4D BOLD fMRI simulation shows that the reconstructed source map is different from the original image and also that the task-correlation-based functional mapping method is susceptible to noise.

**Conclusion**: BOLD fMRI simulation offers a means to understand the single-voxel MR magnitude and phase signals, 3D multivoxel images, and 4D functional movies for a predefined BOLD $\chi$ source with respect to various parameter settings. It also allows us to separate the intravascular/extravascular signals and numerically characterize spin diffusion effect. The 3D BOLD fMRI simulation shows the source-image mismatch, which motivates the benefits of $\chi$ source reconstruction by solving an inverse MRI problem. The 4D BOLD fMRI simulation shows the noise dependence of the task-correlated functional map extraction.

**Keywords:** magnetic resonance imaging (MRI), blood oxygenation level dependence (BOLD), magnetic susceptibility source, dipole effect, voxelization, complex-valued magnetic resonance signal (image), intravoxel dephasing signal, multivoxel image, BOLD fMRI simulation, task correlation

## 1. Introduction

Magnetic resonance imaging (MRI) is a versatile non-invasive imaging technology that has been widely accepted for brain imaging (probing a magnetic state of brain interior). When applied to brain functional imaging, MRI produces a timeseries of images that are construed as an image representation of a brain functional activity. It is believed that any brain activity incurs a cerebral blood oxygenation level dependent (BOLD) magnetic state change that can be detected by MRI [1–4]. Brain functional imaging based on MRI and the endogenous BOLD contrast is termed BOLD fMRI.

In principle, the MRI output is a complex-valued image consisting of a pair of magnitude and phase [5]. Nevertheless, only the MR magnitude image has been exploited for brain imaging (structural or functional). Recent research shows that neither the MR magnitude nor the phase could faithfully represent the brain magnetic state. This is due to a cascade of MRI transformations (including linear dipole-convolved magnetization and nonlinear complex modulo/argument operations [6]). Consequently, conventional BOLD fMRI that is based on MR magnitude imaging may deviate from the underlying brain magnetic source change due to nonlinear data transformations associated with MR magnitude image formation. Since there is a lack of analytic formulation for describing the imaging aspects of BOLD fMRI, we conduct numeric simulations to understand the BOLD fMRI model.

In the past decades, there have been reports on single-voxel BOLD signal simulations [7–9] and multivoxel 3D BOLD imaging simulations [6, 10, 11]. In this chapter, we first provide a tutorial on the numeric simulations of single-voxel signals and multivoxel images and move forward to address implementing 4D BOLD fMRI simulations.

## 2. Models and methods

An overview of a brain BOLD fMRI model is diagramed in **Figure 1**, which consists of a cascade of three modules (stages). Specifically, the "**Source Magnetism**" module provides the phenotypical $\chi$ expression of a brain functional biophysiological state, which serves as the source of the "**MRI technology**" module that produces a complex-valued MR image. Upon data acquisition of a 4D fMRI, a postprocessing stage of "**Statistic image analysis**" is performed to extract the brain functional map (fmap). A complete BOLD fMRI simulation implements the three cascaded stages in **Figure 1** by numerical representations and computations.

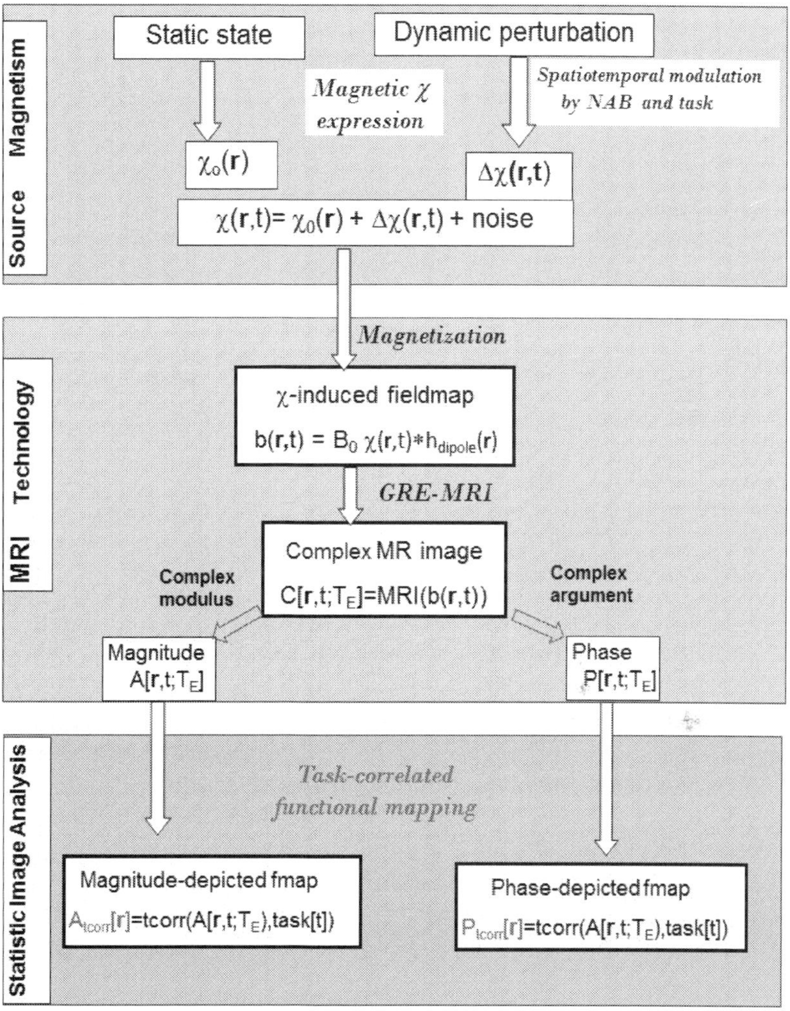


**Figure 1.** A BOLD fMRI model consists of three stages. The stage of "Source Magnetism" provides a dynamic magnetic susceptibility source for the stage of "MRI Technology". The MRI detection produces a 4D complex-valued fMRI dataset, which are used for functional imaging and mapping by "Statistical Image Analysis".

### 2.1. Definition of 3D vasculature and magnetic susceptibility source ($\chi$)

The initial step of BOLD fMRI simulation is to configure a $\chi$-expressed BOLD activity, thereby providing a BOLD $\chi$ source for fMRI. We define a brain cortex volume of interest (VOI) with a tissue background and fill it with a cortex vasculature, thus simulating a brain cortex region.

Let $\chi_0(\mathbf{r})$ denote a static 3D $\chi$ distribution of parenchymal tissue in VOI and $\Delta\chi(\mathbf{r},t)$ the vascular blood $\chi$ change associated with a BOLD activity, with $\mathbf{r} = (x,y,z)$ denoting the spatial coordinates in VOI, then the dynamic 4D $\chi$ source is given by

$$\begin{aligned} &\chi(\mathbf{r},t) = \chi_0(\mathbf{r}) + \Delta\chi(\mathbf{r},t) + \text{noise} \\ &\text{with} \\ &\chi_0(\mathbf{r}) = \chi_{\text{static}}(\mathbf{r}) \qquad \text{(parenchymal tissue)} \\ &\Delta\chi(\mathbf{r},t) = Hct \cdot \chi_{\text{do}} \cdot (1 - Y(t)) \cdot NAB(\mathbf{r}) \cdot V(\mathbf{r},t) \quad \text{(BOLD activity)} \end{aligned} \tag{1}$$

where *Hct* denotes the blood hemocrit ($Hct = 0.4$ for normal blood), $\chi_{\text{do}}$ the magnetic susceptibility difference between deoxygenated and oxygenated blood tissues ($\chi_{\text{do}} = 0.27 \times 4\pi$ ppm (in SI unit)), $Y(t)$ the blood oxygenation level ($Y \in [0,1]$), NAB($\mathbf{r}$) the local neuroactive blob distribution, and $V(\mathbf{r},t)$ the vasculature geometry in VOI. The explicit $t$ variable indicates a possible change during a BOLD activity, such as cerebral blood volume change in $V(\mathbf{r},t)$ and oxygenation level change in $Y(t)$. For the sake of simulating fMRI signals, a pure BOLD activity is expressed by a dynamic blood magnetic susceptibility change, $\Delta\chi(\mathbf{r},t)$, which serves as the magnetic source for BOLD MRI simulation. In practice, the BOLD activity provides an additive term, $\Delta\chi(\mathbf{r},t)$ (a perturbation term), on a background distribution $\chi_0(\mathbf{r})$ in Eq. (1).

A local functional activity is defined by a 3D spatial distribution of NAB($\mathbf{r}$) (a neuroactive blob centered at $\mathbf{r}$ in VOI). For the sake of numerical representation, we assume a NAB by a Gaussian-shaped blob (with soft boundary) or a ball-shaped blob (with hard boundary). A NAB defines a local activity distribution in VOI, which presents with an ON state (active state) and vanishes with an OFF state (resting state) by a temporal modulation of a designed task paradigm. We may define an excitatory activity by a positive distribution (NAB($\mathbf{r}$) > 0) or an inhibitory activity by a negative distribution (NAB($\mathbf{r}$) < 0), in relation to the static background distribution. For the numerical simulation of a BOLD activity, we define a BOLD $\chi$ response by a spatiotemporal modulation model in Eq. (1). A brain active state gives rise to $\Delta\chi(\mathbf{r},t) \neq 0$ in NAB and at a task "ON" epoch, and a brain resting state is numerically characterized by $\Delta\chi(\mathbf{r},t) = 0$ over the VOI in Eq. (1).

It is mentioned that the BOLD $\chi$ expression in a brain activity is simply simulated by a spatial modulation model in Eq. (1), where a neuronal activity is defined by a local blob that shapes a local blood $\Delta\chi$ map by a spatial multiplication. We also simplify the BOLD $\chi$ source simulation by ignoring the hemodynamic response function (hrf), which otherwise could be accounted for by convoluting $\Delta\chi(\mathbf{r},t)$ with a kernel of hrf (usually adopting a canonical hrf that is characteristic of a high upshoot followed by a small undershoot).

A BOLD $\chi$ change happens inside the vascular blood stream. We need to configure the vasculature geometry $V(\mathbf{r},t)$ by filling the VOI with cluttered vessels with a blood volume fraction (*bfrac*), as expressed by

$$V(\mathbf{r},t)=\begin{cases}1, & \mathbf{r}\in \text{vessel}\\ 0, & \text{otherwise}\end{cases} \quad \text{s.t.}\ \ bfrac(t)=\frac{\sum_{(x,y,z)} V(\mathbf{r},t)}{\text{size}(V)} \tag{2}$$

where the $t$ variable is reserved to incorporate the change in cerebral blood volume as a result of vasodilation/vasoconstriction in a BOLD activity. A static vasculature is included as a binary volume $V(\mathbf{r})$ that remains stationary during a BOLD activity. The random vascular geometry is generated under a control of $bfrac = [0.02, 0.04]$ for cortex vasculature simulation [1, 8, 11–13].

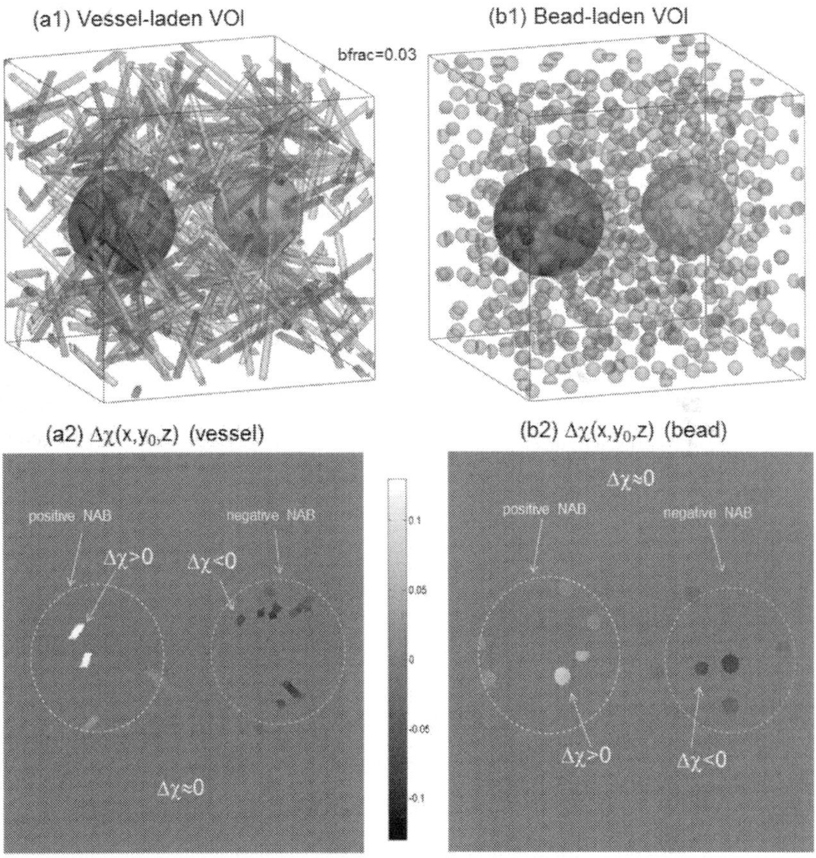


**Figure 2.** Illustrations of VOI vasculature and BOLD $\Delta\chi$ source. The VOI is filled with (a1) random vessels (cylindrical segments) and (b1) spheric beads. The NAB-modulated $\Delta\chi$ distributions are shown in (a2) and (b2), respectively, with a $y_0$-slice. It is noted $\Delta\chi$ may assume positive and negative values in local NAB regions.

In order to maintain a control of constant *bfrac* for cortex vasculature over different regions or across multiresolution subregions, we may fill a VOI with random beads instead of cluttered vessels. In **Figure 2** (**a1,b1**) are illustrated two brain local vasculature geometries with cluttered cylinders and random beads, under local stimuli by an excitatory blob (in red) and an inhibitory blob (in green). The NAB-modulated BOLD $\chi$ response distributions (in an active ON state) are shown in **Figure 2 (a2, b2)** with a $y_0$-slice in which the inactive regions (far from NAB) have little or no BOLD responses ($\Delta\chi \approx 0$).

In order to numerically depict the vasculature geometry, we need to define the VOI with a large finely gridded 3D matrix with a tiny grid element (gridel) at a scale of micronmeter [14]. For example, a matrix of 2048 × 2048 × 2048 gridels, where a gridel = 2 × 2 × 2 μm$^3$, is used to represent a small VOI of 4.1 × 4.1 × 4.1 mm$^3$. The large matrix resulting from VOI gridel sampling offers a quasi-continuous representation of a continuous distribution over VOI. A gridel represents a spin packet (or isochromat) that contains numerous identical proton spins, serving as a mesoscopic representation (at micronmeter scale) between microscopic structure (at atomic and molecular angstrom scale) and macroscopic structure (at millimeter scale of MRI voxels) [15, 16].

### 2.2. Calculation of χ-induced fieldmap

Upon determining the brain $\chi$ source configuration, we calculate the $\chi$-induced magnetic field map (fieldmap for short) by a 3D spatial convolution with a dipole kernel. This is to simulate the brain tissue magnetization process in a main field $B_0$ that produces an inhomogeneous fieldmap. Let b(*x,y,z*) represent the z-component of $\chi$-induced 3D vector field; it is given by [10, 11]

$$\begin{aligned} b(x,y,z) &= B_0\chi(x,y,z) * h_{\text{dipole}}(x,y,z) \\ \text{with } h_{\text{dipole}}(x,y,z) &= \frac{1}{4\pi}\frac{3z^2-(x^2+y^2+z^2)^{3/2}}{(x^2+y^2+z^2)^{5/2}} \end{aligned} \tag{3}$$

where * denotes spatial convolution, and $h_{\text{dipole}}$ a 3D dipole field [17]. In a Fourier domain, the 3D dipole convolution can be efficiently implemented by multiplicative spatial filtering, as expressed by [18]

$$\begin{aligned} FT\{b(x,y,z\} &= H_{\text{dipole}}(k_x,k_y,k_z)\cdot FT\{\chi(x,y,z)\}\cdot B_0 \\ \text{with } H_{\text{dipole}}(k_x,k_y,k_z) &\equiv FT\{h_{\text{dipole}}(x,y,z)\} = \frac{1}{3}-\frac{k_z^2}{k_x^2+k_y^2+k_z^2} \end{aligned} \tag{4}$$

where ($k_x$,$k_y$,$k_z$) denotes the coordinates in the Fourier domain. The fieldmaps induced by the $\Delta\chi$ distribution in a main field $B_0$ are illustrated in **Figure 3** (displayed with a $y_0$-slice), which shows a conspicuous dipole effect in a manifestation of bipolar-valued quadruple lobes around vessels (with an orientation dependence [19]).

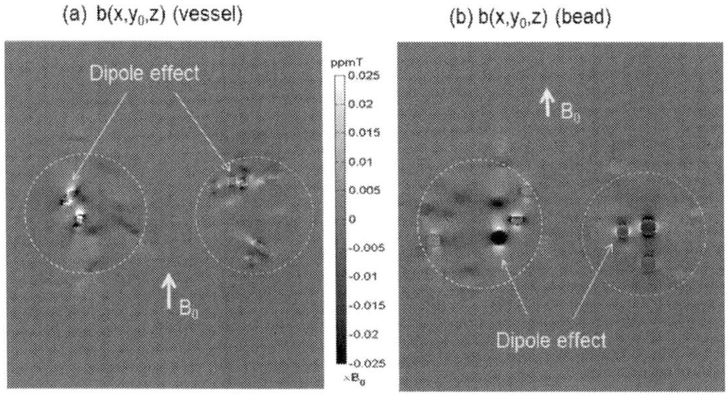


**Figure 3.** The fieldmaps calculated from the $\Delta\chi$ distributions in **Figure 2(a2, b2)**. It is noted that the $\Delta\chi$-induced fieldmap takes on a continuous inhomogenous bipolar-valued distribution over VOI, bearing a conspicuous dipole effect around large vessels (beads).

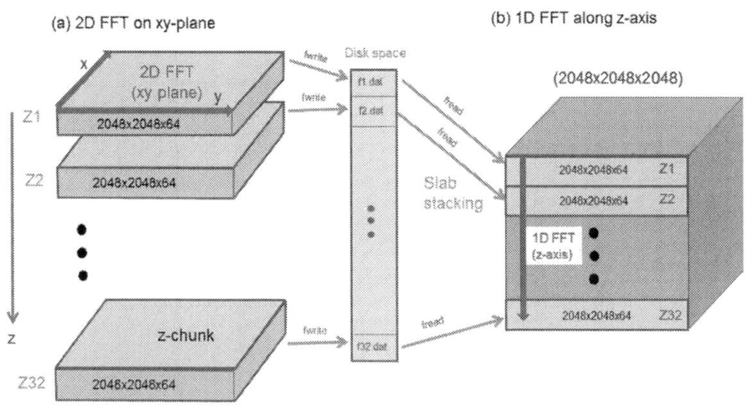


**Figure 4.** 3D FFT implementation by 2D FFT and 1D FFT. The 3D FFT of a large 3D matrix (e.g., 2048 × 2048 × 2048) is achieved by first performing 2D FFT on each $z$-slice ($xy$-plane) and then 1D FFT along $z$ columns. A large 3D matrix is decomposed into a number of small $z$-chunks to reduce the data file management (*fwrite* and *fread*).

In computation implementation, the 3D FFT for fieldmap calculation for a finely-gridded 3D $\chi$ distribution matrix (e.g., 2048 × 2048 × 2048 gridels) may encounter an "out-of-memory" problem. We propose to solve this problem by decomposing 3D FFT into 2D FFT and 1D FFT. Specifically, we first conduct 2D FFT on each $z$-slice (or $xy$-plane) and save the data as data files, and then conduct 1D FFT along each of the $z$-axis columns of a 3D volume that is stacked from $z$-slices (processed by 2D FFT and saved in files). In order to reduce the data file management (*fwrite* and *fread*) of the 3D FFT decomposition, we decompose the 3D matrix into a handful of z-chunks (z-slabs) that each consists of multiple z-slices. The number of z-chunks is dependent upon the available computer RAM (random access memory). As illustrated in **Figure 4**, we only need to manage (*fwrite* and *fread*) a number of 32 z-chucks (each consists of 64 z-slices in a matrix of 2048 × 2048 × 64), instead of 2048 individual z-slices.

### 2.3. Multivoxel partition of VOI

An MRI output is a discrete multivoxel image with the voxel size at a macroscopic millimeter scale, which implies that the MRI scanning process partitions a brain VOI into a small array of macroscopic voxels. We simulate a multivoxel MR image by rebinning mesoscopic gridels (at micronmeter scale) into macroscopic voxels (at millimeter scale). For example, we can reduce a large matrix of 2048 × 2048 × 2048 gridels to a small image matrix of 64 × 64 × 64 voxels with a voxel of 32 × 32 × 32 gridels. The multivoxel partition of VOI is in fact a spatial sampling by voxels, called voxelization. We denote the gridel-sampled representation of a continuous distribution over VOI by a spatial variable "(**r**)", and the voxel-sampled discrete representation by an index variable "[**r**]". Let Ω denote a voxel space, and |Ω| the voxel size (in terms of a number of gridels in Ω). The VOI voxelization is represented by

$$V[x,y,z]=\frac{1}{|\Omega|}\sum_{(x',y',z')\in\Omega(x,y,z)}V(x',y',z') \tag{5}$$

The VOI voxelization (voxel sampling) is necessary for MRI to produce a multivoxel image, due to the band limit of coil transmission and reception, which is designed as a parameter of voxel size in MRI protocol. The voxel size also represents a parameter of spatial resolution. In the MRI output, a high-resolution (corresponding to small voxel size) produces a large image matrix, and vice versa.

### 2.4. Calculation of intravoxel dephasing signals (Monte Carlo method)

An MRI voxel signal (or a NMR signal) is formed by an intravoxel spin precession dephasing in a χ-induced fieldmap. A quadrature detection produces a complex-valued voxel signal, denoted by C[*x*,*y*,*z*] that is formulated by [5]

$$\begin{aligned}&C[x,y,z;X]=\frac{1}{|\Omega|}\sum_{(x',y'.z')\in\Omega(x,y,z)}e^{i\gamma b(x',y',z')T_E}\\&\text{with } X=\{'T_E','B_0','|\Omega|','vesselsize',\cdots\}\end{aligned} \tag{6}$$

where γ denotes the gyromagnetic ratio, and the auxiliary variable 'X' is reserved to explicitly include the dependence of NMR signal upon a diverse set of factors. We are always concerned with the factors of echo time ($T_E$), field strength ($B_0$), spatial resolution (voxel size |Ω|), and vessel geometry in particular.

A voxel contains a number of gridels that each represents a spin packet. The voxel signal calculation in Eq. (6) counts all the spin packets in the voxel space. For a voxel that contains a large number of gridels, we may select a smaller number of gridels to calculate the voxel signal and reduce the computation burden. The intravoxel dephasing signal calculation made by counting the spin packets is a Monte Carlo simulation, which is expressed by

$$C[x,y,z;X] = \frac{1}{N}\sum_{n=1}^{N<|\Omega|} e^{i\gamma b(x_n,y_n,z_n)T_E} \text{ for } (x_n,y_n,z_n) \in \Omega(x,y,z) \tag{7}$$

For example, a voxel of 32 × 32 × 32 gridels consists of 32,768 spin packets, from which we may randomly select 3000 for the intravoxel average computation in Eq. (7) at a small computation cost of 10% (≈3000/32,768). It is noted that $C[x,y,z;X]$ denotes a complex voxel signal at $[x,y,z]$ in VOI, and we also use $C[x,y,z;X]$ to represent a multivoxel complex-valued image in the context that $[x,y,z]$ addresses all the voxels in VOI.

From a complex signal (image), we can calculate its magnitude and phase components by

$$\begin{cases} A[x,y,z;X] = 1 - |C[x,y,z;X]| & \text{(magnitude loss)} \\ P[x,y,z;X] = \angle C[x,y,z;X] & \text{(phase accrual)} \end{cases} \tag{8}$$

It is also noted that we use the magnitude loss and phase accrual to represent the pair of complex signal components and that the magnitude and phase calculations are different nonlinear operations.

### 2.5. Intravascular (IV) and extravascular (EV) signal separation

In an MRI experiment, it is difficult to separate intravascular (IV) signal from extravascular (EV) signal in an NMR signal. In numerical simulation, we can calculate the IV and EV signals separately based on the binary partition of voxel space according to the vessel geometry. Let $\Omega^{IV}$ and $\Omega^{EV}$ denote the IV and EV subspaces in a voxel space, which are partitioned by the vessel geometry by

$$\begin{aligned} &\Omega^{IV}(x,y,z) = \begin{cases} 1 & (x,y,z) \in vessel \\ 0 & \text{otherwise} \end{cases} \\ &\Omega^{EV}(x,y,z) = \begin{cases} 1 & (x,y,z) \notin vessel \\ 0 & \text{otherwise} \end{cases} = 1 - \Omega^{IV}(x,y,z) \\ &\text{with} \quad \Omega = \Omega^{IV} \cup \Omega^{EV} \text{ and } |\Omega| = |\Omega^{IV}| + |\Omega^{EV}| \end{aligned} \tag{9}$$

Then, we calculate the IV signal by only counting the gridels that are within vessel space ($\Omega^{IV}$), and the EV signal by the gridels in $\Omega^{EV}$. That is, the IV and EV signals are given by

$$
\begin{aligned}
C^{IV}[x,y,z;X] &= \frac{1}{|\Omega^{IV}|} \sum_{(x',y'.z')\in\Omega^{IV}(x,y,z)} e^{i\gamma b(x',y',z')T_E} \\
C^{EV}[x,y,z;X] &= \frac{1}{|\Omega^{EV}|} \sum_{(x',y'.z')\in\Omega^{EV}(x,y,z)} e^{i\gamma b(x',y',z')T_E} \\
\text{with} \quad \Omega &= \Omega^{IV} \cup \Omega^{EV}
\end{aligned}
\tag{10}
$$

In **Figure 5** are illustrated the IV/EV partition of a voxel space for IV/EV signal simulations. It is mentioned that the $\Omega^{IV}$ only occupies a small fraction of $\Omega$ and the BOLD $\chi$ change is confined in $\Omega^{IV}$.

Although a BOLD $\Delta\chi$ change is confined in $\Omega^{IV}$ in a NAB, the vascular blood magnetization process in $B_0$ establishes a long-range magnetic field distribution, not only in $\Omega^{IV}$ but also in $\Omega^{EV}$, with a distant decay ($\propto 1/r^3$) and a spatial modulation by NAB (see **Figures 2** and **3**). Obviously, a BOLD activity causes an IV signal and an EV signal simultaneously, which are generated from different field values over the IV and EV spaces, respectively. In **Figure 5(a)** is illustrated the IV/EV signal formations from spin particles in the IV/EV partition spaces.

A voxel NMR signal is formed from its IV and EV signals by a convex combination according to the IV/EV occupancies, as represented by

$$
\begin{aligned}
C[x,y,z;X] &= bfrac \cdot C^{IV}[x,y,z;X] + (1-bfrac) \cdot C^{EV}[x,y,z;X] \\
\text{with} \quad bfrac &= \frac{|\Omega^{IV}|}{|\Omega|}
\end{aligned}
\tag{11}
$$

Consequently, the IV signal contribution is greatly suppressed by a small weight of *bfrac* (<<1), as will be demonstrated later.

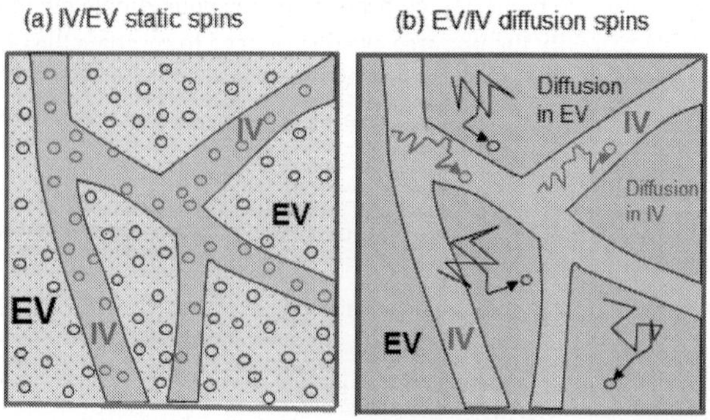


**Figure 5.** Illustration of extravascular (EV) and intravascular (IV) space partition in a voxel for intravoxel spin dephasing signal simulations (a) in absence of spin diffusions (static spins) and (b) in the presence of spin diffusions. A voxel space is partitioned by its intravoxel binary vasculature into IV (vessel=1) and EV (vessel=0) subspaces.

### 2.6. Diffusion effect

An NMR signal is formed via the carrier of hydrogen protons in tissue water. Since the water molecules undergo random motions, the water protons are non-stationary. We describe the proton random motion in 3D space by a trajectory **r**($t$), which is represented by [9, 20]

$$
\begin{aligned}
&\mathbf{r}(t) = x(t)\hat{x} + y(t)\hat{y} + z(t)\hat{z} \\
&x(t+\delta t) = Gauss(x(t), \sigma_d) \\
&y(t+\delta t) = Gauss(y(t), \sigma_d) \\
&z(t+\delta t) = Gauss(z(t), \sigma_d) \\
&\text{with } \ \sigma_d = \sqrt{2 \cdot D \cdot \delta t} \\
&D = \begin{cases} 1.5 \times 10^{-5} cm^2 / s & (x,y,z) \in vessel \\ 0.75 \times 10^{-5} cm^2 / s & (x,y,z) \notin vessel \end{cases}
\end{aligned}
\tag{12}
$$

where $\delta t$ denotes the time interval of the random motion of water molecules ($\delta t$ = 2 ms in simulation), $D$ the diffusion coefficient (different for diffusions in IV and EV), and Gauss a Gaussian distribution of the random motions (with a standard deviation of $\sigma_d$). It is noted that water proton diffusion in IV space is twice faster than in EV space. In **Figure 5(b)** are illustrated the diffusion IV and EV signal simulations.

### 2.7. Volumetric BOLD fMRI simulation

Based on individual voxel signal calculation, we implement 3D volumetric BOLD fMRI simulation by calculating the voxel signals at a multivoxel image array. Given a 3D $\chi$ source, the 3D BOLD fMRI simulations produce a 3D complex-valued multivoxel image $C[x,y,z; X]$; here, we are concerned with the spatial pattern comparison between the $\chi$ source and the magnitude image. Since the phase image bears a conspicuous dipole effect that dooms the morphological mismatch with the $\chi$ source, we do not need to compare the phase image with the $\chi$ source. However, the phase image is directly related to the $\chi$-induced fieldmap, and the phase image has been used for the fieldmap reconstruction in an inverse MRI solver [11, 21, 22]. In particular, in a small phase angle regime, the phase conforms the fieldmap with a difference of constant scale. In large phase angle scenarios, the unwrapped phase image resembles the fieldmap very well (albeit with somewhat nonlinear distortions). Therefore, we are also concerned with pattern comparison between MR phase image and the fieldmap. We suggest the spatial pattern comparisons by spatial correlations, which are defined by

$$
\begin{aligned}
\mathrm{corr}(A,\chi) &= \frac{\mathrm{cov}(A[\mathbf{r}], \chi[\mathbf{r}])}{\mathrm{std}(A[\mathbf{r}]) \cdot \mathrm{std}(\chi[\mathbf{r}])} \\
\mathrm{corr}(P,b) &= \frac{\mathrm{cov}(P[\mathbf{r}], b[\mathbf{r}])}{\mathrm{std}(P[\mathbf{r}]) \cdot \mathrm{std}(b[\mathbf{r}]}
\end{aligned}
\tag{13}
$$

It is noted that the spatial pattern correlations are applied to the multivoxel matrices (in notation of [**r**]) of the $\chi$ source, the fieldmap, and the images, which are all discretized at a spatial resolution of the same voxel size.

### 2.8. 4D BOLD fMRI simulation

It is straightforward to implement 4D BOLD fMRI simulation based on the repetition of volumetric BOLD fMRI simulations for each snapshot capture over a BOLD activity. First, we need to define a task-evoked 4D BOLD $\chi$ change, as illustrated in **Figure 6**. Specifically, we configure a 3D vasculature-laden VOI and provide a 3D $\chi$ distribution for a brain VOI state. A local $\chi$ change is simulated with a spatiotemporal modulation by a NAB and a task paradigm (in Eq. (1)). For the weak BOLD response detection, the task paradigm is usually designed as a boxcar waveform for repetition measurement of BOLD signals. We may define a positive NAB for an excitatory BOLD response and a negative NAB for an inhibitory response. The static background $\chi_0$ may be assigned to a water pool ($\chi_0 = \chi_{water}$) or be empty ($\chi_0 = 0$) with an additive Gaussian noise.

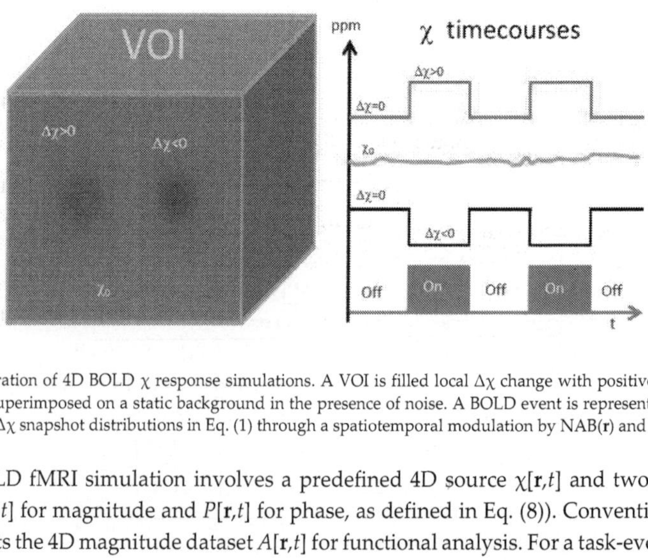


**Figure 6.** Illustration of 4D BOLD $\chi$ response simulations. A VOI is filled local $\Delta\chi$ change with positive and negative $\Delta\chi$ responses superimposed on a static background in the presence of noise. A BOLD event is represented by a timeseries of the 3D $\Delta\chi$ snapshot distributions in Eq. (1) through a spatiotemporal modulation by NAB(**r**) and task($t$).

The 4D BOLD fMRI simulation involves a predefined 4D source $\chi[\mathbf{r},t]$ and two output 4D images ($A[\mathbf{r},t]$ for magnitude and $P[\mathbf{r},t]$ for phase, as defined in Eq. (8)). Conventional BOLD fMRI exploits the 4D magnitude dataset $A[\mathbf{r},t]$ for functional analysis. For a task-evoked BOLD fMRI simulation, the functional activity map can be extracted from a 4D dataspace, $\Lambda[\mathbf{r},t] = \{\chi[\mathbf{r},t], A[\mathbf{r},t], P[\mathbf{r},t]\}$ by a temporal correlation (*tcorr)* map that is defined by

$$\Lambda_{tcorr}[x,y,z] = tcorr\left(\Lambda[x,y,z,t],\ task[t]\right) \equiv \frac{\operatorname{cov}(\Lambda[x,y,z,t], task[t])}{std_t(\Lambda[x,y,z,t])\, std(task[t])} \tag{14}$$
$$\text{with}\quad \Lambda = \{'A', 'P', '\chi^{true}', '\chi^{recon}'\}$$

where $std_t$ denotes the standard deviation of the data with respect to the $t$ variable, $\chi^{true}$ the predefined $\chi$ source, and $\chi^{recon}$ the reconstructed $\chi$ source (by solving the inverse problem of MRI data). It is noted that the correlation coefficient is invariant to signal strength. Therefore, a strong response signal may have the same correlation value as a weak response does as long as the strong and weak responses take on the same timecourse profiles. Consequently, the scale invariance of correlation leads to correlation saturation ($tcorr$ = 1 at regions with different response strengths). Nevertheless, the correlation saturation can be ruined by the presence of noise. Herein, by noise we mean any pattern difference between the response signal timecourse and task timecourse. In reality, the BOLD $\chi$ responses are subject to various noises (biological noise, physiological noise, detection noise) that spoil the task correlations at weak response regions. Only strong responses are immune to noise spoilage. It is the noise in the voxel response timecourse (extracted from a 4D dataset at a specific voxel) that shapes the $tcorr$ map according to the response signal strength.

# 3. Simulation results

## 3.1. Single voxel signal simulations

### *3.1.1. EV/IV signal separation*

By calculating the EV and IV signal portions separately and their convex linear combination in Eq. (11), we present the EV/IV signal behaviors with respect to a span of echo time ($T_E$=[0,

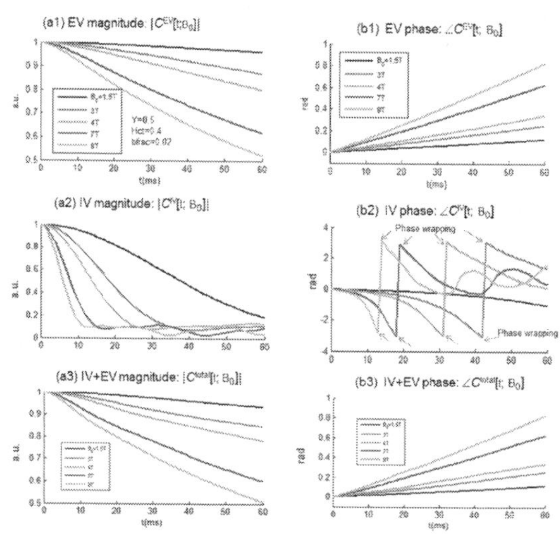


**Figure 7.** Intravascular (IV) and extravascular (EV) voxel signal simulations. The IV signal evolves drastically for a long $T_E$ and its contribution to the full voxel signal is relatively small.

60] ms) and for a range of field strength ($B_0$=[1.5, 3, 4, 7, 9] Tesla). It is seen in **Figure 7** that the IV signal changes quickly with a long echo time. However, the drastic IV signal changes are greatly suppressed in the voxel signals by the dominant EV signals. In particular, the IV signal may be developed into phase wrapping phenomenon for a long echo time (see **Figure 7(b2)**). With the dominance of EV signals in a large voxel, a voxel signal remains as a linear phase accrual with echo time (see **Figure 7(b3)**).

### 3.1.2. *Multiresolution voxel signal behavior*

As a voxel size decreases, the voxel space contains less (or none) vessels, and there is less voxel average effect. In **Figure 8**, the four-level voxel subdivision and multiresolution voxel signal behaviors are demonstrated. At level =1, the parent voxel contains a clutter of vessels where the complex voxel signal appears as a short line-segment trajectory (with respect to $T_E$). As the voxel is decomposed into an 8 × 8 × 8 array at level = 4, the subvoxel only contains a single vessel, and the voxel signal becomes turbulent due to the high field values for rapid Larmor precession [14, 23].

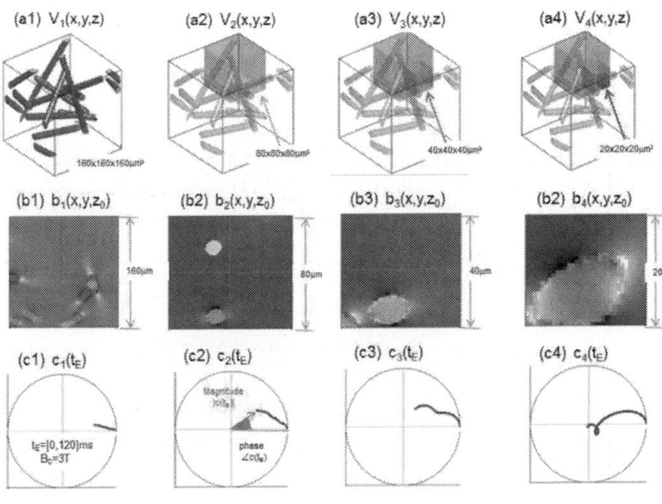


**Figure 8.** Multiresolution complex-valued voxel signals due to voxel subdivision. As the voxel size is dyadically reduced, the smaller voxels contain less vessels, and the voxel signal may become turbulent at vessel boundary (Adapted from [23]).

### 3.1.3. *Diffusion effects on magnitude and phase signals*

The numerical simulations on the diffusion effect on MR magnitude and phase are presented in **Figure 9** for a span of $T_E$ = [0, 60] ms with different field strengths (in terms of $\Delta\chi B_0$ = [0.1, 3] ppmT). The results show that the diffusion has more effect on low field magnitude than on high field magnitude [20]. Nevertheless, the diffusion has little effect on MR phase signals.

http://dx.doi.org/10.5772/63313

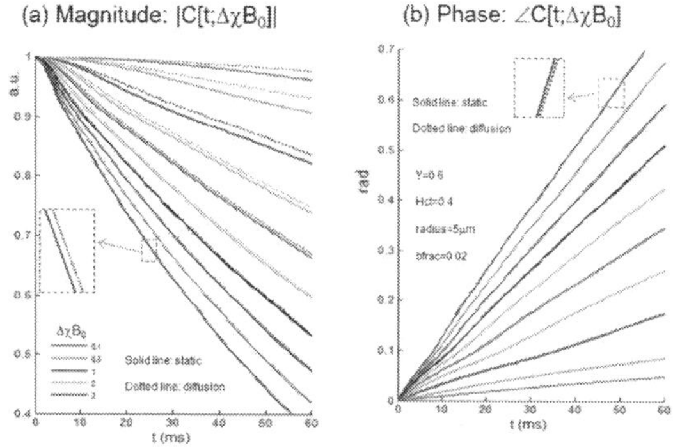


**Figure 9.** Effects of diffusion and field strength on voxel signal magnitude and phase. It is seen that the diffusion has more effects on magnitude signal than on phase signal and that the diffusion effect decreases as the field strengths increases (Adapted from [20]).

## 3.2. Volumetric BOLD fMRI simulations

### *3.2.1. Cortex VOI configuration and voxelization*

We define a cortex VOI in a large matrix and fill it with random beads (radius = 3 μm, *bfrac* = 0.03), and simulate local BOLD response by a Gaussian-shaped NAB, which modulates the local χ distribution by a spatial multiplication. The VOI is partitioned into a coarse matrix by grouping the gridels into voxels. As a result of voxelization, we represent a distribution over

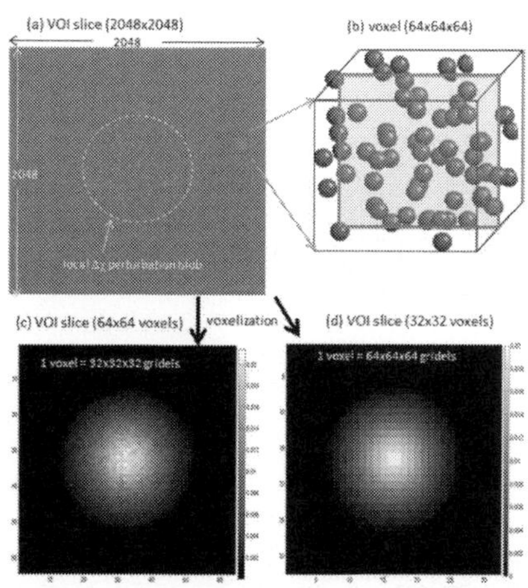


**Figure 10.** Illustration of VOI configuration and voxelization. A VOI is represented by a large matrix for subvoxel structure representation. The VOI voxelization produces a small multivoxel matrix, depending on the voxel size.

VOI by a multivoxel image matrix. The voxelization with a large voxel size produces a small image matrix, and vice versa. **Figure 10** shows a VOI that is represented by a large matrix in gridel sampling **(a)** with a zoomed region for substructure visualization **(b)**. The VOI voxelization by a voxel of 32 × 32 × 32 gridels produces a matrix of 64 × 64 × 64 voxels **(c)** and produces a matrix of 32 × 32 × 32 voxels **(d)** by a voxel of 64 × 64 × 64 gridels. It is seen that a larger voxel size is comprised of more spatial smoothing.

### *3.2.2. Multivoxel image calculation*

Given a 3D $\chi$ distribution in **Figure 11(a)**, we calculated the $\chi$-induced fieldmap by Eq. (2) and presented the results **(b)**. In the absence of diffusion, we calculated the complex-valued T2* images (**c**, **d**). In the presence of diffusion (Eq. (12)), we recalculated the complex-valued T2* images (**e**, **f**). The diffusion simulation on multivoxel fMRI shows that the diffusion effect is insignificant on image formation.

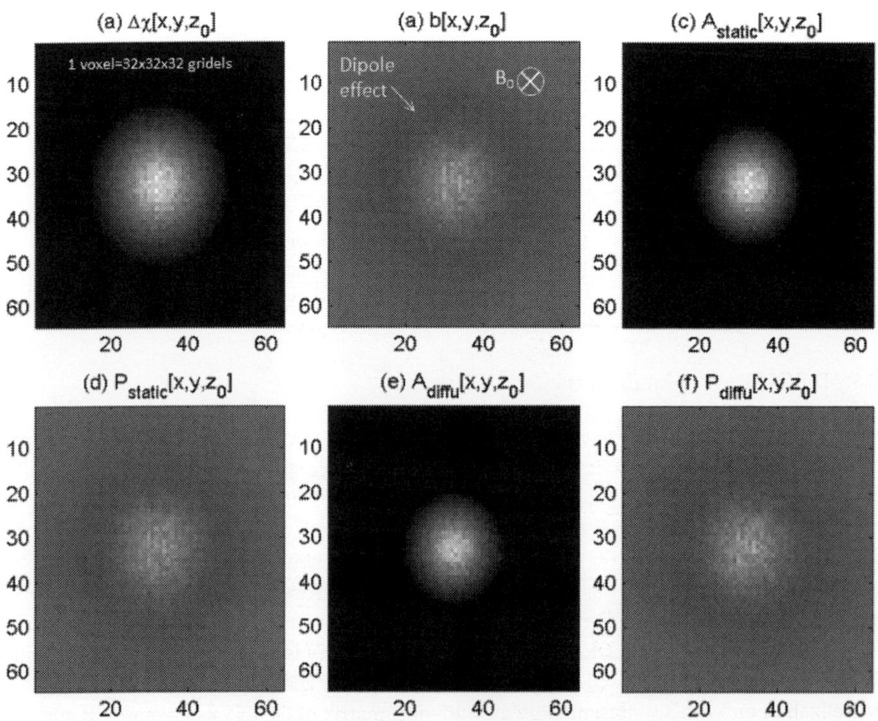


**Figure 11.** Illustration of volumetric BOLD fMRI simulation, displayed with a z-slice (with $B_0$//z-axis). (a) 3D $\Delta\chi$ source (in a matrix of 64 × 64 × 64 voxels resulting from a VOI of 2048 × 2048 × 2048 gridels); (b) the $\Delta\chi$-induced fieldmap; (c, d) the magnitude and phase images with static spins (at $T_E$= 30 ms); and (e, f) the magnitude and phase images with diffusion spins.

http://dx.doi.org/10.5772/63313

### 3.2.3. *Morphological distortions associated with 3D BOLD fMRI*

We performed volumetric BOLD fMRI simulations for a span of echo times ($T_E$= [0, 30] ms) with different parameter settings with respect to voxel size, field strength, and with and without diffusion. With the datasets of numerical BOLD fMRI simulations, we compared the magnitude images with the predefined $\chi$ source and the phase images with the fieldmaps. The results are presented in **Figure 12**. Note that the pattern correlations are plotted in a small display window ([0.9, 1]) out of the full range of *corr* $\in$ [−1, 1] for scrutiny.

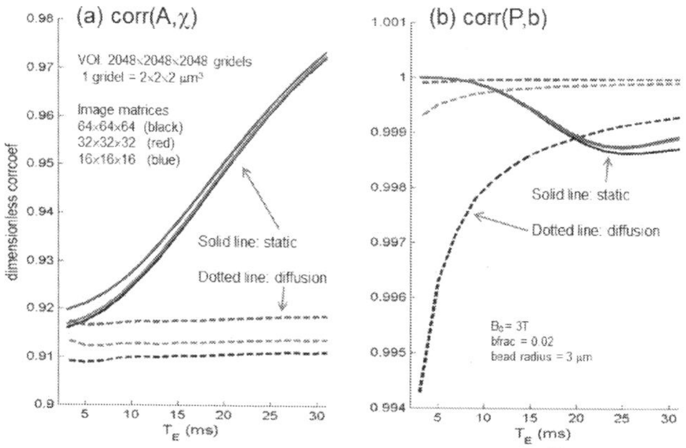


**Figure 12.** Spatial correlation measurements (a) between $\chi$ source and magnitude image and (b) between $\chi$-induced fieldmap and phase image, for static intravoxel dephasing and diffusive intravoxel dephasing. Note the small display windows for corr values in the range of [−1,1] (Adapted from [11]).

### 3.3. 4D BOLD fMRI simulations

The 4D BOLD fMRI simulations are presented in **Figures 13** through **15**. Specifically, in **Figure 13** are shown **(a)** the VOI configuration with two local neuroactive blobs (NAB), **(b)** the NAB-modulated BOLD $\chi$ distribution at an ON state (or active state), and **(c)** the NAB-absent $\chi$ distribution at an OFF state (or resting state), displayed with a $y_0$-slcie. We designed a task paradigm by a pattern of 5 ON states and 5 OFF states, simulating the brain active state measurement by 5 repetitions and the brain resting state measurement by another 5 repetitions. (In practice, a multiple repetition of the "ON/OFF" pattern is used to design the task paradigm). The bead-represented vasculature structure in a voxel in VOI is shown in zoom **(d)** with a 3D display. It is noted that the VOI is represented in a matrix of 2048 × 2048 × 2048 gridels **(a)**, the voxelization on VOI is represented by a multivoxel matrix of 64 × 64 × 64 voxels **(b)** and **(c)** with a voxel = 32 × 32 × 32 gridels **(d)**, and that the cortex vasculature in a VOI is simulated by a uniform random distribution (background) that is independent of the BOLD NAB and task paradigm. The 4D $\chi(\mathbf{r},t)$ representation for a local BOLD activity is related to the NAB and the task through a spatiotemporal model in Eq. (1).

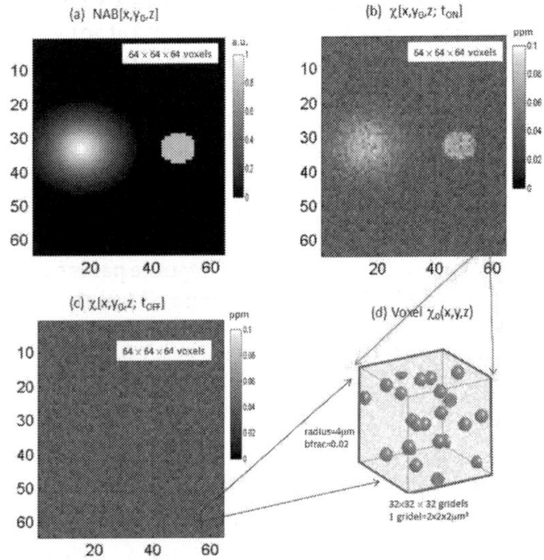


**Figure 13.** Numerical representation of a local BOLD activity in terms of 4D $\chi(\mathbf{r},t)$. (a) A Gaussian-shaped NAB and a ball-shaped NAB in VOI; (b) an ON state $\chi[\mathbf{r},t_{ON}]$; (c) an OFF state $\chi[\mathbf{r},t_{OFF}]$; and (d) the bead-laden structure in a voxel.

Upon the numerical representation of 4D $\chi(\mathbf{r},t)$, we performed 4D BOLD fMRI simulations by repeating the 3D BOLD fMRI simulation for each snapshot time point (there are 10 timepoints for the task pattern of 5 ONs and 5 OFFs), with the settings ($T_E$= 30 ms, $B_0$ = 3 T, VOI matrix =

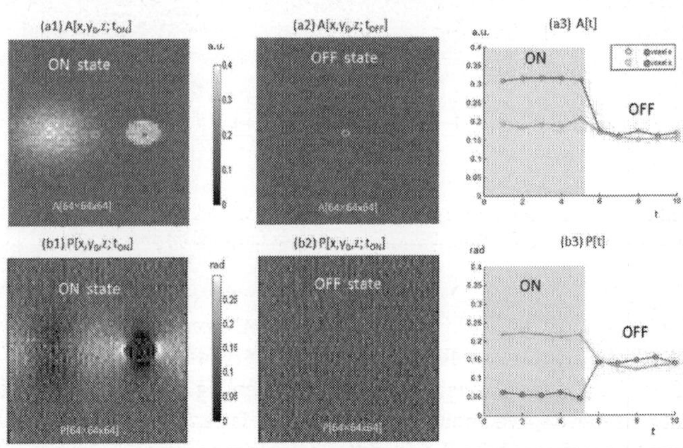


**Figure 14.** Numerical simulations of 4D BOLD fMRI data acquisition. (a1, a2) BOLD magnitude images captured at an ON and OFF state and (a3) the magnitude signal timecourses at two voxels (marked by x and *o* (a1, a2), extracted from the 4D magnitude dataset $A[\mathbf{r},t]$). (b1, b2, b3) for the BOLD phase images in $P[\mathbf{r},t]$ and the voxel phase timecourses.

64 × 64 × 64 voxels, 1 voxel = 32 × 32 × 32 gridels, 1 gridel = 2 × 2 × 2 μm³). **Figure 14** shows (**a1**, **a2**) the magnitude images, (**b1**, **b2**) the phase images captured at an ON and OFF state, and (**a3**, **b3**) the timecourses of magnitude signal changes, and phase signal changes at two voxels: one voxel inside an active blob (marked by "x" in (**a1**)) and another outside the active at blob (marked by "o"). It is noted the ripples in the signal timecourses in (**a3**, **b3**) are attributed to the additive Gaussian random noise in the data acquisition simulations.

By arranging the timeseries of images according to the task timecourse, we can play a movie for a BOLD activity. In reality, the BOLD response is too weak and noisy to be perceived between an ON and OFF state. For the sake of BOLD response pattern representation, we need to extract the BOLD activity blobs from the timeseries of images by statistical parameter mapping method, which consists of an essential task correlation map as defined in Eq. (14).

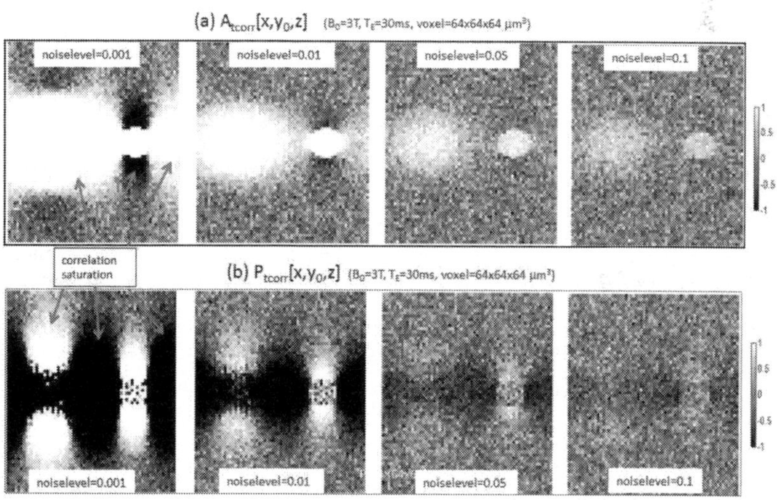


**Figure 15.** Numerical simulations of fmap extractions from 4D BOLD fMRI datasets in the presence of additive Gaussian noises at different noise level = {0.001,0.01,0.05,0.1}. (a) Magnitude fmap and (b) phase fmap.

Upon the completion of 4D BOLD magnitude and phase image datasets ($A[\mathbf{r},t]$, $P[\mathbf{r},t]$), we calculated the task- correlated fmap using Eq. (14). In the results, we obtained 3D $A_{tcorr}$ for BOLD magnitude fmap from the 4D magnitude image dataspace, and a 3D $P_{tcorr}$ for BOLD phase fmap from the 4D phase image dataspace. By repeating the 4D BOLD fMRI simulations with different noise levels, we show that $A_{tcorr}$ or $P_{tcorr}$ is sensitive to the additive Gaussian noise. In **Figure 15** are showed the $A_{tcorr}$ and $P_{tcorr}$ (displayed with a $y_0$-slice out of the 64 × 64 × 64 matrix volume) for the Gaussian noise at different noise levels = {0.001, 0.01, 0.05, 0.1}. It is seen that either the magnitude or phase fmap suffers from correlation saturation in little noise (noise level < 0.01) or tends to be buried in severe noises (noise level > 0.05) for our spatiotemporal modulation model in Eq. (1). In particular, our simulation shows the correlation saturation in extreme cases of little noise or noiseless settings; this phenomenon may be explained by the scale invariance of correlation coefficient. On the other extreme case, a severe noise may destroy the task-correlated activity blob; this explains the pursuit on high-SNR image acquisition.

Our 4D BOLD fMRI simulations show that the predefined BOLD NAB in **Figure 13(a)** could be largely reproduced by a task-correlation magnitude fmap ($A_{tcorr}$ in **Figure 15(a)**) as extracted from a 4D BOLD fMRI magnitude dataset, thus justifying the BOLD fMRI experiment for brain functional mapping. In comparison, the phase fmap (in $P_{tcorr}$) is spatially dissimilar to the predefined BOLD NAB due to the conspicuous dipole effect in the phase images [6, 11]. Nevertheless, our 4D BOLD fMRI simulations also show that the imaging noise has a strong effect on the fmap extracted from the magnitude or phase image dataset due to the simplified spatiotemporal modulation model for numerical BOLD $\chi$ expressions.

## 4. Discussion

The data acquisition of BOLD fMRI is not analytically tractable due to the involvement of diversified parameters. The BOLD fMRI simulations provide a means to observe the effect of MRI transformations on the MR data acquisition; spatial distortions between the underlying magnetic source and MR images; and reproducibility of functional activity extraction from a 4D BOLD fMRI dataset.

Since MRI is designed to measure a magnetic field distribution, the BOLD fMRI only measures the $\chi$-expressed BOLD response during a functional activity, a phenotypic numeric expression of a biophysiological brain functional activity in terms of tissue magnetism. It is believed that a functional activity causes IV blood magnetism change in terms of oxygenated and deoxygenated blood magnetic susceptibility change. Therefore, our simulation begins with a configuration of magnetic source by a vasculature-laden VOI with a 3D $\chi$ source distribution. Through a spatiotemporal modulation by a predefined local neuroactive blob (numerically NAB($\mathbf{r}$)) and a task paradigm (numerically task($t$)), we define a dynamic $\chi$ source to represent a $\chi$-expressed BOLD activity (in Eq. (1)). It is pointed out in Eq. (1) that the BOLD $\chi$ response may incorporate the factors of cerebral metabolic rate of oxygen consumption ($CMRO_2$), cerebral blood volume (CBV), and cerebral blood flow (CBF) through the parameters of $Y(\mathbf{t})$ and $V(\mathbf{r},t)$, thereby enabling the numeric simulations of MRI-detected BOLD activity. In reality, the biophysiological aspects for neurovascular coupling are far more complicated than the spatiotemporal modulation model in Eq. (1), which deserves a long-term exploration.

Upon a predefined $\chi$ source map, we implement 3D BOLD fMRI numerical simulation based on MRI principles. In the results, we are concerned with pattern comparison between the source distribution and the output images (magnitude and phase). Our simulations show that neither the magnitude image nor the phase image is a faithful representation of the $\chi$ source distribution. In the context of volumetric medical imaging, the MRI output image is not a tomographic reproduction (quantitative spatial mapping) of the $\chi$ source. Since the source-image mismatch is due to a cascade of MRI transformations that cause distortions during data acquisition, this inspires us to reconstruct the $\chi$ source by solving an inverse MRI problem [21, 22].

In NMR principle, a voxel signal is formed from numerous hydrogen proton precessions in a magnetic field. The signal formation involves a huge space scale span from a microscopic atomic scale to macroscopic millimeter scale. For numerical simulations, we implement the mesoscopic micrometer scale through gridel sampling [14, 15]. A gridel is a tiny grid element (at micronmeter scale) smaller than vessel size with which we may digitally depict a vessel geometry. On the other hand, a gridel consists of numerous protons at microscopic atomic scale. The collective proton spins in a gridel are denoted by a spin packet [14, 15]. We define a cortex VOI in a large finely-gridded matrix and partition the VOI into a coarse multivoxel matrix, with each voxel containing an adequate number of gridels for subvoxel structure representation. The VOI partition and gridel rebinning for multivoxel image formation is a topic of multiresolution BOLD signal analysis [15, 23].

In the past decades, the BOLD fMRI mechanism was numerically simulated with signal voxel signals, [7–9], offering an understanding of BOLD fMRI signal formation with respect to a diverse set of parameter settings. However, the single-voxel signal simulation cannot reveal the spatial context for source-image mapping study. Therefore, we were motivated to use multivoxel image simulations for revealing the spatial mismatches between the source and the image [9–11]. Based on 3D BOLD fMRI simulations, it is a straightforward process to implement 4D BOLD fMRI simulations. Our 4D BOLD fMRI simulations for a task-evoked brain functional activity, based on a simple spatiotemporal modulation model in Eq. (1), show that the fmap extraction from a 4D BOLD fMRI dataset is sensitive to the additive Gaussian noise. The noise dependence of the task-correlation-based fmap extraction is attributed to the scale invariance of the correlation coefficient.

One factor for the source-image mismatch is the dipole effect that is introduced during the tissue magnetization in a main field $B_0$, which is unavoidable for MRI data acquisition. The dipole effect is introduced to the $\chi$-induced fieldmap, which is propagated to the MR magnitude and phase images (signals) via different data transformations. The dipole effect on the $\chi$-induced fieldmap manifests bipolar-valued quadruple lobes around vessels. Upon MRI data acquisition, the magnitude image is a nonnegative nonlinear spatial mapping of the fieldmap and the phase image is an *arctan* nonlinear spatial mapping. It is interesting to show in our numeric simulations that the nonnegative magnitude image resembles the predefined $\chi$ source distribution, except for the negative inversions at negative $\chi$ regions (not reported herein), and we have found that the (unwrapped) bipolar-valued phase image conforms very well with the bipolar-valued fieldmap [6, 11]. The phase image bears a conspicuous dipole effect that makes a striking difference between the phase image and the predefined $\chi$ source.

BOLD fMRI simulation is a time-consuming computation job. In a computer cluster (a Kernel Linux system with 16 CPUs and 252 GB memory), the single-voxel signal simulation requires about 1 hour, and 3D multivoxel simulation requires more than 10 hours, and 4D BOLD fMRI simulation requires a few days, depending on the sizes of gridel, voxel, and VOI. The computation burden may be greatly reduced by a Bloch technique [24], which implements intravoxel dephasing signal calculation by a linear approximation. The fast Bloch simulation method is good for MR phase image simulation, but not good for MR magnitude simulation due to an accentuated edge effect. Moreover, the IV and EV signal separation and the diffusion simulations are not implementable by the Bloch method.

## 5. Conclusion

We conclude our numerical BOLD fMRI simulations by the following findings (albeit qualitative):

1. Both the MR magnitude and the phase images are spatially different from the predefined magnetic susceptibility distribution. This image-source distortion is due to the inevitable data transformations associated with MRI data.
2. By numerical simulation, we can separate the intravascular (IV) signal from the extravascular (EV) signal in a voxel signal. The IV signal is much stronger than the EV signal as a result of a BOLD $\chi$ change. However, the drastic IV signal evolution is usually greatly suppressed in a voxel signal by a small proportion of blood volume fraction ($bfrac \approx [0.02, 0.04]$).
3. As voxel size decreases, the voxel signals evolve more drastically and turbulently inside and around the large vessels.
4. The proton diffusion effect due to nonstationary water molecules in brain tissues incurs more MR magnitude signal decays in a low field than in a high field. In comparison, the proton diffusion has little effect on MR phase signals.
5. The numerical simulation on 4D BOLD fMRI for task-evoked functional mapping shows that the functional activity extraction by a task correlation technique is sensitive to data noise.

Overall, the numerical simulations on BOLD fMRI allow us to look into the insights of a single-voxel signal, a multivoxel image, and a video of brain functional BOLD activity with respect to various parameter settings. The finding in source-image mismatch inspires us to seek for the underlying magnetic source of BOLD fMRI for more accurate brain functional mapping. The finding in the noise sensitiveness of task-correlated fmap raises a caveat to the correlation-based functional mapping.

## Abbreviations:

1D: one dimensional; 2D: two dimensional; 3D: three dimensional (spatial); 4D: four dimensional (spatiotemporal); BOLD: blood oxygenation level dependent; MR: magnetic resonance; MRI: magnetic resonance imaging; fMRI: functional MRI; FFT: fast Fourier transform; NAB: neuroactive blob; VOI: volume of interest; IV: intravascular; EV: extravascular; gridel: grid

http://dx.doi.org/10.5772/63313

element; bfrac: blood volume fraction; fmap: functional map; corr: correlation (coefficient); tcorr: temporal correlation or task correlation.

## Author details

Zikuan Chen[1*] and Vince Calhoun[1,2]

*Address all correspondence to: zchen@mrn.org

1 The Mind Research Network and LBERI, Albuquerque, New Mexico, USA

2 University of New Mexico, ECE Department, Albuquerque, New Mexico, USA

## References

[1] J. L. Boxerman, L. M. Hamberg, B. R. Rosen *et al.*, "MR contrast due to intravascular magnetic susceptibility perturbations," *Magn Reson Med,* vol. 34, no. 4, pp. 555-66, Oct, 1995.

[2] S. Ogawa, R. S. Menon, D. W. Tank *et al.*, "Functional brain mapping by blood oxygenation level-dependent contrast magnetic resonance imaging. A comparison of signal characteristics with a biophysical model," *Biophys J,* vol. 64, no. 3, pp. 803-12, Mar, 1993.

[3] S. Ogawa, D. W. Tank, R. Menon *et al.*, "Intrinsic signal changes accompanying sensory stimulation: functional brain mapping with magnetic resonance imaging," *Proc Natl Acad Sci U S A,* vol. 89, no. 13, pp. 5951-5, Jul 1, 1992.

[4] O. J. Arthurs and S. Boniface, "How well do we understand the neural origins of the fMRI BOLD signal?" *Trends Neurosci,* vol. 25, no. 1, pp. 27-31, Jan, 2002.

[5] E. M. Haacke, R. Brown, M. Thompson *et al.*, Magnetic Resonance Imaging Physical Principles and Sequence Design, John Wiley & Sons, Inc, 1999.

[6] Z. Chen and V. Calhoun, "Nonlinear magnitude and linear phase behaviors of T2* imaging: theoretical approximation and Monte Carlo simulation," *Magn Reson Imaging,* vol. 33, no. 4, pp. 390-400, May, 2015.

[7] J. L. Boxerman, P. A. Bandettini, K. K. Kwong *et al.*, "The intravascular contribution to fMRI signal change: Monte Carlo modeling and diffusion-weighted studies in vivo," *Magn Reson Med,* vol. 34, no. 1, pp. 4-10, Jul, 1995.

[8] J. Martindale, A. J. Kennerley, D. Johnston *et al.*, "Theory and generalization of Monte Carlo models of the BOLD signal source," *Magn Reson Med,* vol. 59, no. 3, pp. 607-18, Mar, 2008.

[9] A. P. Pathak, B. D. Ward, and K. M. Schmainda, "A novel technique for modeling susceptibility-based contrast mechanisms for arbitrary microvascular geometries: the finite perturber method," *Neuroimage,* vol. 40, no. 3, pp. 1130-43, Apr 15, 2008.

[10] Z. Chen, and V. Calhoun, "Volumetric BOLD fMRI simulation: from neurovascular coupling to multivoxel imaging," *BMC medical imaging,* vol. 12, pp. 8, 2012.

[11] Z. Chen, and V. Calhoun, "Understanding the morphological mismatch between magnetic susceptibility source and T2* image," *Magnetic Resonance Insights,* vol. 6, pp. 65-81, 2013.

[12] Z. Chen, A. Caprihan, and V. Calhoun, "Effect of surrounding vasculature on intravoxel BOLD signal," *Medical physics,* vol. 37, no. 4, pp. 1778-87, Apr, 2010.

[13] W. M. Spees, D. A. Yablonskiy, M. C. Oswood *et al.*, "Water proton MR properties of human blood at 1.5 Tesla: magnetic susceptibility, T(1), T(2), T*(2), and non-Lorentzian signal behavior," *Magn Reson Med,* vol. 45, no. 4, pp. 533-42, Apr, 2001.

[14] Z. Chen, and V. D. Calhoun, "Magnitude and phase behavior of multiresolution BOLD signal," *Concepts Magn Reson,* vol. 37B, no. 3, pp. 129-35, 2010.

[15] Z. Chen, and V. Calhoun, "A computational multiresolution BOLD fMRI model," *IEEE Trans. BioMed. Eng,* vol. 58, no. 10, pp. 2995-9, 2011.

[16] D. A. Yablonskiy, "Quantitation of intrinsic magnetic susceptibility-related effects in a tissue matrix. Phantom study," *Magn Reson Med,* vol. 39, no. 3, pp. 417-28, Mar, 1998.

[17] J. R. Reitz, F. J. Milford, and R. W. Christy, Foundations of Electromagnetic Theory, New York: Addison-Wisley, 1993.

[18] J. P. Marques and R. Bowtell, "Application of a Fourier-based method for rapid calculation of field inhomogeneity due to spatial variation of magnetic susceptibility," *Concepts Magn. Reson,* vol. B 25, pp. 65-78, 2005.

[19] Z. Chen and V. Calhoun, "Effect of object orientation angle on T2* image and reconstructed magnetic susceptibility: numerical simulations," *Magn. Reson. Insight,* vol. 6, pp. 23-31, 2013.

[20] Z. Chen and V. Calhoun, "Computed diffusion contribution in the complex BOLD fMRI signal," *Conc. Magn. Reson. Part A,* vol. 40A, no. 3, pp. 128-145, 2012.

[21] Z. Chen and V. Calhoun, "Computed inverse resonance imaging for magnetic susceptibility map reconstruction," *J. Comp. Assist. Tomo,* vol. 36, no. 2, pp. 265-74, Mar, 2012.

[22] Z. Chen and V. Calhoun, "Reconstructing brain magnetic susceptibility distributions from T2* phase images by TV-reguarlized 2-subproblem split Bregman iterations," *Rep. Med. Imag,* vol. 7, pp. 41-53, 2014.

[23] Z. Chen, Z. Chen, and V. Calhoun, "Blood oxygenation level-dependent functional MRI signal turbulence caused by ultrahigh spatial resolution: numerical simulation and theoretical explanation," *NMR Biomed,* vol. 26, no. 3, pp. 248-64, Mar, 2013.

[24] P. Latta, M. L. Gruwel, V. Jellus *et al.*, "Bloch simulations with intra-voxel spin dephasing," *J. Magn. Reson,* vol. 203, no. 1, pp. 44-51, Mar, 2010.

Chapter 2

# Basics of Multibody Systems: Presented by Practical Simulation Examples of Spine Models

Bauer Sabine

Additional information is available at the end of the chapter

http://dx.doi.org/10.5772/62864

**Abstract**

Computer modeling is a widely used method to determine the biomechanical behavior of a system. The aim of our biomechanical multibody simulation computer modeling is to consider the characteristics of a musculoskeletal system through the use of knowledge from the fields of mechanics, anatomy, and physiology in the model in an appropriate manner, in order to obtain as accurately as possible a realistic simulation of the biomechanical behavior of the system. Various application examples of a lumbar spine model that takes the spinal structures with their specific material properties into account are presented: effects of different spine alignments in standing position, effects of overweight on the spinal biomechanics, and application possibilities of biomechanical computer models in medicine.

**Keywords:** multibody simulation, lumbar spine model, biomechanical behavior, load determination, preoperative planning

## 1. Introduction

According to the World Health Organization (WHO), back pain of the lower spine has reached epidemic proportions, being reported by about 80% of people at some time in their life [1]. Hoy notes that lower back pain causes more global disability than any other condition [2]. The causes of back pain are manifold. Reasons may be degenerative changes of intervertebral discs, spinal stenosis, spondylolisthesis, spinal stenosis, traumatic injury, skeletal irregularities, and osteoporosis. But there is also a correlation between increased body weight and low back pain [3–5]. These overloads may result in sequelae such as instability or dysesthesia with narrowing of the spinal canal and compression of the associated nerve roots may be a consequence. If a conservative treatment does not achieve a pain relief anymore, only a surgically induced stabilization like a therapeutic option remains. Mayer [6] indicates that no validated results exist about the success of these operations over a period of two years, and thus provide clear evidence of reduced adjacent segment degeneration. Furthermore, statements about the sustainability of clinical and radiological results with respect to a reconstruction of the segmental mobility are still missing. A modern non-invasive method for assessing the effect of medical operational measures is the load determination in various spinal structures by means of computer modeling.

To capture the load distribution of the lumbar spine, highly developed so-called finite-element (FE) models [7–11] can be used which allow a very detailed calculation of force and torque transmission—both in the rigid bones and in the elastic proportions as intervertebral discs, ligaments, and implants. The complexity of the models, however, requires high computing times for each load case. Is the aspect of the holistic approach of the human movement in the focus of interest, the multibody simulation (MBS) is a suitable simulation method? Due to the highly efficient short computation times, even complex motion sequences can be simulated.

## 2. Basics of model building and simulation

Computer modeling is a widely used method for determining the biomechanical behavior of a system. A distinction is made between the FE modeling and MBS modeling. Both simulation methods are used to aid engineers and researchers in investigating and analyzing mechanical and mechatronic systems in various fields such as the car, railway, engine, aerospace industries, and medical applications. The difference between the FE modeling and MBS modeling lies in the basic model structure, and thus in the field of application. For analyzing highly sophisticated problems, the FE modeling is the appropriate modeling method. Within this mathematical method, based on the numerical solution of partial differential equations, the system is divided into a finite number of simple geometric elements, the finite elements [12]. An FE model is composed of geometric elements starting with points in space, which are linked to each other by so-called edges. Three points define a triangular plane. The corners are called vertices. Connected triangles result in faces which have a contour defined by a sequence of vertices, which is called a polygon. For visualization purposes, the faces can be colored and

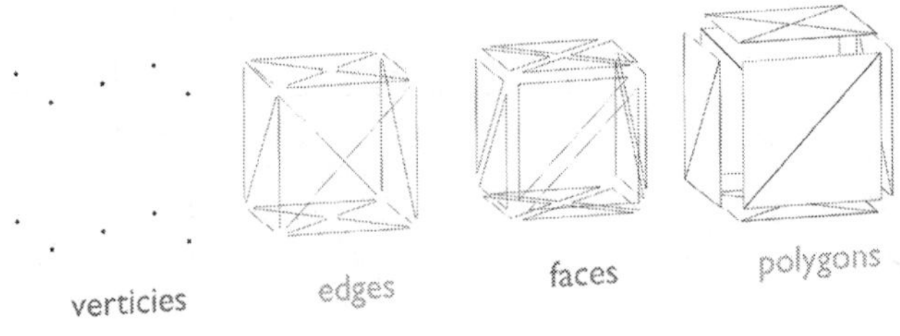


**Figure 1.** Different elements of polygon mesh modeling.

textured. This information is attached to the vertices, as it is common in computer graphics (**Figure 1**).

For each junction of elements, the so-called nodes, boundary, and transition conditions are defined in accordance with a specific material law [13]. In this way, highly detailed analyses of material properties can be carried out by an FE model. However, FE modeling requires a relatively long computational time. According to Berkley [14], the model's accuracy increases with the number of finite elements that are used to describe the geometry. But each additional element also means additional computational time. Solving such large numbers of FE equations leads to an enormously time-consuming calculation as in [15, 16]. The accuracy of the system and the expected computing time must therefore be carefully matched. A much faster calculation method is the MBS. The MBS describes the interaction of individual bodies with each other and with their environment, that is, the forces and torques acting on the bodies and between the bodies as well as the resulting movements [17].

The modeled bodies are assumed to be rigid and thus not deformable. The different bodies are linked through massless joints and kinematic constraints, which allow certain relative motions and restrict others [12]. Each body has a specific mass and a moment of inertia. This mass and inertia characteristics are associated with a single point, the center of gravity of the body. Thereby, every rigid body is provided with its own coordinate system (reference system). Based on this coordinate system, the exact location in space can be determined with respect to the inertial frame.

The degrees of freedom (DoF) of a rigid body are described by independent coordinates. A rigid body has a maximum of six DoF. It can move along the $x$-, $y$-, and $z$-axis (**Figure 2**, left), and rotate about these axes (**Figure 2**, right).

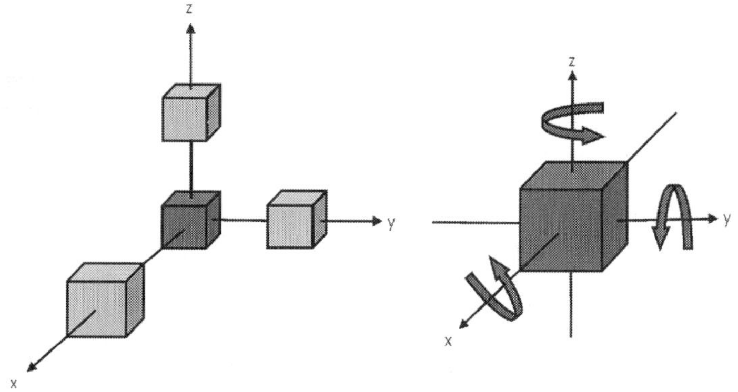


**Figure 2.** Degrees of freedom of a rigid body [18]: A rigid body is free to move along the $x$-, $y$-, and $z$-axis (left) and rotate about the $x$-, $y$-, and $z$-axis (right).

Possible translations and rotations relative to the inertial system can be realized through the implementation of appropriate joint types. If a model is composed of two or more rigid bodies, they are connected by a massless joint. The joints provide certain DoF. Depending on the definition of joint type, the joint

1. allows bodies or a body and a reference frame to be connected to each other with no DoF,
2. provides free movement to the body, with six DoF,
3. applies kinematic excitations to a body, as a rheonomic joint.

Furthermore, it is possible that forces and torques can be transferred between two body markers, which are generally located on different bodies, by a so-called force element. The type of interaction depends on the implemented force law. According to [19], the DoF of a model are determined by a number of independent state variables, which characterize the movement of the body. Furthermore, the movement of the MBS system depends on the inertial properties of its bodies, masses, inertia tensors, and its centers of gravity. The kinematics of the model is defined by a system of coupled differential equations. These equations of motion give the relation between motion and forces. For this reason, they can be solved in two ways: the forward or direct dynamics and the inverse dynamics. In the case of forward dynamics, the movement is determined by known internal forces or torques, whereas the reconstruction of the internal forces or torques from movements and external forces, like the gravity, is called inverse dynamics [20].

It should be noted that the presented modeling styles MBS and FE can be used independently of each other, but can also be combined with each other.

## 3. MBS lumbar spine models

The aim of our biomechanical computer modeling is to consider the characteristics of a musculoskeletal system through the use of knowledge from the fields of mechanics, anatomy, and physiology in the model in an appropriate manner, in order to obtain as accurately as possible a realistic simulation of the biomechanical behavior of the system. In the following, various application examples of a lumbar spine model that takes all spinal structures with their specific material properties into account are presented.

### 3.1. Structure of the spine model

The MBS models of the lumbar spine consist of vertebrae L1–L5, os sacrum and os ilium. These bony parts are connected by joints with appropriate DoF and ligament structures, which are attached to characteristic points of the skeletal parts. The facet joints are realized as three-dimensional (3D) contact areas, so that the acting contact forces avoid the penetration of two corresponding joint surfaces. All the individual structures are modeled with specific material properties in order to simulate their realistic mechanical behavior.

### 3.2. Surface generation

The 3D surface models of the vertebral bodies are based on computed tomography (CT) data sets of artificial vertebrae of Europeans. These data sets are generated through the use of segmentation and visualization plugins to visualize the data sets and make them available for simulation as Computer Aided Design (CAD) data sets (**Figure 3**) [21, 22].

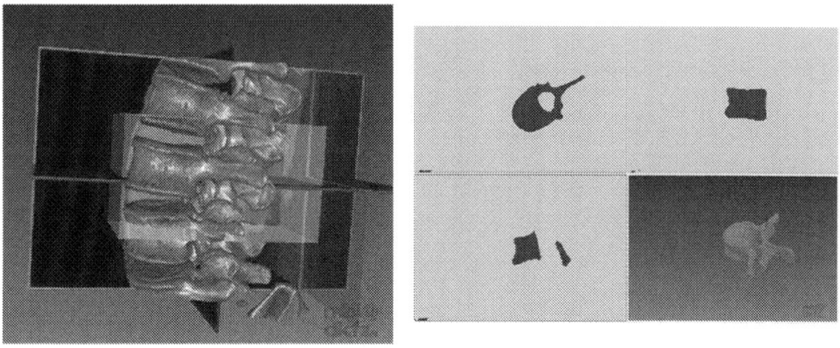

**Figure 3.** Surface generation through segmentation (left) and visualization (right) plugins [29].

### 3.3. Modeling of the biomechanical behavior of the spinal structures

The surface models are extended to biomechanical models by adding specific biomechanical properties to all spinal structures. The biomechanical property of the translational movement of the intervertebral discs is described by a force law, which is composed of a geometry-based stiffness term and a damping term [18, 23]. Most movements of the intervertebral discs do not consist of purely translational movements but also of intervertebral rotations. If the disc is deflected from its initial position, a deflection-dependent reaction torque will be developed [24].

As already said, in the model also the anterior and posterior longitudinal ligament (ALL/PLL), the ligamentum flavum (LF), the capsular ligament (CL), the interspinous ligament (ISL), the supraspinous ligament (SSL) as well as the intertransverse ligament (ITL) are implemented. Because a ligament can be defined only between two points, broad ligament structures are realized by a bundle of several fibers. The biomechanical properties of the ligaments are represented by characteristic curves of appropriate literature [25].

In the following models, the facet joints are simulated by a 3D contact surface whose dimensions and orientation are directed to the inclinations of the facet joints of the surface model. In this way, the modeling considers the different individual dimensions and specific orientations of the facet joints in all lumbar levels. Is exclusively a detailed analysis of the load behavior of the facet joints in focus, the facet surfaces are simulated by a 3D layer of cartilage (see Section 4). It should be noted that a detailed modeling of the facet surfaces is accompanied by a large increase of computation time. Therefore, prior to the model building a specific question should be defined, in order to decide whether such a detailed facet joint modeling is needed.

A further important structure to stabilize the human body in upright position is the musculature. According to [7], the four muscle groups, left and right musculus erector spinae and left and right rectus abdominis muscle, are modeled. The force representing the musculus erector spinae is varied so, that additional torque on the upper endplate of the vertebra L1 is no longer necessary to maintain the lumbar spine in a state of equilibrium. The model parameters used for muscles are taken from [7, 26]. These muscular structures are implemented at the moment just in the models of Chapter 4.1. A comparison of the different spine models with the corresponding muscle models is performed (see Section 4).

### 3.4. Validation and sensitivity analysis of the model

For the validation process, there is the difficulty of developing a suitable method, which confirms the accuracy of the modeling. An established method compares the simulation results with results from accepted publications. But it has to be mentioned that not all parameters which may have a significant influence on the result are always published. If such a factual circumstance is known, which is at the same time the model limitation, this has to be considered in the discussion of the model validity.

The model validation was performed by comparing the simulation results with FE results and in-vivo data as found in references [7, 27–29]. A detailed presentation of the validation is to be taken from reference [24]. Another difficulty lies in the selection of suitable input parameters from the literature. The values of these parameters differ significantly in some cases [30]. The validation and modeling cannot be seen as complete, and are successively continued to develop MBS models that get closer to the reality.

## 4. Practical application examples of simulation

To gain an insight into the practical applications of computer modeling in the field of biomechanical modeling of human structures, selected examples of different spinal simulation cases are shown below. In the first examples, the effects of different spinal alignments and obesity in adults and children on the lumbar spine are discussed. Subsequently practical examples of possible use of computer models in medicine will be introduced.

### 4.1. Effects of different spine alignments in the standing position

Due to different physical constitution and daily physical stress, an individual characteristic alignment of the spine is developed in the course of life. Therefore, the double-S shape of the human spine is subject to a wide range of variations [31–34]. To investigate the effects of such different spinal curvatures on the intradiscal pressure, five models of the lumbar spine with different lordosis angles are created (**Figure 4**). In this work, the lordosis angle is defined by the line through the upper endplate of L1 and the endplate of os sacrum.

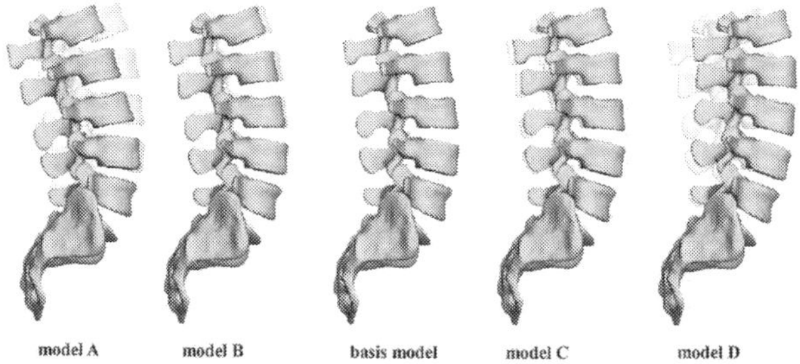


**Figure 4.** MBS lumbar spine models with different alignments: The model located in the middle has to be understood as a basic model concerning the anthropometrical and biomechanical properties for the further models A, B, C, and D. The basic model has a lumbar angle of 60°, model A of 64°, model B of 61°, model C of 59°, and model D 56°. It should be noted that the proportions in this figure should be understood as an approximation to the real model dimensions. Therefore, deviations can occur from the model.

Upright standing of a normal-weight person is chosen as simulation case because it represents the natural load case. The models are applied with the weight of the upper body. The force application point is located in the center of gravity. This gravitational force causes a deformation of the intervertebral discs, and a corresponding reaction force in the intervertebral discs is built. Therefore, the average intervertebral disc force, calculated from the different values of corresponding functional spinal units (FSUs) of the five models, increases from the lowest FSU to the uppermost FSU. In this context, the term FSU is understood as the smallest physiological motion unit consisting of two adjacent vertebrae, the corresponding intervertebral disc and all adjoining ligament [25].

**Figure 5** shows the intradiscal pressure of all functional spine units of the different aligned models in comparison. Because of the different spine alignments, it could be assumed that also the intradiscal pressures of the various models should greatly differ from each other. But this

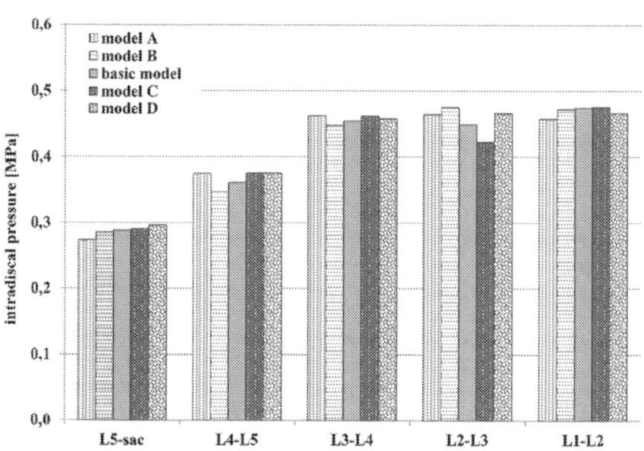


**Figure 5.** Interdiscal pressure of the differed aligned lumbar spinal models.

assumption is not immediately evident from **Figure 5**. However, the percentage difference of the maximum and minimum intradiscal pressure value of an FSU is determined, and the percentage difference of the FSUs L5-Sac and L4-L5 is 8% and of the FSU L2-L3 even 13%. For the intervertebral discs, the resulting percentages of L3-L4 and L1-L2 are 3% and 5% respectively.

To sum up, it can be stated that the individual spinal alignment has an impact on the load distribution of the intervertebral disc.

### 4.2. Effects of overweight on the spinal biomechanics

The WHO called being overweight and obesity the leading chronic health problems [35]. In the world more than 1.9 billion adults, 18 years and older, were overweight in 2014 and of these over 600 million were obese [36]. Overweight and obesity are contributing factors for many ailments and can lead to the development of chronic diseases, like diabetes, cardiovascular disease, coronary heart disease, or osteoarthritis [37–39]. While there are a large number of studies on the effects of these factors on the cardiovascular system and the psyche of the concerned person [40, 41], the potential consequences of orthopedic damage, particularly of the spine, associated with obesity are hardly known yet. In [3–5], a direct correlation between back pain and obesity is described. The exact load changes within the various spinal structures have not been sufficiently explored yet. With the help of computer modeling, the effects of obesity on the kinematics and kinetics of various spine structures can be analyzed. In the following the potential effects of obesity of an adult and an adolescent human are illustrated by specific MBS models exemplary.

Example 1: Simulation of the effects on the spinal structures of body weight of a normal-weight and an overweight adult male

The modeling was carried out in three steps: step 1 is the creation of an MBS model of the lumbar spine, step 2 the creation of a suitable surface models of the two weight classes, including the determination of their anthropometric characteristics, and step 3 the fusion of the MBS lumbar spine model with the surface model [42]. In this example, the force application point is also located in the center of gravity. Taking into account the body weight, body height (1.85 m), sex (male), age (37), and the original two surface models, a normal-weight man (75 kg) and an obese man (127 kg, grade II) are created with the help of an open-source software for the creation of human 3D surfaces. By means of the mass-distribution model of Zatsiorskj [43], the mass distribution of the individual body segments is determined. All other model parameters are identical in both models. By fusing the surface models with the detailed biomechanical model of the lumbar spine, two new simulation models are built up, so that the effects of a normal-weight and obese man on the spinal structures can be analyzed.

Due to the body weight, the intervertebral discs are deformed. In the case of the normal-weight person, in general the intervertebral deformations in all FSUs are very small (**Figure 6**). The cranial located intervertebral discs are more deformed than the caudal intervertebral discs. Comparing the deformation values of the obese with those of normal weight, it can be seen that they are about 1.7 times greater. The validation of the deformation values is difficult, because we are not aware of studies, whose study design corresponds exactly to ours. Brinkmann investigated the fatigue fracture of human lumbar vertebra under cyclic axial compression and presented an example of force versus deformation curve of a specimen with material properties characterized as "tough" [44]. The force versus deformation curve indicates that a force of 500 N causes a deformation of about 0.025 cm and a force of 750 N a deformation of 0.044 cm. Because the simulated acting weight force of the upper body segments is in the case of normal body weight approximately 460 N, and in the case of overweight approximately 780 N and the deformations are in the range of 0.025 cm–0.04 cm (normal weight) and between 0.042 cm and 0.068 cm (obese), it is seen that the magnitude of this values corresponds to those of Brinkmann.

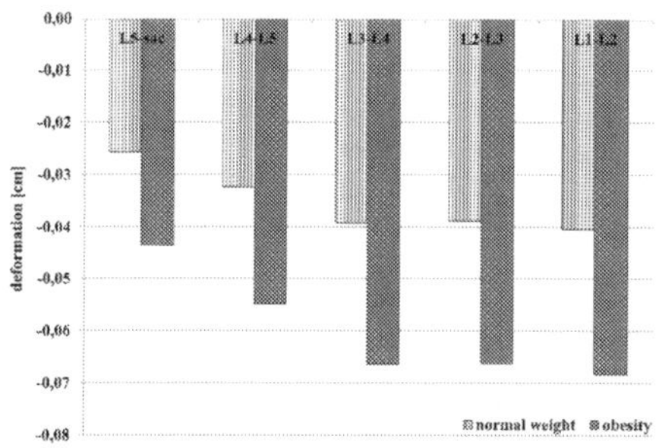


**Figure 6.** Deformations of the intervertebral discs.

Each intervertebral disc develops a disc force, which depends on the deformation and deformation velocity of the corresponding FSU. **Figure 7** shows the force component acting

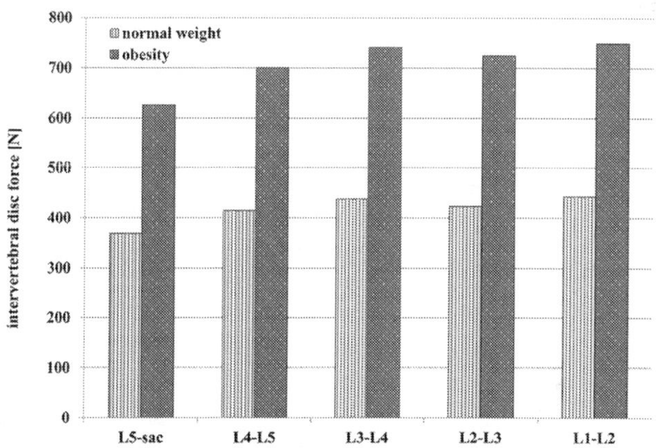


**Figure 7.** Intervertebral disc force of the different FSUs.

perpendicular to the disc. It can be clearly seen that the intervertebral discs of the obese are much more stressed than those of normal weight. The intervertebral disc force of the obese is, as well as in the above-discussed case of deformation, 1.7 times higher than the intervertebral disc force of the normal weighted. It could therefore be concluded that the deformation value, as opposed to the deformation velocity (see Section 3.3), has a great impact on the intervertebral disc force.

**Figure 8** shows the intersegmental rotations of the intervertebral discs. Whereas all intervertebral discs of the obese person perform flexions, the intervertebral discs of the normal-weight person are deflected in different directions. The lowest two intervertebral discs of normal-weight person perform flexion. The FSU L4-L3 and L2-L1 rotate backwards and the uppermost FSU L2-L1 rotates forward. Particularly evident is the high rotation values of the obese person. The FSU L1-L2 performs with about 17°, the largest rotational movement. In the literature [45, 46], the maximum range of motion (RoM) of FSU L1-L2 is specified by values between 2 and 13°. Consequently, our simulation values differ from these values. But the difference is relativized by the therein given standard deviations of about 2.5°. Further, it has to be analyzed whether the model of the obese person sufficiently reflects the reality, because identical biomechanical parameters are used in both simulation models. It is necessary to investigate in further work whether the biomechanical properties of the spinal structures are adapted in reality to the body weight, in order to avoid such rotations and prevent overloading or degenerative damage. Moreover, in this model, the stabilizing muscles are not considered, which could prevent such rotation.

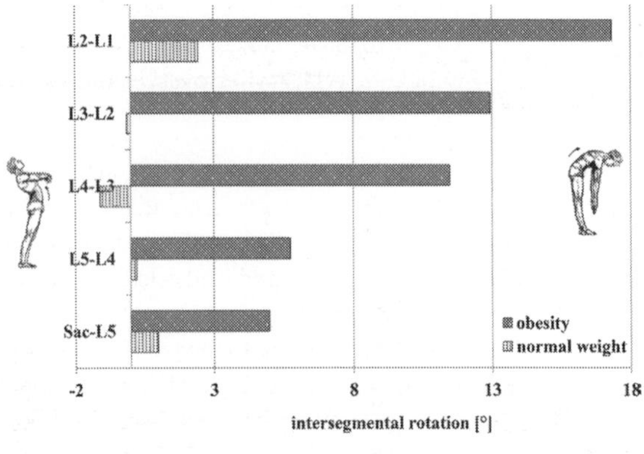


**Figure 8.** Intervertebral rotations of the different FSUs: Positive rotation angles represent flexion and negative rotation angles extension movements.

The movements of the FSUs can affect the biomechanical behavior of posterior located facet joints (**Figure 9**). It is striking that the loads of the FSU L1-L2 respectively L2-L3 are not loaded. Further it can be seen, that in the case of obesity the loads decrease to cranial. A possible reason may be, in this section, the pure ventral directed rotations. The two corresponding joint surfaces of the facets are distracted, and thus no contact force is build. To achieve a complete clarification of this, a model specification in the form of a sophisticated 3D facet joints modeling is required (see Section 5).

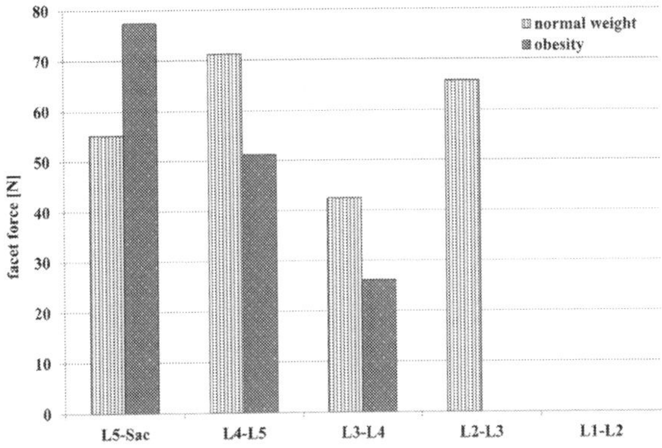


**Figure 9.** Contact forces of the facet joints.

Example 2: Simulation of the effects on the spinal structures of body weight of a normal-weight, an overweight, and an obese child

More than 42 million children under the age of five were overweight in 2013 worldwide [35]. According to Deckelbaum [47], not only in the USA the number of overweight children and adolescents has doubled in the last two to three decades but also the similar doubling rates are being observed worldwide. Therefore, the WHO called overweight and obesity as the leading chronic health problem [35].

Three MBS models of the child's lumbar spine were created to quantify the effects of normal-weight, overweight, and obese children to the kinematics and transmitted forces and torques of the different spinal structures. With the help of these 3D models, dynamic movements and static situations can be simulated. For simulation and load calculation of the effects of different weight classes, the masses of the body segments are adapted to these weight classes [48]. Therefore, the first lumbar vertebra L1 is loaded with the weight of the upper body segments of a normal weight, an overweight, and an obese child in different simulations. The total mass fractions of the segment parts is $m_{\text{normal}} = 22.91$ kg for normal-weight child, $m_{\text{overweight}} = 27.73$ kg for overweight child, and $m_{\text{obese}} = 32.56$ kg for obese child. In the case of overweight and obesity, the intervertebral discs are more heavily loaded in comparison to the normal-weight child. In both cases, the intervertebral discs of the FSU L4-L5 are most loaded (**Figure 10**). The slightest load undergoes the FSU L1-L2. The increase in body weight has a direct influence on the loading structure of the intervertebral discs. If the normal-weight child would become overweight, the loads of the intervertebral discs would rise by an average of 1.5 times. In the case of obesity, the intervertebral discs are more than 2.3 times higher loaded.

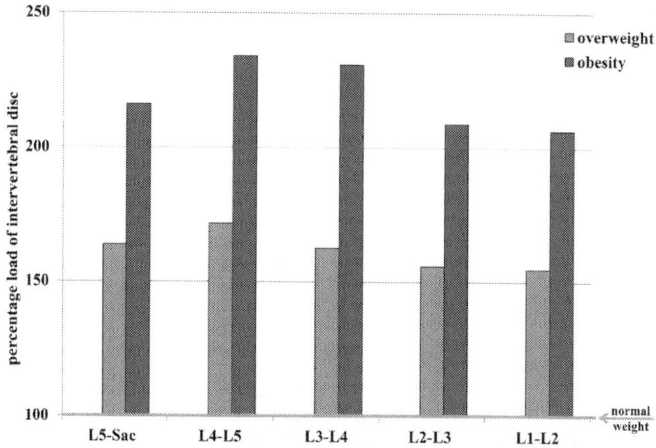


**Figure 10.** Percentage load of the intervertebral disc.

Through the increased body weight, the intervertebral discs perform pure flexion (**Figure 11**). Here, the amount of flexion of the obese child is mostly more than doubled compared with the movement of the normal-weight child. Particularly obvious is the difference in the FSU L3-L4. In the case of obesity, this FSU is deflected more than 3.5 times larger from its initial position (normal weight).

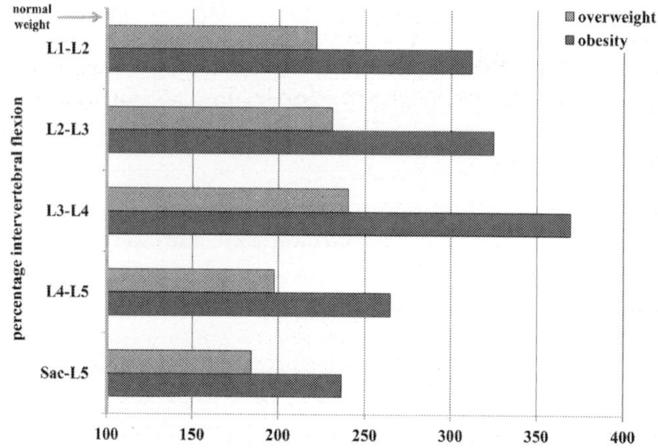


**Figure 11.** Percentage intersegmental rotation.

Through the forward rotations of the intervertebral discs, the approach and origin points of the posterior ligaments move away from each other. As a result, the corresponding ligaments are stretched and develop in an opposite direction acting as reaction force (**Figure 12**). In the case of an obese child, the posterior ligaments are 2 to 2.5 times more loaded than under normal body weight. Under obesity, a particularly extreme ligament load occurs in the FSU L3-L4. This more than 4 times larger load may result from the above-described extensive intersegmental rotations in these FSU.

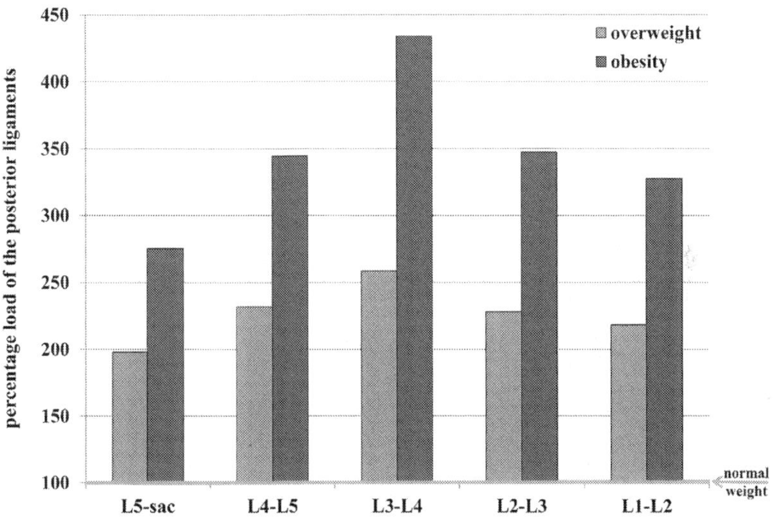


**Figure 12.** Percentage load of the posterior ligaments.

It seems to be evident that by the increase of body weight, the loads of the internal structures rise to the same extent. This correlation, which can be predicted even before the simulation, was confirmed by the simplest load case, the upright standing. Further investigations, such as the analysis of load distribution in different structures of an overweight or obese child during everyday activities or during highly dynamic movements, like they occur in sports, can give additional insights into the effects of obesity on the musculoskeletal system.

### 4.3. Application possibilities of biomechanical computer models in medicine

Because the MBS features very short computation times and surgical planning is increasingly computer-based, preoperative simulations can be used to predict the effects of different surgical methods and to identify the best possible surgical option. Furthermore, in future a transfer of topographic and kinematic simulation data of implants in 3D planning and navigation procedures is conceivable. In this process, coordinates of the implants from the computer model and the 3D model data of the spine may be transferred to the navigation system in the appropriate data format. It should be noted that the MBS modeling of the biomechanical properties of the intervertebral disc represents an initial approach. Therefore, the implementation of FE parts is indispensable to simulate patient-specific biomechanical properties.

To demonstrate the medical application possibilities of the simulation, the effect of a spinal fusion under different load cases is exemplified by an appropriate computer model (**Figure 13**). For that the mechanical properties of the MBS model were adjusted, so that no residual movement in FSU L4-L5 is possible. Thus, two models of the lumbar spine were created [49]. As in previous models, the upright position is used as the load case in this simulation, and also an external load of 600 N and 700 N is applied at the center of the vertebral endplate of L1.

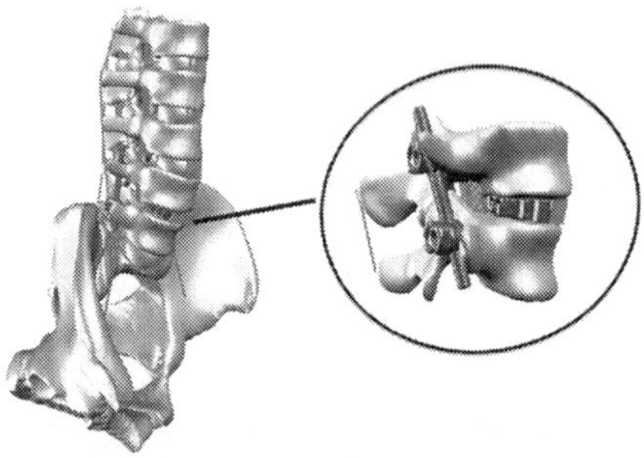

**Figure 13.** Detailed MBS lumbar spine model with fused FSU L4-L5.

Considering only the disc force of the model without fused FSU L5-L4, it can be seen that the pressures in all FSUs increase with higher external force (**Figure 14**). Comparing the pressure of the intervertebral discs of both models, the disc loads of the FSU L1-L2 are almost the same. A deviation results for the other functional units. The pressure in the FSU's L5-Sac to L2-L3, of the model with fused FSU L4-L5, is lower than without fusion.

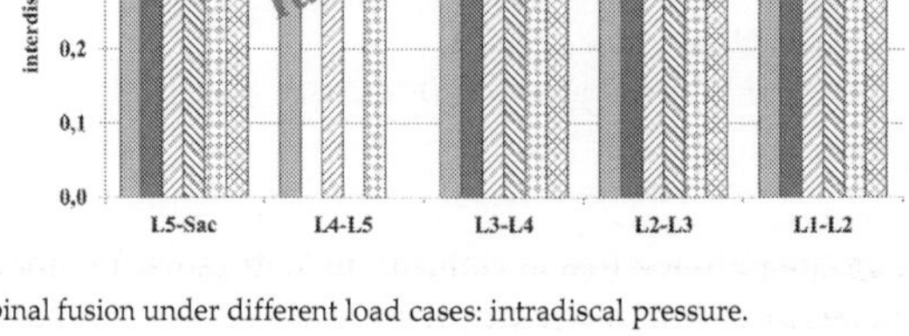


**Figure 14.** Effect of a spinal fusion under different load cases: intradiscal pressure.

In this case, a spinal fusion affects especially the loads of the facet joints. **Figure 15** clearly shows that after fusion, the forces in the facet joints are particularly higher in the upper FSU. Through such an increased load situation degenerative changes can be caused in the facet joints in long term.

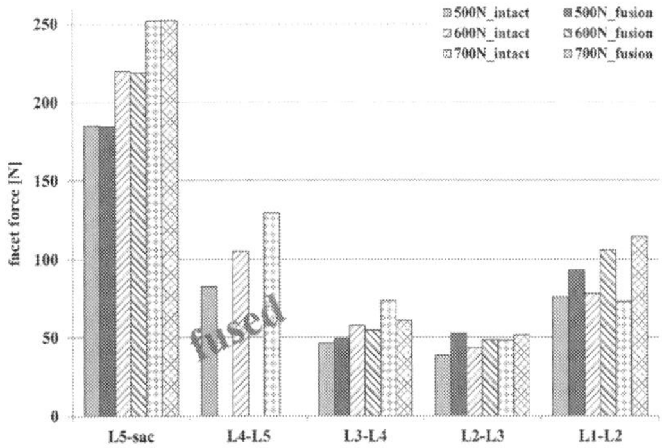


**Figure 15.** Effect of a spinal fusion on the facet loads.

Comparing the intersegmental rotation of the discs (**Figure 16**) with and without fused L4-L5 disc, it can be seen that the discs of the fused model perform less deflection in the FSUs L5-Sac to L2-L3. The lower lumbar spine thus has lower mobility than in the non-fused state. This means that after an intervertebral disc stiffening, the lower lumbar spine would have a lower mobility than in a non-fused state.

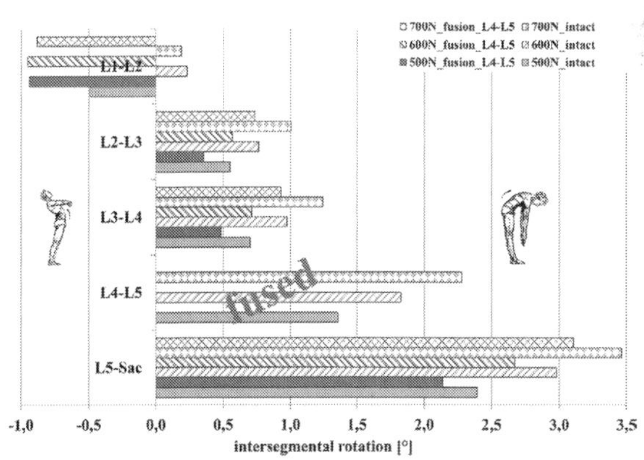


**Figure 16.** Effect of a spinal fusion on the intersegmental rotation.

In summary, it can be stated that a fusion can lead to load redistribution. In this simulation case, especially the posterior structures that are located above the fused FSUs are stressed more than the ventrally located structures. A further example in the field of medicine is studying the effects of different body weights on selected surgical procedures.

## 5. Meaningfulness and limitation of MBS modeling

It is clearly pointed out that modeling has to be understood as an approximation to the reality. In near future, it will probably not be possible that all influencing factors can be simulated completely as in reality. Often, input parameters based on literature data representing the average of a specific cohort. Because each person has a very specific anthropometric and morphological characteristic, the standard deviations of such investigations may be relatively large. For example, the standard deviation for geometric parameters that describe the sagittal alignment of the spine is partially enormous. The deviation from average of the pelvic incidence is partly more than 20% [31], of the pelvic tilt 53% [32] respectively 70% [33], and of the total lumbosacral lordosis 19% [34], etc. But based on sensitivity analysis, the exact influence of individual parameters can be determined. However, because of the complexity of the models, it is very important to know the exact configuration of the model and the limitations of its input parameters. Therefore, the modeling and the validation process should to be understood as an evolving process and will be advanced in future research.

Opportunities for improvement and expansion of the different model components will be summarized in the following:

In the presented models, the biomechanics of the intervertebral disc is defined by a force law, which can be understood as an initial approach. To precise the biomechanical properties of the annulus fibrosis and nucleus pulposus, a 3D hybrid model consisting of MBS and FE units will be built. The aim is to analyze whether the implementation of FE-disc features contributes to a significant gain of knowledge concerning load distribution of the intervertebral discs and the adjacent spinal structures.

Currently, a highly accurate modeled individual cartilaginous contact layer for all facet joints is in development. These individually formed layers of cartilage (**Figure 17**) allow us to do a 3D calculation of the resulting forces.

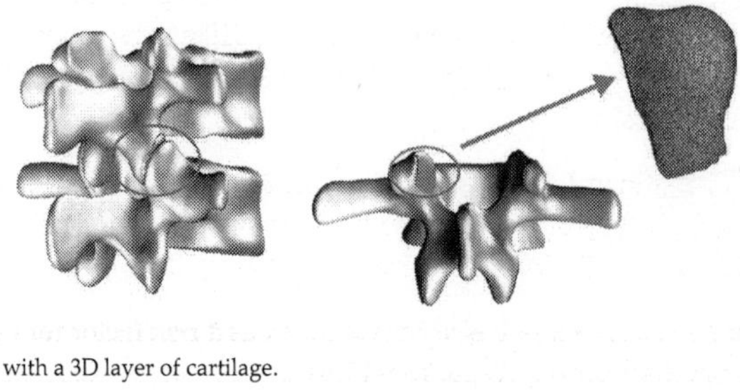

**Figure 17.** Facet joints with a 3D layer of cartilage.

An extremely important spinal structure that describes the dynamics of the musculoskeletal system is the spinal musculature. Up to now, the muscle groups of the erector spinae and the rectus abdominis implemented in the models are very rudimentary. In focus of current work are corresponding muscle models that describe the dynamics of muscle contraction in an appropriate manner [50, 51].

The aim of our research is the creation of patient-specific 3D hybrid computer models of the human spine for preoperative planning in neurosurgical and orthopedic stabilizing spinal operations. Known and alternative surgical procedures are simulated and a comparison of these possible surgical procedures is presented to determine the biomechanical effects. The simulation is realized highly efficient with short computation times, which will allow a later use in real systems. That means, the 3D coordinates of the optimized implant position can be exported out of the individual models as data sets and can be transferred, to position the implants very accurately, to a navigation system.

## Author details

Bauer Sabine

Address all correspondence to: bauer@uni-koblenz.de

MTI Mittelrhein, Institute for Medical Engineering and Information Processing, University Koblenz-Landau, Campus Koblenz, Germany

## References

[1] World Health Organization Scientific Group on the Burden of Musculoskeletal Conditions at the Start of the New Millennium: The burden of musculoskeletal conditions at the start of the new millennium. WHO Technical Report. Series 919, 2003: 1–218. //apps.who.int/iris/handle/10665/42721

[2] Hoy D, March L, Brooks P, Blyth F, Woolf A, Bain C, Williams G, Smith E, Vos T, Barendregt J, Murray C, Burstein R, Buchbinder R: The global burden of low back pain: Estimates from the Global Burden of Disease 2010 study. Annals of the Rheumatic Diseases, 2014. http://ard.bmj.com/content/early/2014/02/14/annrheumdis-2013-204428.abstract

[3] Mikkonen P, Laitinen J, Remes J, Tammelin T, Taimela S, Kaikkonen K, Zitting P, Korpelainen R, Karppinen J: Association between overweight and low back pain. Spine. 38 (12), 2013: 1026–1033. DOI 10.1093/aje/kwp356

[4] Heuch I, Hagen K, Zwart J-A: Body mass index as a risk factor for developing chronic low back pain. Spine. 38 (2), 2013: 133–139. DOI 10.1097/BRS.0b013e3182647af2

[5] Kaila-Kangas L, Leino-Arjas P, Riihimäki H, Luukkonen R, Kirjonen J: Smoking and overweight as predictors of hospitalization for back disorders. Spine. 28 (16), 2003: 1860–1868. DOI 10.1097/01.BRS.0000083284.47176.80

[6] Mayer C, Siems W. 100 Pathologies in physiotherapy. 1st ed. Springer: Berlin Heidelberg; 2011. 244 p. DOI 10.1007/978-3-642-17267-0

[7] Rohlmann A, Zander T, Rao M, Bergmann G: Applying a follower load delivers realistic results for simulating standing. Journal of Biomechanics. 42 (10), 2009: 1520–1526. DOI 10.1016/j.jbiomech.2009.03.048

[8] Rohlmann A, Nabil Boustani H, Bergmann G, Zander T: Effect of a pedicle-screw-based motion preservation system on lumbar spine biomechanics: A probabilistic finite element study with subsequent sensitivity analysis. Journal of Biomechanics. 43 (15), 2010: 2963–2969. DOI 10.1016/j.jbiomech.2010.07.018

[9] Rohlmann A, Zander T, Schmidt H, Wilke H-J, Bergmann G: Analysis of the influence of disc degeneration on the mechanical behaviour of a lumbar motion segment using the finite element method. Journal of Biomechanics. 39 (13), 2006: 2484–2490. DOI 10.1016/j.jbiomech.2005.07.026

[10] Schmidt H, Heuer F, Simon U, Kettler A, Rohlmann A, Claes L, Wilke H-J: Application of a new calibration method for a three-dimensional finite element model of a human lumbar annulus fibrosus. Clinical Biomechanics. 21 (4), 2006: 337–344. DOI 10.1016/j.clinbiomech.2005.12.001

[11] Schmidt H, Heuer F, Claes L, Wilke H-J: The relation between the instantaneous center of rotation and facet joint forces—A finite element analysis. Clinical Biomechanics. 23 (3), 2008: 270–278. DOI 10.1016/j.clinbiomech.2007.10.001

[12] Schwertassek R, Wallrapp O: Dynamics of flexible multibody systems. Methods of Mechanics for computer-aided design and analysis of mechatronic systems. Wiesbaden: Vieweg+Teubner; 1999. 476 p. DOI 10.1007/978-3-322-93975-3

[13] Grote K-H, Feldhusen J. editors. Dubbel - Paperback for engineering. 24th. ed. Berlin, Heidelberg, New York: Springer; 2014. 2072 p. DOI 10.1007/978-3-642-38891-0

[14] Berkley J, Turkiyyah G, Berg D, Ganter M, Weghorst S: Real-time finite element modeling for surgery simulation: An application to virtual suturing. IEEE Transactions on Visualization and Computer Graphics. 10 (3), 2004: 314–325. DOI 10.1109/TVCG.2004.1272730

[15] Chomphan S, Leekitwattana M: A reduced finite element model for analyzing the transverse shear stiffness of truss-like core sandwich beam. Journal of Computer Science. 7 (10), 2011: 1474–1477. DOI 10.3844/jcssp.2011.1474.1477

[16] Zhang X, Kneupner K, Kuhlenkötter B: A new force distribution calculation model for high quality production processes. The International Journal of Advanced Manufacturing Technology. 27 (7–8), 2006: 726–732. DOI 10.1007/s00170-004-2229-x

[17] Lehner S: Development and validation of biomechanical computer models and their use in sports science [thesis]. Koblenz: University Koblenz-Landau; 2007.

[18] Juchem S: Development of a computer model of the lumbar spine for the determination of mechanical loads [thesis]. Koblenz: University Koblenz-Landau; 2009.

[19] SIMPACK 9.9 Documentation. Copyright by SIMPACK GmbH ©2001–2015.

[20] Otten E: Inverse and forward dynamics: Models of multi-body systems. Philosophical Transactions of the Royal Society of London B: Biological Sciences. 358 (1437), 2003: 1493. http://rstb.royalsocietypublishing.org/content/358/1437/1493, isbn:0962–8436

[21] Reimche P: Segmentation of computer tomography data of the spine [thesis]. Koblenz: University Koblenz-Landau; 2010.

[22] Nowack S: Visualization of the spine using segmented computer tomography data for further use in SIMPACK [thesis]. Koblenz: University Koblenz-Landau; 2010.

[23] Gruber K, Juchem S: Realisation of physical properties in a computer model of the lumbar spine. 16th Congress of the European Society of Biomechanics, Luzern, Schweiz. Journal of Biomechanics. 41 (1), 2008: 358.

[24] Bauer S, Buchholz U. Biomechanical effects of spinal fusion to adjacent vertebral segments. In: UKSim-AMSS Seventh European Modelling Symposium on Computer Modelling and Simulation, 20–22 Nov. 2013; Manchester: IEEE Computer Society; pp. 158–163.

[25] White A, Panjabi M: Clinical biomechanics of the spine. Lippincott; 1990.

[26] Rohlmann A, Bauer L, Zander T, Bergmann G, Wilke H-J: Determination of trunk muscle forces for flexion and extension by using a validated finite element model of the lumbar spine and measured in vivo data. Journal of Biomechanics. 39 (6), 2006: 981–989. DOI 10.1016/j.jbiomech.2005.02.019

[27] Wilke H-J, Neef P, Caimi M, Hoogland T, Claes L: New in vivo measurement of pressure in the intervertebral disc in daily life. Spine. 24 (8), 1999: 755–762. DOI 10.1097/00007632-199904150-00005

[28] Sato K, Kikuchi S, Yonezawa T: In vivo intradiscal pressure measurement in healthy individuals and in patients with ongoing back problems. Spine. 24 (23), 1999: 2468–2474. DOI 10.1097/00007632-199912010-00008

[29] Wood K, Kos P, Schendel M, Persson K: Effects of position on the sagittal-plane profile of the thoracolumbar spine. Journal of Spinal Disorders. 9 (2), 1996: 165–169. DOI 10.1186/1749-799X-9-11

[30] Bauer S, Paulus D: How does the intervertebral discs parameter variation affect the biomechanical behavior of spinal structures? Results of a detailed study of multibody simulation sensitivity. International Journal of Engineering and Applied Sciences. 2 (9), 2015: 37–42. DOI 10.1515/cdbme-2015-0092

[31] Roussouly P, Gollogly S, Berthonnaud E, Dimnet J: Classification of the normal variation in the sagittal alignment of the human lumbar spine and pelvis in the standing position. Spine. 30 (3), 2005: 346–353 DOI 10.1097/01.brs.0000152379.54463.65

[32] Boulay C, Tardieu C, Hecquet J, Benaim C, Mouilleseaux B, Marty B, Prat-Pradal D, Degaye J, Duval-Beaupère G, Pélissier J: Sagittal alignment of spine and pelvis regulated by pelvic incidence: Standard values and prediction of lordosis. European Spine Journal. 15 (4), 2006: 415–422. DOI 10.1007/s00586-005-0984-5

[33] Legaye J, Duval-Beaupère G, Hecquet J, Marty C: Pelvic incidence: A fundamental pelvic parameter for three-dimensional regulation of spinal sagittal curves. European Spine Journal. 7 (2), 1998: 99–103. DOI 10.1007/s005860050038

[34] Jackson R, Hales C: Congruent spinopelvic alignment on standing lateral radiographs of adult volunteers. Spine. 25 (21), 2000: 2808–2815. DOI 10.1097/00007632-200011010-00014

[35] World Health Organization Consultation on Obesity, editors. Obesity: Preventing and managing the global epidemic. Report of a WHO consultation. Geneva: World Health Organization; 2000. p. 252. DOI 10665/42330

[36] Obesity and Overweight. Fact sheet N°311 2015 [Internet]. Available from: http://www.who.int/mediacentre/factsheets/fs311/en [Accessed 2016-01-06].

[37] Ludwig D: The glycemic index—physiological mechanisms relating to obesity, diabetes, and cardiovascular disease. Journal of the American Medical Association. 287 (18), 2002: 2414–2423. DOI 10.1001/jama.287.18.2414

[38] Hauner H: Health risks of obesity and weight gain. Deutsches Ärzteblatt 93 (51–52), 1996: A-3405. Available from: http://www.aerzteblatt.de/int/article.asp?id=4496

[39] Kahn B, Flier J: Obesity and insulin resistance. The Journal of Clinical Investigation. 106 (4), 2000: 473–481. DOI 10.1172/JCI10842

[40] Atlantis E, Baker M: Obesity effects on depression: Systematic review of epidemiological studies. International Journal of Obesity. 32 (6), 2008: 881–891. DOI 10.1038/ijo.2008.54

[41] Goodman E, Whitaker R: A prospective study of the role of depression in the development and persistence of adolescent obesity. Pediatrics. 110 (3), 2002: 497–504. DOI 10.1542/peds.110.3.497

[42] Bauer S, Keller E, Paulus D. Back pain caused by obesity? Biomechanical MBS modeling of the load situation of the lumbar spine with different body weights. In: Bildverarbeitung für die Medizin 2015, Algorithmen Systeme Anwendungen, Proceedings Workshops 15–17 March 2015; Lübeck. Berlin, Heidelberg: Springer Vieweg, pp. 323–328.

[43] Zatsiorsky V, Ariun S, Selujanov V: Mass geometry of the human body. Theorie und Praxis Körperkultur. 31 (6), 1982: 416–423.

[44] Brinckmann P, Biggemann M, Hilweg D: Fatigue fracture of human lumbar vertebrae. Clinical Biomechanics. 3 (Supplement), 1988: S1–S23. Available from: http://www.sciencedirect.com/science/article/pii/S0268003388800019, ISBN: 0268–0033

[45] Alam W: Radiological evaluation of lumbar intervertebral instability. Indian Journal of Aerospace Medicine. 46 (2), 2002: 48–53. Available from: http://medind.nic.in/iab/t02/i2/iabt02i2c.shtml

[46] Cook D, Yeager M, Cheng B: Range of Motion of the intact lumbar segment: A multivariate study of 42 lumbar spines. International Journal of Spine Surgery. 9 (5), 2015: 1–8. DOI 10.14444/2005

[47] Deckelbaum R, Williams C: Childhood obesity: The health issue. Obesity Research. 9 (4), 2001: 239–243. DOI 10.1038/oby.2001.125

[48] Bauer S, Wasserhess C, Paulus D: Quantification of loads on the lumbar spine of children with different body weight—a comparative study with the help of computer modelling. In: Biomedical engineering, 2014. Berlin, Boston: Walter de Gruyter, 28 884–888. DOI 10.1515/bmt-2014-5012

[49] Bauer S, Paulus D: Analysis of the biomechanical effects of spinal fusion to adjacent vertebral segments of the lumbar spine using multi body simulation. International Journal of Simulation. 15 (2), 2014: 8–13. DOI 10.5013/IJSSST.a.15.02.01

[50] Rockenfeller R, Götz T: Optimal control of isometric muscle dynamic. Journal of Mathematical and Fundamental Sciences. 47 (1), 2015: 12–30.

[51] Rockenfeller R, Günther M, Schmitt S, Götz T: Comparative sensitivity analysis of muscle activation dynamics. Computational and Mathematical Methods in Medicine. 2015, 2015: 1℃16. Article ID 585409, http://dx.doi.org/10.1155/2015/585409 in press. Available from: http://www.hindawi.com/journals/cmmm/aip/585409

Chapter 3

# Simulation of Neural Behavior

Tatsuo Kitajima, Zonggang Feng and Azran Azhim

Additional information is available at the end of the chapter

http://dx.doi.org/10.5772/64028

**Abstract**

The brain is an organ that takes the central role in advanced information processing. There exist great many neurons in our brain, which build complicated neural networks. All information processing in the brain is accomplished by neural activity in the form of neural oscillations. In order to understand the mechanisms of information processing, it is necessary to clarify functions of neurons and neural networks. Although the current progress of experiment technology is remarkable, only experiments by themselves cannot uncover the behavior of only a single neuron. Computational neuroscience is a research field, which fills up the deficiency in experiments. By modeling the essential features of a neuron or a neural network, we can analyze their fundamental properties by computer simulation. In this chapter, one aspect of computational neuroscience is described. At the first, the cell membrane and a neuron can be modeled by using an RC circuit. Next, the Hodgkin-Huxley model is introduced, which has the function of generation of action potentials. Furthermore, many neurons show the subthreshold resonance phenomena, and the cell membrane is necessary to be modeled by an RLC circuit. Finally, some simulation results are shown, and properties of such neuronal behaviors are discussed.

**Keywords:** cell membrane, action potential, neural oscillation, subthreshold resonance phenomenon, RLC circuit

## 1. Introduction

Our brain is an extraordinary microsome and has been completely shrouded in mystery. However, its mystery has been just a little bit by bit solved owing to recent advances in experimental technologies and tremendous development of computers. Many people can simply say "brain," but it is a general term for a collection of six main regions, that is, cerebrum, diencephalon, midbrain, cerebellum, pons, and medulla oblongata. The brain is an organ that takes the central role in advanced information processing, such as visual, auditory, speech or language faculties, motion control, recognition, emotion, and so on. According to advances of experiment and computer technology, the research of brain science or neuroscience has been made not only in the fields of medicine, biology, biochemistry, pharmacology, and psychology but also in the field of engineering.

The present-day computers have outstanding processing capacity. For example, they can find the data that satisfy some requirements among huge quantities of data (database) or can calculate over five trillion figures of pi($\pi$). Therefore, many people are inclined to think that our brain will be able to be replaced by computer in near future. Surely, computers excel at processing of digitized data and processing by following a standard algorithm. However, it can hardly execute processing, such as recognition of ambiguity figures (such as illusionism) or inference based on imperfect information, which our brain can instantaneously carry out. Reason for this comes from differences in ways of information processing of the computer and our brain. The current computers, called von Neumann computer, are grounded in sequential processing by using central processing units (CPUs) and memory storages, while on the other hand, our brain bases on parallel and distributed processing through neural networks whose components are neurons.

There exist tens of billions of neurons in our brain, which build neural networks in complicated arrangement. All information processing in the brain is accomplished by neural activity in the form of neural oscillations that cause cortical oscillations (delta, theta, alpha, beta, or gamma oscillation). In order to clarify the mechanisms of advanced information processing in the brain, such as learning and memory, it is necessary to understand functions and features of neurons and neural networks. Although the current progress in experiment technology and measuring system is remarkable, only experiments by themselves cannot uncover the behavior of only a single neuron, because even a single neuron has complex biophysical characteristics and never stops growth. Computational neuroscience is a research field which fills up such a deficiency in experiments. By modeling the essential features of a neuron or a neural network at multiple spatial-temporal scales, we can capture and analyze the fundamental properties of a neuron or a neural network by computer simulation. Moreover, we can even offer some suggestions to experimental study by taking into account the probable results obtained from the simulation.

## 2. Neuron model with a low-pass filter property

### 2.1. Electrical circuit model of the cell membrane

Neurons play a key role in almost all brain functions. Fundamental function of neurons is to generate action potentials when they received sufficient stimuli from the environment. Once action potentials are generated, they are transmitted to other neurons so as to communicate information from one neuron to another. There exist many types of neurons in the brain, such as pyramidal neurons in the hippocampus and neocortex (**Figure 1(a)**), motor neurons in motor cortex (**Figure 1(b)**), or Purkinje cells in the cerebellum (**Figure 1(c)**) [1]. Although their shapes are different, they have basically the same structure. As shown in **Figure 2(a)**, a neuron is composed of three parts, that is, the soma (cell body) where action potentials are generated, the dendrite that receives inputs from other neurons, and the axon along which action potentials are transmitted to axon terminals. One thing especially worth mentioning, the dendrite of a neuron has hundreds to thousands of spines, on which axon terminals of other neurons connect. This junction is called a synapse, through which information are transmitted from one neuron to another (**Figure 2(b)**). Actually, there exist two kinds of synapses, one of which is an electric synapse and the other is a chemical synapse [1]. The former is a junction where neurons are directly contacted each other and information are electrically conducted from one neuron to another. This junction is also called a gap junction. On the other hand, the latter one is a junction with a cleft, called a synaptic cleft, into which neurochemical transmitters are released from the axon terminal and they bind to receptors on the spine head. Electrical synapses are found at the sites that require the fastest possible response, such as nociceptive reflex, whereas chemical synapses are found in almost all neurons of the brain. **Figure 2(b)** shows an example of a chemical synapse. Both synapses have a very important role in signal processing between neurons.

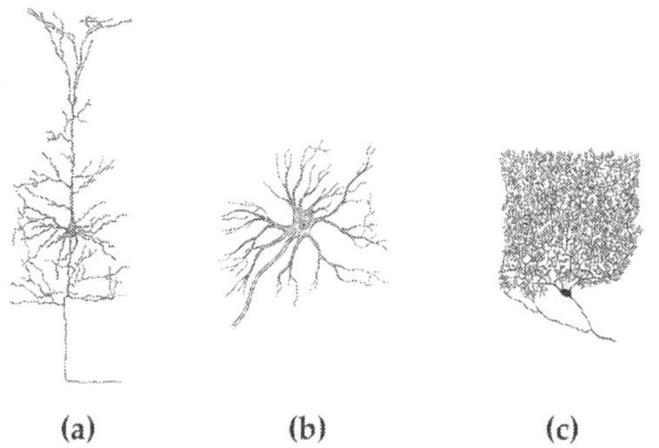


**Figure 1.** Various types of neurons. (a) Pyramidal neuron (cortex), (b) motor neuron (spinal cord),and (c) Purkinje cell (cerebellum).

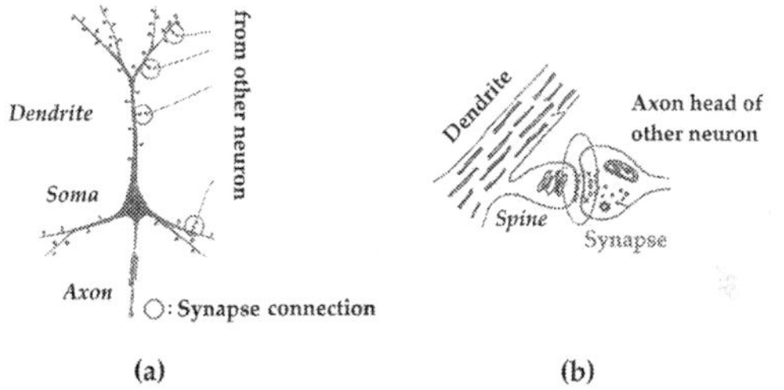


**Figure 2.** (a) Schematic neuron (Structure of neuron). (b) Synaptic connection at the synapse.

Surfaces of a neuron are covered with the cell membrane, which separates the interior of cell from the exterior environment. The cell membrane is composed of protein, lipid, and carbohydrate [1]. As shown in **Figure 3(a)**, it is composed of two layers of phospholipid molecules, each of which has a hydrophilic head (circle) and hydrophobic tail (two waved lined), and both hydrophobic tails face each other inside the cell membrane. This structure is called lipid bilayer. Furthermore, the concentration of the extracellular ions, such as $Na^+$, $Cl^-$, or $Ca^{2+}$, is higher than the intracellular one. Contrarily, the concentration of intracellular ion, such as $K^+$, is higher than the extracellular one. In addition, many types of ion channels (protein) are penetrating the cell membrane. Those ion channels are normally closed. If neurochemical transmitters released from the presynaptic axon terminal bind to receptors of the corresponding ion channels on the spine head, those ion channels are activated and open. Subsequently, specific ion flow occurs according to their ionic gradients. At the resting state, those channels are closed and no ionic flows occur except for small leakage.

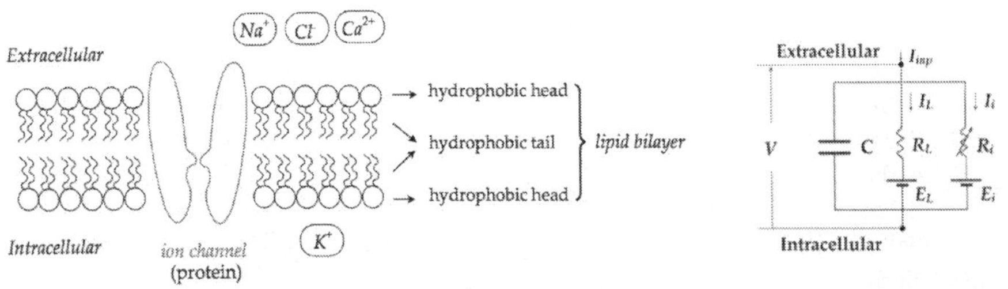


(a)

(b)

**Figure 3.** Cell membrane. (a) Cross section of a cell membrane lipid bilayer and (b) equivalent RC circuit model of cell membrane.

Based on the above properties, the cell membrane has the following electrical properties:

**a.** It is lipid bilayer, that is, it is composed of two parallel plates. Thus, the cell membrane has characteristics similar to "capacitance," $C$.

**b.** The difference between intracellular and extracellular ion concentrations corresponds to "power source," $E_i$ ($i = Na^+, K^+, Cl^-$ or $Ca^{2+}$).

**c.** The ionic flowability of opening ion channels is thought of as "resistance" $R_i$ or "conductance" $1/R_i$.

**d.** The corresponding flows of $Na^+$, $K^+$, $Cl^-$, or $Ca^{2+}$ through ion channels are "current," $I_{Na}$, $I_K$, $I_{Cl}$, or $I_{Ca}$.

With these points in mind, the cell membrane can be modeled by an equivalent RC circuit, which is shown in **Figure 3(b)**. Once an RC circuit is obtained, we can obtain its dynamics by using Ohm's law, Kirchhoff's law, or other knowledge of electrical circuit theory. From **Figure 3(b)**, the following equation is obtained:

$$C\frac{dV}{dt} = -\frac{1}{R_L}\cdot(V - E_L) - \frac{1}{R_i}\cdot(V - E_i) + I_{inp}, \tag{1}$$

where $V$ is the membrane potential of the cell membrane, $C$ is the membrane capacitance, $R_L$ is the leakage resistance, $E_L$ is the reversal potential, $R_i$ is the flowability of ion $i(i = Na^+, K^+, Cl^-$, or $Ca^{2+})$, $E_i$ is the corresponding ionic equilibrium potential, and $I_{inp}$ is the specific input current given to the cell membrane. As a neuron is covered with the cell membrane, a synapse or a soma can be also expressed by using an RC circuit. Accordingly, we can study the synaptic properties or neuronal characteristics by using computer simulations.

### 2.2. Generation of action potentials (Hodgkin-Huxley model)

In this section, we give one model that can generate an action potential, which is the basic function of a neuron. When a dendritic spine receives stimuli from an axon terminal of other neuron, the membrane potential of a spine head changes depending on that stimulus. Those potential changes are transmitted to the soma (strictly speaking, the axon hillock in the neighborhood of the soma) through dendrites and integrated there. If the accumulated potential of the soma exceeds the threshold, an action potential is generated. Generated action potentials are transmitted to axon terminals along the axon. Based on this knowledge, McCulloch and Pitts expressed a neuron as a product-sum threshold element in 1943 [2]. Their model is a formal neuron model, called McCulloch-Pitts model, and is shown in **Figure 4**.

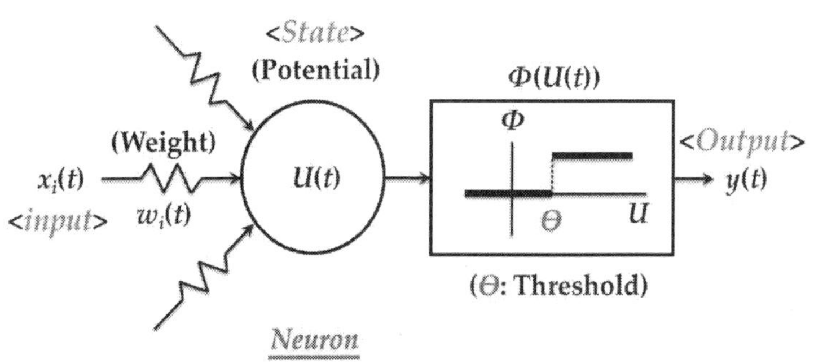


**Figure 4.** Formal neuron model (The McCulloch-Pitts model).

The McCulloch-Pitts model is expressed as follows:

$$u(t) = \sum_{i=1}^{N} w_i(t) \cdot x_i(t), \tag{2}$$

$$y(t) = \Phi(u(t)) = \begin{cases} 1 & : u(t) \geq \theta \\ 0 & : u(t) < \theta \end{cases}, \tag{3}$$

where $x_i(t)$ is an input from $i$th neuron, $w_i(t)$ is a weight from a neuron $i$, $u(t)$ is a state (potential) of a neuron, $y(t)$ is its output, and $\theta$ is a threshold. In this model, if a state $u(t)$ exceeds a threshold $\theta$, output 1 is send to other neurons. Notice that, however, McCulloch-Pitts model does not consider a refractory period, during which neurons cannot or find it hard to generate the next action potential.

As the McCulloch-Pitts model was a very easy model for engineers to understand the mechanism of generation of action potentials, many engineers have applied this model to study basic neuronal behaviors. The most prominent example is the application to the perceptron, which was known as one of the powerful tools for some kinds of pattern recognition problems. Although there exist many variations of the McCulloch-Pitts model, one of them uses a sigmoid function instead of a step function expressed by Eq. (3). This kind of model is applied to the back propagation algorithm and recently the deep learning method, because a sigmoid function is a differentiable function. However, the practical neurons are not so simple as the McCulloch-Pitts model and the back propagation algorithm. Therefore, more profound considerations were necessary to describe complicated neuronal behaviors.

In 1952, Hodgkin and Huxley developed one mathematical model that explains the generation of an action potential (impulse or spike) based on physiological experiments for a squid giant axon [3]. As described in the previous section, the extracellular concentration of $Na^+$ is higher than the intracellular one, and the intracellular concentration $K^+$ is higher than the extracellular one, and the cell membrane has both $Na^+$ permeable channel ($Na$ channel) and $K^+$ permeable channel ($K$ channel). Hodgkin and Huxley found that both $Na$ and $K$ channels are voltage-dependently activated, that is, the activation and inactivation of these channels are affected by the membrane potential of the cell membrane. They also elucidated that action potentials are generated by increased or decreased activation and inactivation of $Na$ channel and increased or decreased activation of $K$ channel. Based on the results of physiological experiments for a squid giant axon, they showed that an action potential is generated whenever the cell membrane is depolarized over the threshold. They proposed a schematic electrical circuit model that can explain the mechanism for generation of action potentials, called the Hodgkin-Huxley model (HH model).

http://dx.doi.org/10.5772/64028

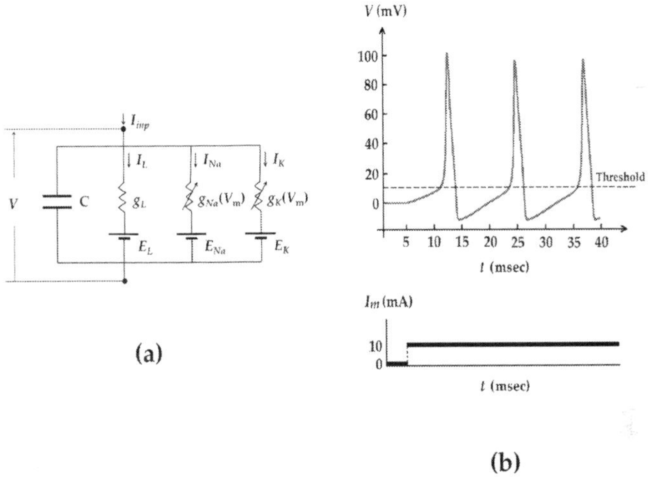


**Figure 5.** The Hodgkin-Huxley model. (a) Conductance-based electrical circuit of the Hodgkin-Huxley model and (b) simulation result.

**Figure 5(a)** shows the HH model and its dynamics is given as follows:

$$I_{inp} = C\frac{dV}{dt} + I_L + I_{Na} + I_K, \tag{4}$$

where $V$ is the membrane potential of the cell, $C$ is the capacitance, $I_L$ is the leak current, $I_{Na}$ and $I_K$ are currents through *Na* channel and *K* channel, respectively, and $I_{inp}$ is the input current. They proposed the empirical formulae, which appropriately indicate activation and inactivation properties of *Na* channel and activation properties of *K* channel, that is, the change of ionic permeability of $Na^+$ and $K^+$. Currents $I_L$, $I_{Na}$, and $I_K$ are given as follows [3]:

$$I_L = \bar{g}_L \cdot (V - E_L), \tag{5}$$

$$I_{Na} = \bar{g}_{Na} \cdot m(V,t)^3 \cdot h(V,t) \cdot (V - E_{Na}), \tag{6}$$

$$I_K = \bar{g}_K \cdot n(V,t)^4 \cdot (V - E_K), \tag{7}$$

where $\bar{g}_L$ is the leakage conductance, $\bar{g}$ and $\bar{g}_K$ are the amplitude of *Na* channel conductance and *K* channel conductance, respectively, $E_L$ is the resting potential, and $E_{Na}$ and $E_K$ are equilibrium potentials of *Na* channel and K *channel*. $m(V, t)$ and $h(V, t)$ are activation and inactivation variables of *Na* channel, and $n(V,t)$ is an activation variable of *K* channel. They gave the following empirical formula:

$$\frac{dx(V,t)}{dt} = \alpha_x(V)\cdot(1-x(V,t)) - \beta_x(V)\cdot x(V,t), \quad (x = m,h,n) \tag{8}$$

$$\alpha_m(V) = \frac{0.1\,(25-V)}{\exp\left(\frac{25-V}{10}\right)-1}, \quad \beta_m(V) = 4\exp(-\frac{V}{18}), \tag{9}$$

$$\alpha_h(V) = 0.07\exp\left(-\frac{V}{20}\right), \quad \beta_h(V) = \frac{1}{\exp\left(\frac{30-V}{10}\right)+1}, \tag{10}$$

$$\alpha_n(V) = \frac{0.01\,(10-V)}{\exp\left(\frac{10-V}{10}\right)-1}, \quad \beta_m(V) = 0.125\exp\left(-\frac{V}{80}\right). \tag{11}$$

**Figure 5(b)** shows one example of computer simulation results for the HH model. When a continuous DC input is given to the HH model, action potentials can be generated at certain interval, that is, with a refractory period. Regardless of the strength of inputs, action potentials have the same shape and size. All differential equations were solved by the fourth-order Rung-Kata method by using C++. Parameters used here were as $C$ = 1μF/cm², $\bar{g}_L$ =0.3 mS/cm², $\bar{g}$ =0.3 mS/cm², $\bar{g}_K$ =0.3 mS/cm², $E_{Na}$= 115 mV, $E_K$=−12 mV, $I_{inp}$ = 10 mA/cm², and the resting potential = 0 mV.

## 3. Neuron model with a band-pass filter property

### 3.1. Subthreshold resonance phenomenon

As described in Section 2.2, neurons can generate action potentials depending on the strength of DC input stimuli. As shown in **Figure 6(a)**, for small DC inputs (dark blue, light blue, dashed red lines), action potentials are not generated by reason that membrane potentials do not exceed the threshold. However, if a larger input (red line) is given to a neuron, the membrane potential can exceed the threshold and as a result, an action potential is generated. On the contrary, when AC inputs are given to a neuron, outputs of a neuron are unlike the cases of DC inputs, apart from whether the membrane potential exceeds the threshold or not. We consider three AC inputs (blue, red, and green in **Figure 6(b)**), whose amplitudes are equal but their frequencies are different ($f_1$<$f_2$<$f_3$). By using an AC input with frequency $f_1$(blue), the membrane potential (blue line) is assumed to be obtained under the threshold level, that is, in a subthreshold level. If the input frequency increases from $f_1$ to $f_2$ (red), the membrane potential (red line) is still in a subthreshold level, but its amplitude becomes larger than that of frequency $f_1$ (blue line). However, if the input frequency further increases to $f_3$ (green), the amplitude of the membrane potential (green line) reduces and becomes smaller than that of frequency $f_2$ (red line). Instead of AC inputs with a single frequency, let an AC input whose frequency increases with time be given to this neuron. This kind of AC is called a chirp current. Then, its membrane potential has the shape with an expanded center section as shown in **Figure 6(c)**, that is, the membrane potential takes the maximum at a specific frequency, however, remains at a subthreshold level. As its FFT shows, this neuron has a band-pass property, that is, frequency selectivity. These kinds of oscillatory phenomena in a subthreshold level are called the subthreshold resonance phenomena.

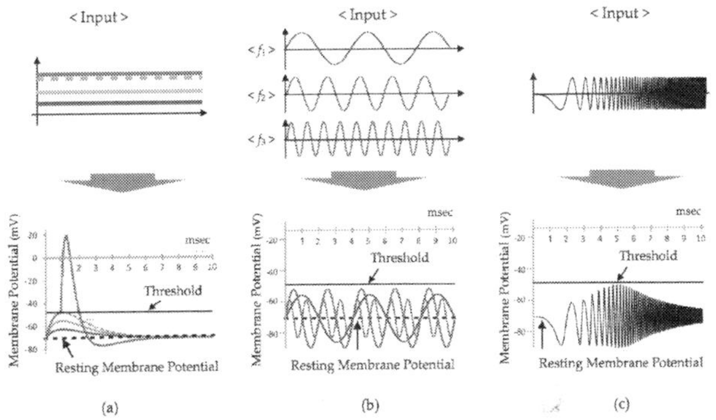


**Figure 6.** Subthreshold resonance phenomena. (a) DC inputs with different amplitudes, (b) AC inputs with different frequencies, and (c) a chirp current input whose frequency increases as time increases.

Subthreshold resonance oscillations have been found in many excitatory and/or inhibitory neurons in the whole brain. Mauro et al. first reported a subthreshold resonance oscillation in squid giant axon [4]. Koch discussed these resonance oscillations in relation to the cable theory [5]. Since then, these resonance phenomena have been observed in many neurons in various regions of the brain, such as trigeminal root ganglion [6], inferior olive [7], and thalamus [8, 9]. These subthreshold resonance phenomena have been also reported in cortical neurons [10–14], and in the 2000s, also in hippocampal neurons in CA1 [15, 16]. Although it is suspected that frequency selectivity of neurons should play an important role in behavioral or perceptual functions in animals, their practical roles have still been unclear. Recently, Narayanan and Johnston [17] reported that subthreshold resonance oscillations in hippocampal CA1 neurons are closely related to the long-term synaptic plasticity, which is currently considered as one of possible foundations of learning and memory [18, 19]. So, it is very interesting and attractive to study those resonance oscillatory features, in order to clarify the mechanisms of higher information processing functions in the brain, such as learning, short-term memory, or working memory.

As already described, the cell membrane is usually modeled by an RC circuit. However, if a chirp current is given to an RC circuit, a membrane potential shows only a property of low-pass filter shown in **Figure 7(a)**. On electrical circuit theory, resonance circuit must contain inductive elements, that is, inductance $L$. Indeed, if a chirp current is given to an RLC circuit, a membrane potential shows a band-pass property shown in **Figure 7(b)**. Having many neurons, the subthreshold resonance phenomena indicate that those neurons must have some kind of inductive factor. So exactly, what is a distinguishing major role of such inductive characteristics in the cell membrane? By advances of experimental technique, it has been reported that many kinds of voltage-dependent ion channels have an important role in subthreshold phenomena. Such ion channels involved in the subthreshold resonance phenomena are different from neuron to neuron that belongs to brain regions. Among them, slow non-inactivating $K^+$ channel (*Krs* channels) [10], hyperpolarization-activated cationic channel (*h* channel) [12], and persistent $Na^+$ channels (*NaP* channel) [13] are well known. In addition to these channels, voltage-dependent $Ca^{2+}$ channels in neurons and/or dendritic spines [8] are also concerned in the subthreshold resonance oscillation.

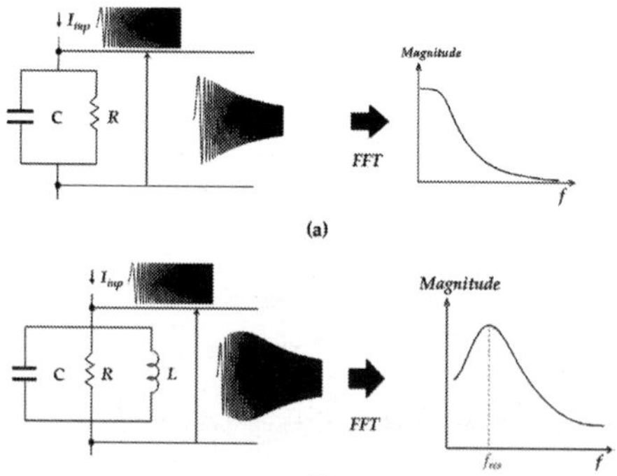


**Figure 7.** Calculated membrane potential for a chirp current and its magnitude of FFT. (a) RC circuit and (b) RLC circuit.

### 3.2. Inductive property of voltage-dependent ion channels

A hyperpolarization-activated cation channel (*h* channel) and a persistent sodium channel (*NaP* channel) are known to mediate the subthreshold resonance oscillation observed in entorhinal cortical neurons [12, 14]. In this section, we show how such voltage-dependent ion channels have inductive properties. We consider a compartment neuron model with h channel and *NaP* channel as shown in **Figure 8**. Its dynamics are expressed by the following conductance-based equations [13]:

$$C\frac{dV}{dt} = -I_L - I_h - I_{NaP} - I_{inp}, \tag{12}$$

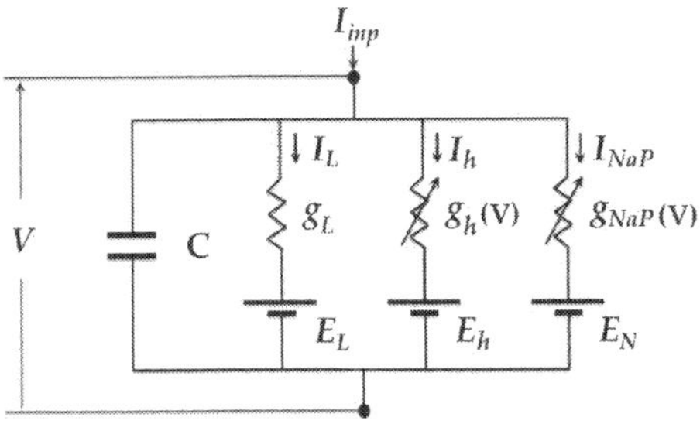


**Figure 8.** A compartmental neuron model with h channel and NaP channel.

where $V$ is the membrane potential, $I_L$ is the leak current, $I_h$ and $I_{NaP}$ are the currents through $h$ channel and $NaP$ channel, respectively, and $I_{inp}$ is the input current. The leak current $I_L$ is given by

$$I_L = \bar{g}_L \cdot (V - E_L). \tag{13}$$

where $\bar{g}_L$ is the leak conductance and $E_L$ is the resting potential. Currents $I_h$ and $I_{NaP}$ are given as follows:

$$I_h = g_h(V) \cdot (V - E_h) = \bar{g}_h \cdot \{0.65\, m_{hf}(V) + 0.35\, m_{hs}(V)\} \cdot (V - E_h). \tag{14}$$

$$I_{NaP} = g_{NaP}(V) \cdot (V - E_N) = \bar{g}_{NaP} \cdot m_{NaP}(V) \cdot (V - E_N). \tag{15}$$

where $g_h(V)$ and $g_{NaP}(V)$ are, respectively, the $h$ channel conductance and the $NaP$ channel conductance, $\bar{g}_h$ and $\bar{g}$ are, respectively, the maximum amplitude of $g_h(V)$ and $g_{NaP}(V)$, and $E_h$ and $E_N$ are the equilibrium potentials for $K^+$ through $h$ channel and $Na^+$ for $NaP$ channel, respectively. $m_{hf}(V)$ and $m_{hs}(V)$ are, respectively, the fast activation and slow activation variables of $h$ channel, and $m_{NaP}(V)$ is an activation variable of $NaP$ channel. They satisfy the following equations:

$$\frac{dm_x}{dt} = \frac{1}{\tau_x} \cdot (m_{x\infty} - m_x), \quad (x = hf, hs, NaP) \tag{16}$$

$$m_{hf} = \frac{1}{1 + \exp\left(\frac{V + 79.2}{9.78}\right)}, \quad \tau_{hf} = 1 + \frac{0.51}{\exp\left(\frac{V - 1.7}{10}\right) + \exp\left(-\frac{V + 340}{52}\right)}, \tag{17}$$

$$m_{hf} = \frac{1}{1+\exp\left(\dfrac{V+71.3}{7.9}\right)}, \quad \tau_{hs} = 1 + \frac{5.6}{\exp\left(\dfrac{V-1.7}{14}\right)+\exp\left(-\dfrac{V+260}{43}\right)}, \tag{18}$$

$$m_{NaP\infty} = \frac{1}{1+\exp\left(-\dfrac{V+38}{6.5}\right)}, \quad \tau_{NaP} = 0.15\,\text{ms}. \tag{19}$$

### 3.2.1. *Equivalent admittance (impedance) of h channel*

Let $V^*$ be the equilibrium potential, $I_h^*$ be the $h$-current at $V^*$. From Eq. (14), $I_h^*$ satisfies the following relation:

$$I_h^* = \bar{g}_h \cdot \{0.65\, m_{hf}(V^*) + 0.35\, m_{hs}(V^*)\} \cdot (V^* - E_h). \tag{20}$$

When the membrane potential $V(t)$ changes from $V^*$ to $V^* + \delta V(t)$, where $\delta V(t)$ is a small variation of the membrane potential from $V^*$, the current $I_h(t)$ also changes from $I_h^*$ to $I_h^* + \delta I_h^*(t)$, where $\delta I_h(t)$ is a small variation of $h$ current caused by $\delta V(t)$. $I_h^* + \delta I_h(t)$ satisfies the following relation:

$$I_h^* + \delta I_h(t) = \bar{g}_h \cdot \{0.65\, m_{hf}(V^* + \delta V(t)) + 0.35\, m_{hf}(V^* + \delta V(t))\} \cdot (V^* + \delta V(t) - E_h). \tag{21}$$

Let $m_{hf}(V^* + \delta V)$ approximate by $m_{hf}(V^*) + \delta m_{hf}$ and $m_{hs}(V^* + \delta V)$ by $m_{hs}(V^*) + \delta m_{hs}$ for a small variation $\delta V$. Then, Eq. (21) can be expressed by the following equation:

$$\begin{aligned} I_h^* + \delta I_h(t) &= \bar{g}_h \cdot \{0.65\, m_{hf}(V^*) + 0.35\, m_{hs}(V^*)\} \cdot (V^* - E_h) \\ &+ \bar{g}_h \cdot \{0.65\, \delta m_{hf} + 0.35\, \delta m_{hs}\} \cdot (V^* - E_h) \\ &+ \bar{g}_h \cdot \{0.65\, m_{hf}(V^*) + 0.35\, m_{hs}(V^*)\} \cdot \delta V(t) \\ &+ \bar{g}_h \cdot \{0.65\, \delta m_{hf} + 0.35\, \delta m_{hs}\} \cdot \delta V(t). \end{aligned} \tag{22}$$

By subtracting Eq. (20) from Eq. (22) and dropping the higher-order variation terms than the second, which appeared on the right-hand side of Eq. (22), the following equation is obtained:

$$\delta I_h \approx \bar{g}_h \cdot \{0.65\, \delta m_{hf} + 0.35\, \delta m_{hs}\} \cdot (V^* - E_h) + \bar{g}_h \cdot \{0.65\, m_{hf*} + 0.35\, m_{hs*}\} \cdot \delta V. \tag{23}$$

As an activation variable $m_{hf}(V)$ satisfies Eq. (16), $m_{hf}(V^*)$ and $m_{hf}(V^* + \delta V)$ must satisfy the following equations:

$$\frac{dm_{hf}(V^*)}{dt} = \frac{1}{\tau_{hf}(V^*)} \cdot \{m_{hf\infty}(V^*) - m_{hf}\}, \tag{24}$$

$$\frac{dm_{hf}(V^* + \delta V)}{dt} = \frac{1}{\tau_{hf}(V^* + \delta V)} \cdot \{m_{hf\infty}(V^* + \delta V) - m_{hf}(V^* + \delta V)\}, \tag{25}$$

where left terms of Eqs. (24) and (25), $dm(V^*)/dt$ and $dm(V^* + \delta V)/dt$, represent the quantity $dm/dt$ evaluated at $V^*$ and $V^* + \delta V$, respectively. By approximating also $\tau(V^* + \delta V)$ by $\tau(V^*) + \delta\tau_{hf}$, where $\delta\tau$ is a small variation caused by $\delta V$, Eq. (25) is written as follows:

$$\begin{aligned} \frac{d[m_{hf}(V^*) + \delta m_{hf}]}{dt} &\approx \frac{1}{\tau_{hf}(V^*) + \delta\tau_{hf}} \cdot \{m_{hf\infty}(V^*) + \delta m_{hf\infty} - (m_{hf}(V^*) + \delta m_{hf})\} \\ &\approx \frac{1}{\tau_{hf}(V^*)}[1 - \frac{\delta\tau_{hf}}{\tau_{hf}(V^*)} + \ldots] \cdot \{m_{hf\infty}(V^*) + \delta m_{hf\infty} - (m_{hf}(V^*) + \delta m_{hf})\}. \end{aligned} \tag{26}$$

By dropping the higher-order variation terms than the second and subtracting Eq. (24) from Eq. (26), the following equation is obtained:

$$\frac{d\delta m_{hf}}{dt} \approx \frac{1}{\tau_{hf}(V^*)} \cdot \{\delta m_{hf\infty} - \delta m_{hf}\}. \tag{27}$$

Furthermore, as a small variation $\delta m_\infty$ may be approximately expressed by $[dm_\infty(V^*)/dV] \cdot \delta V$, Eq. (27) becomes as follows:

$$\frac{d\delta m_{hf}}{dt} \approx \frac{1}{\tau_{hf}(V^*)} \cdot \left\{ \frac{dm_{hf\infty}(V^*)}{dV} \cdot \delta V - \delta m_{hf} \right\}. \tag{28}$$

Using the differential operator $\boldsymbol{p}$ instead of time derivative (d/d$t$), Eq. (28) can be written as follows:

$$\left(p+\frac{1}{\tau_{hf}(V^*)}\right)\cdot\delta m_{hf}=\frac{1}{\tau_{hf}(V^*)}\cdot\left(\frac{dm_{hf\infty}(V^*)}{dV}\right)\cdot\delta V. \tag{29}$$

From this relation, a small variation $\delta m_{hf}$ is definitely expressed by $\delta V$ as follows:

$$\delta m_{hf}=\frac{\frac{1}{\tau_{hf}(V^*)}\cdot\frac{\mathrm{d}m_{hf\infty}(V^*)}{\mathrm{d}V}}{p+\frac{1}{\tau_{hf}(V^*)}}\cdot\delta V. \tag{30}$$

Notice that $\mathrm{d}m_{hf\infty}(V^*)/\mathrm{d}V$ in the numerator of the right-hand side can be directly calculated from Eq. (17), that is, it is given by

$$\frac{\mathrm{d}m_{hf\infty}(V^*)}{\mathrm{d}V}=\frac{1}{9.78}\cdot\frac{\exp\left(\frac{V^*+79.2}{9.78}\right)}{\left\{1+\exp\left(\frac{V^*+79.2}{9.78}\right)\right\}^2}. \tag{31}$$

Exactly in the same way, a small variation $\delta m_{hs}$ is expressed by $\delta V$ as follows:

$$\delta m_{hs}=\frac{\frac{1}{\tau_{hs}(V^*)}\cdot\frac{\mathrm{d}m_{hs\infty}(V^*)}{\mathrm{d}V}}{p+\frac{1}{\tau_{hs}(V^*)}}\cdot\delta V. \tag{32}$$

By substituting Eqs. (30) and (32) into Eq. (23), $\delta I_h$ is finally expressed by $\delta V(t)$ as follows:

$$\begin{aligned}\frac{\delta I_h}{\delta V}&\approx\bar{g}_h\cdot\{0.65\,m_{hf*}+0.35\,m_{hs*}\}\\&+\bar{g}_h\cdot\left\{0.65\frac{\frac{1}{\tau_{hf}(V^*)}\cdot\frac{\mathrm{d}m_{hf\infty}(V^*)}{\mathrm{d}V}}{p+\frac{1}{\tau_{hf}(V^*)}}+0.35\frac{\frac{1}{\tau_{hs}(V^*)}\cdot\frac{\mathrm{d}m_{hs\infty}(V^*)}{\mathrm{d}V}}{p+\frac{1}{\tau_{hs}(V^*)}}\right\}\cdot(V^*-E_h).\end{aligned} \tag{33}$$

As $\delta I(t)/\delta V(t)$ represents admittance, Eq. (33) shows an equivalent admittance of $h$ channel for a small variation $\delta V$ and its admittance can be expressed by parallel coupling circuits of one conductance and two admittances. That is, the first term of Eq. (33) represents a conductance of $h$ channel, which is expressed by the inverse of a pure resistance $R_h$; the second term is an admittance of a fast activation variable $Y_{hf}$, which can be expressed by the inverse of series coupling of an inductance $L_{hf}$ and a resistance $R_{hf}$, that is, $Y_{hf} = 1/(R_{hf} + p \cdot L_{hf})$; and the third term is an admittance element of a slow activation variable $Y_{hs}$, which is also expressed by the inverse of series coupling of an inductance $L_{hs}$ and a resistance $R_{hs}$, that is, $Y_{hs} = 1/(R_{hs} + p \cdot L_{hs})$. **Figure 9** shows an equivalent RLC circuit of $h$ channel, where $R_h$, $R_{hf}$, $R_{hf}$, $R_{hs}$, and $L_{hs}$ are given as follows:

$$R_h = \frac{1}{\bar{g}_h \cdot \{0.65\, m_{hf*} + 0.35\, m_{hs*}\}}, \tag{34}$$

$$R_{Lf} = \frac{1}{0.65\, \bar{g}_h \cdot \frac{dm_{hf\infty}(V*)}{dV} \cdot (V* - E_h)}, \quad L_f = \tau_{hf}{}^* \cdot R_{Lf}, (35) \tag{35}$$

$$R_{hs} = \frac{1}{0.35\, \bar{g}_h \cdot \frac{dm_{hs\infty}(V*)}{dV} \cdot (V* - E_h)}, \quad L_{hs} = \tau_{hs}{}^* \cdot R_{hs}. \tag{36}$$

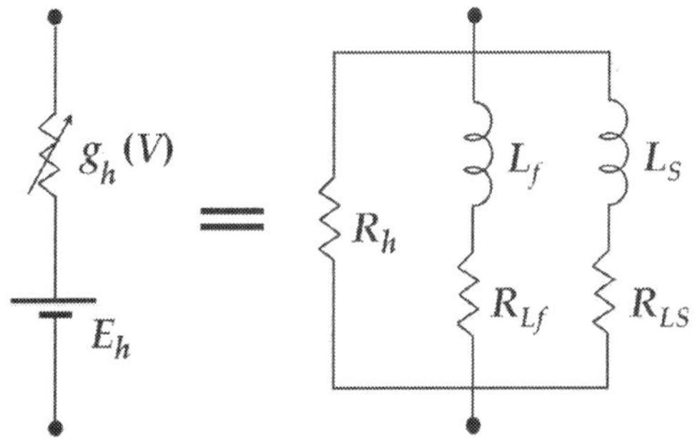


**Figure 9.** An equivalent RLC circuit for $h$ channel.

### 3.2.2. *Equivalent admittance (impedance) of NaP channel*

As in the case of with $h$ channel, let $V^*$ be the equilibrium potential and $I^*$ be the $NaP$ current at $V^*$. From Eq. (15), $I^*$ satisfies the following relation:

$$I_{NaP}^* = \bar{g}_{NaP} \cdot m_{NaP}(V*) \cdot (V* - E_N). \tag{37}$$

When the membrane potential $V(t)$ changes from $V^*$ to $V^*+\delta V(t)$, the current $I_{NaP}(t)$ also changes from $I^*_{\mathrm{NaP}}$ to $I^*_{\mathrm{NaP}}+\delta I_{\mathrm{NaP}}(t)$, where $\delta I_{NaP}(t)$ is a small variation of $NaP$ current caused by $\delta V(t)$. Then, $I^*_{\mathrm{NaP}}+\delta I_{\mathrm{NaP}}(t)$ satisfies the following relation:

$$I^*_{NaP} + \delta I_{NaP}(t) = \bar{g}_{NaP} \cdot m_{NaP}(V* + \delta V(t)) \cdot (V* + \delta V(t) - E_N). \tag{38}$$

Let $m_{NaP}(V^* + \delta V)$ approximate by $m_{NaP}(V^*) + \delta m_{NaP}$ for a small variation $\delta V$. Then, Eq. (38) can be expressed by the following equation:

$$\begin{aligned} I^*_{NaP} + \delta I_{NaP}(t) = \bar{g}_{NaP} \cdot m_{NaP}(V*) \cdot (V* - E_N) + \bar{g}_{NaP} \cdot \delta m_{NaP} \cdot (V* - E_N \\ + \bar{g}_{NaP} \cdot m_{NaP}(V*) \cdot \delta V(t) + \bar{g}_{NaP} \cdot \delta m_{NaP} \cdot \delta V(t). \end{aligned} \tag{39}$$

By subtracting Eq. (37) from Eq. (39) and dropping the higher-order variation terms than the second, which appeared on the right-hand side of Eq. (39), the following equation is obtained:

$$\delta I_{NaP} \approx \bar{g}_{NaP} \cdot \delta m_{NaP} \cdot (V* - E_N) + \bar{g}_{NaP} \cdot m^*_{NaP} \cdot \delta V. \tag{40}$$

By following the same procedure from Eq. (24) to Eq. (26) except that $\tau_{NaP}$ is constant (0.15 ms), a small variation $\delta m_{NaP}$ can be expressed as follows:

$$\frac{\mathrm{d}\delta m_{NaP}}{\mathrm{d}t} \approx \frac{1}{0.15} \cdot \{\delta m_{NaP\infty} - \gamma m_{NaP}\}. \tag{41}$$

By approximating a small variation $\delta m_{NaP\infty}$ by $[\mathrm{d}m_{NaP\infty}(V^*)/\mathrm{d}V] \cdot \delta V$, Eq. (41) becomes

$$\frac{\mathrm{d}\delta m_{NaP}}{\mathrm{d}t} \approx \frac{1}{0.15} \left\{ \frac{\mathrm{d}\delta m_{NaP\infty}(V*)}{\mathrm{d}V} \cdot \delta V - \delta m_{NaP} \right\}. \tag{42}$$

By using the differential operator $p$, a small variation $\delta m_{NaP}$ can be expressed by $\delta V$ as follows:

$$\delta m_{NaP} = \frac{\frac{1}{0.15} \cdot \frac{\mathrm{d}m_{NaP\infty}(V^*)}{\mathrm{d}V}}{p + \frac{1}{0.15}} \cdot \delta V. \tag{43}$$

By substituting Eq. (43) into Eq. (40), $\delta I_{NaP}$ is finally expressed by $\delta V(t)$ as follows:

$$\frac{\delta I_{NaP}}{\delta V} \approx \bar{g}_{NaP} \cdot m_{NaP}(V^*) + \bar{g}_{NaP} \cdot \frac{\frac{1}{0.15} \cdot \frac{\mathrm{d}m_{NaP\infty}(V^*)}{\mathrm{d}V}}{p + \frac{1}{0.15}} \cdot (V^* - E_N). \tag{44}$$

Eq. (44) shows an equivalent admittance of *NaP* channel for a small variation $\delta V$, and it can be expressed by parallel coupling circuits of one conductance and one admittance. That is, the first term of Eq. (44) represents a conductance of *NaP* channel, which is expressed by the inverse of a pure resistance $R_{NaP}$, and the second term is an admittance of an activation variable $Y_{NaP}$, which is expressed by the inverse of series coupling of an inductance $L_P$ and a resistance $R_P$, that is, $Y_{NaP} = 1/(R_P + p \cdot L_P)$. **Figure 10** shows an equivalent RLC circuit of *NaP* channel, where $R_{NaP}$, $R_P$, and $L_P$ are given as follows:

$$R_{NaP} = \frac{1}{\bar{g}_{NaP} \cdot m_{NaP}(V^*)}, \tag{45}$$

$$R_P = \frac{1}{\frac{1}{0.15} \bar{g}_{NaP} \cdot \frac{\mathrm{d}m_{NaP\infty}(V^*)}{\mathrm{d}V} \cdot (V^* - E_N)}, \quad L_P = 0.15 \cdot R_P, \tag{46}$$

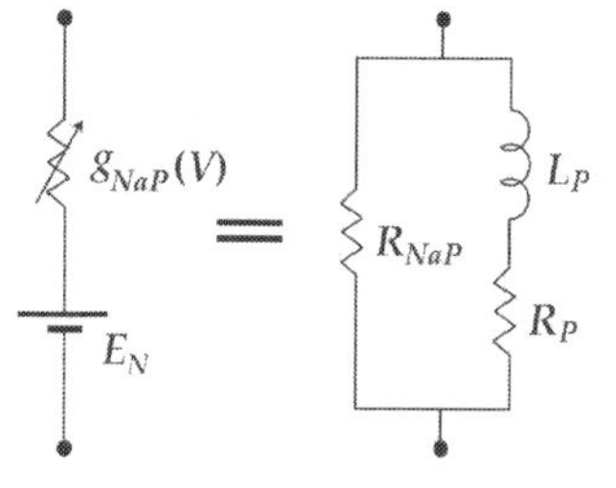


**Figure 10.** An equivalent RLC circuit for *NaP* channel.

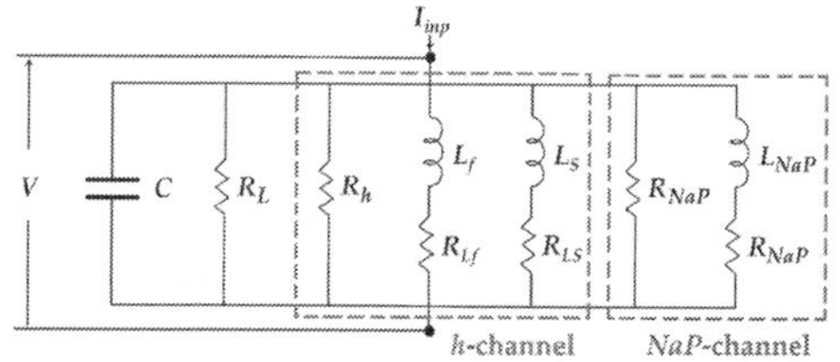


**Figure 11.** An equivalent RLC circuit for a compartment model with *h* channel and *NaP* channel.

### 3.2.3. *Equivalent RLC circuit of a neuron with h channel and NaP channel*

By combining the results of Sections 3.2.1 and 3.2.2, an equivalent RLC circuit for a neuron model with *h* channel and *NaP* channel is obtained. **Figure 11** shows its equivalent RLC circuit. In this section, we show some simulation results for a compartment neuron model (**Figure 8**) and its equivalent RLC circuit(**Figure 11**). A chirp current given to both a compartment neuron model and its equivalent RLC circuit is described as follows:

$$I_{inp} = A_{inp} \sin(\omega(t) \cdot t) + id, \quad \omega(t) = 2\pi f \frac{t}{T}, \tag{47}$$

where the angular frequency $\omega(t)$ increases from 0 to $2\pi f$ over the period $[0, T]$. $i_d$ is a DC bias current, which is set to zero in this subsection. The following parameter values were used in simulations; $C = 1.5\ \mu F/cm^2$, $\bar{g}_L = 0.15\ mS/cm^2$, $E_L = -65\ mV$, $\bar{g}_{NaP} = 0.5\ mS/cm^2$, $\bar{g}_h = 1.5\ mS/cm^2$, $E_N = 55\ mV$, $E_K = -90\ mV$, $E_h = -20 mV$.

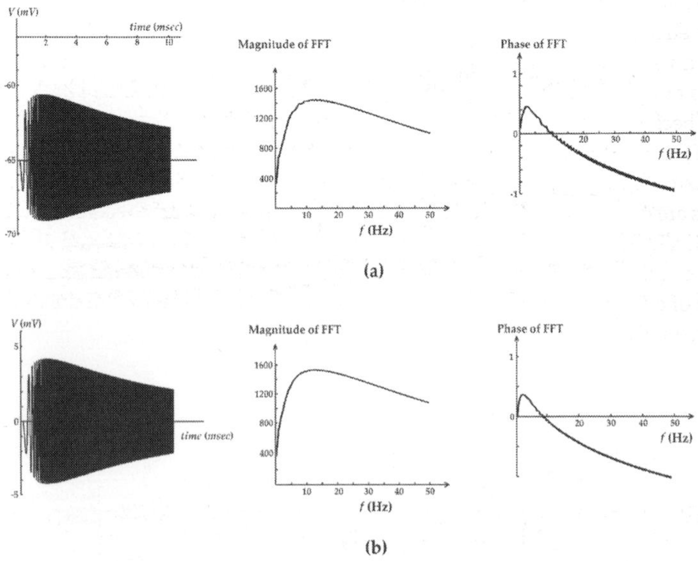


**Figure 12.** Membrane potential and the magnitude and the phase of its FFT. Simulation result for (a) a compartment model (**Figure 8**) and (b) its equivalent RLC circuit (**Figure 11**).

**Figure 12(a)** shows one simulation result for a compartment model with *h* channel and *NaP* channel. The membrane potential *V* and the amplitude and the phase of its FFT are shown. As the magnitude of FFT shows, this neuron model has a band-pass property. **Figure 12(b)** shows the simulation result for its equivalent RLC circuit. Comparing **Figure 12(a)** and **(b)**, the membrane potentials and their FFTs are exactly similar. This fact indicates that the derived RLC circuit represents almost the same properties of a compartment neuron model within a small variation of the membrane potential. In other words, voltage-dependent *h* channel and *NaP* channel may surely have inductive properties and contribute to the subthreshold resonance phenomena.

### 3.3. Properties of voltage responses to oscillatory current inputs

A neuron can generate action potentials whenever its membrane potential exceeds the threshold except during a refractory period. If the membrane potential of a neuron stays in a subthreshold level, a neuron cannot generate action potentials. However, as described in the previous section, many neurons in the brain have the subthreshold resonance properties. This fact indicates that a neuron may be able to generate an action potential when AC inputs whose frequencies are close to the resonance frequency of a neuron are given, because the resulting membrane potential for that input has the potential to exceed the threshold by the effects of the subthreshold resonance property. Actually, this fact has been observed in neurons of the brain. For example, Hutcheon et al. studied subthreshold voltage responses to AC inputs in neurons from the sensorimotor cortex of rats [11]. **Figure 13** shows one of their results. Cases 1–3 show effects of the input amplitude: (Case 1) if a chirp current with a small amplitude is given to a neuron, the membrane potential does not exceed the threshold and no action potentials are generated; (Case 2) if its input amplitude increases a little bit, the membrane potential becomes larger but it still stays in a subthreshold level and no action potentials are generated; and (Case 3) if its amplitude increases more, the membrane potential exceeds for AC inputs with frequencies close to a resonance frequency of a neuron. As a result, action potentials are generated around that frequency. Cases 4 and 5 show effects of a DC bias input: (Case 4) if a DC-bias in the input current increases a little bit from 0μA/cm$^2$, the membrane potential cannot exceed the threshold and no action potentials are generated and (Case 5) if the value of a DC bias is raised more, the membrane potential can exceed the threshold and action potentials are generated.

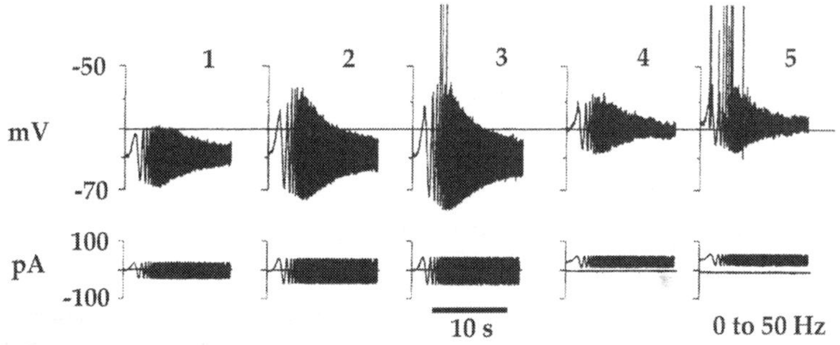


**Figure 13.** Experimental results: Subthreshold voltage responses for a chirp current input with different amplitudes and DC bias currents observed in sensory cortex of rats [11].

We consider here a compartment neuron model with $h$ channel and $NaP$ channel described in the previous section, into which the HH model is incorporated in order to generate action potentials. **Figure 14** shows its integrated neuron model, and the following equation is obtained:

$$C\frac{dV}{dt} = -I_L - I_h - I_{NaP} - I_{Na} - I_K + I_{inp}. \tag{48}$$

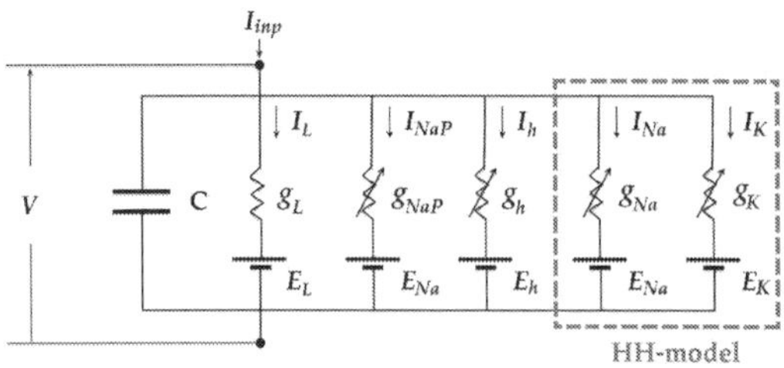


**Figure 14.** A compartment model with $h$ channel and $NaP$ channel into which the Hodgkin-Huxley model (the HH-model) is incorporated.

Eq. (48) is an extension form of Eq. (12), into which two currents $I_N$ and $I_K$ of the HH model are added. Detail dynamics of $I_L$, $I_h$, and $I_{NaP}$ are given by Eqs. (13)–(15) in Section 3.2. Dynamics of $I_{Na}$ and $I_K$ are also given by Eqs. (6) and (7) in Section 2.2. In addition to parameter values shown in the previous section, the following values were used in simulations: $\bar{g}_{Na}$=52 mS/cm$^2$, $\bar{g}_K$=52 mS/cm$^2$, $E_N$ = 55 mV, and $E_K$ = −90 mV.

**Figure 15(a)** shows the membrane potential for a chirp current input with $A_{inp}$ = 2.5 μA/cm$^2$ and $i_d$ = 0 μA/cm$^2$. For this input, the membrane potential cannot exceed the threshold, and no action potentials are generated. However, if the amplitude of AC input ($A_{inp}$) increases, the situation changes. **Figure 15(b)** shows the membrane potentials for a chirp current input whose amplitude increases to 3.3 μA/cm$^2$. In this case, the membrane potential exceeds the threshold for the input frequency close to the resonance frequency of this neuron model. As shown in **Figure 12**, it is 13 Hz in this neuron model. On the other hand, **Figure 15(c)** shows the membrane potential for a chirp input with $A_{inp}$ = 2.5 μA/cm$^2$ and increased $i_d$ = 1 μA/cm$^2$. Almost the same response as **Figure 12(b)** is obtained. However, resulting membrane potentials in **Figures 13** and **15** are not completely identical, because neurons used in experiments by Hutcheon et al. and a neuron model used in this simulations are different. However, simulation results follow a similar tendency as experimental results by Hutcheon et al.[11].

By computer simulations, effects of the amplitude of AC input, its frequency, and a DC-bias current on the membrane potential were studied [20]. Some results are shown here. **Figure 16** shows the membrane potentials for the AC inputs with a single frequency, setting $A_{inp}$ = 3.3 μA/cm$^2$. **Figure 16(a)** shows the results for 2 Hz input frequency. In this case, no action potentials are generated, because the membrane potential cannot exceed the threshold at all.

http://dx.doi.org/10.5772/64028

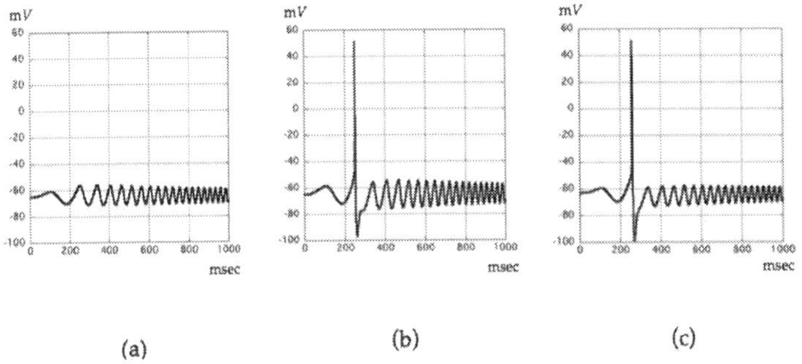


**Figure 15.** Simulated membrane potential for a chirp current input with different amplitude and DC bias current. (a) Response for $A_{inp}$ = 2.5 μA/cm$^2$ and $i_d$ = 0 μA/cm$^2$. (b) Response for $A_{inp}$ = 3.3 μA/cm$^2$ and $i_d$ = 0 μA/cm$^2$. (c) Response for $A_{inp}$ = 2.5 μA/cm$^2$ and $i_d$ = 1 μA/cm$^2$.

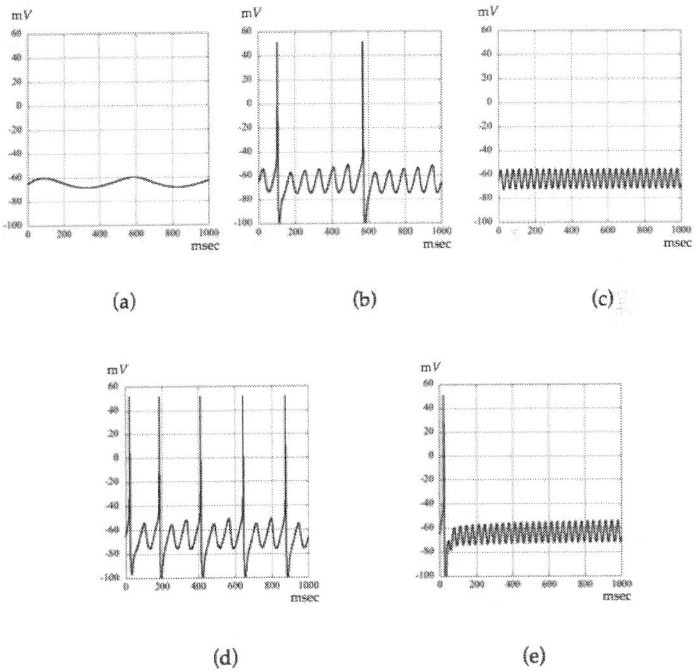


**Figure 16.** Simulated membrane potential for an AC input with a single frequency ($A_{inp}$ is fixed to 2.5 μA/cm$^2$). (a) Response for $i_d$ = 0 μA/cm$^2$ and $f$ = 2 Hz. (b) Response for $i_d$ = 0 μA/cm$^2$ and $f$ = 13 Hz. (c) Response for $i_d$ = 0 μA/cm$^2$ and $f$ = 30 Hz. (d) Response for $i_d$ = 1 μA/cm$^2$ and $f$ = 13 Hz. (e) Response for $i_d$ = 1 μA/cm$^2$ and $f$ = 30 Hz.

**Figure 16(b)** shows that action potentials are generated, because the input frequency is 13 Hz, which is close to the resonance frequency of this neuron model. Thus, the maximum amplitude of membrane potentials exceeds the threshold by the effect of the subthreshold resonance property. In the case of **Figure 16(c)**, for 30 Hz input frequency, no action potentials are generated, because the membrane potential is less than the threshold. On the other hand, if a DC bias current input increases to 1μA/cm$^2$, as **Figure 16(d)** shows, more action potentials are generated for 13 Hz input frequency input than the case of no DC bias input. This indicates the effect of a DC bias current on generation of action potentials. Comparing **Figure 16(b)** and **(d)**, it is clarified that the more spikes are observed than the case of no DC bias current input. For the case of $i_d$= 1 μA/cm$^2$,a neuron model can also generate an action potential for 30Hz input frequency, as shown in **Figure 16(e)**. As no action potential is generated for the case of $i_d$= 0 μA/cm$^2$, this is also caused by the effect of a DC bias current input.

## 4. Conclusion

Until now, it has been mainly proposed that the cell membrane and neurons are modeled by an RC circuit. However, from the fact that many neurons in various regions of the brain have band pass properties, a neuron should be modeled by an RLC circuit. In this chapter, an equivalent RLC circuit was developed for a neuron model with *h* and *NaP* channels, and it was clarified that the subthreshold resonance property of this neuron model comes from inductive properties of *h* and *NaP* channels, especially, *h* channel. Furthermore, by incorporating the Hodgkin-Huxley dynamics into this neuron model, we showed the relation between the subthreshold resonance oscillation and the generation of action potentials. By computer simulations, it was shown that the amplitude of an AC input and a DC bias current input strongly play a role in the generation of action potentials, coupled with AC input frequencies.

It is presumed that the subthreshold resonance phenomena may relate closely to various practical neuron activities and behaviors in our brain, such as the sensitivity to external noises in sensory system. So, it is very important and interesting to study firing patterns of a neuron or properties of burst oscillations by using computer simulations, in order to clarify the mechanisms of higher information processing in the brain.

Needless to say, mutual collaboration of experimental research and modeling research is of large significance, in order to create more sophisticated models based on the most recent findings from experiments, and in order to develop new experimental methods to verify the facts suggested from simulation results.

## Acknowledgements

We thank Mr. Babak V. Ghaffari for preparing figures.

## Author details

Tatsuo Kitajima[1*], Zonggang Feng[2] and Azran Azhim[3]

*Address all correspondence to: tatsuo.kitajima@gmail.com

1 Malaysia-Japan International Institute of Technology (MJIIT), UTM KL Campus, Kuala Lumpur, Malaysia

2 Yamagata University, Yonezawa-shi, Yamagata, Japan

3 International Islamic University Malaysia, Kuantan Campus, Kuantan, Malaysia

## References

[1] Nicholls JG, Martin AR, Wallace BG, Fuchs PA: From Neuron to Brain (4th edition). Sinauer Associates Inc., Massachusetts, USA; 2001; 25 p.

[2] McCulloch WS, Pitts WJ: A logical calculus of the ideas immanent in nervous activity. Bull. Math. Biophys. 1943; 7; 115–133.

[3] Hodgkin AL, Huxley AF: A quantitative description of membrane current and its application to conduction and excitation in nerve. J. Physiol. 1952; 177; 500–544.

[4] Mauro A, Conti F, Dodge F, Shor R: Subthreshold behavior and phenomenological impedance of the squid giant axon. J. Gen. Physiol. 1970; 55; 497–523.

[5] Koch C: Cable theory in neurons with active linearized membrane. Biol. Cybern. 1984; 50; 15–33.

[6] Puil E, Gimbarzevsky B, Spigelman I:Primary involvement of K+ conductance in membrane resonance of trigeminal root ganglion neurons. J. Neurophysiol. 1988; 59; 77–89.

[7] Lampl I, Yarom Y: Subthreshold oscillations of the membrane potential: A functional synchronizing and timing device. J. Neurophysiol. 1993; 70; 2181–2186.

[8] Hutcheon B, Miura RM, Yarom Y. Puil E: Low-threshold calcium current and resonance in thalamic neurons: A model of frequency preference. J. Neurophysiol. 1994; 71; 583–594.

[9] Puil E, Meiri H, Yarom Y: Resonant behavior and frequency preferences of thalamic neurons. J. Neurophysiol. 1994; 71; 575–582.

[10] Gutfreund Y, Yarom Y, Segev I: Subthreshold oscillations and resonant frequency in guinea-pig cortical neurons. J. Physiol. 1995; 483; 621–640.

[11] Hutcheon B, Miura RM, Puil E: Subthreshold membrane resonance in neocortical neurons. J. Neurophysiol. 1996; 76; 683–697.

[12] Dickson CT, Magistretti J, Shalinsky MH, Fransen E, Hasselmo MH, Alomso A: Properties and role of $I_h$ in the pacing of subthreshold oscillations in enrorhinal cortex layer II neurons. J. Neurophysiol. 2000; 83; 2562–2579.

[13] Acker CD, Kopell N, White JA: Synchonization of strongly coupled excitatory neurons: Relating network behavior to biophysics. J. Comput. Neurosci. 2003; 15; 71–90.

[14] Rotstein HG, Opperman T, White JA, Kopell N: The dynamic structure underlying subthreshold oscillatory activity and the onset of spikes in a model of medial entorhinal cortex stellate cells. J. Comput. Neurosci. 2006; 21;271–292.

[15] Leung LS, Yu H-W: Theta-frequency resonance in hippocampal CA1 neurons in vitro demonstrated by sinusoidal current injection. J. Neurophysiol. 1998; 79; 1592–1596.

[16] Pike FG, Goddard RS, Suckling M, Ganter P, Kasthuri N, Paulsen O: Distinct frequency preferences of different types of rat hippocampal neurones in response to oscillatory input currents. J. Physiol. 2000;529; 205–213.

[17] Narayanan R, Johnston D: Long-term potentiation in rat hippocampal neurons is accompanied by spatially widespread changes in intrinsic oscillatory dynamics and excitability. Neuron. 2007; 56; 1061–1075.

[18] Kitajima T, Hara K: A generalized Hebbian rule for activity-dependent synaptic modification. Neural Netw. 2000; 13; 445–454.

[19] Johnston D, Christie BR, Frick A, Gray R, Hoffman DA, Schexnayder LK, Watanabe S, Yuan LL: Active dendrites, potassium channels and synaptic plasticity. Phil. Trans. R. Soc. Lond. B. 2003; 358; 667–674.

[20] Kitajima, T, Feng, Z: Subthreshold Resonance Oscillation and Generation of Action Potential, 19th IFAC World Congress, Cape Town, South Africa, FrB07.3, 11818–11823; August, 2014.

Chapter 4

# Numerical Simulations of Dynamics Behaviour of the Action Potential of the Human Heart's Conduction System

Beata Jackowska-Zduniak

Additional information is available at the end of the chapter

http://dx.doi.org/10.5772/63017

**Abstract**

A proposed model consisting of two coupled van der Pol models is considered as a description of the heart action potential. A system of ordinary differential equations is used to recreate pathological behaviour in the conducting system of the heart such as Wolff-Parkinson-White (WPW) syndrome and the most common tachycardia: atrioventricular nodal reentrant tachycardia (AVNRT). Part of the population has abnormal accessory pathways: fast and slow. These pathways in the atrioventricular node (AV node) are anatomical and functional excipients of supraventricular tachycardia. However, the appearance of two pathways in the AV node may be an excipient of arrhythmia—the WPW syndrome. The difference in the conduction time between these pathways is the most important factor. This is the reason to introduce three types of couplings and delay to our system in order to reproduce different types of the AVNRT. In our research, the result of introducing the feedback loops and couplings entails the creation of waves which can correspond to the re-entry waves which occur in the AVNRT. Our main aim is to study solutions of the equations of the system and to take into consideration the influence of feedback and delays which occur in the pathological modes. The proposed models made it possible to reproduce the most important physiological properties of the discussed pathologies. Since the model is phenomenological, the results are accurate as far as a simple model can describe the potential found in one of the more complex oscillators found in biology.

**Keywords:** van der Pol model, ordinary differential equations, delay, feedback, couplings, action potential, WPW syndrome, AVNRT, numerical analysis

## 1. Introduction

In this chapter, the research on the electrical conduction system of the human heart is concerned. The parts of this system are pacemaker centres made of special cells similar to embryonic cells which form the following concentrations: sino-atrial node (SA), atrioventricular node (AV) and His-Purkinje system [1]. The key elements of the conduction system considered include SA node and AV node. Modelling the formation and conduction of electrical impulses in the heart is one of the most developed areas of mathematical biology. For years, the most popular models of action potentials which occur in the heart have included the Hodgkin-Huxley model and the Purkinje cells model. These models, even though very effective, are not very suitable for studying the dynamics of the system, which is described in view of high dimensionality of the phase space and very broad spatial parameters. In this chapter, we propose ordinary differential system which is based on the van der Pol models and which makes it possible to reconstruct pathological behaviours in the system of the heart, such as the WPW syndrome and different types of AVNRT. The motivation for writing this chapter was that there is a problem with making the appropriate diagnosis and therefore with treating the disease effectively. This kind of problem is observed mainly in different types of AVNRT. The reasons of those problems are not fully known and the mechanisms of these pathologies are not fully understood. Also, the symptoms are often mistakenly taken for other heart diseases. It should be emphasized that the clinical pictures of these disease are also non-specific. In the past few years, we understood that the structure of the AV node has a multi-level architecture in which there may be many pathways (slow and fast) at different locations in the AV node [2, 3]. This helped to recognize many types of AVNRT, which previously were understood as one, although the mechanisms of action were different. In literature, there are no mathematical models that would specifically model the various types of AVNRT. There were attempts to model AVNRT only as a single pathology having the slow and fast pathways [4, 5]. Part of the population has abnormal accessory pathways: fast and slow, cf. [1, 6]. The pathways in the AV node are anatomical and functional contributions of the most popular supraventricular tachycardia, which is a re-entry tachycardia from the AV node. The atrioventricular nodal re-entrant tachycardia is caused by re-entries. A condition for AVNRT to occur is that two electric pathways occur in and around the AV node (for example, slow and fast pathways). This gives way to the occurrence of re-entry. We can distinguish five different forms of the AVNRT (typical: slow/fast, atypical: fast/slow and other forms: slow/slow, more than two re-entries waves, one fast pathway with depolarization of slow pathway) [7, 8, 9]. This depends on the multi-level architecture of the AV node. The AVNRT circuit involves larger areas including atrioventricular junction, adjacent atrial structures and in particular so-called atrial inputs including at least antero-superior and postero-inferior entries, and sometimes also the left atrial entry. Based on the van der Pol equation, we study the influence of feedback which occurs in the normal heart action mode as well as in pathological modes. Particularly, it is important to introduce the time delay into this feedback. Delay values used in our research correspond to those which occur in the electrical conduction system, for example, in the case of an accessory conducting pathway, so-called Wolff-

Parkinson-White syndrome. In the conduction system of the heart, the only correct electrical conduction pathway between atria and ventricles is the bundle of His. Part of the population has abnormal accessory pathways through which electrical pulses are directly conducted from atria to ventricles. The extra electrical pathway is presented at birth and is fairly rare. The WPW syndrome is detected in about 4 out of every 100000 people. People of all ages, including infants, can experience the symptoms related to the WPW syndrome. Additional path conducts electrical impulses to the ventricles in the case of WPW. This conduction takes place without proper synchronization. Usually, this extra conduction pathway does not cause serious disturbances. Sometimes, however, there is a reflection of the electrical impulse, and it returns to the atria after each heartbeat. This causes the coupling in which each atrial contraction is followed by chambers contraction and then atrial contraction again. The heart rate can reach about 200 beats per minute when the normal rhythm at rest is about 72 beats per minute.

As already mentioned, synchronization is very important for a correctly functioning heart in the sense of cardiovascular conduction. The impact of different types of couplings related to the pathologies which are presented in this research and how do they affect the synchronization of the two oscillators will be discussed in this chapter. The analysis of synchronization of various modifications of the van der Pol model has been considered in many works. For example, paper [10] presents synchronization areas near the main parametric resonance and transition conditions from regular to chaotic motion. In paper [11], authors analyse the phenomenon of complete synchronization in a network of four coupled oscillators. Reference [12] considered mechanisms of various bifurcation phenomena occurring in Bonhoffer van der Pol neurons coupled with a time delay through the characteristics of synaptic transmissions. The phenomenon of synchronization in van der Pol oscillators coupled by a time-varying resistor is researched in ref. [13]. However, in these papers there are no examples of application of this model for recreating a pathological behaviour of the electrical-conduction system of the human heart, and therefore the considered ranges of parameters are wider than those which can be used in medical applications. The van der Pol oscillator provides rich dynamical behaviour [14] and also synchronization phenomena. In order to better understand the mechanisms that cause these arrhythmias in paper are proposed models of AVNRT and WPW syndrome.

## 2. Modelling techniques

The van der Pol model was used in this research because it is a two-dimensional model with small number of parameters and it is a relaxation oscillator. The van der Pol equation is often used to describe an action potential occurring in the heart. The model with a delay and often with a term including a coupling coefficient has been a topic of many articles, e.g. [15–17]. However, in these articles there are no exact examples of application of this model for recreating a pathological behaviour of the electrical conduction system of the human heart such as the AVNRT and the WPW, and therefore the range of parameters considered by them is wider than that which can be used in medical applications. Below, the author will present one of the most important existing mathematical models of the action potential. Basing on the knowledge of van der Pol model given below will be carried out construction of the proposed models.

### 2.1. Van der Pol model

Since every node is a self-exciting pacemaker, it can be described using the van der Pol oscillator which is the relaxation oscillator. It was first introduced by van der Pol and van der Mark as a model in the electronic circuit theory in 1927, [19]:

$$\ddot{x} + a\left(x^2 - 1\right)\dot{x} + x = 0 \tag{1}$$

where

$$f\left(x\right) = 0.5a\left(x^2 - 1\right) \tag{2}$$

$f(x)$ is a damping coefficient, which is negative for $|x| < 1$ and positive for $|x| > 1$. Nevertheless, the van der Pol model requires some changes to be introduced in order to reproduce features of heart's action potential. In paper [20], Postnov substituted a linear term by a non-linear cubic force called the Duffing term

$$\ddot{x} + a\left(x^2 - \mu\right)\dot{x} + \frac{x\left(x+d\right)\left(x+2d\right)}{d^2} = 0 \tag{3}$$

where $a$, $\mu$, $d$ are positive control parameters.

In this way, he introduced modifications which allowed maintaining the required structure of the phase space. Such model can be applied to model either SA or AV node. The main property of a modified relaxation oscillator is the mutual interaction of a limit cycle which is presented around an unstable focus with a saddle and a stable node. This allows reproducing correctly the refraction period and non-linear phase sensitivity of an action potential of node cells.

A solution of Eq. (3) in time presents the action potential whereas a solution in velocity makes it possible to obtain very important phase portrait. We can easily see that the main qualitative difference between Eqs. (1) and (3) is the appearance of two additional steady states, $x_2 = -d$ and $x_3 = -2d$. As before, $x_1 = 0$ is an unstable node or a focus surrounded by a stable unique limit cycle, $x_2 = -d$ is a saddle and $x_3 = -2d$ forms a focus or a node and can be either stable or unstable, depending on the sign of $4d^2 - \mu$. In the case considered by Postnov [20], the first steady state is an unstable focus, the third one is a stable node. In the considered model (5), the problem is the adjustment of the position of stationary states in the phase space. In order to reproduce behaviour of the heart, a new parameter $e$ is added. For better regulation of the frequency, the

$e \cdot d$ factor is substituted with an independent coefficient $f$ corresponding to harmonic oscillator's frequency, [20]. We present the final version of the model in its two variable first-order form that reads [20]:

$$\begin{aligned}\dot{x} &= y,\\ \dot{y} &= -a\left(x^2-1\right)y - fx\left(x+d\right)\left(x+e\right)\end{aligned} \tag{4}$$

The system that we use as a reference one is given in following form:

$$\begin{aligned}\dot{x}_1 &= y_1\\ \dot{y}_1 &= -a_1\left(x_1^{\,2}-1\right)y_1 - f_1x_1\left(x_1+d_1\right)\left(x_1+e_1\right)\\ \dot{x}_2 &= y_2\\ \dot{y}_2 &= -a_2\left(x_2^{\,2}-1\right)y_2 - f_2x_2\left(x_2+d_2\right)\left(x_2+e_2\right)\end{aligned} \tag{5}$$

where $a_1=a_2=5;\ f_1=f_2=3;\ d_1=d_2=3;\ e1=7;\ e2=4.5$ are control parameters. In the next part of this paper, a modified van der Pol system with delayed feedback and couplings describes various pathologies observed in heart action, for example, WPW syndrome and different types of AVNRT pathology.

## 3. Construction and analysis of proposed models

In this section we turn to constructing new models for specific pathologies we would like to describe. All the models we propose below consist of two modified van der Pol models. The system with delayed feedback describes various pathologies observed in the heart action, e.g. WPW syndrome and different types of AVNRT.

A numerical model was created using Dynamics Solver and a program which was written in C++. The explicit Runge-Kutta formula with a variable integration step was used. Results were confirmed and plots were made with Matlab standard dde23 solver.

For the single node model (Eq. (4)) of an electrical conduction system with no feedback, a periodic potential and the corresponding limit cycle (with a transient state) are obtained like in **Figures 1** and **2**. Potential period equals 1.4.

The reference parameters have values which are given below:

$$\mathrm{a}_1=\mathrm{a}_2=5,\ \mathrm{d}_1=\mathrm{d}_2=3,\ \mathrm{e}_1=7, \mathrm{e}_2=4.5,\ \mathrm{f}_1=\mathrm{f}_2=3. \tag{6}$$

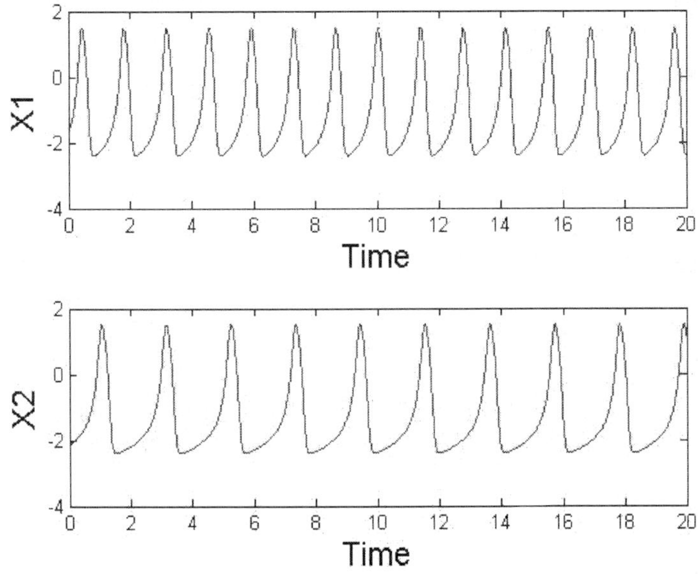


**Figure 1.** Time series for reference model without feedback and delay, see Eq. (5).

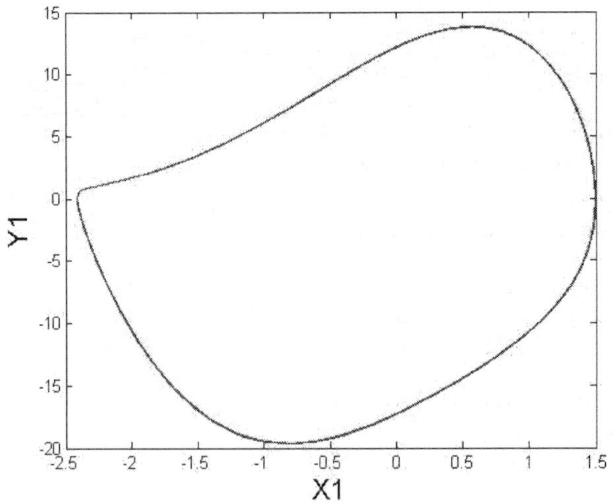


**Figure 2.** Phase portrait for reference model without feedback and delay, see first part of Eq. (5).

The addition of coupling (especially feedback with delay) to the $x_1$ term allows modelling the re-entry wave which causes the exceptional situation when AV node is the master for SA node. Such situation takes place in case of WPW syndrome, this situation is presented by the following equations:

$$\dot{x}_1 = y_1 + k(x_1(t-\tau) - x_1)$$
$$\dot{y}_1 = -a_1(x_1{}^2 - 1)y_1 - f_1 x_1(x_1 + d_1)(x_1 + e_1)$$

Parameters have the following values: $k = 2$, $\tau = 0.25$ and other parameters are the same as in the reference system. In the time series of the modified model with feedback, there is a 'delayed impulse'. The result of introducing feedback to the system is the creation of a wave similar to the initial wave—action potential, but delayed. It can be assumed that such a feedback can be treated as an external, periodic excitation of the wave. In **Figure 3** we can observe a kind of tachycardia which is a typical symptom of the Wolff-Parkinson-White syndrome. The period of oscillations is about 0.9 whereas the reference period of physiological action potential is 1.4.

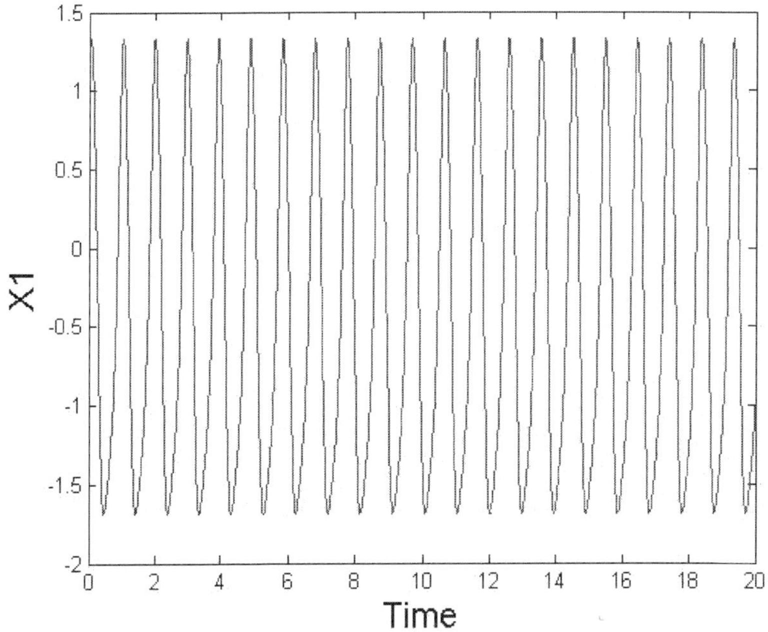


**Figure 3.** Dynamics of action potential during WPW syndrome.

Now we consider the AVNRT pathology. We would like to propose a mechanism which reproduces the dynamics of action potential occurring at the phenomenon of AVNRT. In this case, we have a coexistent conduction by two or more pathways: slow and fast. In this model, we assume that the fast pathway is described by the first van der Pol model, but the slow pathway is treated as an action potential in other characteristic, so we use the second model of van der Pol to describe the pathway.

Next, we focus on such a type of AVNRT in which only one fast pathway with depolarization of slow pathway occurs. The conduction is only out of the fast pathway, because descending depolarization of slow pathway prevents conduction. To describe that situation, we add only one unidirectional coupling to our model. This coupling does not change the main rhythm $x_1$ (see **Figure 4**). In this case, the model could be written in the following form:

$$\begin{cases} \dot{x}_1 = y_1 \\ \dot{y}_1 = a_1\left(x_1^2 - 1\right)y_1 - f_1 x_1\left(x_1 + d_1\right)\left(x_1 + e_1\right) \\ \dot{x}_2 = y_2 + kx_1 \\ \dot{y}_2 = a_2\left(x_2^2 - 1\right)y_2 - f_2 x_2\left(x_2 + d_2\right)\left(x_2 + e_2\right) \end{cases} \tag{7}$$

where $k$ is the coupled coefficient, $\tau$ is the delay and other parameters are fixed as $a$=5, $f$=3, $d$=3, $e$=7.

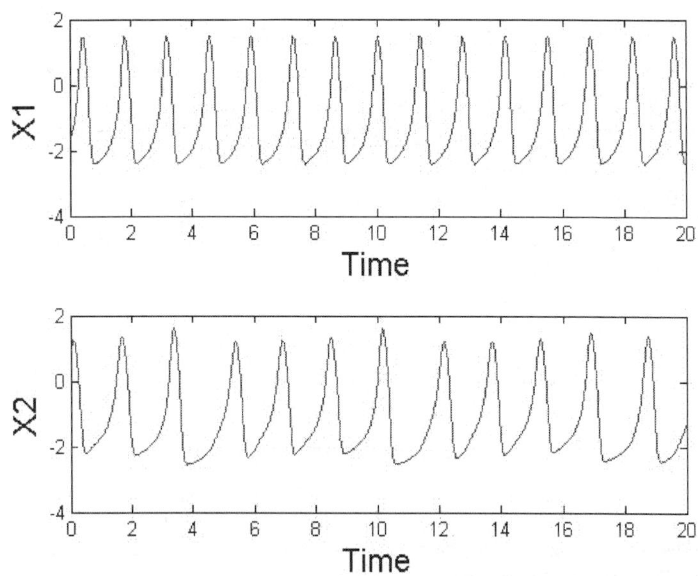


**Figure 4.** Time series for fast type of AVNRT.

Now, we consider a situation where the difference in the refractive state of both pathways leads to an excitation of one of them causing the re-entry wave [20]. In **Figure 5**, the result for a typical AVNRT (fast/slow) is presented. This type of AVNRT is described by the following system:

$$\begin{cases} \dot{x}_1 = y_1 - k\left(x_1\left(t-\tau\right) - x_1\right) \\ \dot{y}_1 = a_1\left(x_1^2 - 1\right)y_1 - f_1 x_1\left(x_1 + d_1\right)\left(x_1 + e_1\right) \\ \dot{x}_2 = y_2 \\ \dot{y}_2 = a_2\left(x_2^2 - 1\right)y_2 - f_2 x_2\left(x_2 + d_2\right)\left(x_2 + e_2\right) \end{cases} \tag{8}$$

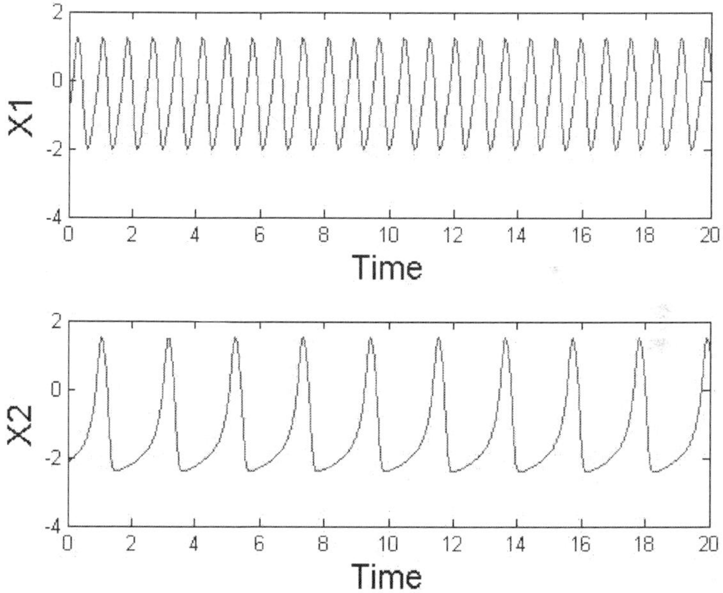


**Figure 5.** Dynamics of action potential for a typical AVNRT, given in Eq. (8).

The mechanism of the typical AVNRT is similar to this which is observed in the WPW syndrome. Also, we have a feedback with delay in the first part of the given model.

The atypical AVNRT (slow/fast type of AVNRT) is described in the following way:

$$\begin{cases} \dot{x}_1 = y_1 - k_1\left(x_2\left(t-\tau\right) - x_1\right) \\ \dot{y}_1 = a_1\left(x_1^2 - 1\right)y_1 - f_1x_1\left(x_1 + d_1\right)\left(x_1 + e_1\right) \\ \dot{x}_2 = y_2 - k_2\left(x_1 - x_2\left(t-\tau\right)\right) \\ \dot{y}_2 = a_2\left(x_2^2 - 1\right)y_2 - f_2x_2\left(x_2 + d_2\right)\left(x_2 + e_2\right) \end{cases} \tag{9}$$

In both of those types of AVNRT (fast/slow and slow/fast) we obtain regular fast rhythm, which is a typical behaviour for this kind of pathology (during this type of tachycardia, the rhythm of the heart is about 35% more frequent than normal rhythm, which is in accordance with our results).

The last case is for the situation where there are two re-entry waves but both go through slow pathways (slow/slow type of AVNRT), which we reflect by the following system of equations:

$$\begin{cases} \dot{x}_1 = y_1 - k_1\left(x_2\left(t-\tau\right) - x_1\right) \\ \dot{y}_1 = a_1\left(x_1^2 - 1\right)y_1 - f_1x_1\left(x_1 + d_1\right)\left(x_1 + e_1\right) \\ \dot{x}_2 = y_2 - k_2\left(x_1 - x_2\left(t-\tau_1\right)\right) - k_3\left(x_1 - x_2\left(t-\tau_2\right)\right) \\ \dot{y}_2 = a_2\left(x_2^2 - 1\right)y_2 - f_2x_2\left(x_2 + d_2\right)\left(x_2 + e_2\right) \end{cases} \tag{10}$$

In this variant, we also observe shortening (like in **Figure 5**) of the period of oscillations. In this pathology, the presence of more than two conduction paths is possible which is associated with more re-entry waves. Increasing the number of feedbacks modelling re-entry waves of slow pathways causes a progressive shortening of the period of oscillation, while the rhythm remains regular. The conclusion is that a regular excitation may evoke a regular answer.

After examining the influence of excitation with modified van der Pol oscillator wave, we have analysed behaviour of the modified van der Pol oscillator with feedback excited with a single rectangular pulse. In this way, two excitations co-exist in the system—the wave brought by the oscillator's feedback and the one from the external pulse. The pulse is defined by a step function H for the amplitude $A$=4 and the length of pulse $L$ =0.05 and it is applied to the oscillator with $k$=1 and $T$=1. The function H is defined as:

$$H_{A,L}\left(t\right) = \begin{cases} A, \ 0 < t < L \\ 0, \ otherwise \end{cases}$$

Influence of the pulse is treated as an appearance of the accessory current in the system. For this reason, this pulse is introduced to the equation describing the potential change (the $x$ variable):

$$\dot{x} = y(t) + k\left(x(t-T) - x(t)\right) + H_{A,L}\left(t - t_p\right),$$
$$\dot{y} = -a\left(x^2(t) - 1\right)y(t) - fx(t)\left(x(t) + d\right)\left(x(t) + e\right)$$

where *tp* denotes the moment in time when the pulse starts.

The influence of the pulse, which results in the period length change, depends on in which phase of oscillations it is applied. As mentioned before, the excitation influences the system having the regular behaviour.

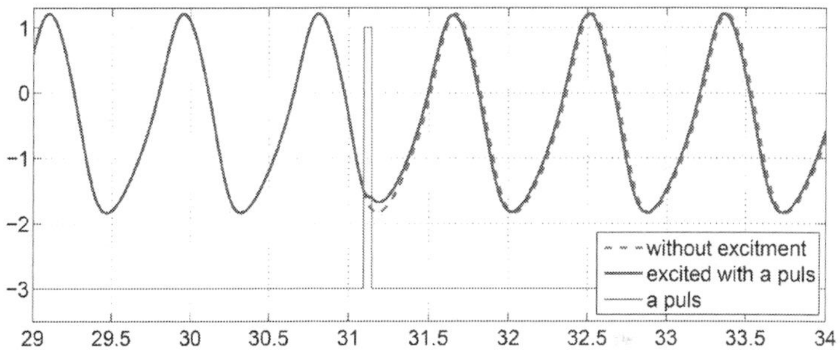


**Figure 6.** Numerical solution of the system with feedback ($k = 1,\ T = 0.5$), excited with the rectangular pulse.

Numerical solution of the system with feedback ($k=1$, $T=0.5$), excited with the rectangular pulse is presented in **Figure 6**. Red colour presents modified van der Pol model with feedback, whereas blue one shows the modified van der Pol model with feedback, which is additionally excited with the rectangular pulse. In this case application of the external pulse does not influence oscillator's period length, oscillations are stable. There are phase ranges for which oscillations are sensitive to a disturbance. Phase response curves for modified van der Pol system without feedback and for two cases with feedback ($k=1$, $T=1$ and $k=1$, $T=0.5$) which are excited with the rectangular pulse ($A=4$, $L=0.05$) are shown in **Figure 7**. A phase response curve is a graphic presentation of the influence of excitation for oscillation phases of modified van der Pol system. Its shape depends on in which phase of oscillation the excitation is exerted. This curve describes the dependence between the change of length of one cycle of oscillation and the excitation phase $\varphi$. For example, the application of the excitation in a moment when the system abides in the refraction state does not change the behaviour of the system.

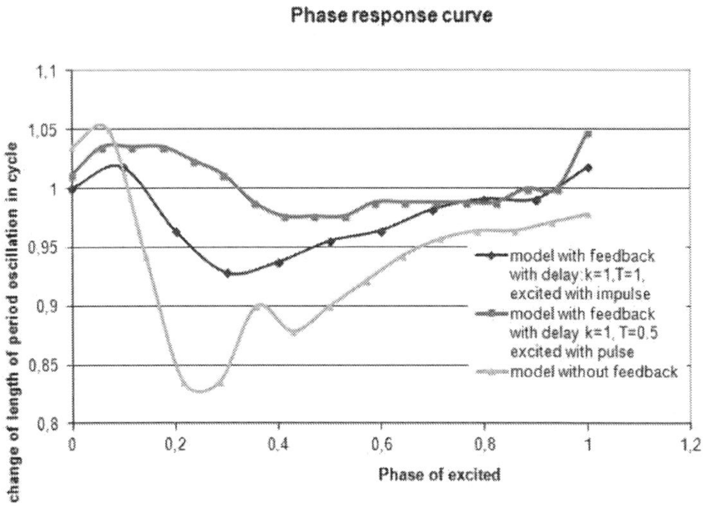


**Figure 7.** Phase response curves for models with rectangular pulse.

The system is phase-sensitive, and that, depending on the phase, excitation may change the potential period length. Models with feedback are much less phase-sensitive, **Figure 7**. The feedback strongly modifies the properties of the modified van der Pol model.

The human heart rhythm with feedback about AV node is low-variable. The results of this study were consulted with the medical doctor from the Institute of Cardiology in Anin near Warsaw, who confirmed that the very stable heart rhythm is typical for patients with AV nodal re-entrant tachycardia.

One of the most important features of oscillators is synchronization. The behaviour of cardiac pacemaker cells resembles those relaxation oscillators. A characteristic property of relaxation oscillators is that they may be synchronized by an external signal, if the latter has a periodicity similar to spontaneous frequency of the oscillator [14]. We investigate a phenomenological model for the heartbeat which consists of two coupled van der Pol oscillators. The coupling between these oscillator (action potential) can be either unidirectional or bidirectional, with or without feedback. Below, we present our model with possible couplings and feedbacks and try to analyse all of them for behaviour of given system and its synchronization.

$$\begin{cases} \dot{x}_1 = y_1 - k_1\left(x_2(t-\tau) - x_1\right) \\ \dot{y}_1 = a_1\left(x_1^2 - 1\right)y_1 - f_1 x_1\left(x_1 + d_1\right)\left(x_1 + e_1\right) + s_1\left(x_2 - x_1\right) \\ \dot{x}_2 = y_2 - k_2\left(x_1 - x_2(t-\tau)\right) \\ \dot{y}_2 = a_2\left(x_2^2 - 1\right)y_2 - f_2 x_2\left(x_2 + d_2\right)\left(x_2 + e_2\right) + s_2\left(x_1 - x_2\right) \end{cases} \tag{11}$$

If we consider physiological coupling between nodes, then the $s_2$ coupling is introduced to our system. It means that the SA node directs AV node. For small value of $s_2$ (in **Figure 8**, $s_2=1$, $k_1=0$, $s_1=0$, $k_2=0$) the result is similar to ref. [1], **Figure 8**.

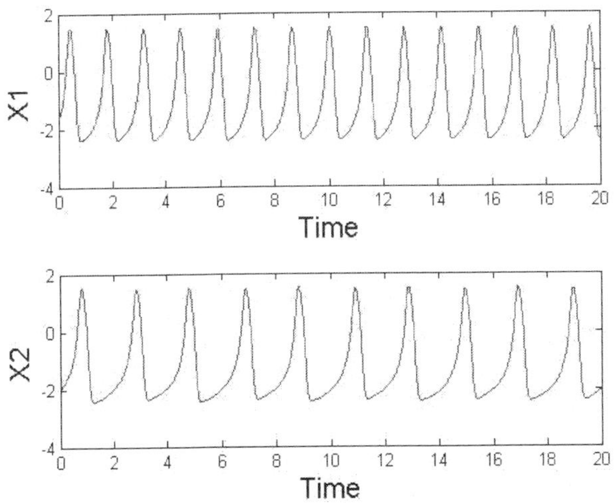


**Figure 8.** Time series: physiological coupling between nodes, the parameters are given in Eq. (9).

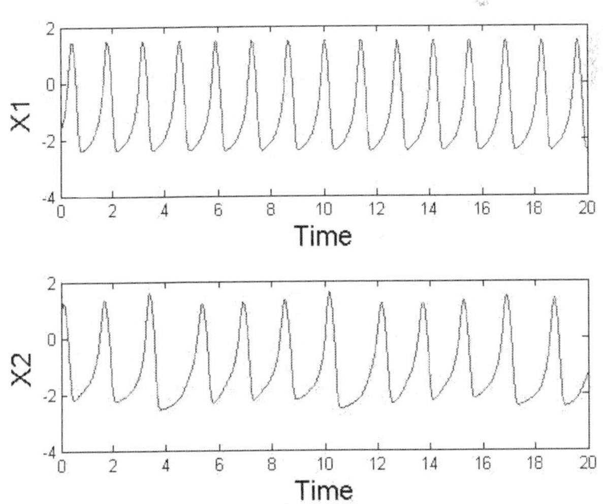


**Figure 9.** Time series: physiological coupling for $s_2=5$.

But for bigger value (e.g. 10 or 100), parts of amplitudes are synchronized in-phase with $x_1$ and aperiodic behaviour appears, which is presented in **Figures 9** and **10**.

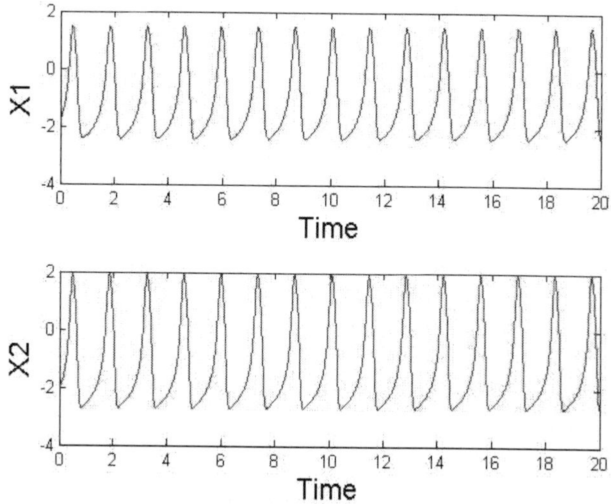


**Figure 10.** Time series: physiological coupling for $s_2 = 100$.

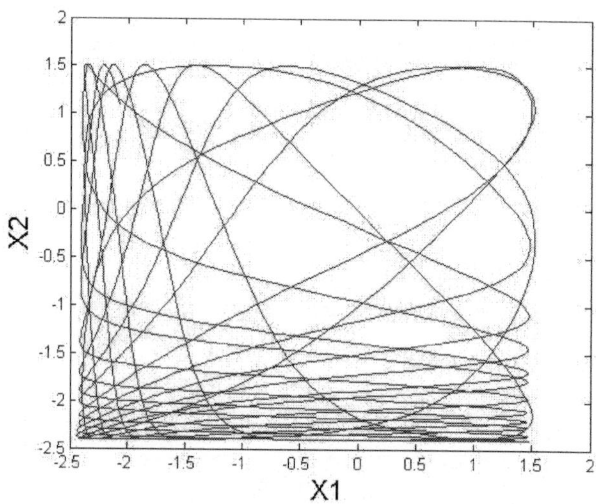


**Figure 11.** Projection of the phase space for $s1 = 1$.

This causes the attempt of fitting the AV frequency to SA which slows down the heart rate.

We study here the synchronization properties of such an association with respect to the nature and intensity of coupling.

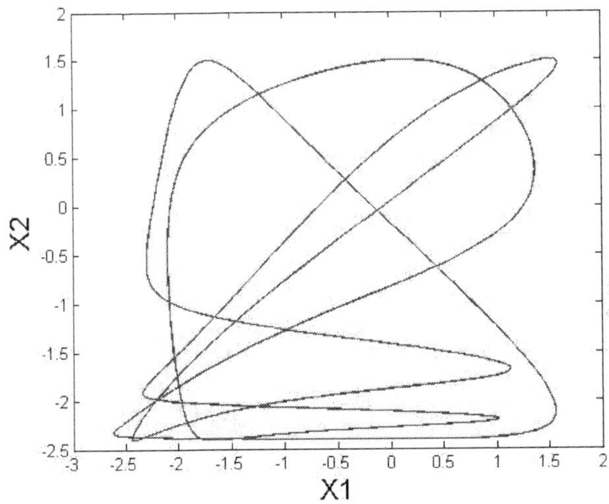


**Figure 12.** Projection of the phase space for $s1 = 10$.

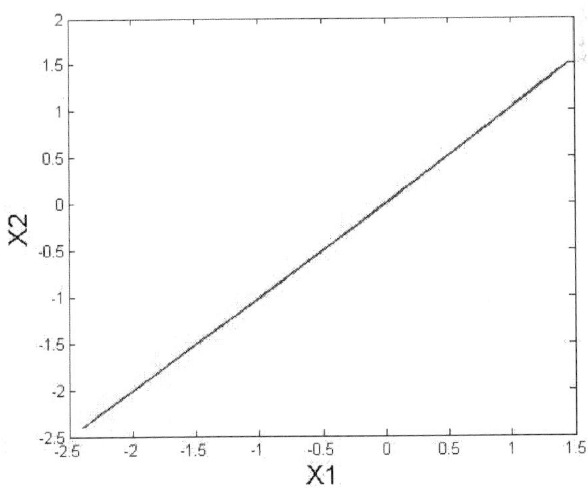


**Figure 13.** Projection of the phase space for $s1 = 1000$.

In **Figures 11–13**, we can observe an influence of unidirectional coupling for strength of synchronization of given oscillators (Eq. (11)). We must remember that complete synchronization of oscillators, characterized by $x_1(t)=x_2(t)$ and $y_1(t)=y_2(t)$, is unlikely to be observed in practice, due to the non-similarity of the coupled oscillators [21]. But oscillators, which are considered, are similar. In case when there is added unidirectional coupling to the system ($s_1 \neq 0$ *or* $s_2 \neq 0$), it is assumed that the coupling coefficient is a variable parameter in the analysed system. This parameter denotes the strength of the unidirectional coupling, all the remaining parameters being held constant. For small $s_1$ there is no synchronization, but for large $s1$ there is complete synchronization, which is shown in **Figure 13**. Similar results are obtained for $s_2$. When bidirectional coupling occurs in the system ($s_1 \neq 0$ *and* $s_2 \neq 0$), it can also obtain complete synchronization but there must be big asymmetry of value of coupling coefficients: $s_1 \ll s_2$ *or* $s_1 \gg s_2$.

Finally, the influence of the bidirectional coupling for behaviour of the model was studied. It would seem that the bidirectional coupling should operate so that when we enter it in relation 2:1 between oscillators, the rhythm of the fast pathway should be slowed down, while the rhythm of the fast pathway should accelerate.

In the model without feedback, periodic potential $x_1$ and $x_2$ are obtained, which is a dynamics of a physiological rhythm. But there is no synchronization for these parameters. When coupling coefficients are added to the system: $k_1 \neq 0$ *and* $k_2 \neq 0$, we obtain a set of projections of the phase space for different values of couplings, **Figures 14–16**.

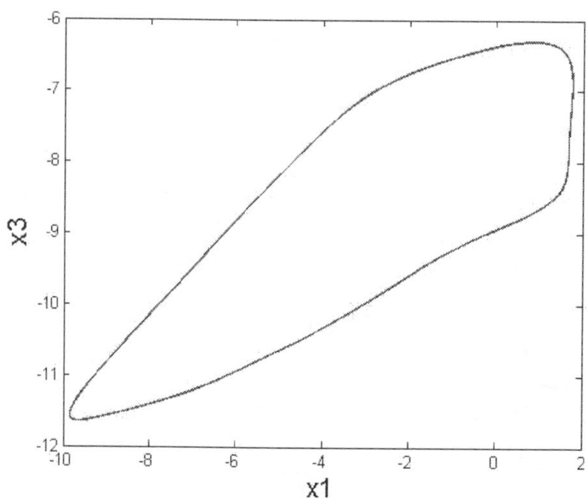


**Figure 14.** Projection of the phase space for $k1=2$ and $k2=1$.

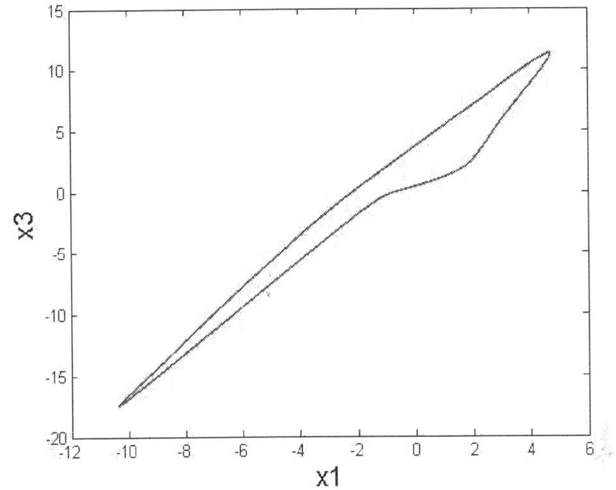


**Figure 15.** Projection of the phase space for k1=5 and k2=10..

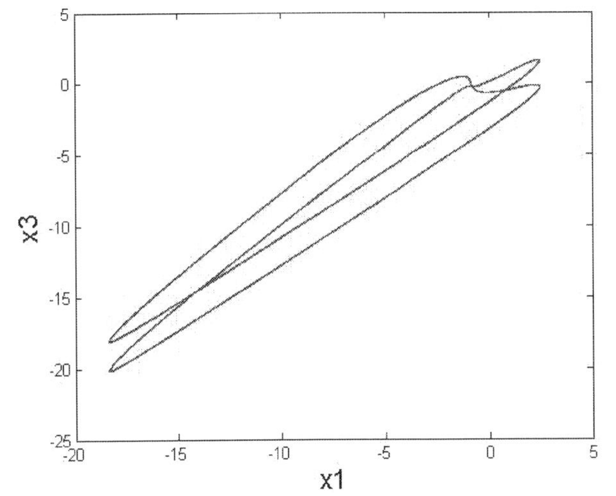


**Figure 16.** Projection of the phase space for k1=10 and k2=10.

However, with bigger values of $k_1$, $k_2$, a partial synchronization can be found in the system, **Figure 15**. Further increasing the value of the coefficients causes, however, the most significant changes in the portrait of the phase space. We can observe partial synchronization, but this synchronization has asymmetric character, **Figure 16**.

We investigated the synchronization between oscillators themselves despite that the generation of cardiac dysrhythmias are associated with a lack of synchronization between autonomous pacemakers [22]. But we showed that we can obtain certain types of synchronization: phase synchronization, partial synchronization or lag synchronization. This depends on the strength of coupling coefficients. Corresponding large coefficient may cause synchronization, but often setpoints are not the values of the physiological range.

## 4. Conclusions

Main aim of the paper was to propose the system of differential equations describing the dynamics of action potential that accompanies the WPW syndrome and five different forms of AVNRT. In this work, by using the proposed models we were able to reproduce the most important physiological properties of the discussed pathologies. In literature, there are no mathematical models of AVNRT. By using one of the proposed models, we can try to add an equation which is responsible for modelling the pharmacological treatment of the pathologies of our interest. These type of models then can help to determine an optimal treatment. On the other hand, we should keep in mind that the proposed models are phenomenological, so the results are accurate as far as a simple model can describe the potential found in one of the more complex oscillators appearing in real biological phenomena. We can continue the validation of these models with the use of medical data. However, to collect the necessary data, only the invasive methods can be used, which constitutes an important difficulty.

## Author details

Beata Jackowska-Zduniak

Address all correspondence to: beata.zduniak@wp.pl

Warsaw University of Life Sciences, Warsaw, Poland

## References

[1] S. Konturek, editor.The human physiology. The cardiovascular system.II. Cracow: Jagiellonian University Press; 2001.

[2] D. G. Katritsis, M. E. Josephson. Classification of electrophysiological types of atrioventricular nodal re-entrant tachycardia: a reappraisal. Europace. 2013;15:1231-1240.

[3] K. Malaczynska, K. Blaszczyk. Atrioventricular nodal reentrant tachycardia. Polish review of the Cardiology. 2012;14:196-203.

[4] B. Zduniak, M. Bodnar, U. Foryś. A modified van der Pol equation with delay in a description of the heart action. Int. J. Appl. Math. Comput. Sci. 2014;24:853-863.

[5] P. Podziemski, J. J. Żebrowski,. A simple model of the right atrium of the human heart with the sinoatrial and atrioventricular nodes included. J Clin Monit Comput. 2013;27:481-498.

[6] A. Fujiki. Junctional rhythm associated with ventriculoatrial block during slow pathway ablation in atypical atrioventricular nodal re-entrant tachycardia. Europace. 2008;10:928-987.

[7] B.Dabrowska, P. Gajewski. Postepowanie u chorych z nadkomorowymi zaburzeniami rytmu Wytyczne American College of Cardiology, American Heart Association European Society of Cardiology. Medycyna Praktyczna. 2004;6:1-62.

[8] R.A. Freedman, J.W. Mason. Sustained ventricular tachycardia, clinical aspects. Cardiac Pacing and Electrophysiology. Third Edition. P. Samet and N. El. Sherif, eds., Philadelphia: W. B. Sanders Co. 1991; 247-264.

[9] W. G. Stevenson. Exploring postinforction reentrant ventrivular tachycardia with entertainment mapping. J. Am. Coll. Cardiol. 1997;29: 1180-1189.

[10] J. Warminski. Synchronization effects and chaos in the Van der Pol-Mathieu oscillator. J. Theoretical. Appl. Mechanics. 2001;4(39): 861-884.

[11] P. Perlikowski, A. Stefanski, T. Kapitaniak. Discontinuous synchrony in an array of Van der Pol oscillators. Int. J. Non-Linear. Mechanics. 2010;45:895-901.

[12] K. Tsumoto, T. Yoshinaga, H. Kawakami. Bifurcations of synchronized responses in synaptically coupled Bonhoffer Van der Pol neurons. Phys. Rev. E. 2002;65: 036330-1-036230-9.

[13] Y. Uwate, Y. Nishio. Synchronization phenomena in van der Pol oscillators coupled by a time-varying resistor. Int. J. Bifurc. Chaos. 2007;17(10):3565-3569.

[14] L. Henk van der Tweel, F. L. Meijler, F. J. L. van Capelle. Synchronization of the heart. J. Appl. Physiol. 1973;34(2): 283-287.

[15] A. Maccari. The response of a parametrically excited van der Pol oscillator to a time delay state feedback. Nonlinear Dynamics. 2001;26:105-119.

[16] J. Xu, K.W. Chung. Effects of time delayed position feedback on a van der Pol – Duffing oscillator. Physica D. 2003;180(1):17-39.

[17] D.V. Ramana Reddy, A. Sen, G.L. Johnston. Experimental evidence of time-delay-induced death in coupled limit-cycle oscillators. Phys. Rev. Lett.. 2000;85:3381–3384.

[18] A. Hodgkin, A.F. Huxley. A quantitative description of membrane current and its application to conduction and excitation in nerve. J. Physiol. 1952;117: 500-544.

[19] Ch. Letellier, editor. Chaos in Nature. New Jersey: World Scientific Publishing Co. Ltd.; 2013. pp. 1-377.

[20] D. Postnov, S. K. Han, H. Kook. Synchronization of diffusively coupled oscillators near the homoclinic bifurcation. Phys. Rev. E. 1999;60(3): 2799-2807.

[21] K. Grudziński. Modeling the Electrical Activity of the Heart Conduction [thesis]. Warsaw, Poland; 2007.

[22] S.Bocaletti, J. Kurthus, G. Osipov, D. Valladares, C.S. Zhou. The synchronization of chaotic systems. Phys. Rep. 2002;366(1):1-101.

Section 2

# Mathematical and Numerical Methods

Chapter 5

# Numerical Simulation Using Artificial Neural Network on Fractional Differential Equations

Najeeb Alam Khan, Amber Shaikh,
Faqiha Sultan and Asmat Ara

Additional information is available at the end of the chapter

http://dx.doi.org/10.5772/64151

**Abstract**

This chapter offers a numerical simulation of fractional differential equations by utilizing Chebyshev-simulated annealing neural network (ChSANN) and Legendre-simulated annealing neural network (LSANN). The use of Chebyshev and Legendre polynomials with simulated annealing reduces the mean square error and leads to more accurate numerical approximation. The comparison of proposed methods with previous methods confirms the accuracy of ChSANN and LSANN.

**Keywords:** neural network, fractional Riccati, Legendre polynomial, Chebyshev polynomial, simulated annealing

## 1. Introduction

During the last few decades, fractional calculus has gained massive attention of physicists and mathematicians because of its numerous interdisciplinary applications. Many recent researches are ended up demonstrating the significance of fractional-order differential equations as valuable instruments to model several physical phenomena such as the non-linear oscillation of earthquake and the fluid dynamics traffic can be elegantly modelled with fractional derivatives [1, 2]. Various physical processes show fractional-order behaviour that might change with respect to time or space. The adoption of fractional calculus concepts is well known in many scientific areas such as physics, diffusion and wave propagation, heat transfer, viscoelasticity and damping, electronics, robotics, electromagnetism, signal processing, telecommunications, control systems, traffic systems, system identification, chaos and fractals, biology, genetic algorithms, filtration, modelling and identification, chemistry, irreversibility, as well as economy and finance [3–5].

Modelling of different physical phenomena gave rise to a special differential equation known as Riccati differential equation that was named after an Italian mathematician Count Jacopo Francesco Riccati. Due to many applications of fractional Riccati differential equations such as in stochastic controls and pattern formation, many researchers studied it to get the exact or approximate solutions. Such as fractional variational iteration method was applied in [6] to give an approximate analytical solution of non-linear fractional Riccati differential equation. His modified homotopy perturbation method (MHPM) was used on quadratic Riccati differential equation of fractional order [7]. The results of fractional Riccati differential equation were also obtained on the basis of Taylor collocation method [8]. Fractional Riccati differential equations were solved by means of variational iteration method and homotopy perturbation Pade technique [9, 10], and the numerical results were attained by using Chebyshev finite difference method [11]. Adomian decomposition method was presented for fractional Riccati differential equation [12], the problem was described by means of Bernstein collocation method [13], and enhanced homotopy perturbation method (EHPM) was used to study this problem [14]. Recently, artificial neural network and sequential quadratic programming have been utilized to obtain the solution of Riccati differential equation [15]. The problem was also explained by Legendre wavelet operational matrix method [16] and the results of fractional Riccati differential equation by new homotopy perturbation method (NHPM) [17] were obtained.

In recent years, artificial neural network (ANN) is one of the methods that are attaining massive attention of researchers in the area of mathematics as well as in different physical sciences. The concept of ANN started to develop in 1943 when a neurophysiologist and a young mathematician [18] gave the idea on working of a neuron with the help of an electric circuit. Later, a book [19] was written to clarify the working of neurons then in 1949. Bernard Widrow and Marcian Hoff developed a model MEDALIN that was used to study the first real-world problem of neural network. Researchers continued to study the single-layered neural network, but in 1975, the concept of multilayer perceptron (MLP) was introduced, which was computationally exhaustive due to multilayer architecture. The excessive training time and high computational complexity of MLP gave rise to functional neural network by which the complexity of multilayers was overcome by introducing variable functions [20]. Functional link neural network has been implemented to several problems such as modified functional link neural network for denoising of image [21], active control of non-linear noise processes through functional link neural network [22], and the problem of channel equalization in a digital communication system was solved by functional link neural network [23]. Due to less computational effort with easy to implement procedure, functional link neural network was also implemented to solve differential equations [24, 25].

## 2. Definitions and preliminaries

The Riemann-Liouville, Grünwald-Letnikov and Caputo definitions of fractional derivatives of order $\alpha>0$ are used more frequently among several definitions of fractional derivatives and integrals, but in this chapter, the Caputo definition will be used for working out the fractional derivative in a subsequent procedure. The definitions of commonly used fractional differential operators are discussed in the study of Sontakke and Shaikh [26].

**Definition 1:** The Riemann-Liouville fractional derivative operator can be defined as follows:

$$D^{\alpha}g(x)=\frac{1}{\Gamma(\xi-\alpha)}\frac{d^{\xi}}{dx^{\xi}}\int_{a}^{x}\frac{g(\beta)}{(x-\beta)^{\alpha+1-\xi}}d\beta,\quad \xi\text{-}1<\alpha<\xi$$

where here $\alpha>0,\ x>a,\ \alpha,\ a$ and $x\in R$.

**Definition 2:** The definition of fractional differential operator was introduced by Caputo in late 1960s that can be defined as follows [27]:

$$D_{*}^{\alpha}g(x)=\frac{1}{\Gamma(\xi-\alpha)}\int_{a}^{x}\frac{g^{(\xi)}(\beta)}{(x-\beta)^{\alpha+1-\xi}}d\beta,\quad \xi\text{-}1<\alpha<\xi$$

where here $\alpha>0,\ x>a,\ \alpha,\ a$ and $x\in R$.

The Caputo fractional derivative satisfies the important attribute of being zero when applied to a constant. In addition, it is attained by computing an ordinary derivative followed by the fractional integral, while the Riemann-Liouville is acquired in the contrary order.

## 3. ChSANN and LSANN

### 3.1. Methodology

The functional mapping of (LSANN) and (ChSANN) is shown in **Figure 1** demonstrating the structure of both methods, but for the convenience of the reader, a stepwise explanation of both the methods is also presented.

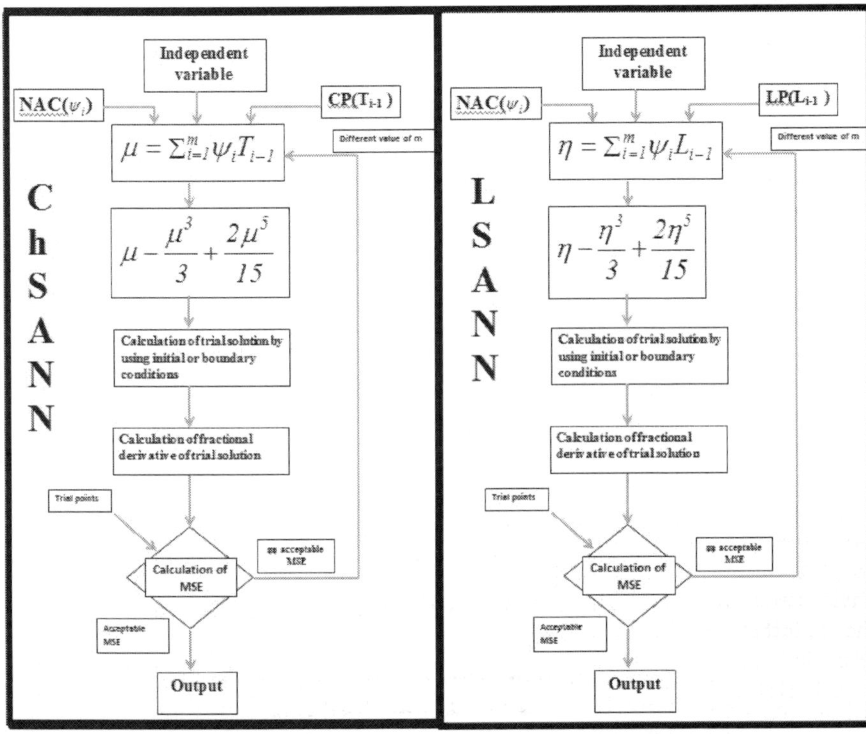


**Figure 1.** Model diagram of ChSANN and LSANN.

The combined steps for both the methods are explained because of the structural similarity in them, except the polynomial basis that affects the accuracy of the results.

Step 1: The summation of the product of network adaptive coefficients (NAC) and Chebyshev or Legendre polynomials is calculated for the independent variable of fractional differential equation for an arbitrary value of $m$ as shown in **Figure 1**.

Step 2: The activation of $\mu$ or $\eta$ will be performed by the first three terms of the series of tangent hyperbolic function tanh ( • ), these terms have been mentioned in **Figure 1**.

Step 3: The trial solution will be calculated by using initial conditions as in the study of Lagaris and Fotiadis [28].

Step 4: Required derivatives of the trial solution will be calculated.

Step 5: The optimization of mean square error (MSE) or learning of NAC will be executed by the thermal minimization methodology known as simulated annealing. The equation used to calculate MSE would be discussed in next section. Before optimization, the independent variable will be discretized by an array of trial points.

Step 6: If the value of MSE is in an acceptable range, then the values of trial points and NAC will be replaced in trial solution to get the output. On the other hand, the procedure will be repeated from step 1 with a different value of $m$.

### 3.2. Implementation on fractional Riccati differential equation

In this section, the ChSANN and LSANN are employed for the fractional Riccati differential equation of the type:

$$\frac{d^\alpha y(t)}{dt^\alpha} = f(t,y), \quad y(0) = A\ , \quad 0 < \alpha \leq 1 \tag{1}$$

For implementing both methodologies, Eq. (1) can be written in the following form:

$$\nabla^\alpha y_{tr}(t,\psi) - F(t, y_{tr}(t,\psi)) = 0, \quad t \in [0,1] \tag{2}$$

$y_{tr}(t, \psi)$ can be defined as trial solution, where $\psi$ is defined as NAC, generally known as weights, and $\nabla$ is defined as differential operator. Trial solution will be obtained by applying Taylor series on the activation of $\mu$ by using the initial conditions, while $\mu$ being the sum of the product of network adaptive coefficients and Chebyshev polynomials. For obtaining the trial solution of LSANN, the above procedure will be pursued, but $\eta$ will be calculated in spite of $\mu$, that is the sum of the product of NAC and Legendre polynomials. Here, tanh ( • )is used as activation function, but for fractional derivative based on Caputo sense, first three terms of the Taylor series of tanh ( • ) are considered that are given for ChSANN as follows:

$$N = \mu - \frac{\mu^3}{3} + \frac{2\mu^5}{15} \tag{3}$$

while for ChSANN, $\mu$ can be defined as follows:

$$\mu = \sum_{i=1}^{m} \psi_i T_{i-1} \tag{4}$$

where here $T_{i-1}$ are Chebyshev polynomials with the following recursive formula:

$$T_{m+1}(x) = 2xT_m(x) - T_{m-1}(x), \ m \geq 2 \tag{5}$$

while hile $T_0(x)=1$ and $T_1(x)=x$.

For LSANN, the activation function and $\eta$ can be defined as follows:

$$N = \eta - \frac{\eta^3}{3} + \frac{2\eta^5}{15} \tag{6}$$

$$\eta = \sum_{i=1}^{m} \psi_i L_{i-1} \tag{7}$$

whereas hereas $L_{i-1}$ are the Legendre polynomials with the recursive formula:

$$L_{m+1} = \frac{1}{(m+1)} (2m+1)\, x\, L_m(x) - \frac{1}{(m+1)} m\, L_{m-1}(x), \;\; m \geq 2 \tag{8}$$

where here $L_0(x)=1$ and $L_1(x)=x$, and value of $m$ is adjustable to reach the utmost accuracy. For Eq. (1), the trial solution can be written as defined in the study of Lagaris and Fotiadis [28], but $N$ will be used according to the method.

$$y_{tr}(t,\psi) = A + t\, N \tag{9}$$

Trial solution can be written in expanded form for ChSANN at $m=2$ as follows:

$$y_{tr}(t,\psi) = A + t\left( \psi_1 + t\psi_2 - \frac{1}{3}(\psi_1 + t\psi_2)^3 + \frac{2}{15}(\psi_1 + t\psi_2)^5 \right) \tag{10}$$

Fractional derivative in Caputo sense of Eq. (10) is as follows:

$$\begin{aligned} \nabla^\alpha y_{tr}(t,\psi) = & \frac{\Gamma 2}{\Gamma(2-\alpha)} t^{1-\alpha}\left( \psi_1 - \frac{\psi_1^3}{3} + \frac{2\psi_1^5}{15} \right) + \left(\frac{2}{3}\right)\frac{\Gamma 6}{\Gamma(7-\alpha)} t^{5-\alpha}\left(\psi_1\psi_2^4\right) \\ & + \left(\frac{2}{15}\right)\frac{\Gamma 7}{\Gamma(7-\alpha)} t^{6-\alpha}\left(\psi_2^5\right) + \frac{\Gamma 3}{\Gamma(3-\alpha)} \; t^{2-\alpha}\left( \psi_2 - \psi_1^2\psi_2 + \frac{2}{3}\psi_1^4\psi_2 \right) \\ & + \frac{\Gamma 4}{\Gamma(4-\alpha)} t^{3-\alpha}\left( \frac{4}{3}\psi_1^3\psi_2^2 - \psi_1\psi_2^2 \right) + \frac{\Gamma 5}{\Gamma(5-\alpha)} t^{4-\alpha}\left( \frac{4}{3}\psi_1^2\psi_2^3 - \frac{\psi_2^3}{3} \right) \end{aligned} \tag{11}$$

The mean square error (MSE) of the Eq. (1) will be calculated from the following:

$$MSE(\psi_i) = \sum_{j=1}^{n} \frac{1}{n}\left( \nabla^\alpha y_{tr}\left(t_j,\psi_i\right) - F\left(t_j, y_{tr}\left(t_j,\psi_i\right)\right) \right)^2, \quad t \in [0,1] \tag{12}$$

whereas here as $n$ can be defined as number of trial points. The learning of NAC will be performed from Eq. (10) by minimizing the MSE to the lowest possible acceptable minimum value. The thermal minimization methodology and simulated annealing is applied here for the learning of NAC. The process of simulated annealing can be described as a physical model of annealing, where a metal object is first heated and then slowly cooled down to minimize the system energy. Here, we have implemented the procedure by Mathematica 10, but the interested readers can learn the details of simulated annealing from the study of Ledesma et al. [29].

***Example 1:***

Consider the following Riccati differential equation with initial condition as:

$$\frac{d^{\alpha}y(t)}{dt^{\alpha}}+y^{2}(t)-1=0,\quad y(0)=0\,,\ 0<\alpha\leq 1$$

The exact solution for $\alpha=1$ is given by the following:

$$y(t)=\frac{e^{2t}-1}{e^{2t}+1}$$

The above fractional Riccati differential equation is solved by implementing the ChSANN and LSANN algorithms for various values of $\alpha$ and the results are compared with several methods to exhibit the strength of proposed neural network algorithms. The ChSANN and LSANN methods are employed on the above equation for $\alpha=1$ with 20 equidistant training points and 6 NAC and attained the mean square error up to $5.501631\times10^{-9}$and $1.21928\times10^{-9}$ for ChSANN and LSANN, respectively. **Figure 2** shows the combined results of ChSANN for different

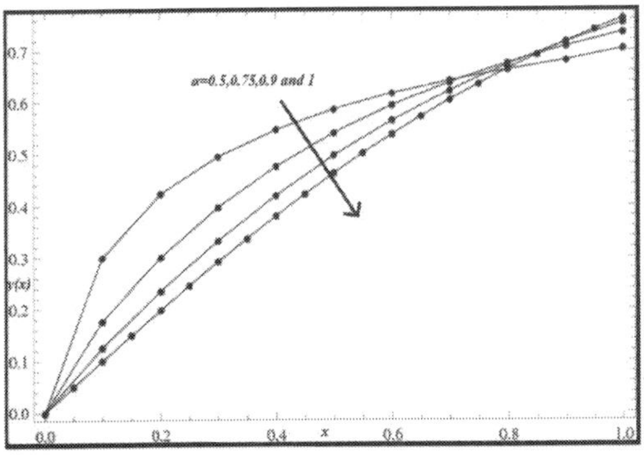


**Figure 2.** ChSANN results at different values of $\alpha=1$.

values of $\alpha$. **Table 1** depicts the comparison of results obtained from both the methods with exact solution and the absolute error values for both the methods. Absolute error (AE) values for ChSANN and LSANN can be viewed in **Table 1** but can be better visualized in **Figure 3**. Implementation of ChSANN and LSANN for $\alpha = 0.75$ with 10 equidistant training points and 6 NAC on the above equation gave the mean square error up to $1.66032 \times 10^{-7}$ for ChSANN and $4.8089 \times 10^{-7}$ for LSANN. **Table 2** shows the numerical comparison for $\alpha = 0.75$ with 10 equidistant training points of ChSANN and LSANN with the methods in [13, 14], while **Tables 3** and **4** demonstrate the numerical comparison of the proposed methods with the methods in [7, 13, 14] for $\alpha = 0.5$and $\alpha = 0.9$ correspondingly. Numerical values of ChSANN for $\alpha = 1$ at $t = 1$ are presented in **Table 5**.

| $x$ | Exact | ChSANN | LSANN | AE of ChSANN | AE of LSANN |
|---|---|---|---|---|---|
| 0.05 | 0.049884 | 0.0499572 | 0.0499441 | $1.20167 \times 10^{-6}$ | $1.49267 \times 10^{-5}$ |
| 0.10 | 0.099668 | 0.0996676 | 0.0996552 | $4.32269 \times 10^{-6}$ | $1.27675 \times 10^{-5}$ |
| 0.15 | 0.148885 | 0.148884 | 0.148876 | $1.13944 \times 10^{-6}$ | $9.07723 \times 10^{-6}$ |
| 0.20 | 0.197375 | 0.197372 | 0.197367 | $2.91448 \times 10^{-6}$ | $7.92946 \times 10^{-6}$ |
| 0.25 | 0.244919 | 0.244915 | 0.244909 | $4.13612 \times 10^{-6}$ | $9.23796 \times 10^{-6}$ |
| 0.30 | 0.291313 | 0.291309 | 0.291301 | $3.63699 \times 10^{-6}$ | $1.12070 \times 10^{-5}$ |
| 0.35 | 0.336376 | 0.336374 | 0.336363 | $1.41863 \times 10^{-6}$ | $1.22430 \times 10^{-5}$ |
| 0.40 | 0.379949 | 0.379949 | 0.379937 | $1.42762 \times 10^{-6}$ | $1.17881 \times 10^{-5}$ |
| 0.45 | 0.421899 | 0.421902 | 0.421889 | $3.33093 \times 10^{-6}$ | $1.03088 \times 10^{-5}$ |
| 0.50 | 0.462117 | 0.462117 | 0.462108 | $3.05535 \times 10^{-6}$ | $8.76900 \times 10^{-6}$ |
| 0.55 | 0.500520 | 0.500521 | 0.500512 | $3.81254 \times 10^{-6}$ | $7.95700 \times 10^{-6}$ |
| 0.60 | 0.537055 | 0.537046 | 0.537042 | $3.62984 \times 10^{-6}$ | $8.00729 \times 10^{-6}$ |
| 0.65 | 0.571670 | 0.571663 | 0.571662 | $6.95133 \times 10^{-6}$ | $8.33268 \times 10^{-6}$ |
| 0.70 | 0.604368 | 0.604360 | 0.604360 | $7.47479 \times 10^{-6}$ | $8.04113 \times 10^{-6}$ |
| 0.75 | 0.635149 | 0.635145 | 0.635142 | $4.22458 \times 10^{-6}$ | $6.62579 \times 10^{-6}$ |
| 0.80 | 0.664037 | 0.664038 | 0.664032 | $1.57001 \times 10^{-6}$ | $4.48924 \times 10^{-6}$ |
| 0.85 | 0.691069 | 0.691076 | 0.691067 | $6.23989 \times 10^{-6}$ | $2.58549 \times 10^{-6}$ |
| 0.90 | 0.716298 | 0.716303 | 0.716298 | $5.13615 \times 10^{-6}$ | $2.66632 \times 10^{-7}$ |
| 0.95 | 0.739783 | 0.739780 | 0.739793 | $3.29187 \times 10^{-6}$ | $9.67625 \times 10^{-6}$ |
| 1.00 | 0.761594 | 0.761584 | 0.761644 | $9.94216 \times 10^{-6}$ | $4.97369 \times 10^{-5}$ |

**Table 1.** Numerical comparisons of ChSANN and LSANN values with exact values for fractional Riccati differential equation.

http://dx.doi.org/10.5772/64151

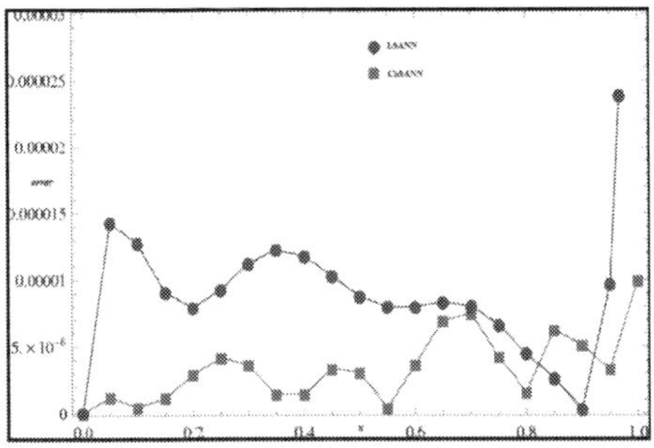


**Figure 3.** Absolute error of ChSANN and LSANN at $\alpha = 1$ for test example 1.

| $x$ | ChSANN | LSANN | IABMM [14] | EHPM [14] | MHPM [7] | Bernstein [13] |
|---|---|---|---|---|---|---|
| 0 | 0 | 0 | 0 | 0 | 0 | 0 |
| 0.2 | 0.30018 | 0.29937 | 0.3117 | 0.3214 | 0.3138 | 0.30997 |
| 0.4 | 0.47512 | 0.47486 | 0.4885 | 0.5077 | 0.4929 | 0.48163 |
| 0.6 | 0.59334 | 0.59320 | 0.6045 | 0.6259 | 0.5974 | 0.59778 |
| 0.8 | 0.67572 | 0.67571 | 0.6880 | 0.7028 | 0.6604 | 0.67884 |
| 1.0 | 0.73748 | 0.73430 | 0.7478 | 0.7542 | 0.7183 | 0.73683 |

**Table 2.** Numerical comparison for $\alpha = 0.75$.

| $x$ | ChSANN | LSANN | MHPM [7] |
|---|---|---|---|
| 0 | 0 | 0 | 0 |
| 0.1 | 0.299658 | 0.299416 | 0.273875 |
| 0.2 | 0.422837 | 0.422808 | 0.454125 |
| 0.3 | 0.494204 | 0.494145 | 0.573932 |
| 0.4 | 0.545856 | 0.545773 | 0.644422 |
| 0.5 | 0.585660 | 0.585619 | 0.674137 |
| 0.6 | 0.616648 | 0.616647 | 0.671987 |
| 0.7 | 0.641558 | 0.641543 | 0.648003 |
| 0.8 | 0.662486 | 0.662452 | 0.613306 |
| 0.9 | 0.681101 | 0.681237 | 0.579641 |
| 1.0 | 0.702813 | 0.703857 | 0.558557 |

**Table 3.** Numerical comparison for $\alpha = 0.5$.

| $x$ | ChSANN | LSANN | IABMM [14] | EHPM [14] | MHPM [7] | Bernstein [13] |
|---|---|---|---|---|---|---|
| 0 | 0 | 0 | | | | |
| 0.2 | 0.234602 | 0.236053 | 0.2393 | 0.2647 | 0.2391 | 0.23878 |
| 0.4 | 0.419229 | 0.419898 | 0.4234 | 0.4591 | 0.4229 | 0.42258 |
| 0.6 | 0.563627 | 0.564474 | 0.5679 | 0.6031 | 0.5653 | 0.56617 |
| 0.8 | 0.672722 | 0.673241 | 0.6774 | 0.7068 | 0.6740 | 0.67462 |
| 1.0 | 0.753188 | 0.755002 | 0.7584 | 0.7806 | 0.7569 | 0.75458 |

**Table 4.** Numerical comparison for $\alpha = 0.9$.

| No of NAC | No of training points | Mean square error | $y(t)$ | Absolute error |
|---|---|---|---|---|
| 4 | 10 | $9.7679 \times 10^{-5}$ | 0.760078 | $1.51570 \times 10^{-3}$ |
| 5 | 20 | $2.3504 \times 10^{-7}$ | 0.761644 | $5.02121 \times 10^{-5}$ |
| 6 | 20 | $5.5016 \times 10^{-9}$ | 0.761584 | $9.94216 \times 10^{-6}$ |

**Table 5.** Numerical values of ChSANN at $t = 1$ and for $\alpha = 1$.

*Example 2:*

Consider the nonlinear Riccati differential equation along with the following initial condition:

$$\frac{d^{\alpha} y(t)}{dt^{\alpha}} + y^2(t) - 2y(t) - 1 = 0, \quad y(0) = 0\,, \quad 0 < \alpha \le 1$$

The exact solution when $\alpha = 1$ is given by [7]:

$$y(t) = 1 + \sqrt{2}\tanh\left(\sqrt{2}\,t + \frac{1}{2}\log\left(\frac{\sqrt{2}-1}{\sqrt{2}+1}\right)\right)$$

ChSANN and LSANN algorithms are executed on the above test experiment with 6NAC, $\alpha = 1$ and 20 equidistant points that gave the mean square error up to $1.6127 \times 10^{-7}$and $4.68641 \times 10^{-6}$ for ChSANN and LSANN, respectively. **Table 6** shows the absolute errors and the numerical comparison with exact values for both the methods, while graphical comparison can be better envisioned through **Figure 4**. **Tables 7** and **8** display the numerical comparison of the proposed methods with the results obtained in [7] for $\alpha = 0.75$and [13] for $\alpha = 0.9$, respectively, whereas the mean square error, number of training points, and NAC for different values of $\alpha$ are presented in **Table 9**. The effects on accuracy of results with variable NAC and training points can be understood through **Table 10**.

| $x$ | ChSANN | LSANN | Exact | AE of ChSANN |
|---|---|---|---|---|
| 0.05 | 0.052620 | 0.053034 | 0.052539 | $8.0725 \times 10^{-5}$ |
| 0.10 | 0.110385 | 0.110899 | 0.110295 | $8.9742 \times 10^{-5}$ |
| 0.15 | 0.173488 | 0.173936 | 0.173419 | $6.8944 \times 10^{-5}$ |
| 0.20 | 0.242027 | 0.242359 | 0.241977 | $5.0509 \times 10^{-5}$ |
| 0.25 | 0.315977 | 0.316226 | 0.315926 | $5.0577 \times 10^{-5}$ |
| 0.30 | 0.395175 | 0.395419 | 0.395105 | $6.9946 \times 10^{-5}$ |
| 0.35 | 0.479313 | 0.479634 | 0.479214 | $9.9086 \times 10^{-5}$ |
| 0.40 | 0.567937 | 0.568390 | 0.567812 | $1.2488 \times 10^{-4}$ |
| 0.45 | 0.660455 | 0.661048 | 0.660318 | $1.3690 \times 10^{-4}$ |
| 0.50 | 0.756146 | 0.756840 | 0.756014 | $1.3149 \times 10^{-4}$ |
| 0.55 | 0.854184 | 0.854907 | 0.854071 | $1.1284 \times 10^{-4}$ |
| 0.60 | 0.953657 | 0.954329 | 0.953566 | $9.0888 \times 10^{-5}$ |
| 0.65 | 1.053601 | 1.054165 | 1.053524 | $7.6914 \times 10^{-5}$ |
| 0.70 | 1.153027 | 1.153472 | 1.152949 | $7.8337 \times 10^{-5}$ |
| 0.75 | 1.250962 | 1.251332 | 1.250867 | $9.4552 \times 10^{-5}$ |
| 0.80 | 1.346479 | 1.346852 | 1.346364 | $1.1576 \times 10^{-4}$ |
| 0.85 | 1.438740 | 1.439172 | 1.438614 | $1.2625 \times 10^{-4}$ |
| 0.90 | 1.527024 | 1.527452 | 1.526911 | $1.1292 \times 10^{-4}$ |
| 0.95 | 1.610762 | 1.610859 | 1.610683 | $7.8852 \times 10^{-5}$ |
| 1.00 | 1.689559 | 1.688555 | 1.689498 | $6.1063 \times 10^{-5}$ |

**Table 6.** Numerical comparison of ChSANN and LSANN values with exact values at $\alpha = 1$ for fractional Riccati differential equation test example 2.

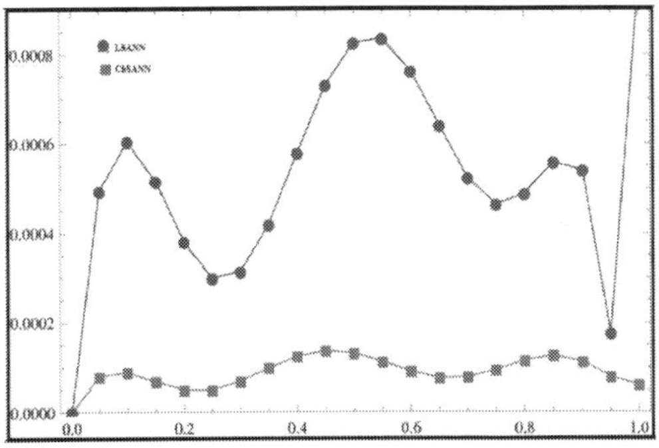


**Figure 4.** Absolute error of ChSANN and LSANN at $\alpha = 1$ for test example 2.

| $x$ | ChSANN | LSANN | MHPM [7] |
|---|---|---|---|
| 0 | 0 | 0 | 0 |
| 0.1 | 0.22983 | 0.21885 | 0.216866 |
| 0.2 | 0.46136 | 0.45018 | 0.482292 |
| 0.3 | 0.69478 | 0.68545 | 0.654614 |
| 0.4 | 0.92279 | 0.91423 | 0.891404 |
| 0.5 | 1.13531 | 1.12664 | 1.132763 |
| 0.6 | 1.32357 | 1.31532 | 1.370240 |
| 0.7 | 1.48314 | 1.47660 | 1.594278 |
| 0.8 | 1.61485 | 1.61045 | 1.794879 |
| 0.9 | 1.72401 | 1.71972 | 1.962239 |
| 1.0 | 1.81844 | 1.80882 | 2.087384 |

**Table 7.** Numerical comparison for $\alpha = 0.75$.

| $x$ | ChSANN | LSANN | Reference [13] |
|---|---|---|---|
| 0.2 | 0.31018 | 0.30567 | 0.314869 |
| 0.4 | 0.69146 | 0.68661 | 0.697544 |
| 0.5 | 0.89758 | 0.89230 | 0.903673 |
| 0.6 | 1.10220 | 1.09708 | 1.107866 |
| 0.8 | 1.47288 | 1.46889 | 1.477707 |
| 1.0 | 1.76276 | 1.76355 | 1.765290 |

**Table 8.** Numerical comparison for $\alpha = 0.9$.

| $\alpha$ | ChSANN | | | LSANN | | |
|---|---|---|---|---|---|---|
| | NAC | Training points | MSE | NAC | Training points | MSE |
| 1 | 6 | 20 | $1.6127 \times 10^{-7}$ | 6 | 20 | $4.68641 \times 10^{-6}$ |
| 0.9 | 6 | 10 | $7.2486 \times 10^{-6}$ | 6 | 10 | $7.36985 \times 10^{-6}$ |
| 0.75 | 6 | 20 | $6.9229 \times 10^{-5}$ | 6 | 10 | $1.91318 \times 10^{-5}$ |

**Table 9.** Value of mean square error at different values of $\alpha$.

| No. of NAC | No of training points | MSE | $y(t)$ | AE |
|---|---|---|---|---|
| 4 | 10 | $1.1531 \times 10^{-5}$ | 1.67997 | $9.52973 \times 10^{-3}$ |
| 5 | 10 | $4.9226 \times 10^{-7}$ | 1.69016 | $6.61306 \times 10^{-4}$ |
| 6 | 20 | $1.6127 \times 10^{-7}$ | 1.68956 | $6.10629 \times 10^{-5}$ |

**Table 10.** Numerical values of ChSANN at $t = 1$ and for $\alpha = 1$.

## 4. Results and discussion

In this chapter, two new algorithms have been developed and verified for the Riccati differential equation with fractional order, based on the functional neural network, Chebyshev and Legendre polynomials and simulated annealing for fractional differential equations. Substantiation of the methods is carried out by examining two benchmark examples that were already solved by some previously renowned methods. The numerical evaluation with previously obtained results for fractional-order derivative exhibited the achievement of proposed methods.

For test example 1, better results with less value of mean square error were obtained for each method. Comparison of the mean square errors $5.501631 \times 10^{-9}$ and $1.21928 \times 10^{-9}$ for ChSANN and LSANN, respectively, showed that the mean square error is less for LSANN when $\alpha = 1$. However, it can be observed from **Table 1** and **Figure 2** that ChSANN gave the better results with slightly more mean square error than LSANN. It can be noted from **Table 5** that better results can be attained with variable number of weights and training points, while the trend witnessed from **Table 5** indicated that for ChSANN, decreasing value of mean square error is directly proportional to the absolute error for $\alpha=1$.

The test example 2 showed quite similar trends as of example 1. **Tables 6** and **9** exhibited that for $\alpha=1$, less mean square error for ChSANN than LSANN was noted due to which, more accurate results were achieved by ChSANN at $\alpha=0.9$ as compared to LSANN that can be viewed in **Figure 4**. The results obtained for fractional values of derivatives are compared with MHPM for $\alpha=0.75$ and a collocation-based method of Bernstein polynomials for $\alpha=0.9$ as presented in **Tables 7** and **8**. The comparison showed that the results achieved by ChSANN and LSANN are quite similar to the results obtained by MHPM and collocation-based method of Bernstein polynomials. However, according to the observations from the case of $\alpha=1$, it can be assumed that the results obtained for $\alpha=0.75$ will be accurate up to 2–3 decimal places because the MSE was detected up to $6.9229 \times 10^{-5}$ for ChSANN and $1.91318 \times 10^{-5}$ for LSANN. While the results achieved for $\alpha=0.9$ will be accurate up to 3–4 decimal places as the MSE was noticed up to $7.2486 \times 10^{-6}$ for ChSANN and $7.36985 \times 10^{-6}$ for LSANN.

The methods proposed in this study are capable of handling highly non-linear systems. Both the proposed neural architectures are less computational and exhaustive than MLP. With ease of computation, the suggested activation function has made fractional differential equations possible to solve. Training of NAC by simulated annealing with Chebyshev and Legendre neural architecture minimized the MSE up to a tolerable level that leads to more accurate numerical approximation. Simulated annealing is a probabilistic procedure that is mostly free of initial values and can easily escape from local optimum to global optimum unlike other methods. As well as it can successfully optimize the functions with crests and plateaus. The methods can be enhanced by introducing more advanced optimization techniques. The motivation behind the work is the successful implementation of neural algorithms in the field of calculus that gave the solution of fractional differential equations a new direction with ease of implementation.

## 5. Conclusion

In this chapter, ChSANN and LSANN have been developed for fractional differential equations and successfully employed on two benchmark examples of Riccati differential equations. The proposed methods gave the excellent numerical approximation of the Riccati differential equation of fractional order. The most remarkable advantage of the proposed methods is the accurate prediction of the result for the fractional values of derivative. These procedures are easy to implement and can be used to find the exact solution in the fractional values of derivative. ChSANN displayed more accurate results than LSANN for the similar applied conditions. Both the proposed algorithms are non-iterative and can be implemented through mathematical software and Mathematica 10 was used in this study to obtain all the results displayed in **Tables 1–10** and **Figures 2–4**.

## Author details

Najeeb Alam Khan[1*], Amber Shaikh[1], Faqiha Sultan[2] and Asmat Ara[3]

*Address all correspondence to: njbalam@yahoo.com

1 Department of Mathematics, University of Karachi, Karachi, Pakistan

2 Department of Sciences and Humanities, National University of Computer and Emerging Sciences, Karachi, Pakistan

3 Department of Computer Science, Mohammad Ali Jinnah University, Karachi, Pakistan

## References

[1] He JH. Nonlinear oscillation with fractional derivative and its applications. International Conference on Vibrating Engineering. 1998;98:288–91.

[2] He JH. Some applications of nonlinear fractional differential equations and their approximations. Bulletin of Science, Technology & Society. 1999;15(2):86–90.

[3] Grigorenko I, Grigorenko E. Chaotic dynamics of the fractional Lorenz system. Physical Review Letters. 2003;91(3):034101.

[4] Podlubny I. Fractional differential equations: an introduction to fractional derivatives, fractional differential equations, to methods of their solution and some of their applications. Academic Press; 1998. ISBN 0125588402.

[5] Podlubny I. Geometric and physical interpretation of fractional integration and fractional differentiation. Fractional Calculus and Applied Analysis. 2002;5(4):367–86.

[6] Merdan M. On the solutions fractional Riccati differential equation with modified Riemann-Liouville derivative. International Journal of Differential Equations. 2012;2012:1–17.

[7] Odibat Z, Momani S. Modified homotopy perturbation method: application to quadratic Riccati differential equation of fractional order. Chaos, Solitons & Fractals. 2008;36(1):167–74.

[8] Öztürk Y, Anapalı A, Gülsu M, Sezer M. A collocation method for solving fractional Riccati differential equation. Journal of Applied Mathematics. 2013;2013:1–8.

[9] Jafari H, Tajadodi H. He's variational iteration method for solving fractional Riccati differential equation. International Journal of Differential Equations. 2010;2010:1–8.

[10] Jafari H, Tajadodi H, Baleanu D. A modified variational iteration method for solving fractional Riccati differential equation by Adomian polynomials. Fractional Calculus and Applied Analysis. 2013;16(1):109–22 .

[11] Khader MM. Numerical treatment for solving fractional Riccati differential equation. Journal of the Egyptian Mathematical Society. 2013;21(1):32–7.

[12] Momani S, Shawagfeh N. Decomposition method for solving fractional Riccati differential equations. Applied Mathematics and Computation. 2006;182(2):1083–92.

[13] Yüzbaşı Ş. Numerical solutions of fractional Riccati type differential equations by means of the Bernstein polynomials. Applied Mathematics and Computation. 2013;219(11):6328–43.

[14] Hosseinnia SH, Ranjbar A, Momani S. Using an enhanced homotopy perturbation method in fractional differential equations via deforming the linear part. Computers & Mathematics with Applications. 2008;56(12):3138–49.

[15] Raja MAZ, Manzar MA, Samar R. An efficient computational intelligence approach for solving fractional order Riccati equations using ANN and SQP. Applied Mathematical Modelling. 2015;39(10–11):3075–93.

[16] Balaji S. Legendre wavelet operational matrix method for solution of fractional order Riccati differential equation. Journal of the Egyptian Mathematical Society. 2015;23(2): 263–70.

[17] Khan NA, Ara A, Jamil M. An efficient approach for solving the Riccati equation with fractional orders. Computers & Mathematics with Applications. 2011;61(9):2683–9.

[18] McCulloch WS, Pitts W. A logical calculus of the ideas immanent in nervous activity. Bulletin of Mathematical Biophysics. 1943;5:115–33.

[19] Hebb DO. The organization of behavior: A neuropsychological theory. New York: Wiely; 1949.

[20] Pao Y-H, Phillips SM, Sobajic DJ. Neural-net computing and the intelligent control of systems. International Journal of Control. 1992;56(2):263–89.

[21] Pandey C, Singh V, Singh O, Kumar S. Functional link artificial neural network for denoising of image. Journal of Electronics and Communication Engineering. 2013;4(6): 109–15.

[22] Panda G, Das DP. Functional link artificial neural network for active control of nonlinear noise processes. International Workshop on Acoustic Echo and Noise Control. 2003;2003:163–6.

[23] Patra JC, Pal RN, editors. Functional link artificial neural network-based adaptive channel equalization of nonlinear channels with QAM signal. Systems, Man and Cybernetics, 1995 Intelligent Systems for the 21st Century, IEEE International Conference on; 22–25 October 1995.

[24] Mall S, Chakraverty S. Comparison of artificial neural network architecture in solving ordinary differential equations. Advances in Artificial Neural Systems. 2013;2013:1–12.

[25] Mall S, Chakraverty S. Chebyshev Neural Network based model for solving Lane-Emden type equations. Applied Mathematics and Computation. 2014;247:100–14.

[26] Sontakke BR, Shaikh AS. Properties of Caputo operator and its applications to linear fractional differential equations. International Journal of Engineering Research and Applications. 2015;5(5):22–7.

[27] Caputo M. Linear models of dissipation whose Q is almost frequency independent-II. Geophysical Journal International. 1967;13(5):529–39.

[28] Lagaris IE, Fotiadis DI. Artificial neural networks for solving ordinary and partial differential equations. IEEE Transactions on Neural Networks. 1998;9(5):987–1000.

[29] Ledesma S, Aviña G, Sanchez R. Practical considerations for simulated annealing implementation. In: Tan CM, editor. Simulated Annealing: InTech; 2008. ISBN 9789537619077.

Chapter 6

# Numerical Simulations of Some Real-Life Problems Governed by ODEs

N. H. Sweilam and T. A. Assiri

Additional information is available at the end of the chapter

http://dx.doi.org/10.5772/63958

**Abstract**

In this chapter, some real-life model problems that can be formulated as ordinary differential equations (ODEs) are introduced and numerically studied. These models are the variable-order fractional Hodgkin–Huxley model of neuronal excitation (VOFHHM) and other models with the variable-order fractional (VOF) time delay, such as the 4-year life cycle of a population of lemmings model, the enzyme kinetics with an inhibitor molecule model, and the Chen system model. A class of numerical methods is used to study the above-mentioned models such as non-standard finite difference (NSFD) and Adams-Bashforth-Moulton (ABM) methods. Numerical test examples are presented.

**Keywords:** Ordinary differential equations, Variable and fractional order real-life mathematical models, Adams-Bashforth-Moulton method, Non-standard finite difference method, Error analysis in numerical computations

## 1. Numerical simulations for VOFHHM of neuronal excitation

### 1.1. Introduction

Hodgkin and Huxley proposed the famous Hodgkin–Huxley equations which quantitatively describe the generation of action potential of squid giant axon [1].

$$C_m \frac{dV_m}{dt} = I_{ext} - I_{ionic}, \tag{1}$$

where $C_m$ is the membrane capacitance, $V_m$ is the intracellular potential, $t$ is the time, Iionic is the net ionic current flowing across the membrane, and $I_{ext}$ is the externally applied current [2].

The ionic current described in Hodgkin and Huxley's giant squid axon can be divided into three different cases: sodium current, potassium current, and leakage current, for example, voltage-gated persistent $K^+$ current with four activation gates (resulting in the term $n^4$, where n is the activation variable for $K^+$), voltage-gated transient $Na^+$ current with three activation gates and one inactivation gate (the term $m^3 \hbar$) [3].

The total ionic current is therefore

$$I_{ionic} = \overbrace{G_{Na}(V - E_{Na})}^{I_{Na}} + \overbrace{G_K(V - E_K)}^{I_K} + \overbrace{G_L(V - E_L)}^{I_L}, \tag{2}$$

where $I_{Na}$ and $I_K$ are the currents through $Na^+$ and $K^+$ channels, respectively. The current $I_L$ is the leak current and denotes all the residue currents through a cell membrane other than $Na^+$ and $K^+$ currents. G denotes conductance value for each individual ionic component, and E is an equilibrium potential.

Hodgkin and Huxley defined the probability for a gate that can be found in its permissive state to depend on the membrane potential, therefore incorporating the voltage-dependent conductance [4, 5]. A probability $p$ ranging from 0 to 1 can be defined for each gate, but since a large population of channels (and therefore gates) has to be considered, this leads to the following:

$$1 - p(t) = {}^{\beta_p}_{\alpha_p} p(t)$$

where 1−p(t) is the fraction in non-permissive state, p(t) is the fraction in permissive state, and $\alpha_p$ and $\beta_p$ are called rate functions.

Transitions between permissive and non-permissive states are assumed to obey the relation:

$$\frac{dp}{dt} = \alpha_p(V)(1-p) - \beta_p(V)p, \qquad p = m, n, \hbar, \tag{3}$$

where m and n are the activation variables for the sodium and the potassium, respectively, and represent the sodium de-inactivation.

In the literature, Alan Lloyd Hodgkin and Andrew Huxley authored a succession of five papers describing the nonlinear ODEs that model how action potentials can be initiated and propagated through an axon [1–5]. HHM can be considered one of the most successful mathematical models in quantity lively describing biological phenomena, and it is the method which can be used in deriving the model of a squid that is directly applicable to many kinds of neurons and other excitable cells [5–7].

Action potentials occur in excitable cells, including neurons, muscle cells, and endocrine cells. It is known that the brain is a complicated network of a tremendous number of neurons. A neuron has a very special shape, which is much different from usual sphere-shaped or disk-like cells [8]. A soma is the main body of neuron from which a long cable called an axon is extended. Neurons transmit and exchange electric signals called action potentials or spikes. Then, the electric signals or information is transmitted in the direction from a dendrite to an axon, see **Figure 1** [8].

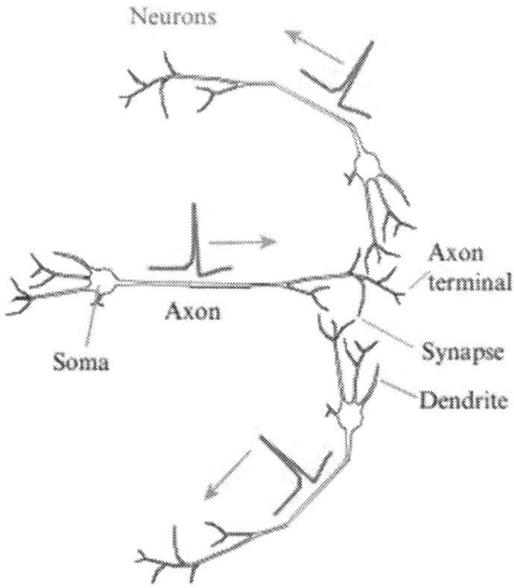


**Figure 1.** Neurons cells.

Doi et al. [8] have briefly explained the framework of the Hodgkin–Huxley formalism to model the action potential generation of neuron sand of other excitable cells. In 2012, Siciliano [9] has studied different numerical methods to solve the HHM. Six different numerical methods are first introduced and compared using a simple and arbitrary ODE. In 2014, Sweilam and Nagy [6] have presented numerical method for solving fractional Hodgkin–Huxley model (FHHM), described as follows:

$$CD^{\eta}V = I_{ext} - \bar{g}_{Na}m^3h(V - E_{Na}) - \bar{g}_K n^4 h(V - E_K) - g_L(V - E_L),$$
$$D^{\eta}p = \alpha_p(V)(1-p) - \beta_p(V)p, p = m, n, \hbar,$$

where $0 < \eta \leq 1$.

In this work, the above-described model in [6] will be extended to VOFHHM, which is more general than fractional model.

The main aim of studying the VOFHHM is to show the behavior of the action potential when the derivative expressed as the VOF in order to explain the extent of this impact on the gating variables.

### 1.2. VOFHHM

It is well known that HHM is based on the parallel thought of a simple circuit with batteries, resistors, and capacitors [9]. Current can be carried through the circuit as ions passing through the membrane (resistors) or by charging the capacitors of the membrane. In this circuit, current flow across the membrane has two major components: one, $I_C$ (μA cm$^{-2}$) associated with charging the membrane capacitance C(μF cm$^{-2}$) and, the other, $I_{ionic}$ associated with the movement of specific types of ions across the membrane.

For the VOF model, we suggest that:

$$I_C = CD^{\eta(t)}V, \tag{4}$$

where $V$ is the membrane voltage ((mV), measured in volts), $0 < \eta\ (t) \leq 1$, and $D^{\eta(t)}$ is defined by Grünwald–Letinkov approximation for the VOF derivative as follows:

$$D^{\eta(t)}y(t) = \lim_{h\to 0} h^{-\eta(t)} \sum_{i=0}^{\frac{[t]}{h}} (-1)^i \binom{\eta(t)}{i} y(t-ih), \tag{5}$$

where $[t]$ denotes the integer part of $t$ and $h$ is the step size.

Substituting (4) into (1), we obtain:

$$CD^{\eta(t)}V = I_{ext} - I_{ionic}(t). \tag{6}$$

Transitions between permissive and non-permissive states are assumed to obey the relation:

$$D^{\eta(t)}p = \alpha_p(V)(1-p) - \beta_p(V)p, \qquad p = m, n, \hbar, \tag{7}$$

The conductance for each current component can be written in the form [5]:

$$G_{Na} = \bar{g}_{Na} m^3 h, G_{Na} = \bar{g}_K n^4, G_L = g_L, \tag{8}$$

where $\bar{g}_{Na}$ and $\bar{g}_K$ are the maximal conductance of sodium and potassium, respectively, and $g_L$ is a constant. Substituting (2) and (8) into (6), we obtain:

$$CD^{\eta(t)}V = I_{ext} - \bar{g}_{Na}m^3h(V - E_{Na}) - \bar{g}_K n^4 h(V - E_K) - g_L(V - E_L). \tag{9}$$

Eqs. (9) with (7) are a generalization of HHM [5], and it can be described as follows:

$$CD^{\eta(t)}V = I_{ext} - \bar{g}_{Na}m^3h(V - E_{Na}) - \bar{g}_K n^4 h(V - E_K) - g_L(V - E_L),$$

$$D^{\eta(t)}p = \alpha_p(V)(1-p) - \beta_p(V)p, \qquad p = m, n, \hbar.$$

The variable $p$ approaches the steady-state value [5]:

$$p^*(V) = \frac{\alpha_p}{\alpha_p + \beta_p}, \qquad p = m, n, \hbar, \tag{10}$$

when the membrane potential $V$ remains constant.

### 1.3. Discretizations of the model using NSFD method

The aim of this part is to introduce numerical discretization for Eqs. (7) and (9). The NSFD method [10–17] is used where the step size h in the FDM is replaced by a function $\psi(h)$. Also, the Grünwald–Letinkov definition will be used with $V(t_k)$=$V_k$, $p(t_k)$, $p(t_k) = p_k$, and then, we claim

$$\sum_{i=0}^{k=1} c_i^{\eta(t)} p_{k+1-i} = \alpha_p V_k (1 - p_k) - \beta_p V_k p_k, \qquad p = m, n, \hbar, \tag{11}$$

$$C\sum_{i=0}^{k+1} c_i^{\eta(t)} V_{k+1-i} = I_m - \bar{g}_{Na} m_{k-1}^2 m_k \hbar (V_k - E_{Na}) - \bar{g}_K n_{k-1}^3 n_k \hbar (V_k - E_K) - g_L(V_k - E_L). \tag{12}$$

Doing some algebraic manipulation to Eqs. (11) and (12) yields the following equations:

$$\mathrm{p}_{k+1} = \frac{-\sum_{i=1}^{k+1} c_i^{\eta(t)} \mathrm{p}_{k+1-i} + \alpha_p \mathrm{V}_k (1 - \mathrm{p}_k) - \beta_p \mathrm{V}_k \mathrm{p}_k}{c_0^{\eta(t)}}, \qquad \mathrm{p} = \mathrm{m}, \mathrm{n}, \hbar, \tag{13}$$

$$V_{k+1} = \frac{I_{ext} - \sum_{i=1}^{k+1} c_i^{\eta(t)} V_{k+1-i} - \bar{g}_{Na} m_{k-1}^2 m_k \hbar (V_k - E_{Na}) - \bar{g}_K n_{k-1}^3 n_k \hbar (V_k - E_K) - g_L(V_k - E_L)}{C c_0^{\eta(t)}} \tag{14}$$

where $c_0^{\eta(t)} = \psi(h)^{-\eta(t)}$, $\psi(h) = e^h - 1$.

### 1.4. Numerical experiments

VOFHHM can be summarized neatly into four separate variable-order fractional ODEs with some supporting functions. These equations are described in Eqs. (7) and (9), where the rate functions are listed below [5]:

$$\alpha_n(\mathrm{V}) = 0.01(\mathrm{V}+1)\left[exp\left(\frac{V+10}{10}\right)\right]^{-1}, \beta_n(V) = 0.125\,exp\left(\frac{V}{80}\right),$$

$$\alpha_m(\mathrm{V}) = 0.1(\mathrm{V}+25)\left[exp\left(\frac{V+25}{10}\right)\right]^{-1}, \beta_m(V) = 4\,exp\left(\frac{V}{18}\right),$$

$$\alpha_h(\mathrm{V}) = 0.07\,exp\left(\frac{V}{20}\right), \beta_h(V) = \left[exp\left(\frac{V+30}{10}\right)\right]^{-1},$$

and

$\bar{g}_{\mathrm{Na}}=120\mathrm{mS/cm}^2$, $\bar{g}_{\mathrm{K}}=36\mathrm{mS/cm}^2$, $g_L=0.3\mathrm{mS/cm}^2$, $E_{Na}=120\mathrm{mV}$, $E_K=-12\mathrm{mV}$, $E_L=10.6\mathrm{mV}$, with the initial conditions $V(0) = V_0$, and $p(0) = p_0 = p^*(V_0)$. The behavior of the neuron can be simulated for different initial values of $V$. **Figure 2** shows an action potential simulated by the solver ode45, i.e., fourth-order Runge–Kutta method, and NSFD method at $\eta(t) = 1$, of the variable-order Hodgkin–Huxley equations for zero $\mathrm{I}_{ext}$, and $V_0 = -40$ mV. Also, in this figure, all parts of the action potential are presented including the rapid upraise, downfall, and unexcitable phase, according to the number sequence as follows:

**i.** Number 1 means that the action potential begins to fire, the sodium channels are now open, and an influx of sodium occurs.

**ii.** Number 2 means that the membrane becomes more positive at this point due to sodium entering the cell. Now, the potassium channels open and leave the cell.

**iii.** Number 3 means that the sodium channels have now become refractory and no more sodium is allowed to enter.

**iv.** Number 4 means that the sodium channel is still in its refractory stage and only the potassium ions are passing through the membrane. As the potassium ions continue to leave the cell, the membrane potential moves toward the resting value.

**v.** Number 5 means that the potassium channels close and the sodium channels begin to leave the refractory phase and reset to its resting phase.

http://dx.doi.org/10.5772/63958

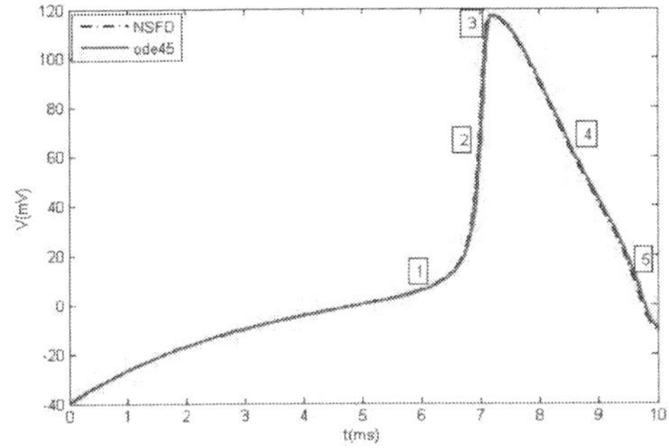


**Figure 2.** An action potential created by using ode45 and NSFD method at $\eta$ (t) = 1.

Finally, the potassium returns to its resting value where it can wait another action potential (for more details see [8, 9]). Moreover, in **Figure 3**, the gating variables are correctly constrained between 0 and 1 as expected using ode45 and NSFD method, respectively.

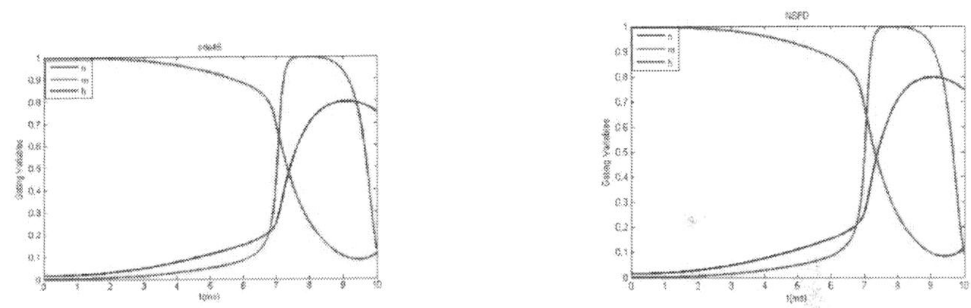


**Figure 3.** Plot of the different gating variables using ode45 (left) and NSFD method (right) at $\eta$ (t) = 1.

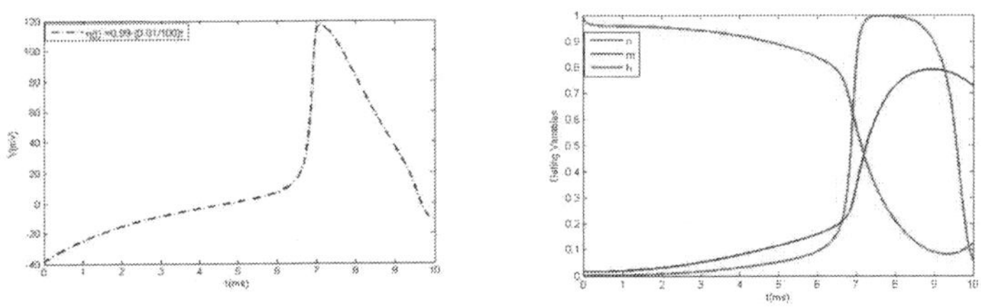


**Figure 4.** The approximated action potential (left) and the gating variables (right) using the NSFD method at $(t) = 0.99 - (0.01/100)t$.

**Figures 4–8** show the approximated action potential and the gating variables using the NSFD method obtained for different values of $(t)$, where $\eta(t) = 0.99 - (0.01/100)t$, $\eta(t) = 0.87 -$

$(0.01/100)t$, $\eta(t)$ =0.79 – $(0.001)t$, and $\eta(t)$ = 0.67 – $(0.001)t$, respectively. These figures show an example of a numerically solved solution of the Hodgkin–Huxley equations. **Figures 4–8** (left) are a waveform of the membrane potential. A pulsatile input applied at a time t = 5 ms ((ms) time measured in second) induces an action potential. **Figures 4–7** (right) show the dynamics of all three gating variables m, n, and h. Sodium activation, m, changes much more rapidly than either h or n. **Figure 9** (left) describes the relationship between the variables n and h, where n is the activation variable of potassium channel expressed in a dark color, while h is inactivation variable of sodium channel expressed in a light color. The action potential, n, be in stillness stage and begins to enter the cell until it reaches the highest activity, unlike the action potential, h, at the top of its activity. Step by step, the action potential, h, decreases its activities and continues to leave the cell and moves toward the resting value. At a certain moment in time, the intersection between them are occurred, where n increased while h decreased. **Figure 9** (right) describes the relationship between the variables m and h, where m is the activation variable of potassium channel expressed in a dark color, while h is inactivation variable of sodium channel expressed in a light color. The dynamics variables m and h have the same dynamics similar to n and h, where m increased while h decreased. **Figure 10** describes the dynamics of gating variables n and m in 3D. The variables n and m are the activation variables of $K^+$ and $Na^+$ ionic channels, respectively. They are expressed in a dark color and a light color, respectively. They are in stillness stage and begin to enter the cell until they reach the highest activity, where they are in the case of increasing.

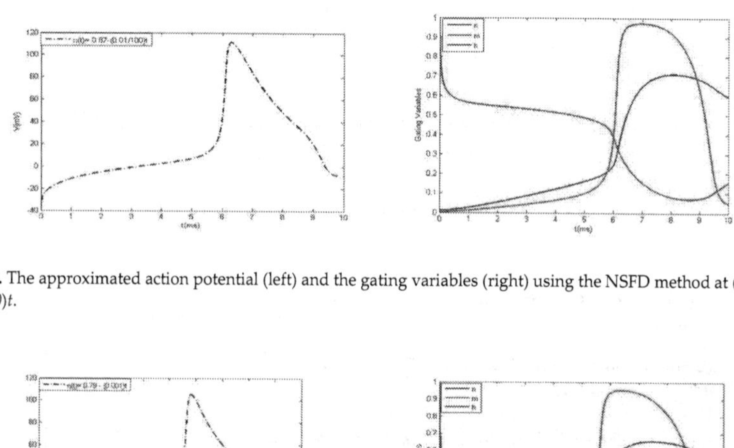

**Figure 5.** The approximated action potential (left) and the gating variables (right) using the NSFD method at *(t) = 0.87 – (0.01/100)t.*

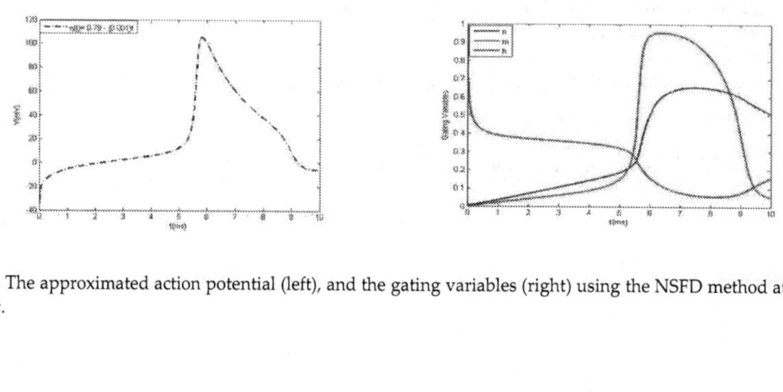

**Figure 6.** The approximated action potential (left), and the gating variables (right) using the NSFD method at *(t) = 0.79 – (0.001)t.*

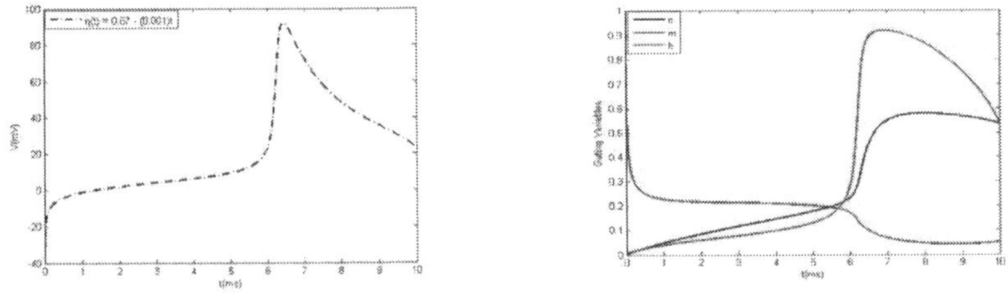


**Figure 7.** The approximated action potential (left) and the gating variables (right) using the NSFD method at $(t) = 0.67 - (0.001)t$.

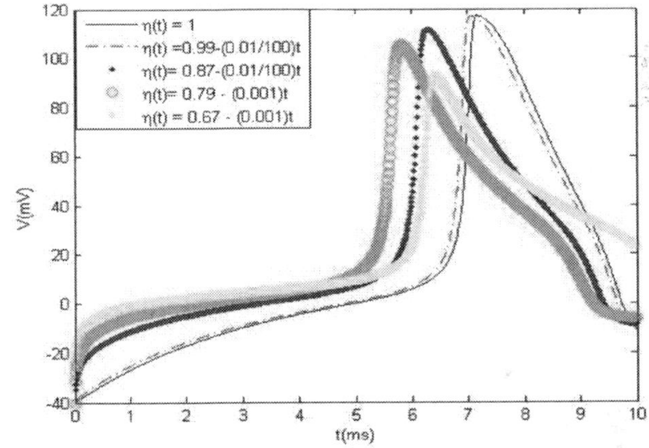


**Figure 8.** An action potential created from the NSFD method using different values of $\eta$ (t).

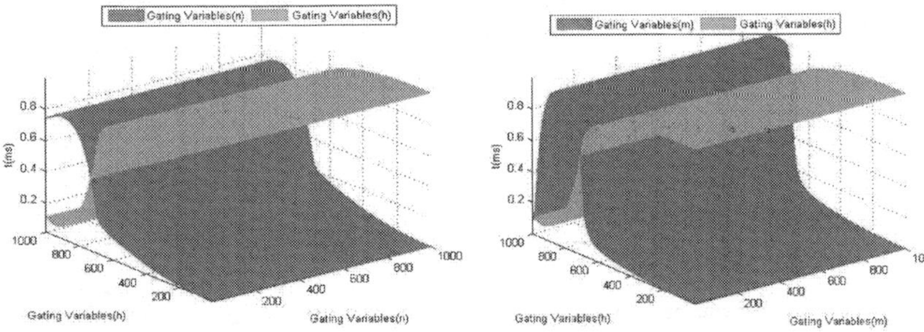


**Figure 9.** The waveforms of the gating variables n and h (left), and m and h (right) in 3D.

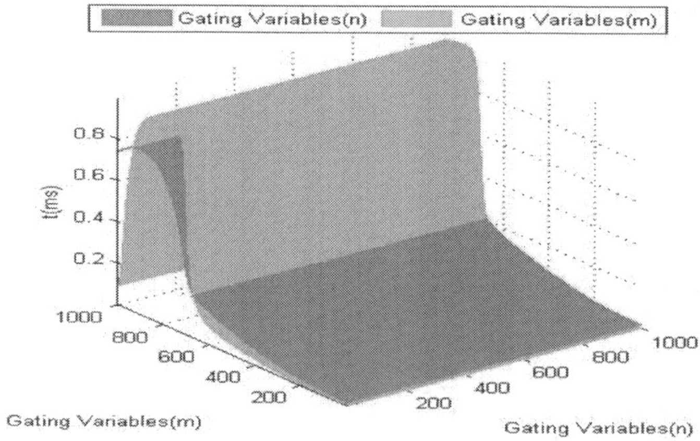


**Figure 10.** The waveforms of the gating variables n and m in 3D.

## 2. Real-life models governed by nonlinear delay differential equations (DDEs)

### 2.1. Introduction

DDEs are differential equations in which the derivatives of some unknown functions at present time are dependent on the values of the functions at previous times. In real-world systems, delay is very often encountered in many practical systems, such as control systems [18], lasers, traffic models [19], metal cutting, epidemiology, neuroscience, population dynamics [20], and chemical kinetics [21]. Recent theoretical and computational advancements in DDEs reveal that DDEs are capable of generating rich and plausible dynamics with realistic parameter values. Naturally, occurrence of complex dynamics is often generated by well-formulated DDE models. This is simply due to the fact that a DDE operates on an infinite-dimensional space consisting of continuous functions that accommodate high-dimensional dynamics.

For example, the Lotka–Volterra predator prey model [22] with crowding effect does not produce sustainable oscillatory solutions that describe population cycles. However, the Nicholson's blowflies model [23] can generate rich and complex dynamics. Delayed fractional differential equations (DFDEs) are correspondingly used to describe dynamical systems [23]. In recent years, DFDEs begin to arouse the attention of many researchers [7, 19, 20, 25–27]. Simulating these equations is an important technique in the research, and accordingly, finding effective numerical methods for the DFDEs is a necessary process. Several methods based on Caputo or Riemann–Liouville definitions [28] have been proposed and analyzed. For instance, based on the predictor–corrector scheme, Diethelm et al. introduced the ABM algorithm [29–31] and mean while some error analysis was presented to improve the numerical accuracy. In

2011, Bhalekar and Daftardar-Gejji [25] have been extended the ABM algorithm to solve DDEs of fractional order and presented numerical illustrations to demonstrate utility of the method. In 2012, Ma et al. [32] have presented the numerical solution of a VOF financial system which is calculated by using the ABM method.

This section presents class of numerical method for solving the variable-order fractional nonlinear delay differential equations (VOFDDEs). The main aim of this part is to study VOFDDEs numerically.

## 2.2. ABM method for the VOFDDEs

In this section, the ABM algorithm has been extended to study the VOFDDEs, where the derivative is defined in the Caputo VOF sense. Special attention is given to prove the error estimate of the proposed method. Numerical test examples are presented to demonstrate utility of the method. Chaotic behaviors are observed in variable-order one-dimensional delayed systems.

In the following, we apply the ABM predictor–corrector method to implement the numerical solution of VOFDDEs.

Let us consider the following VOF system:

$$D_t^{\alpha(t)}y(t)=f\big(t,y(t),y(t-\tau)\big),\qquad t\in[o,T],0<\alpha(t)\leq 1. \tag{15}$$

$$y(t)=g(t),\qquad t\in[-\tau,0], \tag{16}$$

where $f$ is in general a nonlinear function.

Also, consider a uniform grid $\{t_n = nh: n = -k, -k+1,\ldots, -1,0,1,\ldots, N\}$ where $k$ and $N$ are integers such that $h = \tau/k$. Let

$$y_h(t_j)=g(t_j),\qquad j=-k,-k+1,\ldots,-1,0, \tag{17}$$

and note that

$$y_h(t_j-\tau)=y_h(jh-kh)=y_h(t_{j-k}),\qquad j=0,1,2,\ldots,N. \tag{18}$$

Applying the integral $J_{t_{n+1}}^{\alpha(t_{n+1})}$, which is defined by the Riemann–Liouville variable-order integral as

$$J_x^{\alpha(x)} f(x) = \frac{1}{\Gamma(\alpha(x))} \int_a^x (x-t)^{\alpha(x)-1} f(t)\,dt, \tag{19}$$

on both sides of (15) and using (16), we claim to:

$$y(t_{n+1}) = g(0) + \frac{1}{\Gamma(\alpha(t_{n+1}))} \int_0^{t_{n+1}} (t_{n+1}-\zeta)^{\alpha(t_{n+1})-1} f(\zeta, y(\zeta), y(\zeta-\tau))\,d\zeta. \tag{20}$$

Further, the integral in Eq. (20) is evaluated using product trapezoidal quadrature formula [29–31, 33]. Then, we have the following corrector formula:

$$y_h(t_{n+1}) = g(0) + \frac{h^{\alpha(t_{n+1})}}{\Gamma(\alpha(t_{n+1})+2)} f(t_{n+1}, y_h(t_{n+1}), y_h(t_{n+1}-\tau)) +$$
$$\frac{h^{\alpha(t_{n+1})}}{\Gamma(\alpha(t_{n+1})+2)} \sum_{j=0}^{n} a_{j,n+1} f(t_j, y_h(t_j), y_h(t_j-\tau)),$$

or

$$y_h(t_{n+1}) = g(0) + \frac{h^{\alpha(t_{n+1})}}{\Gamma(\alpha(t_{n+1})+2)} f(t_{n+1}, y_h(t_{n+1}), y_h(t_{n+1-k})) +$$
$$\frac{h^{\alpha(t_{n+1})}}{\Gamma(\alpha(t_{n+1})+2)} \sum_{j=0}^{n} a_{j,n+1} f(t_j, y_h(t_j), y_h(t_{j-k})), \tag{21}$$

where

$$a_{j,n+1} = \begin{cases} n^{\alpha(t_{n+1})+1} - (n-\alpha(t_{n+1}))(n+1)^{\alpha(t_{n+1})}, & j=0, \\ (n-j+2)^{\alpha(t_{n+1})+1} + (n-j)^{\alpha(t_{n+1})+1} - 2(n-j+1)^{\alpha(t_{n+1})+1}, & 1 \le j \le n, \\ 1, & j = n+1, \end{cases} \tag{22}$$

$$y_h(t_{j-k}) \approx v_{n+1} = \begin{cases} \delta_{y_{n-m+1}} + (1-\delta)_{y_{n-m+1}}, & if \quad m>1, \\ \delta_{y_{n+1}^p} + (1-\delta)_{y_n}, & if \quad m=1, \end{cases} \tag{23}$$

$0 \le \delta < 1$ and the unknown term $y_h(t_{n+1})$ appears on both sides of (21).

Due to nonlinearity off, Eq. (21) cannot be solved explicitly for $y_h(t_{n+1})$, so we replace the term $y_h(t_{n+1})$ on the right-hand side by an approximation $y_h^p(t_{n+1})$, which is called predictor. The product rectangle rule is used in (20) to evaluate the predictor term

$$y_h^p(t_{n+1}) = g(0) + \frac{1}{\Gamma(\alpha(t_{n+1}))}\sum_{j=0}^{n} b_{j,n+1} f(t_j, y_h(t_j), y_h(t_j-\tau),$$

or

$$y_h^p(t_{n+1}) = g(0) + \frac{1}{\Gamma(\alpha(t_{n+1}))}\sum_{j=0}^{n} b_{j,n+1} f(t_j, y_h(t_j), y_h(t_{j-k}), \tag{24}$$

where $b_{j,n+1} = \frac{h^{\alpha(t_{n+1})}}{\alpha(t_{n+1})}((n-j+1)^{\alpha(t_{n+1})} + (n-j)^{\alpha(t_{n+1})}$.

### 2.3. Error analysis of the algorithm

In this subsection, we aim to introduce the following lemma, which will be used in the proof of main theorem.

Lemma 2.1. [31] (a) Let $z \in C^1[0, T]$, then

$$\left|\int_0^{t_{n+1}} (t_{n+1}-t)^{\alpha(t_{n+1})-1} z(t)\,dt - \sum_{j=0}^{n} b_{j,n+1} z(t_j)\right| \le \frac{1}{\alpha(t_{n+1})}\|z'\|_\infty t_{n+1}^{\alpha(t_{n+1})} h. \tag{25}$$

(b) Let $z \in C^2[0, T]$, then

$$\left|\int_0^{t_{n+1}} (t_{n+1}-t)^{\alpha(t_{n+1})-1} z(t)\,dt - \sum_{j=0}^{n+1} a_{j,n+1} z(t_j)\right| \le C_{\alpha(t_{n+1})}^{T_r}\|z''\|_\infty t_{n+1}^{\alpha(t_{n+1})} h. \tag{26}$$

Proof. To prove statement (a), by construction of the product rectangle formula, we find that the quadrature error has the representation [31]

$$\int_0^{t_{n+1}} (t_{n+1}-t)^{\alpha(t_{n+1})-1} z(t)\,dt - \sum_{j=0}^{n} b_{j,n+1} z(t_j) = \sum_{j=0}^{n} \int_{jh}^{(j+1)h} (t_{n+1}-t)^{\alpha(t_{n+1})-1} \left(z(t) - z(t_j)\right)dt.$$

Apply the mean value theorem of differential calculus to the second factor of the integrand on the right-hand side of the above equation

$$\left|\int_0^{t_{n+1}} (t_{n+1}-t)^{\alpha(t_{n+1})-1} z(t)dt - \sum_{j=0}^{n} b_{j,n+1} z(t_j)\right|$$

$$\leq \|z'\|_\infty \sum_{j=0}^{n} \int_{jh}^{(j+1)h} (t_{n+1}-t)^{\alpha(t_{n+1})-1} (t-jh)dt,$$

$$= \|z'\|_\infty \frac{h^{1+\alpha(t_{n+1})}}{\alpha(t_{n+1})} \sum_{j=0}^{n} \left(\frac{1}{1+\alpha(t_{n+1})}[(n+1-j)^{1+\alpha(t_{n+1})}\right.$$

$$\left.-(n-j)^{1+\alpha(t_{n+1})}] - (n-j)^{\alpha(t_{n+1})}\right),$$

$$= \|z'\|_\infty \frac{h^{1+\alpha(t_{n+1})}}{\alpha(t_{n+1})} \left(\frac{(n+1)^{1+\alpha(t_{n+1})}}{1+\alpha(t_{n+1})} - \sum_{j=0}^{n} j^{\alpha(t_{n+1})}\right),$$

$$= \|z'\|_\infty \frac{h^{1+\alpha(t_{n+1})}}{\alpha(t_{n+1})} \left(\int_0^{t_{n+1}} j^{\alpha(t_{n+1})}dt - \sum_{j=0}^{n} j^{\alpha(t_{n+1})}\right).$$

Here, the term in parentheses is simply the remainder of the standard rectangle quadrature formula, applied to the function $t^{\alpha(t_{n+1})}$ and taken over the interval [0, n + 1]. Since the integrand is monotonic, we may apply some standard results from quadrature theory to find that this term is bounded by the total variation of the integrand, thus

$$\left|\int_0^{t_{n+1}} (t_{n+1}-t)^{\alpha(t_{n+1})-1} z(t)dt - \sum_{j=0}^{n} b_{j,n+1} z(t_j)\right| \leq \frac{1}{\alpha(t_{n+1})} \|z'\|_\infty (n+1)^{\alpha(t_{n+1})} h^{1+\alpha(t_{n+1})}. \quad \square$$

Similarly, we can prove (b).

Now, let us consider that $f(\cdot)$ in (15) satisfies the following Lipschitz conditions with respect to its variables

$$|f(t,y_1,u) - f(t,y_2,u)| \leq L_1 |y_1 - y_2|,$$

$$|f(t,y,u_1) - f(t,y,u_2)| \leq L_2 |u_1 - u_2|, \tag{27}$$

where $L_1$ and $L_2$ are positive constants.

Theorem 1. Suppose the solution y(t) ∈ $C^2$ [0, T], of the Eqs. (15) and (16), satisfies the following two conditions:

$$\left| \begin{array}{l} \int_0^{t_{n+1}} (t_{n+1}-t)^{\alpha(t_{n+1})-1} D_t^{\alpha(t_{n+1})} y(t)\,dt - \\ \sum_{j=0}^{n} b_{j,n+1} D_t^{\alpha(t_{n+1})} y(t_j) \end{array} \right| \le C t_{n+1}^{\gamma_1} h^{\delta_1}, \tag{28}$$

$$\left| \begin{array}{l} \int_0^{t_{n+1}} (t_{n+1}-t)^{\alpha(t_{n+1})-1} D_t^{\alpha(t_{n+1})} y(t)\,dt - \\ \sum_{j=0}^{n} a_{j,n+1} D_t^{\alpha(t_{n+1})} y(t_j) \end{array} \right| \le C t_{n+1}^{\gamma_2} h^{\delta_2},$$

with some $\gamma_1, \gamma_2 \ge 0$, and $\delta_1$, $\delta_2 < 0$, then for some suitable $T > 0$, we have

$$\max_{0\le j\le N} \left| y(t_j) - y_h(t_j) \right| = O(h^q),$$

where $q = \min(\delta_1 + \alpha(t), \delta_2)$, $N = [T/h]$, and $C$ is a positive constant.

Proof. We will use the mathematical induction to prove the result. Suppose that the conclusion is true for j = 0, 1,…, n, then we have to prove that the inequality also holds for j = n + 1. To do this, we first consider the error of the predictor $y_{n+1}^p$. From (27), we have

$$\begin{array}{l} \left| f(t_j, y(t_j), y(t_j-\tau)) - f(t_j, y_j, \upsilon_j) \right| \le \left| f(t_j, y(t_j), y(t_j-\tau)) - f(t_j, y_j, y(t_j-\tau)) \right| + \\ \left| f(t_j, y_j, y(t_j-\tau)) - f(t_j, y_j, \upsilon_j) \right| \le L_1 h^q + L_2 h^q = (L_1 + L_2) h^q. \end{array}$$

So

$$\left| y(t_{n+1}) - y_{n+1}^p \right| = \frac{1}{\Gamma(\alpha(t_{n+1}))} \left| \int_0^{t_{n+1}} (t_{n+1}-t)^{\alpha(t_{n+1})-1} f(t, y(t), y(t-\tau))\,dt - \sum_{j=0}^{n} b_{j,n+1} f(t_j, y_j, \upsilon_j) \right|$$

$$\leq \frac{1}{\Gamma(\alpha(t_{n+1}))}\left|\int_0^{t_{n+1}} (t_{n+1}-t)^{\alpha(t_{n+1})-1} D_t^{\alpha(t_{n+1})} y(t)dt - \sum_{j=0}^{n} b_{j,n+1} D_t^{\alpha(t_{n+1})} y(t_j)\right| +$$
$$\frac{1}{\Gamma(\alpha(t_{n+1}))}\sum_{j=0}^{n} b_{j,n+1}\left|f(t_j, y(t_j), y(t_j-\tau)) - f(t_j, y_j, y(t_j-\tau))\right| +$$
$$\left|f(t_j, y_j, y(t_j-\tau)) - f(t_j, y_j, \upsilon_j)\right|$$
$$\leq \frac{Ct_{n+1}^{\gamma_1}}{\Gamma(\alpha(t_{n+1}))} + \frac{1}{\Gamma(\alpha(t_{n+1}))}\sum_{j=0}^{n} b_{j,n+1}(L_1+L_2)Ch^q,$$

and from

$$\sum_{j=0}^{n} b_{j,n+1} = \sum_{j=0}^{n}\int_{\mathrm{jh}}^{(\mathrm{j}+1)\mathrm{h}} (t_{n+1}-t)^{\alpha(t_{n+1})-1}dt = \frac{1}{\alpha(t_{n+1})}t_{n+1}^{\alpha(t_{n+1})} \leq \frac{1}{\alpha(t_{n+1})}T^{\alpha(t_{n+1})},$$

we have

$$\left|y(t_{n+1} - y_{n+1}^p)\right| \leq \frac{CT^{\gamma_1}}{\Gamma(\alpha(t_{n+1}))}h^{\delta_1} + \frac{CT^{\alpha(t_{n+1})}}{\Gamma(\alpha(t_{n+1})+1)}h^q.$$

Since

$$\sum_{j=0}^{n} a_{j,n+1} \leq \sum_{j=0}^{n} \frac{h^{\alpha(t_{n+1})}}{\alpha(t_{n+1})(\alpha(t_{n+1})+1)}$$
$$[(k-j+2)^{\alpha(t_{n+1})+1} - (k-j+1)^{\alpha(t_{n+1})+1} - (k-j+1)^{\alpha(t_{n+1})+1} + (k-j)^{\alpha(t_{n+1})+1}],$$

$$= \int_0^{t_{n+1}} (t_{n+2}-t)^{\alpha(t_{n+1})}dt - \int_0^{t_{n+1}} (t_{n+1}-t)^{\alpha(t_{n+1})}dt,$$
$$= \frac{1}{\alpha(t_{n+1})}\int_0^{t_{n+1}} \left[(t_{n+1}-t)^{\alpha(t_{n+1})}\right](t)'dt,$$
$$= \frac{1}{\alpha(t_{n+1})}t_{n+1}^{\alpha(t_{n+1})} \leq T^{\alpha(t_{n+1})},$$

we have

$$\left|y(t_{n+1})-y_{n+1}^{p}\right|=\frac{1}{\Gamma(\alpha(t_{n+1}))}\left|\begin{array}{l}\int_0^{t_{n+1}}(t_{n+1}-t)^{\alpha(t_{n+1})-1}f(t,y(t),y(t-\tau))dt-\\ \sum_{j=0}^{n}a_{j,n+1}f(t_j,y_j,\upsilon_j)-a_{n+1,n+1}f(t_{n+1},y_{n+1}^{p},\upsilon_{n+1})\end{array}\right|,$$

$$\leq\frac{1}{\Gamma(\alpha(t_{n+1}))}[\left|\begin{array}{l}\int_0^{t_{n+1}}(t_{n+1}-t)^{\alpha(t_{n+1})-1}f(t,y(t),y(t-\tau))dt\\ -\sum_{j=0}^{n}a_{j,n+1}f(t_j,y_j,y(t_j-\tau))\end{array}\right|+$$

$$\sum_{j=0}^{n}a_{j,n+1}\left|f(t_j,y_j,y(t_j-\tau))-f(t_j,y_j,\upsilon_j)\right|+$$

$$a_{n+1,n+1}\left|f(t_{n+1},y(t_{n+1}),y(t_{n+1}-\tau))-f(t_{n+1},y_{n+1}^{p},\upsilon_{n+1})\right|]$$

$$\leq\frac{1}{\Gamma(\alpha(t_{n+1}))}[Ct_{n+1}^{\gamma_2}h^{\delta_2}+Ch^{q}\sum_{j=0}^{n}a_{j,n+1}+$$

$$a_{n+1,n+1}L\left(h^{q}+\frac{CT^{\gamma_1}}{\Gamma(\alpha(t_{n+1}))}h^{\delta_1}+\frac{CT^{\alpha(t_{n+1})}}{\Gamma(\alpha(t_{n+1})+1)}h^{q}\right)]$$

$$\leq\frac{1}{\Gamma(\alpha(t_{n+1}))}[CT^{\gamma_2}+$$

$$\frac{Lh^{h}}{\alpha(t_{n+1})(\alpha(t_{n+1})+1)}+$$

$$\frac{CLT^{\gamma_1}}{\Gamma(\alpha(t_{n+1})+2)}+$$

$$\frac{CLT^{\alpha(t_{n+1})}h^{\alpha(t_{n+1})}}{\alpha(t_{n+1})\Gamma(\alpha(t_{n+1})+2)}]h^{q}=Ch^{q}.$$

### 2.4. Numerical examples

We present the purpose of this subsection to show that the proposed scheme designed provides good approximations for VOFDDEs. Throughout this subsection, we discuss four examples and their numerical solutions.

Example 2.1. Consider a VOFDDE:

$$D_t^{\alpha(t)}y(t)=\frac{2y(t-2)}{1+y(t-2)^{9.65}}-y(t),$$

$$y(t)=0.5,\qquad t\leq 0 \tag{29}$$

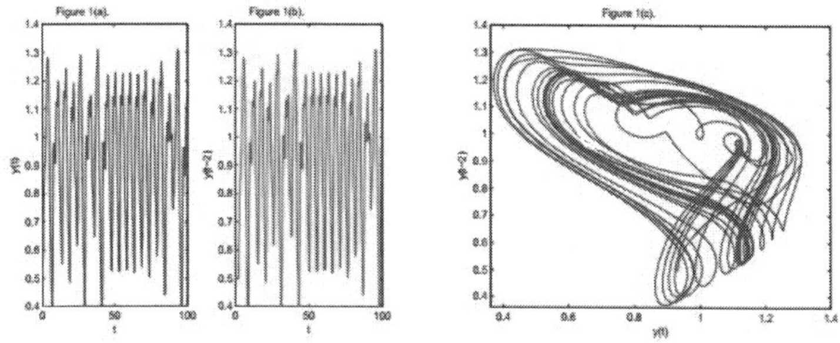

**Figure 11.** The numerical behavior of system (29) and chaotic attractors at $\alpha = 1$.

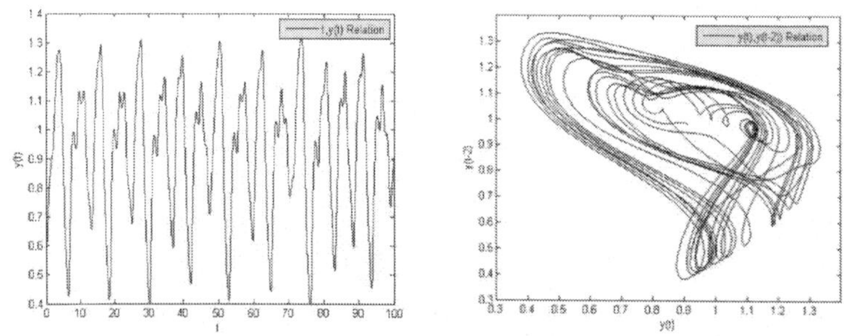

**Figure 12.** The numerical behavior of system (29) and chaotic attractors at $\alpha(t) = 0.97$.

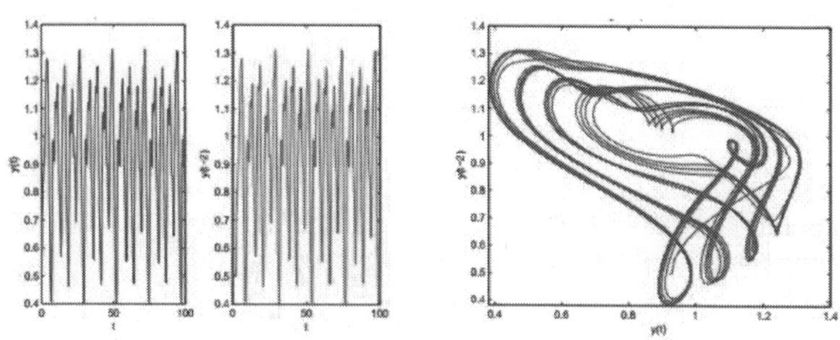

**Figure 13.** The numerical behavior of system (32) and chaotic attractors at $\alpha(t) = 0.99 - (0.01/100)t$.

In **Figures 11** and **1(a, b)** show the solutions $y(t)$ and $y(t-2)$ of the system (29), for $\alpha = 1$ and h = 0.1, whereas **Figure 1(c)** shows phase portrait of the system, i.e., plot of y(t) versus y(t – 2) for the same value of $\alpha$. In this figure, it observed that the system (29) shows aperiodic chaotic behavior. Moreover, **Figure 12** shows the plot of the numerical solutions $y(t)$ and the plot of $y(t)$ versus $y(t-2)$, respectively, at $\alpha(t) = 0.97$. In the following, we choose different cases for $\alpha(t)$. **Figures 13** and **14** show the solutions y(t) and y(t − 2) of the given system for $a(t) = 0.99 - (0.01/100)t$ and $\alpha(t) = 0.95 - (0.01/100)t$, respectively. The chaotic portrait for these values of $\alpha(t)$ is shown. In **Figure 15**, we have decreased the value of $\alpha(t)$, where $\alpha(t) = 0.85 - (0.01/100)t$, and observed that the system becomes periodic.

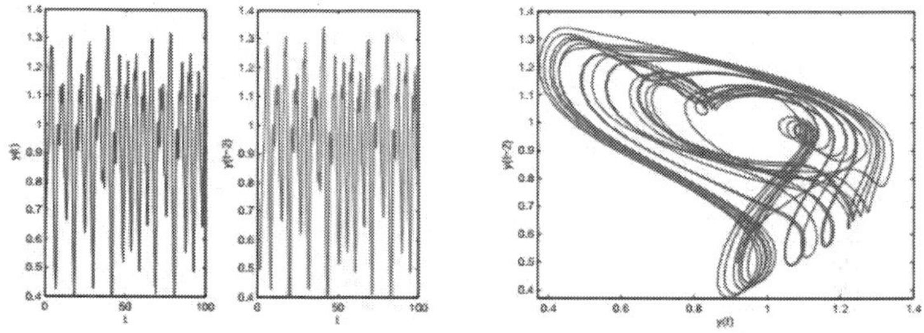

**Figure 14.** The numerical behavior of system (29) and chaotic attractors at $\alpha(t) = 0.95 - (0.01/100)t$.

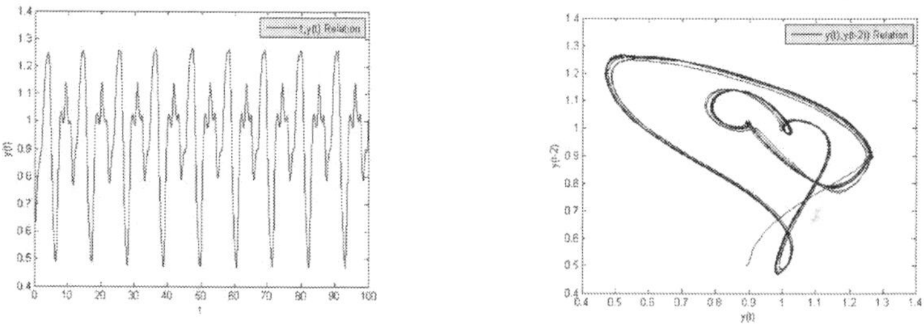

**Figure 15.** The numerical behavior of system (29) and chaotic attractors at $\alpha(t) = 0.85 - (0.01/100)t$.

## 2.5. The four-year life cycle of a population of lemmings model

Lemmings are small rodents, usually found in or near the Arctic, in tundra biomes. It used to be that every three to 4 years, there were massive numbers of lemmings in the mountains and then the next year it was gone. Therefore, it has been an interesting thing to try to find out why. Are there factors that affect the lemming population such as climate, temperature, precipitation, and the like, that is, what we refer to as the lemming cycle. The modern scientific study of lemmings started with work carried out by the Norwegian Professor of Zoology Robert Collett, who at the end of the nineteenth century gathered a great deal of information about lemmings. To try to understand why lemmings fluctuate both regularly and extensively is indeed an important problem in ecology [34]. In [27], Tavernini has solved a model of the 4-year life cycle of a population of lemmings in an integer order. In [25], Bhalekar and Daftardar-

Gejji have studied the model in a fractional order. In the following example [27], we study the extension of the lemming model:

Example 2.2. Consider the variable-order version of the four-year life cycle of a population of lemmings

$$D_t^{\alpha(t)}y(t)=3.5y(t)\left(1-\frac{y(t-0.74)}{19}\right), y(0)-19.00001, \qquad y(t)=19, \qquad t<0. \qquad (30)$$

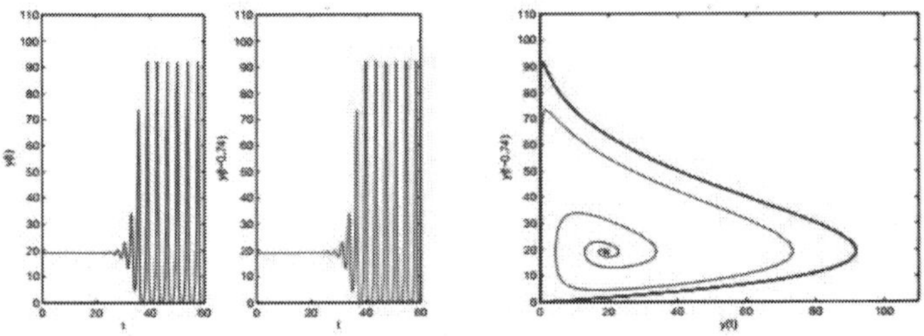

**Figure 16.** The numerical behavior of system (33) and plots of the $(t)$, $y(t-0.74)$ relation for $\alpha = 1$.

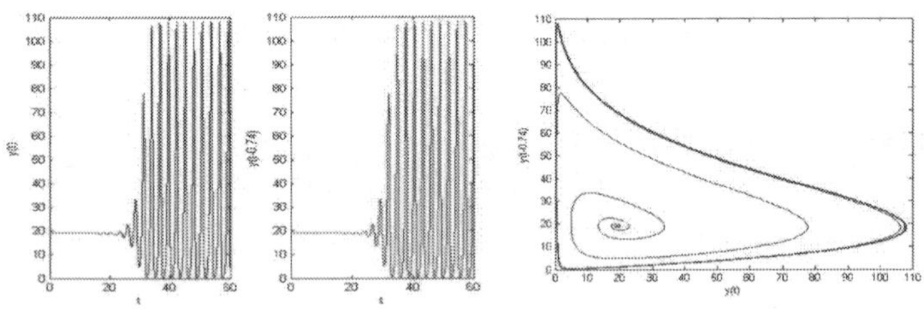

**Figure 17.** The numerical behavior of system (33), and plots of the $y(t)$, $y(t-0.74)$ relation for $\alpha(t) = 0.97$.

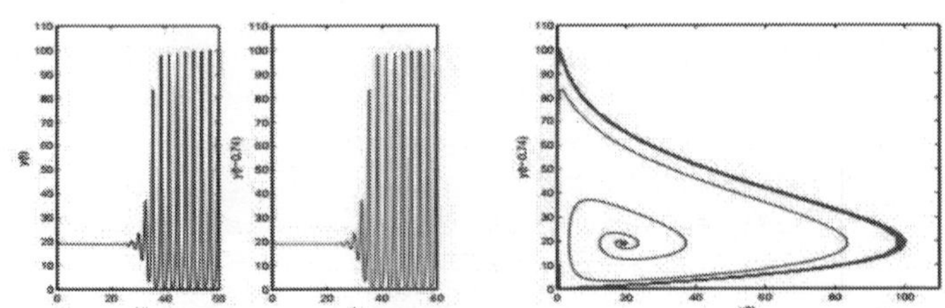

**Figure 18.** The numerical behavior of system (33) and the stretching phenomena for $\alpha(t) = 0.99 - (0.01/100)t$.

**Figure 16** shows the solutions $y(t)$ and $y(t-0.74)$ of system (33) for $\alpha = 1$ and h = 0.1 and shows phase portrait of $y(t)$ versus y(t − 0.74) for the same value of $\alpha$. **Figure 17** shows the plot of the numerical solutions $y(t)$ and the plot of $y(t)$ versus $y(t-0.74)$, respectively, at $(t) = 0.97$. The numerical results for VOFDDEs at different values of $\alpha(t)$ are given in **Figures 18–22**. These figures show the stretching phenomena between the numbers of lemmings in y(t) versus y(t − 2), for the values $\alpha(t) = 0.99 - (0.01/100)_t$, $\alpha(t) = 0.98 - (0.02/100)_t$; $\alpha(t) = 0.95 - (0.01/100)_t$, $\alpha(t) = 0.87 - (0.02/100)_t$, and $\alpha(t) = 0.85 - (0.01/100)_t$, respectively. It is observed that the phase portrait gets stretched as the value of α(t) decreases, and this stretching is towards positive side of the axis.

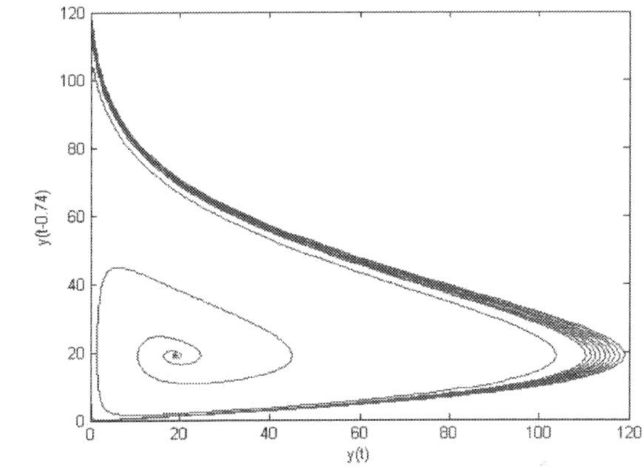


**Figure 19.** The stretching.

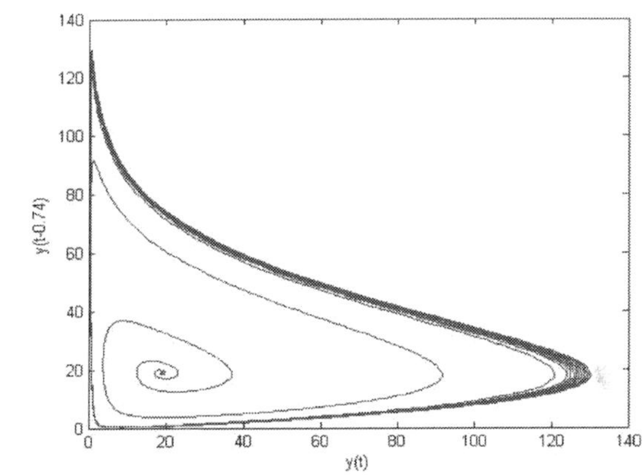


**Figure 20.** The stretching phenomena for $\alpha(t) = 0.98 - (0.02/100)t$. Phenomena for $\alpha(t) = 0.95 - (0.01/100)t$.

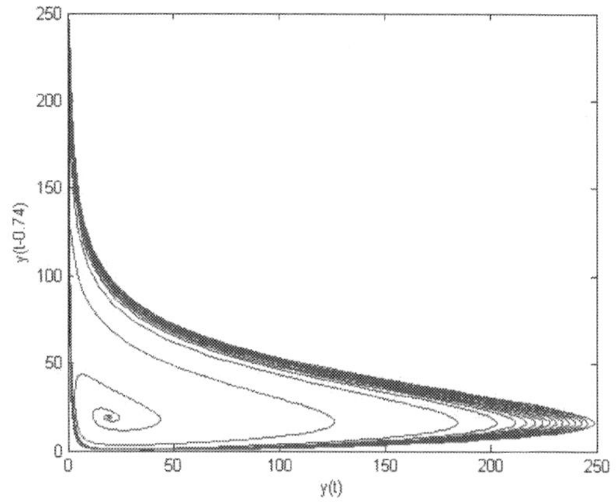


**Figure 21.** The stretching phenomena for $\alpha(t) = 0.87 - (0.02/100)t$.

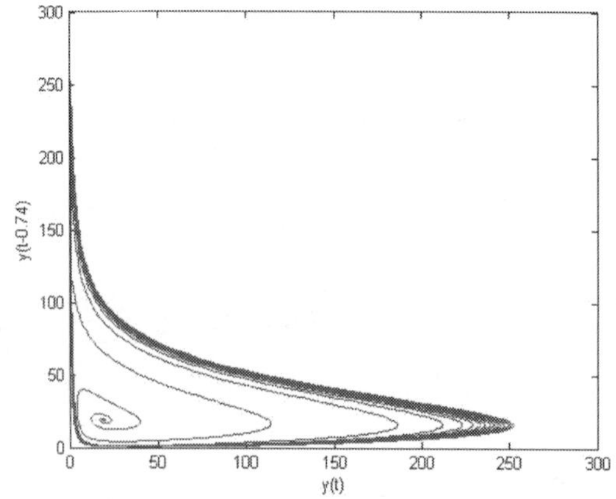


**Figure 22.** The stretching phenomena for $\alpha(t) = 0.85 - (0.01/100)t$.

## 2.6. The enzyme kinetics with an inhibitor molecule model

An enzyme inhibitor is a molecule that binds to an enzyme and decreases its activity or completely inhibits the enzyme catalytic activity. It is well known that all these inhibitors follow the same rule to interplay in enzyme reaction. Furthermore, there are many factors that affect enzyme's activity, such as temperature and pH. Many drug molecules are enzyme inhibitors, so their discovery and improvement are an active area of research in biochemistry and pharmacology to protect enzyme from any change. Therefore, studying the enzyme kinetics and structure–function relationship is vital to understand the kinetics of enzyme inhibition that in turn is fundamental to the modern design of pharmaceuticals in industries [35]. The frequency conversion mechanism in enzymatic feedback systems has been investigated with computer simulations in 1984 by Okamoto and Hayashi [36]. In [25], Bhalekar and Daftardar-Gejji have been study the enzyme kinetics with an inhibitor molecule model in a fractional order. In the following, we will study the model in [25] in general form where the derivative is given in a VOF.

Example 2.3. Consider the variable-order version of four-dimensional enzyme kinetics with an inhibitor molecule

$$D_t^{\alpha(t)} y_1(t) = 10.5 - \frac{y_1(t)}{1 + 0.0005 y_4^3(t-4)},$$

$$D_t^{\alpha(t)} y_2(t) = \frac{y_1(t)}{1 + 0.0005 y_4^3(t-4)} - y_2(t),$$

$$D_t^{\alpha(t)} y_3(t) = y_2(t) - y_3(t),$$

$$D_t^{\alpha(t)} y_4(t) = y_3(t) - 0.5 y_4(t),$$

$$y(t) = [60, 10, 10, 20]^T, t \leq 0. \tag{31}$$

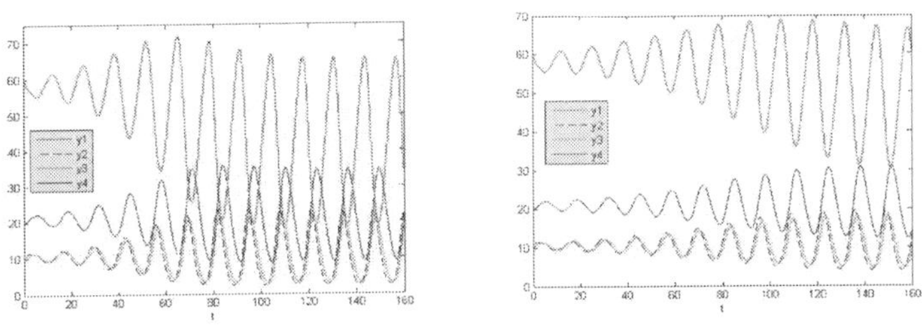

**Figure 23.** The numerical behavior of system (34) at $\alpha = 1$ (left) and $\alpha = 95$ (right).

**Figure 23** shows the solutions $y(t)$, $(1 \leq i \leq 4)$, with step size h= *1*, for = *1*, and $\alpha = 95$, respectively. Whereas **Figures 24–26** show the numerical results in case of variable order at $(t) = 0.99 - (0.01/100)t$, $\alpha(t) = 0.95 - (0.01/100)t$, $\alpha(t) = 0.91 - (0.01/100)t$, and $\alpha(t) = 0.83 - (0.01/100)t$, respectively. For $0.90 < \alpha(t) \leq 1$, the height of oscillations of the solutions increases as t increases as shown in **Figures 24** and **25**, while in **Figure 26**, the system settles down for sufficiently large t, for $\alpha(t) < 90$.

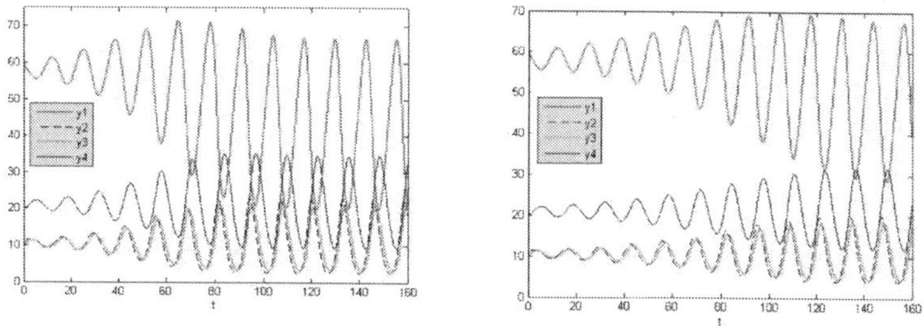


**Figure 24.** The numerical behavior of system (34) at $\alpha(t) = 0.99 - (0.01/100)t$ (left) and $\alpha(t) = 0.95 - (0.01/100)t$ (right).

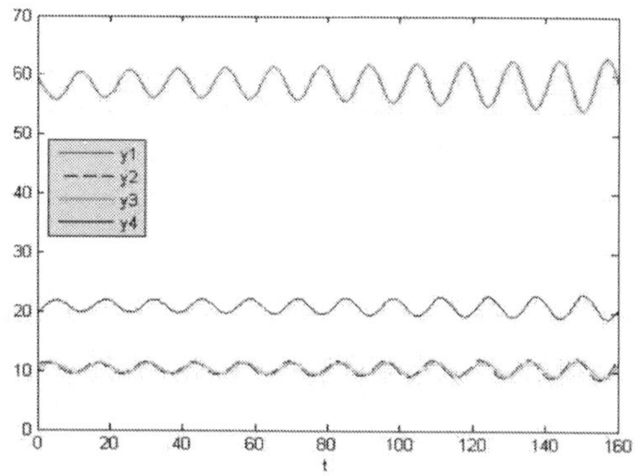


**Figure 25.** The numerical behavior of system (34) at $\alpha(t) = 0.91 - (0.01/100)t$.

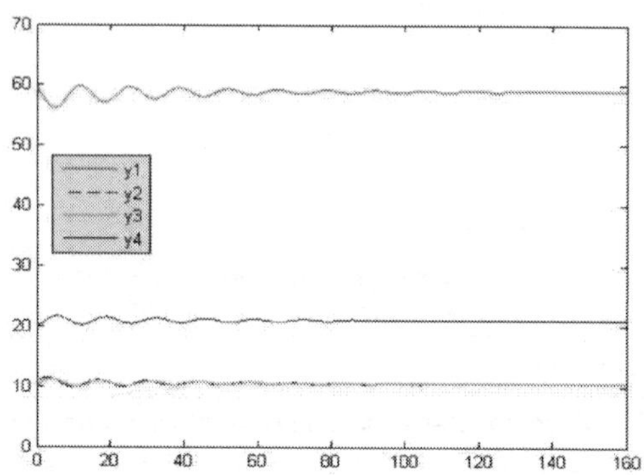


**Figure 26.** The numerical behavior of system (34) at $\alpha(t) = 0.83 - (0.01/100)t$.

### 2.7. The Chen system model

The atmosphere is a layer of gases surrounding the planet Earth that has, at each altitude above each point of the Earth's surface, a density, a pressure, a temperature, etc., and all these vary over time. It is of course unthinkable to know all this infinite number of data and to understand something about it. Approximations must be made. Edward Norton Lorenz (1917–2008) is a pioneer of chaos theory. He introduced the strange attractor notion and coined the term butterfly effect. In 1963 [37], he developed a simplified mathematical model for atmospheric convection when he studied the atmospheric convection. His model of the atmosphere was reduced to only three numbers x, y, and z and the evolution of the atmosphere to a tiny equation, where each point x, y, and z in space symbolizes a state of the atmosphere and the evolution follows a vector field. Later, several dynamical systems exhibiting chaos have been presented in various branches of science [24]. For example, in 1999, Chen and Ueta found another simple three-dimensional autonomous system, which is not topologically equivalent to Lorenz's system and which has a chaotic attractor [38]. In [39], Chen proved that "The Chen system is a special case of the Lorenz system." In 2004, Li and Peng [40] have presented Chen system with a fractional order. In 2012, Bhalekar et al. [41] proposed the fractional-order Chen system with time delay. In the following example, we will extend Chen system to a VOF, which can be more general.

Example 2.4. Consider the generalization of the delay fractional-order version of the Chen system [3] which involves the variable order:

$$D_t^{\alpha(t)}x(t) = a(y(t) - x(t-\tau)),$$

$$D_t^{\alpha(t)}y(t) = (c-a)x(t-\tau) - x(t)z(t) + cy(t),$$

$$D_t^{\alpha(t)}z(t) = x(t)y(t) - bz(t-\tau),$$

$$x(t) = 0.2, y(t) = 0, z(t) = 0.5 \, for t \in [-\tau, 0], \tag{32}$$

on the interval *[0,30]* and with step size $h = 0.001$.

At= *1*, **Figure 27** shows the numerical solution for $\tau = 0.005$ and shows chaotic *yz* phase portrait for this case. **Figure 28** shows the numerical solution and chaotic *yz* phase portrait at $\alpha = 0.97$ and $\tau = 0.005$. Moreover, for the variable order, we choose different cases for $\alpha(t)$:

At $\alpha(t) = 0.97 - (0.01/100)t$, **Figure 29** shows the numerical solution $y(t)$ and chaotic *yz* phase portrait of this example for $\tau = 0.005$. When we increase the value of τ to 0.015, the results of the numerical solution and chaotic *yz* phase portrait become stable as shown in **Figure 30**. At $\alpha(t) = 0.94 - (0.01/100)t$, **Figure 31** shows the numerical solution for $\tau = 0009$, and a limit cycle phase portrait was observed. When we increase the value of τ to 0.011, the chaotic *yz* phase portrait becomes stable as shown in **Figure 32. Figure 33** shows the numerical solution for $\tau = 0.005$ and chaotic $yz$ phase portrait at $\alpha(t) = 89 - (0.01/100)t$. It is observed that even in one-dimensional delayed systems of variable order, chaotic behavior can be shown, and subjected to some critical order, the system changes its nature and becomes periodic. In some cases, it is observed that the phase portrait gets stretched as the order of the derivative is reduced. According to the numerical test examples, it can be concluded that the proposed numerical technique is a powerful technique to calculate approximate solution of VOFDDEs.

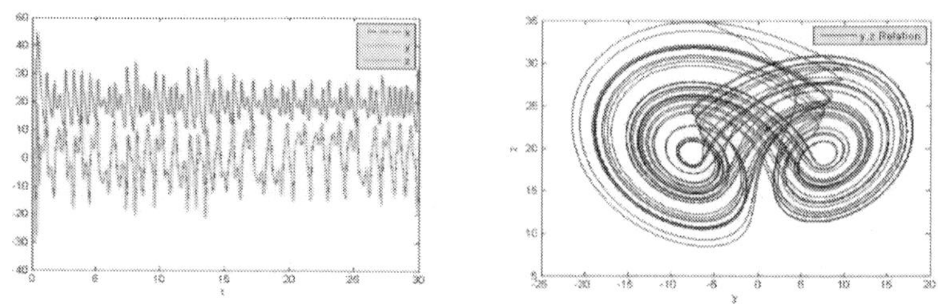

**Figure 27.** The numerical behavior and chaotic attractors for = $1$, and $\tau = 0.005$.

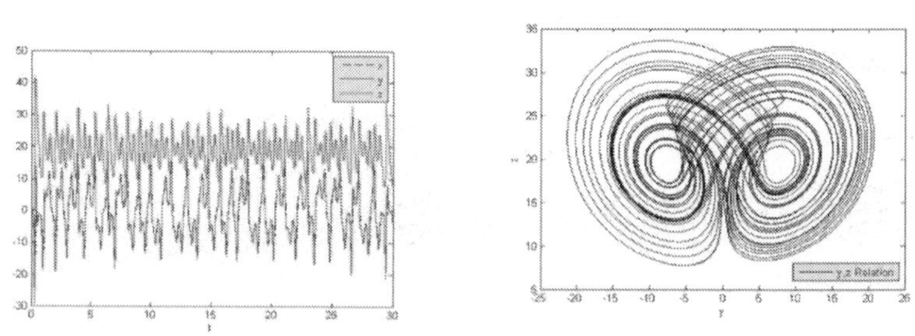

**Figure 28.** The numerical behavior and chaotic attractors for $\alpha = 0.97$ and $\tau = 0.005$.

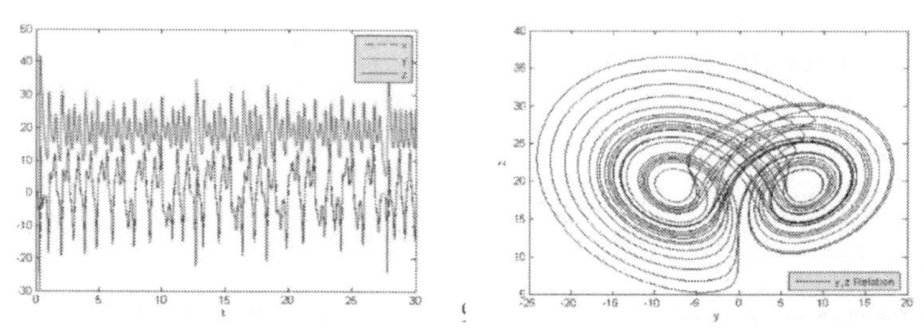

**Figure 29.** The numerical behavior and chaotic attractors for $\alpha(t) = 0.97 - (0.01/100)t$ and $\tau = 0.005$.

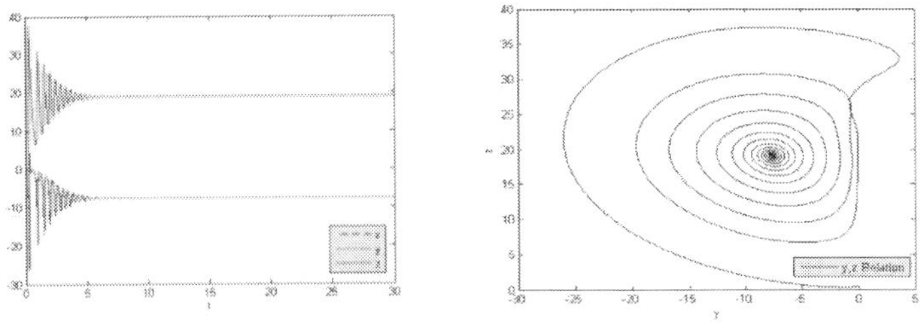

**Figure 30.** The numerical behavior and chaotic attractors for $\alpha(t) = 0.97 - (0.01/100)t$ and $\tau = 0.015$.

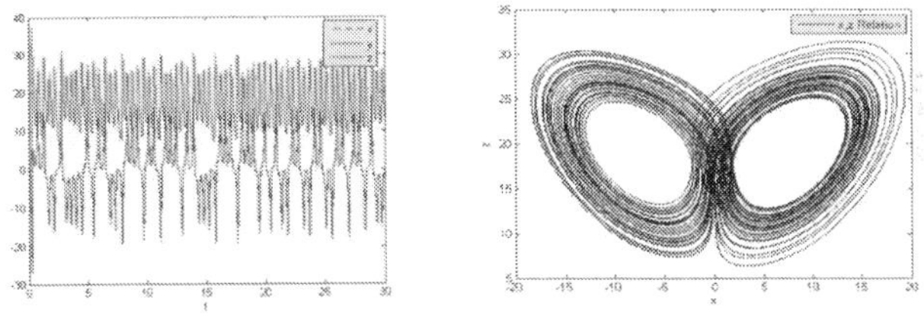

**Figure 31.** The numerical behavior and chaotic attractors for $\alpha(t) = 0.94 - (0.01/100)t$ and $\tau = 0.009$.

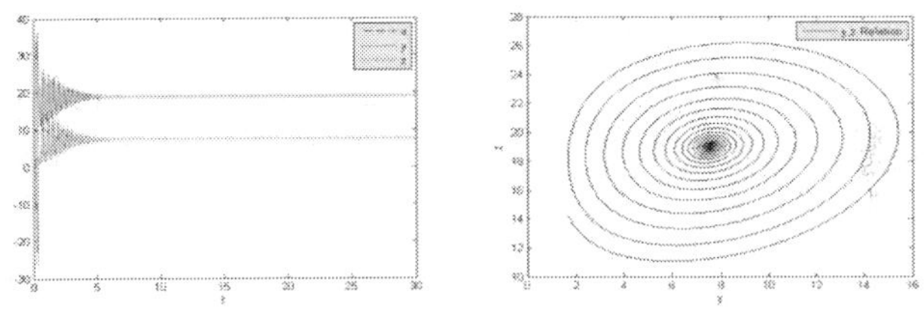

**Figure 32.** The numerical behavior and chaotic attractors for $\alpha(t) = 0.94 - (0.01/100)t$ and $\tau = 0.011$.

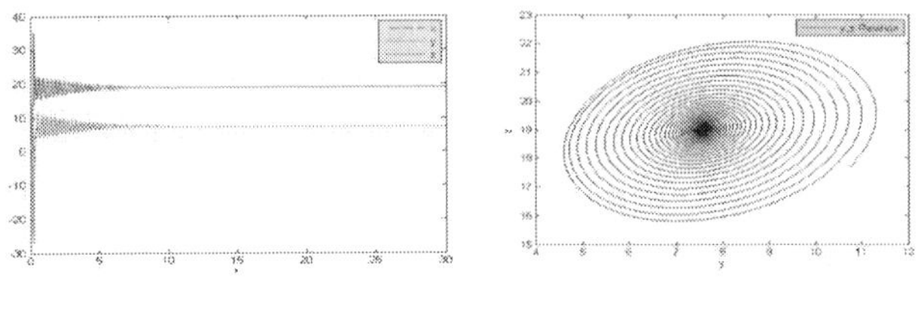

**Figure 33.** The numerical behavior and chaotic attractors for $\alpha(t) = 0.89 - (0.01/100)t$ and $\tau = 0.005$.

## Author details

N. H. Sweilam[1*] and T. A. Assiri[2]

*Address all correspondence to: nsweilam@sci.cu.edu.eg

1 Department of Mathematics, Faculty of Science, Cairo University, Giza, Egypt

2 Department of Mathematics, Faculty of Science, Umm Al-Qura University, Saudi Arabia

## References

[1] A. L. Hodgkin, A. F. Huxley, B. Katz, Measurement of current-voltage relations in the membrane of the giant axon of Loligo, J. Physiol, 116, 4, 424–448, 1952.

[2] A. L. Hodgkin, A. F. Huxley, Currents carried by sodium and potassium ions through the membrane of the giant axon of Loligo, J. Physiol, 116, 4, 449–472, 1952.

[3] A. L. Hodgkin, A. F. Huxley, The components of membrane conductance in the giant axon of Loligo, J. Physiol, 116, 4, 473–496, 1952.

[4] A. L. Hodgkin, A. F. Huxley, The dual effect of membrane potential on sodium conductance in the giant axon of Loligo, J. Physiol, 116, 4, 497–506, 1952.

[5] A. L. Hodgkin, A. F. Huxley, A quantitative description of membrane current and its application to conduction and excitation in nerve, J. Physiol, 117, 500–544, 1952.

[6] N. H. Sweilam, A. M. Nagy, An efficient method for solving fractional Hodgkin-Huxley model, Phys. Lett. A, 378, 1980–1984, 2014.

[7] N. H. Sweilam, T. A. Assiri, Numerical study for the general Hodgkin Huxley model of neuronal excitation, Appl. Math. Inf. Sci. 4, 8, 1–8, 2014.

[8] S. Doi, J. Inoue, Z. Pan, K. Tsumoto, Computational electrophysiology, Springer, 2010.

[9] Siciliano, Ryan. (2012). "The Hodgkin-Huxley Model – Its Extensions, Analysis and Numerics." McGill University. Web. April 9th, 2013.

[10] R. E. Mickens, Non-standard finite difference model of differential equations, World Scientific, Singapore, 1994.

[11] R. E. Mickens, Application of non-standard finite difference schemes, World Scientific Publishing Co. Pte. Ltd., Singapore, 2000.

[12] R. E. Mickens, Non-standard finite difference schemes for reactions-diffusion equations, Numerical Methods Partial Differential Equations Fractals, 15, 201–214, 1999.

[13] R. E. Mickens, Numerical integration of population models satisfying conservation laws: NSFD methods, Biol. Dyn. 1, 4, 1751–1766, 2007.

[14] R. E. Mickens, Calculation of denominator functions for non-standard finite difference schemes for differential equations satisfying a positivity condition, Numerical Methods for Partial Differential Equations, 23, 672–691, 2007.

[15] R. E. Mickens, Finite difference models of ordinary differential equations: influence of denominator functions, J. Franklin Inst., 327, 143–149, 1990.

[16] R. E. Mickens, A non-standard finite difference scheme for a fisher PDF having non-linear diffusion, Comput. Math. Appl., 45, 429–436, 2003.

[17] R. E. Mickens, A non-standard finite difference scheme for the Lotka-Volterra system, Appl. Numer. Math., 45(2–3), 309–314, 2003.

[18] E. Fridman, L. Fridman, E. Shustin, Steady modes in relay control systems with time delay and periodic disturbances, J. Dyn. Syst., Measur., Control, 122, 4, 732–737, 2000.

[19] L. C. Davis, Modification of the optimal velocity traffic model to include delay due to driver reaction time, Physica A, 319, 557–567, 2002.

[20] Y. Kuang, Delay differential equations with applications in population biology, Academic Press, Boston, San Diego, New York, 1993.

[21] I. Epstein, Y. Luo, Differential delay equations in chemical kinetics, non-linear models: the cross-shaped phase diagram and the originator, J. Chem. Phys., 95, 244–254, 1991.

[22] P. Liu, S. Elaydi, Discrete competitive and cooperative methods of Lotka-Volterra type, Comput. Appl. Analysis, 3, 53–73, 2001.

[23] E. Braverman, D. Kinzebulatov, Nicholson's blowflies equation with a distributed delay, Can. Appl. Math. Quart., 14, 2, 2006.

[24] T. K. Alligood, T. D. Sauer, J. A. Yorke, Chaos: an introduction to dynamical systems, Springer, 2008.

[25] S. Bhalekar, V. Daftardar-Gejji, A predictor-corrector scheme for solving non-linear delay differential equations of fractional order, J. Fract. Calculus Appl., 1, 5, 1–9, 2011.

[26] K. S. Miller, B. Ross, An introduction to the fractional calculus and fractional differential equations, Wiley-Interscience, New York, NY, USA, 1993.

[27] N. H. Sweilam, T. A. Assiri, A. M. Nagy, N. Y. Ali, Numerical simulations for variable order fractional non- linear delay differential equations, J. Fract. Calculus Appl., 6, 1, 71–82, 2015.

[28] F. Liu, P. Zhuang, V. Anh, I. Turner, A fractional order implicit difference approximation for the space-time fractional diffusion equation, ANZIAM J., 47(EMAC2005), 48–68, 2006.

[29] K. Diethelm, The analysis of fractional differential equations, Springer, Berlin, Germany, 2010.

[30] K. Diethelm, N. J. Ford, A. D. Freed, A predictor-corrector approach for the numerical solution of fractional differential equations, Non-Linear Dynamics, 29, 3–22, 2002.

[31] K. Diethelm, N. J. Ford, A. D. Freed, Detailed error analysis for a fractional Adams method, Numer. Algor., 36, 1, 31–52, 2004.

[32] S. Ma, Y. Xu, W. Yue, Numerical solutions of a variable order fractional financial system, J. Appl. Math., 2012, 14, 2012 (Article ID 417942).

[33] K. Diethelm, N. J. Ford, A. D. Freed, Yu. Luchko, Algorithms for the fractional calculus: a selection of numerical methods, Comput. Methods Appl. Mech. Energy, 194, 743–773, 2005.

[34] R. Boonstra, C. J. Krebs, N. C. Stenseth, Population cycles in small mammals: the problem of explaining the low phase, Ecology, 79, 1479–1488, 1998.

[35] A. J. Sami, A. R. Shakoor, Cellulase activity inhibition and growth retardation of associated bacterial strains of Aulacophora foviecollis by two glycosylated flavonoids isolated from Magnifier indicia leaves, J. Med. Plants Res., 5, 2, 184–190, 2011.

[36] M. Okamoto, K. Hayashi, Frequency conversion mechanism in enzymatic feedback systems, J. Theoret. Biol., 108, 4, 529–537, 1984.

[37] N. E. Lorenz, Deterministic non-periodic flow, J. Atmos. Sci., 20, 1, 130–141, 1963.

[38] G. Chen, T. Ueta, Yet another chaotic attractor, Int. J. Bifurc. Chaos, 9, 7, 1465–1466, 1999.

[39] G. Chen, Comments on "Chen's attractor exists if Lorenz repulse exists: The Chen system is a special case of the Lorenz system", CHAOS, 23, 033108, 2013.

[40] C. Li, G. Peng, Chaos in Chen's system with a fractional order, Chaos, Solitons and Fractals, 22, 443–50, 2004.

[41] S. Bhalekar, V. Daftardar-Gejji, P. Gade, Dynamics of fractional ordered Chen system with delay, PRAMANA-J. Phys., 79, 1, 61–69, 2012.

Chapter 7

# A Multi-Domain Spectral Collocation Approach for Solving Lane-Emden Type Equations

Motsa Sandile Sydney, Magagula Vusi Mpendulo,
Goqo Sicelo Praisegod, Oyelakin Ibukun Sarah and
Sibanda Precious

Additional information is available at the end of the chapter

http://dx.doi.org/10.5772/63016

**Abstract**

In this work, we explore the application of a novel multi-domain spectral collocation method for solving general non-linear singular initial value differential equations of the Lane-Emden type. The proposed solution approach is a simple iterative approach that does not employ linearisation of the differential equations. Spectral collocation is used to discretise the iterative scheme to form matrix equations that are solved over a sequence of non-overlapping sub-intervals of the domain. Continuity conditions are used to advance the solution across the non-overlapping sub-intervals. Different Lane-Emden equations that have been reported in the literature have been used for numerical experimentation. The results indicate that the method is very effective in solving Lane-Emden type equations. Computational error analysis is presented to demonstrate the fast convergence and high accuracy of the method of solution.

**Keywords:** Multi-domain, Lame-Emden, Spectral Relaxation method, Collocation, Astrophysics

## 1. Introduction

In the most general form, Lane-Emden type equations are given as

$$y'' + \frac{\gamma}{x} y' + f(x, y) = g(x), \quad x \in [0, \infty), \quad y(0) = \alpha_0, \; y'(0) = \beta_0 \tag{1}$$

where the prime denotes differentiation with respect to $x$, $f(x, y)$ is a non-linear function, $g(x)$ is a prescribed function and $\gamma$, $\alpha_0$, $\beta_0$ are known constants. In recent years, problems described by this class of differential equations have been widely investigated by many researchers because of their applications in astronomy, mathematical biology, mathematical physics, non-Newtonian fluid mechanics, and other areas of science and engineering. From a solution method viewpoint, it has been observed that, owing to the singularity at $x = 0$, Lane-Emden type equations are not trivial to solve. For this reason, the equations are normally used as benchmark equations for testing the effectiveness and robustness of new analytical and numerical methods of solution.

Analytical approaches that have recently been used in solving the Lane-Emden equations are mostly based on truncated series expansions. Examples include the Adomian decomposition method [1–3], differential transformation method [4, 5], Laplace transform [6, 7], homotopy analysis method [8–10], power series expansions [11–14] and variational iteration method [15–17]. Being power series based, the above methods have a small region of convergence and are not suitable for generating solutions in very large values of $x$. For this reason, most analytical approaches have only reported solutions of Lane-Emden type equations on small interval $[0,1]$ on $x$ axis. Despite this limitation, analytical approaches have been found to be desirable because they easily overcome the difficulty caused by the singularity at $x = 0$.

To overcome the limitations of analytical solution methods, several numerical approaches have been proposed for the solution of Lane-Emden type equations. Numerical methods based on spectral collocation have been found to be particularly effective. Collocation methods that have been reported recently for the solution of Lane-Emden type equations include the Bessel collocation method [18, 19], Jacobi-Gauss collocation method [20], Legendre Tau method [21], Sinc-collocation method [22], Chebyshev spectral methods [23], quasi-linearisation based Chebyshev pseudo-spectral method [24, 25] and a collocation method based on radial basis functions [26]. The discretisation scheme of collocation based methods is only implemented on interior nodes of the discretised domain. This property makes it possible for these collocation methods to overcome the difficulty of dealing with the singular point.

In this work, we present a multi-domain spectral collocation method for solving Lane-Emden equations. The method is based on the innovative idea of reducing the governing non-linear differential equations to a system of first-order equations which are solved iteratively using a Gauss-Seidel–like relaxation approach. The domain of the problem is divided into smaller non-overlapping sub-intervals on which the Chebyshev spectral collocation method is used to solve the iteration scheme. The continuity condition is used to advance the solution across neighbouring sub-intervals. The advantage of the approach is that it does not use Taylor-series based linearisation methods to simplify the non-linear differential equations. The method is free of errors associated with series truncation. The algorithm is also very easy to develop and yields very accurate results using only a few discretisation nodes. The accuracy of the method is validated against known results from the literature. The aim of the study is to explore the applicability of the multi-domain spectral collocation method to Lane-Emden type equations over semi-infinite domains. The results confirm that the method is suitable for solving all types of Lane-Emden equations.

## 2. A multi-domain pseudospectral relaxation method

In this section, we describe the development of the multi-domain collocation algorithm for the solution of Lane-Emden type equations. This algorithm addresses some limitations of standard collocation methods. Without loss of generality, we express the second-order generalised Lane-Emden Eq. (1) as a system of first-order ordinary differential equations (ODEs). If we let $h - y_0$, the initial value problem (1) transforms to

$$y'(x) = h(x), \quad y(0) = \alpha_0, \tag{2}$$

$$h'(x) + \frac{\gamma}{x}h + f(x,y) = g(x), \quad h(0) = \beta_0, \tag{3}$$

where $y'(x) = h(x)$. The following iterative scheme for solving (2) and (3) is introduced:

$$y'_{i+1}(x) = h_i(x), \quad y_{i+1}(0) = \alpha_0, \tag{4}$$

$$h'_{i+1}(x) + \frac{\gamma}{x}h_{i+1}(x) + f(x, y_{i+1}) = g(x), \qquad h_{i+1}(0) = \beta_0. \tag{5}$$

Assuming that an initial approximation $h_0(x)$ is given, Eq. (4) can be solved for $y_{i+1}(x)$ and the solution can be used immediately in Eq. (5) which is, in turn, solved for $h_{i+1}$. Thus, at each iteration level $i + 1$, Eqs. (4) and (5) form a pair of linear decoupled first-order differential equations. The solution procedure is discussed below.

Below, we describe the development of the multi-domain approach for solving the system of first-order Eqs. (4) and (5). The multi-domain technique approach assumes that the main interval can be decomposed into $p$ non-overlapping sub-intervals. Let $x \in \Lambda$, where $\Lambda = [a, b]$ is the interval where the solution of Eq. (1) exists. The sub-intervals are defined as

$$\Lambda_k = (x_{k-1}, x_k), \quad k = 1, 2, \cdots, p, \quad \text{with,} \quad a = x_0 < x_1 < x_2 < \cdots < x_p = b. \tag{6}$$

The solution procedure assumes that the solution at each sub-interval $\Lambda_k$, denoted by $y^{(k)}(x)$, can be approximated by a Lagrange interpolation polynomial of the form

$$y^{(k)}(x) \sim \sum_{s=0}^{N} y^{(k)}(x_s) L_s(x), \tag{7}$$

which interpolates $y^{(k)}(x)$ at selected points, chosen to be the Chebyshev-Gauss-Lobatto, defined by

$$\{\tau_s\}_{s=0}^{N} = \left\{ \cos\left(\frac{\pi s}{N}\right) \right\}_{s=0}^{N}. \tag{8}$$

The choice of the interpolation function (7) with Lagrangre polynomial basis and grid points (8) enables the use of simple formulas for converting the continuous derivatives to discrete matrix-vector form at the collocation points $\tau_s$. The function $L_s(x)$ is the characteristic Lagrange cardinal polynomial defined as

$$L_s(x) = \prod_{\substack{s=0 \\ s \neq k}}^{M} \frac{x - x_k}{x_s - x_k}, \tag{9}$$

that obey the Kronecker delta equation:

$$L_s(x_k) = \delta_{sk} = \begin{cases} 0 & \text{if } s \neq k \\ 1 & \text{if } s = k. \end{cases} \tag{10}$$

The solution method seeks to solve each of the system of first-order ODEs independently in each $k_{th}$ sub-interval $\Lambda_k$ using the solutions obtained in the preceding interval $\Lambda_{k-1}$ as initial conditions. In the first interval the solution is computed on $[x_0, x_1]$ and is labelled $y^{(1)}(x)$. The value of the solution at the last node $y^{(1)}(x_1)$ is used as an initial condition when seeking a solution in the second sub-interval $\Lambda_2$. This procedure is repeated in each $\Lambda_k$ interval with the solutions marched across each interval using the following continuity condition:

$$y^{(k)}(x_{k-1}) = y^{(k-1)}(x_{k-1}), \quad h^{(k)}(x_{k-1}) = h^{(k-1)}(x_{k-1}). \tag{11}$$

Therefore, in each sub-interval $\Lambda_k$, the following system of ODEs is solved:

$$\frac{dy_{i+1}^{(k)}(x)}{dx} = h_i^{(k)}(x), \quad y_{i+1}^{(k)}(x_{k-1}) = \alpha_{k-1} \tag{12}$$

http://dx.doi.org/10.5772/63016

$$\frac{dh_{i+1}^{(k)}(x)}{dx}+\frac{\gamma}{x}h_{i+1}^{(k)}(x)=g(x)-f(x,y_{i+1}^{(k)}),\quad h_{i+1}^{(k)}(x_{k-1})=\beta_{k-1},\tag{13}$$

where

$$\alpha_{k-1}=y^{(k-1)}(x_{k-1}),\quad \beta_{k-1}=h^{(k-1)}(x_{k-1}),\quad k=1,2,\ldots,p.$$

Eqs. (12) and (13) cannot be solved exactly because of the non-linear function $f(x, y)$. Accordingly, we employ the spectral collocation at the grid points $x_j$ for $j=0,1,2,\cdots,N$ for each sub-interval $\Lambda_k$. Before the spectral method is applied, each sub-interval $[x_{k-1}, x_k]$ is transformed to $[-1,1]$ using the linear transformation:

$$x=\frac{x_k-x_{k-1}}{2}\tau+\frac{x_k+x_{k-1}}{2},\quad \tau\in[-1,1].\tag{14}$$

The derivatives at the collocation points are evaluated as

$$\left.\frac{dy^{(k)}}{dx}\right|_{x=x_j}=\sum_{s=0}^{N}y^{(k)}(x_s)\frac{dL_s(x_j)}{dx}=\frac{2}{\Delta x_k}\sum_{s=0}^{N}y^{(k)}(\tau_s)\frac{dL_s(\tau_j)}{d\tau}=\sum_{s=0}^{N}D_{js}y^{(k)}(\tau_s),\tag{15}$$

where $\Delta x_k=x_k-x_{k-1}$, $\mathbf{D}_{js}=\frac{2}{\Delta x_k}D_{js}$ with $D_{js}=\frac{dL_s(\tau_j)}{d\tau}$ being the $j$th and $s$th entry of the standard first derivative Chebyshev differentiation matrix of size $(N+1)\times(N+1)$ as defined in [27]. Evaluating Eqs. (12) and (13) at the grid points $\tau_j$ for $j=0,1,2,\cdots,N$ gives

$$\sum_{s=0}^{N}\mathbf{D}_{js}y_{i+1}^{(k)}(\tau_s)=h_i^{(k)}(\tau_j),\quad y_{i+1}^{(k)}(\tau_N)=\alpha_{k-1},\tag{16}$$

$$\sum_{s=0}^{N}\mathbf{D}_{js}h_{i+1}^{(k)}(\tau_s)+\frac{\gamma}{x_j}h_{i+1}^{(k)}(\tau_j)=g(x_j)-f(x_s,y_{i+1}^{(k)}(\tau_j)),\quad h_{i+1}^{(k)}(\tau_N)=\beta_{k-1}.\tag{17}$$

Including the relevant initial conditions in Eqs. (16) and (17) yields

$$\sum_{s=0}^{N-1}\mathbf{D}_{js}y_{i+1}^{(k)}(\tau_s)=V_i^{(k)}(\tau_j),\tag{18}$$

$$\sum_{s=0}^{N-1} \mathbf{D}_{js} h_{i+1}^{(k)}(\tau_s) + \frac{\gamma}{x_j} h_{i+1}^{(k)}(\tau_j) = W_i^{(k)}(\tau_j). \tag{19}$$

where

$$V_i^{(k)}(\tau_j) = h_i^{(k)}(\tau_j) - \mathbf{D}_{jN} y_{i+1}^{(k)}(\tau_N), \tag{20}$$

$$W_i^{(k)}(\tau_j) = g(x_j) - f(x_j, y_{i+1}^{(k)}(\tau_j)) - \mathbf{D}_{jN} h_{i+1}^{(k)}(\tau_N), \tag{21}$$

Eqs. (18) and (19) can be expressed in matrix form as follows:

$$\mathbf{D}\mathbf{Y}_{i+1}^{(k)} = \mathbf{V}_i^{(k)}, \tag{22}$$

$$(\mathbf{D} + \zeta)\mathbf{H}_{i+1}^{(k)} = \mathbf{W}_i^{(k)}, \tag{23}$$

where the vectors $\mathbf{Y}^{(k)}$, $\mathbf{H}^{(k)}$, $\mathbf{V}^{(k)}$ and $\mathbf{W}^{(k)}$ are respectively given by

$$\mathbf{Y}^{(k)} = [y^{(k)}(\tau_0), y^{(k)}(\tau_1), y^{(k)}(\tau_2), \cdots, y^{(k)}(\tau_{N-1})]^T, \tag{24}$$

$$\mathbf{H}^{(k)} = [h^{(k)}(\tau_0), h^{(k)}(\tau_1), h^{(k)}(\tau_2), \cdots, h^{(k)}(\tau_{N-1})]^T, \tag{25}$$

$$\mathbf{V}^{(k)} = [v^{(k)}(\tau_0), v^{(k)}(\tau_1), v^{(k)}(\tau_2), \cdots, v^{(k)}(\tau_{N-1})]^T, \tag{26}$$

$$\mathbf{W}^{(k)} = [w^{(k)}(\tau_0), w^{(k)}(\tau_1), w^{(k)}(\tau_2), \cdots, w^{(k)}(\tau_{N-1})]^T, \tag{27}$$

and $T$ denotes the transpose of the vector. The $N \times N$ diagonal matrix $\zeta$ is given by

$$\zeta = \begin{bmatrix} \frac{\gamma}{x_0} & & & \\ & \frac{\gamma}{x_1} & & \\ & & \ddots & \\ & & & \frac{\gamma}{x_{N-1}} \end{bmatrix}. \tag{28}$$

http://dx.doi.org/10.5772/63016

The approximate values of $y^{(k)}(x)$ and $\frac{dy^{(k)}(x)}{dx}$ are obtained by iteratively solving Eqs. (22) and (23), respectively, for $i=0,1,2,\dots$, starting from suitable initial approximation.

## 3. Numerical experiments

In this section, we discuss the numerical experiments to be used to demonstrate the accuracy and general performance of the multi-domain pseudospectral relaxation method. In these numerical experiments, we have selected equations with known exact solutions, and to determine the accuracy of the method, we find the relative error. The relative error is defined as

$$E_j = \frac{|y_e(x_j) - y_a(x_j)|}{|y_e(x_j)|} \tag{29}$$

where $E_j$ is the relative error at a grid point $x_j$, $y_e(x_j)$ and $y_a(x_j)$ are the exact and approximate solutions at a grid point $x_j$, respectively.

### Example 1

We first consider the linear, homogeneous Lane-Emden equation, with variable coefficients:

$$y'' + \frac{2}{x}y' - 2(2x^2+3)y = 0, \;\; x>0, \quad \text{subject to} \quad y(0)=1 \quad \text{and} \quad y'(0)=0, \tag{30}$$

which has the exact solution:

$$y(x) = e^{x^2}.$$

Eq. (30) has been solved by various researchers using different techniques such as the variational iteration method and the homotopy-pertubation method [16, 28, 29].

### Example 2

Secondly, the non-linear, homogeneous Lane-Emden equation, with variable coefficients is considered:

$$y'' + \frac{2}{x}y' + 4(2e^y + e^{y/2}) = 0, \;\; x>0, \quad \text{subject to} \quad y(0)=0 \quad \text{and} \quad y'(0)=0 \tag{31}$$

which has the exact solution:

$$y(x) = -2\ln(1+x^2).$$

Eq. (31) has been solved by [29, 30, 31] using the lie symmetry, the homotopy-pertubation method and the variational iteration method.

**Example 3**

In this example, we consider the non-linear, variable coefficients, homogeneous Lane-Emden equation:

$$y'' + \frac{2}{x}y' - 6y = 4y\ln(y), \quad x > 0, \quad \text{subject to} \quad y(0) = 1 \quad \text{and} \quad y'(0) = 0 \tag{32}$$

which has the exact solution:

$$y(x) = e^{x^2}.$$

Ramos [28] solved Eq. (32) using the variation iteration method, while Yildirim [16] solved the same equation using the linearisation method.

**Example 4**

We consider the non-linear, homogeneous Lane-Emden equation:

$$y'' + \frac{6}{x}y' + 2y(7 + \ln(y^2)) = 0, \quad x > 0, \quad \text{subject to} \quad y(0) = 1 \quad \text{and} \quad y'(0) = 0 \tag{33}$$

which has the exact solution [32]:

$$y(x) = e^{-x^2}.$$

This example was solved by Wazwaz [32] using the Adomian decomposition method.

**Example 5**

We consider the non-linear, homogenous Lane-Emden equation, which represent an infinite circular cylinder in astrophysics:

$$y'' + \frac{2}{x}y' + y^3 - 6 - x^6 = 0, \quad x > 0, \quad \text{subject to} \quad y(0) = 0 \quad \text{and} \quad y'(0) = 0, \tag{34}$$

which has the exact solution [33]:

$$y(x) = x^2.$$

This example was solved by Yin et al. [33] using the modified Laplace decomposition method.

**Example 6**

Lastly, we consider the Lane-Emden equation with the general form:

$$y'' + \frac{2}{x}y' + y^m = 0, \; x > 0, \quad \text{subject to} \quad y(0) = 1 \quad \text{and} \quad y'(0) = 0. \tag{35}$$

Eq. (35) is the standard Lane-Emden equation that models the thermal behaviour of a spherical cloud of glass acting under the mutual attraction of its molecules and subject to classical laws of thermodynamics [34]. The values of $m$ in the interval $[0,5]$ are most physically interesting to study. The equation is linear when $m = 0$ and $m = 1$ and non-linear for values of $m>1$. Wazwaz [35] gave the general solution of Eq. (35) in series form as

$$\begin{aligned} y(x) = 1 - \frac{1}{6}x^2 + \frac{m}{120}x^4 - \frac{m(8m-5)}{3.7!}x^6 + \frac{m(70-183m+122m^2)}{9.9!}x^8 \\ + \frac{m(3150-1080m+12642m^2-5032m^3)}{45.11!}x^{10} + \ldots. \end{aligned} \tag{36}$$

Analytical solutions for $m=0,1$ and $m=5$ are given as [35]

$$y(x) = 1 - \frac{1}{3!}x^2, \qquad y(x) = \frac{\sin x}{x}, \qquad \text{and} \qquad y(x) = \left(1 + \frac{x^2}{3}\right)^{-\frac{1}{2}}, \tag{37}$$

respectively. In this example, we consider the Lane-Emden Eq. (35) for $m = 5$. We therefore consider the equation:

$$y'' + \frac{2}{x}y' + y^5 = 0, \; x > 0, \quad \text{subject to} \quad y(0) = 1 \quad \text{and} \quad y'(0) = 0 \tag{38}$$

with the exact solution:

$$y(x) = \left(1 + \frac{x^2}{3}\right)^{-1/2}. \tag{39}$$

## 4. Results and discussion

In this section, we discuss and present the results obtained using the proposed algorithm. We used the six examples in the previous section. The results were generated using MATLAB 2013. To validate the accuracy, computational time and general performance of the method, we computed relative errors and computational time of each of the numerical examples. The level of accuracy of the algorithm at a particular level is determined by the relative error $R_k$ defined by

$$R_k = \frac{|y_e(x_k) - y_a(x_k)|}{|y_e(x_k)|}, \quad 0 \le k \le N, \tag{40}$$

where $N$ is the number of grid points, $y_a(x_k)$ is the approximate solution and $y_e(x_k)$ is the exact solution at the grid point $x_k$. The graphs were all generated using $N = 4$. For each numerical experiment, we present the relative error and the corresponding approximate solution for $N = 4$ and $N = 6$ in a tabular form. The central processing unit computational time is displayed. Graphs showing an excellent agreement between the analytical and approximate solutions are presented for each numerical experiment. These graphs validate the accuracy of the method. Error graphs showing the distribution of the relative errors are also presented. These error graphs are in excellent agreement with the results presented in the tables for all the numerical experiments used in this chapter.

| | | N = 4 | | N = 6 | |
|---|---|---|---|---|---|
| $x$ | Exact | Approximate | Relative error | Approximate | Relative error |
| 0.2 | 1.060313 | 1.060313 | 1.884728e−14 | 1.060313 | 4.251109e−014 |
| 0.4 | 1.140018 | 1.140018 | 3.505912e−14 | 1.140018 | 6.505415e−014 |
| 0.6 | 1.371416 | 1.371416 | 7.852585e−14 | 1.371416 | 1.066980e−013 |
| 0.8 | 1.787189 | 1.787189 | 1.413886e−13 | 1.787189 | 1.474757e−013 |
| 1.0 | 2.522988 | 2.522988 | 2.355112e−13 | 2.522988 | 1.864022e−013 |
| 1.2 | 3.858367 | 3.858367 | 3.776361e−13 | 3.858367 | 2.234047e−013 |
| 1.4 | 6.391979 | 6.391979 | 5.987445e−13 | 6.391979 | 2.591455e−013 |
| 1.6 | 11.471251 | 11.471251 | 9.227679e−13 | 11.471251 | 2.937560e−013 |
| 1.8 | 22.301278 | 22.301278 | 1.396995e−12 | 22.301278 | 3.316738e−013 |
| 2.0 | 46.966942 | 46.966942 | 2.066546e−12 | 46.966942 | 3.633883e−013 |
| CPU Time (sec) | 0.659414 | 0.629082 | | 0.659414 | |

**Table 1.** Analytical, approximate solutions and relative errors for Example 1.

**Table 1** shows the exact, approximate solution and the relative error for Eq. (30). For $N = 4$, the multi-domain spectral relaxation method gives a relative error of approximately $10^{-12}$ and for $N = 6$, the relative error is on average $10^{-13}$. Increasing the number of grid points results in a more accurate solution. The results obtained from the multi-domain spectral relaxation method are remarkable since few grid points give accurate results in a large domain. Using a few grid points ensures that the numerical method converges within few seconds.

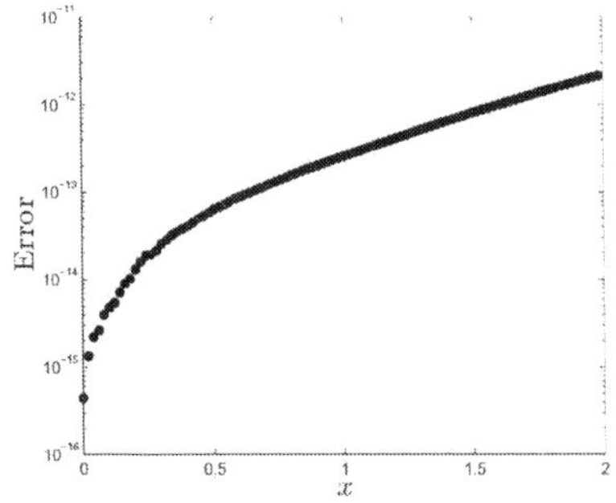


**Figure 1.** Error graph.

**Figure 1** shows the relative error displayed in **Table 1** for $N = 4$. The results in **Figure 1** are in excellent agreement with those in **Table 1**. **Figure 2** shows the analytical and approximate solutions. Since the approximate solution is superimposed on the exact solutions, this implies that the multi-domain pseudospectral relaxation method converged to the exact solution over the domain $x \in [0,2]$. **Table 1** and **Figures 1** and **2** validate the accuracy and computational efficiency of the multi-domain pseudospectral relaxation method for Eq. (30).

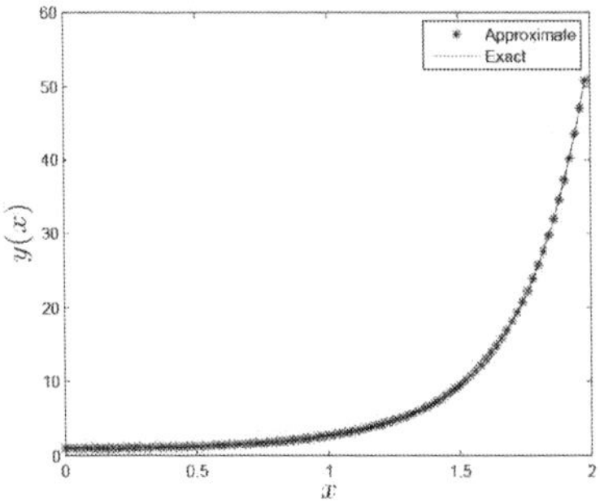


**Figure 2.** Comparison of analytical and approximate solutions for Example 1.

The results obtained from approximating the solution to Eq. (31) using the multi-domain pseudospectral relaxation method are shown in **Table 1** and **Figures 3** and **4**. In **Table 2**, we display the exact solution, approximate solution and the relative error of Eq. (31) in Example 2. For $N = 4$, the multi-domain spectral relaxation method gives a relative error of approximately $10^{-11}$. For $N = 4$ the relative error is approximately $10^{-13}$. We observe that increasing the number of grid points decreases the relative error. The multi-domain pseudospectral relaxation method uses a few grid points to achieve accurate results in the domain $x \in [0,20]$. A maximum of $N = 6$ grid points ensured that the numerical method converged to an error of $10^{-13}$ within a fraction of a second.

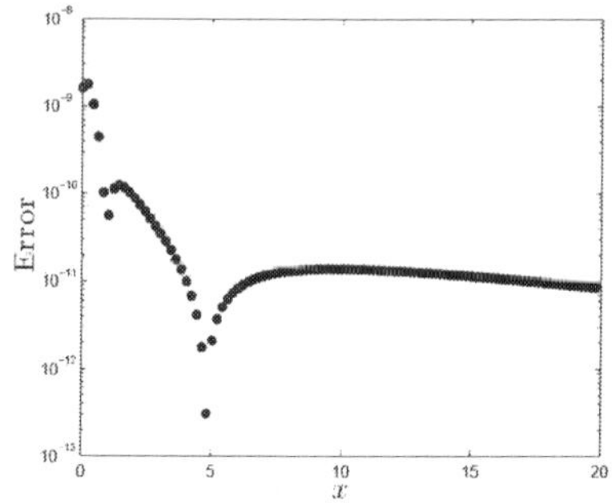


**Figure 3.** Error graph.

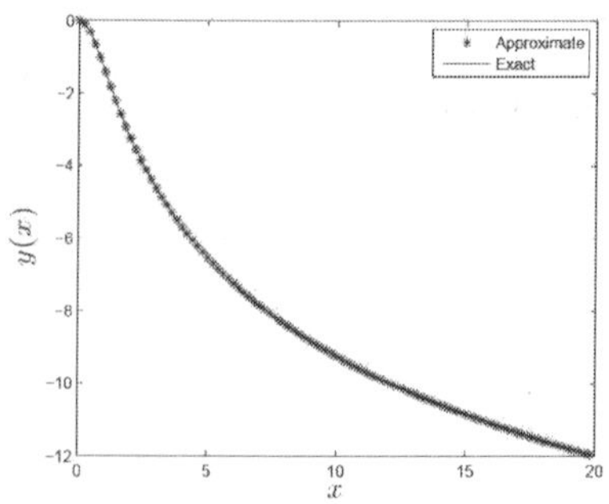


**Figure 4.** Comparison of analytical and approximate solutions for Example 2.

**Figure 3** shows the relative error displayed in **Table 2** for $N = 4$. The results in **Figure 3** are in excellent agreement with those in **Table 2**. **Figure 4** shows the analytical and approximate solutions of Eq. (31). The approximate solution superimposed on the exact solutions shows that the multi-domain pseudospectral relaxation method converged to the exact solution over the domain $x \in [0,20]$. The match between the exact and approximate solutions in **Table 2** and **Figures 3** and **4** validates the accuracy and computational efficiency of the multi-domain pseudospectral relaxation method for Eq. (31).

| | | N = 4 | | N = 6 | |
|---|---|---|---|---|---|
| $x$ | Exact | Approximate | Relative error | Approximate | Relative error |
| 2 | −3.271943 | −3.271943 | 8.810376e−011 | −3.271943 | 2.704972e−014 |
| 4 | −5.697684 | −5.697682 | 1.000287e−011 | −5.697684 | 6.202217e−014 |
| 6 | −7.243401 | −7.243399 | 8.316853e−012 | −7.243401 | 2.136148e−014 |
| 8 | −8.365152 | −8.365151 | 1.308867e−011 | −8.365152 | 3.825343e−015 |
| 10 | −9.243421 | −9.243420 | 1.383787e−011 | −9.243421 | 4.807193e−015 |
| 12 | −9.964487 | −9.964487 | 1.318604e−011 | −9.964487 | 5.172115e−015 |
| 14 | −10.575872 | −10.575872 | 1.205994e−011 | −10.575872 | 6.720993e−015 |
| 16 | −11.106445 | −11.106445 | 1.080384e−011 | −11.106445 | 3.199792e−016 |
| 18 | −11.575028 | −11.575028 | 9.561315e−012 | −11.575028 | 6.293749e−015 |
| 20 | −11.927621 | −11.927622 | 8.504839e−012 | −11.927621 | 1.738910e−014 |
| CPU Time (sec) | 0.649135 | 0.602359 | | 0.649135 | |

**Table 2.** Analytical, approximate solutions and relative errors for Example 2.

The results obtained from approximating the solution to Eq. (32) are given in **Table 3** and **Figures 5** and **6**. **Table 3** shows the exact solution, the approximate solution and the relative error of Eq. (32). For $N = 4$, the multi-domain spectral relaxation method gives a relative error of approximately $10^{-12}$, while for $N = 6$, the relative error is approximately $10^{-13}$. We observe that increasing the number of grid points decreases the relative error and hence increases the accuracy of the method. This pseudospectral method uses a few grid points to achieve accurate results in the domain $x \in [0,2]$. $N = 6$ grid points ensured that the numerical method converged to an error of $10^{-13}$ within few seconds.

| | | N = 4 | | N = 6 | |
|---|---|---|---|---|---|
| $x$ | Exact | Approximate | Relative error | Approximate | Relative error |
| 0.2 | 1.029322 | 1.029322 | 2.502345e−014 | 1.029322 | 1.682611e−014 |
| 0.4 | 1.146713 | 1.146713 | 1.316722e−013 | 1.146713 | 4.124439e−014 |
| 0.6 | 1.383892 | 1.383892 | 3.732052e−013 | 1.383892 | 6.915367e−014 |
| 0.8 | 1.809228 | 1.809228 | 8.178657e−013 | 1.809228 | 1.078787e−013 |
| 1.0 | 2.562286 | 2.562286 | 1.581696e−012 | 2.562286 | 1.493997e−013 |
| 1.2 | 3.931024 | 3.931024 | 2.814656e−012 | 3.931024 | 1.883216e−013 |
| 1.4 | 6.53322 | 6.53322 | 4.761036e−012 | 6.53322 | 2.300241e−013 |
| 1.6 | 11.762306 | 11.762306 | 7.722919e−012 | 11.762306 | 2.750095e−013 |
| 1.8 | 22.940410 | 22.940410 | 1.211045e−011 | 22.940410 | 3.176323e−013 |
| 2.0 | 48.467816 | 48.467816 | 1.845750e−011 | 48.467816 | 3.667955e−013 |
| CPU Time (sec) | 1.069773 | 1.010628 | | 1.069773 | |

**Table 3.** Analytical, approximate solutions and relative errors for Example 3.

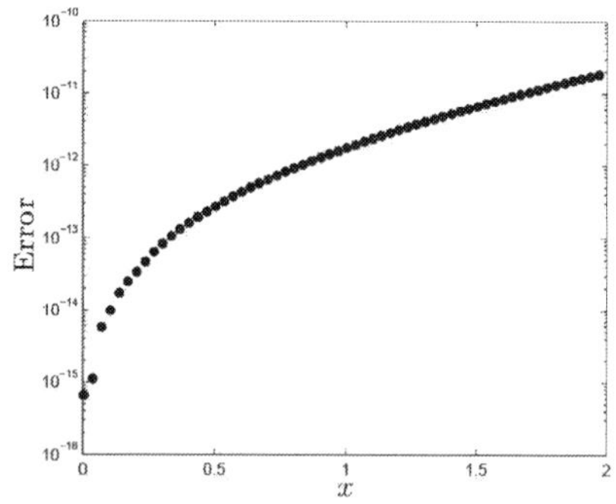


**Figure 5.** Error graph.

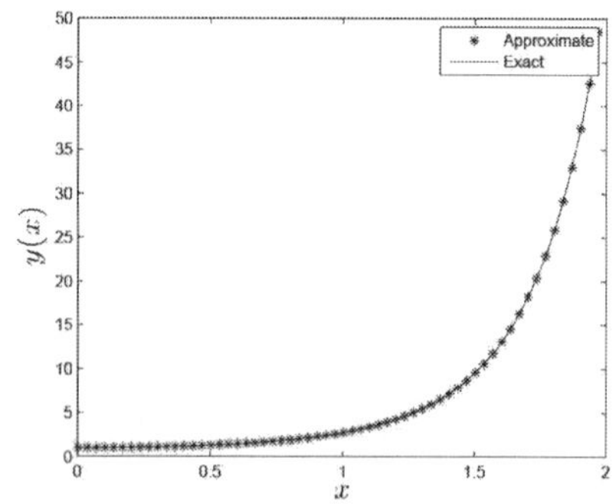


**Figure 6.** A comparison of analytical and approximate solutions in Example 3.

The relative error shown in **Table 3** is displayed in **Figure 5**. The results in **Figure 5** are in excellent agreement with those in **Table 3**. **Figure 6** shows the analytical and approximate solutions of Eq. (32). The approximate solution being superimposed on the exact solutions implies that the multi-domain pseudospectral relaxation method converged to the exact solution over the domain $x \in [0,2]$. The match between the exact and approximate solutions in **Table 3** and **Figures 5** and **6** validates the accuracy and computational efficiency of the multi-domain pseudospectral relaxation method for Eq. (32).

The results obtained from approximating the solution to Eq. (33) are given in **Table 4** and **Figures 7** and **8**. **Table 4** shows the exact solution, the approximate solution and the relative error of Eq. (33). For $N = 4$, the multi-domain spectral relaxation method gives a relative error of approximately $10^{-13}$. For $N = 6$, the relative error is also approximately $10^{-13}$. Increasing the number of grid points decreases the relative error. Thus, a maximum of $N = 6$ grid points ensures convergence of the method. $N = 6$ grid points ensured that the numerical method converged to an error of $10^{-13}$ in a fraction of seconds.

http://dx.doi.org/10.5772/63016

| | | N = 4 | | N = 6 | |
|---|---|---|---|---|---|
| $x$ | Exact | Approximate | Relative error | Approximate | Relative error |
| 0.2 | 0.974097 | 0.974097 | 7.978218e−015 | 0.974097 | 2.803774e−014 |
| 0.4 | 0.877179 | 0.877179 | 1.215047e−014 | 0.877179 | 6.999178e−014 |
| 0.6 | 0.729173 | 0.729173 | 1.248514e−014 | 0.729173 | 1.079508e−013 |
| 0.8 | 0.559538 | 0.559538 | 1.805602e−014 | 0.559538 | 1.341305e−013 |
| 1.0 | 0.396355 | 0.396355 | 3.221242e−014 | 0.396355 | 1.606419e−013 |
| 1.2 | 0.259177 | 0.259177 | 6.232707e−014 | 0.259177 | 1.756296e−013 |
| 1.4 | 0.156446 | 0.156446 | 1.011254e−013 | 0.156446 | 1.754615e−013 |
| 1.6 | 0.087174 | 0.087174 | 1.525094e−013 | 0.087174 | 1.404105e−013 |
| 1.8 | 0.044840 | 0.044840 | 1.897188e−013 | 0.044840 | 3.528213e−014 |
| 2.0 | 0.021292 | 0.021292 | 1.404623e−013 | 0.021292 | 2.123230e−013 |
| CPU Time (sec) | 1.080828 | 1.046274 | | 1.080828 | |

**Table 4.** Analytical, approximate solutions and relative errors for Example 4.

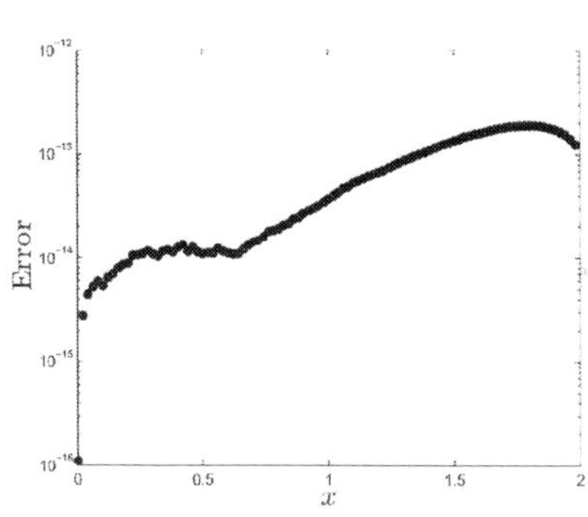


**Figure 7.** Error graph.

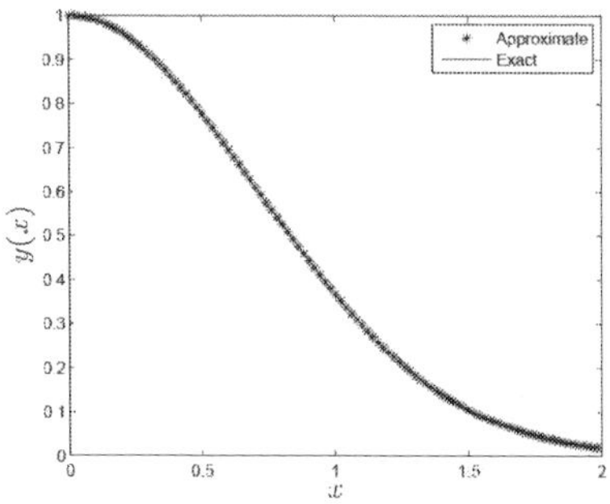


**Figure 8.** A comparison of analytical and approximate solutions in Example 4.

**Figure 7** shows the relative error displayed in **Table 4** for $N = 4$. The results in **Figure 7** are in excellent agreement with those in **Table 4. Figure 8** shows the analytical and approximate solutions. Since the approximate solution is superimposed on the exact solutions, this implies that the multi-domain pseudospectral relaxation method converged to the exact solution over the domain $x \in [0,2]$. **Table 4** and **Figures 7** and **8** validate the accuracy and computational efficiency of the multi-domain pseudospectral relaxation method for Eq. (33).

The results obtained from approximating the solution to Eq. (34) are given in **Table 5** and **Figures 9** and **10. Table 5** shows the exact solution, the approximate solution and the relative error of Eq. (34). The multi-domain pseudospectral relaxation method gives a relative error of approximately $10^{-14}$. For $N = 6$, the relative error is approximately $10^{-14}$. Increasing the number of grid points decreases the relative error and thus implying that the numerical method converged to the exact solution. The pseudospectral collocation method uses a few grid points to achieve accurate results in the domain $x \in [0,2]$. The numerical method converged to an error of $10^{-14}$ in a fraction of a second.

| | | N = 4 | | N = 6 | |
|---|---|---|---|---|---|
| $x$ | **Exact** | **Approximate** | **Relative error** | **Approximate** | **Relative error** |
| 0.2 | 0.026244 | 0.026244 | 4.759186e−015 | 0.026244 | 1.692155e−014 |
| 0.4 | 0.131044 | 0.131044 | 1.397903e−014 | 0.131044 | 3.473577e−014 |
| 0.6 | 0.315844 | 0.315844 | 2.495721e−014 | 0.315844 | 5.518706e−014 |
| 0.8 | 0.580644 | 0.580644 | 3.537301e−014 | 0.580644 | 6.864276e−014 |
| 1.0 | 0.925444 | 0.925444 | 4.138845e−014 | 0.925444 | 8.445643e−014 |
| 1.2 | 1.350244 | 1.350244 | 3.880967e−014 | 1.350244 | 9.981979e−014 |
| 1.4 | 1.855044 | 1.855044 | 4.093663e−014 | 1.855044 | 1.098825e−013 |
| 1.6 | 2.439844 | 2.439844 | 3.749517e−014 | 2.439844 | 8.700337e−014 |
| 1.8 | 3.104644 | 3.104644 | 2.445989e−014 | 3.104644 | 4.706026e−014 |
| 2.0 | 3.849444 | 3.849444 | 4.614580e−016 | 3.849444 | 6.575777e−015 |
| CPU Time (sec) | 0.705910 | 0.638383 | | 0.705910 | |

**Table 5.** Analytical, approximate solutions and relative errors for Example 5.

**Figure 9** shows the relative error displayed in **Table 5** for $N = 4$. The results in **Figure 9** are in excellent agreement with those in **Table 5. Figure 10** shows the analytical and approximate solutions. Since the approximate solution is superimposed on the exact solutions, this implies that the multi-domain pseudospectral relaxation method converged to the exact solution over the domain $x \in [0,2]$. **Table 5** and **Figures 9** and **10** validate the accuracy and computational efficiency of the multi-domain pseudospectral relaxation method for Eq. (34).

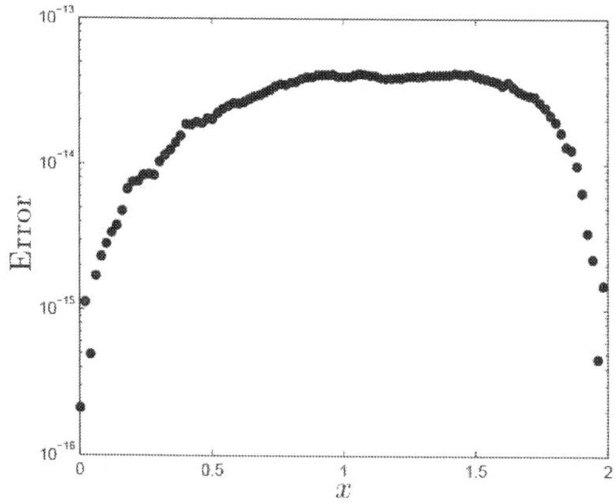


**Figure 9.** Error graph.

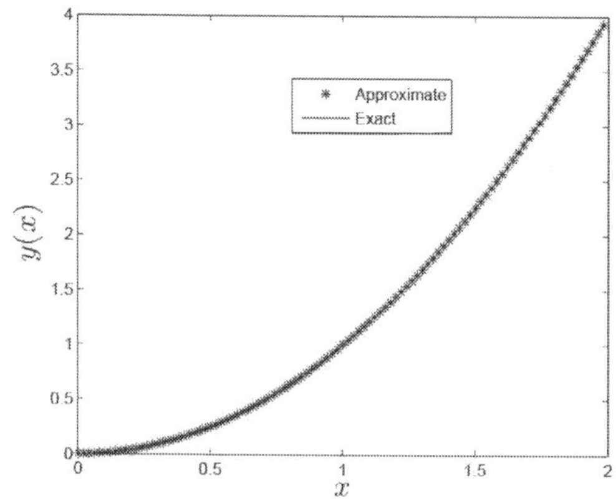


**Figure 10.** A comparison of analytical and approximate solutions in Example 5.

The results obtained from approximating the solution to Eq. (38) are given in **Table 6** and **Figures 11, 12** and **13**. **Table 6** shows values obtained for the exact and approximate solution together with the respective relative error values of Eq. (38). For $N = 4$ the multi-domain pseudospectral collocation method gives a relative error of approximately $10^{-11}$ and $10^{-13}$ for $N = 6$. An increase in the number of grid points results in a decrease in the relative error. This implies that the numerical method converges to the exact solution of Eq. (38). The multi-domain pseudospectral relaxation method used a few grid points to achieve accurate results in the domain $x \in [0,20]$. $N = 6$ grid points ensured that the numerical method converged to an error of $10^{-13}$ within a few seconds as shown in **Table 6**.

| | | N = 4 | | N = 6 | |
|---|---|---|---|---|---|
| $x$ | Exact | Approximate | Relative error | Approximate | Relative error |
| 2 | 0.650926 | 0.650926 | 1.991857e–011 | 0.650926 | 3.189482e–014 |
| 4 | 0.395693 | 0.395693 | 2.135316e–011 | 0.395693 | 3.745701e–014 |
| 6 | 0.276499 | 0.276499 | 6.204217e–012 | 0.276499 | 5.842239e–014 |
| 8 | 0.211100 | 0.211100 | 8.877991e–012 | 0.211100 | 1.519920e–013 |
| 10 | 0.170333 | 0.170333 | 2.323778e–011 | 0.170333 | 2.328536e–013 |
| 12 | 0.142624 | 0.142624 | 3.707619e–011 | 0.142624 | 3.096185e–013 |
| 14 | 0.122609 | 0.122609 | 5.055364e–011 | 0.122609 | 4.021536e–013 |
| 16 | 0.107492 | 0.107492 | 6.378059e–011 | 0.107492 | 4.983484e–013 |
| 18 | 0.095677 | 0.095607 | 7.683911e–011 | 0.095677 | 5.994828e–013 |
| 20 | 0.087057 | 0.087057 | 8.847457e–011 | 0.087057 | 6.926360e–013 |
| CPU Time (sec) | 1.199892 | 1.046417 | | 1.199892 | |

**Table 6.** Analytical, approximate solutions and relative errors for Example 6.

**Figure 11** shows the plot for different values of $m$. The results are in good agreement with those obtained by [25, 26]. **Figure 12** displays the relative error graph of Eq. (38). The results in **Figure 12** are in excellent agreement with those obtained in **Table 6**. The comparison between the exact solution and approximate solution of Eq. (38) is shown in **Figure 13**. The superimposition of the approximate solution on the exact solution implies that the multi-domain pseudospectral relaxation method converged to the exact solution over the domain $x \in [0,20]$. **Table 6** and **Figures 11, 12** and **13** give a validation of the accuracy and computational efficiency of the multi-domain pseudospectral relaxation method for Eq. (38).

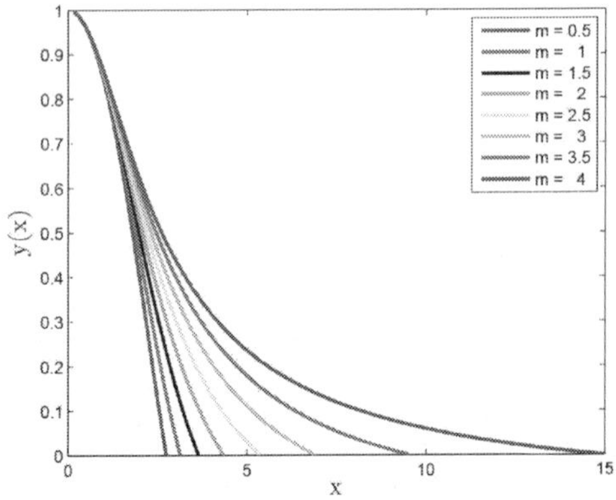


**Figure 11.** Plot showing solutions to Eq. (35) for some values of $m$.

http://dx.doi.org/10.5772/63016

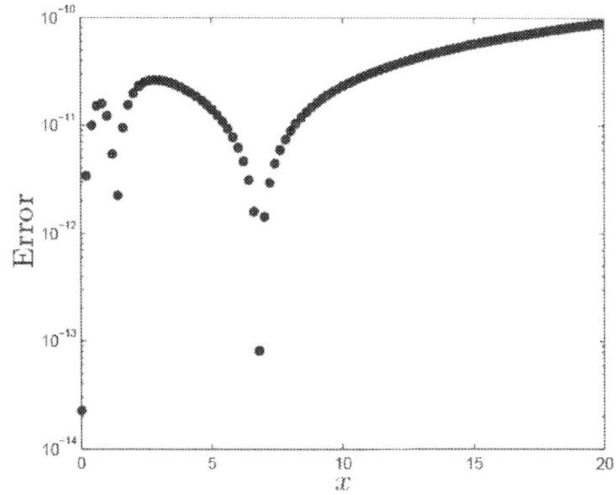


Figure 12. Error graph.

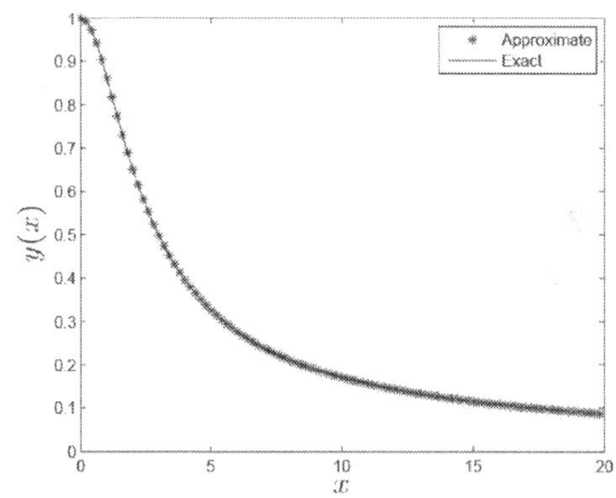


Figure 13. A comparison of analytical and approximate solutions in Example 6.

## 5. Conclusion

In this work, we presented a multi-domain spectral collocation method for solving Lane-Emden equations. This numerical method was used to solve six Lane-Emden equations. The results obtained were remarkable in the sense that using few grid points, we were able to achieve accurate results. We were able to compute the results using minimal computational time. The approximate solutions were in excellent agreement with the exact solutions in all the numerical experiments. We presented error graphs, approximate and exact solution graphs to show accuracy of the method. Tables showing relative errors were also generated to show accuracy and computational efficiency of the numerical method presented.

This approach is useful for solving other nonlinear, singular initial value problems. This approach is an alternative to the already existing list of numerical methods that can be used to solve such equations. This numerical approach can be extended to solve time-dependent Lane-Emden equations and other singular value type of equations.

## Acknowledgements

This work is based on the research supported in part by the National Research Foundation of South Africa (Grant No: 85596).

## Author details

Motsa Sandile Sydney*, Magagula Vusi Mpendulo, Goqo Sicelo Praisegod, Oyelakin Ibukun Sarah and Sibanda Precious

*Address all correspondence to: sandilemotsa@gmail.com

School of Mathematics, Statistics & Computer Science, University of KwaZulu-Natal, Scottsville, Pietermaritzburg, South Africa

## References

[1] S.G. Hosseini, S. Abbasbandy, Solution of Lane-Emden type equations by combination of the spectral method and adomian decomposition method, Mathematical Problems in Engineering, vol. 2015, 10 p., 2015, Article ID 534754. doi:10.1155/2015/534754

[2] A.M. Wazwaz, A new method for solving singular initial value problems in the second-order ordinary differential equations, Applied Mathematics and Computation, vol. 128, no. 1, pp. 45–57, 2002.

[3] A.M. Wazwaz, Adomian decomposition method for a reliable treatment of the Emden-Fowler equation, Applied Mathematics and Computation, vol. 161, no. 2, pp. 543–560, 2005.

[4] V.S. Ertürk, Differential transformation method for solving differential equations of Lane-Emden type, Mathematical & Computational Applications, vol. 12, no. 3, pp. 135–139, 2007.

[5] Y. Khan, Z. Svoboda, Z. Šmarda, Solving certain classes of Lane-Emden type equations using the differential transformation method, Advances in Difference Equations, vol. 2012, p. 174, 2012. doi:10.1186/1687-1847-2012-174

[6] F. Yin, J. Song, F. Lu, H. Leng, A coupled method of Laplace transform and Legendre wavelets for Lane-Emden-type differential equations, Journal of Applied Mathematics, vol. 2012, 16 p., 2012, Article ID 163821. doi:10.1155/2012/163821

[7] F. Yin, W. Han, J. Song, Modified Laplace decomposition method for Lane-Emden type differential equations, International Journal of Applied Physics and Mathematics, vol. 3, no. 2, 2013. doi:10.7763/IJAPM.2013.V3.184

[8] A.S. Bataineh, M.S.M. Noorani, I. Hashim, Homotopy analysis method for singular IVPs of Emden-Fowler type, Communications in Nonlinear Science and Numerical Simulation, vol. 14, no. 4, pp. 1121–1131, 2009.

[9] S. Liao, A new analytic algorithm of Lane-Emden type equations, Applied Mathematics and Computation, vol. 142, no. 1, pp. 1–16, 2003.

[10] O.P. Singh, R.K. Pandey, V.K. Singh, An analytic algorithm of Lane-Emden type equations arising in astrophysics using modified Homotopy analysis method, Computer Physics Communications, vol. 180, no. 7, pp. 1116–1124, 2009.

[11] A. Aslanov, Determination of convergence intervals of the series solutions of Emden-Fowler equations using polytropes and isothermal spheres, Physics Letters A, vol. 372, no. 20, pp. 3555–3561, 2008.

[12] C. Hunter, Series solutions for polytropes and the isothermal sphere, Monthly Notices of the Royal Astronomical Society, vol. 328, no. 3, pp. 839–847, 2001.

[13] C. Mohan, A.R. Al-Bayaty, Power-series solutions of the Lane-Emden equation, Astrophysics and Space Science, vol. 73, no. 1, pp. 227–239, 1980.

[14] I.W. Roxburghm, L.M. Stockman, Power series solutions of the polytrope equations, Monthly Notices of the Royal Astronomical Society, vol. 303, no. 3, pp. 466–470, 1999.

[15] J.H. He, Variational approach to the Lane-Emden equation, Applied Mathematics and Computation, vol. 143, no. 2–3, pp. 539–541, 2003.

[16] A. Yildirim, T. Öziş, Solutions of singular IVPs of Lane-Emden type by the variational iteration method, Nonlinear Analysis, vol. 70, no. 6, pp. 2480–2484, 2009.

[17] A.M. Wazwaz, The variational iteration method for solving the Volterra integro-differential forms of the Lane-Emden equations of the first and the second kind, Journal of Mathematical Chemistry, vol. 52, no. 2, pp. 613–626, 2014.

[18] S. Yüzbasi, A numerical approach for solving the high-order linear singular differential-difference equations, Computers and Mathematics with Applications, vol. 62, pp. 2289–2303, 2011.

[19] S. Yüzbasi, M. Sezer, An improved Bessel collocation method with a residual error function to solve a class of Lane-Emden differential equations, Mathematical and Computer Modelling, vol. 57, pp. 1298–1311, 2013.

[20] A.H. Bharwy, A.S. Alofi, A Jacobi-Gauss collocation method for solving nonlinear Lane-Emden type equations, Communications in Nonlinear Science and Numerical Simulation, vol. 17, pp. 62–70, 2012.

[21] K. Parand, M. Razzaghi, Rational legendre approximation for solving some physical problems on semi-infinite intervals, Physica Scripta, vol. 69, no. 5, pp. 353–357, 2004.

[22] K. Parand, A. Pirkhedri, Sinc-collocation method for solving astrophysics equations, New Astronomy, vol. 15, no. 6, pp. 533–537, 2010.

[23] J.P. Boyd, Chebyshev spectral methods and the Lane-Emden problem, Numerical Mathematics: Theory, Methods and Applications, vol. 4, no. 2, pp. 142–157, 2011.

[24] S.S. Motsa, P. Sibanda, A new algorithm for solving singular IVPs of Lane-Emden type, in Proceedings of the 4th International Conference on Applied Mathematics, Simulation, Modelling (ASM'10), pp. 176–180, Corfu Island, Greece, July 2010.

[25] S.S. Motsa, S. Shateyi, A successive linearization method approach to solve Lane-Emden type of equations, Mathematical Problems in Engineering, vol. 2012, 14 p., 2012, Article ID 280702. doi:10.1155/2012/280702

[26] K. Parand, S. Abbasbandy, S. Kazem, A.R. Rezaei, An improved numerical method for a class of astrophysics problems based on radial basis functions, Physica Scripta, vol. 83, no. 1, 2011, Article ID 015011.

[27] L.N. Trefethen, Spectral methods in MATLAB, SIAM, Philadelphia, 2000.

[28] J.I. Ramos, Linearization techniques for singular initial-value problems of ordinary differential equations, Journal of Applied Mathematics and Computation, vol. 161, pp. 525–542, 2005.

[29] M.S.H. Chowdhury, I. Hashim, Solution of a class of singular second-order IVPs by homotopy-perturbation method, Physics Letters A, vol. 365, pp. 439–447, 2007.

[30] C.M. Khalique, P. Ntsime, Exact solutions of the Lane-Emden-type equation, New Astronomy, vol. 13, no. 7, pp. 476–480, 2008.

[31] K. Parand, M. Dehghan, A.R. Rezaei, S.M. Ghaderi, An approximation algorthim for the solution of the nonlinear Lane-Emden type equation arising in Astorphisics using Hermit functions Collocation method, Computer Physics Communications, vol. 181, pp. 1096–1108, 2010.

[32] A.M. Wazwaz, A new method for solving singular initial value problems in second-order ordinary differential equations, Applied Mathematics and Computation, vol. 128, pp. 45–57, 2002.

[33] F.K. Yin, W.Y. Han, J.Q. Song, Modified Laplace decomposition method for Lane-Emden type differential equations, International Journal of Applied Physics and Mathematics, vol. 3, pp. 98–102 no. 2, March 2013.

[34] N. T. Shawagfeh, Nonperturbative approximate solution of Lane-Emden equation, Journal of Mathematical Physics, vol. 34, pp. 4364–4369, 1993.

[35] A.M. Wazwaz, A new algorithm for solving differential equations of Lane-Emden type, Applied Mathematics and Computation, vol. 118, pp. 287–310, 2001.

Chapter 8

# Numerical Solution of System of Fractional Differential Equations in Imprecise Environment

Najeeb Alam Khan, Oyoon Abdul Razzaq,
Asmat Ara and Fatima Riaz

Additional information is available at the end of the chapter

http://dx.doi.org/10.5772/64150

**Abstract**

Fractional calculus and fuzzy calculus theory, mutually, are highly applicable for showing different aspects of dynamics appearing in science. This chapter provides comprehensive discussion of system of fractional differential models in imprecise environment. In addition, presenting a new vast area to investigate numerical solutions of fuzzy fractional differential equations, numerical results of proposed system are carried out by the Grünwald-Letnikov's fractional derivative. The stability along with truncation error of the Grünwald-Letnikov's fractional approach is also proved. Moreover, some numerical experiments are performed and effective remarks are concluded on the basis of efficient convergence of the approximated results towards the exact solutions and on the depictions of error bar plots.

**Keywords:** fuzzy-valued functions, fuzzy differential equations, fractional differential equations, Grünwald-Letnikov's derivative

## 1. Introduction

It is worthwhile mentioning, since last few decades, the theory of fractional calculus has gained significant importance in almost every branch of science, for having the capability to consider integrals and derivatives of any arbitrary order. The characteristic feature of generalizing the classic integer-order differentiation and n-fold integration to arbitrary fractional order have broadened its application in modeling several phenomena of physics, mathematics, and engineering. The differential models of fractional order, due to the nonlocal properties of fractional operator, are excellent instruments for providing information about the current as well as the historical state of the system. For these reasons, it is intensively developed and advanced, and existence of its solution is studied by well-known authors, Euler, Laplace, Liouville, Riemann, Fourier, Abel, Caputo, etc., to further widen its scope in describing various real-world problems of science, for instance see [1–6]. Another wide-spreading exploration of mathematics is theory of fuzzy calculus, which has a lot of interesting applications in physics, engineering, mechanics, and many others. It is the theory of a particular type of interval-valued functions, in which mapping is made in such a way that it takes all the possible values in $[0, 1]$ and not only the crisp values as found in usual interval-valued functions. After the inception of fuzzy set theory by Zadeh [7], its attributes have been extended and established to overcome impreciseness of parameters and structures in mathematical modeling, reasoning, and computing [8–12].

Advanced development of mathematical theories and techniques has gained very high standard. On the basis of classical theories, new theories are pioneered by undergoing its inadequacies and widening its scope in many disciplines. In a similar manner, the aforementioned theories have been brought together in modeling different aspects of applied sciences, to analyze the change in the respective system at each fractional step with the uncertain parameters. Agarwal et al. [13] initiatively incorporated uncertainty into dynamical system, modeled fractional differential equations with uncertainty, and studied its possible solutions. Ahmad et al. [14] described the situation of impreciseness of initial values of fractional differential equations and discussed its solutions by utilizing Zadeh's extension principle. In [15, 16], authors considered the concept of Caputo and Riemann fractional derivative, respectively, together with the Hukuhara differentiability and demonstrated the fuzzy fractional differential equations and a lot of others [17–23].

In light of noteworthy applications of above-mentioned theories, in this chapter, we demonstrate fractional order dynamical models in fuzzy environment to depict unequivocal fractional differential equations of dynamical system. Moreover, we investigate its numerical solutions using the well-known Grünwald-Letnikov's fractional definition. This definition is widely applicable as a numerical scheme to solve linear and nonlinear differential equations of fractional order [24–26]. It is considered as an extended form of the classical Euler method. Here it will be utilized, for the first time, to solve fractional differential equations of imprecise functions. Sequentially, this chapter features description of fuzzy theory and fuzzy-valued functions for the explanation of impreciseness, modeling of system of nonlinear fractional order differential equations with imprecise functions, deliberation of Grünwald-Letnikov's fractional approach in conjunction with its truncation error for the proposed system, tabulated and pictorial investigations of some examples, and conclusive remarks of the undergone experiments and findings of the whole manuscript.

## 2. Basic descriptions

Fuzzy calculus theory is the branch of mathematical analysis that deals with the interval analysis of imprecise functions. This section comprises some rudiments of fuzzy calculus theory and acquaints the necessary notations that are prerequisite for the whole paper. All the below-mentioned descriptions are widely elaborated and used in literature, for instance [13–23].

### 2.1. Fuzzy numbers

Let $\mathcal{E}$ be the set of subsets of the real axis $\mathcal{R}$. If $\tau \in \mathcal{E}$ and $\tau:[0, 1] \to \mathcal{R}$ such that, $\tau$ is normal, fuzzy convex, upper semi-continuous membership function and compactly supported on the real axis $\mathcal{R}$, then $\mathcal{E}$ is said to be the space of fuzzy numbers $\tau$. Any $\tau \in \mathcal{E}$ can be represented in level sets explicitly, i.e. $[\tau]^{\lambda} = [\underline{\tau}(\lambda), \bar{\tau}(\lambda)]$ for $\lambda \in [0,1]$, where $\underline{\tau}(\lambda)$ and $\bar{\tau}(\lambda)$ signify as the lower and upper branches of $\tau$, respectively, that satisfy the following conditions:

a. $\bar{\tau}(\lambda)$ is bounded non-decreasing lower function, left continuous on $(0, 1]$ and right continuous at $\lambda = 0$

b. $\underline{\tau}(\lambda)$ is bounded non-increasing upper function, left continuous on $(0, 1]$ and right continuous at $\lambda = 0$

c. $\underline{\tau}(\lambda) \le \bar{\tau}(\lambda)$

The sum and scalar product of any fuzzy number is the consequence of Zadeh's extension principal. Let $\oplus$, $\bullet$ and $\Theta$ be the symbols of addition, multiplication and subtraction, accordingly, for fuzzy numbers, which will be greatly used throughout the paper, then, for $\lambda \in [0,1]$:

i. $$[\tau \oplus \upsilon]^{\lambda} = [\tau]^{\lambda} \oplus [\upsilon]^{\lambda} = [\underline{\tau}(\lambda) + \underline{\upsilon}(\lambda), \bar{\tau}(\lambda) + \bar{\upsilon}(\lambda)] \qquad \tau, \upsilon \in \mathcal{E}$$

ii. For $$a \in \mathcal{R},\ [a\tau]^{\lambda} = a\,[\tau]^{\lambda} = \begin{cases} [a\underline{\tau}(\lambda), a\bar{\tau}(\lambda)] & \text{if } a > 0 \\ \{0\} & \text{if } a = 0 \\ [a\bar{\tau}(\lambda), a\underline{\tau}(\lambda)] & \text{if } a < 0 \end{cases}$$

iii. $$[\tau \bullet \upsilon]^{\lambda} = \begin{bmatrix} \min\{\underline{\tau}(\lambda)\underline{\upsilon}(\lambda), \underline{\tau}(\lambda)\bar{\upsilon}(\lambda), \bar{\tau}(\lambda)\underline{\upsilon}(\lambda), \bar{\tau}(\lambda)\bar{\upsilon}(\lambda)\}, \\ \max\{\underline{\tau}(\lambda)\underline{\upsilon}(\lambda), \underline{\tau}(\lambda)\bar{\upsilon}(\lambda), \bar{\tau}(\lambda)\underline{\upsilon}(\lambda), \bar{\tau}(\lambda)\bar{\upsilon}(\lambda)\} \end{bmatrix}$$

iv. $$\tau \Theta \upsilon = [\min\{\underline{\tau}(\lambda) - \underline{\upsilon}(\lambda), \bar{\tau}(\lambda) - \bar{\upsilon}(\wp)\}, \max\{\underline{\tau}(\lambda) - \underline{\upsilon}(\lambda), \bar{\tau}(\lambda) - \bar{\upsilon}(\lambda)\}]$$

The distance between any two fuzzy numbers $\tau$ and $\upsilon$ is given by the Hausdorff metric $\mathbf{D}$ as:

$$\mathbf{D}(\tau,\upsilon) = \sup_{\lambda\in[0,1]} \mathbf{D}\left([\tau]^{\lambda},[\upsilon]^{\lambda}\right) = \sup_{\lambda\in[0,1]} \max\left\{ \left|\underline{\tau}(\lambda)-\underline{\upsilon}(\lambda)\right|, \left|\overline{\tau}(\lambda)-\overline{\upsilon}(\lambda)\right| \right\} \tag{1}$$

Thus, ($\mathcal{E}$, **D**) defines a complete metric space with the properties of Hausdorff metric for fuzzy numbers.

## 2.2. Fuzzy-valued Function and its fractional derivative

Any interval-valued function $\tilde{\mathcal{F}}$ is said to be a fuzzy-valued function if $\tilde{\mathcal{F}}$ is defined as $\tilde{\mathcal{F}}:\mathcal{R}\to\mathcal{E}$. Its $\lambda$-level set can be represented by real-valued functions $\underline{\mathcal{F}}(t;\lambda)$ and $\overline{\mathcal{F}}(t;\lambda)$ as its lower and upper branches, accordingly, i.e. $\tilde{\mathcal{F}}(t)=\left[\underline{\mathcal{F}}(t;\lambda),\overline{\mathcal{F}}(t;\lambda)\right]$, $\forall t\in\mathcal{R}$ and $\lambda\in[0,1]$. Moreover, if $\lim_{t\to t_0}\underline{\mathcal{F}}(t;\lambda)$ and $\lim_{t\to t_0}\overline{\mathcal{F}}(t;\lambda)$ exist as finite fuzzy numbers, then $\lim_{t\to t_0}\tilde{\mathcal{F}}(t)$ exists. Consequently, let $\mathcal{C}$ be the space of continuous fuzzy-valued functions, then $\tilde{\mathcal{F}}(t)\in\mathcal{C}$ if $\underline{\mathcal{F}}(t;\lambda)$ and $\overline{\mathcal{F}}(t;\lambda)$ are continuous. The arithmetic for any two fuzzy-valued functions $\tilde{\mathcal{F}}$ and $\tilde{\mathcal{G}}$ can be defined as previously mentioned in Section 2.1 for fuzzy numbers. Subsequent to existence of limit and continuity of $\tilde{\mathcal{F}}$, the fuzzy-valued function $\tilde{\mathcal{F}}(t)$ is said to be differentiable at each $t_0\in[a, b]$, if $\tilde{\mathcal{F}}'(t_0)\in\mathcal{E}$ exists, such that

$$\tilde{\mathcal{F}}'(t_0) = \lim_{h\to 0}\frac{\tilde{\mathcal{F}}(t_0+h)\ominus\tilde{\mathcal{F}}(t_0)}{h} \tag{2}$$

where $h$ is taken in a way that $(t_0+h)\in(a, b)$. For $\tilde{\mathcal{F}}(t)=\left[\underline{\mathcal{F}}(t;\lambda),\overline{\mathcal{F}}(t;\lambda)\right]$, $\tilde{\mathcal{F}}(t)$ is said to be differentiable at $t\in[a, b]$ if its lower function $\underline{\mathcal{F}}(t;\lambda)$ and upper function $\overline{\mathcal{F}}(t;\lambda)$ are differentiable at $t\in[a, b]$, i.e. for all $\lambda\in[0, 1]$,

$$\tilde{\mathcal{F}}'(t)=\left[\min\left\{\frac{d}{dt}\underline{\mathcal{F}}(t;\lambda),\frac{d}{dt}\overline{\mathcal{F}}(t;\lambda)\right\},\max\left\{\frac{d}{dt}\underline{\mathcal{F}}(t;\lambda),\frac{d}{dt}\overline{\mathcal{F}}(t;\lambda)\right\}\right] \tag{3}$$

In a similar manner, fractional order differential of $\tilde{\mathcal{F}}(t)$ can be defined as, for all $\lambda\in[0, 1]$, if $\underline{\mathcal{F}}(t;\lambda)$ and $\overline{\mathcal{F}}(t;\lambda)$ are differentiable of order $\omega>0$, then $\tilde{\mathcal{F}}(t)$ is differentiable of order $\omega>0$, i.e.

$$\mathcal{D}_t^{\omega}\tilde{\mathcal{F}}(t)=\left[\min\left\{D_t^{\omega}\underline{\mathcal{F}}(t;\lambda),D_t^{\omega}\overline{\mathcal{F}}(t;\lambda)\right\},\max\left\{D_t^{\omega}\underline{\mathcal{F}}(t;\lambda),D_t^{\omega}\overline{\mathcal{F}}(t;\lambda)\right\}\right] \tag{4}$$

where $\mathcal{D}_t^{\omega}$ can be either fuzzy Riemann-Liouville fractional differential operator or fuzzy Caputo-type fractional differential operator [15, 16, 19, 22, 23]. Here it is considered as fuzzy Caputo-type fractional derivative that is approximated by Grünwald-Letnikov's approach, illustrated in the next sequel.

### 2.3. System of fractional order fuzzy differential equations

In particular, modeling of differential equations of fractional order in imprecise characteristics is obtained by encompassing fuzzy-valued functions. Let $\tilde{\mathcal{X}}(t):\mathcal{R}\to\mathcal{E}$, then fuzzy differential equation of fractional order $\omega\in(0, 1]$, subjected to initial conditions, is structured as:

$$\mathcal{D}_t^{\omega}\tilde{\mathcal{X}}(t)=\Psi\left(t,\tilde{\mathcal{X}}(t)\right) \tag{5}$$

$$\tilde{\mathcal{X}}(t_0)=\tilde{\mathcal{U}}_0 \tag{6}$$

where the unknown fuzzy-valued function $\tilde{\mathcal{X}}(t)$ can be written in form of $\lambda$-levels as, for all $\lambda\in[0, 1]$, $\tilde{\mathcal{X}}(t)=\left[\underline{\mathcal{X}}(t;\lambda),\overline{\mathcal{X}}(t;\lambda)\right]$, where as $\Psi\left(t,\tilde{\mathcal{X}}(t)\right)$ can be linear or nonlinear term in the form of fuzzy-valued function and $\tilde{\mathcal{U}}_0$ is the fuzzy number, which can also be expressed as $\tilde{\mathcal{U}}_0=\left[\underline{\mathcal{U}_0}(\lambda),\overline{\mathcal{U}_0}(\lambda)\right]$, for all $\lambda\in[0,1]$. Concisely, Eq. (5) is considered to have a unique and stable solution, for the reason that $\Psi\left(t,\tilde{\mathcal{X}}(t)\right)$ is continuous and satisfies the Lipschitz condition, i.e. there exists $L>0$ such that for $\Psi:\mathcal{R}\to\mathcal{E}$

$$\mathbf{D}\left(\Psi\left(t,\tilde{\mathcal{X}}\right),\Psi\left(t,\tilde{\mathcal{W}}\right)\right)\leq L.\mathbf{D}\left(\tilde{\mathcal{X}},\tilde{\mathcal{W}}\right)\quad\forall\left(t,\tilde{\mathcal{X}}\right),\left(t,\tilde{\mathcal{W}}\right)\in\mathcal{R},\ \tilde{\mathcal{X}},\tilde{\mathcal{W}}\in\mathcal{E} \tag{7}$$

Many papers [14, 15, 22] comprise the theorems of stability and uniqueness of the solution of Eq. (5).

Here, we consider the system of fractional order fuzzy differential equations of the following form:

$$\begin{aligned}\mathcal{D}_t^{\omega_1}\tilde{\mathcal{X}}_1(t)&=\Psi\left(\tilde{\mathcal{X}}_1(t),\tilde{\mathcal{X}}_2(t),\cdots,\tilde{\mathcal{X}}_n(t)\right)\\ \mathcal{D}_t^{\omega_2}\tilde{\mathcal{X}}_2(t)&=\Psi\left(\tilde{\mathcal{X}}_1(t),\tilde{\mathcal{X}}_2(t),\cdots,\tilde{\mathcal{X}}_n(t)\right)\end{aligned} \tag{8}$$

$$\mathcal{D}_t^{\omega_n} \tilde{\mathscr{X}}_n(t) = \Psi\left(\tilde{\mathscr{X}}_1(t), \tilde{\mathscr{X}}_2(t), \cdots, \tilde{\mathscr{X}}_n(t)\right)$$

with the initial conditions,

$$\tilde{\mathscr{X}}_1(t_0) = \tilde{v}_1, \tilde{\mathscr{X}}_2(t_0) = \tilde{v}_2, \ldots, \tilde{\mathscr{X}}_n(t_0) = \tilde{v}_n \tag{9}$$

where $\tilde{v}_1, \tilde{v}_2, \ldots, \tilde{v}_n$ are the fuzzy numbers that can be written as, for all $\lambda \in [0,1], \tilde{v}_n(\lambda) = \left[\underline{v}_n(\lambda), \overline{v}_n(\lambda)\right]$, $n \geq 1$, $\omega_1, \omega_2, \ldots, \omega_n$ are the fractional orders such that $\omega_n \in (0, 1]$ and the right hand side of Eq. (8) represent a system of fuzzy nonlinear equations with crisp coefficients $k_{ij}$, $i \geq 1$, $j \leq n$, i.e.

$$\Psi\left(\tilde{\mathscr{X}}_1(t), \tilde{\mathscr{X}}_2(t), \cdots, \tilde{\mathscr{X}}_n(t)\right) = \sum_{j=1}^{n} k_{ij} \tilde{\mathscr{X}}_j^m(t), \qquad m \geq 1 \tag{10}$$

Therefore, Eq. (8) can be remodeled as:

$$\begin{aligned}
\mathcal{D}_t^{\omega_1} \tilde{\mathscr{X}}_1(t) &= \sum_{j=1}^{n} k_{1j} \tilde{\mathscr{X}}_j^m(t) = k_{11} \tilde{\mathscr{X}}_1^m(t) \oplus k_{12} \tilde{\mathscr{X}}_2^m(t) \oplus \cdots \oplus k_{1n} \tilde{\mathscr{X}}_n^m(t), \\
\mathcal{D}_t^{\omega_2} \tilde{\mathscr{X}}_2(t) &= \sum_{j=1}^{n} k_{2j} \tilde{\mathscr{X}}_j^m(t) = k_{21} \tilde{\mathscr{X}}_1^m(t) \oplus k_{22} \tilde{\mathscr{X}}_2^m(t) \oplus \cdots \oplus k_{2n} \tilde{\mathscr{X}}_n^m(t), \\
&\vdots \\
\mathcal{D}_t^{\omega_n} \tilde{\mathscr{X}}_n(t) &= \sum_{j=1}^{n} k_{nj} \tilde{\mathscr{X}}_j^m(t) = k_{n1} \tilde{\mathscr{X}}_1^m(t) \oplus k_{n2} \tilde{\mathscr{X}}_2^m(t) \oplus \cdots \oplus k_{nn} \tilde{\mathscr{X}}_n^m(t)
\end{aligned} \tag{11}$$

And as mentioned earlier, $\mathcal{D}_t^{\omega_n}, n \geq 1$, are taken as the fuzzy Caputo-type fractional differential operators and are numerically interpreted using Grünwald-Letnikov's fractional derivative definition.

## 3. Grünwald-Letnikov's fractional derivative

This section comprises the description of Grünwald-Letnikov's fractional derivative in conjunction with the algorithm to solve the system of Eq. (11) and undergoes some requisite theorem and lemma of the governing approach.

http://dx.doi.org/10.5772/64150

Consider a function $\varphi(t)$ in finite interval [0, T], let the interval be divided into equidistant grids of step size $h$ as:

$$0 = \eta_0 < \eta_1 < \cdots < \eta_\sigma = t = \sigma h \quad \text{with } \eta_\sigma - \eta_{\sigma-1} = h \tag{12}$$

$$^{GL}D_t^\omega \varphi(t) = \lim_{h \to 0} \frac{1}{h^\omega} \sum_{i=0}^{\left[\frac{t}{h}\right]} (-1)^i \binom{\omega}{i} \varphi(t - ih) \tag{13}$$

where $\binom{\omega}{i}$ are the binomial coefficients that are obtained by the formula:

$$\binom{\omega}{i} = \frac{\Gamma(\omega+1)}{i!\Gamma(\omega - i + 1)} \tag{14}$$

and $\left[\frac{t}{h}\right]$ represents the integral part.

### 3.1. Lemma

Let $\varphi(t)$ be a smooth function in $[0, T]$, such that it can be expressed as a power series for $[t] < T$, where $[t]$ is the integral part of $t$, then the Grünwald-Letnikov's approximation for each $0 < t < T$, a series of step size $h$ and $t = \sigma h$ can be stated as:

$$^{GL}D_t^\omega \varphi(t) = \frac{1}{h^\omega} \sum_{i=0}^{\sigma} (-1)^i \binom{\omega}{i} \varphi(t_{\sigma-i}) + O(h) \qquad (h \to 0) \tag{15}$$

This definition is considered to be equivalent to the definition of Riemann-Liouville fractional derivative and for equivalence to Caputo's fractional definition the following term of initial value is added to the right hand side of Eq. (15), i.e.

$$^{GL}D_t^\omega \varphi(t) = \frac{1}{h^\omega} \sum_{i=0}^{\sigma} (-1)^i \binom{\omega}{i} \varphi(t_{\sigma-i}) - \frac{t_\sigma^{-\omega}}{\Gamma(1-\omega)} \varphi(0) \tag{16}$$

That becomes zero if initial values of Caputo-type differential equations are homogeneous and again reduces to that of Riemann-Liouville definition. Since here the fuzzy Caputo-type fractional differential equations are considered with inhomogeneous initial values, the definition in Eq. (16) will be used for the approximation of Eq. (11).

Now let $\tilde{\mathcal{F}}$ be a fuzzy-valued function such that $\tilde{\mathcal{F}}:\mathcal{R}\rightarrow\mathcal{E}$, then Grünwald-Letnikov's fractional derivative of $\tilde{\mathcal{F}}(t)$ is expressed as:

$$ {}^{GL}\mathcal{D}_t^{\omega}\tilde{\mathcal{F}}(t)=\frac{1}{h^{\omega}}\sum_{i=0}^{\sigma}(-1)^i\binom{\omega}{i}\tilde{\mathcal{F}}(t_{\sigma-i})\Theta\frac{t_{\sigma}^{-\omega}}{\Gamma(1-\omega)}\tilde{\mathcal{F}}(0) \tag{17} $$

and in $\lambda$-level sets it is sorted out as, for all $\lambda\in[0, 1]$,

$$ {}^{GL}\mathcal{D}_t^{\omega}\tilde{\mathcal{F}}(t)=\begin{bmatrix}\frac{1}{h^{\omega}}\sum_{i=0}^{\sigma}(-1)^i\binom{\omega}{i}\underline{\mathcal{F}}(t_{\sigma-i},\lambda)-\frac{t_{\sigma}^{-\omega}}{\Gamma(1-\omega)}\underline{\mathcal{F}}(0,\lambda),\\ \frac{1}{h^{\omega}}\sum_{i=0}^{\sigma}(-1)^i\binom{\omega}{i}\overline{\mathcal{F}}(t_{\sigma-i},\lambda)-\frac{t_{\sigma}^{-\omega}}{\Gamma(1-\omega)}\overline{\mathcal{F}}(0,\lambda)\end{bmatrix} \tag{18} $$

Next consider the fractional system in Eq. (11), for the cases of inhomogeneous initial values. Assume the uniform grids $t_{\sigma}=\sigma h$, where $\sigma=1,\ \ldots,\ M$, such that $Mh=T$, $M\in\mathcal{N}$. Applying Grünwald-Letnikov's fractional derivative on left hand sides of Eq. (11) we get,

$$ \begin{aligned}&\frac{1}{h^{\omega_1}}\sum_{i=0}^{\sigma}(-1)^i\binom{\omega_1}{i}\tilde{\mathcal{X}}_1((\sigma-i)h)\Theta\frac{(\sigma h)^{-\omega_1}}{\Gamma(1-\omega_1)}\tilde{\mathcal{X}}_1(0)=\sum_{j=1}^{n}k_{1j}\tilde{\mathcal{X}}_j^m(\sigma h),\\ &\frac{1}{h^{\omega_2}}\sum_{i=0}^{\sigma}(-1)^i\binom{\omega_2}{i}\tilde{\mathcal{X}}_2((\sigma-i)h)\Theta\frac{(\sigma h)^{-\omega_2}}{\Gamma(1-\omega_2)}\tilde{\mathcal{X}}_2(0)=\sum_{j=1}^{n}k_{2j}\tilde{\mathcal{X}}_j^m(\sigma h),\\ &\qquad\vdots\\ &\frac{1}{h^{\omega_n}}\sum_{i=0}^{\sigma}(-1)^i\binom{\omega_n}{i}\tilde{\mathcal{X}}_n((\sigma-i)h)\Theta\frac{(\sigma h)^{-\omega_n}}{\Gamma(1-\omega_n)}\tilde{\mathcal{X}}_n(0)=\sum_{j=1}^{n}k_{nj}\tilde{\mathcal{X}}_j^m(\sigma h)\end{aligned} \tag{19} $$

Solving above system fuzzy-valued functions of respective fuzzy functions are generated at different grid points.

### 3.2. Theorem: truncation error

Let fuzzy-valued functions $\tilde{\mathcal{X}}_1(t_{\sigma}),\tilde{\mathcal{X}}_2(t_{\sigma}),\cdots,\tilde{\mathcal{X}}_n(t_{\sigma})$ be the approximations to the true solutions $\tilde{X}_1(t_{\sigma})$, $\tilde{X}_2(t_{\sigma})$, $\cdots$, $\tilde{X}_n(t_{\sigma})$, respectively and consider $\Psi$ satisfies Lipchitz condition, then the local truncation error of the proposed numerical approach is $O(h^{1+\omega_n})$, for $n\geq 1$, i.e.

$$\begin{aligned}
&\tilde{\mathscr{X}}_1(t_\sigma)\Theta\tilde{X}_1(t_\sigma)=O\left(h^{1+\omega_1}\right),\\
&\tilde{\mathscr{X}}_2(t_\sigma)\Theta\tilde{X}_2(t_\sigma)=O\left(h^{1+\omega_2}\right),\\
&\quad\vdots\\
&\tilde{\mathscr{X}}_n(t_\sigma)\Theta\tilde{X}_n(t_\sigma)=O\left(h^{1+\omega_n}\right).
\end{aligned}\tag{20}$$

**Proof:**

Assume the $n$th equation of the system (19) and on applying Grünwald-Letnikov's fractional derivative we have,

$$\frac{1}{h^{\omega_n}}\sum_{i=0}^{\sigma}(-1)^i\binom{\omega_n}{i}\tilde{\mathscr{X}}_n(t_{\sigma-i})\Theta\frac{t_\sigma^{-\omega_n}}{\Gamma(1-\omega_n)}\tilde{\mathscr{X}}_n(0)=\Psi\left(\tilde{\mathscr{X}}_1(t_\sigma),\tilde{\mathscr{X}}_2(t_\sigma),\cdots,\tilde{\mathscr{X}}_n(t_\sigma)\right)\tag{21}$$

for $n\geq 1$ and from Lemma 3.1 we can attain,

$$\frac{1}{h^{\omega_n}}\sum_{i=0}^{\sigma}(-1)^i\binom{\omega_n}{i}\tilde{X}_n(t_{\sigma-i})\Theta\frac{t_\sigma^{-\omega_n}}{\Gamma(1-\omega_n)}\tilde{X}_n(0)+O(h)=\Psi\left(\tilde{X}_1(t_\sigma),\tilde{X}_2(t_\sigma),\cdots,\tilde{X}_n(t_\sigma)\right)\tag{22}$$

Subtracting Eq. (22) from Eq. (21),

$$\begin{aligned}
&\frac{1}{h^{\omega_n}}\sum_{i=0}^{\sigma}(-1)^i\binom{\omega_n}{i}\tilde{X}_n(t_{\sigma-i})\Theta\frac{t_\sigma^{-\omega_n}}{\Gamma(1-\omega_n)}\tilde{X}_n(0)\Theta\frac{1}{h^{\omega_n}}\sum_{i=0}^{\sigma}(-1)^i\binom{\omega_n}{i}\tilde{\mathscr{X}}_n(t_{\sigma-i})\\
&\qquad\oplus\frac{t_\sigma^{-\omega_n}}{\Gamma(1-\omega_n)}\tilde{\mathscr{X}}_n(0)+O(h)=\Psi\left(\tilde{X}_1(t_\sigma),\tilde{X}_2(t_\sigma),\cdots,\tilde{X}_n(t_\sigma)\right)\\
&\qquad\Theta\Psi\left(\tilde{\mathscr{X}}_1(t_\sigma),\tilde{\mathscr{X}}_2(t_\sigma),\cdots,\tilde{\mathscr{X}}_n(t_\sigma)\right)
\end{aligned}\tag{23}$$

Let, for $i=0, 1, \ldots\sigma-1$, $\tilde{\mathscr{X}}_n(t_\sigma)=\tilde{X}_n(t_\sigma)$, then on further manipulation we get,

$$\begin{aligned}
&\frac{1}{h^{\omega_n}}\left[\tilde{X}_n(t_\sigma)\Theta\tilde{\mathscr{X}}_n(t_\sigma)\right]+O(h)=\Psi\left(\tilde{X}_1(t_\sigma),\tilde{X}_2(t_\sigma),\cdots,\tilde{X}_n(t_\sigma)\right)\\
&\qquad\Theta\Psi\left(\tilde{\mathscr{X}}_1(t_\sigma),\tilde{\mathscr{X}}_2(t_\sigma),\cdots,\tilde{\mathscr{X}}_n(t_\sigma)\right)
\end{aligned}\tag{24}$$

or it can be rearranged as:

$$\left[\tilde{\mathcal{X}}_n(t_\sigma)\Theta\tilde{X}_n(t_\sigma)\right]=h^{\omega_n}\mathbf{D}\left[\Psi\left(\tilde{\mathcal{X}}_1(t_\sigma),\tilde{\mathcal{X}}_2(t_\sigma),\cdots,\tilde{\mathcal{X}}_n(t_\sigma)\right),\Psi\left(\tilde{X}_1(t_\sigma),\tilde{X}_2(t_\sigma),\cdots,\tilde{X}_n(t_\sigma)\right)\right]+O\left(h^{1+\omega_n}\right) \tag{25}$$

where $\mathbf{D}$ defines Hausdroff distance. On using Lipschitz condition, i.e. Eq. (7), proof is completed by obtaining the following equation:

$$\left(1-L_n h^{\omega_n}\right)\left[\tilde{\mathcal{X}}_n(t_\sigma)\Theta\tilde{X}_n(t_\sigma)\right]\le O\left(h^{1+\omega_n}\right)\quad\forall\, n\ge 1 \tag{26}$$

## 4. Numerical illustrations

Subsequent to the algorithm demonstrated in Section 3, here numerical experiments of some system of fuzzy fractional differential equations are presented. Results for fuzzy-valued functions are depicted in tabular form in the finite interval [0, 1] at different values of $\omega\in(0,1]$. In addition, error bar pictorials are given for each respective example. All the exact values and calculations are carried out through *Mathematica 10.*

### 4.1. Example 1

Following nonlinear fractional system is solved in [27] using homotopy analysis method, here the system is restructured with imprecise functions $\tilde{\mathcal{X}}_1(t)$ and $\tilde{\mathcal{X}}_2(t)$ as:

$$\mathcal{D}_t^{\omega_1}\tilde{\mathcal{X}}_1(t)=0.5\tilde{\mathcal{X}}_1(t)$$

$$\mathcal{D}_t^{\omega_2}\tilde{\mathcal{X}}_2(t)=\tilde{\mathcal{X}}_2(t)\oplus\tilde{\mathcal{X}}_1^2(t) \tag{27}$$

with $\omega_1$, $\omega_2\in(0,1]$ and subjected to initial conditions

$$\tilde{\mathcal{X}}_1(0)=\left[0.75+0.25\lambda,1.125-0.125\lambda\right],\quad\tilde{\mathcal{X}}_2(0)=\left[\lambda-1,1-\lambda\right] \tag{28}$$

On applying Grünwald-Letnikov's fractional definition on left hand side of Eq. (27) and following the algorithm, the differential equations are reduced to nonlinear algebraic equations as:

$$\frac{1}{h^{\omega_1}}\sum_{i=0}^{\sigma}(-1)^i\binom{\omega_1}{i}\tilde{\mathscr{X}_1}((\sigma-i)h)\Theta\frac{(\sigma h)^{-\omega_1}}{\Gamma(1-\omega_1)}\tilde{\mathscr{X}_1}(0)=0.5\tilde{\mathscr{X}_1}(\sigma h),$$

$$\frac{1}{h^{\omega_2}}\sum_{i=0}^{\sigma}(-1)^i\binom{\omega_2}{i}\tilde{\mathscr{X}_2}((\sigma-i)h)\Theta\frac{(\sigma h)^{-\omega_2}}{\Gamma(1-\omega_2)}\tilde{\mathscr{X}_2}(0)=\tilde{\mathscr{X}_2}(\sigma h)\oplus\tilde{\mathscr{X}_1}^2(\sigma h) \tag{29}$$

which on expanding to ƛ-levels of $\tilde{\mathscr{X}_1}(t)$ and $\tilde{\mathscr{X}_2}(t)$ convert into system of four nonlinear equations, i.e. for all ƛ $\in[0, 1]$,

$$\frac{1}{h^{\omega_1}}\sum_{i=0}^{\sigma}(-1)^i\binom{\omega_1}{i}\underline{\mathscr{X}_1}((\sigma-i)h;ƛ)-\frac{(\sigma h)^{-\omega_1}}{\Gamma(1-\omega_1)}\underline{\mathscr{X}_1}(0;ƛ)=0.5\underline{\mathscr{X}_1}(\sigma h;ƛ),$$

$$\frac{1}{h^{\omega_1}}\sum_{i=0}^{\sigma}(-1)^i\binom{\omega_1}{i}\overline{\mathscr{X}_1}((\sigma-i)h;ƛ)-\frac{(\sigma h)^{-\omega_1}}{\Gamma(1-\omega_1)}\overline{\mathscr{X}_1}(0;ƛ)=0.5\overline{\mathscr{X}_1}(\sigma h;ƛ),$$

$$\frac{1}{h^{\omega_2}}\sum_{i=0}^{\sigma}(-1)^i\binom{\omega_2}{i}\underline{\mathscr{X}_2}((\sigma-i)h;ƛ)-\frac{(\sigma h)^{-\omega_2}}{\Gamma(1-\omega_2)}\underline{\mathscr{X}_2}(0;ƛ)=\underline{\mathscr{X}_2}(\sigma h;ƛ)+\underline{\mathscr{X}_1^2}(\sigma h;ƛ),$$

$$\frac{1}{h^{\omega_2}}\sum_{i=0}^{\sigma}(-1)^i\binom{\omega_2}{i}\overline{\mathscr{X}_2}((\sigma-i)h;ƛ)-\frac{(\sigma h)^{-\omega_2}}{\Gamma(1-\omega_2)}\overline{\mathscr{X}_2}(0;ƛ)=\overline{\mathscr{X}_2}(\sigma h;ƛ)+\overline{\mathscr{X}_1^2}(\sigma h;ƛ) \tag{30}$$

| ƛ | $\tilde{\mathscr{X}_1}(t)=[\underline{\mathscr{X}_1}(t;ƛ),\overline{\mathscr{X}_1}(t;ƛ)]$ | | |
|---|---|---|---|
| | **Exact solutions** | **Approx. solutions** | **Absolute error** |
| 0 | [0.7881, 1.1821] | [0.7881, 1.1821] | [$9.7543\times10^{-6}$, $1.4632\times10^{-5}$] |
| 0.2 | [0.8406, 1.1558] | [0.8406, 1.1558] | [$1.0404\times10^{-5}$, $1.4307\times10^{-5}$] |
| 0.4 | [0.8931, 1.1296] | [0.8931, 1.1296] | [$1.1055\times10^{-5}$, $1.3982\times10^{-5}$] |
| 0.6 | [0.9457, 1.1033] | [0.9457, 1.1033] | [$1.1705\times10^{-5}$, $1.3656\times10^{-5}$] |
| 0.8 | [0.9982, 1.0770] | [0.9982, 1.0770] | [$1.2355\times10^{-5}$, $1.3331\times10^{-5}$] |
| 1 | [1.0508, 1.0508] | [1.0508, 1.0508] | [$1.3006\times10^{-5}$, $1.3006\times10^{-5}$] |

**Table 1.** Numerical results and absolute errors of $\tilde{\mathscr{X}_1}(t)$ for Example 1 at $\omega_1=1$, $\omega_2=1$, $h=0.001$ and $t=1$.

Solving this system, numerical approximations of Eq. (27) are obtained. **Tables 1** and **2** represent absolute error of $\tilde{\mathscr{X}_1}(t)$ and $\tilde{\mathscr{X}_2}(t)$, respectively, for $\omega_1=\omega_2=1$, $h=0.001$, $t=1$ and at different values of $\lambda$, whereas **Table 3** shows the approximations of $\widetilde{\mathcal{X}}_1(t)$ and $\widetilde{\mathcal{X}}_2(t)$ for $\omega_1=0.95$, $\omega_2=0.87$, $h=0.1$ and $t=1$, at different values of $\lambda$. In **Figures 1** and **2**, the pointwise error variations of $\widetilde{\mathcal{X}}_1(t)$ and $\widetilde{X}_2(t)$, accordingly, at each time within the given interval for $\omega_1=\omega_2=1$, $h=0.1$ and $\lambda=0.6$, are plotted. In these graphs, each approximated point is plotted against the value of $\sigma$ in a discrete manner and each bar line on respective approximated point illustrates the measure of the absolute error at that point. Absolute error is obtained by taking the point-to-point difference between exact and the solutions calculated by Grünwald-Letnikov's fractional approach. Since these variations show small differences, this implies our results are in good agreement with the exact solutions.

| $\lambda$ | $\widetilde{\mathcal{X}}_2(t)=[\underline{\mathcal{X}}_2(t;\lambda),\overline{\mathcal{X}}_2(t;\lambda)]$ | | |
|---|---|---|---|
| | **Exact solutions** | **Approx. solutions** | **Absolute error** |
| 0 | [-1.0426, 1.2424] | [-1.0426, 1.2426] | [$9.1289\times10^{-6}$, $1.9828\times10^{-4}$] |
| 0.2 | [-0.8133, 1.0155] | [-0.8133, 1.0157] | [$2.8859\times10^{-5}$, $1.8104\times10^{-4}$] |
| 0.4 | [-0.5835, 0.7888] | [-0.5834, 0.7889] | [$4.9162\times10^{-5}$, $1.6393\times10^{-4}$] |
| 0.6 | [-0.3531, 0.5621] | [-0.3530, 0.5623] | [$7.0025\times10^{-5}$, $1.4696\times10^{-4}$] |
| 0.8 | [-0.1222, 0.3356] | [-0.1221, 0.3358] | [$9.1457\times10^{-5}$, $1.3014\times10^{-4}$] |
| 1 | [0.1093, 0.1093] | [0.1094, 0.1094] | [$1.1346\times10^{-4}$, $1.1346\times10^{-4}$] |

**Table 2.** Numerical results and absolute errors of $\widetilde{\mathcal{X}}_2(t)$ for Example 1 at $\omega_1=1$, $\omega_2=1$, $h=0.001$ and $t=1$.

| $\lambda$ | $\widetilde{\mathcal{X}}_1(t)=[\underline{\mathcal{X}}_1(t;\lambda),\overline{\mathcal{X}}_1(t;\lambda)]$ | $\widetilde{\mathcal{X}}_2(t)=[\underline{\mathcal{X}}_2(t;\lambda),\overline{\mathcal{X}}_2(t;\lambda)]$ |
|---|---|---|
| 0 | [1.2745, 1.9117] | [-1.0584, 8.2274] |
| 0.2 | [1.3594, 1.8692] | [-0.1017, 7.3564] |
| 0.4 | [1.4444, 1.8267] | [0.8747, 6.4903] |
| 0.6 | [1.5294, 1.7842] | [1.8707, 5.6291] |
| 0.8 | [1.6143, 1.7418] | [2.8863, 4.7728] |
| 1 | [1.6993, 1.6993] | [3.9215, 3.9215] |

**Table 3.** Approximations of $\widetilde{\mathcal{X}}_1(t)$ and $\widetilde{\mathcal{X}}_2(t)$ of Example 1 for $\omega_1=0.95$, $\omega_2=0.87$, $h=0.1$ and $t=1$.

http://dx.doi.org/10.5772/64150

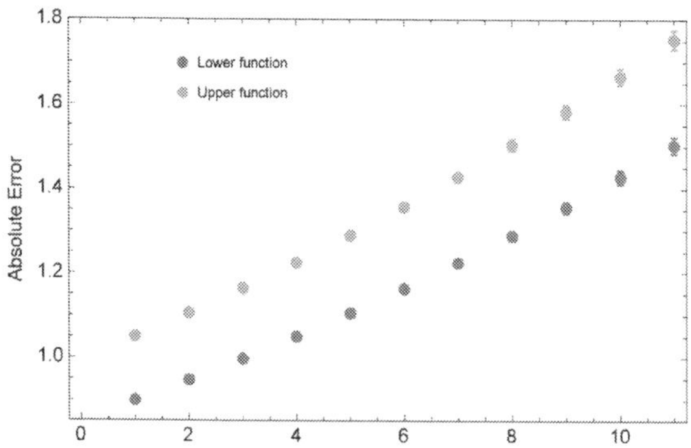


**Figure 1.** Bar plot of $\sigma$ of of Example 1 for $h = 0.1$, $\omega_1 = \omega_2 = 1$ and $ƛ = 0.6$.

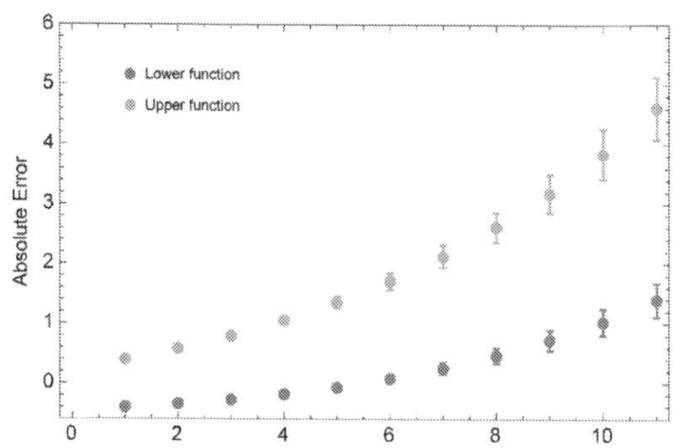


**Figure 2.** Bar plot of approximate solutions and absolute error versus $\sigma$ of $\tilde{\mathcal{X}}_2(t)$ of Example 1 for $h = 0.1$, $\omega_1 = \omega_2 = 1$ and $ƛ = 0.6$.

## 4.2. Example 2

Consider the following nonlinear fractional system [27] with imprecise functions $\tilde{\mathcal{X}}_1(t), \tilde{\mathcal{X}}_2(t)$ and $\tilde{\mathcal{X}}_1(t)$ as:

$$\mathcal{D}_t^{\omega_1} \tilde{\mathcal{X}}_1(t) = \tilde{\mathcal{X}}_1(t),$$

$$\mathcal{D}_t^{\omega_2} \tilde{\mathcal{X}}_2(t) = 2\tilde{\mathcal{X}}_1^2(t)$$

$$\mathcal{D}_t^{\omega_3}\tilde{\mathcal{X}}_3(t)=3\tilde{\mathcal{X}}_1(t)\bullet\tilde{\mathcal{X}}_2(t) \tag{31}$$

with $\omega_1$, $\omega_2$, $\omega_3 \in (0, 1]$ and subjected to initial conditions

$$\tilde{\mathcal{X}}_1(0)=\tilde{\mathcal{X}}_2(0)=[0.75+0.25ƛ,1.125-0.125ƛ],\quad \tilde{\mathcal{X}}_3(0)=[ƛ-1,1-ƛ] \tag{32}$$

On employing Grünwald-Letnikov's approach, the differential equations are converted into nonlinear algebraic equations as:

$$\frac{1}{h^{\omega_1}}\sum_{i=0}^{\sigma}(-1)^i\binom{\omega_1}{i}\tilde{\mathcal{X}}_1((\sigma-i)h)\Theta\frac{(\sigma h)^{-\omega_1}}{\Gamma(1-\omega_1)}\tilde{\mathcal{X}}_1(0)=\tilde{\mathcal{X}}_1(\sigma h),$$

$$\frac{1}{h^{\omega_2}}\sum_{i=0}^{\sigma}(-1)^i\binom{\omega_2}{i}\tilde{\mathcal{X}}_2((\sigma-i)h)\Theta\frac{(\sigma h)^{-\omega_2}}{\Gamma(1-\omega_2)}\tilde{\mathcal{X}}_2(0)=2\tilde{\mathcal{X}}_1^2(\sigma h)$$

$$\frac{1}{h^{\omega_3}}\sum_{i=0}^{\sigma}(-1)^i\binom{\omega_3}{i}\tilde{\mathcal{X}}_3((\sigma-i)h)\Theta\frac{(\sigma h)^{-\omega_3}}{\Gamma(1-\omega_3)}\tilde{\mathcal{X}}_3(0)=3\tilde{\mathcal{X}}_1(\sigma h)\bullet\tilde{\mathcal{X}}_2(\sigma h) \tag{33}$$

and in ƛ-levels of $\tilde{\mathcal{X}}_1(t)$, $\tilde{\mathcal{X}}_2(t)$, and $\tilde{X}_3(t)$ the system above converts into six nonlinear equations, i.e. for all $ƛ \in [0,1]$,

$$\frac{1}{h^{\omega_1}}\sum_{i=0}^{\sigma}(-1)^i\binom{\omega_1}{i}\underline{\mathcal{X}_1}((\sigma-i)h;ƛ)-\frac{(\sigma h)^{-\omega_1}}{\Gamma(1-\omega_1)}\underline{\mathcal{X}_1}(0;ƛ)=\underline{\mathcal{X}_1}(\sigma h;ƛ),$$

$$\frac{1}{h^{\omega_1}}\sum_{i=0}^{\sigma}(-1)^i\binom{\omega_1}{i}\overline{\mathcal{X}_1}((\sigma-i)h;ƛ)-\frac{(\sigma h)^{-\omega_1}}{\Gamma(1-\omega_1)}\overline{\mathcal{X}_1}(0;ƛ)=\overline{\mathcal{X}_1}(\sigma h;ƛ),$$

$$\frac{1}{h^{\omega_2}}\sum_{i=0}^{\sigma}(-1)^i\binom{\omega_2}{i}\underline{\mathcal{X}_2}((\sigma-i)h;ƛ)-\frac{(\sigma h)^{-\omega_2}}{\Gamma(1-\omega_2)}\underline{\mathcal{X}_2}(0;ƛ)=2\underline{\mathcal{X}_1^2}(\sigma h;ƛ),$$

$$\frac{1}{h^{\omega_2}}\sum_{i=0}^{\sigma}(-1)^i\binom{\omega_2}{i}\overline{\mathcal{X}_2}((\sigma-i)h;ƛ)-\frac{(\sigma h)^{-\omega_2}}{\Gamma(1-\omega_2)}\overline{\mathcal{X}_2}(0;ƛ)=2\overline{\mathcal{X}_1^2}(\sigma h;ƛ),$$

$$\frac{1}{h^{\omega_3}}\sum_{i=0}^{\sigma}(-1)^i\binom{\omega_3}{i}\underline{\mathcal{X}_3}((\sigma-i)h;ƛ)-\frac{(\sigma h)^{-\omega_3}}{\Gamma(1-\omega_3)}\underline{\mathcal{X}_3}(0;ƛ)=3\underline{\mathcal{X}_1}(\sigma h;ƛ)\underline{\mathcal{X}_2}(\sigma h;ƛ)$$

$$\frac{1}{h^{\omega_3}}\sum_{i=0}^{\sigma}(-1)^i\binom{\omega_3}{i}\overline{\mathcal{X}_3}((\sigma-i)h;\lambda)-\frac{(\sigma h)^{-\omega_3}}{\Gamma(1-\omega_3)}\overline{\mathcal{X}_3}(0;\lambda)=3\overline{\mathcal{X}_1}(\sigma h;\lambda)\overline{\mathcal{X}_2}(\sigma h;\lambda) \quad (34)$$

Thus, numerical results of Eq. (31) are obtained from the above system. **Tables 4–6** present absolute error of $\tilde{\mathcal{X}}_1(t)$, $\tilde{\mathcal{X}}_2(t)$, and $\tilde{X}_3(t)$, respectively, for $\omega_1=\omega_2=\omega_3=1$, $h=0.001$, $t=1$ and at different values of $\lambda$. In **Table 7**, the approximations of $\tilde{\mathcal{X}}_1(t)$, $\tilde{\mathcal{X}}_2(t)$, and $\tilde{X}_3(t)$ are rendered for $h=0.1$, $\omega_1=0.95$, $\omega_2=0.87$, $\omega_3=0.79$ and $t=1$, at different values of $\lambda$. Additionally, the pointwise error variations between approximated and exact solutions of $\tilde{\mathcal{X}}_1(t)$, $\tilde{\mathcal{X}}_2(t)$, and $\tilde{X}_3(t)$ at each time within the given interval for $\omega_1=\omega_2=\omega_3=1$ and $\lambda = 0.6$ are plotted in **Figures 3–5**, respectively. It is to be noted that the small length of bar lines on each point is illustrating small differences between the exact and the result obtained by the proposed approach that shows the acceptable convergence of the solution towards the exact values.

| $\lambda$ | $\tilde{\mathcal{X}}_1(t)=\left[\underline{\mathcal{X}_1}(t;\lambda),\overline{\mathcal{X}_1}(t;\lambda)\right]$ | | |
|---|---|---|---|
| | Exact solutions | Approx. solutions | Absolute errors |
| 0 | [0.8281, 1.2421] | [0.8281, 1.2421] | [$4.1012\times10^{-5}$, $6.1521\times10^{-5}$] |
| 0.2 | [0.8832, 1.2145] | [0.8833, 1.2145] | [$4.3747\times10^{-5}$, $6.0154\times10^{-5}$] |
| 0.4 | [0.9384, 1.1869] | [0.9385, 1.1869] | [$4.6482\times10^{-5}$, $5.8788\times10^{-5}$] |
| 0.6 | [0.9937, 1.1593] | [0.9937, 1.1593] | [$4.9217\times10^{-5}$, $5.7421\times10^{-5}$] |
| 0.8 | [1.0489, 1.1317] | [1.0489, 1.1317] | [$5.1952\times10^{-5}$, $5.6054\times10^{-5}$] |
| 1 | [1.1041, 1.1041] | [1.1041, 1.1041] | [$5.4688\times10^{-5}$, $5.4688\times10^{-5}$] |

**Table 4.** Numerical results and absolute errors of $\tilde{\mathcal{X}}_1(t)$ for Example 2 at $\omega_1=\omega_2=\omega_3=1$, $h=0.001$ and $t=1$.

| $\lambda$ | $\tilde{\mathcal{X}}_2(t)=\left[\underline{\mathcal{X}_2}(t;\lambda),\overline{\mathcal{X}_2}(t;\lambda)\right]$ | | |
|---|---|---|---|
| | Exact solutions | Approx. solutions | Absolute errors |
| 0 | [0.8732, 1.4021] | [0.8733, 1.4024] | [$1.2956\times10^{-4}$, $2.9153\times10^{-4}$] |
| 0.2 | [0.9401, 1.3649] | [0.9403, 1.3652] | [$1.4742\times10^{-4}$, $2.7872\times10^{-4}$] |
| 0.4 | [1.0082, 1.3280] | [1.0084, 1.3283] | [$1.6644\times10^{-4}$, $2.6619\times10^{-4}$] |
| 0.6 | [1.0774, 1.2914] | [1.0776, 1.2917] | [$1.8658\times10^{-4}$, $2.5397\times10^{-4}$] |
| 0.8 | [1.1476, 1.2551] | [1.1478, 1.2553] | [$2.0789\times10^{-4}$, $2.4202\times10^{-4}$] |
| 1 | [1.2189, 1.2189] | [1.2192, 1.2192] | [$2.3036\times10^{-4}$, $2.3036\times10^{-4}$] |

**Table 5.** Numerical results and absolute errors of $\tilde{\mathcal{X}}_2(t)$ for Example 2 at $\omega_1=\omega_2=\omega_3=1$, $h=0.001$ and $t=1$.

| $\lambda$ | $\tilde{\mathcal{X}}_3(t)=[\underline{\mathcal{X}}_3(t;\lambda),\overline{\mathcal{X}}_3(t;\lambda)]$ | | |
|---|---|---|---|
| | **Exact solutions** | **Approx. solutions** | **Absolute errors** |
| 0 | [-0.8102, 1.4429] | [-0.8099, 1.4438] | [$2.6067\times10^{-4}$, $7.7596\times10^{-4}$] |
| 0.2 | [-0.5829, 1.2225] | [-0.5827, 1.2232] | [$3.0938\times10^{-4}$, $7.2979\times10^{-4}$] |
| 0.4 | [-0.3538, 1.0026] | [-0.3534, 1.0032] | [$3.6373\times10^{-4}$, $6.8548\times10^{-4}$] |
| 0.6 | [-0.1226, 0.7831] | [-0.1222, 0.7838] | [$4.2389\times10^{-4}$, $6.4299\times10^{-4}$] |
| 0.8 | [0.1106, 0.5642] | [0.1111, 0.5648] | [$4.9030\times10^{-4}$, $6.0228\times10^{-4}$] |
| 1 | [0.3458, 0.3458] | [0.3464, 0.3464] | [$5.6330\times10^{-4}$, $5.6330\times10^{-4}$] |

**Table 6.** Numerical results and absolute errors of $\tilde{\mathcal{X}}_3(t)$ for Example 2 at $\omega_1=\omega_2=\omega_3=1$, $h=0.001$ and $t=1$.

| $\lambda$ | $\tilde{\mathcal{X}}_1(t)=[\underline{\mathcal{X}}_1(t;\lambda),\overline{\mathcal{X}}_1(t;\lambda)]$ | $\tilde{\mathcal{X}}_2(t)=[\underline{\mathcal{X}}_2(t;\lambda),\overline{\mathcal{X}}_2(t;\lambda)]$ | $\tilde{\mathcal{X}}_3(t)=[\underline{\mathcal{X}}_3(t;\lambda),\overline{\mathcal{X}}_3(t;\lambda)]$ |
|---|---|---|---|
| 0 | [2.2517, 3.3776] | [5.9374, 12.7914] | [16.8425, 57.0920] |
| 0.2 | [2.4018, 3.3025] | [6.7016, 12.2538] | [20.5781, 53.4113] |
| 0.4 | [2.5519, 3.2274] | [7.5119, 11.7278] | [24.7487, 49.8770] |
| 0.6 | [2.7020, 3.1524] | [8.3682, 11.2134] | [29.3793, 46.4859] |
| 0.8 | [2.8522, 3.0773] | [9.2705, 10.7104] | [34.4950, 43.2349] |
| 1 | [3.0023, 3.0023] | [10.2189, 10.2189] | [40.1209, 40.1209] |

**Table 7.** Approximations of $\tilde{\mathcal{X}}_1(t)\tilde{\mathcal{X}}_2(t)$, and $\tilde{\mathcal{X}}_3(t)$ of Example 2 for $\omega_1=0.95$, $\omega_2=0.87$ $\omega_3=0.79$, $h=0.1$ and $t=1$.

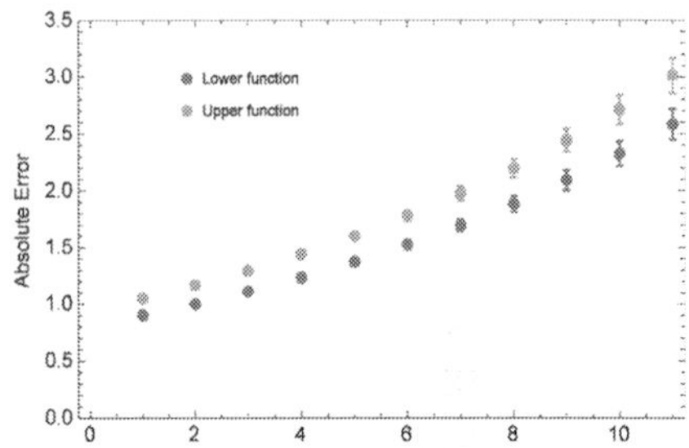


**Figure 3.** Bar plot of approximate solutions and absolute error versus $\sigma$ of $\tilde{\mathcal{X}}_1(t)$ of Example 2 for $h=0.1$, $\omega_1=\omega_2=\omega_3=1$ and $\lambda=0.6$.

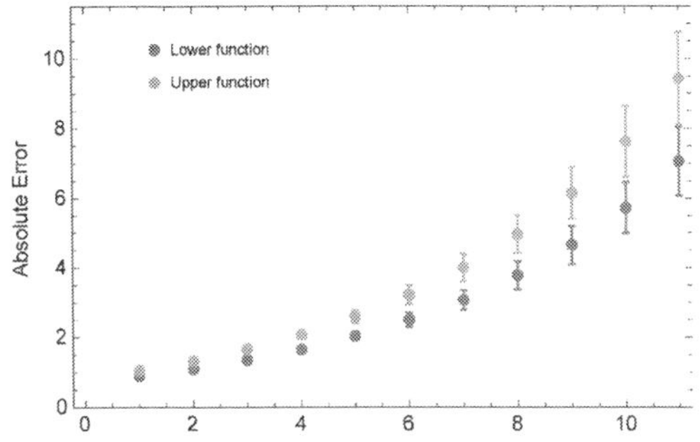


**Figure 4.** Bar plot of approximate solutions and absolute error versus $\sigma$ of $\widetilde{\mathscr{X}}_2(t)$ of Example 2 for $h=0.1$, $\omega_1=\omega_2=\omega_3=1$ and $\lambda=0.6$.

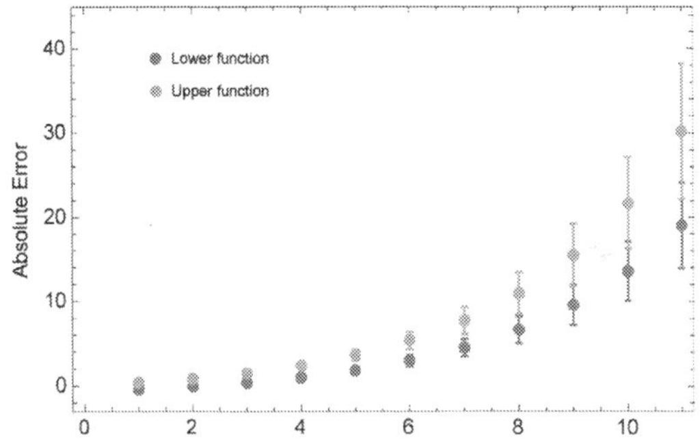


**Figure 5.** Bar plot of approximate solutions and absolute error versus $\sigma$ of $\widetilde{X}_3(t)$ of Example 2 for $h=0.1$, $\omega_1=\omega_2=\omega_3=1$ and $\lambda=0.6$.

## 5. Conclusion

In this chapter, system of fractional differential equations with fuzzy-valued functions was constructed to study the system in imprecise environment. We assessed numerical interpretations of the system using Grünwald-Letnikov's fractional derivative scheme, which has not been considered for fuzzy differential equations in literature hitherto. In addition, we illustrated the stability of the scheme for the system of fuzzy fractional differential equations. Furthermore, we conducted experiment on some nonlinear fuzzy fractional systems and successfully attained the approximated solutions. From the entire discussion and analysis, collectively, we come up with the following remarks:

- Scrutinizing differential models with arbitrary fractional order in combination with fuzzy theory is effectively advantageous to analyze the change in the system at each fractional step with imprecise parameters rather than crisp values.
- Grünwald-Letnikov's fractional definition is equivalent to either Riemann-Liouville fractional definition or Caputo-type fractional definition in case of homogeneous and inhomogeneous initial values, respectively. Since Riemann-Liouville fractional definition and Caputo-type fractional definition are greatly applicable for defining fractional derivative of fuzzy-valued functions, so is Grünwald-Letnikov's fractional definition found to be.
- Approximations of examples attained by undertaking Grünwald-Letnikov's fractional derivative approach are efficaciously convergent towards the exact solutions that prove the method to be appropriate for the solutions of fuzzy differential equations of fractional order to a great extent.
- Pointwise explanation of errors through bar graph is conspicuously helpful in locating the error between exact and calculated solutions at each time by simply measuring the length of the bar at the respective point.

## Author details

Najeeb Alam Khan[1*], Oyoon Abdul Razzaq[1], Asmat Ara[2] and Fatima Riaz[1]

*Address all correspondence to: njbalam@yahoo.com

1 Department of Mathematics, University of Karachi, Karachi, Pakistan

2 Department of Computer Science, Mohammad Ali Jinnah University, Karachi, Pakistan

## References

[1] Podlubny I. Fractional-order systems and fractional-order controllers. Kosice: Institute of Experimental Physics, Slovak Academy of Sciences; 1994:12.

[2] Panagiotopoulos PD, Panagouli OK. Fractal geometry in contact mechanics and numerical applications. In Fractals and Fractional Calculus in Continuum Mechanics: Springer Vienna; 1997: 109–171.

[3] Oldhman K, Spanier J. The fractional calculus: theory and applications of differentiation and integration to arbitrary order. New York: Academic Press; 1974.

[4] Miller KS, Ross B. An introduction to the fractional calculus and fractional differential equations: Wiley New Jersey; 1993.

[5] Gorenflo R, Mainardi F. Fractional calculus. Springer Vienna; 1997.

[6] Podlubny I. Fractional differential equations: an introduction to fractional derivatives, fractional differential equations, to methods of their solution and some of their applications: Academic press San Diego; 1998.

[7] Zadeh LA. Fuzzy sets. Information and Control. 1965;8(3):338–53.

[8] Puri ML, Ralescu DA. Differentials of fuzzy functions. Journal of Mathematical Analysis and Applications. 1983;91(2):552–8.

[9] Kandel A. Fuzzy dynamical systems and the nature of their solutions. Fuzzy Sets: Springer US; 1980: 93–121.

[10] Kaleva O. Fuzzy differential equations. Fuzzy sets and systems. 1987;24(3):301–17.

[11] Dubois D, Prade H. Towards fuzzy differential calculus part 3: Differentiation. Fuzzy Sets and Systems. 1982;8(3):225–33.

[12] Bede B, Gal SG. Generalizations of the differentiability of fuzzy-number-valued functions with applications to fuzzy differential equations. Fuzzy Sets and Systems. 2005;151(3):581–99.

[13] Agarwal RP, Lakshmikantham V, Nieto JJ. On the concept of solution for fractional differential equations with uncertainty. Nonlinear Analysis: Theory, Methods & Applications. 2010;72(6):2859–62.

[14] Ahmad M, Hasan MK, Abbasbandy S. Solving fuzzy fractional differential equations using Zadeh's extension principle. The Scientific World Journal. 2013;2013: Article ID 454969, 11 pages.

[15] Salahshour S, Allahviranloo T, Abbasbandy S, Baleanu D. Existence and uniqueness results for fractional differential equations with uncertainty. Advances in Difference Equations. 2012;2012(1):1–12.

[16] Allahviranloo T, Abbasbandy S, Shahryari MRB, Salahshour S, Baleanu D. On solutions of linear fractional differential equations with uncertainty. Abstract and Applied Analysis. 2013;2013:13.

[17] Varazgahi HR, Abbasbandy S. Modified fractional Euler method for solving Fuzzy sequential Fractional Initial Value Problem under H-differentiability. Journal of Fuzzy Set Valued Analysis. 2015;2015(2):110–21.

[18] Shahriyar M, Ismail F, Aghabeigi S, Ahmadian A, Salahshour S. An eigenvalue eigenvector method for solving a system of fractional differential equations with uncertainty. Mathematical Problems in Engineering. 2013;2013: Article ID 579761, 11 pages.

[19] Ngo VH. Fuzzy fractional functional integral and differential equations. Fuzzy Sets and Systems. 2015;280:58–90.

[20] Khan NA, Riaz F, Razzaq OA. A comparison between numerical methods for solving Fuzzy fractional differential equations. Nonlinear Engineering. 2014;3(3):155–62.

[21] Ghaemi F, Yunus R, Ahmadian A, Salahshour S, Suleiman M, Saleh SF, editors. Application of fuzzy fractional kinetic equations to modelling of the acid hydrolysis reaction. Abstract and Applied Analysis. 2013;2013: Article ID 610314, 19 pages.

[22] Arshad S, Lupulescu V. On the fractional differential equations with uncertainty. Nonlinear Analysis: Theory, Methods & Applications. 2011;74(11):3685–93.

[23] Khan NA, Riaz F, Abdul Razzaq O. An operator method for finding the solution of linear fractional order fuzzy differential equations. Progress in Fractional Differentiation and Applications. 2016;2(1):41–54.

[24] Scherer R, Kalla SL, Tang Y, Huang J. The Grünwald–Letnikov method for fractional differential equations. Computers & Mathematics with Applications. 2011;62(3):902–17.

[25] Murio DA. Stable numerical evaluation of Grünwald–Letnikov fractional derivatives applied to a fractional IHCP. Inverse Problems in Science and Engineering. 2009;17(2): 229–43.

[26] Khader M, Sweilam N, Mahdy A. Two computational algorithms for the numerical solution for system of fractional differential equations. Arab Journal of Mathematical Sciences. 2015;21(1):39–52.

[27] Zurigat M, Momani S, Odibat Z, Alawneh A. The homotopy analysis method for handling systems of fractional differential equations. Applied Mathematical Modelling. 2010;34(1):24–35.

Section 3

# Heat Transfer with Fluids

Chapter 9

# Analysis of Heat Transfer in an Experimental Heat Exchanger Using Numerical Simulation

Laura L. Castro, Alfredo Aranda and
Gustavo Urquiza

Additional information is available at the end of the chapter

http://dx.doi.org/10.5772/63957

**Abstract**

In this chapter, an analysis of convection heat transfer in an experimental heat exchanger using experimental data and numerical simulation data (by means **computational fluid dynamics** (CFD)) is presented. Work was realized in four stages. In the first stage, experimental data were obtained from a heat exchanger installed in Thermohydraulic Laboratory from CIICAp. Analytic calculus with experimental data was realized in the second stage to establish proper values in boundary and operation conditions for numerical simulation. The third stage includes numerical simulation using CFD of the heat exchanger domain with both working fluids (air-water). At the fourth stage, an analysis of the results was performed.

The obtained results are a fair representation of theoretical behavior since phenomena such as thermal and hydrodynamic boundary layers can be observed, which are in function of the flow, either laminar or turbulent. The production of vortices in the case of air in the area of wake is also observed, all this information is useful for optimization and to propose other arrangements that are to be studied in order to achieve improvements in efficiency of heat exchanger. The averaged errors between analytical calculus estimated using experimental data and numerical simulations did not exceed 20%. The ratio between simulation and real heat exchange is 85%.

**Keywords:** Heat Exchanger, Heat Transfer, computational fluid dynamics, CFD

## 1. Introduction

Analysis of heat transfer is necessary for optimization and better use of energy resources of the heat exchangers; we provide the necessary information in terms of the behavior of fluids in certain areas or arrangements to which more heat is transferred so that the more information about the process is known; it will be possible to have a device with lower maintenance costs or energy supply. Currently, computational fluid dynamics (CFD) has been emerged as a powerful tool for the analysis of various processes that deal with fluids, and in the case of heat exchangers it is widespread and has proven to be a reliable tool for analysis. An example is the study by Z.C. Liu and W. Liu. about the geometry of the pipes used in heat exchangers of shell and tube type, which has been shown to modifying the geometry of the tube and modifying the fluid flow patterns, which results in variations in heat transfer as well as the various flow regimes, and that as the fluid velocity increases thereby increasing the turbulence the heat transfer also increases [1].

The study of the loss of efficiency in heat exchangers because of corrosion or malfunction of the system is also important, as presented in the work of Torres-Tamayo et al., which explains how it affects resource consumption; in this work the coefficients of heat transfer by convection are determined as well as the impact of this corrosion decreased the system efficiency because it showed a decrease in the thermal efficiency of 70% in heat exchangers due to such problems [2, 3].

### 1.1. Experimental heat exchanger

The experimental heat exchanger is of tubular type, cross flow occurs at 90°, it comprises vertical tubes placed in a 10 × 4 matrix in an arrangement of square type [4] as shown in **Figure 1**.

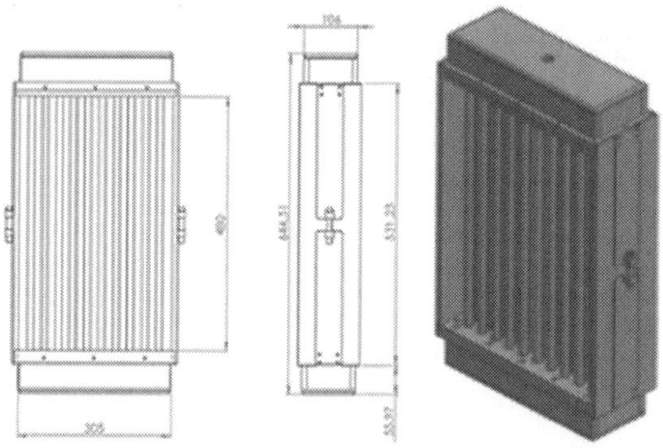

**Figure 1.** Frontal, lateral, and isometric view from heat exchanger (dimension in millimeters).

The heat exchanger is provided with an acrylic duct that is used to conduct the air to the tube arrangement (**Figure 2**). Water flows through 40 tubes vertically and constantly by means of a recirculation circuit which comprises a pump and a reservoir, and the air is supplied by a vertical fan.

http://dx.doi.org/10.5772/63957

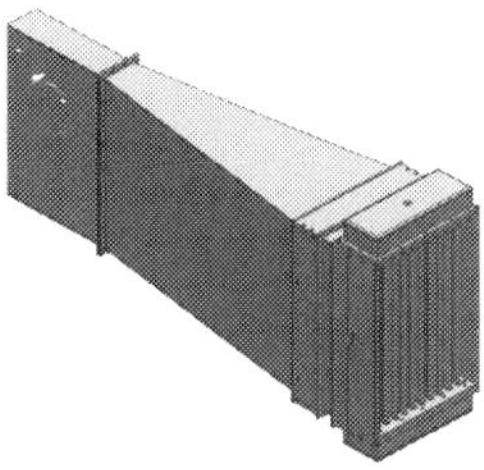

**Figure 2.** Isometric view of air duct and heat exchanger.

## 1.2. Instrumentation

The experimental heat exchanger is implemented with 32 fixed thermocouples, a flow meter is used to measure the flow of water, and readings of air velocity are taken during the test with an anemometer. Thirty-two thermocouples are connected to a data acquisition system in which the analogic signals received are changed to digital signals and then processed and captured in a computer using the LAB-VIEW software. In **Figure 3**, a diagram of the device with basic instrumentation installed therein to monitor the variables of interest is shown.

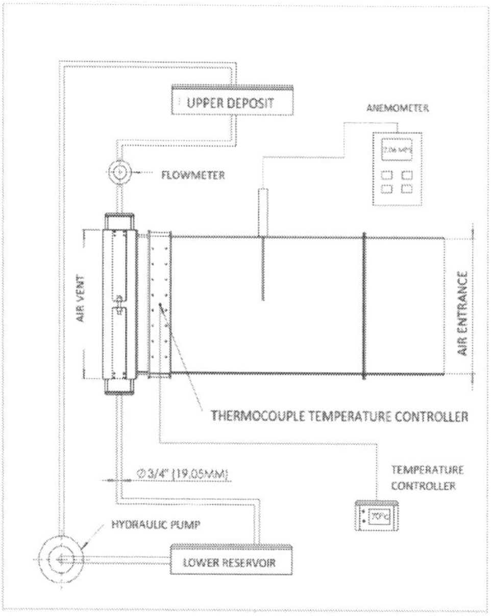


**Figure 3.** Diagram of instrumentation.

An anemometer was used to measure the velocity of the air entering to feed channel to heat exchanger (**Figure 4**).

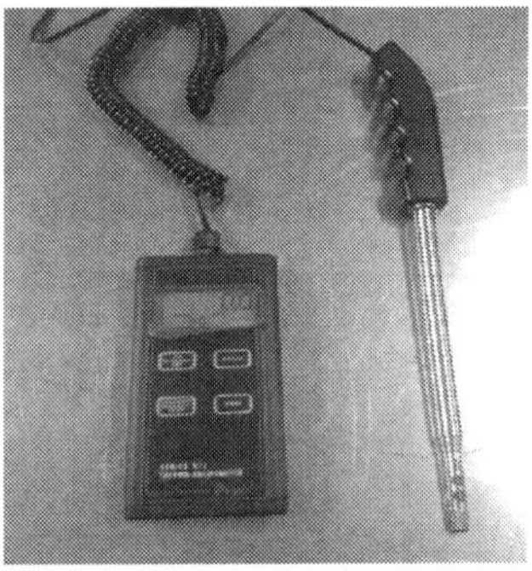

**Figure 4.** Hot-wired anemometer.

A flowmeter is installed in the water supply pipe before entering into the arrangement of heat exchanger tubes (**Figure 5**).

**Figure 5.** Turbine flow meter installed in the water supply pipe.

The procedure for data collection is as follows:

1. Ingress of air.

2. Ingress of water (just to fill pipes).

3. Resistances are turned on for heating the air.
4. Temperatures are expected to stabilize and begin to measure air velocity in anemometer.
5. Water circulation starts and flow meter readings are taken.
6. Once the desired output and inlet temperatures on heat exchanger are achieved, about 15 min of data are taken.

| **Temperatures** | | |
|---|---|---|
| **Water** | | |
| Variable | °C | K |
| T inlet | 18.8000 | 291.9500 |
| Inner wall (calculated) | 28.9000 | 302.1500 |
| T outlet | 20.1600 | 293.3100 |
| **Air** | | |
| T inlet | 63.1600 | 336.3100 |
| T outer wall (action) | 29.0000 | 302.1500 |
| T outlet | 32.8900 | 306.0400 |
| **Operation data** | | |
| Water flow rate | $1.99 \times 10^{-04}$ | $m^3/s$ |
| Air speed | 1.2835 | m/s |

**Table 1.** Averaged variables from experimental measurements.

| **Water properties at 19°C (average)** | | |
|---|---|---|
| Density | 998.8800 | $kg/m^3$ |
| Cp | 4184.4000 | J/kg K |
| K | 0.5962 | W/m K |
| Viscosity | $1.11 \times 10^{-03}$ | kg/m s |
| Pr | 7.8740 | |
| **Air properties at 48°C (average)** | | |
| Density | 1.0970 | $kg/m^3$ |
| Cp | 1007 | J/kg K |
| K | 0.0272 | W/m K |
| Viscosity | $1.95 \times 10^{-05}$ | kg/m s |
| Pr | 0.7233 | |

**Table 2.** Averaged properties of fluids.

On the completion of the measurements and obtaining the data needed, these are organized and averages are computed, which are used for numerical simulation. The averages of the main variables measured are presented in **Table 1**. With the acquired data and obtaining the properties of both fluids, it is possible to calculate the rate of heat transfer and convective coefficients, and then they are used to perform numerical simulation. It is also necessary to calculate the average of fluid properties (**Table 2**).

### 1.3. Theoretical approach

The aim of the presented calculations is to obtain heat transfer and convective coefficients for both fluids. In reality, the convection phenomenon is complex and a constant numerical value for the heat convective coefficient is obtained; while stationary the heat transfer phenomenon is impossible; however, it is possible to obtain a representative average performing theoretical assumptions that are valid; in this case, the variables will be obtained with a theoretical model in which the same amount of heat is transferred with constant convective coefficients per unit average value area along the entire contact surface for both fluids [5]. The nomenclature of variables used on analytical calculation can be found in **Table 3**.

| Variable | Symbol | Units |
|---|---|---|
| Density | $\rho$ | kg/m$^3$ |
| Specific heat | $Cp$ | J/kg K |
| Thermal conductivity coefficient | $k$ | W/m K |
| Dynamic viscosity | $\mu$ | kg/m s |
| Prandtl number | $Pr$ | – |
| Temperature | $T$ | K |
| Heat transfer | $Q$ | W |
| Velocity | $v$ | m/s |
| Volumetric flow | $\acute{v}$ | m$^3$/s |
| Mass flow | $\dot{m}$ | kg/s |
| Temperature gradient | $\Delta T$ | K |
| Convective coefficient | $h$ | W/m$^2$ K |
| Nusselt number | $Nu$ | – |
| Reynolds number | $Re$ | - |
| Transversal section area | $A_{ST}$ | m$^2$ |
| Heat transfer area | $A_{TC}$ | m$^2$ |
| Inner diameter | $D_i$ | m |

| Variable | Symbol | Units |
|---|---|---|
| Outer diameter | $D_e$ | m |
| Diagonal passage | $S_D$ | m |
| Longitudinal passage | $S_L$ | m |
| Transversal passage | $S_T$ | m |
| Thickness | $l$ | m |
| Hydrodynamic inlet length | $L_H$ | m |
| Thermal inlet length | $L_T$ | m |

**Table 3.** Nomenclature.

Subindex 1: Property or variable belonging to air.

Subindex 2: Property or variable belonging to water.

From equation for energy balance:

$$Q = \dot{m}_2 Cp_2 \Delta T_{2\,balance} \tag{1}$$

The total water mass flow:

$$\dot{m}_2 = \acute{\upsilon}_2 \, \rho_2 \tag{2}$$

The temperature gradient for the energy balance is:

$$\Delta T_{2\,balance} = T_{2\,outlet} - T_{2\,inlet} \tag{3}$$

As the heat transfer rate is known, the heat transfer coefficient can be obtained from:

$$Q_{2\,conv} = h_2 A_{T2} \left( \Delta T_{C2} \right) \tag{4}$$

$\Delta T_{C2}$ can be obtained from:

$$\Delta T_{C2} = T_{inner\,wall} - T_{water\,average}$$

where

$$T_{water\ average} = \frac{T_{2\ \text{outlet}} + T_{2\ \text{inlet}}}{2}$$

the temperature of the inner wall is not known; however, the temperature of the outer wall, the tube thickness 1 mm, and thermal conductivity of copper tube, which is 380 W/m K and also has 40 tubes, are known; and as $Q_{cond} = Q_{convection} = Q_2$ it follows that:

$$T_{innerwall} = T_{outterwall} - \frac{\left(\frac{1}{40}\right)\left(Q_{conduction}\right)\ln\left(\frac{r_{outter}}{r_{inner}}\right)}{2\pi Lk} \tag{5}$$

As the temperature of the inner wall and the average water temperature are known, it is possible to obtain the heat transfer coefficient, which from Eq. (4) yields

$$h_2 = \frac{Q_{2\ convection}}{A_{T2}\left(\Delta T_{2C}\right)}$$

Now we can calculate the energy balance for air. First, the volumetric flow must be obtained:

$$\acute{v}_1 = v_1 A_{st1} \tag{6}$$

The air mass flow is calculated with the following equation:

$$\dot{m}_1 = \acute{v}_1 \rho_1 \tag{7}$$

Then, $Q_2 = Q_1$ and it is possible to obtain the heat transfer coefficient of air, using $h$ from Eq. (4):

$$h_1 = \frac{Q_2}{A_{1T}\left(\Delta T_{1C}\right)}$$

The area for convection transfer to the air is

$$A_{T1} = 40\pi D_o L$$

And the temperature gradient $\Delta T_{1C}$ would be

$$\Delta T_{1C} = T_{airaverage} - T_{outterwall}$$

As the temperature of the outer wall is known, the average temperature is obtained as follows:

$$T_{(average\ air)} = \frac{\left(T_{(inletair)} + T_{(\ outletair)}\right)}{2}$$

All the above calculations are based on energy balances, but it is possible based on Nusselt numbers for comparison calculations. To calculate the Nusselt number for water, first obtain the Reynolds number to determine the conditions of the fluid:

$$Re_2 = \frac{\rho_2 v_2 D_i}{\mu_2} \tag{8}$$

The water velocity is given by

$$v_2 = \frac{\acute{v}_2}{A_{st2}} \tag{9}$$

The area $A_{ST\ 1}$ of the cross section for the flow of water is

$$A_{st2} = 40\left(\frac{\pi D_o^{\ 2}}{4}\right)$$

The Reynolds number describes the flow rate of fluids according to their size, and flow in a tube is considered laminar if it holds that $Re < 2300$. It is considered in transition if $2300 < Re < 4000$. And it is considered turbulent if $Re > 4000$ [5, 6].

The Nusselt number for a constant flow of heat per unit area for a fully developed flow and laminar flow along a circular pipe is 4.36. In this case, the water has a laminar flow and therefore the Nusselt number for this fluid is already known.

The heat transfer coefficient would be described by the following equation:

$$h_2 = \frac{Nu_2 k_2}{D_i} \tag{10}$$

And the heat transfer is obtained from Eq. (4):

$$Q_{2\,conv} = h_2 A_{T2} \left( \Delta T_{C2} \right)$$

where

$$A_{T2} = 40 \pi D_i L$$

Now the mass coefficient is calculated based on the Nusselt number for air leaving the heat transferred by air which is absorbed by water $Q_2 = Q_1$.

It is necessary to know the hydraulic diameter of the cross section that crosses in air:

$$D_h = L_c = \frac{4 A_C}{P} \tag{11}$$

As the air flows through the matrix or tube bank, the speed will remain unchanged because the volume of air flow will be lower in the area where this is in contact with the tubes, and to maintain flow mass, the speed increases accordingly. Then, it is interesting to know the maximum speed reached by the air; this is the type of arrangement of the tube bank, and this case is rectangular arrangement type and the equation for the maximum speed is defined as

$$v_{max} = v \frac{S_T}{S_T - D_o} \tag{12}$$

And the Reynolds number according to Eq. (8) is

$$Re_2 = \frac{\rho v_{max} L_c}{\mu} \tag{13}$$

If the Reynolds number is the turbulent regime as in this case, the equation determined by Churchill and Bernstein can be applied, which is valid for all Reynolds numbers [6]:

$$Nu_1 = \frac{h D_o}{k} = 0.3 + \frac{0.62 Re^{1/2} Pr^{1/3}}{\left( 1 + \left( \frac{0.4}{Pr} \right)^{2/3} \right)^{1/4}} \left( 1 + \left( \frac{Re}{282{,}000} \right)^{5/8} \right)^{4/5} \tag{14}$$

As the thermal conductivity of air is known from Eq. (10), it is possible to know the mass coefficient:

$$h_1 = \frac{Nu_1 k_1}{D_o}$$

## 2. Numerical simulation

The geometry used for the analysis has exactly the same dimensions as that of the heat exchanger installed on the laboratory (1:1 scale) in order to obtain data and represent both volumes of fluid (water and air) within the domain. This geometry was formed using the Solid Works software. Once completed, it is exported to the ICEM CFD software that is used to discretize the domain and to assign the name of the frontiers or boundaries of the total domain.

The discretization of the model is the partition or geometry in small elements called control volumes, where the Navier-Stokes equations will be evaluated, which govern fluid dynamics. For discretization, it is necessary to define the existing volumetric bodies; in this case, there are total 41 bodies; 40 of them are tubes, which represent the total volume of water, and the remaining body represents the air passing through them.

The discretization or (or mesh) selected was unstructured. Then, the parameters for the partition of the total volume into smaller volumes are set; these parameters are set in order to have the maximum size and the minimum size that can have the volume or item in a specific area.

Once meshed, the next step is to establish the boundary conditions in the domain; these conditions are very important because the solution is based on them and must be known before carrying out numerical simulation as these represent the actual phenomenon being simulated; and if they are not representative, it is impossible to validate such a simulation.

### 2.1. Preprocessing

For numerical simulation, the software ANSYS CFX was used, which is generally used to provide the numerical solution of differential equations of fluid dynamics. For solving such equations, the first step is known as preprocessing; at this stage, the discrete model is loaded and disclosed to the program boundary conditions, and to the parameters for the convergence of the solution. It was decided to separate the model into two domains as there are two fluids: one represents the total volume of water and the other the total volume of air as well as the respective boundaries. The boundary conditions are presented in **Table 4**.

### 2.2. Processing

At this stage, the Navier-Stokes equations are solved for each subdomain global system of equations.

1. The partial differential equations are integrated into all generated control volumes; the Navier-Stokes and models of thermal energy and turbulence are assigned to each node of each element or subdomain.

2. These integral equations become a global system of equations because each control volume is connected to the adjacent nodes.

3. The global system of equations is solved iteratively; this is necessary because of the nonlinear nature of the equations, and then the exact solution is approached for the solution. That is, the numerical solution obtained by each iteration should converge toward and approach a condition previously considered.

| Zone | Boundary type | Condition | Variables | |
|---|---|---|---|---|
| **External domain (turbulent air)** | | | **Magnitude** | **Temperature** |
| Case | Wall | Adiabatic no slip | – | – |
| Air inlet | Inlet | Mass flow | $\dot{m} = 0.1284\,kg/s$ | 336.3100 K |
| Air outlet | Outlet | Pressure | 0 Pa | 306.0400 K |
| Outer tube wall | Wall | Convection No slip | $h_1 = 77.6200 W/m^2 K$ | 302.1500 K |
| **Internal domain (laminar water)** | | | **Condition** | **Temperature** |
| Water inlet | Inlet | Mass flow | $\dot{m} = 0.1987$ kg/s | 291.9500 K |
| Water outlet | Outlet | Pressure | 0 Pa | 293.3100 K |
| Inner tube wall | Wall | Convection no slip | $h_2 = 184.1873\,W/m^2 K$ | 302.0400 K |

**Table 4.** Boundary conditions for numerical simulation.

### 2.3. Postprocessing

Postprocessing is the final stage of CFD simulation, which allows visualizing the results of flow behavior inside the domain. There are several options to observe it, for example, contours, streamlines, and vectors. In the next section, the examples of post-processing are presented.

## 3. Results

As the results of the numerical simulation, fluids behave as expected according to the theory; for the case of water, as has flow within pipes, it is expected that the hydrodynamic and thermal layers are fully formed and have a length region input and a fully developed area.

As can be seen from **Figure 6**, tubes have an overall length sufficient for the water flow developing hydrodynamically and with a predominance of the fully developed flow as established in the calculations in Section 1.3.

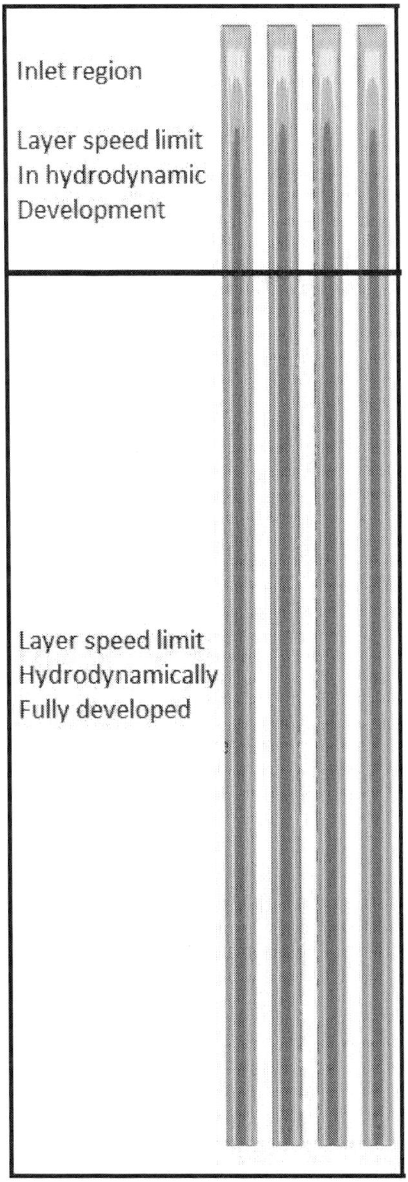


**Figure 6.** Formation and development of the hydrodynamic boundary layer, velocity vectors in the inlet region, and development of the velocity boundary layer in the total length tubes.

The temperature of tubes wall is not constant for the thermal boundary layer, and, therefore, the thermal boundary layer has different temperatures at the interface of the tube wall and the fluid; as can be observed, it behaves correctly. **Figure 7** shows that the fluid cooler is located at the center of the tube, and the fluid is at a higher temperature at the boundary.

Theoretically, the air velocity should be higher where the circulating cross section (**Figure 8**) is reduced; wake vortices should also be formed, generated by the effect of separation of the hydrodynamic boundary layer in the tube wall (**Figure 9**).

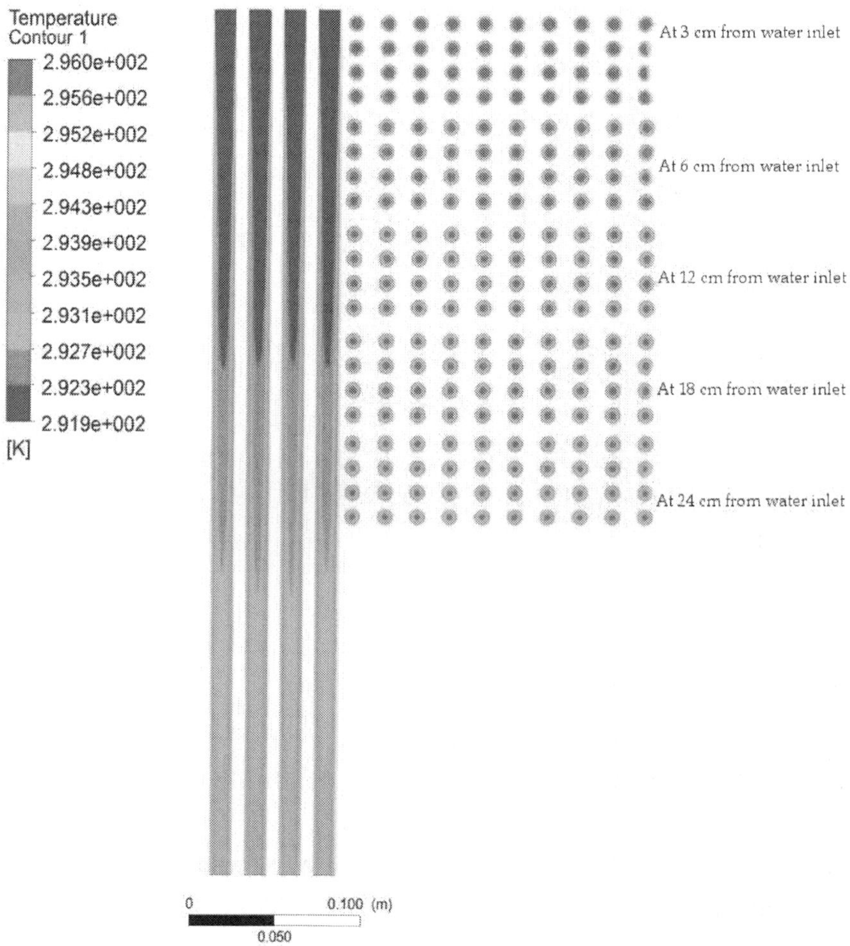


**Figure 7.** Development of thermal boundary layer: middle plane of tubes and transversal plane at different heights.

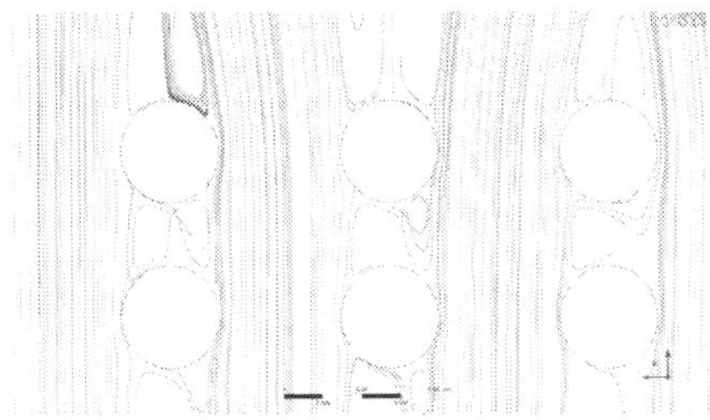

Figure 8. Air velocity contour in a cross section cut of 24 cm of the water inlet to the arrangement of pipes.

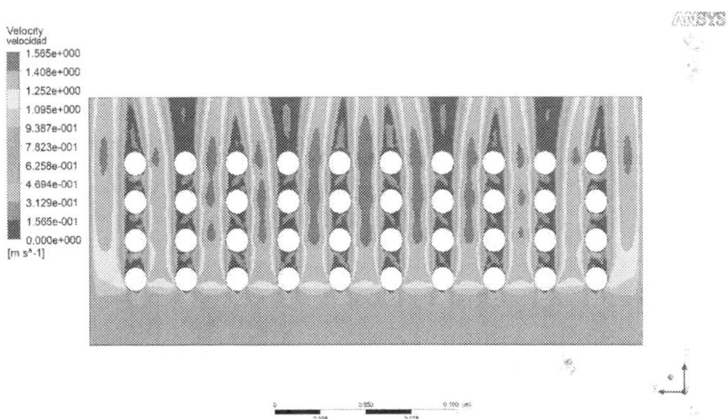


Figure 9. Close-up view of streamlines of airflow at the transversal plane.

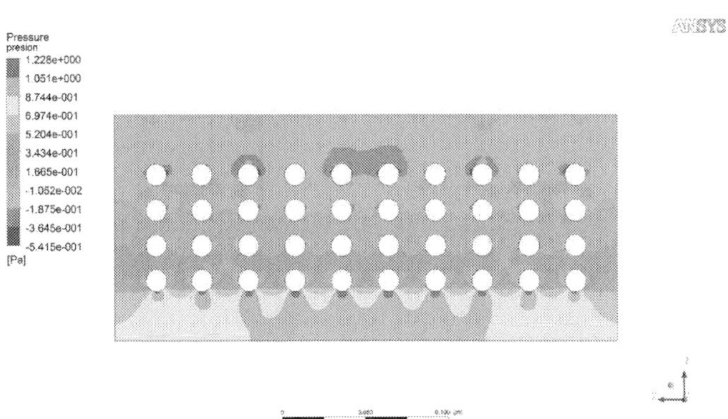


Figure 10. Contour static gauge pressure in the matrix of tubes.

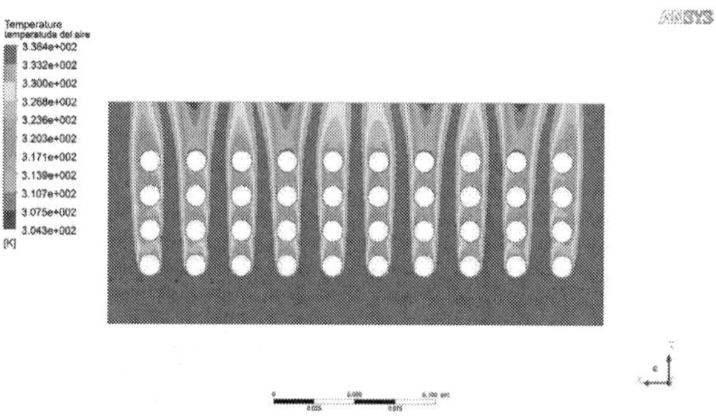


**Figure 11.** Outline temperature air flowing through the tube arrangement.

The maximum speed calculated theoretically was 1.711 m/s and from simulation it is 1.565 m/s, which represents a percentage error of 8.5% that can be considered small due to the complexity of the phenomenon. In the simulation results, it is possible to observe the formation of high-pressure areas where air directly enters the wall of the tube and low-pressure zones where the hydrodynamic wake zone (**Figure 10**) is generated.

For air temperatures, in a manner analogous to the water, the lower temperature is found at the boundary between the outer tube wall and the fluid as shown in **Figure 11**.

The average temperature difference in the tubes is approximately 4°C between numerical simulation and experimentally obtained (**Figure 12**) whereas the average temperature difference at the air outlet is about 6°C (**Figure 13**).

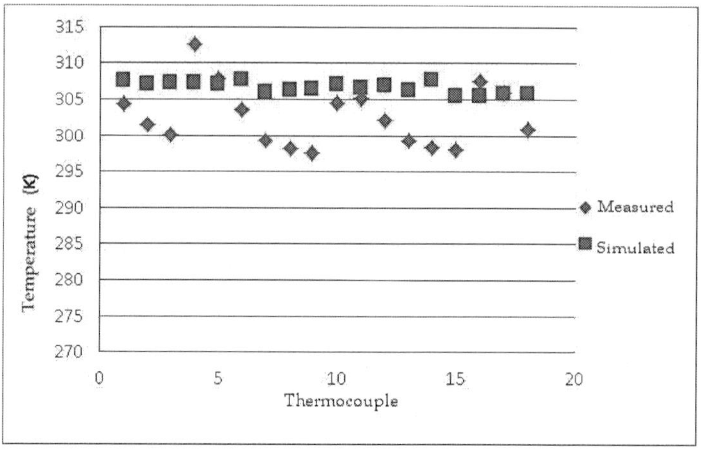


**Figure 12.** Temperatures measured vs. numerically simulated in the outer wall of tubes from the heat exchanger.

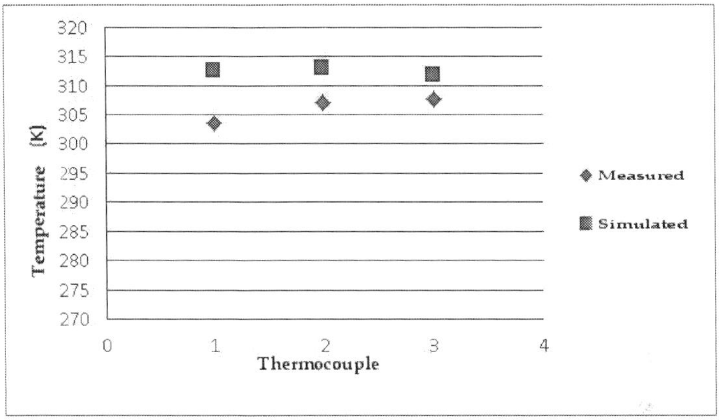


**Figure 13.** Temperatures measured vs. numerically simulated in the air outlet of the heat exchanger.

Although temperatures are not exactly the same, the differences are relatively small as well as the behavior is expected theoretically; it should also be noted that when working with heat transfer convection errors in physical quantities will usually be larger than with phenomena such as conduction, which is a complex phenomenon, as there are a greater number of variables involved.

**Table 5** shows the results of calculus of heat transfer rate from both working fluids that are obtained by energy balances. In addition, the Nusselt number was calculated to subsequently obtain the convective coefficients of both fluids.

| | Magnitude | Error |
|---|---|---|
| $Q_{Water}$ | **1131.1976 W** | **15.1500 %** |
| $Q_{air}$ | **1333.1700 W** | |
| $Nu_{Water}$ | **1489.5220 W** | **19.0130 %** |
| $Nu_{air}$ | **1839.2200 W** | |

**Table 5.** Comparison of the magnitudes of the rate of heat transfer test analyzed.

In order to represent the efficiency of numerical simulations, the following ratio was calculated:

$$\eta = \frac{Q_{Real}}{Q_{Simulation}} = \frac{1131.19}{1333.17} = 0.85$$

which is quite acceptable for such heat transfer problems.

## 4. Conclusion

Numerical simulations were performed using different operational parameters for various measurements with experimental data in order to have a comprehensive approach to the analysis and comparison of experimental and simulated data.

The results of the numerical simulations were validated with calculations and the data obtained by measurements on the heat exchanger, with the average errors of 19% and 15%, respectively, for heat transfer calculus, considering that the phenomenon of convection is difficult to simulate perfectly because the equations and assumptions made to be represented analytically are not accurate enough.

Theoretically, the behavior of fluids and heat transfer was as expected. That is, it was possible to find out the results of the simulation of all phenomena involved in the convection generation of hydrodynamic and thermal boundary layers, the wake regions and production of vortices, and the areas of high and low pressures.

## Author details

Laura L. Castro*, Alfredo Aranda and Gustavo Urquiza

*Address all correspondence to: lauracg@uaem.mx

Research Center on Engineering and Applied Science (CIICAp), from the Autonomous University of Morelos State (UAEM), Morelos, Mexico

## References

[1] Z.C. Liu, W. Liu.. 3D numerical study on shell side heat transfer and flow characteristics of rod-baffle heat exchangers with spirally corrugated tubes. International Journal of Thermal Sciences.. 2015;(89):34–42. DOI: doi:10.1016/j.ijthermalsci.2014.10.011

[2] Enrique Torres-Tamayo, Luís E. Quintana-Charlot, Orlando Vega-Arias, Yoalbys Retirado-Mediaceja. Coeficientes de transferencia de calor y pérdida de eficiencia en intercambiadores de calor de placas durante el enfriamiento del licor amoniacal. Minería y Geología. 2011;27(2):67–83.

[3] Agnieszka Flaga-Maryanczyk, Jacek Schnotale, Jan Radon, Krzysztof Was. Experimental measurements and CFD simulation of a ground source heat exchanger operating at a cold climate for a passive house ventilation system. Energy and Buildings. 2014;(68): 562–570. DOI: doi:10.1016/j.enbuild.2013.09.008

[4] Erick Omar Castañeda Magadán. Simulación Numérica y Construcción de un Intercambiador de Calor Experimental [ [thesis]. Universidad Autónoma del Estado de Morelos:2015. 145 pp.

[5] Yunus A. Cengel, Afshin J. Ghajar. Heat and Mass Transfer. 4th ed. McGraw-Hill, USA; 2011. 921 pp.

[6] KakaÇ or Kakac, H. Liu. Heat Exchangers: Selection Rating and Thermal Design. 2nd ed. CRC, USA; 2002.

Chapter 10

# Solving Inverse Heat Transfer Problems When Using CFD Modeling

Paweł Ludowski, Dawid Taler and Jan Taler

Additional information is available at the end of the chapter

http://dx.doi.org/10.5772/63807

**Abstract**

The chapter presents solving steady-state inverse heat transfer problems using Computational Fluid Dynamics (CFD) software. Two examples illustrate the application of the proposed method. As the first inverse problem determining the absorbed heat flux to water walls in furnaces of steam boilers is presented in detail. Three different measurement devices (flux tubes) were designed to identify steady-state boundary conditions in water wall tubes of combustion chambers. The first meter is made of a short eccentric tube in which four thermocouples on the fire side below the inner and outer tube surfaces are installed. The fifth thermocouple is situated at the rear of the tube on the housing side of the water wall tube. The second meter has two longitudinal fins that are welded to the bare eccentric tube. In the third option of the instrument, the fins are attached to the water wall tubes but not to the flux tubes as in the second version of the flux tubes. The first instrument is used to measure the heat flux to water walls made from bare tubes, while another two heat flux tubes are designated for measuring the heat flux to membrane walls. Unlike the existing devices, the flux tube is not attached to neighboring water-wall tubes. The absorbed heat flux on the outer surface and the heat transfer coefficient at the inner surface of the flux tube are determined from temperature measurements at internal points. The thermal conductivity of the flux-tube material is a function of temperature. The nonlinear inverse problem of heat conduction (IHCP) is solved using the least-squares method. Three unknown parameters are determined using the Levenberg–Marquardt method. In each iteration, the temperature distribution in the cross section of the heat flux instrument is determined using the ANSYS/CFX software.

Another inverse heat transfer problem will be a CFD simulation carried out for the platen superheater placed in the combustion chamber of the circulating fluidized bed (CFB) boiler. Velocity, pressure, and temperature of the steam, as well as the temperature of the tube wall with the complex cross section, were computed using the ANSYS/CFX software. The direct and inverse problems were solved. In the first inverse problem, the heat transfer coefficient on the flue-gas side was determined based on the measured steam temperature at the inlet and outlet of the three pass steam superheater. In the second inverse problem, the inlet steam temperature and the heat transfer coefficient on the flue-gas side were estimated using measured steam temperatures at selected locations of the superheater. The Levenberg–Marquardt method was also used to solve the second inverse problem. At every iteration step, a direct conjugate heat transfer problem was solved using the ANSYS/CFX software. The CFX program was called and controlled by an external program written in Python language. The Levenberg–Marquardt algorithm was also included in the Python program.

**Keywords:** CFD modeling, inverse heat transfer problem, heat flux measurement, pulverized coal-fired boiler, furnace, water wall, circulating fluidized bed boiler, platen superheater

---

## 1. Introduction

The aim of direct conjugate heat transfer problems was determining the distribution of pressure, velocity, and temperature of the fluid and solid in the analyzed area when boundary conditions are known. In inverse problems, based on temperature measurements at chosen points located within the analyzed domain, boundary conditions are determined. Nonlinear inverse problems are solved iteratively. At every iteration, the direct problem is solved. When analyzed domain has a complex shape, then it is necessary to apply CFD software to solve the direct problem. In particular, when conjugate boundary problem is solved, that is, when the temperature fields in the liquid and solid are determined simultaneously, use of CFD software becomes indispensable. Two inverse problems are solved in this chapter. Identification of boundary conditions in the tube of membrane water wall was carried out in the first example. The subject of the second inverse problem is to identify the temperature of the steam entering the superheater and the identification of the heat transfer coefficient on the outer surface of the superheater. The Levenberg–Marquardt method was used to solve both inverse problems. At every iteration step, a direct conjugate heat transfer problem was solved using the ANSYS/CFX software. The CFX program was called and controlled by an external program written in Python language. The Levenberg–Marquardt method that was used for solving nonlinear least squares problem was also included in the Python program. This chapter is based mainly on two papers published earlier [1, 2].

## 2. Measurements of heat flux absorbed by water walls in combustion chambers

Measurements of steady-state heat flux and heat transfer coefficient are subject of many current studies [3–10]. Heat flux measurements absorbed by the water walls of the combustion chamber are used in the design of the steam boilers or in the control systems of the soot blowers. A method for online measurement of the heat flux to the refractory lining in steam generators of municipal solid waste incinerators is presented in [9, 10]. The heat flux measurement can be used for the online monitoring of the refractory lining as well as for determining the build up of deposits on the membrane walls [9, 10]. Various methods are used for solving inverse heat conduction problem (IHCP) to estimate surface heat flux or heat transfer coefficient. A proper understanding of combustion and heat transfer in furnaces and heat exchange on the water-steam side in tubes needs an accurate measurement of heat flux which is taken over by membrane furnace walls [1, 8–23]. Identification of boundary conditions has also great practical meaning in boiler superheaters [2]. There are three wide categories of heat flux measurements of the boiler water-walls: (1) portable heat flux devices inserted in inspection ports [11–15], (2) Gardon-type heat flux meters welded to the sections of the boiler tubes [11–14], (3) tubular-type instruments located between two neighboring boiler tubes [1, 2, 7, 8, 16–21]. Tubular-type and Gardon meters placed on the furnace tube wall in intense slagging areas can be important boiler diagnostic device for monitoring of slag deposition [2, 22–24]. If a heat flux instrument is to measure the absorbed heat flux accurately, it must be similar to the boiler tube as closely as possible. It is crucial for radiant heat exchange between the flame and measuring instruments. Two main factors in this respect are the emissivity and the temperature of the absorbing surface. Because the instrument will almost always be coated with ash, mainly the properties of the ash and not the instrument dominate the situation. Due to the significant variation of the thermal conductivity, accurate measurements can be performed only if the deposit on the meter is corresponding to that on the surrounding tubes. The tubular-type instruments known also as flux tubes satisfy this requirement. In these devices, the measured heat flux tube temperatures are used for indirect measurement of heat flux.

The measuring tube is equipped with two thermocouples in holes of known radial locations $r_1$ and $r_2$. The thermocouples are led out to the junction box where they are connected differentially to give a flux-related electromotive force.

The use of the one-dimensional heat conduction equation for determining temperature distribution in the tube wall gives the simple relationship:

$$q_m = \frac{k(f_1 - f_2)}{r_o \ln(r_1 / r_2)} \tag{1}$$

where $f_1$ and $f_2$ are measured wall temperatures at the locations $r_1$ and $r_2$, respectively, and $r_o$ is the outer radius of the tube. The symbol $k$ denotes the thermal conductivity of the tube material. The accuracy of this equation is low because of the circumferential heat conduction in the tube wall.

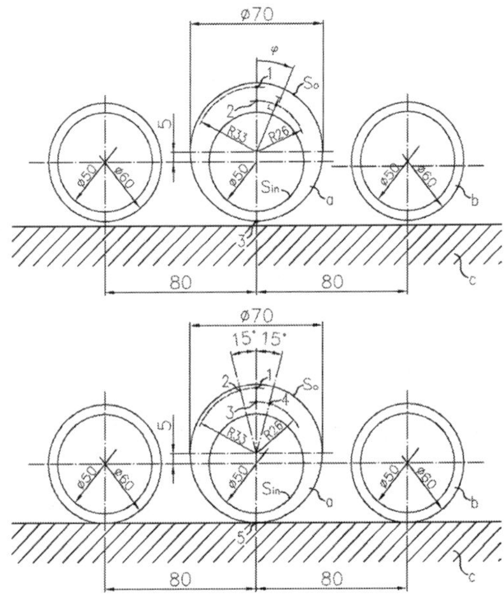


**Figure 1.** Flux tubes made of bare tubes; (a) flux tube with three temperature sensors, (b) flux tube with five temperature sensors.

Therefore, the measurement of the heat flux absorbed by water-walls with satisfactory accuracy is a challenging task. Considerable work has been done in recent years in this field [1, 2, 9–21, 24]. Previous studies to precisely measure the local heat flux to membrane water walls in steam boilers failed due to unknown water-side heat transfer coefficients. The heat flux can be only determined accurately if the water-side heat transfer coefficient will be identified experimentally [7, 8, 15–18]. In this section, a numerical method for determining the heat flux in boiler furnaces, based on measured interior flux-tube temperatures, is presented. The tubular type device has been designed (**Figures 1** and **2**) to provide a highly accurate measurement of absorbed heat flux $q_m$, water-side heat transfer coefficient $h_f$, and water-steam temperature $T_f$. The number of thermocouples is greater than or equal to three. Unlike existing devices, the developed flux tubes are manufactured from bare or longitudinally finned tubes which are not welded to adjacent water-wall tubes. Temperature distribution in the flux tube is symmetric and not distorted by different temperature fields in neighboring tubes. Significant differences in water temperature can occur in the neighboring water wall tubes of sub- and supercritical once-through boilers due to the nonuniform heat flux distribution across the width of the combustion chamber wall. For this reason, the flux tubes presented in the chapter are especially useful for measurements in the once-through boilers. The thermal conductivity of the flux-tube material depends on temperature. The meter is made from a short piece of the eccentric tube. It contains two or four thermocouples on the fireside below the inner and outer surfaces of the tube. The third (**Figure 1a**) or the fifth thermocouple (**Figures 1b**, **2a**, and **2b**) is located at the rear of the tube (on the casing side). The boundary conditions on the outer and inner surfaces of the water flux tube must then be determined from temperature measurements at the interior locations. Two (**Figure 1a**) or four (**Figures 1b** and **2**) K-type sheathed thermocouples, 1 mm in diameter, are inserted into holes, which are parallel to the tube axis, that is, parallel to the direction of flow of the water–steam mixture. The end of the sheathed thermocouple, where the hot junction is situated, was bonded to the bottom of the hole using ceramic adhesive to reduce the contact resistance between the thermocouple jacket and tube flux material. The heat transfer by conduction along the thermocouple is minimized because the thermocouples pass through isothermal holes with a depth of 60 mm. The thermocouples are brought to the rear of the tube in the slot machined in the tube wall. An austenitic guard strip with a thickness of 3 mm—welded to the tube—is used to protect the thermocouples from the incident flame radiation. A K-type sheathed thermocouple with a pad is used to measure the temperature at the rear of the flux tube. This temperature is very close to the water-steam temperature. Because the heat flux on the rear surface of the measuring tube is zero (membrane water-walls are perfectly insulated) or very small (bare tube water-walls), the rear part of the tube is almost unheated. For this reason, there is very little difference in temperature between the wall and the fluid in the rear part of the flux tube. This was proved both, by experiments and computer calculations.

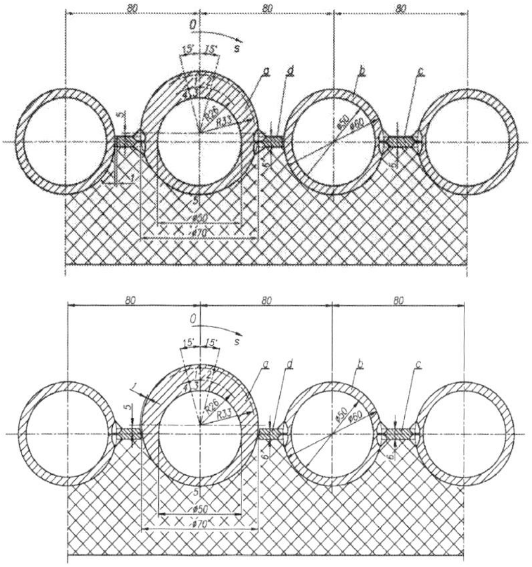

**Figure 2.** Flux tubes for membrane water walls; (a) fins welded to the flux tube, (b) fins welded to adjacent water wall tubes.

An IHCP was solved using the least squares method. Three unknown parameters were determined using the Levenberg–Marquardt method. At every iteration step, the temperature distribution in the cross section of the heat flux tube was computed using the ANSYS/CFX software [25]. Test calculations were conducted to estimate the accuracy of the presented method. The uncertainty in determined parameters was calculated using the Gauss uncertainty propagation rule. The technique presented in this chapter is appropriate for water walls made of bare tubes (**Figure 1a** and **b**) and membrane water-walls (**Figure 2a** and **b**). The new technique has advantages in view of the simplicity and accuracy.

The method can be used to determine the resistance of scale or iron oxide on the inner surface of the water wall tubes. The thermal resistance $R$ of deposits on the inner surface of the measuring device can be determined experimentally using the following relationship

$$R = \frac{1}{h_f} - \frac{1}{h_c}, \tag{2}$$

where the symbol $h_f$ stands for the equivalent heat transfer coefficient for the tube inner surface with a scale layer.

The thermal resistance $R_s = \delta_s/k_s$ of the scale layer can be determined analytically, but the thickness $\delta_s$ and thermal conductivity $k_s$ of the scale layer are difficult to measure in practice.

The heat transfer coefficient $h_c$ can be identified after the beginning of the boiler operation when the tube inner surface is clean. Also, the value of $h_c$ can be estimated after chemical cleaning of the tube internal surfaces. An equivalent heat transfer coefficient $h_f$ is monitored online during the boiler operation. Another measure of scale presence on the tube inner surface is the maximum temperature of the outer surface of the heat flux tube, which increases with the growth of scale thickness on the inner surface. If the thermal resistance of the scale and the maximum temperature of the heat flux tube is greater than the limit values, the boiler should be cleaned chemically.

### 2.1. Theory

The water walls can be made of plain tubes or tubes which are welded together with steel flat bars (longitudinal fins) to form membrane wall panels. The water walls are insulated on the rear side and exposed on the front side to radiation from a combustion chamber. The thermometric inserts were manufactured in the laboratory and then securely welded to the water wall tubes at various levels in the combustion chamber of the steam boiler.

The following assumptions in a heat conduction model of the flux tube are made:

- the temperature distribution is two dimensional and steady state,
- the thermal conductivity of the flux tube and membrane wall may depend on temperature,
- the heat transfer coefficient $h_c$ and the scale thickness $\delta_s$ are uniform on the inner tube circumference.

The temperature distribution $T$ is governed by the nonlinear partial differential equation

$$\nabla \cdot [k(T)\nabla T] = 0 \tag{3}$$

The unknown boundary conditions may be expressed as

$$\left[k(T)\frac{\partial T}{\partial n}\right]\Big|_{S} = q(s) \tag{4}$$

where $q(s)$ is the radiation heat flux absorbed by the exposed flux tube and membrane wall surface. The local heat flux $q(s)$ is a function of the view factor $\psi(s)$

$$q(s) = q_m \psi(s) \tag{5}$$

where $q_m$ is measured heat flux (thermal loading of the heating surface), and $s$ denotes the coordinate along the boundary (**Figure 2**). The view factor $\psi(s)$ from the infinite flame surface to the differential element on the membrane wall surface $ds$ can be determined graphically [17], or numerically [25].

In this chapter, $\psi(s)$ was evaluated analytically for bare tubes and numerically for membrane water-walls using the finite element program ANSYS/CFX [25] as a function of extended coordinate $s$.

The boundary condition on the inner surface of the tube $S_{in}$ is defined by Newton's law of cooling

$$-\left[k(T)\frac{\partial T}{\partial n}\right]\Big|_{S_{in}} = h_f(T|_{S_{in}} - T_f) \tag{6}$$

where $T_f$ designates the temperature of the water–steam mixture.

The rear side of the membrane water wall is perfectly insulated. Instead of the boundary condition on the outer surface of the water wall tube, measured values $f_i$ of metal temperature at internal locations of the flux tubes are known

$$T_e(\mathbf{r}_i) = f_i, \quad i = 1, \ldots, m \tag{7}$$

where $m = 3$ or $m = 5$ designates the number of thermocouples (**Figures 1** and **2**). The unknown parameters: $x_1 = q_m$, $x_2 = h_f$, and $x_3 = T_f$ were estimated using the least-squares method. The symbol $r_{in} = d_f/2 = d_t/2$ stands for the inner tube radius. The symbols $d_f$ and $d_t$ designate the inner diameter of the flux and water wall tube, respectively. Unknown parameters $\mathbf{x} = (x_1, \ldots, x_n)^{tr}$ for $n = 3$ are selected so that computed temperatures $T(\mathbf{x}, \mathbf{r}_i)$ agree within certain limits with the experimentally measured temperatures $f_i$. The location of the thermocouple is defined by the position vector $\mathbf{r}_i$. This may be expressed as

$$T(\mathbf{x},\mathbf{r}_i) - f_i \cong 0, \quad i = 1,\ldots,m. \tag{8}$$

The least-squares method is used to determine parameters $\mathbf{x}$. The sum of squares

$$S(\mathbf{x}) = \sum_{i=1}^{m} [f_i - T(\mathbf{x},\mathbf{r}_i)]^2 \tag{9}$$

can be minimized by a general unconstrained method.

However, the properties of (9) make it worthwhile to use methods designed specifically for the nonlinear least-squares problem. In this work, the Levenberg–Marquardt method [26, 27] is used to determine the parameters $x_1$, $x_2$ and $x_3$. The Levenberg–Marquardt method performs the $k$-th iteration as

$$\mathbf{x}^{(k+1)} = \mathbf{x}^{(k)} + \delta^{(k)} \tag{10}$$

where

$$\delta^{(k)} = [(\mathbf{J}^{(k)})^{tr} \mathbf{J}^{(k)} + \mu \mathbf{I_n}]^{-1} (\mathbf{J}^{(k)})^{tr} [\mathbf{f} - \mathbf{T}(\mathbf{x}^{(k)})], \quad k = 0,1,\ldots \tag{11}$$

where $\mu$ is the multiplier, and $I_n$ is the identity matrix. The Levenberg–Marquardt method is a combination of the Gauss–Newton method ($\mu^{(k)} \to 0$) and the steepest-descent method ($\mu^{(k)} \to \infty$). The latter method is used far from the minimum, changing continuously to the former as the minimum is approached. Initially, a small positive value of $\mu$ was selected, for example, $\mu^{(1)} = 0.01$. If, at the $k$th iteration, the step $\boldsymbol{\delta}^{(k)}$ of (10) reduces S($\mathbf{x}$), then $\mu^{(k)}$ is decreased by a factor of 10 and trial solution is updated, that is, $\mathbf{x}^{(k+1)} = \mathbf{x}^{(k)} + \boldsymbol{\delta}^{(k)}$. In this way, the algorithm is pushed closer to Gauss–Newton method. If within the $k$th iteration, the step $\boldsymbol{\delta}^{(k)}$ does not reduce S($\mathbf{x}$), $\mu^{(k)}$ is progressively increased by a factor of 10, for example, $\mu^{(k)} = 10\mu^{(k)}$, each time recomputing $\boldsymbol{\delta}^{(k)}$ until a reduction in S($\mathbf{x}$) is achieved. The $m \times n$ Jacobian matrix $\mathbf{J}$ of $T(\mathbf{x}^{(k)}, \mathbf{r}_i)$ is defined as

$$\mathbf{J}^{(k)} = \frac{\partial \mathbf{T}(\mathbf{x})}{\partial \mathbf{x}^{tr}}\Big|_{\mathbf{x}=\mathbf{x}^{(k)}} = \begin{bmatrix} \frac{\partial T_1}{\partial x_1} & \cdots & \frac{\partial T_1}{\partial x_n} \\ \cdots & \cdots & \cdots \\ \cdots & \cdots & \cdots \\ \cdots & \cdots & \cdots \\ \cdots & \cdots & \cdots \\ \frac{\partial T_m}{\partial x_1} & \cdots & \frac{\partial T_m}{\partial x_n} \end{bmatrix}_{\mathbf{x}=\mathbf{x}^{(k)}}, \tag{12}$$

where $\mathbf{T}(\mathbf{x}^{(k)}) = (T_1^{(k)}, \ldots, T_m^{(k)})^{tr}$. A finite-difference method was used to estimate the Jacobian matrix at the approximate solution. The sensitivity coefficient defined in Eq. (12) is important indicators of the ability to estimate the unknown parameters. Very small sensitivities indicate the parameters difficult to estimate. The inverses of the sensitivities appear in the variance propagation rule given by Eq. (16). Although the unknowns $x_1$, $x_2$, and $x_3$, are not of the same order of magnitude, the normalized and not normalized vector **x** gave the same solutions. Therefore, the vector **x** was not normalized prior to the solution of the problem. The iterative procedure is continued until the variations in $x_i^{(k)}$, $i = 1, \ldots, n$ are less than a small preset tolerance $\varepsilon$. At every $k$-th iteration step, the temperature distribution $\mathbf{T}(\mathbf{x}^{(k)}, \mathbf{r}_i)$ is calculated using the element-based FVM method.

The estimates for the initial values of the parameters $x_1^{(1)}$, $x_2^{(1)}$, and $x_3^{(1)}$ are

$$x_1^{(1)} = \frac{k^{(1)}}{r_o} \frac{0.5(f_1 + f_2) - 0.5(f_3 + f_4)}{\ln(r_1 / r_2)} \tag{13}$$

$$x_2^{(1)} = \frac{x_1^{(1)} r_o}{r_{in}} \frac{1}{0.5(f_3 + f_4) - (x_1^{(1)} r_o / k^{(1)}) \ln\{r_2 / [r_2 - 0.8(r_2 - r_{in})]\} - x_3^{(1)}} \tag{14}$$

$$x_3^{(1)} = f_5 \tag{15}$$

where the radii are: $r_o = 0.035$ m, $r_{in} = 0.020$ m, $r_1 = 0.033$ m, $r_2 = 0.026$ m. The thermal conductivity $k^{(1)}$ is evaluated at the mean temperature:

$$f_m = (f_1 + f_2 + f_3 + f_4)/4, i.g. k^{(1)} = k(f_m).$$

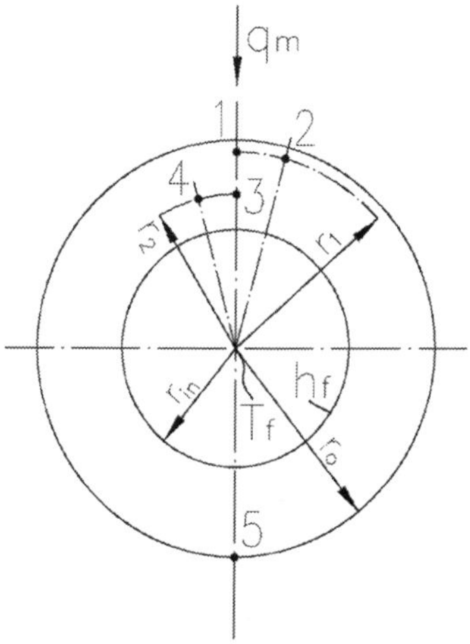


**Figure 3.** Flux tube with constant thickness used to determine initial values of unknown sought parameters.

The relationships (13)–(15) were derived assuming one-dimensional temperature distribution in the heat flux tube with constant thickness (**Figure 3**). In the formula (14), the tube wall temperature at the distance: 0.2 $(r_2 - r_{in})$ from the inner surface was taken as the temperature of the tube inner surface, which results in a lower initial value of the heat transfer coefficient $x_2^{(1)}$.

The Levenberg–Marquardt method allows determining the desired parameters even for an inaccurate estimation of their starting values since the steepest-descent method is used at the beginning of the iteration process. The use of Eqs. (13–15) to select the initial values of parameters makes it possible to find quickly a convergent solution with a small number of iterations. By selecting other starting values, the correct solution is also obtained but with a larger number of iterations.

The Levenberg–Marquardt method works very well in practice and has become the standard of nonlinear least-squares procedures [26, 27]. The boundary value problem that is given by Eq. (3) and boundary conditions (4) and (6) was solved at each iteration step by the element based finite volume method using the ANSYS/CFX software. The CFX program was called and controlled by an external program written in Python programming language [28]. The Levenberg–Marquardt algorithm was also incorporated into the Python program.

### 2.2. Uncertainty analysis

The uncertainties of the determined parameters $\mathbf{x}^*$ will be estimated using the error propagation rule of Gauss [29–33]. The propagation of uncertainty in the independent variables:

measured wall temperatures $f_j$, $j$ = 1, …, $m$, thermal conductivity $k$, radial $r_j$ and angular $\phi_j$, $j$ = 1, …, $m$, coordinates of the thermocouples is estimated from the following expression

$$2\sigma_{x_i} = \left\{ \sum_{j=1}^{m} \left[ \left( \frac{\partial x_i}{\partial f_j} 2\sigma_{f_j} \right)^2 + \left( \frac{\partial x_i}{\partial r_j} 2\sigma_{r_j} \right)^2 + \left( \frac{\partial x_i}{\partial \varphi_j} 2\sigma_{\varphi_j} \right)^2 \right] + \left( \frac{\partial x_i}{\partial k} 2\sigma_k \right)^2 \right\}^{\frac{1}{2}}, \quad i = 1,2,3. \tag{16}$$

The symbols,$\sigma_{f_j}^2$, $\sigma_{r_j}^2$, $\sigma_{\varphi_j}^2$, and $\sigma_k^2$ designate variances of measured temperatures, radial, and angular thermocouple locations and thermal conductivity.

The 95% uncertainty in the estimated parameters can be expressed in the form $x_i = x_i^* \pm 2\sigma_{x_i}$, where $x_i = x_i^*$, $i$ = 1, 2, 3 represent the value of the parameters obtained using the least squares method.

The sensitivity coefficients $\partial x_i/\partial f_j$, $\partial x_i/\partial r_j$, $\partial x_i/\partial \phi_j$, and $\partial x_i/\partial k$ in Eq. (16) were approximated by the central difference quotients

$$\frac{\partial x_i}{\partial f_j} = \frac{x_i(f_1,\ldots,f_j+\delta,\ldots,f_m) - x_i(f_1,\ldots,f_j-\delta,\ldots,f_m)}{2\delta}, \quad i = 1,\ldots,n, \qquad j = 1,\ldots,m \tag{17}$$

where δ is a small positive number.

The error propagation rule given by Eq. (16), which is also known as the principle of the variance propagation, is used extensively to assess the uncertainty of indirect steady-state measurements.

### 2.3. Test computations

Four thermometric inserts will be investigated. In the first flux tube (**Figure 1a**) made from a plain eccentric tube, the wall temperature is measured at two locations at different radii on the fire side. The third thermocouple is placed on the outer tube surface on the insulated side of the water wall. In the second flux tube (**Figure 1b**), made also from the bare tube, four thermocouples are placed at the forward tube part. The fifth temperature sensor is situated at the same position as in the first heat flux. The third flux tube (**Figure 2a**) has two longitudinal fins, which are not welded to the adjacent water wall tubes, so the temperature distribution in the measuring device is not disturbed by the water wall tubes. The fourth device (**Figure 2b**) is without fins, which are welded to the neighboring water wall tubes. There are four thermocouples located at different radii and angles in the flux-tube wall on the fire side, and one thermocouple is attached to the outer tube surface on the back side of the water wall.

### 2.3.1. *Flux tube made from bare tube*

First, the temperature distribution in the cross section of the flux tube will be determined. The following data were adopted for the calculation: absorbed heat flux, $q_{m,e}$ = 250 000 W/m$^2$, heat transfer coefficient, $h_{f,e}$ = 30 000 W/(m$^2$ K), and the temperature of the water-steam mixture, $T_{f,e}$ = 318°C. The view factor $\psi(\phi)$ was evaluated analytically and numerically using the ANSYS software. The consistency of analytical and numerical results is quite good (**Figure 4**).

| Temperature, °C | 100 | 200 | 300 | 400 |
|---|---|---|---|---|
| Thermal conductivity, W/(m K) | 50.69 | 48.60 | 46.09 | 42.30 |

**Table 1.** Thermal conductivity k(T) of steel 20G, as a function of temperature.

The view factor at φ = 180° is about 0.08 since a part of the incident radiation heat flux from the combustion chamber passes through spaces between bare tubes and is reflected by the adiabatic boiler refractory. The material of the heat flux tube is 20G steel. The composition of the 20G mild steel is as follows: 0.17–0.24% C, 0.7–1.0% Mn, 0.15–0.40% Si, 60.04% P, 60.04% S. The thermal conductivity of the heat flux tube is assumed to be temperature dependent (**Table 1**).

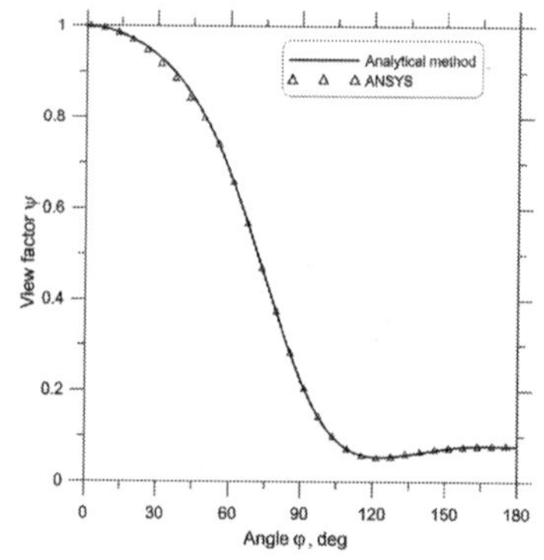


**Figure 4.** Comparison of view factor calculated analytically and numerically using ANSYS/CFX for the flux tubes shown in **Figure 1**. The origin of the cylindrical coordinate system is at the center of the outer flux-tube surface.

The 95% uncertainty interval for thermal conductivity was assumed ±0.5 W/(m K) [34]. The thermal conductivity of the flux-tube material (mild steel 20G) was approximated using a simple linear function

$$k(T) = 53.26 - 0.0238T \tag{18}$$

First, measured temperatures were generated artificially to test the method developed in the chapter. The division of the flux-tube model into finite elements is shown in **Figure 5**. Three different finite element meshes were used to compute the temperature at the locations 1–5. The temperature distribution in the flux tube was calculated using ANSYS/CFX v13.0.

The coordinates of the temperature measuring points 1–5 are as follows:

| | |
|---|---|
| $P_1$ | $r_1 = 33$ mm, $\phi_1 = 0°$, |
| $P_2$ | $r_2 = 33$ mm, $\phi_2 = 15°$, |
| $P_3$ | $r_3 = 26$ mm, $\phi_3 = 0°$, |
| $P_4$ | $r_4 = 26$ mm, $\phi_4 = 15°$, |
| $P_5$ | $r_5 = 35$ mm, $\phi_5 = 180°$, |

The temperature at the points 1–5 obtained for various meshes shown in **Figure 5** are summarized in **Table 2**.

The analysis of the results listed in **Table 2** shows that the temperature calculated using the different grids are very close to each other.

| Measuring point | Temperature, °C | Finite element mesh | | |
|---|---|---|---|---|
| | | Figure 5a | Figure 5b | Figure 5c |
| 1 | $T_1$ | 418.31 | 418.36 | 418.55 |
| 2 | $T_2$ | 415.66 | 415.77 | 415.84 |
| 3 | $T_3$ | 374.08 | 373.75 | 374.14 |
| 4 | $T_4$ | 372.22 | 372.17 | 372.22 |
| 5 | $T_5$ | 321.11 | 321.10 | 321.12 |

**Table 2.** Flux-tube temperature at the points $P_1$–$P_5$ computed for different finite element meshes shown in **Figure 5**.

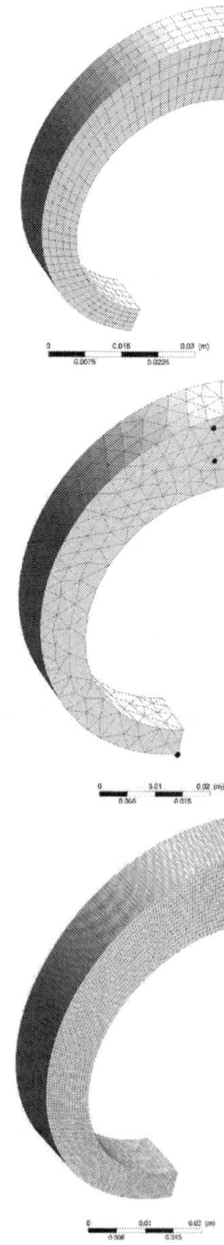

**Figure 5.** Division of geometrical model of the heat flux tube into finite elements; (a) hexahedral mesh–1150 elements hex8, 1692 nodes; (b) tetrahedral mesh—1909 elements tet4, 518 nodes; (c) hexahedral mesh—59520 elements hex8, 66759 nodes.

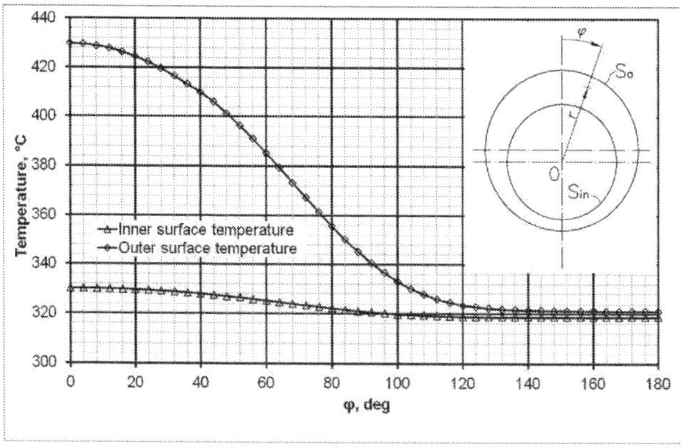


**Figure 6.** Flux-tube temperature at the outer and inner surfaces as a function of angular coordinate $\varphi_1$.

The temperature changes at the inner and outer surface on the flux-tube circumference which were obtained using the mesh shown in **Figure 5a** are depicted in **Figure 6**.

First, the temperatures for the mesh shown in **Figure 5a** were taken as "measured data": $f_1$ = 418.31°C, $f_2$ = 415.66°C, $f_3$ = 374.08°C, $f_4$ = 372.22°C, $f_5$ = 321.11°C (**Table 2**).

Taking the calculated temperatures as measured temperatures and using the same finite element mesh, the following results are obtained:

- For three measuring points: $P_1$, $P_3$, and $P_5$ (**Figure 1a**):

$$q_m = 250000.19\ \mathrm{W/m^2},$$

$$h = 30000.38\ \mathrm{W/(m^2\ K)},$$

$$T_f = 318.00°\mathrm{C}$$

- For five measuring points: $P_1$, $P_2$, $P_3$, $P_4$, and $P_5$ (**Figure 1b**):

$$q_m = 249999.94\ \mathrm{W/m^2},$$

$$h = 30000.16\ \mathrm{W/(m^2\ K)},$$

$$T_f = 318.00°\mathrm{C}.$$

When the temperature values obtained for the mesh illustrated in **Figure 5c** were adopted as "measured data" then an inverse calculation using the mesh shown in **Figure 5a** gives little different results:

- For three measuring points: $P_1$, $P_3$, and $P_5$ (**Figure 1a**):

$$q_m = 250892.94\,/\,\mathrm{m}^2,$$

$$h = 30418.33\,/\,(\mathrm{m}^2\ \mathrm{K}),$$

$$T_f = 318.00°\mathrm{C}.$$

- For five measuring points: $P_1$, $P_2$, $P_3$, $P_4$, and $P_5$ (**Figure 1b**):

$$q_m = 250898.22\,\mathrm{W/m}^2,$$

$$h = 30498.66\,\mathrm{W/(m^2 \cdot K)},$$

$$T_f = 318.01°\mathrm{C}.$$

Analysis of the results demonstrates that for exact "measurement data," the obtained results are in very good agreement with the input values. The impact of measuring point number on the results of the inverse problem solution can be better estimated when the measured temperatures are assumed to be disturbed with pseudorandom errors, which are characterized by the 95% uncertainty intervals: $2\sigma_{f_j} = \pm 0.2\,K; 2\sigma_{r_j} = \pm 0.05\,mm; 2\sigma_{\varphi_j} = \pm 0.5$ , $j = 1, \ldots, 5$; $2\sigma_k = \pm 0.5\,W\,/\,(m \cdot K)$. At first, the uncertainties in the estimated parameters: $x_1 = q_m$, $x_2 = h$, $x_3 = T_f$ will be determined when the flux tube illustrated in **Figure 1a** is used. To estimate uncertainties in determined parameters, Eq. (16) was used. The partial derivatives appearing in Eq. (16) were calculated using the central difference approximation (17). The results are listed in **Table 3**.

The analysis of the results presented in **Table 3** shows that the largest absolute values have the following coefficients: $\partial q_m/\partial f_j$, $\partial h_f/\partial f_j$, $\partial q_m/\partial r_j$, and $\partial h_f/\partial r_j$.

For this reason to obtain small uncertainties in the heat flux $q_m$ and the heat transfer coefficient $h_f$, the random errors in measured temperatures and radial locations of the thermocouples should be small.

Applying Eq. (16) yields: $2\sigma_{(x1)}$= 4073.50 W/m2; $2\sigma_{(x2)}$= 3921.12W/(m2·K); $2\sigma_{(x3)}$= 0.22 K. The 95% uncertainties in the estimated parameters are as follows:

$$q_m = 250\,000.2 \pm 4073.5\,\mathrm{W/m^2},$$

$$h_f = 30\,000.4 \pm 3921.1\,\mathrm{W/(m^2 \cdot K)},$$

$$T_f = 318.0 \pm 0.22°\mathrm{C}.$$

| Thermocouple number, j | $\partial x_i/\partial f_j$ | | |
|---|---|---|---|
| | $\partial q_m/\partial f_j$, W/(m²K) | $\partial h_f/\partial f_j$, W/(m²K²) | $\partial T_f/\partial f_j$<br>– |
| 1 | 2825.19 | 1656.70 | −0.0018 |
| 2 | 2663.14 | 1589.09 | 0.0179 |
| 3 | −2718.39 | −3037.09 | −0.0536 |
| 4 | −2784.89 | −3019.57 | −0.0342 |
| 5 | −119.11 | 2798.77 | 1.0722 |
| **Thermocouple number, j** | $\partial x_i/\partial r_j$ | | |
| | $\partial q_m/\partial r_j$, W/(m²·mm) | $\partial h_f/\partial r_j$, W/(m²·K·mm) | $\partial T_f/\partial r_j$, K/mm |
| 1 | −16347.09 | −9468.39 | 0.0143 |
| 2 | −15136.96 | −8846.43 | −0.1046 |
| 3 | 18012.69 | 27039.19 | 0.3659 |
| 4 | 18156.25 | 26298.52 | 0.2319 |
| 5 | 51.72 | −1268.71 | −0.4674 |
| **Thermocouple number, j** | $\partial x_i/\partial \phi_j$ | | |
| | $\partial q_m/\partial \phi_j$, W/(m²·deg) | $\partial h_f/\partial \phi_j$, W/(m²·K·deg) | $\partial T_f/\partial \phi_j$, K/deg |
| 1 | 114.55 | 133.76 | −0.0002 |
| 2 | −1104.76 | −670.19 | −0.0079 |
| 3 | −134.66 | −150.88 | −0.0027 |
| 4 | 768.36 | 812.51 | 0.0090 |
| 5 | −0.24 | 0.88 | 0.0004 |
| | $\partial x_i/\partial k$ | | |
| | $\partial q_m/\partial k$, K/m | $\partial h_f/\partial k$, 1/m | $\partial T_f/\partial k$, m·K²/W |
| | 5696.11 | 742.42 | −0.0006 |

**Table 3.** Partial derivatives appearing in Eq. (16) for the evaluation of measurement uncertainty.

If the device with five temperature measurement points is used (**Figure 1b**) then the uncertainties become smaller: $2\sigma_{x_1} = 3557.73\ \mathrm{W/m^2}; 2\sigma_{x_2} = 2379.85\mathrm{W/(m^2K)}; 2\sigma_{x_3} = 0.22\ \mathrm{K}$.

The limits of the 95% uncertainty interval are as follows:

$$q_m = 249999.9 \pm 3557.7\ \mathrm{W/m^2},$$

$$h_f = 30000.16 \pm 2379.9\ \mathrm{W/(m^2\ K)},$$

$$T_f = 318.0 \pm 0.22°\mathrm{C}.$$

Inspection of the results demonstrates the good accuracy in both cases. If the number of temperature measurement points is equal five then the uncertainties in the estimated heat flux and heat transfer coefficient become smaller, because an imprecise location of one thermocouple has a smaller influence on the estimated parameters. For two temperature sensors placed at the forward part of the heat flux tube, an inaccurately situated temperature sensor influences to a larger extent the results.

If the standard deviations of the variables measured directly are greater also standard deviations of the determined parameters: $q_m$, $h_f$, and $T_f$ will be greater. If the random errors will be doubled, the standard deviation will also be doubled. This conclusion follows from the analysis of Eq. (16). This has no effect on the convergence of the solution. For larger random errors in measured temperatures, a convergent solution is obtained, but with a slightly larger number of iterations.

To demonstrate the influence of the selection of parameter initial values on the solution convergence and on the number of iterations, the computations will be carried out for five measuring temperature points and using two sets of initial values:

- $q_m^{(1)} = 100\ 000\ \mathrm{W/m^2},\ h_f^{(1)} = 40\ 000\ \mathrm{W/(m^2\ K)},\ T_f^{(1)} = 316°\mathrm{C},$
- $q_m^{(1)} = 400\ 000\ \mathrm{W/m^2},\ h_f^{(1)} = 10\ 000\ \mathrm{W/(m^2\ K)},\ T_f^{(1)} = 317°\mathrm{C},$

Adopting "measured data" from **Table 2** for the mesh shown in **Figure 5a**, the following results were obtained:

- $q_m = 249999.80\mathrm{W/m^2},\ h_f = 29999.78\mathrm{W/(m^2K)},\ T_f = 318.00°\mathrm{C}$ after 27 iterations,
- $q_m = 250000.15\mathrm{W/m^2},\ h_f = 30000.03\mathrm{W/(m^2K)},\ T_f = 318.00°\mathrm{C}$ after 27 iterations.

Because the start values of parameters are far from the input values (exact solution) the number of iteration is large. However, the solution found is correct in both cases.

If one of the temperature measurements is affected by a significant measurement error then the incorrect temperature measurement must be removed from the analysis. It was assumed that the measured temperature at the point 4 is equal to the measured temperature at the point 5 to assess the influence of the large measurement error. Using the finite element mesh depicted in **Figure 5a** and disturbed "measurement data": $f_1$ = 418.31°C, $f_2$ = 415.66°C, $f_3$ = 374.08°C, $f_4$ = 321.11°C, $f_5$ = 321.11°C, the following values of the parameters were found: $q_m$ = 303 248.29 W/m², $h_f$ = 5 705 392.54 W/(m² K), $T_f$ = 306.16°C. One can see that the determined parameters considerably differ from the exact values: $q_m$ = 250 000 W/m², $h_f$ = 30 000 W/(m² K), $T_f$ = 318°C. In practice, it is easy to notice that one of the measuring points is damaged because during correct measurements the temperatures measured at the points 1 and 2 should be similar, as well as temperatures at the points 3 and 4 should be close to each other.

### 2.3.2. *Flux tube for membrane water walls–fins attached to the flux tube*

In combustion chambers with membrane water walls, heat flux tube with longitudinal fins may be used (**Figure 2a**). To eliminate the influence of neighboring water wall tubes on the temperature field in the heat flux tube, the longitudinal fins are not welded to the adjacent tubes.

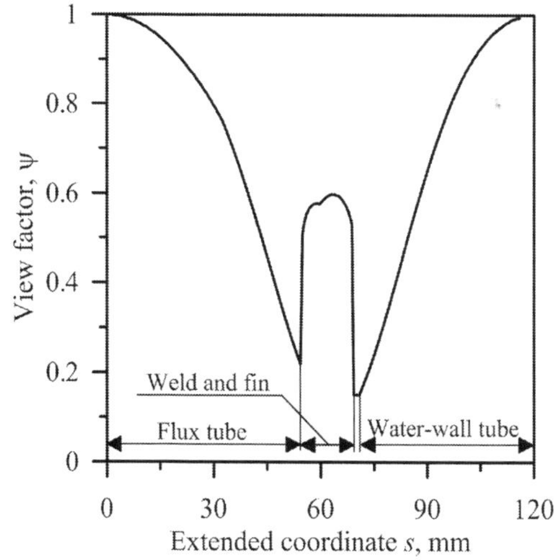


**Figure 7.** View factor distribution on the outer surface of the flux tube and adjacent water-wall tube which are shown in **Figure 2a**.

The distribution of the view factor on the surface of the flux tube, fin, and water wall tube is depicted in **Figure 7**. The origin of the *s* coordinate is shown in **Figure 2**. Because of the symmetry, only the representative water wall section illustrated in **Figure 8** needs to be analyzed.

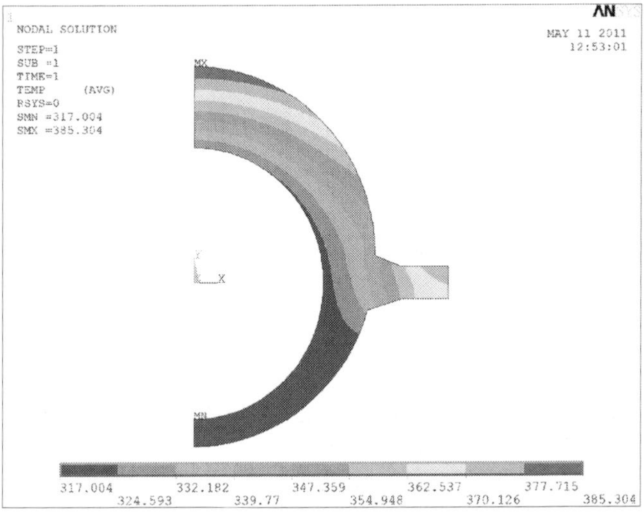


**Figure 8.** Temperature distribution in the flux-tube cross section for: $q_m$ = 150000 W/m$^2$. $T_f$ = 317°C and $h_f$ = 27000 W/(m$^2$ K).

To illustrate that the maximum temperature of the fin tip is lower than the allowable temperature for the 20G steel, the flux-tube temperature was calculated using ANSYS/CFX package [25]. Variations of the view factor on the flux-tube weld and fin surface were also calculated with ANSYS/CFX. An inspection of the results shown in **Figure 8** shows that the maximum temperature of the fin does not exceed 375°C. Next to illustrate the effectiveness of the presented method test calculations were carried out. The thermal conductivity of the 20G steel was approximated by the function (18).

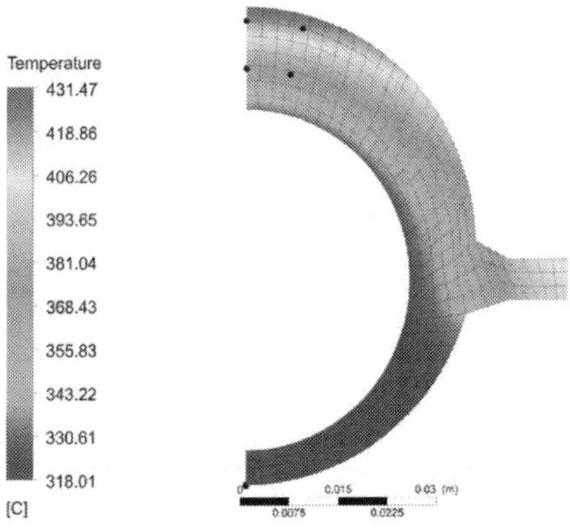

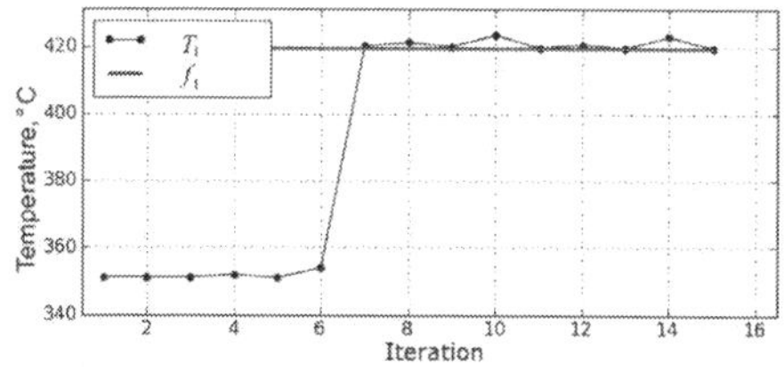


**Figure 9.** Temperature distribution (a) in the flux tube obtained from the solution of the inverse problem for the "exact" data: f1 = 419.66°C. f2 = 417.31°C. f3 = 374.90°C. f4 = 373.19°C. f5 = 318.01°C and iteration number (b) for the temperature T1.

The "measured" temperatures $f_i$, $i = 1, 2, \ldots, 5$ were generated artificially by means of ANSYS/CFX for: $q_m$ = 250 000 W/m$^2$, $h_f$ = 30 000 W/(m$^2$ K) and $Tf$ = 318°C. The following values of "measured" temperatures were obtained $f_1$ = 419.66°C, $f_2$ = 417.31°C, $f_3$ = 374.90°C, $f_4$ = 373.19°C, $f_5$ = 318.01°C. The temperature distribution in the flux-tube cross section reconstructed on the basis of five measured temperatures is shown in **Figure 9a**. The inverse method presented in the chapter is very accurate because the estimated parameters:
$q_m$ = 250 000.063 W/m$^2$, $h_f$ = 30 000.054 W/(m$^2$ K), and $T_f$ = 318.0°C differ slightly from the input values.

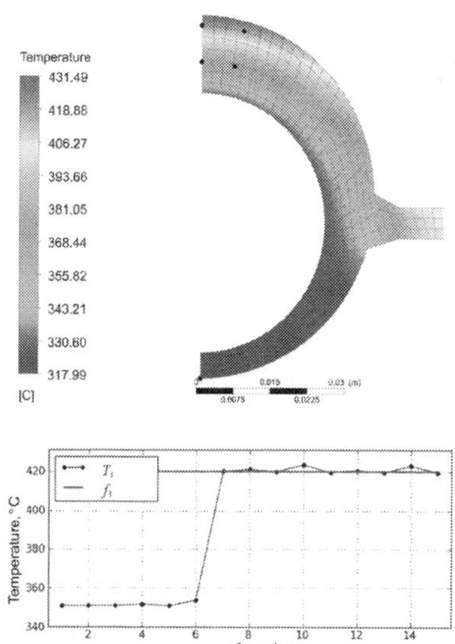


**Figure 10.** Temperature distribution (a) in the flux tube obtained from the solution of the inverse problem for the "perturbed" data: $f_1$ = 420.16°C. $f_2$ = 416.81°C. $f_3$ = 375.40°C. $f_4$ = 372.69°C. $f_5$ = 318.01°C and iteration number (b) for the temperature $T_1$.

To show the influence of the measurement errors on the determined parameters, the 95% confidence intervals were estimated. The following uncertainties of the measured values were assumed (at 95% confidence interval): $2\sigma_{f_j} = \pm 0.4\text{K}$, $2\sigma_{r_j} = \pm 0.10\text{mm}$, $2\sigma_{\varphi_j} = \pm 1.0°$, $j=1, \ldots, 5$, $2\sigma_k = \pm 1.0\text{W}/(\text{mK})$. For these test calculations, the 95% uncertainties in the parameters measured directly were taken two times greater than the uncertainties in the previous case analyzed in Section 4.1. The limits of the 95% uncertainty interval are as follows:

$$q_m = 250000.06 \pm 7102.46\ \text{W/m}^2,$$

$$h_f = 30000.05 \pm 4735.71\ \text{W/(m}^2\ \text{K)},$$

$$T_f = 318.00 \pm 0.41°\text{C}.$$

Despite the doubling of uncertainties, the results are quite good. Larger relative errors in determined the heat transfer coefficient are due to a small difference in temperature between the inner surface of the flux tube and the fluid temperature. For this reason, the impact of the uncertainties in direct measurements on the estimated heat transfer coefficient is greater.

The uncertainties (95% confidence interval) of the coefficients $x_i$ were determined using the error propagation rule (16). The calculated uncertainties are: ±4.1% for $q_m$, ±27.3% for $h_f$ and ±0.1% for $T_f$. The accuracy of the results obtained is acceptable.

Then, the inverse analysis was carried out for perturbed data: $f_1 = 420.16$°C, $f_2 = 416.81$°C, $f_3 = 375.40$°C, $f_4 = 372.69$°C, $f_5 = 318.01$°C. The reconstructed temperature distribution is illustrated in **Figure 10a**. The obtained results are $q_m = 250\ 118.613$ W/m², $h_f = 30\ 050.041$ W/(m² K) and $T_f = 317.99$°C. The influence of the error in the measured temperatures on the estimated parameters is small.

The number of iterations in the Levenberg–Marquardt procedure is small in both cases (**Figures 9b** and **10b**).

## 2.4. Flux tube for membrane water walls—fins attached to the adjacent water wall tubes

The variation of the view factor on the surface of the flux tube, fin, and water wall tube is illustrated in **Figure 11**. The origin of the cylindrical coordinate system is at the center of the outer flux-tube surface (**Figure 2b**). Because of the symmetry, only the half of the flux tube was considered.

The measured temperatures: $f_1 = 418.28$°C, $f_2 = 415.61$°C, $f_3 = 374.05$°C, $f_4 = 372.18$°C, $f_5 = 318.00$°C were generated artificially for the following input data $q_m = 250\ 000$ W/m², $h_f = 30\ 000$ W/(m² K), $T_f = 318.00$°C. The inverse analysis yields the values of unknown parameters: $q_m = 249\ 999.43$ W/m², $h_f = 29\ 999.60$ W/(m² K), $T_f = 318.00$°C, which are very close to the input values. The reconstructed temperature distribution is shown in **Figure 12**. The uncertainty analysis was omitted because the results are very similar to the results obtained in Section 4.2.

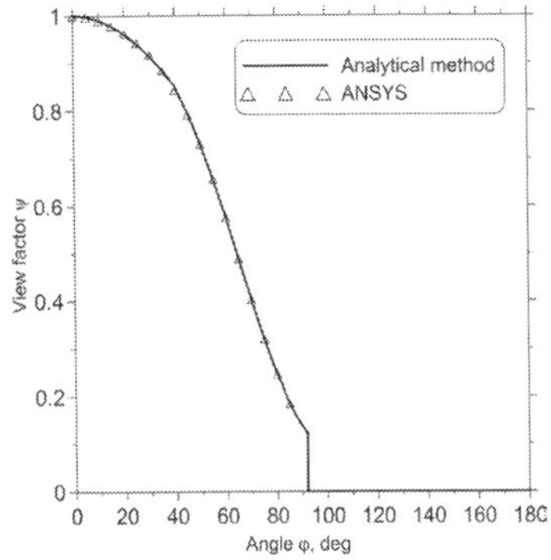


**Figure 11.** Comparison of view factor calculated analytically and by FEM for the flux tube shown in **Figure 2b**.

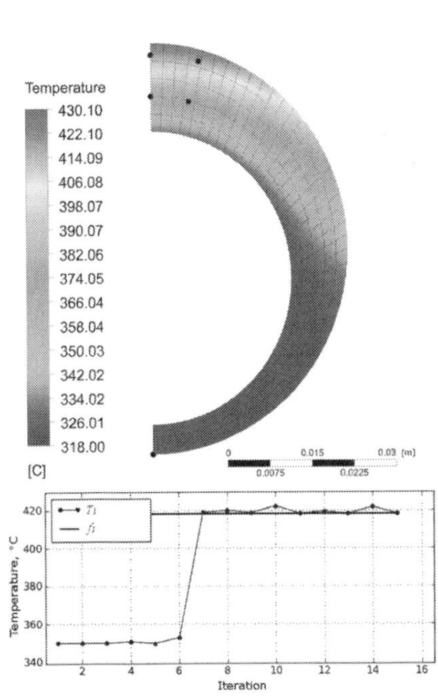


**Figure 12.** Temperature distribution in the flux tube obtained from the solution of the inverse problem for the unperturbed data: $f_1$ = 418.28°C, $f_2$ = 415.61°C, $f_3$ = 374.05°C, $f_4$ = 372.18°C, $f_5$ = 318.00°C; (a) temperature distribution; (b) iteration process.

## 2.5. Boiler test

The pulverized coal-fired boiler produces 58.3 kg/s superheated steam at 11 MPa and 540°C. Experimental studies were conducted in this boiler for a mass flow rate of live steam equal to $210 \cdot 10^3$kg/h. Measuring heat flux tubes were installed in the middle of the water wall at different levels of the boiler combustion chamber. Despite the boiler is operated in a steady state load, slow time variations in the measured temperatures are observed. This phenomenon is characteristic for the combustion of coal in large boilers. However, time changes of the meter temperature are very slow and the temperature distribution in the meter can be considered as a steady state. Temperature measurement results for the heat flux tubes located at a level of

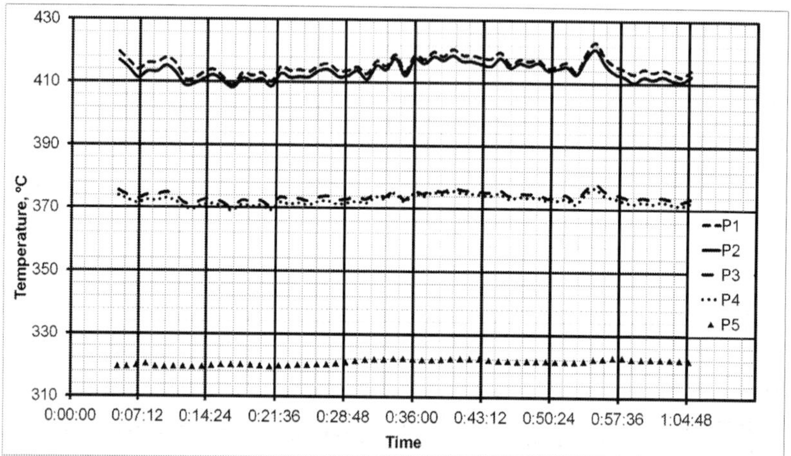


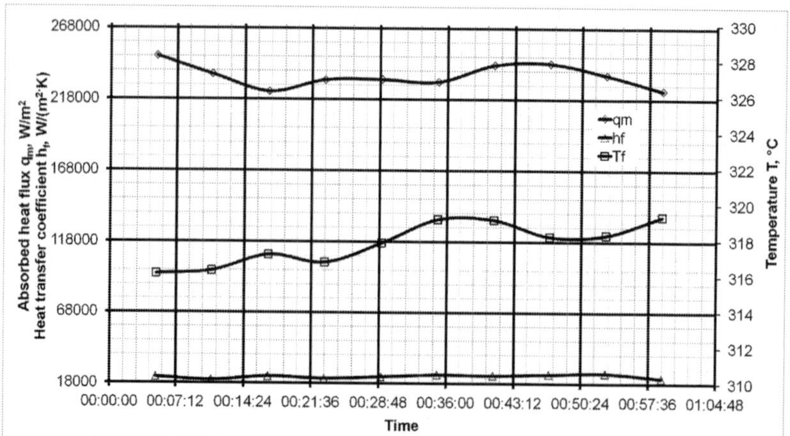


**Figure 13.** Measured temperature histories at five points for heat flux tube located at the level of 15.4 m (a) and estimated parameters: absorbed heat flux $q_m$. Heat transfer coefficient $h_f$ and fluid temperature $T_f$ (b).

15.4 m are depicted in **Figure 11a**, and the estimated parameters as functions of time are depicted in **Figure 11b**.

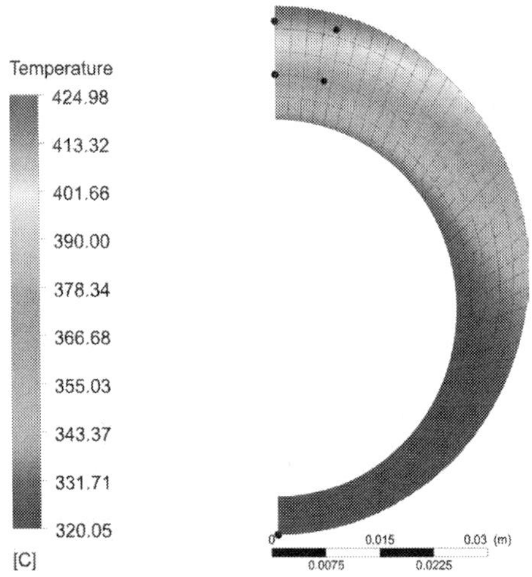


**Figure 14.** Temperature distribution in the cross section of the flux tube located at the level of 15.4 m. which was determined on the basis of measured temperatures: $f_1$ = 413.509°C; $f_2$ = 412.227°C; $f_3$ = 372.855°C; $f_4$ = 372.227°C; $f_5$ = 322.209°C. The estimated parameters are: $q_m$ = 230425.8 W/m²; $h_f$ = 24128.8 W/(m² K); $T_f$ = 319.19°C.

The differences between the measured and computed temperatures for the measurements at the elevation 15.4 m (**Figures 13a** and **14**) are reported in **Table 4**. The time points in the first column of **Table 4** are the same as indicated in **Figure 13a and b**.

| Time | $f_1$, °C | $T_1$, °C | $f_1 - T_1$, K | $f_2$, °C | $T_2$, °C | $f_2 - T_2$, K | $f_3$, °C | $T_3$, °C | $f_3 - T_3$, K |
|---|---|---|---|---|---|---|---|---|---|
| 00:05:00 | 419.55 | 419.58 | −0.03 | 416.89 | 416.88 | 0.01 | 375.53 | 375.67 | −0.15 |
| 00:11:00 | 415.87 | 415.76 | 0.11 | 412.85 | 413.19 | −0.34 | 374.19 | 374.21 | −0.02 |
| 00:17:00 | 408.98 | 409.76 | −0.78 | 408.17 | 407.36 | 0.82 | 370.00 | 370.40 | −0.40 |
| 00:23:00 | 413.61 | 413.79 | −0.18 | 411.39 | 411.27 | 0.12 | 372.83 | 372.93 | −0.10 |
| 00:29:00 | 413.74 | 414.16 | −0.42 | 412.09 | 411.65 | 0.44 | 373.01 | 373.23 | −0.22 |
| 00:35:00 | 413.51 | 414.09 | −0.58 | 412.23 | 411.61 | 0.61 | 372.86 | 373.43 | −0.57 |
| 00:41:00 | 418.98 | 419.28 | −0.30 | 416.99 | 416.67 | 0.32 | 375.99 | 376.46 | −0.47 |
| 00:47:00 | 417.67 | 418.30 | −0.62 | 416.34 | 415.68 | 0.66 | 374.86 | 375.27 | −0.41 |
| 00:53:00 | 413.76 | 414.56 | −0.80 | 412.87 | 412.04 | 0.83 | 372.60 | 373.04 | −0.44 |
| 00:59:00 | 413.05 | 412.94 | 0.10 | 410.38 | 410.51 | −0.13 | 373.15 | 373.39 | −0.24 |

| Time | $f_4$, °C | $T_4$, °C | $f_4$-$T_4$, K | $f_5$, °C | $T_5$, °C | $f_5$-$T_5$, K | S, K$^2$ |
|---|---|---|---|---|---|---|---|
| 00:05:00 | 373.88 | 373.76 | 0.12 | 319.49 | 319.49 | 0.00 | 0.04 |
| 00:11:00 | 372.18 | 372.38 | −0.19 | 319.60 | 319.60 | 0.00 | 0.17 |
| 00:17:00 | 369.06 | 368.69 | 0.38 | 320.18 | 320.20 | −0.02 | 1.58 |
| 00:23:00 | 371.17 | 371.14 | 0.04 | 319.96 | 319.96 | −0.01 | 0.06 |
| 00:29:00 | 371.66 | 371.45 | 0.21 | 320.96 | 320.98 | −0.01 | 0.46 |
| 00:35:00 | 372.23 | 371.67 | 0.56 | 322.21 | 322.23 | −0.02 | 1.35 |
| 00:41:00 | 375.06 | 374.61 | 0.46 | 322.36 | 322.38 | −0.01 | 0.62 |
| 00:47:00 | 373.82 | 373.42 | 0.40 | 321.41 | 321.43 | −0.02 | 1.14 |
| 00:53:00 | 371.67 | 371.26 | 0.42 | 321.36 | 321.38 | −0.02 | 1.69 |
| 00:59:00 | 371.88 | 371.66 | 0.22 | 322.39 | 322.39 | 0.00 | 0.14 |

**Table 4.** The differences between measured and calculated temperatures.

The residuals and the sum of temperature difference squares are small. The obtained results show that the proposed method can be successfully applied to identify the operating conditions of water walls in boilers.

Similar measurements and calculations were performed for the insert located at a height of 19.2 m. The results of measurements and calculations are shown in **Figures 15** and **16**.

Measuring insert at an elevation of 15.4 m is situated directly above the burners which makes the value of absorbed heat flux $q_m$ higher in comparison with the absorbed heat flux at a height of 19.2 m. At the level of 15.4 m, heat flux is approximately 230 000 W/m$^2$ while at the height of 19.2 m is about 168 000 W/m$^2$. It is worth mentioning a very high lifetime of measuring heat flux tubes, which is more than 5 years.

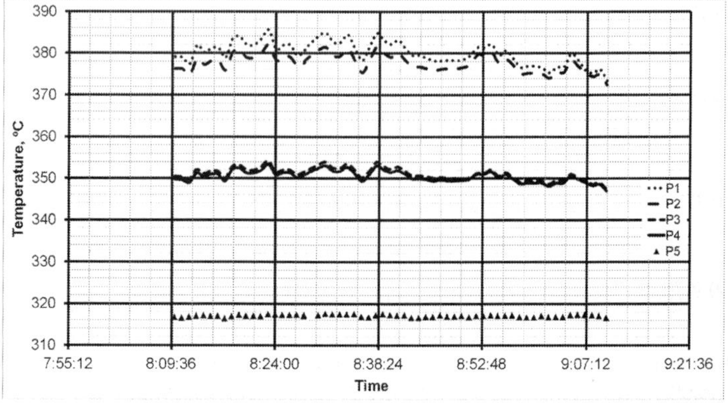

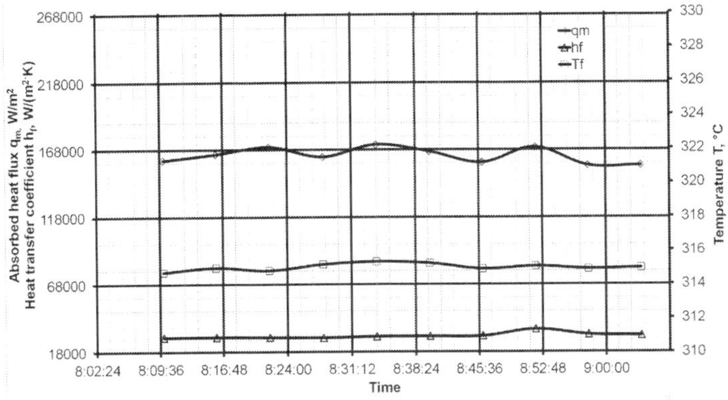


**Figure 15.** Measured temperature histories at five points for heat flux tube located at the level of 19.2 m (a) and estimated parameters: absorbed heat flux $q_m$, heat transfer coefficient $h_f$ and fluid temperature $T_f$ (b).

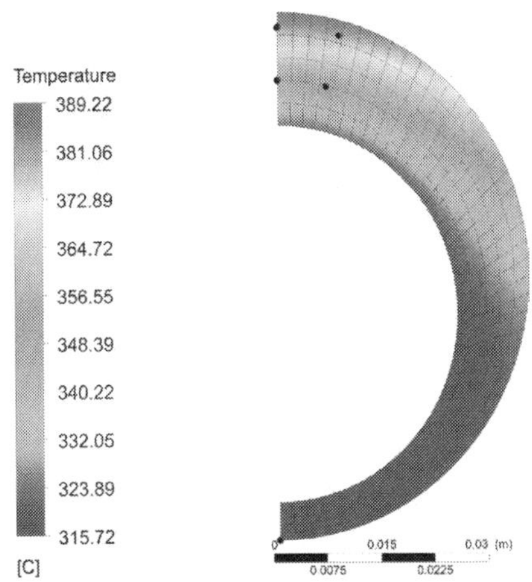


**Figure 16.** Temperature distribution in the cross section of the flux tube located at the level of 19.2 m. which was determined on the basis of measured temperatures: $T_1$ = 382.170°C; $T_2$ = 379.040°C; $T_3$ = 352.270°C; $T_4$ = 351.460°C; $T_5$ = 317.300°C. The estimated parameters are: $q_m$ = 166 577.5 W/m²; $h_f$ = 29 489.5 W/(m² K); $T_f$ = 315.21°C.

## 3. Identification of thermal boundary conditions in heat exchangers of fluidized bed boilers

Circulating fluidized bed (CFB) boilers burning coal or biomass are in use for several years. Fluidized bed combustion is widely used in power boilers due to its impressive environmental performance and also its fuel flexibility. Therefore, the studies of combustion and heat transfer are the subject of many recent investigations aimed at improving the design and operation of CFB boilers. Sun et al. [35] applied wide size biomass and investigated its combustion, heat transfer, and emission characteristics in CFB [35]. They found that co-firing wide screening crushed biomass pellets in CFB may reduce emissions and enhance heat transfer. Sundaresan and Kolar [36] conducted experiments to determine the total surface-average heat transfer coefficients from the tube to suspension for vertical tubes of different heights, which were placed in the core of a square cold CFB riser.

Superheaters and reheaters are the surfaces that achieve the highest temperatures in a boiler and for this reason require a lot of attention in the design, fabrication, operation, and maintenance to ensure that the permissible metal temperatures are never exceeded. A standard method for hydraulic calculation and design of boilers is described in [37]. The hydraulic calculation of superheater aims to provide the safe temperature of superheater tubes, efficient flow arrangement, and determination of pressure losses. Considerable attention has been given to hydraulic maldistribution in steam superheater tubes. A standard method for thermal design of steam boilers, including superheaters, was developed in [38]. Although the boiler standards are extensively used by manufacturers of boilers, they adopt for the calculation of the superheaters procedures which are used in design or performance calculations of usual heat exchangers assuming constant physical fluid properties [37–40]. For superheated steam, a constant value of the specific heat cannot be assumed because of the strong dependence on temperature. The specific heat of the water steam can decrease even twice over the length of the superheater tube.

The basic superheater and reheater design principles are discussed in detail by Rayaprolu [39]. Thermal and flow process in large steam boilers are the subject of the book [40]. Design and performance procedures for calculating of coal-fired boilers were described. Much attention has been paid to analyzing start-ups of steam boilers. Approximately 40% of all boiler failures are caused by damage of steam superheaters due to the overheating of the tube material [41]. Because of this, steam superheaters are modeled mathematically or monitored to avoid overheating of tubes. CFD simulations and optimization results of a 300 MW lignite-fired power boiler are presented by Tzolakis et al. [42]. A heat recovery steam generator (HRSG) was optimized by Behbahaninia using the genetic algorithm [43]. The results show that the thermodynamic optimization is not capable of decreasing significantly the total cost of the HRSG. Mathematical modeling of the boiler superheater was presented in not many publications despite a great interest of boiler manufacturers. This is mainly due to the difficulty of the description of complex flow and heat transfer processes taking place in the steam superheaters both in pulverized coal and fluidized boilers. A numerical method for modeling of the superheaters in pulverized coal-fired boilers was developed in [44, 45]. Much trouble causes the flue-gas temperature unevenness in a duct where a superheater is situated. A thermal load deviation model for the superheater and reheater in a utility boiler is presented by Xu et al. [46]. Many failure analyses on the superheaters were carried out to reveal the causes of tube overheating or tube rapture. The unevenness of the steam temperature is one of the main reasons for boiler tube failures. The 320 MW natural gas-fired boiler was simulated using the

CFD code by Rahimi et al. [47]. The main goal of the computational analysis was to detect the reason for the tube rupture inside the boiler. A new procedure for determining heat flux in superheater and reheater tubes based on the empirical formulas and the finite element modeling is presented by Purbolaksono et al. [48]. The finite element simulations were performed by Othman et al. [49] to find the main reason for superheater tube deformations. It was revealed that the failure of the tubes occurred due to the restriction of the tube deformations. Local short-term overheating of the tubes due to concentrated flue-gas flow was the primary cause of superheater tube failure [50]. A failure analysis was carried out using visual inspections and in situ measurements of hardness the experimental examination was supplemented by finite element analyzes. The rate of corrosive wear in superheaters of supercritical boilers was presented in the paper by Pronobis and Wojnar [51]. The slagging and fouling processes in superheaters influence the efficiency and lifetime of the boiler. Harding and O'Connor used the ten-year database to determine the lost generated through forced outages due to the coal quality or slagging and fouling issues [52]. A computer system for monitoring slagging and fouling of superheaters is described in [24].

Direct and inverse problems in a platen superheater situated in the combustion chamber of a CFB boiler were studied in [2].

The review of the state of the art in the field of superheaters shows that published papers on the superheaters present mostly experimental results and relate to search for the causes of failures of superheater tubes or analyze ash fouling.

In this work, the finite volume modeling of a platen superheater is presented. The fluidized bed boilers steam superheaters are placed in the combustion chamber and are made of tubes with non-circular cross sections, to avoid erosion and slagging (**Figure 17**). Due to the complex shape of the cross section of superheater tubes (**Figure 18**), numerical modeling has been applied to correctly determine the temperature distribution of steam and tube wall. Accurate calculating the superheater tube wall temperature is necessary because of the high prices of alloy steels used in superheater manufacturing.

A CFD simulation will be carried out for the platen superheater located in the combustion chamber of the CFB boiler. The second stage superheater is situated in the upper part of the combustion chamber of a circulating fluidized bed boiler (CFB boiler) with the capacity of 425 $\cdot 10^3$ kg/h steam. The steam boiler with a live steam temperature equal 560°C and a pressure of 16.1 MPa has an atmospheric circulating fluidized bed furnace. The superheater is a three-pass heat exchanger. The water steam flows inside the tubes while the flue gas with a constant temperature flows upwards in a perpendicular direction to the tube axes. Two inverse problems will be solved. First, the flue-gas side heat transfer coefficient $h_g$ will be determined using temperatures measured at the outlet and inlet of the heat exchanger. This coefficient is essential for the proper design of superheaters in fluidized bed boilers. In the second inverse problem, in addition, to the heat transfer coefficient $h_g$ will also be searched the steam temperature at the inlet to the superheater based on the measured steam temperatures at three points located at the ends of the superheater passes. Such inverse problem is encountered in a superheater steam temperature controllers.

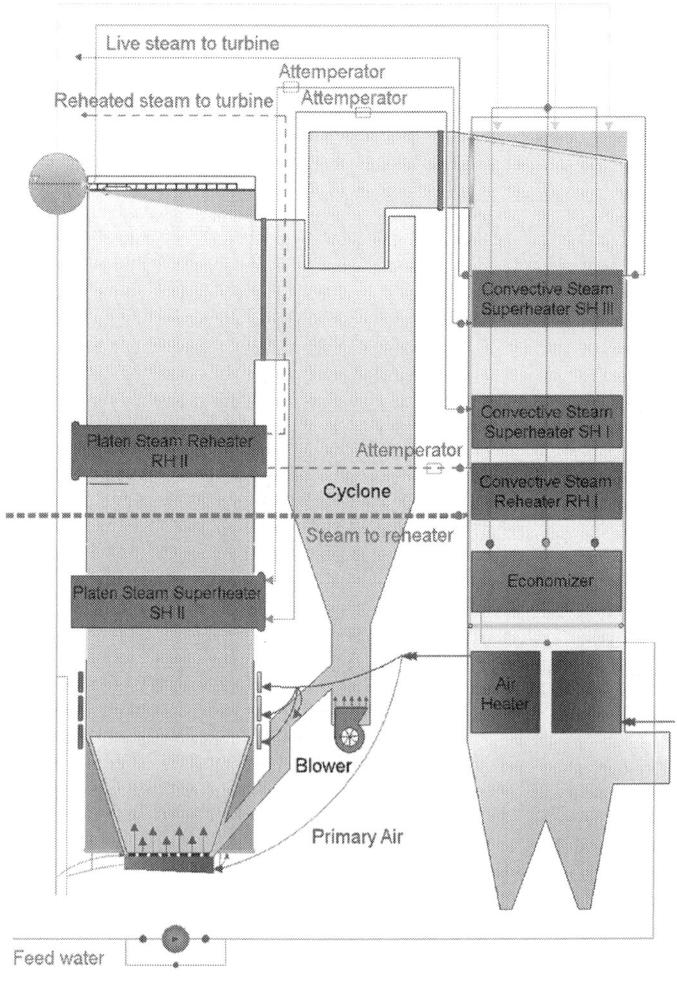


**Figure 17.** The arrangement of heating surfaces in circulating fluidized bed boiler with a steam capacity of $425 \cdot 10^3$ kg/h.

On modern large steam boilers, the temperature must be held close to design values since excessive temperatures have a serious effect on the metal lifetime of all parts of a boiler which are subject to it. The inlet steam temperature will be determined from the solution of the inverse problem. Based on this temperature, a correct flow rate of cooling water to the spray-type desuperheater (attemperator) is calculated. Despite the great practical importance, this type inverse heat transfer problems have not yet been analyzed.

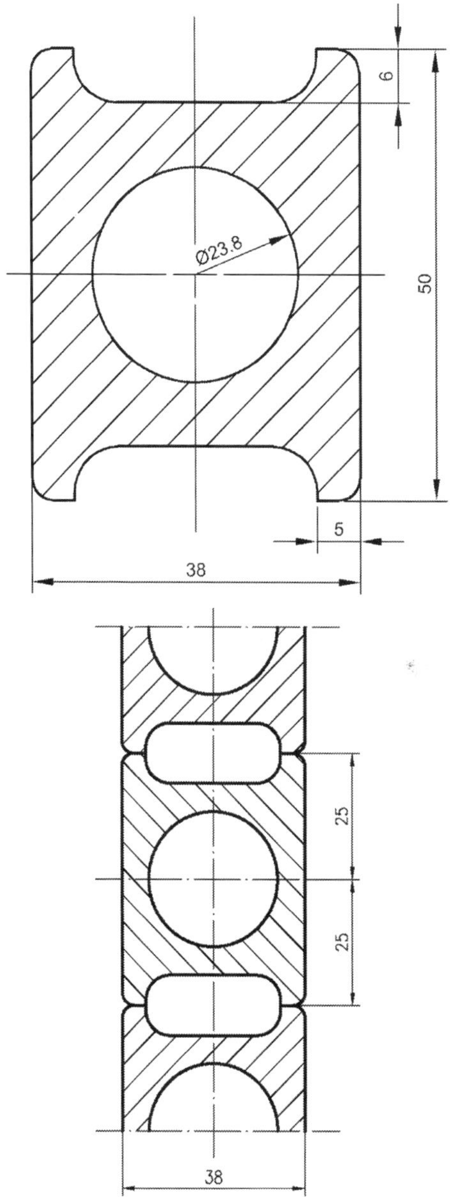


**Figure 18.** Platen superheater made from "omega" tubes; (a) cross section of omega tube, (b) platen superheater cross-section.

## 4. Description of the numerical method

Velocity, pressure, and temperature of the steam, as well as the temperature of the tube wall with the complex cross section, will be computed using the ANSYS/CFX v13.0 software [25].

The direct and inverse problems will be solved. In the inverse problem, the steam temperature at the superheater inlet and the heat transfer coefficient on the flue-gas side will be determined using measured steam temperatures at selected locations in the superheater. If the flue-gas side heat transfer coefficient is determined based on the measured steam temperature at the superheater outlet, the secant method is used. In this case, it is assumed that the inlet steam temperature is also measured. The Levenberg–Marquardt method is used to solve the least squares problem when the inlet steam temperature and the flue-gas side heat transfer coefficient are determined based on the measured steam temperature at the selected points along the steam flow path. At every iteration step, a direct problem was solved using the ANSYS/CFX v13.0 software. Time-averaged three-dimensional equations of conservation of mass, momentum and energy are solved using an element-based finite volume method. The heat transfer in the flowing steam was modeled using equations of mass, momentum, and energy conservation which can be written as follows [25]:

$$\frac{\partial \rho}{\partial t} + \nabla \cdot (\rho \mathbf{U}) = 0 \tag{19}$$

$$\frac{\partial (\rho \mathbf{U})}{\partial t} + \nabla \cdot (\rho \mathbf{U} \otimes \mathbf{U}) = -\nabla p + \nabla \cdot \tau + \mathbf{S_M} \tag{20}$$

$$\frac{\partial (\rho h)}{\partial t} - \frac{\partial p}{\partial t} + \nabla \cdot (\rho \mathbf{U} h) = \nabla \cdot (k \nabla T) + \mathbf{U} \cdot \nabla p + \tau : \nabla \mathbf{U} + \mathbf{S_E} \tag{21}$$

where the stress tensor $\tau$ is related to the strain rate by

$$\tau = \mu(\nabla \mathbf{U} + (\nabla \mathbf{U})^T - \frac{2}{3} \delta \nabla \cdot \mathbf{U}) \tag{22}$$

Temperature distribution in double omega tube walls (**Figure 18**) is governed by the heat conduction equation

$$c_w \rho_w \frac{\partial T_w}{\partial t} = \nabla \cdot [k_w(T_w) \nabla T_w] \tag{23}$$

Two equation turbulence model SST (Shear Stress Transport), which was developed based on the Wilcox $k$–$\omega$ and $k$–$\varepsilon$ turbulence models [53], was used to model the flow turbulence. The baseline $k$–$\omega$ model is a two equations turbulence model that offers a good compromise between numerical effectiveness and computational accuracy. This model is a combination of the $k$–$\omega$ and $k$–$\varepsilon$ models.

The Wilcox $k$–$\omega$ model is given by two equations:

$$\frac{\partial(\rho k)}{\partial t}+\frac{\partial}{\partial x_j}\left(\rho U_j k\right)=\frac{\partial}{\partial x_j}\left[\left(\mu+\frac{\mu_t}{\sigma_{k1}}\right)\frac{\partial k}{\partial x_j}\right]+P_k-\beta'\rho k\omega \tag{24}$$

$$\frac{\partial(\rho\omega)}{\partial t}+\frac{\partial}{\partial x_j}\left(\rho U_j\omega\right)=\frac{\partial}{\partial x_j}\left[\left(\mu+\frac{\mu_t}{\sigma_{\varpi 1}}\right)\frac{\partial\omega}{\partial x_j}\right]+\alpha_1\frac{\omega}{k}P_k-\beta_1'\rho\omega^2 \tag{25}$$

To develop the baseline $k$–$\omega$ turbulence model, the transformed $k$–$\varepsilon$ model is also used:

$$\frac{\partial(\rho k)}{\partial t}+\frac{\partial}{\partial x_j}\left(\rho U_j k\right)=\frac{\partial}{\partial x_j}\left[\left(\mu+\frac{\mu_t}{\sigma_{k2}}\right)\frac{\partial k}{\partial x_j}\right]+P_k-\beta'\rho k\omega \tag{26}$$

$$\begin{aligned}&\frac{\partial(\rho\omega)}{\partial t}+\frac{\partial}{\partial x_j}(\rho U_j\omega)=\\&=\frac{\partial}{\partial x_j}\left[\left(\mu+\frac{\mu_t}{\sigma_{\varpi 2}}\right)\frac{\partial\omega}{\partial x_j}\right]+2\rho\frac{1}{\sigma_{\varpi 2}\,\omega}\frac{\partial k}{\partial x_j}\frac{\partial\omega}{\partial x_j}+\alpha_2\frac{\omega}{k}P_k-\beta_2\rho\omega^2\end{aligned} \tag{27}$$

Multiplying Eqs. (24) and (25) of the Wilcox model by weighting function $F_1$, the transformed $k$–$\varepsilon$ Eqs. (26) and (27) by a weighting function $(1-F_1)$ and adding the transformed equations gives the baseline $k$–$\omega$ model:

$$\frac{\partial(\rho k)}{\partial t}+\frac{\partial}{\partial x_j}(\rho U_j k)=\frac{\partial}{\partial x_j}\left[\left(\mu+\frac{\mu_t}{\sigma_{k3}}\right)\frac{\partial k}{\partial x_j}\right]+P_k-\beta'\rho k\omega+P_{kb} \tag{28}$$

$$\begin{aligned}&\frac{\partial(\rho\omega)}{\partial t}+\frac{\partial}{\partial x_j}(\rho U_j\omega)=\\&=\frac{\partial}{\partial x_j}\left[\left(\mu+\frac{\mu_t}{\sigma_{\omega 3}}\right)\frac{\partial\omega}{\partial x_j}\right]+(1-F_1)2\rho\frac{1}{\sigma_{\omega 2}\,\omega}\frac{\partial k}{\partial x_j}\frac{\partial\omega}{\partial x_j}+\alpha_3\frac{\omega}{k}P_k-\beta_3\rho\omega^2+P_{\omega b}\end{aligned} \tag{29}$$

The baseline $k$–$\omega$ model has the advantages of the Wilcox $k$–$\omega$, and the $k$–$\varepsilon$ but is not able to predict onset and amount of flow separation from smooth surfaces [53]. The main reason for this drawback is neglecting of the transport of the turbulent shear stress. This causes an over-prediction of the eddy-viscosity. In order to eliminate this deficiency, the shear stress transport (SST) turbulence model was developed [53], in which the turbulent viscosity $\nu_t$ is limited by the following equation:

$$\nu_t = \frac{\alpha_1 k}{\max(\alpha_1 \omega, SF_2)} \tag{30}$$

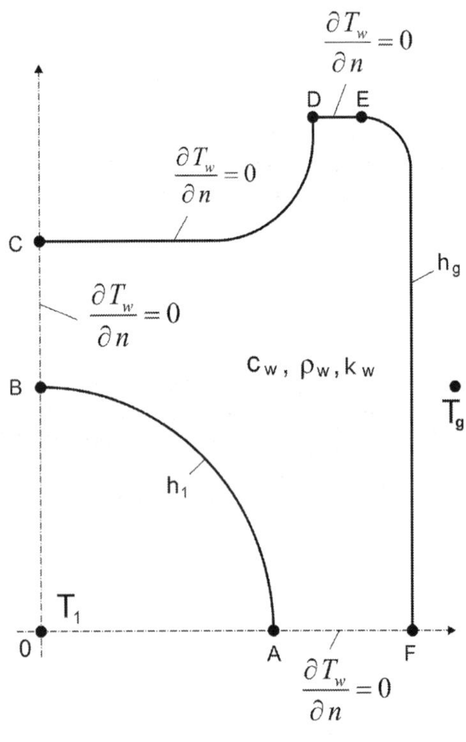


**Figure 19.** One-fourth of a tube cross section.

Because of the symmetry, only one-fourth of a tube cross section was analyzed (**Figure 19**). Heat is transferred by convection from the combustion chamber to the tube through the surface E–F. The surfaces A–F and B–C–D–E are thermally insulated. The tube inner surface A–B is cooled by the flowing live steam. The following boundary conditions were assumed for the tube wall (**Figure 19**):

$$T|_{A-B} = T_w|_{A-B}, \quad k\frac{\partial T}{\partial n}|_{A-B} = -k_w\frac{\partial T_w}{\partial n}|_{A-B} \tag{31}$$

$$k_w\frac{\partial T_w}{\partial n}|_{B-C-D-E} = 0 \tag{32}$$

$$k_w\frac{\partial T_w}{\partial n}|_{E-F} = h_g\left(T_g - T_w|_{E-F}\right) \tag{33}$$

$$k_w\frac{\partial T_w}{\partial n}|_{A-F} = 0 \tag{34}$$

Also, the fluid temperature and the steam mass flow rate or steam velocity are known at the inlet of the tube. The steam pressure is given at the outlet of the tube. The direct conjugate heat transfer problem described by Eqs. (19) and (29) with appropriate boundary conditions was solved using the ANSYS/CFX software.

## 5. Results of the superheater modeling using ANSYS//CFX

The ANSYS CFX commercial software v13.0 [25] was used for the numerical calculations. Computer calculations were carried out for the second stage of the steam superheater which is made of omega tubes from 10CrMo 910 low alloy steel. At first, direct and inverse problems were solved for the single tube representing the first pass of the superheater. A finite element mesh contains 1 233 999 elements and 747 945 finite element nodes. The cross section of the tube is shown in **Figure 18**. The length of the modeled tube is 8 517 mm. Thermal properties of the superheated steam were calculated using the industrial standard IAPWS-IF97 [54]. Changes in thermal conductivity with temperature for the 10CrMo 910 steel are shown in **Figure 20**.

At first, test simulations were performed for the following data:

- $T_{in}$ = 462°C—temperature of the superheated steam at tube inlet,
- $P_{out}$ = 16.5 MPa—pressure of the steam at tube outlet,
- $T_g$ = 850°C—flue-gas temperature in the combustion chamber,
- $h_g$ = 200 W/(m$^2$ K)—heat transfer coefficient on the gas side.

Two different steam inlet velocities $u_{in}$: 16.7 m/s and 10 m/s were assumed at the inlet of the tube to illustrate the influence of the steam side conditions on the steam and tube wall

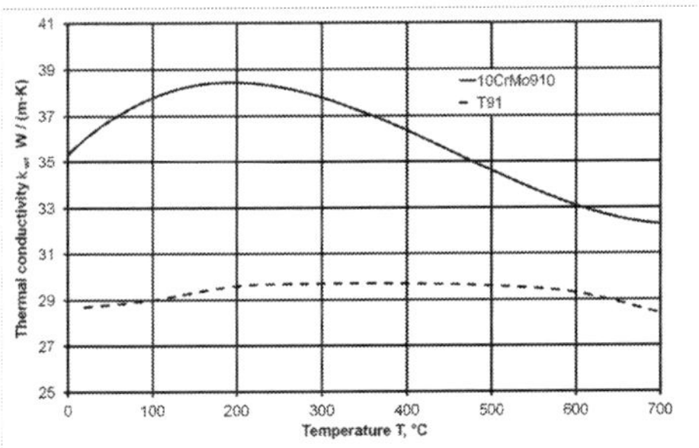


**Figure 20.** The thermal conductivity of 10CrMo 910 and T91 steels as a function of temperature.

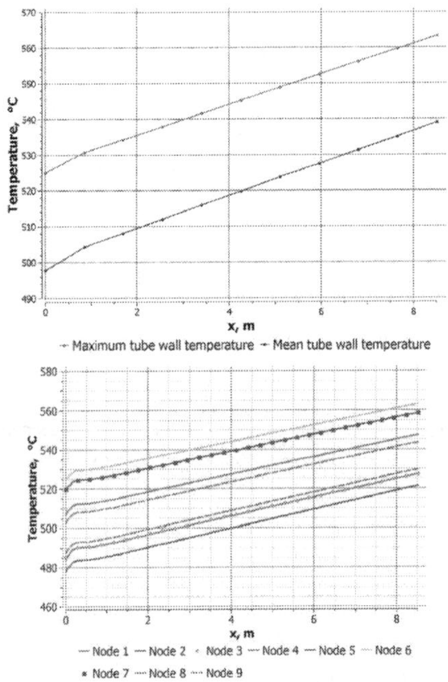


**Figure 21.** Tube wall temperature; (a) changes of mean and maximum tube wall temperature over the tube length, (b) temperature of the tube wall at the nodes: 1, 2, 3, 4, 5, 7, 8, and 9 over the tube length; $u_{in}$ = 16.7 m/s, $h_g$ = 200 W/(m$^2$ K).

temperature. The steam velocity of 16.7 m/s corresponds to 100% boiler load, while the steam velocity equal to 10 m/s corresponds to the partial boiler load. Then, to assess the impact of the gas side heat transfer coefficient $h_g$ on the temperature of the steam and tube, calculations for $u_{in}$ = 16.7 m/s and $h_g$ = 250 W/(m$^2$ K) were also carried out.

The results of the computer simulation for $u_{in}$ = 16.7 m/s and $h_g$ = 200 W/(m$^2$ K) are shown in **Figures 21–23**.

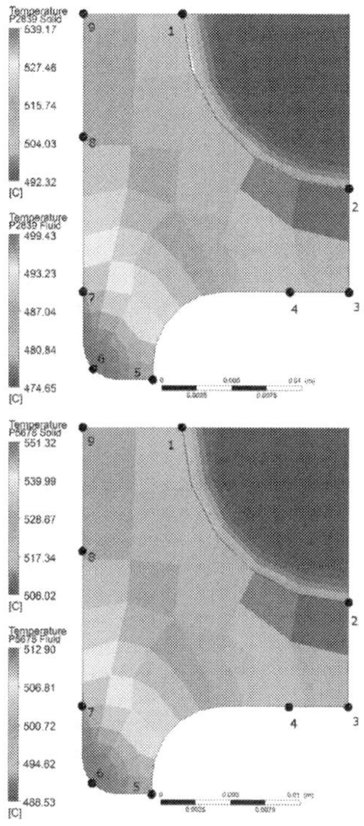

Figure 22. The temperature distribution in the tube wall and steam in two cross sections; (a) at the distance of 2839 mm from the inlet; (b) at the distance of 5678 mm from the inlet; $u_{in}$ = 16.7 m/s, $h_g$ = 200 W/(m$^2$ K).

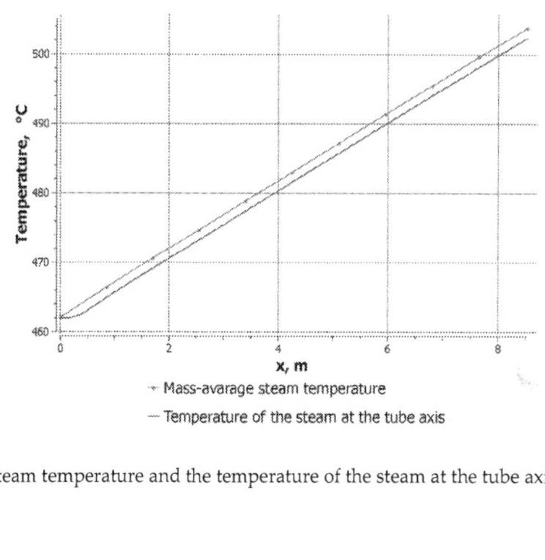


Figure 23. Mass-average steam temperature and the temperature of the steam at the tube axis.

From the analysis of the results shown in **Figure 21a** and **b**, it can be seen that the steam temperature over the tube length grows almost linearly. Only, in the region close to the tube inlet the wall temperature is lower. This is due to much higher heat transfer coefficient in the developing flow which occurs at the inlet region of the tube. The steam in the boundary layer is cool at the inlet section, which contributes to a better cooling tube wall. It should be noted that the difference between the maximum and average temperature over the tube cross section is large but does not exceed 30 K (**Figure 21a**).

The rise of the tube wall temperature is almost linear over a length of the tube due to the constant value of the heat transfer coefficient in the region of the developed flow. At the entrance section of the tube, the heat transfer coefficient is higher because of developing a fluid flow. In this region, the temperature difference over the boundary layer is greater, so the heat flux and heat transfer coefficient are larger, and tube temperature is lower. **Figures 22a** and **6b** show the temperature distribution in the tube wall and steam at two cross sections away from the inlet, respectively at the distance of 2 839 mm and 5 678 mm. The maximum temperature of the wall is at the tube edge (**Figure 22a**). This temperature is 539.2°C at the distance of 2 839 mm and 551.3°C at the distance of 5678 mm from the inlet of the tube. The increase of the mass-average steam temperature over the entire length of the tube is 41 K (**Figure 23**).

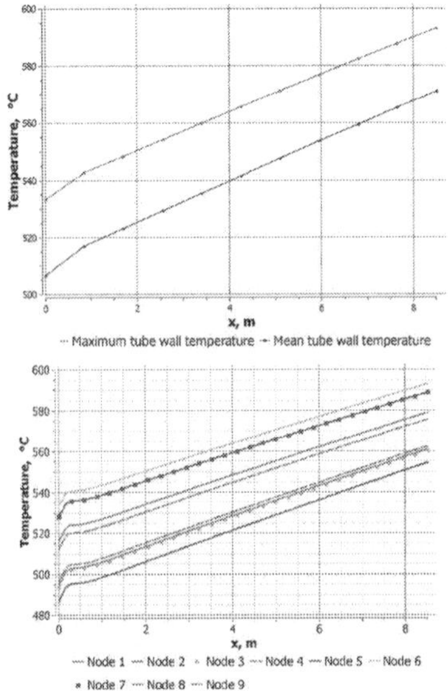


**Figure 24.** Tube wall temperature; (a) changes of mean and maximum tube wall temperature over the tube length, (b) temperature of the tube wall at the nodes: 1, 2, 3, 4, 5, 7, 8, and 9 over the tube length; $u_{in}$ = 10 m/s, $h_g$ = 200 W/(m$^2$ K).

The value obtained from the numerical simulation is in good agreement with the measured rise in the steam temperature. Steam temperature is highest near the inner surface of the tube.

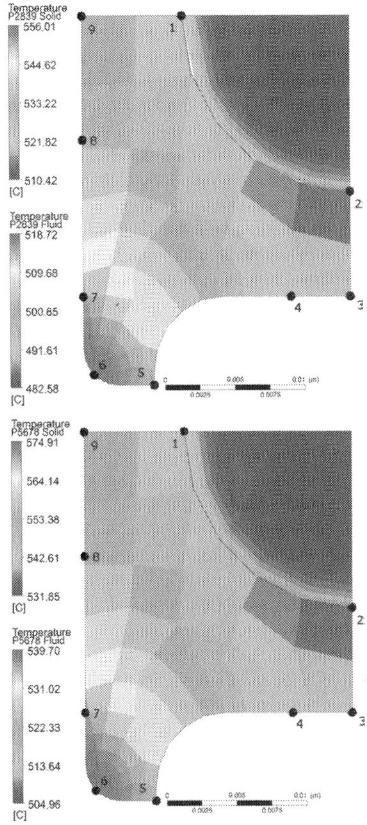


**Figure 25.** The temperature distribution in the tube wall and steam in two cross sections; (a) at the distance of 2839 mm from the inlet; (b) at the distance of 5678 mm from the inlet; $u_{in}$ = 10 m/s, $h_g$ = 200 W/(m²·K).

For the two different steam velocities at the inlet to the pipe: 16.7 m/s and 10 m/s the difference between the mass-average temperature of the steam and temperature in the axis of the tube is small (**Figure 23**). Tube wall temperatures are higher when the steam velocity at the inlet is lower and equal to $u_{in}$ = 10 m/s. The results of the computer simulation for $u_{in}$ = 10 m/s and $h_g$ = 200 W/(m$^2$ K) are shown in **Figures 24** and **25**. A similar effect on the tube wall temperature has the heat transfer coefficient on the flue-gas side. The CFD simulation was thus performed for the velocity of the steam at the tube inlet: $u_{in}$ = 16.7 m/s and the heat transfer coefficient on the gas side: $h_g$ = 250 W/(m$^2$ K), that is, the heat transfer coefficient was increased by 50 W/(m$^2$ K). The CFD simulation results are shown in **Figures 26** and **27**. If the heat transfer coefficient on the gas side is $h_g$ = 250 W/(m$^2$ K) then the steam and tube wall temperature is higher, because the heat flow rate transferred from flue gas to the steam is larger (**Figures 26** and **27**).

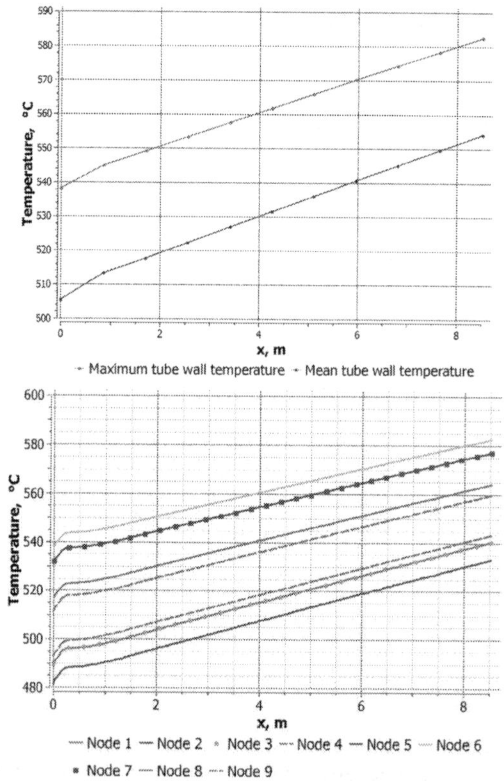


**Figure 26.** Tube wall temperature; (a) changes of mean and maximum tube wall temperature over the tube length, (b) temperature of the tube wall at the nodes: 1, 2, 3, 4, 5, 7, 8, and 9 over the tube length; $u_{in}$ = 16.7 m/s, $h_g$ = 250 W/(m² K).

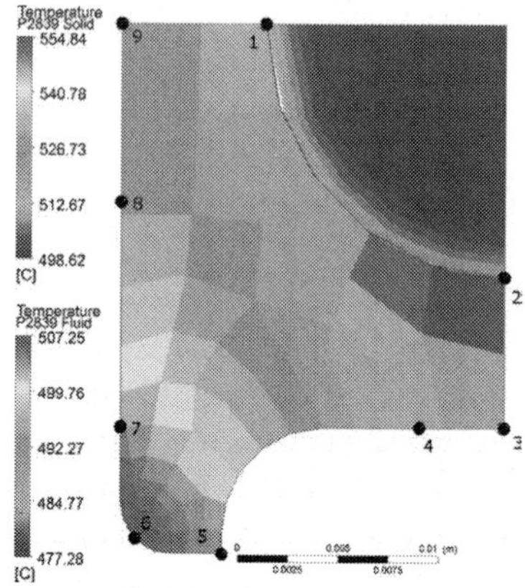

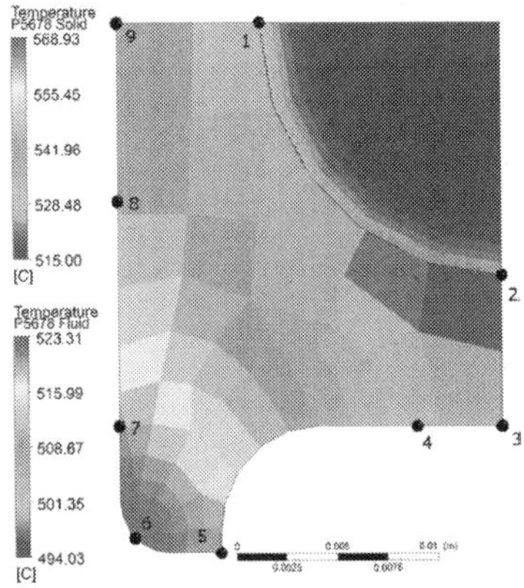

**Figure 27.** The temperature distribution in the tube wall and steam in two cross sections; (a) at the distance of 2839 mm from the inlet; (b) at the distance of 5678 mm from the inlet; $u_{in}$ = 16.7 m/s, $h_g$ = 250 W/(m² K).

The correctness of the results obtained using CFD simulation was examined using the energy balance equation. The heat flow rate $\dot{Q}_{out}$ transmitted through the outer surface of the tube with an area of $A_{out}$, which is given by the integral

$$\dot{Q}_{out} = \int_{A_{out}} \dot{q}_{out} dA \tag{35}$$

should be equal to the heat flow rate $\dot{Q}_{in}$ transmitted through the inner surface

$$\dot{Q}_{in} = \int_{A_{in}} \dot{q}_{in} dA \tag{36}$$

and to the heat flow rate $\dot{Q}_s$ absorbed by the steam

$$\dot{Q}_s = \dot{m}(h_{outlet} - h_{inlet}) \tag{37}$$

where $h_{inlet}$ and $h_{oulet}$ stand for the steam enthalpy at the inlet and the outlet of the superheater tube, respectively, and $\dot{m}$ denotes the steam mass flow rate. The symbols $\dot{q}_{out}$ and $\dot{q}_{in}$ designate the heat flux at the outer and inner tube surface. It has been proved that the solution is independent of the finite volume mesh. Twelve different meshes were examined. The finite element number ranged from 790 179 to 3 789 699. For the CFD simulations presented in the work, the mesh consisting of 1 233 999 elements with the total number of nodes equal to 747 945 was selected. The quality requirements for the finite element mesh, given in the CFX

Reference Guide, were satisfied. The mesh statistics like the orthogonal angle, expansion factor, and aspect ratio were confirmed by the CFX solver that they are correct [25].

For the analyzed case: $u_{in} = 16.7$ m/s, $h_g = 200$ W/(m$^2$ K) and for the mesh consisting of 1 233 999 elements, the following values of the heat flow rate were obtained:

$$\dot{Q}_{out} = \dot{Q}_{in} = =57.266\,\text{kW and}\,57.644\,\text{kW}.$$

The relative difference defined as:

$$\varepsilon_Q = \frac{0.5(\dot{Q}_{in} + \dot{Q}_{out}) - \dot{Q}_s}{0.5(\dot{Q}_{in} + \dot{Q}_{out})} 100, \%$$

is: $\varepsilon_Q = -0.656\%$

If the number of elements was increased to 3 789 699, then the relative difference is almost the same and equal to: $\varepsilon_Q = -0.655\%$.

The consistency of the results is very good. Taking into account that in the inverse problem is solved iteratively, the direct problem is repeatedly solved so the element mesh cannot be too fine because of computing time.

## 6. Inverse problem

Ten platens of the superheater SH II are located at combustion chamber of the circulating fluidized bed boiler (**Figure 17**). Steam temperature is measured outside of the combustion chamber at the points 1–4. Because these points are located outside of a fire region, it is easy to measure steam temperature by attaching the thermocouple to the tube outer surface that is thermally insulated (**Figure 28**).

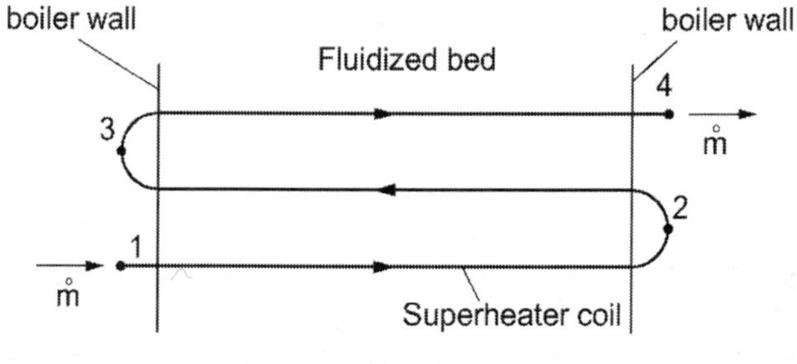


**Figure 28.** Three pass single superheater coil.

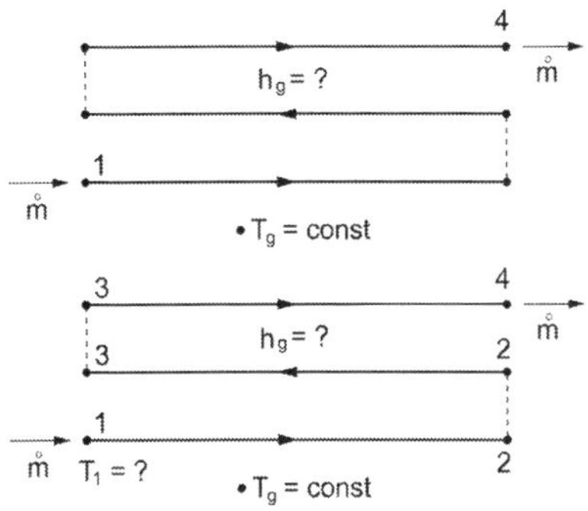


**Figure 29.** Inverse problem for a three pass second stage platen superheater, (a) flue-gas side heat transfer coefficient $\alpha_g$ is determined based on steam temperature measured at point number 4, (b) flue-gas side heat transfer coefficient $h_g$ and inlet steam temperature $T_1$ are determined based on steam temperature measured at points 2, 3, and 4.

| No. | Input data | | | | | Results | |
|---|---|---|---|---|---|---|---|
| | $\dot{m}$, kg/s | $T_g$, °C | $P_4$, MPa | $f_1$, °C | $f_4$, °C | $\alpha_g$, W/(m²K) | $P_1$, MPa |
| 1 | 0.2644 | 812.7 | 8.73 | 366.54 | 508.45 | 115.54 | 8.82 |
| 2 | 0.3148 | 826.78 | 10.12 | 379.35 | 505.74 | 123.83 | 10.22 |
| 3 | 0.4616 | 866.11 | 13.71 | 393.79 | 501.04 | 160.59 | 13.86 |

**Table 5.** Input data and results for the first inverse problem (**Figure 27a**).

Two different inverse problems were solved. The first and second inverse problems are presented in **Figure 29a** and **b**, respectively. At first, a flue-gas side heat transfer coefficient $h_g$ was estimated based on the measured steam temperature at the outlet and at the end of the three pass platen superheater made from omega tubes with the length of 8517 mm (**Figure 29b**). Also flue-gas temperature $T_g$, steam mass flow rate $\dot{m}$ per one tube, and the outlet steam pressure $P_4$ are known from measurements **Figure 27a**. The inverse problem was solved for three data sets (**Table 5**). The heat transfer coefficient $h_g$ was adjusted to obtain the outlet steam temperature $T_4$ equal to the measured value $f_4$. The following nonlinear algebraic equation

$$T_4 - f_4 = 0 \tag{38}$$

was solved iteratively using the secant method [27, 28] to determine the flue-gas side heat transfer coefficient $h_g$. At every iteration step, the temperature distribution in the tube wall and steam was determined using ANSYS/CFX. The three pass steam superheater was divided into finite element mesh which has 3 603 132 finite elements and 2 207 434 nodes (**Figure 30**). The solution of the inverse problem (**Table 6**) was obtained only after a few iterations. The CFD simulation also enabled the determination of pressure $P_1$ at the inlet to the superheater (**Table 5**).

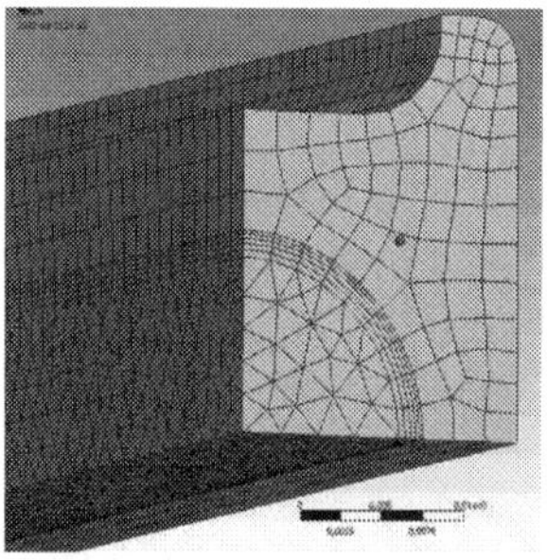

**Figure 30.** Finite volume mesh for a tube quarter.

| No. | Input data | | | | | | Results | | |
|---|---|---|---|---|---|---|---|---|---|
| | $\dot{m}$, kg/s | $T_g$, °C | $P_4$, MPa | $f_2$, °C | $f_3$, °C | $f_4$, °C | $h_g$, W/(m²·K) | $T_1$, °C | $P_1$, MPa |
| 1 | 0.2644 | 812.70 | 8.73 | 414.89 | 463.02 | 508.45 | 114.95 | 365.66 | 8.82 |
| 2 | 0.3148 | 826.78 | 10.12 | 422.43 | 464.00 | 505,74 | 121.65 | 379.68 | 10.22 |
| 3 | 0.4616 | 866.11 | 13.71 | 427.88 | 463.65 | 501.04 | 158.81 | 393.54 | 13.85 |

**Table 6.** Input data and results for the second inverse problem (**Figure 29b**).

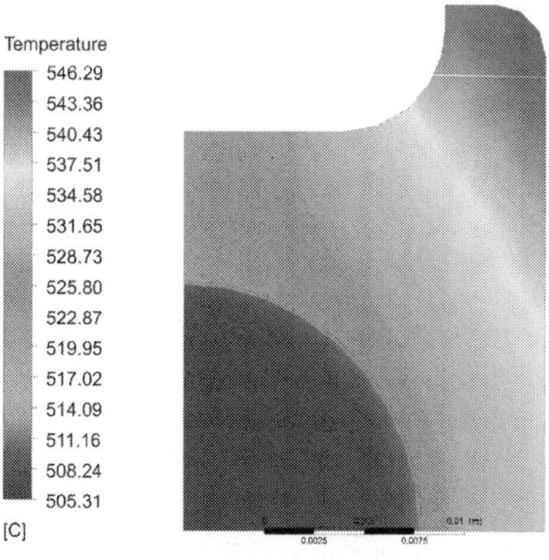


**Figure 31.** Steam and tube wall temperature distribution at the outlet of the three pass superheater for the data set number 1—three measurement points (**Table 6**).

In the second inverse problem, the flue-gas side heat transfer coefficient $x_1 = h_g$ and steam temperature $x_2 = T_1$ at the inlet of the superheater are two unknowns which were determined based on measured steam temperatures $f_2$, $f_3$, and $f_4$ at three points 2, 3, and 4 located at the outlets of each pass (**Figure 29b**). The number of measured temperatures is greater than the number of unknown parameters to increase the accuracy of the solution of the inverse problem. If the number of measuring points is greater, then the effect of random errors in temperature measurements on the results obtained from the solution of the inverse problem is smaller.

The least-squares method was used to determine parameters $h_g$ and $T_1$. The sum of squares

$$S = \sum_{i=2}^{4}(f_i - T_i)^2 \tag{39}$$

was minimized using the Levenberg–Marquardt method [26]. At every $k$-th iteration step, the steam temperature distribution $\mathbf{T}(\mathbf{x}^{(k)}, \mathbf{r}_i)$ is calculated, where $\mathbf{r}_i$designates the position vector of the steam measurements points. The steam and tube wall temperature were calculated at each iteration step using ANSYS/CFX software. The CFX program was called and controlled by an external program written in Python language [28]. The Levenberg–Marquardt algorithm was also included in the Python program. Three data sets were used in the inverse analysis (**Table 6**). From the analysis of the results shown in **Table 7**, it can be seen that the agreement between the calculated and measured steam temperature at the superheater inlet is very satisfactory. Also, the minimum value of the sum of squared temperature differences (39) is very small (**Table 7**). The similar values of the heat transfer coefficients $h_g$ were obtained from the solution of the first and second inverse problems (**Tables 5** and **7**).

The actual measured data were adopted for the inverse analysis: tube material—T91 steel, pass length—8517 mm. The thermal conductivity of T91 steel as a function of temperature is shown in **Figure 20**. The experimental data sets adopted for the inverse analysis and the estimated heat transfer coefficients $\alpha_g$ and steam inlet temperatures $T>_1$ are shown in **Table 6**. The computed temperatures at the measurement locations are very close to the measured values (**Table 7**). The minimum sum of the temperature difference squares is small.

The analysis of the results listed in **Table 7** shows that steam temperature increase is almost the same in each pass. Despite the decreasing temperature difference between the flue gas and steam the increases in steam temperature are: $(T_2 - T_1) = 42.51$ K, $(T_3 - T_2) = 42.31$ K, and $(T_4 - T_3) = 40.98$ K for the first, second, and third pass, respectively (**Table 7**, data set no. 2). The reason for this is a large reduction in the specific heat of the steam with the temperature. To achieve the same steam temperature rise in the third pass, much less heat flow rate is needed in comparison with the first pass.

The uncertainties of the determined parameters $\mathbf{x}^*$ were estimated using the error propagation rule of Gauss [29–33]. The propagation of uncertainty in the independent variables, that is, in measured steam temperatures $f_2$, $f_3$, and $f_4$, is estimated from the following equation:

$$2\sigma_{x_i} = \left[ \sum_{j=2}^{m} \left( \frac{\partial x_i}{\partial f_j} 2\sigma_{f_j} \right)^2 \right]^{\frac{1}{2}}, \quad m = 4, \quad i = 1,2 \tag{40}$$

The 95% uncertainty in the estimated parameters can be expressed in the form $x_i = x_i^* \pm \sigma_{x_i}$, where $x_i = x_i^*$, $i = 1, 2, 3$ represent the value of the parameters obtained using the least squares method.

Assuming that the 95% uncertainty in measured steam temperatures is equal $2\sigma_{fj} = 0.5$ K for $j = 2, 3, 4$ the uncertainties in calculated temperature $T_1$ and heat transfer coefficient $h_g$ are: $2\sigma_{T_1} = 0.74$ K and $2\sigma_{h_g} = 0.99$ W/(m$^2$K). The results are quite satisfactory.

| No. | $f_1$, °C / $T_1$, °C | $f_2$, °C / $T_2$, °C | $f_3$, °C / $T_3$, °C | $f_4$, °C / $T_4$, °C | $e = \frac{f_1 - T_1}{f_1} \cdot 100$, % | $S_{min}$, K$^2$ |
|---|---|---|---|---|---|---|
| 1 | 366.54 | 414.89 | 463.02 | 508.45 | 0.240 | 0.0006 |
| | 365.66 | 414.88 | 463.04 | 508.44 | | |
| 2 | 379.35 | 422.43 | 464.00 | 505.74 | −0.087 | 0.3752 |
| | 379.68 | 422.19 | 464.50 | 505.48 | | |
| 3 | 393.79 | 427.88 | 463.65 | 501.04 | 0.064 | 0.0384 |

**Table 7.** Comparison of measured and calculated steam temperatures at the inlet to the superheater and at measuring points 3, 4, and 5.

## 7. Conclusions

The chapter presents an effective method for solving nonlinear inverse heat transfer problems using CFD software. Application of the method is illustrated by the identification of the boundary conditions in water wall tubes and boundary conditions in a platen superheater of a CFB boiler.

A CFD-based method for determining heat flux absorbed by water-wall tubes, heat transfer coefficient at the inner flux-tube surface and temperature of the water-steam mixture has been presented. New heat flux tubes were proposed. The flux tubes are not welded to the adjacent water-wall tubes, so the temperature distribution in the measuring device is not affected by neighboring water-wall tubes. Based on the measured flux-tube temperatures the nonlinear inverse heat conduction problem was solved. The number of thermocouples placed inside the heat flux tube including the thermocouple on the rear outer tube surface is greater than the number of unknown parameters because additional measurement points reduce the uncertainty in determined parameters. To achieve a good accuracy of measurements, the uncertainties in measured heat flux-tube temperatures and the radial thermocouple locations should be small since they have the largest impact on the accuracy of the parameter estimation. The proposed flux tubes and the inverse procedure for determining absorbed heat flux can be used both when the inner surface of the heat flux tube is clean and when the scale or corrosion deposits are present on the inner surface what can occur after a long time service of the heat flux tube. The flux tubes can work for a long time in the destructive high-temperature atmosphere of a coal-fired boiler.

The CFD simulation of the thermal-hydraulic processes occurring in the platen steam superheater, located in the combustion chamber of the fluidized bed boiler, was carried out.

The temperature distributions in the tube wall of complex shape and the flowing steam were computed. The steam velocity and pressure distributions can be determined with high accuracy. The CFD modeling is a useful tool to explore the real fluid and heat flow phenomena which occur in platen superheaters operating at high thermal loads. It is well known that even a small increase in tube operating temperature over the design temperature will reduce stress rapture life significantly. The CFD simulation allows calculation of the maximum tube wall temperature along the steam flow path for complex cross section shape of the tubes and complicated flow arrangement of the superheater. The detailed CFD prediction makes possible the proper selection of the steel grade for the analyzed superheater stage or superheater pass.

The temperature-dependent physical properties of the steam and tube material can be easily taken into account. The specific heat of water steam decreases significantly with increasing temperature. The calculations show that the temperature rise in each of the three passes is almost the same in spite of decreasing the temperature difference between the flue gas and steam. If the specific heat were constant, the steam temperature increase in the third pass would be much smaller compared to the first pass. It should be stressed, that it would be impossible to calculate accurately the steam and tube wall temperature if the classical methods for heat exchanger calculations, which assume constant physical steam properties, were used.

Accurate calculation of the heat transfer coefficient on the flue-gas side of the platen superheater placed in the boiler furnace is critical for boiler design. The inaccurate calculation of the heat transfer coefficient is the reason for tubes damage due to an excessive steam temperature which frequently happens in power plants. A new method for determining of the flue-gas side heat transfer coefficient was developed.

The flue-gas side heat transfer coefficient or the inlet steam temperature and flue-gas side heat transfer coefficient were determined based on the measured steam temperatures at selected points along the steam flow path. To solve the inverse problems, the secant method was used when only one temperature measurement point was applied, and one unknown, that is, the heat transfer coefficient on the flue-gas side was searched. The Levenberg–Marquardt method was used to solve the over-determined heat transfer problem. For the solution of the direct conjugate heat transfer problem, which is encountered at every iteration step, while the inverse problem is being solved, ANSYS/CFX software was used.

Identifying the flue-gas side heat transfer coefficients for various boiler loads using the inverse method, a simple mathematical model of the platen superheater can be developed and used in the control system of the superheated steam temperature.

The proposed method of solution can be successfully applied to solve other inverse problems occurring in industrial practice.

## Nomenclature

| | |
|---|---|
| $c_w$ | specific heat capacity, J/(kg K) |
| $f_i$ | $i$-th measured steam temperature, K or °C |
| $F$ | weighting function |
| $F_2$ | blending function |
| $h$ | specific enthalpy, J/kg |
| $h_1, h_g$ | heat transfer coefficient on the inner and outer tube surface, W/(m$^2$ K) |
| $\mathbf{I}$ | identity matrix |
| $\mathbf{J}$ | Jacobian matrix |
| $k$ | turbulence kinetic energy, m$^2$/s$^2$ |
| $k_w$ | tube wall thermal conductivity, W/(m K) |
| $m$ | number of temperature measurements points |
| $\dot{m}$ | steam mass flow rate, kg/s |
| $n$ | outward normal, m |
| $n$ | number of unknowns parameters |
| $p$ | pressure, Pa |
| $P_k$ | production rate of turbulence energy, kg/(m s$^3$) |
| $P_\omega$ | turbulent frequency production term, s/m$^2$ |
| $\dot{q}$ | heat flux, W/m$^2$ |
| $\dot{Q}$ | heat flow rate, W/m$^3$ |
| $r$ | radius, m |
| $S$ | invariant measure of the strain rate, 1/s |
| $S_E$ | energy source, kg/(m s$^3$) |
| $S_M$ | momentum source, kg/(m$^2$ s$^2$) |
| $t$ | time, s |
| $T$ | fluid temperature, K or °C |
| $T_g$ | flue-gas temperature |
| $T_w$ | tube wall temperature, K or °C |
| $u$ | steam velocity, m/s |
| $\mathbf{U}$ | vector of velocity |

http://dx.doi.org/10.5772/63807

| | |
|---|---|
| $U_j$ | *j*-th velocity component |
| $x, y, z$ | Cartesian coordinates |
| $x_1, x_2, x_3$ | unknown parameters |
| $x_j$ | *j*th coordinate |

## Greek letters

| | |
|---|---|
| $\alpha, \beta, \beta'$ | model constant in the Wilcox k-ω turbulence model |
| $\delta$ | identity matrix |
| $\varepsilon$ | turbulence eddy dissipation, $m^2/s^3$ |
| $\mu$ | dynamic viscosity, kg/(m·s) |
| $\mu_t$ | turbulent dynamic viscosity, kg/(m·s) |
| $\nu_t$ | turbulent kinematic viscosity, $m^2/s$ |
| $\rho$ | density, $kg/m^3$ |
| $\rho_w$ | tube wall density, $kg/m^3$ |
| $\sigma$ | standard deviation |
| $\sigma_k$ | turbulence model constant in kinetic energy equation |
| $\sigma_\omega$> | k-ω turbulence model constant |
| $\tau$ | stress tensor |
| $\Omega$ | turbulent frequency, 1/s |
| $\nabla$ | gradient operator (nabla) |
| $\otimes$ | dyadic operator (tensor product) |

## Author details

Paweł Ludowski[1*], Dawid Taler[2] and Jan Taler[3]

*Address all correspondence to: pawel.ludowski@gmail.com

1 ABB Corporate Research Center, Cracow, Poland

2 Institute of Thermal Engineering and Air Protection, Cracow University of Technology, Cracow, Poland

3 Institute of Thermal Power Engineering, Cracow University of Technology, Cracow, Poland

## References

[1] Taler J, Taler D, Ludowski P. Measurements of local heat flux to membrane water walls of combustion chambers. Fuel 2014;115:70–83.

[2] Ludowski P, Taler D, Taler J. Identification of thermal boundary conditions in heat exchangers of fluidized bed boilers. Appl Therm Eng 2013;58:194–204

[3] Shimogori M, Mine T, Ohyatsu N, Takarayama N, Matsumura Y. Effects of fine ash particles and alkali metals on ash deposition characteristics at the initial stage of ash deposition determined in 1.5 MWth pilot plant tests. Fuel 2012;97:233–240.

[4] Vainikka P, Enestam S, Silvennoinen J, Taipale R, Yrjas P, Frantsi A, Hannula J, Hupa M. Bromine as an ash forming element in a fluidised bed boiler combusting solid recovered fuel. Fuel 2012;90:1101–1112.

[5] Liang Q, Guo X, Dai Z, Liu H, Gong X. An investigation on the heat transfer behavior and slag deposition of membrane wall in pilot-scale entrained-flow gasifier. Fuel 2012;102:491–498.

[6] Moghari M, Hosseini S, Shokouhmand H, Sharifi H, Izadpanah S. A numerical study on thermal behavior of a D-type water-cooled steam boiler. Appl Therm Eng 2012;37:360–372.

[7] Taler J, Duda P, Węglowski B, Zima W, Grądziel S, Sobota T, Taler D. Identification of local heat flux to membrane water-walls in steam boilers. Fuel 2009;88:305–311.

[8] Duda P, Taler J. A new method for identification of thermal boundary conditions in water wall tubes. Int J Heat Mass Transf 2009;52:1517–1524.

[9] Beckmann M, Krüger S. Online heat flux measurement at membrane walls of steam generators of municipal solid waste incinerators. In: Proceedings of the 24th Annual International Conference on Incineration and Thermal Treatment Technologies, IT3 Conference, Galveston, Texas, USA, May 9–13, 2005. College Park: University of Maryland; 2005, p. 1–18.

[10] Krüger S., Measurement of heat flux in steam generators, Dresden University of Technology, Faculty of Mechanical Engineering 978-3-935317-41-2. Neuruppin: TK Verlag Karl Thomé-Kozmiensky; 2009.

[11] Taler J, Taler D. Measurement of heat flux and heat transfer coefficient in heat flux processes. In: Cirimele G, D'Elia M, editors, Heat flux: processes, measurement techniques and applications, New York: Nova Science Publishers; 2012, p. 1–103.

[12] Seeger M, Taler J. Design and application of portable heat flux probes for measuring of specific thermal load in combustion chambers of steam boilers. Fortschr.-Ber. VDI Zeitschrift. Reihe 6. Nr 129. Düsseldorf: VDI-Verlag; 1983.

[13] Northover EW, Hitchcock JA. A heat flux meter for use in boiler furnaces. J Sci Instrum 1967;44:371–374.

[14] Neal SBHC, Northover EW. The measurement of radiant heat flux in large boiler furnaces-I. Problems of ash deposition relating to heat flux. Int J Heat Mass Transf 1980;23:1015–1022.

[15] Arai N, Matsunami A, Churchill SW. A review of measurements of heat flux density applicable to the field of combustion. Exp Therm Fluid Sci 1996;12:452–460.

[16] Taler J. Measurement of heat flux to steam boiler membrane water walls. VGB Kraftwerkstechnik 1990;70:540–546.

[17] Taler J. A method of determining local heat flux in boiler furnaces. Int J Heat Mass Transf 1992;35:1625–1634.

[18] Fang Z, Xie D, Diao N, Grace JR, Jim Lim C. A new method for solving the inverse conduction problem in steady heat flux measurement. Int J Heat Mass Transf 1997;40:3947–3953.

[19] Luan W, Bowen BD, Lim CJ, Brereton CMH, Grace JR. Suspension-to membrane-wall heat transfer in a circulating fluidized bed combustor. Int J Heat Mass Transf 2000;43:1173–1185.

[20] Sobota T, Taler D. The measurement of radiant heat flux in combustion chambers of large steam boilers. In: 8th World Congress on Computational Mechanics (WCCM8) and 5th European Congress on Computational Methods in Applied Sciences and Engineering (ECCOMAS 2008). Venice. June/July. 2008.

[21] Sobota T, Taler D. A simple method for measuring heat flux in boiler furnaces. Rynek Energii 2010;86:108–114.

[22] Valero A, Cortes C. Ash fouling in coal-fired utility boilers. Monitoring and optimization of on-load cleaning. Prog Energy Combust Sci 1996;22:189–200.

[23] Teruel E, Cortes C, Diez LI, Arauzo I. Monitoring and prediction of fouling in coal-fired utility boilers using neural networks. Chem Eng Sci 2005;60:5035–5048.

[24] Taler J, Trojan M, Taler D. Monitoring of ash fouling and internal scale deposits in pulverized coal fired boilers. In: Malach DE, editor. Advances in mechanical engineering research, Volume 1, New York: Nova Science Publishers; 2011, p. 91–131.

[25] ANSYS CFX 13. ANSYS Inc. Urbana. Illinois. USA. 2010.

[26] Marquardt W. An algorithm for least-squares estimation of nonlinear parameters. J Soc Ind Appl Math, 1963;11(2):431–441.

[27] Press WH, Teukolsky SA, Vetterling WT, Flannery BP. Numerical recipes in Fortran. The art of scientific computing. New York: Cambridge University Press; 2006.

[28] Kiusalaas J, Numerical methods in engineering with Python. second ed. New York: Cambridge University Press; 2010.

[29] ISO. Guide to the expression of uncertainty in measurement. Geneva: International Organization for Standardization; 1993.

[30] Moffat R. ASME Policy on reporting uncertainties in experimental measurements and results. ASME Heat Transf 2000;122:411–413.

[31] Bevington PR. Data reduction and error analysis for the physical sciences. New York: McGraw-Hill; 1969.

[32] Brandt S. Data analysis. Statistical and computational methods for scientists and engineers. 3rd ed. Berlin: Springer; 1999.

[33] Coleman HW, Steele WG. Experimentation, validation, and uncertainty analysis for engineers. 3rd ed. Hoboken: Wiley; 2009.

[34] Richter F. Temperature-dependent physical properties of steels. Düsseldorf: Mannesmann Forschungberichte 930; 1983.

[35] Sun P, Hui S, Gao Z, Zhou Q, Tan H, Zhao Q, Xu T. Experimental investigation on the combustion and heat transfer characteristics of wide size biomass co-firing in 0.2 MW circulating fluidized bed. Appl Therm Eng 2013;52:284–292.

[36] Sundaresan R, Kolar A K. Axial heat transfer correlations in a circulating fluidized bed riser, Appl Therm Eng 2013;50:985–996.

[37] Lokshin V A, Peterson D F, Schwarz A L. Standard Methods of Hydraulic Design for Power Boilers, Hemisphere, Washington, USA, 1988.

[38] Kuznetsov N W, Mitor W W, Dubovski I E, Karasina E S. (editors), Thermal Calculations of Steam Boilers (Standard Method), Second edition, Energia, Moscow, Russia, 1973.

[39] Rayaprolu R. Boiler for power and process, CRC Press-Taylor & Francis Group, Boca–Raton, USA, 2009.

[40] Taler J (Editor). Thermal and flow processes in large steam boilers, Modeling and monitoring, PWN, Warsaw, Poland, 2011 (in Polish).

[41] French DN. Metallurgical failures in fossil fired boilers, second ed., John Wiley & Sons, New York, USA, 1993.

[42] Tzolakis G, Papanikolaou P, Kolokotronis D, Samaras N, Tourlidakis A, Tomboulides A. Simulation of a coal-fired power plant using mathematical programming algorithms in order to optimize its efficiency. Appl Therm Eng 2012;48:256–267.

[43] Behbahani-nia A, Bagheri M, Bahrampoury R. Optimization of the fire tube heat recovery steam generators for cogeneration plants through genetic algorithm. Appl Therm Eng 2010;30:2378–2385.

[44] Taler D, Trojan M, Taler J. Mathematical modeling of cross-flow tube exchangers with the complex flow arrangement. Heat Transf Eng 2014; 11–12 (11–12).

[45] Trojan M, Taler D. Thermal simulation of superheaters taking into account the processes occurring on the side of the steam and flue gas. Fuel 2015;150: 75–87.

[46] Xu L, Khan J A, Chen Z. Thermal load deviation model for superheater and reheater of a utility boiler. Appl Therm Eng 2000;20:545–558.

[47] Rahimi M, Khoshhal A, Shariati S M. CFD modeling of a boiler's tubes rupture. Appl Therm Eng 2006;26:2192–2200.

[48] Purbolaksono J, Khinani A, Rashid AZ, Ali AA, Ahmad J, Nordin BF. A new method for estimating heat flux in superheater and reheater tubes. Nucl Eng Des 2009;239:1879–1884.

[49] Othman H, Purbolaksono J, Ahmad B, Failure investigation on deformed superheater tubes. Eng Fail Anal 2009;16:329–339.

[50] Purbolaksono J, Ahmad J, Beng LC, Rashid AZ, Khinani A, Ali AA. Failure analysis on a primary superheater tube of a power plant. Eng Fail Anal 2010;17: 158–167.

[51] Pronobis M, Wojnar W. The rate of corrosive wear in superheaters of boilers for supercritical parameters of steam. Eng Fail Anal 2012;19:1–12.

[52] Harding NS, O'Connor DC. Ash deposition impacts in the power industry. Fuel Process Technol 2007;88:1082–1093.

[53] Menter FR. Two-equation eddy-viscosity turbulence models for engineering applications. AIAA J 1994;32:1598–1605.

[54] Wagner W, Kretzschmar HJ. International steam tables-properties of water and steam based on the industrial formulation IAPWS-IF97. Berlin. Springer Press. 2008

Chapter 11

# A Numerical Procedure for 2D Fluid Flow Simulation in Unstructured Meshes

António M. G. Lopes

Additional information is available at the end of the chapter

http://dx.doi.org/10.5772/63077

**Abstract**

The present work addresses the numerical simulation of fluid flow for 2D problems. The physical principles and numerical models implemented in the software package EasyCFD are presented in a synthetic and clear way. The 2D form of the Navier-Stokes equations is considered, using the eddy-viscosity concept to take into account turbulence effects upon the mean flow field. The $k$-$\varepsilon$ and the $k$-$\omega$ Shear Stress Transport (SST) turbulence models allow for the calculation of the turbulent viscosity. The numerical model is based on a control volume approach, using the SIMPLEC algorithm on an unstructured quadrilateral mesh. The mesh arrangement is a non-staggered type. The coordinate transformation, integration discretization and solution method for the governing equations are fully described. As an example of application, the airflow around a NACA 0012 airfoil is calculated and the results for the aerodynamic coefficients are compared with available experimental data.

**Keywords:** CFD, SIMPLEC, unstructured mesh, fluid flow, 2D simulation

## 1. Introduction

The software EasyCFD [1] is a 2D simulation tool aimed at an initiation in the field of computational fluid dynamics. The main guiding lines on its development were the simplicity and the intuitiveness of utilization, in a self-contained package. The physical domain is discretized with quadrilateral unstructured meshes, allowing the simulation to deal with complex geometries of any configuration virtually. The present work synthesizes the main physical principles and numerical models implemented for the solution of 2D fluid flow problems, including heat transfer, in arbitrarily shaped geometries.

## 2. Basic transport equations

For the description of the transport equations, the $x$ and $z$ coordinates of the Cartesian system will be taken as the independent variables, to which correspond, for velocity, the $u$ and the $w$ components. The coordinate transformation for the generalized mesh will be presented later on the present work.

The Navier-Stokes equations describe momentum conservation and, for a 2D situation, may be stated as follows:

$$\frac{\partial(\rho u)}{\partial t}+\frac{\partial}{\partial x}\left(\rho u^2\right)+\frac{\partial}{\partial z}(\rho u w)=\frac{\partial}{\partial x}\left[\Gamma\left(2\frac{\partial u}{\partial x}-\frac{2}{3}div\vec{V}\right)\right]+\frac{\partial}{\partial z}\left[\Gamma\left(\frac{\partial u}{\partial z}+\frac{\partial w}{\partial x}\right)\right]-\frac{\partial p}{\partial x} \quad (1)$$

$$\frac{\partial(\rho u)}{\partial t}+\frac{\partial}{\partial x}\left(\rho u^2\right)+\frac{\partial}{\partial z}(\rho u w)=\frac{\partial}{\partial x}\left[\Gamma\left(2\frac{\partial u}{\partial x}-\frac{2}{3}div\vec{V}\right)\right]+\frac{\partial}{\partial z}\left[\Gamma\left(\frac{\partial u}{\partial z}+\frac{\partial w}{\partial x}\right)\right]-\frac{\partial p}{\partial x} \quad (1a)$$

where $p$ [N/m$^2$] stands for pressure and $I$ represents the buoyancy forces. The diffusion coefficient includes the contributions of the dynamic and turbulent viscosity, i.e., $\Gamma=\mu+\mu_t[\mathrm{N\ s/m^2}]$

In turn, the conservation of mass law, or continuity equation, is

$$\frac{\partial \rho}{\partial t}+\frac{\partial}{\partial x}(\rho u)+\frac{\partial}{\partial z}(\rho w)=0 \quad (2)$$

The energy conservation equation is obtained considering the transport equation for the enthalpy $\phi=c_p\,T$, where $c_p$ [J/kg K] is the specific heat and $T$ [K] is its temperature. For a fluid medium, the corresponding equation is

$$\frac{\partial(\rho c_p T)}{\partial t}+\frac{\partial}{\partial x}\left(\rho c_p u T\right)+\frac{\partial}{\partial z}\left(\rho c_p w T\right)=\frac{\partial}{\partial x}\left[\Gamma\frac{\partial T}{\partial x}\right]+\frac{\partial}{\partial z}\left[\Gamma\frac{\partial T}{\partial z}\right]+S_T \quad (3)$$

with the source term $S_T$ representing the heat generation rate per unit volume [W/m$^3$] and $\Gamma=(\mu/\mathrm{Pr}+\mu_t/\mathrm{Pr}_t)c_p$, with Pr and $\mathrm{Pr_t}$ as the laminar and the turbulent Prandtl number. For solid regions, heat transfer is governed by conduction:

$$\frac{\partial(\rho c_p T)}{\partial t}=\frac{\partial}{\partial x}\left(\lambda\frac{\partial T}{\partial x}\right)+\frac{\partial}{\partial z}\left(\lambda\frac{\partial T}{\partial z}\right)+S_T \quad (4)$$

where $\lambda$[W/mK] is the material thermal conductivity. In a multi-component fluid flow situation, different fluids are present, sharing the same velocity, pressure, temperature and turbulence quantities. The concentration of one of the components (the secondary fluid) is computed with a normal transport equation for a scalar:

$$\frac{\partial(\rho\phi_{c2})}{\partial t}+\frac{\partial}{\partial x}(\rho u\phi_{c2})+\frac{\partial}{\partial z}(\rho w\phi_{c2})=\frac{\partial}{\partial x}\left(\Gamma\frac{\partial\phi_{c2}}{\partial x}\right)+\frac{\partial}{\partial z}\left(\Gamma\frac{\partial\phi_{c2}}{\partial z}\right) \tag{5}$$

where $\phi_{c2}$ is the mass fraction, or concentration, of the secondary fluid. The diffusion coefficient is given by

$$\Gamma=\rho D_{\phi_c}+\frac{\mu_t}{Sc_t} \tag{6}$$

where $D_{\phi_c}$[m$^2$/s] is the kinematic diffusivity that characterizes the fluids pair and $Sc_t$ is the turbulent Schmidt number. The concentration of the secondary fluid plays an active role in the flow field since fluid properties depend on the concentration of each component. The mixture properties (such as viscosity, specific heat, etc.) are determined by a weighted average of the properties of the components. Thus, for a generic property $X$, we have

$$X=\phi_{c1}X_1+\phi_{c2}X_2 \tag{7}$$

where the constraint $\phi_{c1}+\phi_{c2}=1$ holds. Exception is made for density, where a simple analysis may prove that the mixture density $\rho$ is given by

$$\rho=\left(\frac{\phi_{c1}}{\rho_1}+\frac{\phi_{c_2}}{\rho_2}\right)^{-1} \tag{8}$$

## 3. Turbulence modelling

Two of the most popular turbulence models are presented next.

### 3.1. The *k*-ε turbulence model

The standard formulation of this turbulence model is described in, e.g., [2]. The turbulent viscosity is given by

$$\mu_t=C_\mu\frac{\rho k^2}{\varepsilon} \tag{9}$$

The turbulence kinetic energy, $k$ [m$^2$/s$^2$], and its dissipation rate, $\varepsilon$ [m$^2$/s$^3$], are computed with the following transport equations:

$$\frac{\partial(\rho k)}{\partial t}+\frac{\partial}{\partial x}(\rho uk)+\frac{\partial}{\partial z}(\rho wk)=\frac{\partial}{\partial x}\left[\left(\mu+\frac{\mu_t}{\sigma_k}\right)\frac{\partial k}{\partial x}\right]+\frac{\partial}{\partial z}\left[\left(\mu+\frac{\mu_t}{\sigma_k}\right)\frac{\partial k}{\partial z}\right]+P_k-\rho\varepsilon+G_T \tag{10}$$

$$\begin{aligned}&\frac{\partial(\rho\varepsilon)}{\partial t}+\frac{\partial}{\partial x}(\rho u\varepsilon)+\frac{\partial}{\partial z}(\rho w\varepsilon)=\\&\frac{\partial}{\partial x}\left[\left(\mu+\frac{\mu_t}{\sigma_\varepsilon}\right)\frac{\partial \varepsilon}{\partial x}\right]+\frac{\partial}{\partial z}\left[\left(\mu+\frac{\mu_t}{\sigma_\varepsilon}\right)\frac{\partial \varepsilon}{\partial z}\right]+\tfrac{\varepsilon}{k}\left(C_1P_k-C_2\rho\varepsilon+C_3G_T\right)\end{aligned} \tag{11}$$

The term $P_k$ represents the production rate of $k$ as the results of the velocity gradients:

$$P_k=\mu_t\left[2\left(\frac{\partial u}{\partial x}\right)^2+2\left(\frac{\partial w}{\partial z}\right)^2+\left(\frac{\partial u}{\partial z}+\frac{\partial w}{\partial x}\right)^2\right] \tag{12}$$

while the term $G_T$ accounts for the production or destruction of $k$ and $\varepsilon$ due to the thermal gradients:

$$G_T=-\beta g\frac{\mu_t}{\mathrm{Pr}_t}\frac{\partial T}{\partial z} \tag{13}$$

with $g$ [m/s$^2$] being the gravity acceleration and $\beta$ [K$^{-1}$] being the fluid dilatation coefficient. The remaining constants are

$$C_\mu=0.09;\ \sigma_k=1.0;\ \sigma_\varepsilon=1.3;\ C_1=1.44;\ C_2=1.92;\ C_3=1.44 \tag{14}$$

In the proximity of a wall, the previous equations should be modified to account for the viscous effects that become predominant. Wall functions ensure the connection between the viscous sub-layer and the inertia layer, at a location established by the $y^+$ value:

$$y^+=\frac{\rho u_\tau y}{\mu}=\frac{\rho C_\mu{}^{0.25}\sqrt{k}\,y}{\mu} \tag{15}$$

where $u_\tau$ represents the friction velocity and $y$ [m] is the distance to the wall. The utilization of wall laws does not require mesh nodes in the viscous sub-layer, which is a major advantage

http://dx.doi.org/10.5772/63077

from the computational standpoint. The momentum flux per unit area along the direction normal to the wall is given by the wall shear stress, which is computed differently depending on the location of the wall neighbour node relatively to the transition between the viscous and the inertia sub-layers. Denoting by $v$ the generic velocity component parallel to the wall (which may, actually, be $u$ or $w$) and by $y$ the distance to the wall, we have

$$y^{+} \leq 11.63 \quad \Rightarrow \quad \tau_0 = \mu \frac{v_0 - v}{y} \tag{16}$$

$$y^{+} > 11.63 \quad \Rightarrow \quad \tau_0 = \mu \frac{\rho C_{\mu}^{0.25} \chi \sqrt{k}}{\ln\left(E^{*} y^{+}\right)} \left(v_0 - v\right) \tag{16a}$$

where $v_0$ is the wall velocity, $E^{*}=9.793$ for smooth walls and $\chi=0.4187$ is the von Karman constant. In the wall neighbourhood, the production term given by Eq. (12) is computed assuming a Couette flow:

$$P_k = \mu_t \left(\frac{\partial v}{\partial y}\right)^2 \tag{17}$$

where, once again, $v$ is the generic velocity component parallel to the wall and $y$ is the generic distance to the wall. Due to its significant variations near the wall, $\varepsilon$ is averaged for the term $\rho\varepsilon$ in Eq. (10):

$$y^{+} \leq 12 \quad \Rightarrow \quad \dot{q} = \frac{\mu c_p}{\Pr y}\left(T_0 - T\right) \tag{18}$$

$$y^{+} > 11.63 \quad \Rightarrow \quad \rho\varepsilon = \rho C_{\mu}^{0.75} k^{1.5} \frac{\ln\left(E^{*} y^{+}\right)}{\chi y} \tag{18a}$$

For the turbulence kinetic energy, a zero flux along the direction perpendicular to the wall is assigned. For the dissipation rate, Eq. (11) is not employed in the node adjacent to the wall. Instead, the dissipation rate is given by

$$\varepsilon_0 = \frac{C_{\mu}^{0.75} k^{1.5}}{\chi y} \tag{19}$$

As for momentum, the energy flux is computed differently depending on the $y^+$ values. In this case, we have

$$y^+ \leq 12 \quad \Rightarrow \quad \dot{q} = \frac{\mu c_p}{\Pr y}(T_0 - T) \tag{20}$$

$$y^+ > 12 \quad \Rightarrow \quad \dot{q} = \frac{\rho c_p C_\mu^{0.25}\sqrt{k}}{\Pr_t \left[\frac{1}{\chi}\ln\left(E^* y^+\right) + P^*\right]}(T_0 - T) \tag{20a}$$

where $T_0$ is the wall temperature and $P^*$ is the so-called Jayatillaka function:

$$P^* = 9.24\left[\left(\frac{\Pr}{\Pr_t}\right)^{0.75} - 1\right]\left[1 + 0.28\ \exp\left(-0.007\frac{\Pr}{\Pr_t}\right)\right] \tag{21}$$

### 3.2. The $k$-$\omega$SST turbulence model

The $k$-$\omega$ SST model [3] represents a combination of the $k$-$\varepsilon$ and the $k$-$\omega$ models. According to Menter et al. [4], the $k$-$\omega$ model is more accurate near the wall but presents a high sensitivity to the $\omega$ values in the free-stream region, where the $k$-$\varepsilon$ model shows a better behaviour. The $k$-$\omega$ SST model represents a blend of the two, through a weighting factor computed based on the nearest wall distance. The governing equations are

$$\frac{\partial(\rho k)}{\partial t} + \frac{\partial(\rho u k)}{\partial x} + \frac{\partial(\rho w k)}{\partial z} = \overline{P_k} - \beta^* \rho \omega k + \frac{\partial}{\partial x}\left((\mu + \sigma_k \mu_t)\frac{\partial k}{\partial x}\right) + \frac{\partial}{\partial z}\left((\mu + \sigma_k \mu_t)\frac{\partial k}{\partial z}\right) \tag{22}$$

$$\frac{\partial(\rho \omega)}{\partial t} + \frac{\partial(\rho u \omega)}{\partial x} + \frac{\partial(\rho w \omega)}{\partial z} = \frac{\partial}{\partial x}\left((\mu + \sigma_\omega \mu_t)\frac{\partial \omega}{\partial x}\right) + \frac{\partial}{\partial z}\left((\mu + \sigma_\omega \mu_t)\frac{\partial \omega}{\partial z}\right) +$$

$$+\frac{\alpha \overline{P_k}}{\nu_t} - \beta \rho \omega^2 + 2(1 - F_1)\rho \sigma_{\omega 2}\frac{1}{\omega}\left(\frac{\partial k}{\partial x}\frac{\partial \omega}{\partial x} + \frac{\partial k}{\partial z}\frac{\partial \omega}{\partial z}\right) \tag{23}$$

where $\omega$ is the frequency of dissipation of turbulent kinetic energy [$s^{-1}$]. The production of turbulent kinetic energy is limited to prevent the build-up of turbulence in stagnant regions:

$$\overline{P_k} = \min\left(P_k, 10\beta^* \rho k \omega\right) \tag{24}$$

The weighting function $F_1$ is given by

$$F_1 = \tanh\left\{\left\{\min\left[\max\left(\frac{\sqrt{k}}{\beta^* \omega y};\frac{500\nu}{y^2\omega}\right);\frac{4\rho\sigma_{\omega 2}k}{CD_{k\omega}y^2}\right]\right\}^4\right\} \tag{25}$$

and

$$CD_{k\omega} = \max\left(2\rho\sigma_{\omega 2}\frac{1}{\omega}\frac{\partial k}{\partial x_j}\frac{\partial \omega}{\partial x_j},10^{-10}\right) \tag{26}$$

where $y$ represents the distance to the neighbour wall and $v$ is the laminar dynamic viscosity. $F_1$ is zero away from the wall ($k$-$\varepsilon$ model) and changes to unit inside the boundary layer ($k$-$\omega$ model) with a smooth transition based on $y$. The turbulent viscosity is computed as

$$\nu_t = \frac{a_1 k}{\max\left(a_1\omega; SF_2\right)} \tag{27}$$

where $S$ is the invariant measure of the strain rate given by

$$S = \sqrt{S_{ij}S_{ij}} \quad ; \quad S_{ij} = \frac{1}{2}\left(\frac{\partial u_i}{\partial x_j}+\frac{\partial u_j}{\partial x_i}\right) \tag{28}$$

and

$$F_2 = \tanh\left\{\left[\max\left(\frac{2\sqrt{k}}{\beta^* \omega y};\frac{500\nu}{y^2\omega}\right)\right]^2\right\} \tag{29}$$

The constants are computed as a blend of the $k$-$\varepsilon$ and $k$-$\omega$ models by the following generic equation:

$$\alpha = F_1\alpha_1 + \left(1-F_1\right)\alpha_2 \tag{30}$$

The constants are $\alpha_1$= 5/9; $\beta_1$= 3/40; $\sigma_{k1}$ = 0.85; $\sigma_{\omega 1}$ = 0.5; $\alpha_2$= 0.44; $\beta_2$ = 0.0828; $\sigma_{k2}$ = 1; $\sigma_{\omega 2}$ = 0.856; $\beta^*$ = 0.09.

The near wall treatment for momentum and turbulence equations follows the proposal described in [5]. The basic principle behind the automatic wall functions is to switch from a low-Reynolds number formulation to a wall function based on the grid nodes proximity to the wall. According to these authors, the automatic wall treatment avoids the deterioration of results typical of low-Reynolds models when applied on too coarse meshes.

The known solutions for $\omega$ in the viscous (linear) and in the logarithmic near wall region are

$$\omega_{vis} = \frac{6\nu}{0.075\, y^2}\ ; \quad \omega_{\log} = \frac{u_\tau}{0.3\,\chi\, y} \tag{31}$$

The imposed value for $\omega$ at the first node close to a wall is

$$\omega_1 = \sqrt{\omega_{vis}^2 + \omega_{\log}^2} \tag{32}$$

For the turbulence kinetic energy, a zero flux along the direction perpendicular to the wall is assigned. In turn, for the momentum equations, a similar reasoning applies, with expressions for the shear velocity in the viscous and in the logarithmic region:

$$u_\tau^{vis} = \frac{U_1}{y^+};\quad u_\tau^{\log} = \frac{\chi U_1}{\ln\left(E\, y^+\right)} \tag{33}$$

with $U_1$ being the fluid velocity relative to the wall velocity. The wall shear stress is computed as follows:

$$u_\tau = \sqrt[4]{\left(u_\tau^{vis}\right)^4 + \left(u_\tau^{\log}\right)^4} \tag{34}$$

## 4. Numerical method

### 4.1. Transformation of coordinates

Discretizationand integration of the transport equations described previously are performed using a non-orthogonal generalized mesh as shown in **Figure 1**. The independent Cartesian coordinates ($x$, $z$), describing the physical domain, are thus replaced by a boundary-fitted coordinate system ($\xi$, $\zeta$), defined by the mesh lines which may have, locally, any orientation and inclination. The computational domain (as opposed to the physical domain) is the space considered in terms of the boundary-fitted coordinate system($\xi$, $\zeta$) as depicted in **Figure 1**. In the computational domain, the mesh spacing is considered, for convenience, as unitary, i.e., $\Delta\xi = \Delta\zeta = 1$, and the mesh lines are always horizontal ($\xi$ lines) or vertical ($\zeta$ lines). The mesh arrangement is of the collocated type (as opposed to the staggered mesh) with the two velocity components and scalar quantities (temperature, pressure, turbulence kinetic energy and its dissipation rate or frequency, as well as concentrations) located at the control volume (CV) centre.

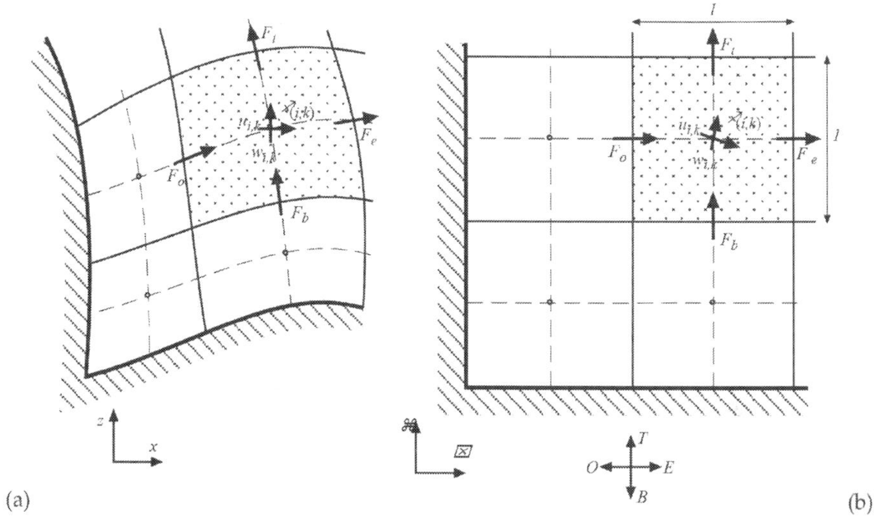

**Figure 1.** The two domains. (a) Physical domain, showing the mesh lines; (b) Computational domain.

Transformation of the original equations is accomplished by replacing the independent variables, using the chain rule, which states that, generically:

$$\frac{\partial \phi}{\partial x} = \frac{\partial \phi}{\partial \xi}\frac{\partial \xi}{\partial x} + \frac{\partial \phi}{\partial \zeta}\frac{\partial \zeta}{\partial x} = \xi_x \frac{\partial \phi}{\partial \xi} + \zeta_x \frac{\partial \phi}{\partial \zeta} \tag{35}$$

The Jacobian of the transformation

$$J = \begin{vmatrix} x_\xi & x_\zeta \\ z_\xi & z_\zeta \end{vmatrix} = x_\xi z_\zeta - x_\zeta z_\xi \tag{36}$$

represents the ratio between the physical size of the control volume and its computational size (unitary). The derivatives $\xi_x$, $\xi_z$, $\zeta_x$ $\zeta_z$ are the contravariant metrics of the transformation. They are computed from the covariant metrics, $x_\xi$, $z_\xi$, $x_\zeta$, $z_\zeta$ as follows:

$$\xi_x = z_\zeta / J; \quad \xi_z = -x_\zeta / J; \quad \zeta_x = -z_\xi / J; \quad \zeta_z = x_\xi / J \tag{37}$$

To obtain the strong conservative form in the boundary-fitted coordinate system ($\xi$, $\zeta$), the transport equations are transformed through the application of the chain rule (35) and multiplied by the Jacobian of the transformation. The metric identity

$$\frac{\partial}{\partial \xi}(J\xi_x) + \frac{\partial}{\partial \zeta}(J\zeta_x) = 0; \quad \frac{\partial}{\partial \xi}(J\xi_z) + \frac{\partial}{\partial \zeta}(J\zeta_z) = 0 \tag{38}$$

is then used to recast some terms. The result, for a generic variable $\phi$, is

$$\begin{aligned} &J\frac{\partial(\rho\phi)}{\partial t} + \frac{\partial}{\partial \xi}(J\rho U\phi) + \frac{\partial}{\partial \zeta}(J\rho W\phi) = \\ &\frac{\partial}{\partial \xi}\left[\Gamma J g^{11}\frac{\partial \phi}{\partial \xi}\right] + \frac{\partial}{\partial \zeta}\left[\Gamma J g^{33}\frac{\partial \phi}{\partial \zeta}\right] + \frac{\partial}{\partial \xi}\left[\Gamma J g^{13}\frac{\partial \phi}{\partial \zeta}\right] + \frac{\partial}{\partial \zeta}\left[\Gamma J g^{13}\frac{\partial \phi}{\partial \xi}\right] + JS_\phi \end{aligned} \tag{39}$$

The terms $g^{11}$, $g^{13}$ and $g^{33}$ are the contravariant metric relations given by

$$g^{11} = \xi_x^2 + \xi_z^2; \quad g^{33} = \zeta_x^2 + \zeta_z^2; \quad g^{13} = \xi_x\zeta_x + \xi_z\zeta_z \tag{40}$$

The non-orthogonal term $g^{13}$ is null if the mesh is locally orthogonal. $U$ and $W$, in Eq. (39), are the contravariant velocities. The terms $J\rho U$ and $J\rho W$ represent mass fluxes through the control volume faces along the computational directions $\xi$ and $\zeta$, respectively, and are computed as follows:

$$F_\xi = J\rho U = \rho\left(z_\zeta u - x_\zeta w\right) \tag{41}$$

$$F_\zeta = J\rho W = \rho\left(x_\xi w - z_\xi u\right) \tag{42}$$

Note that, in this case, the sub-index for the fluxes (such as in $F_\xi$ ) represents the flux direction (and not a derivative, such as for the metrics). Eq. (39) may be rewritten as

http://dx.doi.org/10.5772/63077

$$J\frac{\partial(\rho\phi)}{\partial t}+\frac{\partial}{\partial\xi}\left(F_{\xi}\phi\right)+\frac{\partial}{\partial\zeta}\left(F_{\zeta}\phi\right)=\frac{\partial}{\partial\xi}\left[\Gamma Jg^{11}\frac{\partial\phi}{\partial\xi}\right]+\frac{\partial}{\partial\zeta}\left[\Gamma Jg^{33}\frac{\partial\phi}{\partial\zeta}\right]+J\left(S_{cross}+S_{\phi}\right) \tag{43}$$

where the cross-derivatives were incorporated into the source term $S_{cross}$. A similar procedure is applied to obtain the generalized form of remaining equations, leading to the following form for the Navier-Stokes and continuity equations:

$$\begin{aligned} &J\frac{\partial(\rho u)}{\partial t}+\frac{\partial}{\partial\xi}\left(F_{\xi}u\right)+\frac{\partial}{\partial\zeta}\left(F_{\zeta}u\right)= \\ &\frac{\partial}{\partial\xi}\left[\Gamma Jg^{11}\frac{\partial u}{\partial\xi}\right]+\frac{\partial}{\partial\zeta}\left[\Gamma Jg^{33}\frac{\partial u}{\partial\zeta}\right]-z_{\zeta}\frac{\partial p}{\partial\xi}+z_{\xi}\frac{\partial p}{\partial\zeta}+S_{crossu} \end{aligned} \tag{44}$$

$$\begin{aligned} &J\frac{\partial(\rho w)}{\partial t}+\frac{\partial}{\partial\xi}\left(F_{\xi}w\right)+\frac{\partial}{\partial\zeta}\left(F_{\zeta}w\right)=\frac{\partial}{\partial\xi}\left[\Gamma Jg^{11}\frac{\partial w}{\partial\xi}\right]+\frac{\partial}{\partial\zeta}\left[\Gamma Jg^{33}\frac{\partial w}{\partial\zeta}\right] \\ &+x_{\zeta}\frac{\partial p}{\partial\xi}-x_{\xi}\frac{\partial p}{\partial\zeta}+S_{crossw}+I \end{aligned} \tag{45}$$

$$J\frac{\partial\rho}{\partial t}+\frac{\partial}{\partial\xi}\left[\rho\left(z_{\zeta}u-x_{\zeta}w\right)\right]+\frac{\partial}{\partial\zeta}\left[\rho\left(x_{\xi}w-z_{\xi}u\right)\right]=J\frac{\partial p}{\partial t}+\frac{\partial}{\partial\xi}(J\rho U)+\frac{\partial}{\partial\zeta}(J\rho W)=0 \tag{46}$$

### 4.2. Integration

The integration and solution method for the transport equations are entirely based on the methodology in [6], with some of the suggestions described in [7] and incorporating the necessary modifications for the generalized mesh approach. The general Eq. (43) may be written as

$$J\frac{\partial(\rho\phi)}{\partial t}+\frac{\partial}{\partial\xi}\left(F_{\xi}\phi-\Gamma Jg^{11}\frac{\partial\phi}{\partial\xi}\right)+\frac{\partial}{\partial\zeta}\left(F_{\zeta}\phi-\Gamma Jg^{11}\frac{\partial\phi}{\partial\zeta}\right)=J\left(S_{cross}+S_{\phi}\right) \tag{47}$$

The integration of the previous equation in its control volume leads to

$$\begin{aligned} &J\frac{\partial(\rho\phi)}{\partial t}+\left[F_e\phi_e-D_e\left(\phi_E-\phi_P\right)\right]-\left[F_o\phi_o-D_o\left(\phi_P-\phi_O\right)\right]+ \\ &\left[F_t\phi_t-D_t\left(\phi_T-\phi_P\right)\right]-\left[F_b\phi_b-D_b\left(\phi_P-\phi_B\right)\right]=J\left(S_{1_P}+S_{2_P}\phi_P\right) \end{aligned} \tag{48}$$

where the source term has been written as a linear combination involving $\phi_P$. $F$ and $D$ represent the advective fluxes and the diffusive coefficients, respectively:

$$F_e = F_{\xi e} = \left[\rho\left(z_\zeta u - x_\zeta w\right)\right]_e ; \; F_o = F_{\xi o} = \left[\rho\left(z_\zeta u - x_\zeta w\right)\right]_o$$

$$F_t = F_{\zeta t} = \left[\rho\left(x_\xi w - z_\xi u\right)\right]_t ; \; F_b = F_{\zeta b} = \left[\rho\left(x_\xi w - z_\xi u\right)\right]_b \tag{49}$$

$$D_e = \left(\Gamma Jg^{11}\right)_e ; \; D_o = \left(\Gamma Jg^{11}\right)_o ; \; D_t = \left(\Gamma Jg^{33}\right)_t ; \; D_b = \left(\Gamma Jg^{33}\right)_b \tag{50}$$

In the previous expressions, the subscripts indicate the location relative to the *CV* centre, in the computational domain, with the uppercase denoting neighbour nodes and the lowercase denoting neighbour faces: *E,e*: East; *O,o*: West; *T,t*: Top; *B,b*: Bottom. For simplicity, in Eq. (48), the subscripts $\xi$ and $\zeta$ were dropped from the fluxes $F$ (in fact, fluxes across the eastern and western faces are always along the $\xi$ direction and fluxes across the top and bottom faces are always along the $\zeta$ direction).

For the solution of the equations, it is necessary to evaluate the values of $\phi$ in the *CV* faces (i.e., $\phi_e$, $\phi_o$, $\phi_t$, $\phi_b$). These values are computed as a function of both $\phi_P$ and the values in the neighbour nodes $\phi_E$, $\phi_O$, $\phi_T$, $\phi_B$ according to the adopted advection scheme (to be described later on). Eq. (48) may, then, be written in the following standard form:

$$a_P\phi_P = a_E\phi_E + a_O\phi_O + a_T\phi_T + a_B\phi_B + b \tag{51}$$

or, in a more compact manner,

$$a_P\phi_P = \sum_{nb} a_{nb}u_{nb} + b \tag{51a}$$

with "*nb*" indicating that the sum is to be performed for all the neighbouring locations.

It is necessary to compute the face values $\phi_e$, $\phi_o$, $\phi_t$, $\phi_b$ as a function of $\phi_P$, $\phi_E$, $\phi_O$, $\phi_T$, $\phi_B$ in order to obtain the coefficients $a_E$, $a_O$, $a_T$, $a_B$ of Eq. (51). It is known that a simple arithmetic average is not a physically plausible solution since, due to the presence of a flow, the property $\phi$, being advected, tends to assume a value closer to the upwind value. Several advection schemes may be adopted, being the simplest one the *upwind* scheme. According to this scheme, the property $\phi$ in the CVface takes the upwind value, i.e.,for example, $F_e>0 \Rightarrow \phi_e=\phi_P$; $F_e<0 \Rightarrow \phi_e=\phi_E$ . The complete mathematical formulation for the upwind scheme is

$$
\begin{aligned}
a_E &= D_e + [\![-F_e, 0]\!] \; ; \; a_O = D_o + [\![F_o, 0]\!] \\
a_T &= D_t + [\![-F_t, 0]\!] \; ; \; a_B = D_b + [\![F_b, 0]\!]
\end{aligned}
\tag{52}
$$

Due to its first-order character, the upwind scheme is often not used due to associated numerical diffusion. The Quick scheme is third-order accurate. The deferred correction version of Hayase [8] combines the first-order upwind scheme with a third-order correction, $b_{\text{quick}}$, added to the source term as follows:

$$
\begin{aligned}
&b_{quick} = \\
&\frac{1}{8}[\![F_e, 0]\!](-\phi_O - 2\phi_P + 3\phi_E) - \frac{1}{8}[\![-F_e, 0]\!](3\phi_P - 2\phi_E - 3\phi_{EE}) + \\
&\frac{1}{8}[\![F_o, 0]\!](3\phi_O - 2\phi_P - \phi_E) - \frac{1}{8}[\![-F_o, 0]\!](-\phi_{OO} - 2\phi_O + 3\phi_P) + \\
&\frac{1}{8}[\![F_t, 0]\!](-\phi_B - 2\phi_P + 3\phi_T) - \frac{1}{8}[\![-F_t, 0]\!](3\phi_P - 2\phi_T - 3\phi_{TT}) + \\
&\frac{1}{8}[\![F_b, 0]\!](3\phi_B - 2\phi_P - \phi_T) - \frac{1}{8}[\![-F_b, 0]\!](-\phi_{BB} - 2\phi_B + 3\phi_P) +
\end{aligned}
\tag{53}
$$

The Quick scheme, although third-order accurate, presents oscillations that may lead to some unrealistic behaviour. Total variation diminishing (TVD) schemes, also implemented in the present code, were developed to provide second-order accurate solutions that are free or nearlyfree from oscillations. For further information on this, please refer to, e.g., [9].

### 4.3. Pressure-velocity coupling

EasyCFD adopts the SIMPLEC algorithm (Semi-Implicit Method for Pressure-Linked Equations-Consistent) [7], which is based on the original formulation *SIMPLE* [6]. Due to the non-staggered mesh arrangement (collocated mesh), the Rie-Chow interpolation procedure [10], with the modifications proposed in [11] and [12], is implemented. Let us consider the $u$ momentum conservation Eq. (44). After integration, the evaluation of this equation leads to

$$
a_P u_P = \sum_{nb} a_{nb} u_{nb} - z_\zeta \frac{\partial p}{\partial \xi} + z_\xi \frac{\partial p}{\partial \zeta} + S_{crossu}
\tag{54}
$$

During the iterative process, velocities $u^*$ are computed from the available velocity field $u^m$ and pressure field $p^*$ obtained at the previous step as follows:

$$
a_P\left(1 + \frac{1}{E}\right) u^*_P = \sum_{nb} a_{nb} u^*_{nb} + \frac{a_P}{E} u^m_P - z_\zeta \frac{\partial p^*}{\partial \xi} + z_\xi \frac{\partial p^*}{\partial \zeta} + S_{crossu}
\tag{55}
$$

where $E$ is the under-relaxation factor [7]. During the iterative process, unless convergence is reached, the velocity field $u^*$ obtained from the solution of the momentum equations does not satisfy the continuity requirement unless the correct pressure field $p$ is employed (instead of an incorrect pressure field $p^*$). This means that, if the correct pressure field was employed, a mass-conservative velocity field would be obtained:

$$a_P\left(1+\frac{1}{E}\right)u_P = \sum_{nb} a_{nb}u_{nb} + \frac{a_P}{E}u_P^m - z_\zeta \frac{\partial p}{\partial \xi} + z_\xi \frac{\partial p}{\partial \zeta} + b \tag{56}$$

Thus, the pressure and velocity fields $p^*$ and $u^*$ should be corrected by a certain amount $p'$ and $u'$ :

$$p = p^* + p'; \quad u_P = u_P^* + u'_P \tag{57}$$

Subtracting Eq. (56) from Eq. (55) and taking into account Eq. (57), one obtains

$$a_P\left(1+\frac{1}{E}\right)u'_P = \sum_{nb} a_{nb}u'_{nb} - z_\zeta \frac{\partial p'}{\partial \xi} + z_\xi \frac{\partial p'}{\partial \zeta} \tag{58}$$

The keystone of the SIMPLECalgorithm consists on the subtraction of the term $\sum_{nb} a_{nb}u'_P$ on both sides of the equation and subsequent dropping, leading to

$$\left[a_P\left(1+\frac{1}{E}\right) - \sum_{nb} a_{nb}\right]u'_P = \cancel{\sum_{nb} a_{nb}\left(u'_{nb} - u'_P\right)} - z_\zeta \frac{\partial p'}{\partial \xi} + z_\xi \frac{\partial p'}{\partial \zeta} \tag{59}$$

or, for simplicity:

$$\tilde{a}_P u'_P = -z_\zeta \frac{\partial p'}{\partial \xi} + z_\xi \frac{\partial p'}{\partial \zeta} \tag{60}$$

where

$$\tilde{a}_P = a_P\left(1+\frac{1}{E}\right) - \sum_{nb} a_{nb} \tag{61}$$

http://dx.doi.org/10.5772/63077

The equations for the velocity correction are obtained through the pressure correction field, recurring to the previous equation:

$$u_P^{'} = -\frac{z_\zeta}{\tilde{a}_P}\frac{\partial p^{'}}{\partial \xi} + \frac{z_\xi}{\tilde{a}_P}\frac{\partial p^{'}}{\partial \zeta} \; ; \; w_P^{'} = -\frac{x_\xi}{\tilde{a}_P}\frac{\partial p^{'}}{\partial \zeta} + \frac{x_\zeta}{\tilde{a}_P}\frac{\partial p^{'}}{\partial \xi} \tag{62}$$

leading to

$$u_P = u_P^{*} - \frac{z_\zeta}{\tilde{a}_P}\frac{\partial p^{'}}{\partial \xi} + \frac{z_\xi}{\tilde{a}_P}\frac{\partial p^{'}}{\partial \zeta} \; ; \; w_P = w_P^{*} + \frac{x_\zeta}{\tilde{a}_P}\frac{\partial p^{'}}{\partial \xi} - \frac{x_\xi}{\tilde{a}_P}\frac{\partial p^{'}}{\partial \zeta} \tag{63}$$

### 4.4. The pressure correction equation

As previously stated, the objective of the pressure correction is to produce a pressure field such that the solution of the momentum equations is a mass-conservative velocity field. Consequently, the equations for solving the $p'$ field must be obtained from the continuity equation. The discretized form of this equation is obtained directly from the integration of Eq. (2):

$$J\frac{\rho_P - \rho_P^0}{\Delta t} + \left[\rho\left(z_\zeta u - x_\zeta w\right)\right]_e - \left[\rho\left(z_\zeta u - x_\zeta w\right)\right]_o + \left[\rho\left(x_\xi w - z_\xi u\right)\right]_t - \left[\rho\left(x_\xi w - z_\xi u\right)\right]_b = 0 \tag{64}$$

As one may see, velocities are, now, needed at the control volume faces. Taking Eq. (63), for the $u$ velocity component, at the "$e$" and "$o$" faces and the same equation for the $w$ component at the "$t$" and "$b$" faces, substituting into Eq. (64) and rearranging the terms leads to

$$\begin{aligned} &J\frac{\rho_P - \rho_P^0}{\Delta t} + F_e^* - F_o^* + F_t^* - F_b^* - \left(\frac{\rho g_{33}}{\tilde{a}_P}\frac{\partial p^{'}}{\partial \xi}\right)_e + \left(\frac{\rho g_{33}}{\tilde{a}_P}\frac{\partial p^{'}}{\partial \xi}\right)_o - \left(\frac{\rho g_{11}}{\tilde{a}_P}\frac{\partial p^{'}}{\partial \zeta}\right)_t + \left(\frac{\rho g_{11}}{\tilde{a}_P}\frac{\partial p^{'}}{\partial \zeta}\right)_b + \\ &\left(\frac{\rho g_{13}}{\tilde{a}_P}\frac{\partial p^{'}}{\partial \zeta}\right)_e - \left(\frac{\rho g_{13}}{\tilde{a}_P}\frac{\partial p^{'}}{\partial \zeta}\right)_o + \left(\frac{\rho g_{13}}{\tilde{a}_P}\frac{\partial p^{'}}{\partial \xi}\right)_t - \left(\frac{\rho g_{13}}{\tilde{a}_P}\frac{\partial p^{'}}{\partial \xi}\right)_b = 0 \end{aligned} \tag{65}$$

The terms $g_{ij}$ are the covariant metric relations defined as

$$g_{11} = x_\xi^2 + z_\xi^2 = g^{33}J^2; \; g_{33} = x_\zeta^2 + z_\zeta^2 = g^{11}J^2; \; g_{13} = x_\xi x_\zeta + z_\xi z_\zeta = -g^{13}J^2 \tag{66}$$

The derivatives are evaluated as

$$\left(\frac{\partial p'}{\partial \xi}\right)_e = p'_E - p'_P; \left(\frac{\partial p'}{\partial \xi}\right)_o = p'_P - p'_O; \left(\frac{\partial p'}{\partial \zeta}\right)_t = p'_T - p'_P; \left(\frac{\partial p'}{\partial \zeta}\right)_b = p'_P - p'_B \tag{67}$$

and, for the cross-derivatives,

$$\begin{aligned} \left(\frac{\partial p'}{\partial \xi}\right)_t &= 0.25\left(p'_E + p'_{TE} - p'_O - p'_{TO}\right); \left(\frac{\partial p'}{\partial \xi}\right)_b = 0.25\left(p'_E + p'_{BE} - p'_O - p'_{BO}\right) \\ \left(\frac{\partial p'}{\partial \zeta}\right)_e &= 0.25\left(p'_T + p'_{TE} - p'_B - p'_{BE}\right); \left(\frac{\partial p'}{\partial \zeta}\right)_o = 0.25\left(p'_T + p'_{TO} - p'_B - p'_{BO}\right) \end{aligned} \tag{68}$$

Introducing the discretization expressed by Eqs. (68) and 67 into Eq. (65) allows us to obtain the pressure correction equation:

$$a_P p'_P = a_E p'_E + a_O p'_O + a_T p'_T + a_B p'_B + b \tag{69}$$

where

$$a_E = \left(\frac{g_{33}}{\langle \tilde{a}_P / \rho \rangle}\right)_e; \; a_O = \left(\frac{g_{33}}{\langle \tilde{a}_P / \rho \rangle}\right)_o; \; a_T = \left(\frac{g_{11}}{\langle \tilde{a}_P / \rho \rangle}\right)_t; \; a_B = \left(\frac{g_{11}}{\langle \tilde{a}_P / \rho \rangle}\right)_b \tag{70}$$

$$a_P = a_E + a_O + a_T + a_B \tag{71}$$

$$\begin{aligned} b &= J\frac{\rho_P^0 - \rho_P}{\Delta t} - F_e^* + F_o^* - F_t^* + F_b^* - \\ &\left(\frac{g_{13}}{\langle \tilde{a}_P / \rho \rangle}\frac{\partial p'}{\partial \zeta}\right)_e + \left(\frac{g_{13}}{\langle \tilde{a}_P / \rho \rangle}\frac{\partial p'}{\partial \zeta}\right)_o - \left(\frac{g_{13}}{\langle \tilde{a}_P / \rho \rangle}\frac{\partial p'}{\partial \xi}\right)_t + \left(\frac{g_{13}}{\langle \tilde{a}_P / \rho \rangle}\frac{\partial p'}{\partial \xi}\right)_b \end{aligned} \tag{72}$$

The $\langle\rangle$ symbol denotes a linear interpolation from the control volume centre (where the momentum equations are defined) to the control volume faces (where the fluxes for the continuity equations are needed). The pressure correction field $p'$ obtained from the solution of Eq. (69) is employed for correcting pressure and velocity corrections are obtained from Eq. (63). Note that, since these equations are defined at the control volume centre, $p'$ derivatives are evaluated as

$$\left(\frac{\partial p'}{\partial \xi}\right)_P = 0.5\left(p'_E - p'_O\right);\quad \left(\frac{\partial p'}{\partial \zeta}\right)_P = 0.5\left(p'_T - p'_B\right) \tag{73}$$

One may note that pressure values at the control volume centre are not included in the evaluation of these derivatives (the same applies for the pressure derivatives in the momentum equations). This may lead to the well-known checkerboard pattern for the pressure field. To avoid this effect, the Chie-Row interpolation method proposes that the mass fluxes, to be evaluated at the control volume interfaces for all the transport equations ($F_e$, $F_o$, $F_t$ and $F_b$, in Eq. (48)), be corrected using the pressure correction $p'$ field (instead of being computed from the corrected control volume centre velocities). The correction equations for fluxes are obtained from the correction equations for velocities:

$$F_{e,o} = F_{e,o}^{\ *} - \left[\left\langle\frac{\rho}{\tilde{a}_P}\right\rangle\left(g_{33}\frac{\partial p'}{\partial \xi} - g_{13}\frac{\partial p'}{\partial \zeta}\right)\right]_{e,o} \tag{74}$$

$$F_{t,b} = F_{t,b}^{\ *} - \left[\left\langle\frac{\rho}{\tilde{a}_P}\right\rangle\left(g_{11}\frac{\partial p'}{\partial \zeta} - g_{13}\frac{\partial p'}{\partial \xi}\right)\right]_{t,b} \tag{75}$$

The "starred" fluxes $F^*$ at the control volume interfaces are obtained by interpolating the momentum equation. The keystone of the method is that the pressure gradient is not interpolated, but, instead, is obtained directly from the pressure at contiguous control volume centres. Considering Eq. (55), evaluated in terms of fluxes, one may write

$$F_{e,o}^{\ *} = \frac{F_{e,o}^{m}}{1+E} + \hat{F}_{e,o} + \left\langle\frac{\rho}{\tilde{a}_P}\right\rangle_{e,o}\left(g_{33}\frac{\partial p^*}{\partial \xi} - g_{13}\frac{\partial p^*}{\partial \zeta}\right)_{e,o} \tag{76}$$

$$F_{t,b}^{\ *} = \frac{F_{t,b}^{m}}{1+E} + \hat{F}_{t,b} + \left\langle\frac{\rho}{\tilde{a}_P}\right\rangle_{t,b}\left(g_{11}\frac{\partial p}{\partial \zeta} - g_{13}\frac{\partial p}{\partial \xi}\right)_{t,b} \tag{77}$$

The terms $\hat{F}_{e,o}$ and $\hat{F}_{t,b}$ represent the fluxes

$$\hat{F}_{e,o} = z_\zeta\left\langle\rho\hat{u}\right\rangle_{e,o} - x_\zeta\left\langle\rho\hat{w}\right\rangle_{e,o} \tag{78}$$

$$\hat{F}_{t,b} = x_\xi \langle \rho \hat{w} \rangle_{t,b} - z_\zeta \langle \rho \hat{u} \rangle_{t,b} \tag{79}$$

where the revised velocities $\hat{u}$ and $\hat{w}$ are obtained from the momentum equations as follows:

$$\tilde{a}_P \hat{u}_P = \sum_{nb} a_{nb} \hat{u}_{nb} + \cancel{\frac{a_P}{E} u_P^m} - \cancel{z_\zeta \frac{\partial p^*}{\partial \xi}} + \cancel{z_\xi \frac{\partial p^*}{\partial \zeta}} + b \Rightarrow \hat{u}_P = \frac{\sum_{nb} a_{nb} \hat{u}_{nb} + b}{\tilde{a}_P} \tag{80}$$

$$\tilde{a}_P \hat{w}_P = \sum_{nb} a_{nb} \hat{w}_{nb} + \cancel{\frac{a_P}{E} w_P^m} + \cancel{x_\zeta \frac{\partial p^*}{\partial \xi}} - \cancel{x_\xi \frac{\partial p^*}{\partial \zeta}} + b \Rightarrow \hat{w}_P = \frac{\sum_{nb} a_{nb} \hat{w}_{nb} + b}{\tilde{a}_P} \tag{81}$$

Note that the source term $b$ includes all the contributions (e.g., transient term, cross-derivatives and buoyancy for the $w$ velocity component), except the under-relaxation and pressure gradient.

### 4.5. Solution of the equations

The solution of the equations previously described is carried out with an iterative procedure. For accelerating the convergence rate, two relaxation factors (described next) are applied.

The solution of the equation is sub- or over-relaxed in the following manner:

$$\phi = f \phi_{computed} + (1 - f) \phi_{previous} \tag{82}$$

Values of $f$ lower than unity lead to sub-relaxation, while values greater than unity over-relax the solution process. In the present code, the value $f = 1.1$ is employed for the transport equations, while, for the pressure correction equation, the Point Successive Over Relaxation (PSOR) method [13] combined with the additive correction multigrid method [14] is employed.

The whole flow field calculation is considered to be converged when all the normalized residuals are lower that a predefined value $R_{conv}$ :

$$[\![ R_u, R_w, R_m, R_T, R_k, R_\varepsilon ]\!] < R_{conv} \tag{83}$$

The total normalized residual for the transport equations of $\phi$ ($\phi = u, w, T, k, \varepsilon, \omega$) is determined as follows:

$$R_\phi = \sum_{all}\left(\frac{\left|a_P\phi_P - \sum_{nb} a_{nb}u_{nb} + b\right| J}{a_p\left(\phi_{\max} - \phi_{\min}\right)}\right) / \sum_{all} J \tag{84}$$

where $(\varphi_{max} - \varphi_{min})$ quantifies the amplitude of the variable $\phi$ in the calculation domain.

## 5. Examples of application

To exemplify the numerical method described previously, two test cases are presented next along with a comparison of results with published data.

### 5.1. Flow past an airfoil

A calculation was performed to compute the aerodynamic coefficients of a NACA 0012 airfoil operating at a Reynolds number of $6\times10^6$. The obtained values for the drag and lift coefficients are compared with existing experimental data. The first step is to define the calculation domain, which should be large enough in order to avoid numerical blockage effects. **Figure 2** represents the domain, for a 1 m airfoil cord length. Lateral boundaries are assigned a free slip condition and a uniform velocity profile with 5% turbulence intensity is imposed at the inlet. A mass conservative condition is applied at the outlet boundary. After a mesh independency study, a total of approximately 250,000 mesh nodes were employed, with three mesh refinement regions. Particular care was taken near the airfoil surface, were $y^+$ values ranging from, typically, 0.1 to 6, with an average value of 1.7 all around, were obtained. **Figure 3** depicts the mesh employed.

For the present simulations, both the first-order hybrid [6] and the Quick advection schemes were employed, along with the $k$-$\varepsilon$ and $k$-$\omega$ SST turbulence models. Experimental data are reported by Abbott and Von Doenhoff [15] and Ladson [16].

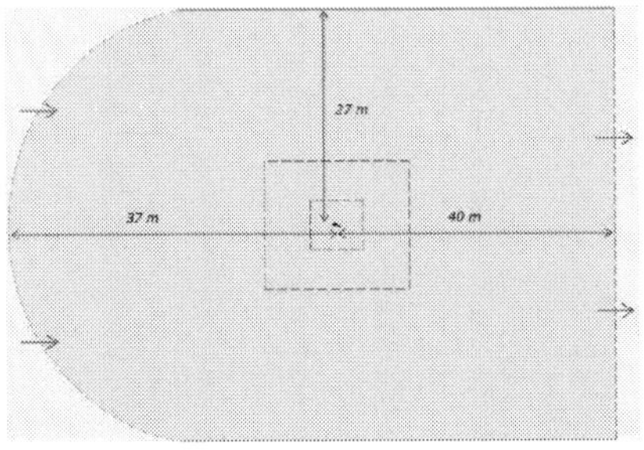


**Figure 2.** Domain dimensions. Airfoil cord is 1 m.

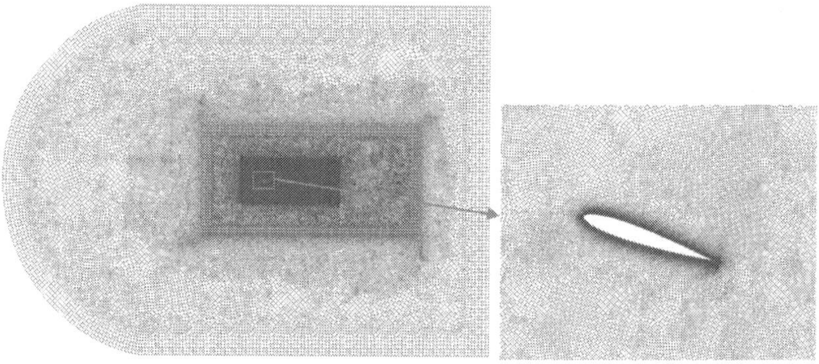

**Figure 3.** Non-structured quadrilateral mesh.

Results for the dependence of the lift coefficient with the airfoil angle of attack $\alpha$ are shown in **Figure 4**. As expected, the lift coefficient presents a linear dependence with the angle of attack $\alpha$ up to the onset of separation, which occurs at $\alpha=16$ . The two advection schemes give similar results up to separation, after which the lift drop in the stall region is more pronounced with the hybrid scheme. Separation is completely established at $\alpha=18$ and for $\alpha \geq 20$ the flow becomes unsteady. Both turbulence models perform very well in the linear region. After separation, data are more spread. The difficulty to obtain reliable experimental data in this circumstance is commonly recognized as the flow is unsteady and presents a 3D behaviour. Comparing the two advection schemes, the Quick scheme performs better, particularly after separation.

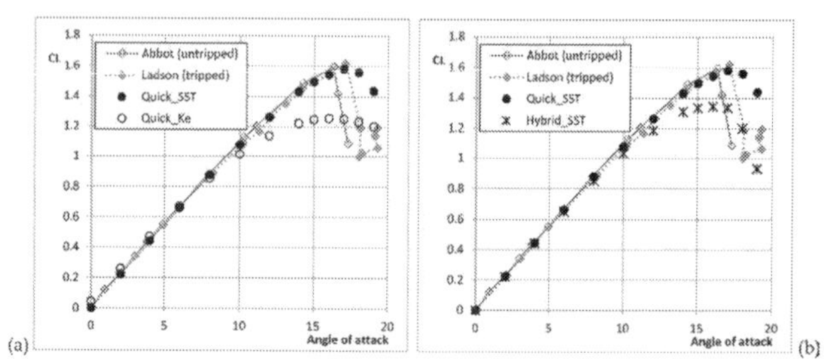


**Figure 4.** Lift coefficient vs. angle of attack. Influence of (a) turbulence modeland (b) advection scheme.

**Figure 5** depicts the relation between lift and drag coefficients. In this case, the *k-ω* SST turbulence model performs substantially better than the *k-ε* model. This is certainly due to the fact that the friction component plays an important role in drag, and thus correctly resolving the boundary layer in the very proximity of the wall is crucial for the drag computation. It is also interesting to note that the advection scheme plays a very important role, with the higher order scheme Quick showing much better than the hybrid scheme, when results are compared with the experimental data.

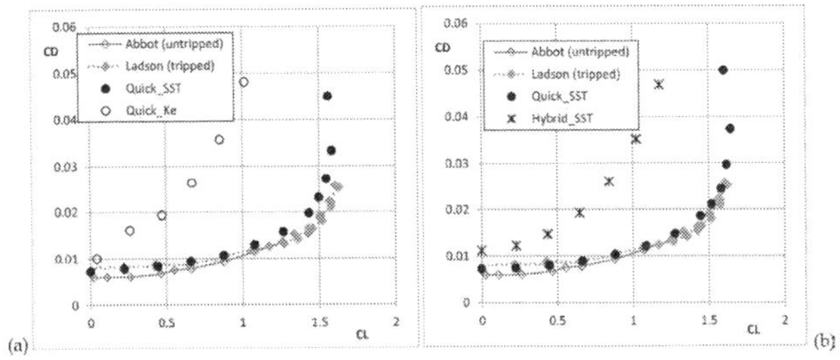


**Figure 5.** Drag coefficient vs. lift coefficient. Influence of (a) turbulence model and (b) advection scheme.

## 5.2. Natural convection inside a cavity

The natural convection flow in a cavity is a classical test for numerical methods in fluid dynamics. The cavity is a square shape (cf. **Figure 6**) with adiabatic horizontal walls. A constant temperature is imposed in each the vertical wall.

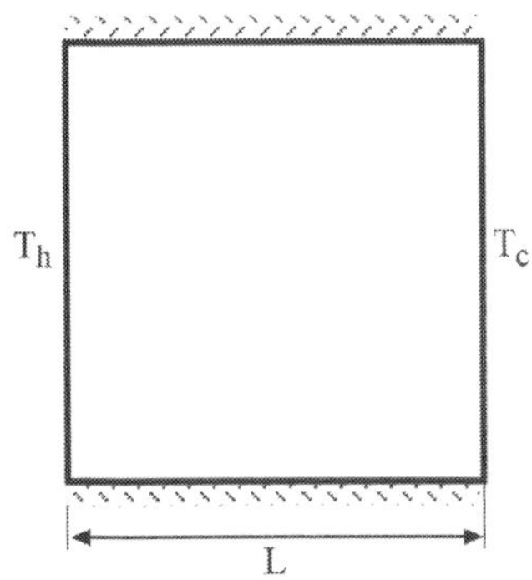


**Figure 6.** Problem definition for the natural convection inside a cavity.

The problem is governed by the following non-dimensional parameters:

$$\text{Prandtl number, } Pr = \frac{\nu}{\alpha} \tag{85}$$

where the thermal diffusivity is $\alpha = \lambda / (\rho c_p)$, $\nu$ is the kinematic viscosity, $\lambda$ is the thermal conductivity, $\rho$ is the density and $c_p$ is the specific heat:

$$\text{Rayleigh number}, Ra = \frac{g\beta \Delta T\, L^3\, \Pr}{\nu^2} \tag{86}$$

where $\beta$ is the thermal expansion coefficient, $g$ is the gravity acceleration and $\Delta T = T_h - T_c$ is the temperature difference between the vertical walls. The transition between laminar and turbulent flow takes place approximately for $Ra = 10^7$. In the present work, simulations were conducted for $Ra = 10^5$ (laminar regime). Air is the operating fluid, for which Pr = *0.71*. The hybrid advection scheme was used and the Boussinesq approximation was adopted. Computations were performed in a non-uniform grid, with 82 × 82 = 6400 nodes. Reference results are reported in [17] and [18] for several Rayleigh numbers in laminar regime, comparing solutions given by several authors. Results for laminar and turbulent flow are also presented in [19].

**Figure 7(a)** and **(b)** displays isothermal lines generated using a constant value spacing between the minimum and the maximum verified within the domain. **Figure 8(a)** and **(b)** shows the flow streamlines. The flow, in the steady-state situation, is characterized by a large vortex filling the cavity, rotating in the clockwise direction. Two small vortices rotating in the same direction are located near the cavity centre. For this case, the minimum and the maximum streamline values used in the visualization do not correspond to the total amplitude of the stream function within the domain. These values were, instead, adjusted in EasyCFD to correspond to those employed in [19]. The agreement between the calculations and those reported in the literature is very good. Vahl Davis and Jones [18] present normalized maximum values for the $u$ and for $w$ components of velocity

$$u^* = \frac{uL}{\alpha}; \quad w^* = \frac{wL}{\alpha} \tag{87}$$

occurring in the vertical and horizontal symmetry lines, respectively. **Table 1** shows the results obtained with EasyCFD, the reference values in [17] and the range of variation for the *37* contributions reported in [18]. This range does not include the minimum and maximum reported values since these clearly fall outside the general trend of the remaining contributions.

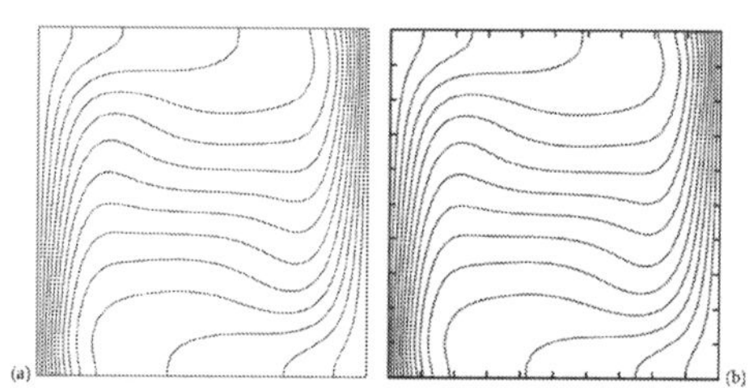

**Figure 7.** Isothermal lines. Ra = $10^5$. (a) EasyCFD and (b) Dixit and Babu [19].

http://dx.doi.org/10.5772/63077

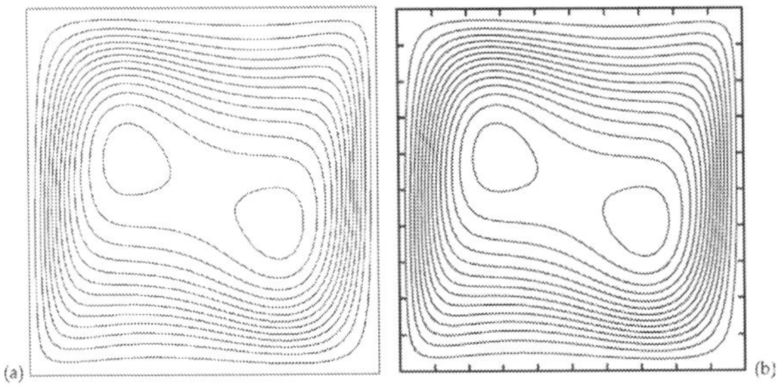

**Figure 8.** Streamlines. Ra = $10^5$. (a) EasyCFD and (b) Dixit and Babu [19].

| EasyCFD | Vahl Davis [17] | Variation range [18] |
|---|---|---|
| 34.44 | 34.81 | 34.2–41.2 |
| 68.21 | 68.68 | 65.8–70.45 |

**Table 1.** Normalized maximum values for the $u$ and $w$ velocity components.

# 6. Concluding remarks

The numerical simulation of fluid flow for 2D problems was addressed. The physical principles and numerical models here presented correspond to the implementation in the software package EasyCFD. Transformation of the original equations to cope with a non-orthogonal generalized mesh is described in detail, along with the coupling of momentum and continuity with an adapted SIMPLEC algorithm for non-staggered meshes. Although not addressed in the present chapter, this software package was developed entirely based on a graphical interface, aiming at an easy and intuitive utilization. With a fast learning curve, this package is very suitable for learning the principles and application methods in computational fluid dynamics and has a great value both as a didactic and an applied tool. Although, at first, the restriction to 2D situations may seem very limitative, a great number of practical situations may be addressed with this approach.

# Author details

António M. G. Lopes

Address all correspondence to: antonio.gameiro@dem.uc.pt

Department of Mechanical Engineering, University of Coimbra, Coimbra, Portugal

## References


[1] Lopes AMG. A 2D software system for expedite analysis of CFD problems in complex geometries. Computer Applications in Engineering Education. 2015;3(2):27–38. DOI: 10.1002/cae.21668.

[2] Launder BE, Spalding DB. The numerical computation of turbulent flows. Computer Methods in Applied Mechanics and Engineering. 1974;3(2):269–289. DOI: 10.1016/0045-7825(74)90029-2.

[3] Menter FR. Zonal two equation kappa-omega turbulence models for aerodynamic flows. AIAA Paper 1993–2906, 24th Fluid Dynamics Conference, 6–9 July 1993; Orlando, Florida.

[4] Menter, Kuntz M, Langtry R. Ten years of industrial experience with the SST turbulence model. Turbulence, Heat and Mass Transfer. 2003;4:625–632.

[5] Menter FR, Ferreira JC, Esch T. The SST turbulence model with improved wall treatment for heat transfer predictions in gas turbines. International Gas Turbine Congress. 2003;(1992):1–7.

[6] Patankar S. Numerical Heat Transfer and Fluid Flow. Series in computational methods in mechanics and thermal sciences; 1980. New York, McGraw-Hill.

[7] Van Doormaal JP, Raithby GD. Enhancements of the SIMPLE method for predicting incompressible fluid flows. Numerical Heat Transfer. 2007;7(2):147–163. DOI: 10.1080/01495728408961817.

[8] Hayase T, Humphrey JA, Greif R. A consistently formulated QUICK scheme for fast and stable convergence using finite-volume iterative calculation procedures. Journal of Computational Physics. 1992;98(1):108–118. DOI: 10.1016/0021-9991(92)90177-Z.

[9] Vertseeg HK, Malalasekera W. An Introduction to Computational Fluid Dynamics. The Finite Volume Method. Pearson Education Limited; Essex, England, 2007.

[10] Rhie CM, Chow WL. Numerical study of the turbulent flow past an airfoil with trailing edge separation. AIAA Journal. 1983;21(11):1525–1532. DOI: 10.2514/3.8284.

[11] Majumdar S. Role of underrelaxation in momentum interpolation for calculation of flow with nonstaggered grids. Numerical Heat Transfer. 1998;13(1):125–132. DOI: 10.1080/10407788808913607.

[12] Shen WZ, Michelsen JA, Sørensen NN, Sørensen JN. An improved SIMPLEC method on collocated grids for steady and unsteady flow computations. Numerical Heat Transfer: Part B. 2003;43:221–239. DOI: 10.1080/713836202.

[13] Ehrlich LW. An ad hoc SOR method. Journal of Computational Physics. 1981;44(1):31–45. DOI: 10.1016/0021-9991(81)90036-X.

[14] Hutchinson BR, Raithby GD. A multigrid method based on the additive correction strategy. Numerical Heat Transfer. 1986;9(5):511–537. DOI: 10.1080/10407788608913491.

[15] Abbott IH, Von Doenhoff AE. Theory of Wing Sections, Including a Summary of Airfoil Data. Dover Publications; New York, 1959.

[16] Ladson CL. Effects of independent variation of Mach and Reynolds numbers on the low-speed aerodynamic characteristics of the NACA 0012 airfoil section. NASA TM 4074, October 1988.

[17] Vahl Davis GD. Natural convection in a square cavity: a benchmark numerical solution. International Journal for Numerical Methods in Fluids. 1983;3:249–264.

[18] Vahl Davis GD, Jones IP. Natural convection in a square cavity: a comparison exercise. International Journal for Numerical Methods in Fluids. 1983;3:227–248.

[19] Dixit HN, Babu V. Simulation of high Rayleigh number natural convection in a square cavity using the lattice Boltzmann method. International Journal of Heat and Mass Transfer. 2006;49:727–739.

Chapter 12

# On a New Numerical Approach on Micropolar Fluid, Heat and Mass Transfer Over an Unsteady Stretching Sheet Through Porous Media in the Presence of a Heat Source/ Sink and Chemical Reaction

Stanford Shateyi, Fazle Mabood and
Gerald Tendayi Marewo

Additional information is available at the end of the chapter

http://dx.doi.org/10.5772/63800

**Abstract**

The problem of MHD micropolar fluid, heat and mass transfer over unsteady stretching sheet through porous medium in the presence of a heat source/sink and chemical reaction is presented in this chapter. By applying suitable similarity transformations, we transform the governing partial differential equations into a system of ordinary differential equations. We then apply the recently developed numerical technique known as the Spectral Quasi-Linearization Method. The validity of the accuracy of the technique is checked against the bvp4c routine method. Numerical results for the surface shear stresses, Nusselt number and the Sherwood number are presented in tabular form. Also numerical results for the velocity, temperature and concentration distribution are presented in graphical forms, illustrating the effects of varying values of different parameters.

**Keywords:** micropolar fluid, unsteady stretching sheet, porous media, heat source/ sink, Spectral Quasi-Linearization Method

## 1. Introduction

The boundary layer flows, heat and mass transfer in a quiescent Newtonian and non-Newtonian fluid driven by a continuous stretching sheet are of significance in a number of industrial engineering processes such as the drawing of a polymer sheet or filaments extruded continuously from a die, the cooling of a metallic plate in a bath, the aerodynamic extrusion of plastic sheets, the continuous casting, rolling, annealing and thinning of copper wires, the wires and fibre coating. During its manufacturing process, a stretched sheet interacts with ambient fluid thermally and mechanically. Both the kinematics of stretching and the simultaneous heating or cooling during such processes have a decisive influence on the quality of the final product. In [1], the effects of chemical reaction and magnetic field on viscous flow over a non-linear stretching sheet were reported. Mabood et al. [2] studied numerically MHD flow and heat transfer of nanofluid over a non-linear stretching sheet. Abel et al. [3] investigated the steady buoyancy-driven dissipative magneto-convective flow from a vertical non-linear stretching sheet. In [4], an analysis of heat transfer over an unsteady stretching sheet with variable heat flux in the presence of heat source or sink was made. Several other studies have addressed various aspects of regular/nanofluids [5–10].

Micropolar fluids are fluids with microstructure and asymmetrical stress tensor. Physically, they represent fluids consisting of randomly oriented particles suspended in a viscous medium. These types of fluids are used in analysing liquid crystals, animal blood, fluid flowing in brain, exotic lubricants, the flow of colloidal suspensions, etc. The theory of micropolar fluids was first proposed by Eringen [11]. In this theory, the local effects arising from the microstructure and the intrinsic motion of the fluid elements are taken into account. The comprehensive literature on micropolar fluids, thermomicropolar fluids and their uses in engineering and technology was presented by Kelson and Desseaux [12]. Gorla and Nakamura [13] discussed the combined convection from a rotating cone to micropolar fluids with an arbitrary variation of surface temperature. Prathap Kumar et al. [14] studied the effect of surface conditions on the micropolar flow driven by a porous stretching sheet. In [15], the case of mixed convection flow of a micropolar fluid past a semi-infinite, steadily moving porous plate with varying suction velocity normal to the plate in the presence of thermal radiation and viscous dissipation was discussed. Mansour et al. [16] studied heat and mass transfer effects on the magnetohydrodynamic (MHD) flow of a micropolar fluid on a circular cylinder. El-Hakiem [17] proposed the dissipation effects on the MHD-free convective flow over a non-isothermal surface in a micropolar fluid. Joule heating and mass transfer effects on the MHD-free convective flow in micropolar fluid are investigated by El-Hakiem et al. [18] and El-Amin [19], respectively. In [20], the derivation of the unsteady MHD-free convection flow of micropolar fluid past a vertical moving porous plate in a porous medium was presented. Many researchers investigated different aspects of micropolar fluid [21–23].

The study of heat source/sink effects on heat transfer is another important issue in the study of several physical problems. The effect of non-uniform heat source, only confined to the case of viscous fluids, was also included in [24–27], while Mabood et al. [28] investigated non-uniform heat source/sink effects and Soret effects on MHD non-Darcian convective flow past a stretching sheet in a micropolar fluid with radiation.

Combined heat and mass transfer problems with chemical reactions are important in many processes of interest in engineering and have received significant attention in recent years. These processes include drying, evaporation at the surface of a water body, energy transfer in a wet cooling tower and the flow in a desert cooler [29]. Chemical reactions are classified as either homogeneous or heterogeneous. A homogeneous reaction is one which occurs uniformly through a given phase, while a heterogeneous reaction takes place in a restricted region or within the boundary of a phase. A reaction is said to be a first-order reaction if the rate of reaction is directly proportional to the concentration [30, 31]. The effect of chemical reaction on thermal radiation for MHD micropolar flow and heat and mass transfer was investigated by Das [32]. Hayat et al. [33] considered MHD flow and mass transfer of an upper-convected Maxwell fluid past a porous shrinking sheet with chemical reaction. The behaviour of chemically reactive solute and distribution in MHD boundary layer flow over a permeable stretching sheet were investigated by Bhattacharyya and Layek [34]. Kandasamy et al. [35] studied the effect of transfer of chemically reactive species in MHD-mixed convective flow past over a porous wedge. The solution for diffusion of chemically reactive species in a flow of a non-Newtonian fluid over a stretching sheet immersed in a porous medium was reported by Afify [36], while Mabood et al. [37] reported the effects of chemical reaction and transpiration on MHD stagnation point flow and heat transfer over a stretching sheet.

The main objective of this chapter is to apply a recently developed numerical technique known as Spectral Quasi-Linearization Method (SQLM) in solving MHD micropolar fluid, heat and mass transfer over an unsteady stretching sheet through porous media in the presence of a heat source/sink and chemical reaction. The SQLM was first implemented by Motsa et al. [38].

## 2. Mathematical formulation

We consider an unsteady two-dimensional, mixed convection flow of a viscous incompressible micropolar fluid, heat and mass transfer over an elastic vertical permeable stretching sheet in the presence of a heat source/sink and chemical reaction. Following [39], the sheet is assumed to emerge vertically in the upward direction from a narrow slot with a velocity,

$$U_w(x,t) = \frac{ax}{1-\alpha t}, \tag{1}$$

where both $a$ and $\alpha$ are positive constants with dimension per unit time. We measure the positive $x$ direction along the stretching sheet with the top of the slot as the origin. We then measure the positive $y$ coordinate perpendicular to the sheet and across the fluid flow. The surface temperature $(T_w)$ and the concentration $(C_w)$ of the stretching sheet vary along the $x$ direction and in time $t$ as

$$T_w(x,t) = T_\infty + \frac{bx}{(1-\alpha t)^2}, \quad C_w(x,t) = C_\infty + \frac{cx}{(1-\alpha t)^2}, \tag{2}$$

where $b$ and $c$ are constants with dimension temperature and concentration respectively, over length. It is noted that the expressions for $U_w(x, t)$, $T_w(x, t)$ and $C_w(x, t)$ are valid only for $t < \alpha^{-1}$. We also remark that the elastic sheet which is fixed at the origin is stretched by applying a force in the $x$-direction and the effective stretching sheet rate $a/(1-\alpha t)$ increases with time. Analogously, the sheet temperature and concentration increase (reduce) if $b$ and $c$ are positive (negative), respectively, from $T_\infty$ and $C_\infty$ at the sheet in the proportion to $x$. We assume that the radiation effect is significant in this study. The fluid properties are taken to be constant except for density variation with temperature and concentration in the buoyancy terms. Under those assumptions and the Boussinesq approximations, the governing two-dimensional boundary layer equations are given as:

$$\frac{\partial u}{\partial x}+\frac{\partial v}{\partial y}=0, \tag{3}$$

$$\frac{\partial u}{\partial t}+u\frac{\partial u}{\partial x}+v\frac{\partial u}{\partial y}=\left(\frac{\mu+\kappa}{\rho}\right)\frac{\partial^2 u}{\partial y^2}+\frac{\kappa}{\rho}\frac{\partial N}{\partial y}+g\beta_t\left(T-T_\infty\right)+g\beta_c\left(C-C_\infty\right)-\frac{\sigma B_0^2 u}{\rho}-\frac{\nu u}{\rho K_p^*}, \tag{4}$$

$$\frac{\partial N}{\partial t}+u\frac{\partial N}{\partial x}+v\frac{\partial N}{\partial y}=\frac{\gamma}{\rho j}\frac{\partial^2 N}{\partial y^2}-\frac{\kappa}{\rho j}\left(2N+\frac{\partial u}{\partial y}\right), \tag{5}$$

$$\frac{\partial T}{\partial t}+u\frac{\partial T}{\partial x}+v\frac{\partial T}{\partial y}=\alpha_0\frac{\partial^2 T}{\partial y^2}+\left(\frac{\mu+\kappa}{\rho c_p}\right)\left(\frac{\partial u}{\partial y}\right)^2\pm\frac{Q}{\rho c_p}\left(T-T_\infty\right), \tag{6}$$

$$\frac{\partial C}{\partial t}+u\frac{\partial C}{\partial x}+v\frac{\partial C}{\partial y}=D\frac{\partial^2 C}{\partial y^2}-\kappa_c\left(C-C_\infty\right). \tag{7}$$

where $u$ and $v$ are the velocity components along the $x$ and$y$ axes, respectively, $T$ is the fluid temperature, $\mu$ is the component of the microrotation vector normal to the $x\ y$ plane, $\gamma$ is the spin gradient viscosity, $\alpha_0$ is the thermal conductivity, $C_p$ is the heat capacity at constant pressure, $g$ is the acceleration due to gravity, $\beta_t$ and $\beta_c$ are the coefficients of thermal expression and concentration expansion, respectively, $\beta_0$ is the transverse magnetic field, $C$ is the concentration of the solutes, $T_\infty$ and $C_\infty$ denote the temperature and concentration far away from the plate, respectively, and $j$ is the microinertia density or microinertia per unit mass. The appropriate boundary conditions for the current model are:

$$u=U_w\left(x,t\right),\ v=V_w,\ N=0,\ T=T_w\left(x,t\right),\ C=C_w\left(x,t\right)\ \text{ at } y=0, \tag{8}$$

$$u=0,\ T\to T_\infty,\ C\to C_\infty\ \text{ as } y\to\infty. \tag{9}$$

## 3. Similarity analysis

In this section, we transform the partial differential equations into ordinary differential equations. Similarity techniques reduce the number of parameters, as well as improve insight into the comparative size of various terms present in the equations.

### 3.1. Transformation of the governing equations

In order to transform the governing Eqs. (3)–(7) into a set of ordinary differential equations, we introduce the following transformation variables [40]:

$$\eta=\sqrt{\frac{a}{\nu(1-\alpha t)}}y,\quad \psi=\sqrt{\frac{a\nu}{(1-\alpha t)}}xf(\eta),\quad N=\sqrt{\frac{a^3}{\nu(1-\alpha t)^3}}xh(\eta),$$
$$\mathrm{T}=T_\infty+\frac{bx}{(1-\alpha t)^2}\theta(\eta),\quad C=C_\infty+\frac{cx}{(1-\alpha t)^2}\phi(\eta),\tag{10}$$

where $\psi(x, y, t)$ is the physical stream function which automatically satisfies the continuity equation. Upon substituting similarity variables into Eqs. (3)–(7), we obtain the following system of ordinary equations:

$$(1+\Delta)f'''+ff''-f'^2-\frac{A}{2}(2f+\eta f')+\Delta h'+\lambda_1\theta+\lambda_2\phi-\left(M_1+\frac{1}{K_p}\right)f'=0,\tag{11}$$

$$\lambda_3 h''+fh'-f'h-\frac{A}{2}(3h+\eta h')-\Delta B(2h+f'')=0,\tag{12}$$

$$\frac{1}{\Pr}\theta''+f\theta'-f'\theta-\frac{A}{2}(4\theta+\eta\theta')+Ec(1+\Delta)f''^2\pm Q_x\theta+0,\tag{13}$$

$$\frac{1}{Sc}\phi''+f\phi'-f'\phi-K\phi-\frac{A}{2}(4\phi+\eta\phi')=0.\tag{14}$$

*Boundary conditions*

The corresponding boundary conditions become:

$$f'(0)=1,\ f(0)=f_w,\ h(0)=0,\ \theta(0)=1,\ \phi(0)=1,\tag{15}$$

$$f'(\infty)=0,\ h(\infty)=0,\ \theta(\infty)=0,\ \phi(\infty)=0. \tag{16}$$

with

$$\begin{gathered}A=\frac{\alpha}{a},\ \Delta=\frac{\kappa}{\mu},\ \lambda_1=\frac{g\beta b}{a^2}=\frac{Gr_x}{\mathrm{Re}_x^2},\ Gr_x=\frac{g\beta(T_w-T_\infty)x^3}{\nu^2},\ \mathrm{Re}_x=\frac{U_w x}{\nu},\alpha_0=\frac{k}{\rho c_p},\\ \lambda_2=\frac{g\beta_c}{a^2}=\frac{Gc_x}{\mathrm{Re}_x^2},\ Gc_x=\frac{g\beta_c(C_w-C_\infty)x^3}{\nu^2},\lambda_3=\frac{\gamma}{\mu j},\ B=\frac{\nu(1-\alpha t)}{ja}=\frac{\nu x}{jU_w},\ \mathrm{Pr}=\frac{\nu}{\alpha},\\ Ec=\frac{U_w^{\ 2}}{c_p(T_w-T_\infty)},M=\frac{\sigma B_0^{\ 2}(1-\alpha t)}{\rho a},\ \frac{1}{K_p}=\frac{\nu(1-\alpha t)}{\rho a K_p^{\ *}},\ Q_x=\frac{Qx}{\rho c_p U_w},\ K=\frac{K_c(1-\alpha t)}{a}.\end{gathered} \tag{17}$$

### 3.2. Quantities of engineering interest

The quantities of engineering interest in the present study are the skin-friction coefficient $C_{fx}$, the local wall couple stress $M_{wx}$, the local Nusselt number $N_{ux}$ and the local Sherwood number $Sh_x$. The quantities are, respectively, defined by:

$$C_{fx}=\frac{2}{\rho U_w^{\ 2}}\left[(\mu+\kappa)\left(\frac{\partial u}{\delta y}\right)_{y=0}+\kappa N|_{y=0}\right]=2(1+\Delta)\mathrm{Re}_x^{\ -1/2}f''(0), \tag{18}$$

$$M_{wx}=\frac{\gamma a}{\nu}\left(\frac{\partial N}{\partial y}\right)_{y=0}=\mathrm{Re}_x^{\ -1}h'(0), \tag{19}$$

$$Nu_x=\frac{-x}{T_w-T_\infty}\left(\frac{\partial T}{\partial y}\right)_{y=0}=-\mathrm{Re}_x^{1/2}\theta'(0), \tag{20}$$

$$Sh_x=\frac{-x}{C_w-C_\infty}\left(\frac{\partial C}{\partial y}\right)_{y=0}=-\mathrm{Re}_x^{1/2}\phi'(0). \tag{21}$$

## 4. Method of solution

In this section, we give a brief overview of the Spectral Quasi-linearization Method (SQLM). The SQLM uses the Newton-Raphson-based quasi-linearization method (QLM) to linearize the governing non-linear equations. The QLM was developed by [41]. The SQLM then integrates the QLM using the Chebyshev Spectral collocation method.

### 4.1. Spectral Quasi-Linearization Method (SQLM)

#### 4.1.1. Main idea

Consider the problem of solving $n$th order non-linear differential equation

$$F\left(u,u',u'',...,u^{(n)}\right)=g(x) \text{ or } F(\mathbf{u})=g(x), \tag{22}$$

subject to prescribed boundary conditions, where $a\leq x\leq b$. The SQLM consists of two basic steps: quasi-linearization and Chebyshev differentiation in that order.

*Quasi-linearization*: If we expand left-hand side of Eq. (22) in Taylor series about $\mathbf{v}(v, v', v'', ..., v^{(n)})=g(x)$ and re-arrange the terms in the resulting equation we get:

$$\mathbf{u}.\nabla F(\mathrm{v})=\mathbf{v}.\nabla F(\mathrm{v})-F(\mathrm{v})+g(x). \tag{23}$$

If $\mathbf{v}$ is given then the previous equation can be used to solve for u. Keeping this in mind, we replace v and u with approximations $\boldsymbol{u}_r$ and $\boldsymbol{u}_{r+1}$ of $\mathbf{u}$ at the end of $r$ and $r$+1 iterations, respectively. This results in the $n$th order linear differential equation

$$a_{0,r}u_{r+1}+a_{1,r}\frac{du_{r+2}}{dx}+a_{2,r}\frac{d^2u_{r+2}}{dx^2}+...+a_{n,r}\frac{d^nu_{r+2}}{dx^n}=R_r \tag{24}$$

Where $a_{m,r}=F_{u^{(m)}}(\mathbf{u}_r)$, $F_{u^{(m)}}=\frac{\partial F}{\partial u^{(m)}}$ and

$$R_r=a_{0,r}u_r+a_{1,r}u_r'+a_{2,r}u_r''+...+a_{n,r}u_r^{(m)}-F(\mathbf{u}_r)+g(x) \tag{25}$$

*Chebyshev differentiation*: To solve the differential Eq. (24) we start by performing the following preliminary steps.

1. Using the linear mapping

$$x(\xi)=\frac{1-\xi}{2}a+\frac{1+\xi}{2}b \tag{26}$$

we transform Eq. (24) on the physical interval [$a$, $b$], say, on the $x$ axis to its equivalent

$$a_{0,r}u_{r+1} + a_{1,r}\beta \frac{du_{r+1}}{d\xi} + a_{2,r}\beta^2 \frac{d^2u_{r+1}}{d\xi^2} + \ldots + a_{n,r}\beta^n \frac{d^nu_{r+1}}{d\xi^n} = R_r \tag{27}$$

on the computational interval [−1, 1] on the $\xi$ axis, where $\beta = \frac{2}{b-a}$.

2. Partition interval [−1, 1] using the collocation points $\xi = \frac{\pi i}{N}$ where $i = 0, 1, 2, \ldots, N$.

Next we calculate differential Eq. (27) at each collocation point $\xi_i$. This is followed by approximating each derivative using the formula:

$$\frac{d^p u_r}{d\xi^p}(\xi_i) = \sum_{j=0}^{N} \left[D^p\right]_{ij} u_r(\xi_i)$$

where D is the $(N+1)\times(N+1)$ Chebyshev differentiation matrix [1]. This process is called Chebyshev differentiation. The differential Eq. (27) is then evaluated at points $\xi_0$, $\xi_1$, .....$\xi_N$ with a linear system

$$A \begin{bmatrix} u_r(\xi_0) \\ u_r(\xi_1) \\ \cdot \\ \cdot \\ \cdot \\ u_r(\xi_N) \end{bmatrix} = \begin{bmatrix} R_r(\xi_0) \\ R_r(\xi_1) \\ \cdot \\ \cdot \\ \cdot \\ R_r(\xi_N) \end{bmatrix}$$

which upon including the boundary conditions and solving for each $r$ generates a sequence $\{\mathbf{u}_r\}$ of approximation which we expect to converge.

### 4.2. Application to current problem

Eq. (14) is of the form

$$F(f, f', \phi, \phi', \phi'') = 0, \tag{28}$$

where

$$F(f, f', \phi, \phi', \phi'') = \frac{1}{Sc}\phi'' + f\phi' - f'\phi - K\phi - \frac{A}{2}(4\phi + \eta\phi'). \tag{29}$$

*Hence quasi-linearization* as directed in Section 4.2.1 replaces non-linear differential Eq. (28) with its linear counterpart

$$d_{0r}f_{r+1}+d_{1r}f'_{r+1}+d_{2r}\phi_{r+1}+d_{3r}\phi'_{r+1}+d_{4r}\phi''_{r+1}=R_r^{(3)} \tag{30}$$

where

$$d_{0r}=\phi'_r,\ d_{1r}=-\phi_r,\ \ d_{2r}=f_r'-K-2A,\ \ d_{3r}=f_r-\frac{A}{2}\eta_r,\ d_{4r}=\frac{1}{Sc},\ R_r^{(3)}=-f_r'\phi_r+f_r\phi_r'.$$

Chebyshev differentiation replaces differential Eq. (30) with a linear system

$$A_{41}=\text{diag}\left\{\boldsymbol{\Phi}_r{}'\right\}-\text{diag}\left\{\boldsymbol{\Phi}_r\right\}\hat{D}, \tag{31}$$

$$A_{44}=\text{diag}\left\{\mathbf{F}_r'\right\}+(-K-2A)I+\text{diag}\left\{\mathbf{F}_r-\frac{A}{2}\eta_r\right\}\hat{D}+\frac{1}{Sc}\hat{D}^2,$$

$$\mathrm{R}_r^{(4)}=-\mathbf{F}_r'\circ\boldsymbol{\Phi}_r+\mathbf{F}_r\circ\boldsymbol{\Phi}_r'$$

$$\mathbf{F}_{r+1}=\left[f_{r+1}(\xi_0)f_{r+1}(\xi_1)\dots f_{r+1}(\xi_N)\right]^T,$$

$$\boldsymbol{\Phi}_{r+1}=\left[\phi_{r+1}(\xi_0)\phi_{r+1}(\xi_1)\dots\phi_{r+1}(\xi_N)\right]^T.$$

Therefore the use of Quasi-linearization followed by Chebyshev differentiation replaces differential Eq. (14) with a linear system (31). Similarly, differential Eqs. (11)–(13) are replaced by linear systems, which if combined with a linear system (30) yield a larger linear system

$$\begin{bmatrix} A_{11} & A_{12} & A_{13} & A_{14}\\ A_{21} & A_{22} & O & O\\ A_{31} & O & A_{33} & O\\ A_{41} & O & O & A_{44}\end{bmatrix}\begin{bmatrix}\mathbf{F}_{r+1}\\ \mathbf{H}_{r+1}\\ \boldsymbol{\Theta}_{r+1}\\ \boldsymbol{\Phi}_{r+1}\end{bmatrix}=\begin{bmatrix}\mathbf{R}_r^{(1)}\\ \mathbf{R}_r^{(2)}\\ \mathbf{R}_r^{(3)}\\ \mathbf{R}_r^{(4)}\end{bmatrix} \tag{32}$$

subject to boundary conditions

$$f_{r+1}(\xi)=f_w,\ \sum_{k=0}^{N}\hat{D}_{Nk}f(\xi)=1,\ h_{r+1}(\xi_N)=\xi_N,\ \theta_{r+1}(\xi_N)=1,\ \phi_{r+1}(\xi_N)=1, \tag{33}$$

$$\sum_{k=0}^{N}D_{0k}f(\xi)=0,\ h_{r+1}(\xi_0)=0,\ \theta_{r+1}(\xi_0)=0,\ \phi_{r+1}(\xi_0)=0, \tag{34}$$

where

$$A_{11}=\text{diag}\left\{\mathbf{F}_r''\right\}+\left(-2\text{diag}\left\{\mathbf{F}_r'\right\}-\left(A+M+\frac{1}{K_p}\right)I\right)\hat{D}+\text{diag}\left\{\mathbf{F}_r-\frac{A}{2}\eta_r\right\}\hat{D}^2+(1+\Delta)\hat{D}^3,$$

$$A_{12}=\Delta\hat{D},\ A_{13}=\lambda_1 I,\ A_{14}=\lambda_2 I,\ \mathbf{R}_r^{(1)}=\mathbf{F}\circ\mathbf{F}_r''-\mathbf{F}_r'\circ\mathbf{F}',$$
$$\text{A}_{21}=\text{diag}\left\{\mathbf{H}_r'\right\}-\text{diag}\{\mathbf{H}_r\}\hat{D}-\Delta B\hat{D}^2,$$

$$A_{22}=-\text{diag}\left\{\mathbf{F}_r'\right\}-\left(\frac{3}{2}A+2\Delta B\right)I+\text{diag}\left\{\mathbf{F}_r-\frac{A}{2}\eta_r\right\}\hat{D}+\lambda_3\hat{D}^2,\ \ \mathbf{R}_r^{(2)}=\mathbf{F}\circ\mathbf{H}_r'-\mathbf{F}_r'\circ\mathbf{H}_r,$$
$$\text{A}_{31}=\text{diag}\left\{\mathbf{\Theta}_r'\right\}-\text{diag}\{\mathbf{\Theta}_r\}\hat{D}+2Ec(1+\Delta)\text{diag}\left\{\mathbf{F}_r''\right\}\hat{D}^2,$$

$$\text{A}_{32}=-\text{diag}\{\mathbf{F}_r\}+(-2A+Q_x)I+\text{diag}\left\{\mathbf{F}_r-\frac{A}{2}\eta_r\right\}\hat{D}+\frac{1}{\text{Pr}}\hat{D}^2,$$
$$\mathbf{R}_r^{(3)}=Ec(1+\Delta)\mathbf{F}_r''+\mathbf{F}\circ\Theta_r'-\mathbf{F}_r'\circ\Theta,$$

$$\text{A}_{41}=\text{diag}\{\mathbf{\Phi}_r'\}-\text{diag}\{\mathbf{\Phi}_r\}\hat{D},$$
$$\text{A}_{42}=-\text{diag}\{\mathbf{F}_r\}-(K+2A)I+\text{diag}\left\{\mathbf{F}_r-\frac{A}{2}\eta_r\right\}\hat{D}+\frac{1}{Sc}\hat{D}^2,$$
$$\mathbf{R}_r^{(4)}=-\mathbf{F}'\circ\Phi_r+\mathbf{F}_r\circ\Phi',$$

$A\ o\ B$ denotes the Hadarmard product (element-wise multiplication) of matrices $A$ and $B$ of the same order, and $I$ and $O$ are the identity and zero matrices, respectively. Boundary conditions (33) and (34) of linear system (32) are in the same manner as done in [2]. This is followed by solution of linear system (32) to get approximations $f_r(\xi_c)$, $h_r(\xi_c)$, $\theta_r(\xi_c)$, $\phi_r(\xi_c)$ for each $r=1, 2, \ldots$ and $c=0, 1, 2, \ldots, N$. However, this last step requires suitable initial approximation for which we choose

$$f_0(\eta) = f_w + 1 - e^{-\eta},\ h_0(\eta) = \eta e^{-\eta},\ \theta_0(\eta) = e^{-\eta},\ \phi_0(\eta) = e^{-\eta},$$

so as to satisfy boundary conditions (33) and (34).

## 5. Results and discussion

The non-linear differential Eqs. (11)–(14) with boundary conditions (15)–(16) depend on several parameters, such as micropolar Δ, unsteadiness $A$, thermal buoyancy $\lambda_1$, solutal buoyancy $\lambda_2$, non-dimensional material $\lambda_3$, magnetic field M, local porous $K_p$, non-dimensional parameter $B$, Eckert number $E_c$, heat generation and/or absorption and chemical reaction. All the SQLM results presented in this work were obtained using $N = 50$ collocation points, and we are glad to highlight that convergence was achieved in just about five iterations. We take the infinity value $\eta_\infty$ to be 40. Unless otherwise stated, the default values for the parameters are taken as:

Pr = 0.71, $B = 0.1$, M = 1, $Ec = 0.1$, $Sc = 0.22$, $\varDelta$ Δ = 0.1, $\lambda_1 = \lambda_2 = 0.5$, $K_p = 1$, $K = 0.5$, f_w = 0.5, $\lambda_3$. In order to validate our numerical method, it was compared to MATLAB routine bvp4c which is an adaptive Lobatto quadrature iterative scheme. This is depicted in **Table 1**. In **Table 1**, we observe that the current results completely agree with the results generated by bvp4c. It is worth noting that convergence of SQLM occurs as early as at the sixth iteration and the method is extremely faster, saving *cpu* time. This gives confidence to our proposed method. We also observe in **Table 1** that the rates of transfers are greatly affected by the micropolar parameter Δ.

| | $-f''(0)$ | | $-\theta'(0)$ | | | $-\phi'(0)$ |
|---|---|---|---|---|---|---|
| Δ | bvp4c | SQLM | bvp4c | SQLM | bvp4c | SQLM |
| 0.1 | 1.51831796 | 1.51831796 | 0.969700948 | 0.96700948 | 2.2273423 | 2.22734623 |
| 0.5 | 1.29335523 | 1.29335523 | 0.89967685 | 0.89967685 | 2.23825301 | 2.23825301 |
| 1 | 1.10530824 | 1.10530824 | 0.82937070 | 0.82937070 | 2.24887626 | 2.24887626 |

**Table 1.** Comparison of the SQLM results of $f$ $-f''(0)$, $-\theta'(0)$, $\phi'(0)$ with those obtained by bvp4c for different values of the micropolar parameter $\varDelta$.

We observe in **Table 2** that the wall stresses, the Nusselt and Sherwood numbers are significantly affected by the changing values of the unsteadiness parameter. The skin-friction coefficient as expected increases with increasing values of the stretching parameter.

| $A$ | $-f''(0)$ | $h'(0)$ | $-\theta'(0)$ | $-\theta'(0)$ |
|---|---|---|---|---|
| 0 | 1.18860026 | 0.03277007 | 0.22581676 | 1.34959740 |
| 1 | 1.51530691 | 0.02767645 | 1.21557294 | 1.75188835 |
| 2 | 1.86832868 | 0.02329578 | 2.06905446 | 2.36549832 |

**Table 2.** The effects of the unsteadiness parameter on $-f''(0)$, $h'(0)$, $-\theta'(0)$, $-\phi'(0)$.

**Table 3** depicts the influence of the thermal buoyancy parameter on the skin friction coefficient, the local couple wall stress, the local Nusselt and Sherwood numbers. Both local wall stresses are reduced as the values of buoyancy parameters are increased but the Nusselt and Sherwood numbers increase with increasing values of the buoyancy parameters.

| $\lambda_1$ | $-f''(0)$ | $h'(0)$ | $-\theta'(0)$ | $-\phi'(0)$ |
|---|---|---|---|---|
| –0.5 | 1.77407269 | 0.03036702 | 1.17144784 | 1.73796915 |
| 0 | 1.64314463 | 0.02897505 | 1.19450881 | 1.74511388 |
| 0.5 | 0.46281664 | 0.01845219 | 1.34838298 | 1.80239822 |

**Table 3.** The influence of the thermal buoyancy parameter on the skin friction coefficient, couple stress and rate of heat and mass transfer coefficient.

| $K_p$ | $-f''(0)$ | $h'(0)$ | $-\theta'(0)$ | $-\phi'(0)$ |
|---|---|---|---|---|
| 0.1 | –0.51158820 | 0.01764248 | 1.36287821 | 1.81467597 |
| 5 | 0.33757366 | 0.01499546 | 1.39049894 | 1.82865098 |
| 10 | 0.63059835 | 0.01202912 | 1.41759309 | 1.84519070 |

**Table 4.** The effects of the local porous parameter on the skin friction coefficient, couple stress, rate of heat and mass transfer coefficient.

| $M$ | $-f''(0)$ | $h'(0)$ | $-\theta'(0)$ | $-\phi'(0)$ |
|---|---|---|---|---|
| 1 | 1.51550691 | 0.02767645 | 1.21557294 | 1.75188835 |
| 3 | 1.91685662 | 0.03972746 | 1.16026663 | 1.73369138 |
| 5 | 2.24935200 | 0.03274343 | 1.11815954 | 1.72039545 |

**Table 5.** The influence of the magnetic field parameter on the skin friction coefficient, couple stress, rate of heat and mass transfer coefficient.

The effect of medium porosity on the wall stresses and the Nusselt and Sherwood numbers is depicted in **Table 4**. Porosity significantly affects the transfer rates. The effect of magnetic field parameter is depicted in **Table 5**. As expected, the presence of the magnetic field has prominent effects on the skin-friction coefficient as well on the heat and mass transfer rates. The drag force that is generated by the presence of magnetic field causes significant resistance to the velocity of the fluid thus increases the wall stresses but reduces the rates of heat and mass transfer.

**Table 6** shows the effects of the micropolar parameter and the non-dimensional material parameter on the wall stress. The micropolar parameter increases the values of the wall couple stress, but the non-dimensional material parameter reduces the values of the wall stress.

| $\Delta$ | $h'(0)$ | $\lambda_3$ | $h'(0)$ |
|---|---|---|---|
| 0.1 | 0.05465849 | 0.1 | 0.22157402 |
| 0.5 | 0.23205149 | 0.2 | 0.08984383 |
| 1 | 0.39106943 | 0.3 | 0.05861008 |

**Table 6.** The effects of the micropolar parameter and the non-dimensional material parameter on the couple stress.

The influence of the micropolar parameter $\Delta$ on the axial velocity is depicted in **Figure 1**. It can be observed in **Figure 1** that axial velocity is an increasing function of the micropolar parameter. Physically, micropolar fluids show reduced drag compared to viscous fluids.

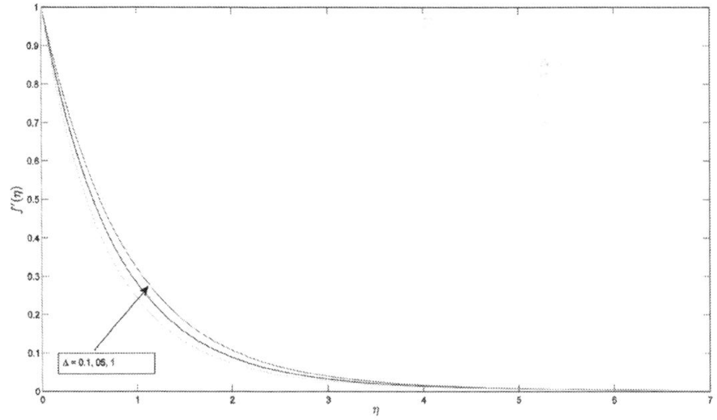


**Figure 1.** Velocity profile for various values of $\Delta$.

In **Figure 2** we display the effect of unsteadiness parameter on the axial velocity $f'(\eta)$ Increasing the values of the unsteadiness parameter ($A$) causes the velocity boundary layer thickness to decrease, thereby reducing the velocity profiles. This is due to increased drag force on the surface. Surface stretching can therefore be used as a stabilizing mechanism in an effort to delay the transition from laminar flow to turbulent fluid flow.

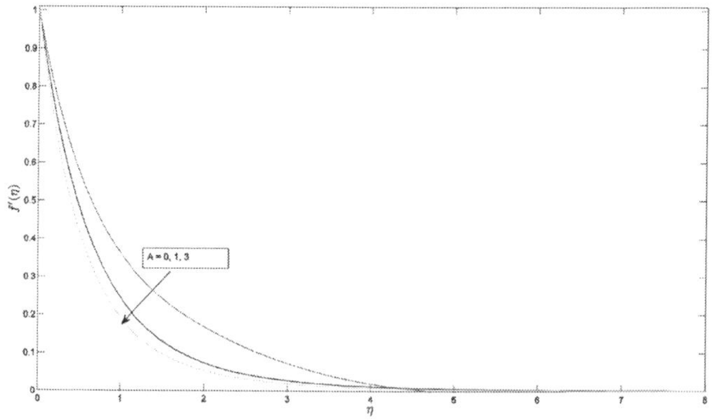


**Figure 2.** Velocity profile with $A$.

The effect of the permeability of the porous medium parameter ($K_p$) on the translational velocity distribution profiles is depicted in **Figure 3**. The translational velocity increases with increasing values of the porosity parameter. Physically, increasing the porosity of the medium implies that the holes of the medium become larger, thereby reducing the resistivity of the medium.

**Figure 4** displays the effect of the thermal buoyancy parameter on the translational velocity distribution. The velocity profiles are reduced for the opposing flows ($\lambda_1$<0). However $\lambda_1$ becomes more positive and favourable pressure gradients are enhanced, thereby accelerating the fluid flow as can be clearly observed in **Figure 4**. It is interesting to note that for large values of the thermal buoyancy parameter, the translational velocity over-shoots near the wall over the moving speed of the sheet. This substantiates the notion that buoyancy accelerates

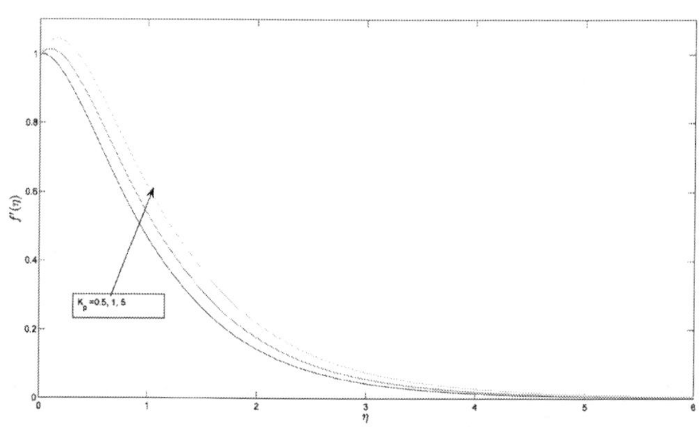


**Figure 3.** Variation of the porosity parameter on the axial velocity.

transition from laminar flow to turbulent flow; therefore, this must always be properly regulated in systems where turbulence is destructive. We also remark that solutal buoyancy as expected has the same effect as thermal buoyancy.

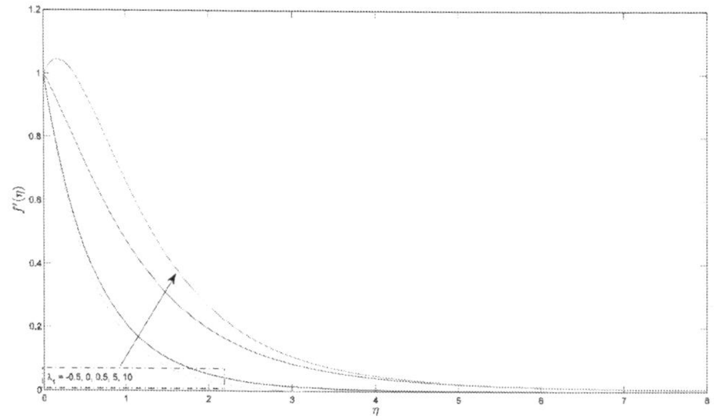


**Figure 4.** The influence of the thermal buoyancy on the axial velocity.

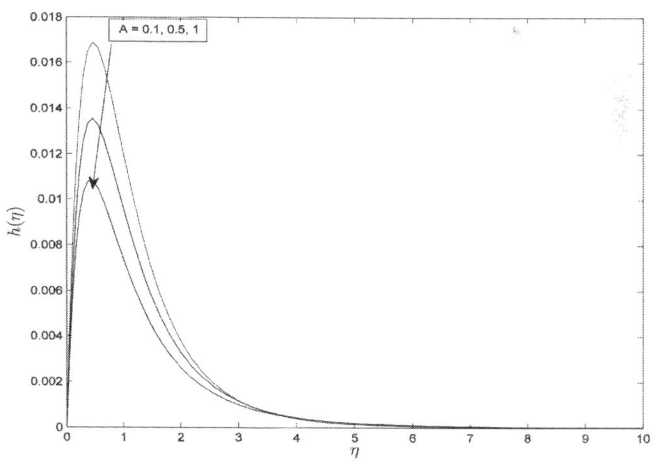


**Figure 5.** Variation of angular velocity with $A$.

The influence of the unsteadiness parameter on the angular velocity $h(\eta)$ is displayed in **Figure 5**. The unsteadiness parameter has pronounced influence on the angular velocity with values of $h(\eta)$ picking up at $\eta=1$, as can be clearly seen in **Figure 5**. However, the angular velocity approaches zero as $\eta$ increases infinitely and the unsteadiness parameter $(A)$ increases.

**Figure 6** shows the effect of the microrotation parameter ($B$) on the angular velocity. We observe that the microrotation effect is more pronounced as expected near the surface. Increasing values of $B$ results in much increasing values of the angular velocity profiles.

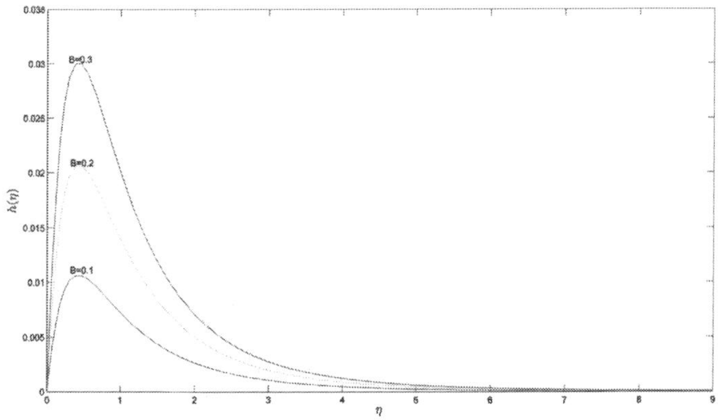


**Figure 6.** Influence of $B$ on the velocity.

We observe in **Figure 7** that the angular velocity is significantly affected by the micropolar parameter ($\Delta$) The angular velocity is greatly induced due to the vortex viscosity effect as $\Delta$ increases.

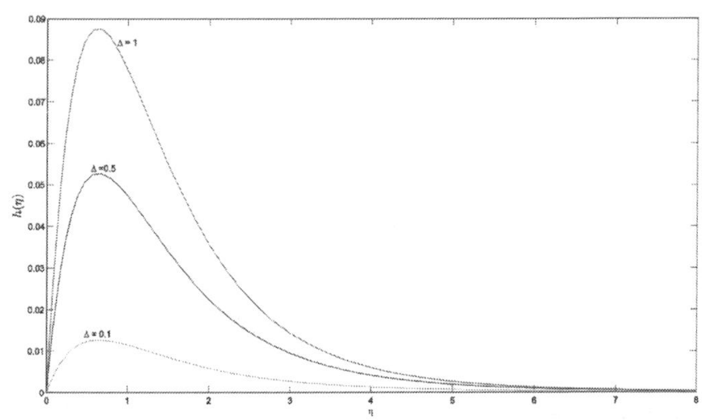


**Figure 7.** Variation of the angular velocity with $\Delta$.

The effect of thermal buoyancy parameter ($\lambda_1$) is displayed in **Figure 8**. We observe that the angular velocity $h(\eta)$ increases with increasing values of the thermal buoyancy parameter $\lambda_1$.

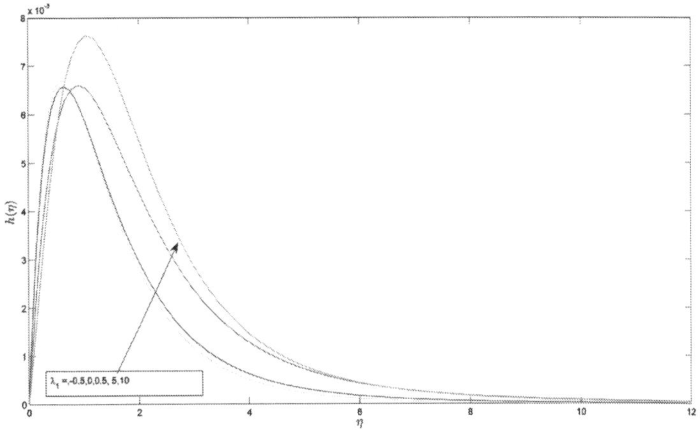


**Figure 8.** Angular velocity profiles for various values of thermal buoyancy.

In **Figure 9**, we display the effect of the metrical parameter on the angular velocity. The angular velocity is greatly reduced by increasing value of $\lambda_3$. This means that either the spin gradient coefficient increases or the microinertia density is reduced.

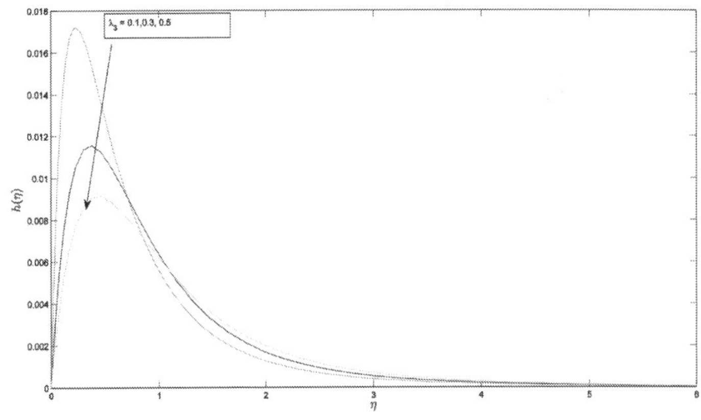


**Figure 9.** Variation of angular velocity with material parameter.

The effect of the unsteadiness parameter is displayed in **Figure 10**. The thermal boundary layer thickness is greatly reduced by increasing values of the unsteadiness parameter thus reducing the fluid temperature distribution

**Figure 11** displays the effect of viscous dissipation on the temperature distribution resulting in increased Eckert number that causes heat energy to be stored in the region as a result of dissipation. This dissipation is caused by viscosity and elastic deformation, thus generating heat due to the frictional heating.

The effect of thermal buoyancy parameter is depleted in **Figure 12**. The thermal boundary layer thickness is reduced when the value of the thermal buoyancy is increased. The fluid temperature is reduced at every point, except at the wall with increasing values of the thermal buoyancy parameter.

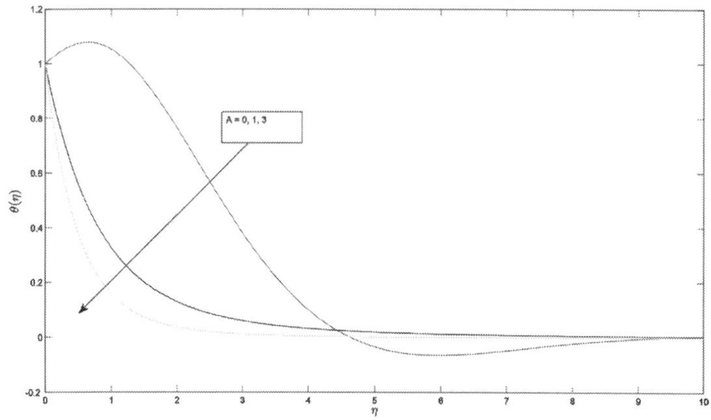


**Figure 10.** Temperature profile for various values of $A$.

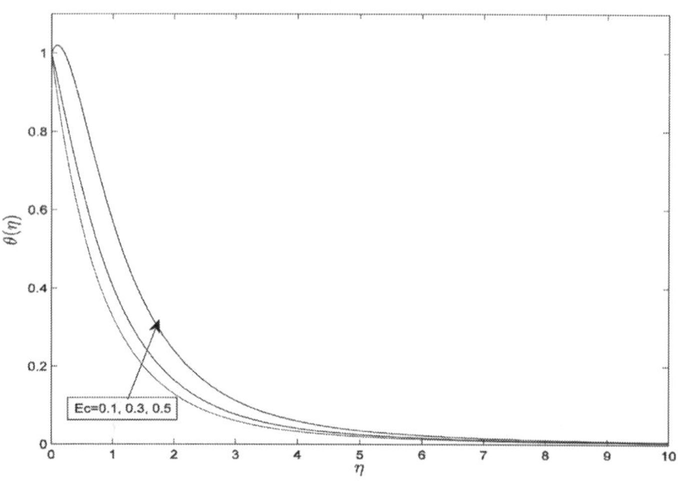


**Figure 11.** Variation of temperature with the Eckert number.

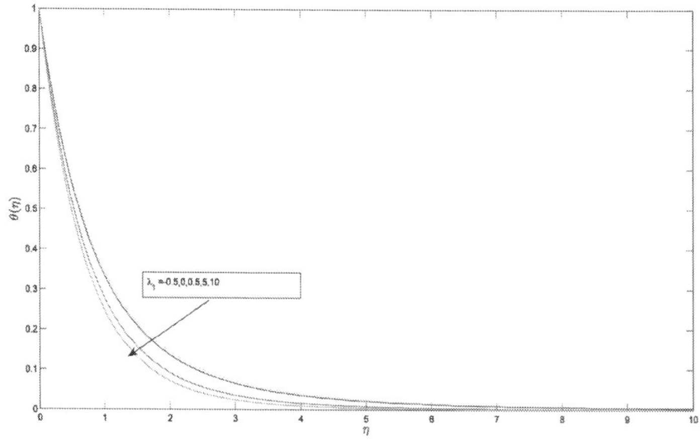


**Figure 12.** Temperature profile for various values of thermal buoyancy.

**Figure 13** displays the variation of temperature distribution within the fluid flow for various values of the heat source/sink parameter. As expected, the fluid temperature increases with increasing values of heat at the source but decreases with increasing values of heat at a sink.

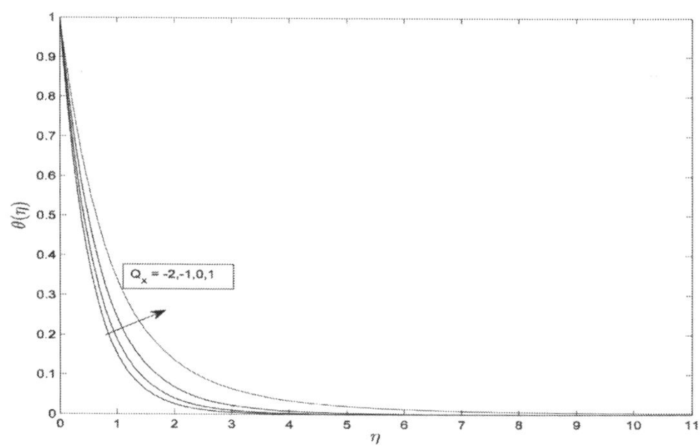


**Figure 13.** Temperature profile for various values of heat source/sink.

**Figure 14** shows the variation of the unsteadiness parameter on the concentration profiles. It is clearly observed that increasing values of $A$ reduces both the solutal boundary layer thickness thus reduces the concentration distributions

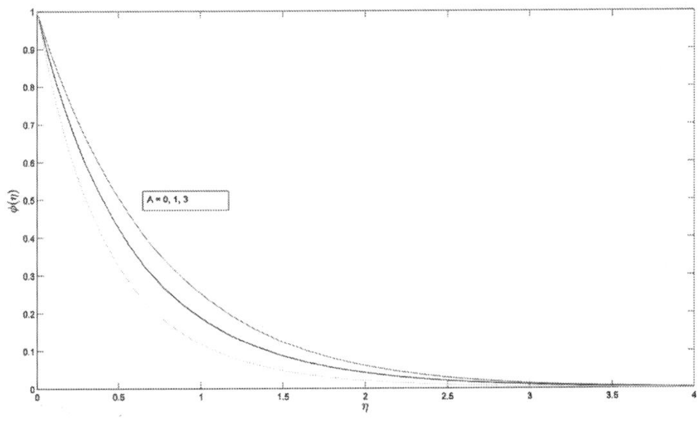


**Figure 14.** Concentration profile for various values $A$

Lastly, the influence of a chemical reaction parameter on the concentration profiles is depicted in **Figure 15**. Physically, the concentration profiles decreases as the chemical reaction parameter increases.

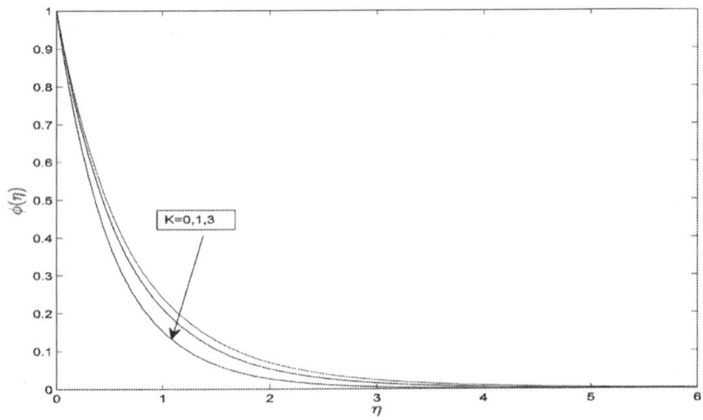


**Figure 15.** Variation.

# 6. Conclusions

The problem of MHD micropolar fluid, heat and mass transfer over unsteadiness stretching sheet through porous medium in the presence of a heat source/sink and chemical reaction is studied in this chapter. By applying suitable similarity transformations, we transformed the governing partial differential equations into a system of ordinary differential equations. We then applied the recently developed numerical technique known as the SQLM to solve the resultant set of non-linear ordinary differential equations. The accuracy of the SQLM was validated against the bvp4c routine method. We observed that the SQLM performs much better than the bvp4c in terms of rate of convergence as well cpu time.

Based on the present study, the following conclusions are made:

1. Buoyancy forces accelerate the fluid flow near the velocity boundary layer in cases of assisting flows but retard the fluid flow in cases of opposing flows.

2. The unsteadiness parameter significantly affects the fluid properties as expected.

3. Both velocity components are increasing functions of the micropolar parameter, while the temperature and concentration distributions are reduced as the micropolar parameter increases.

4. The presence of the viscous dissipation produces heat due to friction between the fluid particles which in turn causes an increase of fluid temperature.

5. The transfer rates of a micropolar fluid are greatly enhanced as either the values of the buoyancy parameter unsteadiness Prandtl or Schmidt number are increased. But these rates are reduced as either the values of the micropolar parameters, magnetic field parameter, Eckert number or chemical reaction parameter are increased.

## Author details

Stanford Shateyi[1*], Fazle Mabood[2] and Gerald Tendayi Marewo[3]

*Address all correspondence to: stanford.shateyi@univen.ac.za

1 University of Venda, Department of Mathematics, Thohoyandou, South Africa

2 Department of Mathematics, University of Peshawar, Pakistan

3 University of Limpopo, Department of Mathematics & Applied Mathematics, Sovenga, South Africa

## References

[1] Rapits A, Perikis C. Viscous flow over a non-linear stretching sheet in the presence of a chemical reaction and magnetic field, Int. J. Non-Linear Mech. 2006; 41: 527–529.

[2] Mabood F, Khan WA, Ismail AIM. MHD boundary layer flow and heat transfer of nanofluids over a nonlinear stretching sheet: a numerical study. J. Magn. Magn. Mater. 2015; 374: 569–576.

[3] Abel MS, Kumar KA, Ravikumara R. MHD flow and heat transfer with effects of buoyancy, viscous and joule dissipation over a nonlinear vertical stretching porous sheet with partial slip. Engineering 2011; 3: 285–291.

[4] Ebashbeshy E, Aldawody DA. Heat transfer over as unsteady stretching surface with variable heat flux in presence of heat source or sink, Comput. Math. Appl. 2010; 60: 2806–2811.

[5] Shateyi S, Prakash J. A new numerical approach for MHD laminar boundary layer flow and heat transfer of nanofluids over a moving surface in the presence of radiation, Boundary Value Probl. 2014; 2014: 2.

[6] Khan WA, Pop I. Boundary layer flow of a nanofluid past a stretching sheet, Int. J. Heat Mass Transfer 2010; 53: 2477–2483.

[7] Makinde OD, Aziz A. Boundary layer flow of a nanofluid past a stretching sheet with a convective boundary condition, Int. J. Therm. Sci. 2011; 50: 1326–1332.

[8] Mustafa M, Hayat T, Obaidat S. Boundary layer flow of a nanofluid over an exponentially stretching sheet with convective boundary conditions, Int. J. Numer. Meth. Heat Fluid Flow 2013; 23: 945–959.

[9] Rashidi MM, Ganesh NV, Abdul Hakeem AK, Ganga B. Buoyancy effect on MHD flow of nanofluid over a stretching sheet in the presence of thermal radiation, J. Mol. Liq. 2014;198: 234–238.

[10] Shateyi S. A new numerical approach to MHD flow of a Maxwell fluid past a vertical stretching sheet in the presence of thermophoresis and chemical reaction, Boundary Value Probl. 2013; 2013: 196.

[11] Eringen AC. Theory of the micropolar fluids, Math. Anal. Appl. J. 1972; 38: 481–496.

[12] Kelson NA, Desseaux A. Effect of surface condition on flow of micropolar fluid driven by a porous stretching sheet, Int. J. Eng. Sci. 2001; 39: 1881–1897.

[13] Gorla RSR, Nakamura S. Mixed convection from a rotating cone to micropolar fluids, Int. J. Heat Fluid Flow 1975; 16: 69–73.

[14] Prathap Kumar J, Umavathi JC, Chamkha AJ, Pop I. Fully developed free convective flow of micropolar and viscous fluids in a vertical channel, Appl. Math. Model. 2010; 34: 1175–1186.

[15] Ibrahim FS, Elaiw AM, Bakr AA. Influence of viscous dissipation and radiation on unsteady MHD mixed convection flow of micropolar fluids, Appl. Math. Inf. Sci. 2008; 2: 143–162.

[16] Mansour MA, El-Hakiem MA, El-Kabeir SM. Heat and mass transfer in magneto hydrodynamic flow of a micropolar fluid on a circular cylinder with uniform heat and mass flux, J. Magn. Magn. Mater. 2000; 220: 259–270.

[17] El-Hakiem MA. Viscous dissipation effects on MHD free convection flow over a nonisothermal surface in a micro polar fluid, Int. Commun. Heat Mass Transfer 2000; 27: 581–590.

[18] El-Hakiem MA, Mohammadein AA, El-Kabeir SMM. Joule heating effects on magneto hydrodynamic free convection flow of a micro polar fluid, Int. Commun. Heat Mass Transfer 1999; 26: 219–227.

[19] El-Amin MF. Magnetohydrodynamic free convection and mass transfer flow in micropolar fluid with constant suction, J. Magn. Magn. Mater. 2011; 234: 567–574.

[20] Kim YJ. Unsteady MHD convection flow of polar fluid past a vertical moving porous plate in a porous medium, Int. J. Heat Mass Transfer 2001; 44: 2791–2799.

[21] Rashidi MM, Mohimanian Pour SA, Abbasbandy S. Analytic approximate solutions for heat transfer of a micropolar fluid through a porous medium with radiation, Commun. Nonlinear Sci. Numer. Simul. 2011; 16: 1874–1889.

[22] Shadloo MS, Kimiaeifar A, Bagheri D. Series solution for heat transfer of continues stretching sheet immersed in a micropolar fluid in the existence of radiation, Int. J. Numer. Methods Heat Fluid Flow 2013; 23: 289–304.

[23] Qasim M, Khan I, Shafie S. Heat transfer in a micropolar fluid over a stretching sheet with Newtonian heating, PLoS ONE 2014; 8: e59393.

[24] Pal D, Chatterjee S. Heat and mass transfer in MHD non-Darcian flow of a micropolar fluid over a stretching sheet embedded in a porous media with non-uniform heat source and thermal radiation, Commun. Nonlinear Sci. Numer. Simul. 2010; 15: 1843–1857.

[25] Pal D, Chatterjee S. Effects of radiation on Darcy–Forchheimer convective flow over a stretching sheet in a micropolar fluid with non-uniform heat source/sink, J. Appl. Fluid Mech. 2015; 8: 207–212.

[26] Bataller RC. Viscoelastic fluid flow and heat transfer over a stretching sheet under the effects of a non-uniform heat source, viscous dissipation and thermal radiation, Int. J. Heat Mass Transfer 2007; 50: 3152–3162.

[27] Subhas AM, Mahesha N. Heat transfer in MHD viscoelastic fluid flow over a stretching sheet with variable thermal conductivity, non-uniform heat source and radiation, Appl. Math. Model. 2008; 32: 1965–1983.

[28] Mabood F, Ibrahim SM, Rashidi MM, Shadloo MS, Lorenzini G. Non-uniform heat source/sink and Soret effects on MHD non-Darcian convective flow past a stretching sheet in a micropolar fluid with radiation. Int. J. Heat Mass Transfer 2016;93: 674–682

[29] Rashad AM, Chamkha AJ, El-Kabeir SMM. Effect of chemical reaction on heat and mass transfer by mixed convection flow about a sphere in a saturated porous media, Int. J. Numer Methods Heat Fluid Flow 2011;21: 418–433.

[30] Magyari E, Chamkha AJ. Combined effect of heat generation or absorption and first-order chemical reaction on micropolar fluid flows over a uniformly stretched permeable surface: the full analytical solution, Int. J. Therm. Sci. 2010; 49: 1821–1828.

[31] Damseh RA, Al-Odat MQ, Chamkha AJ, Shannak BA. Combined effect of heat generation or absorption and first-order chemical reaction on micropolar fluid flows over a uniformly stretched permeable surface, Int. J. Therm. Sci. 2009; 48: 1658–1663.

[32] Das K. Effect of chemical reaction and thermal radiation on heat and mass transfer flow of MHD micropolar fluid in a rotating frame of reference, Int. J. Heat Mass Transfer 2011; 54: 3505–3513.

[33] Hayat T, Abbas Z, Ali N. MHD flow and mass transfer of a upper-convected Maxwell fluid past a porous shrinking sheet with chemical reaction species, Phys. Lett. A 2008; 372: 4698–4704.

[34] Bhattacharyya K, Layek GC. Chemically reactive solute distribution in MHD boundary layer flow over a permeable stretching sheet with suction or blowing, Chem. Eng. Commun. 2010; 197: 1527–1540.

[35] Kandasamy R, Muhaimin I, Khamis AB. Thermophoresis and variable viscosity effects on MHD mixed convective heat and mass transfer past a porous wedge in the presence of chemical reaction, Heat Mass Transfer 2009; 45: 703–712.

[36] Afify A. MHD free convective flow and mass transfer over a stretching sheet with chemical reaction, Heat Mass Transfer 2004; 40: 495–500.

[37] Mabood F, Khan WA, Ismail AIM. MHD stagnation point flow and heat transfer impinging on stretching sheet with chemical reaction and transpiration, Chem. Eng. J. 2015; 273: 430–437.

[38] Motsa SS, Dlamini PG, Khumalo M. Spectral relaxation method and spectral quasilinearization method for solving unsteady boundary layer flow problems, Adv. Math. Phys. 2014, Article ID 341964, 12 p.

[39] Andersson HI, Aarseth JB, Dandapat BS. Heat transfer in a liquid film on unsteady stretching surface, Int. J. Heat Mass Transfer 2000; 43(1): 69–74.

[40] Abd El-Aziz M. Mixed convection flow of a miropolar fluid from an unsteady stretching sheet surface with viscous dissipation, J. Egypt. Math. Soc. 2013, 21, 385–394.

[41] Bellman RE, Kalaba RE. Quasilinearization and Nonlinear Boundary-Value Problems, Elsevier, New York, NY, USA, 1965.

Section 4

# Techniques for Turbulent Flows

Chapter 13

# Computational Fluid Dynamics in Turbulent Flow Applications

Alejandro Alonzo-García,
Claudia del Carmen Gutiérrez-Torres and
José Alfredo Jiménez-Bernal

Additional information is available at the end of the chapter

http://dx.doi.org/10.5772/63831

**Abstract**

This chapter is intended to present to readers a general scope of the technical, theoretical, and numerical applications of computational fluid dynamics using the finite volume method, restricted to incompressible turbulent flows (Ma < 0.3). The main objective of this chapter was to provide readers of a starting point to select an adequate numerical model for the flow regime of interest. Such knowledge could be a key at the moment of extending the analysis to more complex problems, for example, the ones found in heat transfer and fluid flows, multiphase flows, and compressible flows.

**Keywords:** CFD, finite volume technique, circular cylinder, large eddy simulation, conservation equations

## 1. Introduction

Computational fluid dynamics (CFD) is a scientific tool capable of producing information about the main structures of a flowing fluid. As a knowledge area, it finds its origins in the discrete solution of the fundamental equations used in fluid dynamics, such as the mass conservation equation, the momentum conservation equations (based on Newton's second law), and the energy conservation equation (based on the first law of Thermodynamics). All the equations are solved in an approximate way using iterative algorithms to solve lineal algebraic equations systems using matrices [1, 2].

A CFD model has three sequential stages known as preprocessing, solving, and post-processing. In the first stage or preprocessing, the governing equations, properties, and boundary conditions are defined within a domain composed by small interconnected volumetric elements to model the fluid movement. During the second stage or solving process, the adequate selection of discretization schemes (temporal and spatial) for the governing equations is carried out. Also, the convergence criteria or number of iterations, relaxation factors, and pressure and velocity coupling algorithm are set up at this stage. Finally, the post-processing stage involves the analysis and interpretation of the obtained solutions using flow, temperature, and pressures fields [3].

Nowadays, there are different commercial codes developed in a friendly interface, such as ANSYS FLUENT, OPEN FOAM, CFX, X-FLOW, and COMSOL. All of them are capable of helping researchers and engineers at the three aforementioned CFD stages. Generally, the modules of these commercial softwares have been validated comparing the results obtained for specific information such as separation point, circulation length, drag and lift coefficients, and velocities, with experimental and/or analytical results. Very often, the experimental results used for comparison are obtained from carefully controlled experiments about topics such as flow around circular cylinders, flow over forward or backward facing step, flow over a venture, and jet flow, among others [4]. Respecting the programming languages commonly used to develop the CFD codes used in commercial software, the most frequently used are C++, FORTRAN, and lately MATLAB.

## 2. Governing equations in computational fluid dynamics

The governing equations in computational fluid dynamic mathematically express the three fundamental physical principles that describe the movement of any fluid. These equations are as follows:

- Continuity equation or mass conservation principle.
- Newton's second law or momentum conservation principle.
- The first law of thermodynamics or energy conservation principle.

A fluid is a substance that, due to molecular distances, does not present a defined form and adopts the form of the vessel that contains it. Therefore, it is difficult to analyze a fluid from the universal approach used for solids. In general, a fluid can be defined as a substance that deforms continually under the action of a shear stress. If a fluid is in movement, the velocity can be different at different positions within the studied domain, and their particles can rotate and deform at the same time. Considering the fluid as a continuum, there are two approaches that can be used to understand its movement, making it susceptible to be analyzed using the fundamental principles: The first one is based on the study of a volume element of infinitesimal size and fixed in the space with the fluid flowing through it (known as the Eulerian approach) and an infinitesimal fluid element that moves along a streamline with a velocity equal to the local velocity of the flow at each point (Lagrangian approach) [5].

http://dx.doi.org/10.5772/63831

When a differential element of a fluid moving along a streamline, and considering the motion of a particle with a defined velocity through a differential volume defined in a Cartesian space, the governing equations for a compressible viscous flow are as follows:

**(a)** Continuity equation:

$$\frac{\partial \rho}{\partial t}+\nabla \cdot\left(\rho \vec{V}\right)=0 \tag{1.1}$$

**(b)** Navier-Stokes equations:

x-direction component ($\hat{\imath}$)

$$\frac{\partial(\rho u)}{\partial t}+\nabla \cdot\left(\rho u \vec{V}\right)=-\frac{\partial P}{\partial x}+\frac{\partial \tau_{xx}}{\partial x}+\frac{\partial \tau_{yx}}{\partial y}+\frac{\partial \tau_{zx}}{\partial z}+\rho f_x \tag{1.2}$$

y-direction component ($\hat{\jmath}$)

$$\frac{\partial(\rho v)}{\partial t}+\nabla \cdot\left(\rho v \vec{V}\right)=-\frac{\partial P}{\partial y}+\frac{\partial \tau_{xy}}{\partial x}+\frac{\partial \tau_{yy}}{\partial y}+\frac{\partial \tau_{zy}}{\partial z}+\rho f_y \tag{1.3}$$

z-direction component ($\hat{k}$)

$$\frac{\partial(\rho w)}{\partial t}+\nabla \cdot\left(\rho w \vec{V}\right)=-\frac{\partial P}{\partial z}+\frac{\partial \tau_{xz}}{\partial x}+\frac{\partial \tau_{yz}}{\partial y}+\frac{\partial \tau_{zz}}{\partial z}+\rho f_z \tag{1.4}$$

Energy equation:

$$\begin{aligned}\frac{\partial}{\partial t}\left[\rho\left(e+\frac{u^2+v^2+w^2}{2}\right)\right]+\nabla \cdot\left[\rho\left(e+\frac{u^2+v^2+w^2}{2}\right)\vec{V}\right]=\rho\dot{q}+\frac{\partial}{\partial x}\left(k\frac{\partial T}{\partial x}\right)+\frac{\partial}{\partial y}\left(k\frac{\partial T}{\partial y}\right)+\\ \frac{\partial}{\partial z}\left(k\frac{\partial T}{\partial z}\right)-\frac{\partial(uP)}{\partial x}-\frac{\partial(vP)}{\partial y}-\frac{\partial(wP)}{\partial z}+\frac{\partial\left(u\tau_{xx}\right)}{\partial x}+\frac{\partial\left(u\tau_{yx}\right)}{\partial y}+\frac{\partial\left(u\tau_{zx}\right)}{\partial z}+\frac{\partial\left(v\tau_{xy}\right)}{\partial x}+\\ \frac{\partial\left(v\tau_{yy}\right)}{\partial y}+\frac{\partial\left(v\tau_{zy}\right)}{\partial z}+\frac{\partial\left(w\tau_{xz}\right)}{\partial x}+\frac{\partial\left(w\tau_{yz}\right)}{\partial y}+\frac{\partial\left(w\tau_{zz}\right)}{\partial z}+\rho\vec{f}\cdot\vec{V}\end{aligned} \tag{1.5}$$

where $e$ is the internal energy per unit of mass, $\vec{f}$ represents the body forces that act on the centroid of the fluid element (like gravitational, electrical or magnetic forces), "k" is thermal conductivity, P is the static pressure, $\dot{q}$ is the heat transfer rate per unit of mass in the volume element (it can be heat that is a combustion product, a chemical reaction, or an electron flow), $t$ is time, $T$ is temperature, $\rho$ is density, $\tau$ are viscous stresses, and $\nabla = \frac{\partial}{\partial x}\vec{i} + \frac{\partial}{\partial y}\vec{j} + \frac{\partial}{\partial z}\vec{k}$ is the DEL vector operator for Cartesian coordinates. It is necessary to point out that viscous stresses (normal and shear stresses) are related to the deformation rate of the fluid element. Shear stresses are related to the temporal deformation caused by the constant shear force acting on the fluid element. Conventionally, $\tau_{ij}$ represents a stress in the "j" direction, exerted on a plane perpendicular to $i$-axis. Normal stresses are related to the volume change rate in the fluid element (compression or tension); these stresses have in general a lower value than shear stresses.

At the end of the seventeenth century, Isaac Newton established that the shear stress in a fluid is proportional to its temporal deformation rate (velocity gradients, for example). Fluids that follow this behavior are known as Newtonian fluids, and they have many applications in fluid dynamics. For this kind of fluids, Stokes found, in 1845, the following relationships:

$$
\begin{aligned}
\tau_{xy} = \tau_{yx} &= \mu\left(\frac{\partial v}{\partial x} + \frac{\partial u}{\partial y}\right) & \tau_{xx} &= \lambda(\nabla \cdot V) + 2\mu\frac{\partial u}{\partial x} \\
\tau_{xz} = \tau_{zx} &= \mu\left(\frac{\partial w}{\partial x} + \frac{\partial u}{\partial z}\right) & \tau_{yy} &= \lambda(\nabla \cdot V) + 2\mu\frac{\partial v}{\partial y} \\
\tau_{yz} = \tau_{zy} &= \mu\left(\frac{\partial w}{\partial y} + \frac{\partial v}{\partial z}\right) & \tau_{zz} &= \lambda(\nabla \cdot V) + 2\mu\frac{\partial w}{\partial z}
\end{aligned}
\tag{1.6}
$$

where $\mu$ is the molecular viscosity and $\lambda$ is the second viscosity (which is not a term of common use in engineering). For gases, a good approximation can be obtained using the value $\lambda = -2/3\mu$.

Non-Newtonian fluids are those that do not present a linear relationship between stresses and deformation rates due to shear stresses (velocities gradients). A non-Newtonian fluid can present viscoelastic and thixotropic properties as well as different kinds of relationships among density, pressure, and temperature in comparison with a Newtonian fluid. This kind of fluid requires a more specialized treatment to study them, which is out of the scope of this document.

The governing equations presented (1.1)–(1.5) contain seven unknown flow variables expressed in a set of five differential equations. For practical applications, additional equations can be used to "close" the system (equal number of equations and unknowns). For example, in the study of an aerodynamic phenomenon, it is in general possible to assume that a gas behaves as an "ideal gas". For an ideal gas, the state equation is = $\rho RT$, where R is the gas constant. This equation provides the equation system with a sixth equation. It can also be considered a seventh equation to close the equation system using a thermodynamic relationship among state variables, for example: $e = e(T, P)$ For an ideal gas (with constant specific heats), this relationship becomes$e = C_v T$ where $C_v$ is the constant volume-specific heat.

Finally, applying the substantial derivative definition for Cartesian coordinates$D/Dt = \partial/\partial t + u\frac{\partial}{\partial x} + v\frac{\partial}{\partial y} + w\frac{\partial}{\partial z}$ Eqs. (1.1)–(1.5) can be written as follows:

http://dx.doi.org/10.5772/63831

$$\frac{\partial \rho}{\partial t}+\nabla\cdot(\rho V)=0 \tag{1.7}$$

$$\rho\frac{Du}{Dt}=-\frac{\partial P}{\partial x}+\mu\left[\frac{\partial^2 u}{\partial x^2}+\frac{\partial^2 u}{\partial y^2}+\frac{\partial^2 u}{\partial z^2}\right]+\rho f_x \tag{1.8}$$

$$\rho\frac{Dv}{Dt}=-\frac{\partial P}{\partial y}+\mu\left[\frac{\partial^2 v}{\partial x^2}+\frac{\partial^2 v}{\partial y^2}+\frac{\partial^2 v}{\partial z^2}\right]+\rho f_y \tag{1.9}$$

$$\rho\frac{Dw}{Dt}=-\frac{\partial P}{\partial z}+\mu\left[\frac{\partial^2 w}{\partial x^2}+\frac{\partial^2 w}{\partial y^2}+\frac{\partial^2 w}{\partial z^2}\right]+\rho f_z \tag{1.10}$$

$$\begin{aligned}\frac{D}{Dt}\left[\rho\left(e+\frac{u^2+v^2+w^2}{2}\right)\right]&=\rho q+\frac{\partial}{\partial x}\left(k\frac{\partial T}{\partial x}\right)+\frac{\partial}{\partial y}\left(k\frac{\partial T}{\partial y}\right)+\frac{\partial}{\partial z}\left(k\frac{\partial T}{\partial z}\right)\\&-\frac{\partial(uP)}{\partial x}-\frac{\partial(vP)}{\partial y}-\frac{\partial(wP)}{\partial z}+\frac{\partial(u\tau_{xx})}{\partial x}+\frac{\partial(u\tau_{yx})}{\partial y}+\frac{\partial(u\tau_{zx})}{\partial z}+\\&\frac{\partial(v\tau_{xy})}{\partial x}+\frac{\partial(v\tau_{yy})}{\partial y}+\frac{\partial(v\tau_{zy})}{\partial z}+\frac{\partial(w\tau_{xz})}{\partial x}+\frac{\partial(w\tau_{yz})}{\partial y}+\frac{\partial(w\tau_{zz})}{\partial z}+\rho\vec{f}\cdot V\end{aligned} \tag{1.11}$$

The governing equations presented (1.1)–(1.5) or (1.7)–(1.11) are widely known as the Navier–Stokes equations to honor the French physicist Claude Louis Navier and the English mathematician George Gabriel Stokes, who in an independent way, both obtained the equations in the first half of the nineteenth century. Originally, the Navier–Stokes equations terminology was only defined for the momentum equations. However, current CFD literature has been expanded to include the equations of mass and energy conservation. It should be noted that the governing equations can be also expressed in cylindrical and spherical coordinates, or even in generalized curvilinear coordinates.

It has to be kept in mind that these equations were originally formulated to reproduce the physics present in single-phase and non-reactive Newtonian flows. The governing equations for reactive flow systems with multiple components (like the ones found in combustion and multiphase flow problems) can be also established. However, they are more complex because they involve multiple species and phases. It is necessary to note that for this complex flow systems, it becomes a necessity to include approximation models or empirical correlations because several terms are not constant anymore and they become functions for example of temperature, pressure, location, introducing new nonlinearities in the diffusive terms.

The governing equations constitute a coupled nonlinear partial differential equations system; therefore, an analytical solution is difficult to obtain. At the present time, there is not a general solution in a closed form for this equation system. In fact, this is one of the most important reasons of the use of CFD, since it provides numerical approximations to the equations solutions, which have not been found yet using analytical methods, except for idealized cases for one-dimensional or two-dimensional flows in laminar or creeping flows.

The mathematical character of the equations has a significant impact on CFD. First of all, it is very important that the problem is adequately posed, and it means that the solution of the problem exists and it is unique. Furthermore, this solution is only affected by initial and boundary conditions. It is also important to classify the governing equations as elliptical, parabolic, or hyperbolic. Elliptical equations have to be solved simultaneously in the complete flow domain, whereas hyperbolic and parabolic equations propagate from one position to another one.

Mathematically, parabolic and hyperbolic equations are susceptible to be solved using time steps. On the other hand, for the elliptical equations, the flow variables in a given point should be solved simultaneously with the flow variables in other positions. It can be stated that the Navier-Stokes equations have, in general, a mixed nature. They are parabolic in the time domain and elliptical in the space domain [1, 3].

As it was mentioned before, the governing equations can be applied for laminar and turbulent flows by means of the use of additional terms to represent the influence of the fluctuating eddies. In a basic and rigorous way, direct numerical simulation (DNS) works solving numerically these equations to a desired accuracy degree without any additional model or correlation. However, its application is still limited because of the large quantity of resources required to solve the majority of the existent problems, which exceed the capacity of conventional computers.

For turbulent flows, there is a wide spectrum of time and length scales that have to be solved that increase the computational time in DNS simulation. However, from a scientific point of view, the information obtained using DNS is very valuable because it is considered a validation means for turbulent models (with less complexity). The traditional performance of the CFD methods for turbulent flows has been focused on predicting the average influence of the main characteristics of turbulence. Very often, such influence is approached including new transport equations to replicate the effects of generation or dissipation of Reynolds stresses , which represent the transport of momentum in the streamwise direction (x-direction) caused by the turbulent eddies in the "i" and "j" directions. Frequently, average stress models adjust to semi-empirical models, which depend on a number of constants obtained using experimental correlations. These correlations are very often obtained from experiments where the working fluid is air or water, and very frequently, the experimental setup includes a flat plate. In the literature, this kind of closing model is known as a Reynolds Average Navier–Stokes (RANS) turbulence model. This kind of model is the most frequently used for engineering applications today. Unfortunately, for complex turbulent flows there is not a "universal" model that can be applied to any kind of flow, since boundary layer effects can be very different. In fact, the description of what happens within the boundary layer is the main weakness of the RANS models. For many years, RANS models have had success reproducing turbulent zones far away from the wall for fully developed flows. However, they still have problems reproducing unsteady flows or flow separation phenomena (as a result of an adverse pressure gradient) [6, 7]. Even though it is true that for very complex turbulent flows, there exists new and more powerful RANS models, capable of giving useful information to make decisions in an industry for example. Nevertheless, in the scientific world, those models do not seem to have universal validity. Due to that, alternative approaches such as large eddy simulation (LES) and DNS, with the help of the technological evolution of computers, have gained more attention in the last three decades.

## 3. The ANSYS FLUENT software

The software ANSYS FLUENT is one of the most used tools to discretely solve the governing equations in fluid dynamics. It is very useful as a tool oriented to reproduce the behavior and give information for a wide range of fluid flows (compressible or incompressible, laminar or turbulent, steady or unsteady). It also possesses a wide variety of mathematical models for transport phenomena (such as heat transfer and chemical reactions) that can be applied to both simple and more complex geometries. FLUENT can be applied to laminar or turbulent flows within devices, such as heat exchangers, nozzles, complex-shaped ducts, turbomachinery (heat transfer and aerodynamic), heat engine components, external flows, flow through compressors, pumps, fans, and multiphase flows, among others.

In order to make a generalization of the governing equations to include compressibility effects and interactions among different phases, the continuity equation used by FLUENT can be described as follows:

$$\frac{\partial \rho}{\partial t} + \nabla \cdot \left(\rho \vec{V}\right) = S_m \tag{1.12}$$

where the source term $S_m$ represents the mass added to the continuous phase by the disperse phase. Other source terms can be defined by the user.

With respect to the other quantities transported by the fluid, they are modeled based on an integral general equation, where variable $\phi$ can be substituted by different flow variables before being discretized in its matrix form. For that Eq. (1.13), represents a dissipation constant for the transported fluid, which can be, for example, the dynamic viscosity $\mu$ for the momentum transport equations in any direction, or the Eddie viscosity $\mu_t$ associated with the energy production–dissipation models for the turbulent kinetic energy, whose magnitude depends on secondary factors such as turbulent kinetic energy intensity and some semi-empirical correlations.

$$\frac{\partial}{\partial t}\int_V^{\square} \rho\phi dV + \oint_A \rho\phi\vec{V} \cdot dA = \oint_A \Gamma_\phi \nabla\phi \cdot dA + \int_V^{\square} S_\phi dV \tag{1.13}$$

**Table 1** shows some equivalencies associated to the general variable.

| Equation | Variable ($\varphi$) |
|---|---|
| Continuity | 1 |
| X momentum | u |
| Y momentum | v |
| Z momentum | w |
| Transport of turbulent kinetic energy | k |
| Dissipation of the turbulent kinetic energy | $\epsilon$ |

**Table 1.** Different variables used in the general equation.

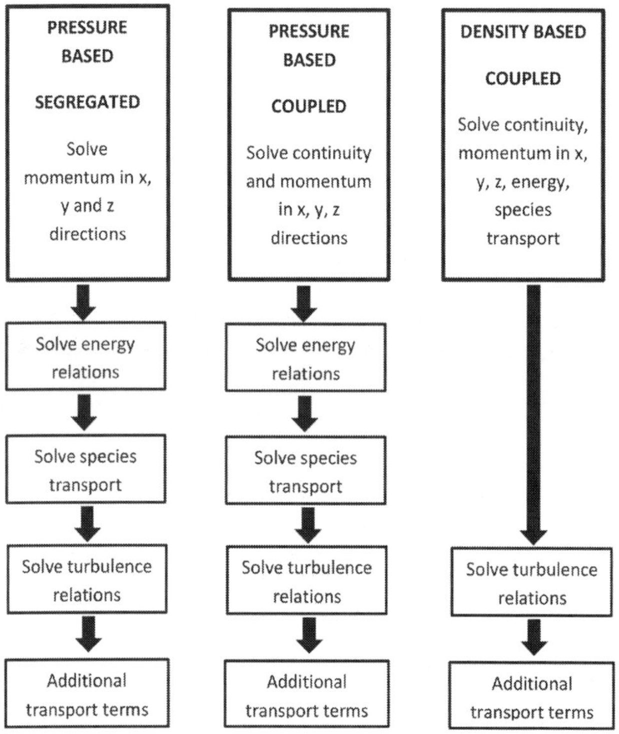


**Figure 1.** The coupled and segregated solvers comparison diagram, adapted with permission from [8].

The FLUENT solvers work based on a logical sequence to solve the discretized equations in two ways, the segregated one or the coupled one [8]. The segregated mode is recommended for flow problems where it can be expected the formation of large velocity gradients. These gradients can be produced by a boundary layer formation with or without flow separation where the compressibility effects are minimal (Mach < 0.3) and with or without temperature gradients at the boundary. Some examples of the application of the segregated solver are as follows: vehicular aerodynamics problems, internal flows, centrifugal pumps velocity fields' analysis, cyclone separator flows, flows in refrigeration ducts, flow pattern in cooling fins, etc. Regarding the coupled solver, it is widely used for the solution of problems related to large compressibility effects in the fluid, such as supersonic flows, hypersonic flows within nozzles combustion chambers, the movement of projectiles, and other objects where the shock waves are produced due to large pressure gradients and density changes.

Numerically speaking, the biggest difference between both solver modes is the way the flow governing equations are solved. The segregated mode solve them sequentially, taking the velocity and pressure equations (or corrected pressure equations) as the main variables, the coupled one solves globally the equations for continuity, momentum, and species exchange. **Figure 1** shows a diagram of both solver modes' performances.

### 3.1. Main parameters and boundary conditions

Although ANSYS FLUENT is a very friendly application, its implementation requires of an adjustment for some predetermined parameters, which will guide the solution process.

Before uploading the mesh associated with the physical domain to be studied, the software requires to define the number of dimensions used to reach the solution; it can be two-dimension (2D) or 3D. To analyze uniform cross sections in bodies with infinite length, it is recommended to use 2D analysis, suppressing the third coordinate because gradients along the depth are not significant. The software offers an option to choose double precision (more significant ciphers). This option is recommended when large gradients in the flow variables are expected, especially at very close nodal position, cells with very large aspect ratio or simply when a better convergence is desirable.

Another important characteristic is the capacity to adjust the number of core processors to be used internally in parallel. This characteristics is especially helpful for problems that require many iterations to be solved (e.g.,, non-stationary models), multiphase and reactive problems, very large grid sizes, and very complex geometries such as airplanes and vehicles.

Finally, this computer program allows to scale the grid physical dimensions to required sizes using both English and international systems. It can be used to work on problems such as the flow between building zones located hundreds of meters from each other or problems related to microfluids. It also allows to select constant values to calculate non-dimensional parameters such as friction coefficient and lift and drag coefficients.

In any CFD model, boundary conditions have to represent faithfully the real conditions at the boundary. According to the mathematical characteristics of the differential equations, boundary conditions can be classified as follows:

**Dirichlet boundary condition:** The value of the flow variable is specified at the boundary. This kind of boundary condition is typically linked to problems involving flow inlets and isothermal walls.

**Neumann boundary condition:** For this kind of boundary condition, the value of the gradient normal to the flow variable is specified. These boundary conditions are often associated with symmetric boundaries and adiabatic walls.

**Mixed boundary conditions:** These are the conditions resulting from a combination of boundary conditions of the kind of Neumann and Dirichlet.

The boundary conditions can be classified by its physical meaning as follows: physical boundaries, such as solid walls, or artificial boundaries, such as outflow. The latter are mathematical approximations to the real behavior of the flow in certain zones. Artificial boundaries can be applied, if the computational domain constitutes part of the total flow field, to research the most interesting region and to reduce computational costs. Artificial boundary conditions require mathematical formulations that are physically significant to the real flow behavior.

Regarding ANSYS FLUENT, there are different types of boundary conditions that can be used to simulate different flow problems. Next, a general description of the most common boundary conditions used in most hydrodynamic studies is presented. The authors recommend readers to consult Ref. [8] for more detailed information.

#### *3.1.1. Velocity inlet*

The "velocity inlet" condition was conceived to prescribe a uniform velocity profile at the entrance of a computational domain (bi-dimensional or tri-dimensional). This boundary condition was created to analyze incompressible flows, such as external flows over complex geometries or internal flows in different sections of piping or machinery. It is not recommended for compressible flows. It also allows to specify the magnitude and the direction of a uniform velocity profile. Other velocity profiles such as parabolic, sinusoidal, and logarithm can be imposed using a user-defined function code (UDF). For turbulent flows, the software allows prescribing the turbulence levels required at the entrance or the domain using different methods. A hydraulic diameter and a value of turbulence intensity can be used to do so for internal flows. For example, for square ducts, the hydraulic diameter can be calculated as 4A/P, where A is the cross section area and P is the perimeter of the same area, also known as the wetted perimeter. For external flows, it is required to provide a characteristic length (for example, the diameter of a cylinder if the flow over a circular cylinder is studied). In this case, the turbulence intensity represents a percentage of the value of the fluctuating values of velocity based on the mean value. For example, if the magnitude of the fluid velocity is 5 m/s and a turbulence level of 10% is prescribed, the inlet velocity would present values from 4.5 to 5.5 m/s. Additionally, different parameters like flow temperatures or heat flux can be established at the entrance of the domain, which are important for energy studies and heat and mass transfer analysis.

http://dx.doi.org/10.5772/63831

### 3.1.2. Pressure inlet

The "pressure inlet" boundary condition is used to define the pressure characteristics at the entrance of the domain for cases where the mass flow or the velocity is unknown at the inlet of the domain. This boundary condition can be used for compressible and incompressible flows. For incompressible flows, the total pressure can be modeled as follows:

$$P_{total} = P_{estatic} + \frac{1}{2}\rho V^2 \tag{1.14}$$

where the total pressure or "gauge total pressure" is known, and it is equivalent to the sum of the static pressure at the inlet, also known as supersonic/initial gauge pressure and a dynamic pressure, which is not necessarily known, but can be manually calculated and compared to the velocity assigned to the normal direction to the boundary condition.

$$P_{total,abs} = P_{estatic}\left[1 + \frac{k-1}{2}M^2\right]^{\frac{k}{k-1}} \tag{1.15}$$

Regarding the compressible flows, Eq. (1.15) is used, where "k" is the specific heats ratio and M is the Mach number.

### 3.1.3. Outflow

The "outflow" boundary condition represents and artificial cut through the flow field, similar to the velocity inlet condition, but set up at the outlet of the flow domain. The outflow conditions are used when the characteristics looked for in the flow are developed at a fraction of the total flow field. When this is true, this boundary condition allows to avoid numerically modeling the complete domain (which can be computationally expensive). In those cases, a distance from the domain inlet is defined as the flow outlet, imposing there the outflow condition. The main difference between an inflow and an outflow condition is that there is not flow information available outside the computational domain for an outflow condition. In contrast, for the inflow condition, there is always information about the entering flow.

The flow variables in an outflow condition have to be approximated in a physically significant way in a manner that does not affect the solution of the governing equations in the computational domain. For an outflow boundary condition, the numerical effects found upstream that are generated have to be eliminated or reduced. Conventionally, in the CFD programming for laminar and steady RANS models, the fully developed conditions in the streamwise direction are expressed by $\partial\varphi/\partial x_i = 0$. However, for more complex cases where recirculating flow structures exist, there can be problems due to the reentrance of mass circulating in a vortex for example. For these cases, a generalized convective boundary condition is used:

$$\left. \frac{\partial \phi}{\partial t} + U_{conv} \frac{\partial \phi}{\partial x_i} \right|_{outlet} = 0 \tag{1.16}$$

The correct use of that equation warrants the vortices can get near or cross the outlet boundary without significantly perturbing the computational solution inside the domain. In the last equation, $x_i$ represents the main flow direction, and $U_{conv}$ denotes the mean convective velocity at the outlet position, approximated using the outlet mass flow value [9].

*3.1.4. Pressure outlet*

The "pressure outlet" boundary condition is conventionally used for the solution of coupled problems (high Mach number values and compressibility effects), where the outflow boundary condition is not convenient. It requires to specify the static pressure (gauge pressure) at the domain outlet. Such value is exclusively respected for subsonic flow cases (M < 1). When the flow is supersonic, the specified pressure will not be used, and a new value will be extrapolated based on previous values.

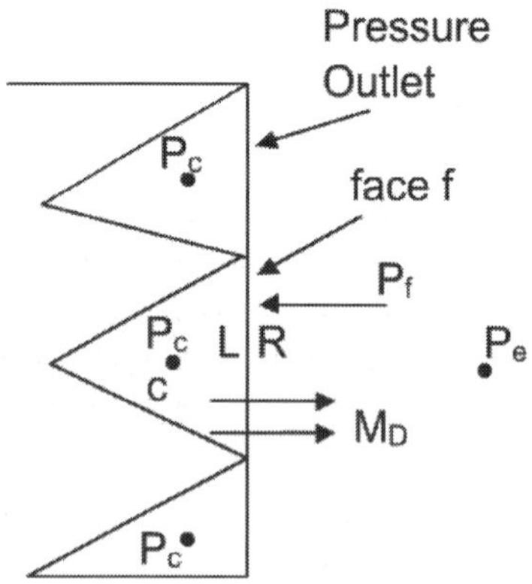


**Figure 2.** Pressure components of the pressure outlet boundary condition, adapted with permission from [10].

To use this boundary condition correctly, it is required to establish a set of flow relations for reversing flow at the outlet during the solution process (a set of backflow relations). Such relations are important because incorrect values for these parameters can cause convergence problems.

Specifically for the coupled solver in the option density based, pressure values at the outlet faces are calculated using a splitting procedure based on the AUSM scheme developed by Liou [11].

For subsonic flow conditions at the outlet, pressure is determined using a weighted average based on the left and right states at the domain boundary (**Figure 2**). This average value is a mix of polynomial adjustments of fifth order based on the Mach number values at the outlet face. Then, the pressure value is finally stated $P_f = f(P_c, P_e, M_n)$ where $P_c$ is the pressure at the pressure value at the inside neighbor cell next the exit face f, being $P_e$ the specified pressure and $M_n$ the Mach number at the normal direction. If there is a supersonic flow, the pressure at the exit face is extrapolated from the inlet cell value. For incompressible flow, the exit face pressure is calculated as an average between the outlets specified pressure and the average pressure value.

$$P_f = \frac{1}{2}\left(P_c + P_e\right) \tag{1.17}$$

The "pressure outlet" boundary condition does not guarantee a constant pressure along the outlet of the domain. However, once the solution of the model converges, the average pressure value at the outlet will tend to reach a value close to the static pressure imposed at the exit.

*3.1.5. Walls*

For viscous flows, the nonslip condition has to be imposed at the walls. This can be attained prescribing $u = v = w = 0$ at the walls, to reproduce the formation of the dynamic boundary layer. In some cases, when solving the flow within the boundary layer is not needed (e.g., in external flows over an immerse body, there is no need to solve the boundary layer on the walls that delimitate the domain), values of shear stresses equal to zero are imposed, which is known as slip walls [12]. In addition to prescribing values for shear stresses, temperature values (Dirichlet type) or normal heat flux values (Neumann type) can be imposed and they are particularly useful for thermal analysis. It is also possible to define wall roughness values, which are especially useful in turbulent flows studies, as well as translational and rotational movement of the walls related to the same frame of reference.

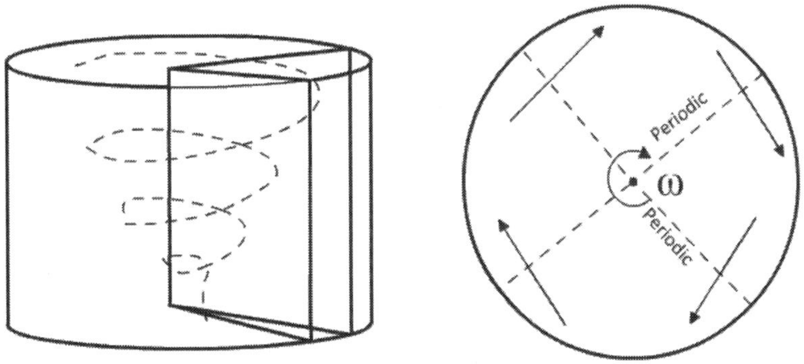


**Figure 3.** Rotational periodicity of a cylindrical recipient, adapted with permission from [10].

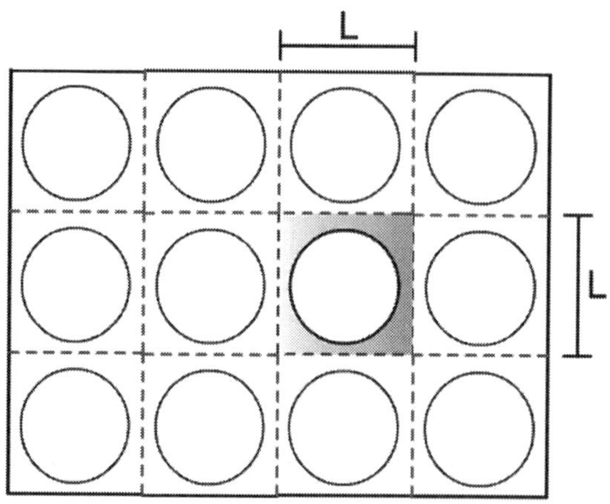


**Figure 4.** Translational periodicity in a heat exchanger array.

*3.1.6. Periodic boundary condition*

Periodic boundary condition is useful to cut down the size of the studied domain, saving simulation time in cases where the geometry of the given problem and the flow pattern have characteristics that are repetitive and periodic along a certain characteristic length "L". The periodic flow behavior can be found in many applications such as heat exchanger channels, flow over pipe banks, and fully developed flow in pipes and ducts. There exist two types of periodicity, such as translational and rotational periodicity (**Figure 3**). For rotational periodicity a constant pressure is defined along the periodicity planes, also defining a rotational axis in the fluid in studies related to turbomachinery.

Regarding translational periodicity, a finite pressure drop can be defined between two periodic Planes (**Figure 4**). Also, a mass flow can be defined.

### 3.2. Some technical suggestions for an adequate solving

To solve adequately a CFD problem, it is recommended a series of best practices whose Application can help to obtain better convergence values for CFD simulations. The first one is to verify that the skewness value of most of the mesh elements is between 0 and 0.5, being the values closest to 0 the most desirable ones. This is to minimize the numerical dissipation for the algorithms responsible of carrying out the flow balances at the cell faces. Another important suggestion to improve initial convergence in fluid, heat transfer, and multiphase flow problems is to first obtain solutions using single precision and first-order discretization models. After that, based on these solutions, change the discretization models to second order models. This should be carried out considering that second-order schemes produce lower error values. From this point, it is recommended to activate the energy equation (if needed) or any multiphase flow or reactive flow parameters (if needed) to obtain adequate convergence. It is also needed to consider that final runs have to be performed using double precision. Finally, having previously obtained convergence, relaxation factor values can be increased to obtain a better solution in each iterative process. It is necessary to remember the importance of the results validation, using for that, experimental values of the same phenomenon in a controlled environment.

### 3.3. Pressure–velocity coupling

In the Navier-Stokes Eqs. (1.7)–(1.10), calculated velocities are related to the momentum transport in two or three dimensions. These velocities should satisfy the mass conservation equation. However, continuity equation does not depend on the pressure as it does the momentum exchange. The convective and dissipative terms of the momentum conservation equation, which depends on the pressure, have second-order, nonlinear terms. When governing equations have to be solved, it is necessary to find the velocity and pressure fields for stationary and time-dependent problems. If the flow is incompressible, continuity equation can be used as a transport equation for density, energy conservation equation represents temperature transport, and the existing pressure gradients can be obtained using equations such as the ideal gas law or any valid state equation. For incompressible flow, however, density has a constant value and there is not a direct link among the governing equations for the mass and momentum transport equations. This situation provokes unpredictable oscillations in the solving process making it considerably difficult.

Regarding the semi-implicit method for pressure-linked equations (SIMPLE) algorithm proposed by Patankar and Spalding in 1972 [13], it has been used for many years as a useful and convenient solving strategy. This algorithm is depicted in **Figure 5**. Unit mass flows go through the faces of the cells, and are evaluated from an initial guessed velocity value in two or three dimensions. From these velocity and pressure fields, a momentum transport equation solution is obtained. Then, from this solution, a corrected pressure is obtained using a series of relationships obtained from the continuity equation.

Finally, such corrected pressure values will be used for the transport and continuity equations solving. The whole process has to be repeated in an iterative manner until a convergence criterion is reached. As it was mentioned before, to reach a solution, it is necessary to initialize the flow using arbitrary values for the velocity and pressure fields. Such values are often selected from meaningful flow quantities such as free stream velocity and the atmospheric pressure for external flows. In the case of an internal flow, the main velocity value(the one with larger magnitude when several inlets are present) and the internal pressure are used.

Nowadays, there are a series of improvements made to the SIMPLE algorithm. One of them is the SIMPLEC algorithm also known as SIMPLE-Consistent [14], which is one of the most popular. This algorithm works similarly to SIMPLE, being its main difference that the momentum conservation equations are modified in a way that allows the velocity correction equations are simplified. The result of this change is that for some cases, the convergence time decreases. This algorithm is optimal to solve laminar flow problems without temperature gradients. It requires less convergence time than the conventional SIMPLE algorithm. Nevertheless, its use is not recommendable to solve turbulent flow, species transport, combustion problems, or any problem involving not only fluid movements, but also a more complex physical problem.

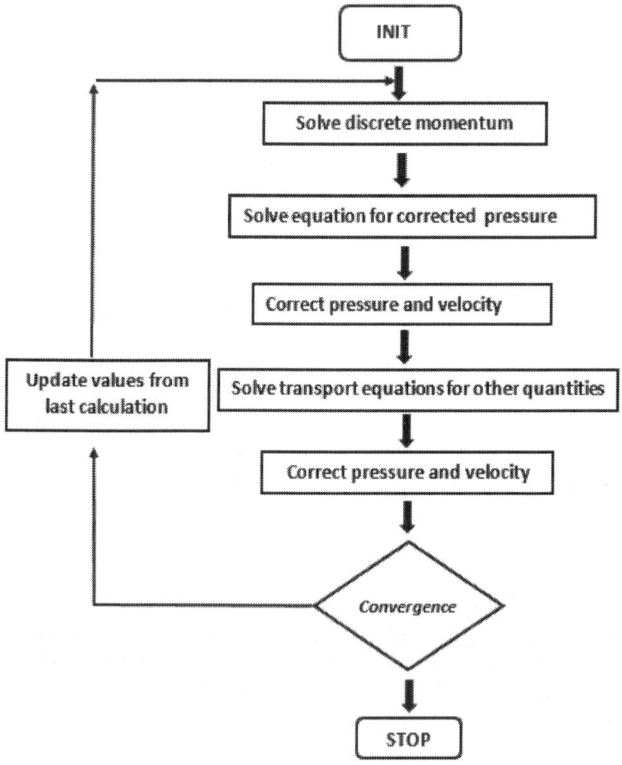


**Figure 5.** Overall stages in the SIMPLE algorithm, adapted with permission from Versteeg and Malalesekera [3].

The pressure implicit with splitting of operators (PISO) algorithm is an improved version of the SIMPLE algorithm. It was created for non-iterative calculations in the numerical solution of non-steady flows. It has been adopted for iterative solution process for steady and non-steady flows, being especially useful for the last ones. This algorithm involves a stage where velocities and pressures are arbitrarily predicted, and two correcting stages. Therefore, it has an additional correcting stage with respect to SIMPLE and SIMPLEC. In the prediction and correction stages, the obtained pressures involve functions that contain within the continuity equation [15].

Even though the PISO algorithm requires additional memory to store the values of the added correction equations, and in general, it requires relaxation factors to stabilize the calculation process, it performs in a quick and efficient way.

http://dx.doi.org/10.5772/63831

In relation to periodic or transient problems, although less popular than PISO and SIMPLE, the fractional step method (FSM) algorithm is a method created as a solving alternative of non-iterative nature (NITA–non-iterative time advancement). Even though its use is less popular than the SIMPLE algorithm and its modifications, due to its formulation, involving a decoupling of the mass and momentum conservation equations using mathematical operators is capable of decreasing the simulation time [16].

Regarding the pressure–velocity coupling algorithm known as COUPLED, it is recommended to solve problems involving steady-state single-phase flows. For this algorithm, the solving process of all flow components is carried out using vectors. This means using a square coefficients matrix derived from flows entering or leaving the control volume through each control surface. This matrix is then algebraically associated with a unidimensional unknown vector. The product of both matrices is then equivalent to a solution vector where boundary conditions are included. The COUPLED algorithm is an alternative to SIMPLE and its spin-offs in the segregated solver, and it is recommended for cases where the domain presents low-quality elements for non-steady problems.

Finally, before starting a solution process, it is recommended to take a careful look into the most adequate coupling schemes for the problem at hand. This can be done considering the most important flow characteristics and looking for a similar case in any classic study case where a benchmark has already been performed (e.g., jets, flow over a flat plate, internal flows).

### 3.4. Turbulent flows CFD

Reynolds number ($Re = \rho\ U\ell/\mu$) is above a certain limit several events take place and cause that the flow behaves in a random manner, and its velocity components fluctuate along the three spatial directions. The flow will also present an unstable nature, promoting large-scale mixing and energy dissipation at small scales. Such regime is known as turbulent regime or turbulence. To include the effect of such fluctuations in the flow, it is necessary to substitute the flow variables that depend on the velocity vector $\vec{V} = f\,(u,\ v,\ w)$, as well as the scalar $P$ for the sum of an average component $\bar{i}$ and is fluctuating counterpart "$i'$" having then:

$$\vec{V} = \bar{\vec{V}} + \vec{V}'u = \bar{u} + u'; \quad v = \bar{v} + v'; \quad w = \bar{w} + w'; \quad P = \bar{P} + p' \tag{1.18}$$

Such decomposition of the different flow variables has to be included in the governing equations, provoking the appearing of three normal stresses and three shear stresses, which, due to its units, are known as the Reynolds stresses, and are Represented as follows:

$$\tau'_{xy} = \tau'_{yx} = -\overline{\rho u'^2}; \quad \tau'_{yy} = -\overline{\rho u'^2}; \quad \tau'_{zz} = -\overline{\rho u'^2}$$

$$\tau'_{xy} = \tau'_{yx} = -\overline{\rho u'v'}; \quad \tau'_{xz} = \tau'_{zx} = -\overline{\rho u'w'}; \quad \tau'_{yz} = \tau'_{zy} = -\overline{\rho v'w'} \tag{1.19}$$

The vector expression for the mass conservation equation and the Navier–Stokes equations are as follows:

$$\frac{\partial \rho}{\partial t} + \nabla \cdot \left( \rho \bar{V} \right) = 0 \tag{1.20}$$

$$\rho \frac{D\bar{V}}{Dt} = \rho \mathbf{g} - \nabla \bar{p} + \nabla \cdot \tau_{ij} \tag{1.21}$$

where:

$$\tau_{ij} = \mu \left( \frac{\partial u_i}{\partial x_j} - \frac{\partial u_j}{\partial x_i} \right) - \overline{\rho u_i' u_j'} \tag{1.22}$$

Laminar Turbulent

It can be noted that the mass conservation equation is practically the same for laminar and turbulent flows. However, it is necessary to point out that this equivalence is valid only for the average values with a significant number of samples, meaning that the average of the fluctuating quantities becomes zero.

Because these stresses vary in their frequencies and sizes as a function of the distance from the walls, turbulent models take into account such variations to solve the closure problem of these extended equations.

## 4. RANS models

In 1972, Jones and Launder [17] proposed a model with two differential equations in addition to the mass and momentum conservation equations. In that model, an equation approximated the effect of the turbulent kinetic energy production rate $k = \frac{1}{2}\left(\overline{u'^2} + \overline{v'^2} + \overline{w'^2}\right)$ and the other one contained the effects of the turbulent kinetic energy dissipation rate "ε". Together, the use of both equations proved to be adequate to obtain good results in turbulent flows whose interest was focused on the study of the influence of average turbulent effects. Both equations are as follows:

$$\frac{Dk}{Dt} \approx \frac{\partial}{\partial x_j}\left[ \frac{v_t}{\sigma_K} \frac{\partial k}{\partial x_j} \right] + v_t \frac{\partial \bar{u}_i}{\partial x_j}\left( \frac{\partial \bar{u}_i}{\partial x_j} + \frac{\partial \bar{u}_i}{\partial x_i} \right) - \epsilon \tag{1.23}$$

http://dx.doi.org/10.5772/63831

$$\frac{D\epsilon}{Dt} \approx \frac{\partial}{\partial x_j}\left[\frac{v_t}{\sigma_\epsilon}\frac{\partial \epsilon}{\partial x_j}\right] + C_1 v_t \frac{\epsilon}{k}\frac{\partial \bar{u}_i}{\partial x_j}\left(\frac{\partial \bar{u}_i}{\partial x_j} + \frac{\partial \bar{u}_j}{\partial x_i}\right) - C_2 \frac{\epsilon^2}{k} \tag{1.24}$$

where $\sigma_K$ and $\sigma$ are the "effective Prandtl numbers", which relate the eddy diffusion of $K$ and to the eddy viscosity: $v_t/v_K$ **and** $\sigma = v_t/v$. Eddy viscosity is modeled as follows:

$$v_t \approx \frac{C_\mu k^2}{\epsilon} \tag{1.25}$$

The five constants of this model are obtained in an experimental way for cases of boundary layer calculations in non-detached flows. They are as follows:

$$C_\mu = 0.09 \quad C_1 = 1.44 \quad C_2 = 1.92 \quad C_\mu = 0.09 \quad \sigma_K = 1.0 \quad \sigma_\epsilon = 1.3 \tag{1.26}$$

Unfortunately, the above presented values cannot be used for any kind of flows (they are not universal). They need to be modified to model the behavior of wakes, jets, and recirculating flows. To deal with this difficulty, different and more sophisticated models have been proposed, which try to reproduce these flow patterns. Some of them are as follows:

1. The $k-$ model, d on the group renormalization, Yakhot y Smith [18].
2. The $k-\omega$ model, Wilcox [19].
3. The $k- -v^2-f$ model, Durbin [20].

## 5. The LES technique

Large eddy simulation is a technique based on the assumption that the largest eddies in a flow are of sizes relative to the characteristic length of the flow, whereas the smallest ones that form on the walls are isotropic and very similar for different kinds of flow, and therefore being more susceptible to be modeled. Under this consideration, the LES technique solve the largest eddies in an explicit way and the effects of the smallest eddies on largest eddies are modeled using a subgrid scale stress model. The justification for both assumptions is that the largest eddies contain the most part of the kinetic energy in a moving fluid, they transport the majority of conservative properties and they vary the most from flow to flow. Meanwhile, the smallest eddies are considered more "universal" and less important in the total flow; therefore, when they are modeled, it is expected that the error introduced is small. Unlike RANS models, LES technique uses a filtering process instead of an averaging process. It means that the information obtained for the largest scales is instantaneous and does not represent an average information. Instead of considering the influence of the velocity fluctuations equal to zero $\overline{u'_{ij}}=0$ like in the RANS models, it has a value that locally influences the solutions, it means

$\overline{u'_{ij}}\neq 0$. In general, the use or the LES technique has produced better results in flow simulations when RANS models usually fail, like turbulent boundary layers subjected to adverse pressure gradients, the prediction of drag coefficients for immerse bodies in periodic regimes [21] and other unsteady flows. Governing equations for the LES model in an incompressible flow are as follows:

$$\frac{\partial \overline{u}_i}{\partial x_i} = 0 \tag{1.27}$$

$$\frac{\partial \overline{u}_i}{\partial t} + \frac{\partial \overline{u}_i \overline{u}_j}{\partial x_j} = -\frac{1}{\rho}\frac{\partial \overline{P}}{\partial x_i} - \frac{\partial \tau_{ij}}{\partial x_j} + \frac{\partial}{\partial x_j}\left[ v \frac{\partial \overline{u}_i}{\partial x_j} \right] \tag{1.28}$$

$$(i = 1,2,3)$$

In the Eqs. (1.27) and (1.28), $\bar{u}_i$ represents the filtered velocity components at different Cartesian positions $x_i$, where $\overline{P}$ represents the filtered pressure component, "$v$" and "$\rho$" represent the kinematic viscosity and density, respectively. Regarding the local influence of the Reynolds stresses, one of the most used models is the classic Smagorinsky model, which is expressed as follows:

$$\tau_{ij} = \overline{u_i u_j} - \overline{u}_i \overline{u}_j \tag{1.29}$$

$$\tau_{ij} - \frac{1}{3}\tau_{kk}\delta_{ij} = -2v_t \overline{S}_{ij} = -2\left(C_s \overline{\Delta}\right)^2 \| S \| \overline{S}_{ij} \tag{1.30}$$

where the strain tensor of the fluid in each cell is $\|S\| = \sqrt{2\overline{S}_{ij}\overline{S}_{ij}}$, being $\bar{S}_{ij}$ the filtered strain tensor, $v_t$ the subgrid scale turbulent viscosity, "$\bar{\Delta}$"the filter characteristic length. Generally, the size of the filter is proportional to the volume "$\Omega$" of the cell $\bar{\Delta}=2(\Omega)^{1/3}$, and the Smagorinsky constant $C_s$ can be varied from 0.05 to 0.1 [22].

## 6. RANS and LES capacities for turbulent flows analysis

Originally, RANS models were conceived to include the turbulence average effect in the Navier–Stokes equations solution. Therefore, they are widely recommended to simulate steady-state fully developed turbulent flows, being especially good reproducing off-wall phenomena. When the problem needed to solve is highly depended on the adequate prediction of pressures and forces on the wall, it is recommended to apply functions for "enhanced wall treatment" and to have at least one nodal element positioned within the viscous sublayer ($y^+ < 5$), with at least ten nodal elements along the whole boundary layer to achieve acceptable results [23]. Another use of RANS models is to provide preliminary results that allow to shorten the simulation time for unsteady problems based on the same technique or the use of LES. Regarding the kind of flows that RANS models have been successful reproducing, it can be said that internal flows, flows over boundary layers, turbulence prediction in a fluid that floats due to density changes, combustion coupled problems, two-phase flows, agitated wall induced turbulence, etc. have had successful results. As for problems where RANS models perform poorly, these are periodic or oscillatory flows, boundary layers affected by large pressure gradients, flow regimes that depend on separation point, and jets.

On the other hand, the LES technique is capable of giving average and instantaneous information about the main structures of turbulent flows without the complete dependence on the average modeling of Reynolds stresses found in the traditional RANS approach. This is advantageous to capture velocities and flow patterns in three dimensional problems. Among the successes of the LES model, it can be mentioned the prediction of separation points and fluctuating forces in external flows for geometries such as circular cylinders, eolic turbines blades, as well as structures and frequencies in jets and atomization systems, etc. Unfortunately, due to the large number of temporal and spatial scales that requires modeling for an acceptable performance, computer time and requirements are still high. The walls produce high demands since it requires the use of grids with nodal elements positioned at $y^+ \approx 1$, very short temporal steps and the size of the eddy scales that the smallest grid elements are capable of capture. This has made impossible the massive application of this technique for flow problems that have many complex geometries and many scales. It results evident that for compressible flows, the Reynolds stresses are more complex than for incompressible flow, being that SGS models for complex flows those that involve multiple phases and reactive flows found in combustions are still in a stage of development and validation [24].

## Author details

Alejandro Alonzo-García[1,2], Claudia del Carmen Gutiérrez-Torres[3*] and José Alfredo Jiménez-Bernal[3]

*Address all correspondence to: claudia2174@yahoo.com

1 Centro de Investigación Científica de Yucatán, A.C, Mexico

2 Tecnológico Nacional de México, Instituto Tecnológico de Mérida, Mexico

3 Instituto Politecnico Nacional, SEPI-ESIME Zacatenco, Mexico City, Mexico

## References

[1] Patankar S. Numerical Heat Transfer and Fluid Flow. 1st ed. USA: CRC Press; 1980. 214 p.

[2] Abbot M., Basco D. Computational Fluid Dynamics: An Introduction to Engineers. 1st ed. UK: Longman Scientific; 1989. 440 p.

[3] Versteeg H., Malalesekera W. An Introduction to Computational Fluid Dynamics. 1st ed. Malaysia: Pearson Prentice Hall; 1995. 272 p.

[4] White F. Viscous Fluid Flow. 2nd ed. USA: McGraw-Hill; 1991. 614 p.

[5] Pritchard, P. Fox and McDonald's Introduction to Fluid Dynamics. 8th ed. USA: John Wiley and Sons Inc.; 2011. 896 p.

[6] Catalano P., Wang M., Iaccarino G., Moin P. Numerical simulation of the flow around a circular cylinder at high Reynolds numbers. Int. J. Heat Fluid Flow. 2003;24:463–469.

[7] Nishino T., Roberts G., Zhang X. Unsteady RANS and Detached-Eddy simulations of flow around circular cylinder in ground effect. J. Fluid Struct. 2008;24:18–33.

[8] Chapter 25. In: Fluent 6.3 User's Guide. 2006. p. 182, Fluent Inc.

[9] Sohankar A., Norberg C., Davidson L. Low-Reynolds flow around a square cylinder at incidence: study of blockage, onset vortices shedding and outlet boundary condition. Int. J. Numer. Methods Fluids. 1998;26:39–56.

[10] Chapter 7. In: Fluent 6.3 User's guide. 2006. p. 236, Fluent Inc.

[11] Liou M. A sequel to AUSM: AUSM+. J. Comput. Phys. 1996;129:364–382.

[12] Kim S. Large eddy simulation of turbulent flow past a circular cylinder in subcritical regime. In: AIAA 44th Aerospace Science Meeting and Exhibit; 2006. pp. 1–18.

[13] Patankar S., Spalding D. A calculation procedure for heat, mass and momentum transfer in three-dimensional parabolic flows. Int. J. Heat Mass Transf. 1972;15:1787–1806.

[14] Van Doormal J., Raithby G. Enhancements of the SIMPLE method for predicting incompressible fluid flows. Numer. Heat Transf. 1984;7:147–163.

[15] Chung T. Computational Fluid Dynamics. 2nd ed. USA: Cambridge University Press. 1058 p.

[16] Armsfield S., Street R. The fractional-step method for the Navier–Stokes equations on staggered grids: accuracy of three variations. J. Comput. Phys. 1999;153:660–665.

[17] Jones P., Launder B. The prediction of laminarization with two-equation model of turbulence. Int. J. Heat Mass Trans. 1972;15:301–314.

http://dx.doi.org/10.5772/63831

[18] Yakhot V., Smith M. The renormalization group, the ε expansion and derivation of turbulence models. J. Sci. Comput. 1992;7:35–61.

[19] Wilcox D. Turbulence modeling for CFD. 2nd ed. USA: DCW Industries; 1998. 540 p.

[20] Durbin O., Petterson R. Separated flow computations with the $k$-$\varepsilon$-$v$^2 model. AIAA J. 1995;33:659–664.

[21] Alonzo-García A., del C. Gutiérrez-Torres C., Jiménez-Bernal J.A., López Aguado-Montes J.L., Barbosa-Saldaña J.A., Mollinedo-Ponce de León H.R. et al. Large eddy simulation of the subcritical flow over a V grooved circular cylinder. Nucl. Eng. Des. 2015;291:35–46.

[22] Sagaut P. Large eddy simulation for incompressible flows and introduction. 3rd ed. Germany: Springer; 2005. 558 p.

[23] Alonzo-García A., del C. Gutiérrez-Torres C., Jiménez-Bernal J.A., Mollinedo-Ponce de León H.R., Martínez-Delgadillo S.A., Barbosa-Saldaña J.G. RANS simulation of the U and V grooves effect in the subcritical flow over four rotated circular cylinders. J. Hydrodyn. 2015;27:569–578.

[24] Gristein F., Margolin L., Rider W. Implicit large eddy simulation: computing turbulent fluid dynamics. 1st ed. New York: Cambridge University Press; 2007. 578 p.

Chapter 14

# Two-Fluid RANS-RSTM-PDF Model for Turbulent Particulate Flows

P. Lauk, A. Kartushinsky, M. Hussainov, A. Polonsky, Ü. Rudi, I. Shcheglov, S. Tisler and K.-E. Seegel

Additional information is available at the end of the chapter

http://dx.doi.org/10.5772/63338

### Abstract

A novel three-dimensional (3D) model based on Reynolds turbulence stress model (RSTM) closure of equations of carrier and particulate phases was elaborated for channel turbulent flows. The essence of the model is the direct calculation of normal and shear components of the Reynolds stresses for the particulate phase similar to the carrier fluid. The model is based on the Eulerian approach, which is applied for the 3D RANS modeling of the carrier flow and the particulate phase and the statistical probability dense function (PDF) approach focusing on the mathematical description of the second moments of the particulate phase.

The obtained numerical results have been verified and validated by comparison with experimental data obtained on turbulent dispersion of solid particles ejected from point source for turbulent uniform linear shear flow. Two cases of spatial orientation of shear of the flow mean velocity were examined: in the direction of gravity and in the direction perpendicular to gravity. Numerical data on turbulent dispersion of particles and spatial displacement of the maximum value of the concentration distribution show satisfactory agreement with experimental results.

**Keywords:** turbulent channel flows, solid particles, closure equations, PDF of particulate phase velocity, shear flow

## 1. Introduction

Turbulent channel particulate flows have numerous engineering applications ranging from pneumatic conveying systems to coal gasifiers, chemical reactor design and are one of the most thoroughly investigated subject in the area of the particulate flows. These flows are very complex and influenced by various physical phenomena, such as particle-turbulence and particle-particle interactions, deposition, gravitational and viscous drag forces, particle rotation and lift forces, turbulent dispersion, etc.

One of the most applicable approaches in computational fluid dynamics (CFD) is the Reynolds-averaged Navier-stokes (RANS) equation approach, which is found in many industrial implementations and is very likely to be claimed and applied in the foreseeable future.

The procedure of analysis of the predicted fluid parameters becomes much more complicated in case of the three-dimensional (3D) dense particulate flows, with additional inclusion of two or/and four coupling phenomena of inter-particle collisions. Within a frame of the RANS modeling, one of the challenging and advantaged theoretical approaches is the Reynolds turbulence stress model (RSTM), since $k$-$\varepsilon$ closure model cannot describe properly the flow of complex geometry.

For the proper modeling of the particulate flows, which may include multifold processes, e.g., the particle-turbulence, or/and particle-particle, and particle-wall interactions and other relevant effects, one can apply the probability dense function (PDF) approach, which gives reasonable formalism for the closure of the governing mass and momentum equations of the particulate phase. Within the PDF approach, the closure of the governing equations of the particulate phase is based on a solution of the differential transport equations written for each particle velocity covariance, taking into account possible mechanisms of the particle-turbulence and particle-particle interactions. Such procedure is similar to the RSTM closure.

Currently, the probability dense function (PDF) approach is widely applied for the numerical modeling of the particulate flows. The PDF models, e.g., [1, 2], contain more complete differential transport equations, which are written for various velocity correlations and consider both the turbulence augmentation and attenuation due to the presence of particles.

As opposed to the round channel flows, the rectangular or/and square channel flows, even in case of unladen flows, are considerably anisotropic with respect to the components of the turbulence energy, that is more expressed near the channel walls and corners being notable for the secondary flows. In addition, the presence of particles enhances such anisotropy. Such particulate flows are studied by RSTM, which are based on the transport equations written for all components of the Reynolds stress tensor-associated with the particulate phase.

The RSTM approach allows to completely analyze the influence of particles on axial, transverse, and spanwise components of the turbulence kinetic energy, including also possible modifications of the cross-correlation velocity moments.

A number of studies based on the RSTM approach showed its good performance and capability for simulation of the complicated flows [3], as well for the turbulent subsonic [4] and supersonic flows [5] and viscoelastic flows [6].

Taulbee [7] used the RSTM approach to calculate the particle-laden shear flow by applying the direct numerical simulation (DNS). The flow Reynolds number was low ($Re$ = 952). Therefore, the method by [7] cannot be applied to the real turbulent flows characterized by considerably higher Reynolds numbers, unlike the present numerical simulation which handles with the flow Reynolds numbers of 56,000 and 140,000.

The RSTM approach was also applied in the model [8]. The only difference was in the fact that the closure of equations of motion of the particulate phase was based on the Boussinesq hypothesis, where the turbulent viscosity of the particulate phase was introduced and calculated using the algebraic expressions obtained in the PDF approach [9]. However, the model [8] was inherently eclectic, since it applied the RSTM closure for a carrier flow and at the same time the Boussinesq hypothesis for the particulate phase.

Recently, Mukin and Zaichik [10] have proposed the nonlinear algebraic Reynolds stress model for the gas flow laden with small heavy particles based on the PDF approach. The original equations written for each component of Reynolds stress were reduced to their general form in terms of the turbulence energy and its dissipation rate with additional effect of the particulate phase. However, the model [10] does not enable a direct solution of the differential transport equations and it applies the $k$-$\varepsilon$ solution.

The study of the particle dispersion that occurs in the velocity uniform shear turbulent flow assumes knowing the internal structure, general relationships, and methods of the flow generation.

Based on the analysis of results of numerous investigations of turbulent dispersion of finite inertia particles, it should be singled out three effects that are of high importance and should be considered: (i) the inertia effect implying that the dispersion of solid particles might exceed the dispersion of the fluid particles in the absence of a body force [11, 12]; (ii) the crossing trajectory effect [13] meaning that in the presence of a drift velocity a finite inertia particle will disperse less than a fluid particle; and (iii) the continuity effect [14] where the dispersion in the direction of the drift velocity exceeds the dispersion in other two directions.

In the mathematical description of the particle turbulent dispersion, there are a number of models and numerical simulations, which can be classified into the Lagrangian and Eulerian (two-fluid) approximations. They relate to the specific flow structures, such as confined flows in pipes and channels or free jets, wakes, and wall boundary flows.

Taylor [15] made the Lagrangian analysis of the dispersion of a particle in a stationary homogeneous turbulence, which showed that turbulent dispersion varies in time and derived the asymptotic expressions of dispersion for short and large times. Later on, the Lagrangian approach for the turbulent dispersion of particles was further developed in [16–21].

One of the most comprehensive numerical research of the particle dispersion in the uniform shear flow, based on the Lagrangian approach, was carried out in [22]. Ahmed and Elghobashi [22] applied DNS to the investigation of the particle inertia effect, effect of direction of gravitation as well as magnitude of a shear number. In particular, Ahmed and Elghobashi [22] have revealed that gravity reduces the particle turbulent dispersion and diffusivity in all directions due to the drift velocity effects.

On the contrary, there are very less studies on the particle turbulent dispersion, which are based on the Eulerian approach. The most significant are the numerical investigations [9, 23], where the statistical PDF models were applied to the particle behavior in the turbulent flows.

The 3D RSTM approach presented here applies the closure of equations of motion of the particulate phase, which is carried out similarly to the closure of the carrier flow, i.e., the equations are written for the normal and shear components of the Reynolds stress. The Reynolds stress equations are derived from the PDF model [9] and presented in a general case. The advantage of the given model is in use of the same closure for both the carrier flow and particulate phase, namely, the Reynolds differential equations.

The given 3D RSTM model has been applied for the turbulent dispersion of solid particles in a turbulent horizontal channel flow imposed to uniform shear.

The obtained numerical results have been verified and validated by comparison with the experimental data.

## 2. Numerical model

The present numerical model being proposed for the evaluation of the particle dispersion is the Eulerian approach, which applies both the 3D RANS modeling of the carrier flow and the particulate phase [24] and the statistical PDF approach focusing on the mathematical description of the second moments of the particulate phase [9]. Within the Eulerian approach, the particulate phase is considered as the diluted medium; therefore, the effect of the particle collision is negligible that means the application of the one-way coupling.

The numerical simulation considered the turbulent dispersion of solid particles in horizontal channel uniform shear turbulent flow for two different cases: i) shear of the mean flow velocity is along the direction of gravity (**Figure 1a**) and ii) shear of the mean flow velocity is directed normally to gravity (**Figure 1b**). Here $u$ is the mean axial velocity of gas.

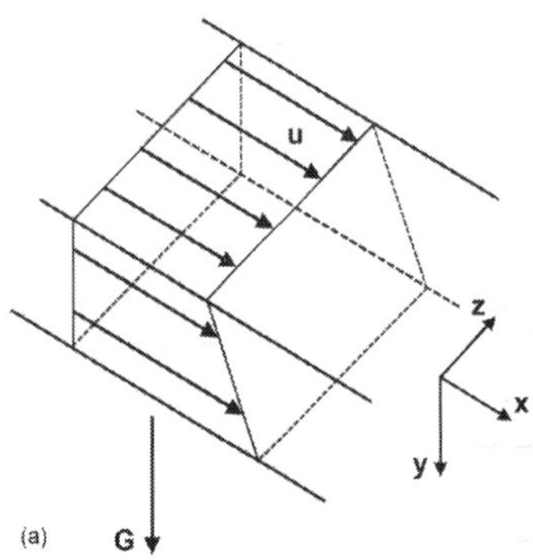

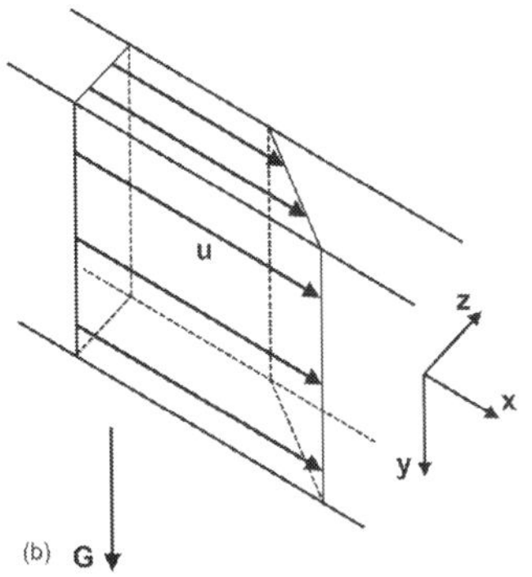


**Figure 1.** Shear of the mean flow velocity in horizontal channel flow. (a) shear of the mean flow velocity is along the direction of gravity; (b) shear of the mean flow velocity is directed normally to gravity.

The particles were brought into the uniform shear gas flow, which has been preliminarily computed to obtain the velocity flow field.

The system of the momentum and closure equations of the gas phase are identical for the unladen flows, while the particle-laden flows are under the impact of the viscous drag force. The Cartesian coordinates are used here.

## 2.1. Governing equations for the particulate phase

The 3D governing equations for the particulate phase are written as follows:

The particle mass conservation equation:

$$\frac{\partial(\alpha u_s)}{\partial x}+\frac{\partial(\alpha v_s)}{\partial y}+\frac{\partial(\alpha w_s)}{\partial z}=\frac{\partial}{\partial x}D_s\frac{\partial \alpha}{\partial x}+\frac{\partial}{\partial y}D_s\frac{\partial \alpha}{\partial y}+\frac{\partial}{\partial z}D_s\frac{\partial \alpha}{\partial z}, \tag{1}$$

$x$-component of the momentum equation:

$$\frac{\partial}{\partial x}\alpha\left[u_s^2-\overline{u_s'^2}\right]+\frac{\partial}{\partial y}\alpha\left[u_s v_s-\overline{u_s' v_s'}\right]+\frac{\partial}{\partial z}\alpha\left[u_s w_s-\overline{u_s' w_s'}\right]=\alpha C_D'\frac{(u-u_s)}{\tau_p}$$
$$+\alpha\ \mathrm{sgn}(g_x)\left(1-\frac{\rho}{\rho_p}\right), \tag{2}$$

$y$-component of the momentum equation:

$$\frac{\partial}{\partial x}\alpha\left[u_s v_s - \overline{u_s' v_s'}\right] + \frac{\partial}{\partial y}\alpha\left[v_s^2 - \overline{v_s'^2}\right] + \frac{\partial}{\partial z}\alpha\left[v_s w_s - \overline{v_s' w_s'}\right] = \alpha C_D' \frac{(v - v_s)}{\tau_p}$$
$$+\alpha \operatorname{sgn}(g_y)\left(1 - \frac{\rho}{\rho_p}\right), \quad (3)$$

z-component of the momentum equation:

$$\frac{\partial}{\partial x}\alpha\left[u_s w_s - \overline{u_s' w_s'}\right] + \frac{\partial}{\partial y}\alpha\left[v_s w_s - \overline{v_s' w_s'}\right] + \frac{\partial}{\partial z}\alpha\left[w_s^2 - \overline{w_s'^2}\right] = \alpha C_D' \frac{(w - w_s)}{\tau_p}, \quad (4)$$

where $u$, $v$, and $w$ are the axial, transverse, and spanwise time-averaged velocity components of gas, respectively; $u_s$, $v_s$ and $w_s$ are the axial, transverse, and spanwise time-averaged velocity components of particulate phase, respectively; $\rho$ is the material density of gas; $\rho_p$ is the material density of particles; $\alpha$ is the particle mass concentration; $g_y$ is the $y$-component of gravity.

The relative friction coefficient $C_D'$ is calculated according to [25].

The closure model for the transport equations of the particulate phase was applied to the PDF model [26], where $D_s$ is the coefficient of the turbulent diffusion of the particulate phase.

The equations for the second-order moments of the fluctuating velocity (turbulent stresses) of the particulate phase are written based on the PDF approach in [9]. These equations describe convective and diffusive transfer, generation of particle velocity fluctuations due to the velocity gradient, generation of fluctuations resulting from particle entrainment into the fluctuating motion of carrier gas flow, and dissipation of turbulent stresses of the particulate phase caused by interfacial forces:

Equation of the $x$-normal component of the Reynolds stress:

$$\frac{\partial}{\partial x}\alpha\left[u_s\overline{u_s'^2} - \tau_p\left(\overline{u_s'^2} + g_u^l\overline{u'^2}\right)\frac{\partial\overline{u_s'^2}}{\partial x}\right] + \frac{\partial}{\partial y}\alpha\left[v_s\overline{u_s'^2} - \frac{\tau_p\left(\overline{v_s'^2} + g_u^n\overline{v'^2}\right)}{3}\frac{\partial\overline{u_s'^2}}{\partial y}\right]$$

$$+\frac{\partial}{\partial z}\alpha\left[w_s\overline{u_s'^2}-\frac{\tau_p}{3}\left(\overline{w_s'^2}+g_u^k\overline{w'}\right)\frac{\partial\overline{u_s'^2}}{\partial z}\right]$$

$$=\frac{\partial}{\partial x}\left\{\alpha\tau_p\left[\left(\overline{u_s'v_s'}+g_u^n\overline{u'v'}\right)\frac{\partial\overline{u_s'^2}}{\partial y}+\left(\overline{u_s'w_s'}+g_u^k\overline{u'w'}\right)\frac{\partial\overline{u_s'^2}}{\partial z}\right]\right\}$$

$$+\frac{\partial}{\partial y}\left\{\frac{\alpha\tau_p}{3}\left[2\left(\overline{u_s'^2}+g_u^l\overline{u'^2}\right)\frac{\partial\overline{u_s'v_s'}}{\partial x}+2\left(\overline{u_s'v_s'}+g_u^n\overline{u'v'}\right)\frac{\partial\overline{u_s'v_s'}}{\partial y}+2\left(\overline{u_s'w_s'}+g_u^k\overline{u'w'}\right)\frac{\partial\overline{u_s'v_s'}}{\partial z}\right.\right.$$

$$\left.\left.+\left(\overline{u_s'v_s'}+g_u^l\overline{u'v'}\right)\frac{\partial\overline{u_s'^2}}{\partial x}+\left(\overline{v_s'w_s'}+g_u^k\overline{v'w'}\right)\frac{\partial\overline{u_s'^2}}{\partial z}\right]\right\}$$

$$+\frac{\partial}{\partial z}\left\{\frac{\alpha\tau_p}{3}\left[2\left(\overline{u_s'^2}+g_u^l\overline{u'^2}\right)\frac{\partial\overline{u_s'w_s'}}{\partial x}\right.\right.$$

$$+2\left(\overline{u_s'v_s'}+g_u^n\overline{u'v'}\right)\frac{\partial\overline{u_s'w_s'}}{\partial y}+2\left(\overline{u_s'w_s'}+g_u^k\overline{u'w'}\right)\frac{\partial\overline{u_s'w_s'}}{\partial z}+\left(\overline{u_s'w_s'}+g_u^l\overline{u'w'}\right)\frac{\partial\overline{u_s'^2}}{\partial x}$$

$$\left.\left.+\left(\overline{v_s'w_s'}+g_u^n\overline{v'w'}\right)\frac{\partial\overline{u_s'^2}}{\partial y}\right]\right\}, \tag{5}$$

Equation of the *y*-normal component of the Reynolds stress:

$$\frac{\partial}{\partial x}\alpha\left[u_s\overline{v_s'^2}-\frac{\tau_p}{3}\left(\overline{u_s'^2}+g_u^l\overline{u'^2}\right)\frac{\partial\overline{v_s'^2}}{\partial x}\right]+\frac{\partial}{\partial y}\alpha\left[v_s\overline{v_s'^2}-\tau_p\left(\overline{v_s'^2}+g_u^n\overline{v'^2}\right)\frac{\partial\overline{v_s'^2}}{\partial y}\right]$$

$$+\frac{\partial}{\partial z}\alpha\left[w_s\overline{v_s'^2}-\frac{\tau_p}{3}\left(\overline{w_s'^2}+g_u^k\overline{w'}\right)\frac{\partial\overline{v_s'^2}}{\partial z}\right]$$

$$=\frac{\partial}{\partial x}\left\{\frac{\alpha\tau_p}{3}\left[2\left(\overline{u_s'v_s'}+g_u^n\overline{u'v'}\right)\frac{\partial\overline{u_s'v_s'}}{\partial x}+2\left(\overline{v_s'^2}+g_u^n\overline{v'^2}\right)\frac{\partial\overline{u_s'v_s'}}{\partial y}\right.\right.$$

$$+2\left(\overline{v_s'w_s'}+g_u^k\overline{v'w'}\right)\frac{\partial\overline{u_s'v_s'}}{\partial z}+\left(\overline{u_s'v_s'}+g_u^n\overline{u'v'}\right)\frac{\partial\overline{v_s'^2}}{\partial y}+\left(\overline{u_s'w_s'}+g_u^k\overline{u'w'}\right)\frac{\partial\overline{v_s'^2}}{\partial z}\Bigg]\Bigg\}$$

$$+\frac{\partial}{\partial y}\left\{\alpha\tau_p\left[\left(\overline{u_s'v_s'}+g_u^l\overline{u'v'}\right)\frac{\partial\overline{v_s'^2}}{\partial x}+\left(\overline{v_s'w_s'}+g_u^k\overline{u'w'}\right)\frac{\partial\overline{v_s'^2}}{\partial z}\right]\right\}$$

$$+\frac{\partial}{\partial z}\left\{\frac{\alpha\tau_p}{3}\left[2\left(\overline{u_s'v_s'}+g_u^l\overline{u'v'}\right)\frac{\partial\overline{v_s'w_s'}}{\partial x}+2\left(\overline{v_s'^2}+g_u^n\overline{v'^2}\right)\frac{\partial\overline{v_s'w_s'}}{\partial y}\right.\right.$$

$$\left.\left.+2\left(\overline{v_s'w_s'}+g_u^k\overline{v'w'}\right)\frac{\partial\overline{v_s'w_s'}}{\partial z}+\left(\overline{u_s'w_s'}+g_u^l\overline{u'w'}\right)\frac{\partial\overline{v_s'^2}}{\partial x}+\left(\overline{v_s'w_s'}+g_u^n\overline{v'w'}\right)\frac{\partial\overline{v_s'^2}}{\partial y}\right]\right\} \quad (6)$$

Equation of the $z$-normal component of the Reynolds stress:

$$\frac{\partial}{\partial x}\alpha\left[u_s\overline{w_s'^2}-\frac{\tau_p}{3}\left(\overline{u_s'^2}+g_u^l\overline{u'^2}\right)\frac{\partial\overline{w_s'^2}}{\partial x}\right]+\frac{\partial}{\partial y}\alpha\left[v_s\overline{w_s'^2}-\frac{\tau_p}{3}\left(\overline{v_s'^2}+g_u^n\overline{v'^2}\right)\frac{\partial\overline{w_s'^2}}{\partial y}\right]$$

$$+\frac{\partial}{\partial z}\alpha\left[w_s\overline{w_s'^2}-\tau_p\left(\overline{w_s'^2}+g_u^k\overline{w'}\right)\frac{\partial\overline{w_s'^2}}{\partial z}\right]=\frac{\partial}{\partial x}\left\{\frac{\alpha\tau_p}{3}\left[2\left(\overline{u_s'w_s'}+g_u^n\overline{u'w'}\right)\frac{\partial\overline{u_s'w_s'}}{\partial x}\right.\right.$$

$$+2\left(\overline{v_s'w_s'}+g_u^n\overline{v'w'}\right)\frac{\partial\overline{u_s'w_s'}}{\partial y}$$

$$\left.\left.+2\left(\overline{w_s'^2}+g_u^k\overline{w'^2}\right)\frac{\partial\overline{u_s'w_s'}}{\partial z}+\left(\overline{u_s'v_s'}+g_u^n\overline{u'v'}\right)\frac{\partial\overline{w_s'^2}}{\partial y}+\left(\overline{u_s'w_s'}+g_u^k\overline{u'w'}\right)\frac{\partial\overline{w_s'^2}}{\partial z}\right]\right\}$$

$$+\frac{\partial}{\partial y}\left\{\frac{\alpha\tau_p}{3}\left[2\frac{\partial\overline{v_s'w_s'}}{\partial x}\left(\overline{u_s'w_s'}+g_u^l\overline{u'w'}\right)\right.\right.$$

$$+2\left(\overline{v_s'w_s'}+g_u^n\overline{v'w'}\right)\frac{\partial\overline{v_s'w_s'}}{\partial y}+2\left(\overline{w_s'^2}+g_u^k\overline{w'^2}\right)\frac{\partial\overline{v_s'w_s'}}{\partial z}$$

http://dx.doi.org/10.5772/63338

$$+\left(\overline{u_s'v_s'}+g_u^l\overline{u'v'}\right)\frac{\partial\overline{w_s'^2}}{\partial x}+\left(\overline{v_s'w_s'}+g_u^k\overline{v'w'}\right)\frac{\partial\overline{w_s'^2}}{\partial z}\Bigg]\Bigg\}$$

$$+\frac{\partial}{\partial z}\left\{\alpha\tau_p\left[\left(\overline{u_s'w_s'}+g_u^l\overline{u'w'}\right)\frac{\partial\overline{w_s'^2}}{\partial x}+\left(\overline{v_s'w_s'}+g_u^n\overline{v'w'}\right)\frac{\partial\overline{w_s'^2}}{\partial y}\right]\right\} \tag{7}$$

Equation of the $xy$ shear stress component of the Reynolds stress:

$$\frac{\partial}{\partial x}\alpha\left[u_s\overline{u_s'v_s'}-\frac{2\tau_p}{3}\left(\overline{u_s'^2}+g_u^l\overline{u'^2}\right)\frac{\partial\overline{u_s'v_s'}}{\partial x}\right]$$

$$+\frac{\partial}{\partial y}\alpha\left[v_s\overline{u_s'v_s'}-\frac{2\tau_p}{3}\left(\overline{v_s'^2}+g_u^n\overline{v'^2}\right)\frac{\partial\overline{u_s'v_s'}}{\partial y}\right]+\frac{\partial}{\partial z}\alpha\left[w_s\overline{u_s'v_s'}-\frac{\tau_p\left(\overline{w_s'^2}+g_u^k\overline{w'^2}\right)}{3}\frac{\partial\overline{u_s'v_s'}}{\partial z}\right]$$

$$=\frac{\partial}{\partial x}\left\{\frac{\alpha\tau_p}{3}\left[2\left(\overline{u_s'v_s'}+g_u^n\overline{u'v'}\right)\frac{\partial\overline{u_s'v_s'}}{\partial y}+2\left(\overline{u_s'w_s'}+g_u^k\overline{u'w'}\right)\frac{\partial\overline{u_s'v_s'}}{\partial z}+\frac{\partial\overline{u_s'^2}}{\partial x}\right.\right.$$

$$\left.\left.\times\left(\overline{u_s'v_s'}+g_u^l\overline{u'v'}\right)+\left(\overline{v_s'^2}+g_u^n\overline{v'^2}\right)\frac{\partial\overline{u_s'^2}}{\partial y}+\left(\overline{v_s'w_w'}+g_u^k\overline{v'w'}\right)\frac{\partial\overline{u_s'^2}}{\partial z}\right]\right\}$$

$$+\frac{\partial}{\partial y}\left\{\frac{\alpha\tau_p}{3}\left[\left(\overline{u_s'^2}+g_u^l\overline{u'^2}\right)\frac{\partial\overline{v_s'^2}}{\partial x}+\frac{\partial\overline{v_s'^2}}{\partial y}\right.\right.$$

$$\times\left(\overline{u_s'v_s'}+g_u^n\overline{u'v'}\right)+\left(\overline{u_s'w_s'}+g_u^k\overline{u'w'}\right)\frac{\partial\overline{v_s'^2}}{\partial z}$$

$$\left.\left.+2\left(\overline{u_s'v_s'}+g_u^n\overline{u'v'}\right)\frac{\partial\overline{u_s'v_s'}}{\partial x}+2\left(\overline{v_s'w_s'}+g_u^k\overline{v'w'}\right)\frac{\partial\overline{u_s'v_s'}}{\partial z}\right]\right\} \tag{8}$$

$$+\frac{\partial}{\partial z}\left\{\frac{\alpha\tau_p}{3}\left[\left(\overline{u_s'^2}+g_u^l\overline{u'^2}\right)\frac{\partial\overline{v_s'w_s'}}{\partial x}+\left(\overline{u_s'v_s'}+g_u^n\overline{u'v'}\right)\frac{\partial\overline{v_s'w_s'}}{\partial y}\right.\right.$$

$$+\left(\overline{u_s'w_s'}+g_u^k\overline{u'w'}\right)\frac{\partial\overline{v_s'w_s'}}{\partial z}+\left(\overline{u_s'v_s'}+g_u^l\overline{u'v'}\right)$$

$$\times\frac{\partial\overline{u_s'w_s'}}{\partial x}+\left(\overline{v_s'^2}+g_u^n\overline{v'^2}\right)\frac{\partial\overline{u_s'w_s'}}{\partial y}+\left(\overline{v_s'w_s'}+g_u^k\overline{v'w'}\right)\frac{\partial\overline{u_s'w_s'}}{\partial z}$$

$$\left.\left.+\left(\overline{u_s'w_s'}+g_u^l\overline{u'w'}\right)\frac{\partial\overline{u_s'v_s'}}{\partial x}+\left(\overline{v_s'w_s'}+g_u^n\overline{v'w'}\right)\frac{\partial\overline{u_s'v_s'}}{\partial y}\right]\right\},$$

Equation of the $xz$ shear stress component of the Reynolds stress:

$$\frac{\partial}{\partial x}\alpha\left[u_s\overline{u_s'w_s'}-\frac{2\tau_p}{3}\left(\overline{u_s'^2}+g_u^l\overline{u'^2}\right)\frac{\partial\overline{u_s'w_s'}}{\partial x}\right]$$
$$+\frac{\partial}{\partial y}\alpha\left[v_s\overline{u_s'w_s'}-\frac{\tau_p}{3}\left(\overline{v_s'^2}+g_u^n\overline{v'^2}\right)\frac{\partial\overline{u_s'w_s'}}{\partial y}\right]$$

$$+\frac{\partial}{\partial z}\alpha\left[w_s\overline{u_s'w_s'}-\frac{2\tau_p}{3}\left(\overline{w_s'^2}+g_u^k\overline{w'^2}\right)\frac{\partial\overline{u_s'w_s'}}{\partial z}\right]$$
$$=\frac{\partial}{\partial x}\left\{\frac{\alpha\tau_p}{3}\left[2\left(\overline{u_s'v_s'}+g_u^n\overline{u'v'}\right)\frac{\partial\overline{u_s'w_s'}}{\partial y}+2\frac{\partial\overline{u_s'w_s'}}{\partial z}\right.\right.$$

$$\times\left(\overline{u_s'w_s'}+g_u^k\overline{u'w'}\right)+\left(\overline{u_s'w_s'}+g_u^l\overline{u'w'}\right)\frac{\partial\overline{u_s'^2}}{\partial x}$$
$$\left.\left.+\left(\overline{v_s'w_s'}+g_u^n\overline{v'w'}\right)\frac{\partial\overline{u_s'^2}}{\partial y}+\left(\overline{w_s'^2}+g_u^k\overline{w'^2}\right)\frac{\partial\overline{u_s'^2}}{\partial z}\right]\right\}$$

$$+\frac{\partial}{\partial y}\left\{\frac{\alpha\tau_p}{3}\left[\left(\overline{u_s'^2}+g_u^l\overline{u'^2}\right)\frac{\partial\overline{v_s'w_s'}}{\partial x}+\left(\overline{u_s'v_s'}+g_u^n\overline{u'v'}\right)\frac{\partial\overline{v_s'w_s'}}{\partial y}\right.\right.$$
$$+\left(\overline{u_s'w_s'}+g_u^n\overline{u'w'}\right)\frac{\partial\overline{v_s'w_s'}}{\partial z}+\left(\overline{u_s'w_s'}+g_u^n\overline{u'w'}\right)$$

$$\times\frac{\partial\overline{u_s'v_s'}}{\partial x}+\left(\overline{v_s'w_s'}+g_u^n\overline{v'w'}\right)\frac{\overline{u_s'v_s'}}{\partial y}+\left(\overline{w_s'^2}+g_u^k\overline{w'^2}\right)\frac{\partial\overline{u_s'v_s'}}{\partial z}$$
$$+\left(\overline{u_s'v_s'}+g_u^l\overline{u'v'}\right)\frac{\partial\overline{u_s'w_s'}}{\partial x}+\left(\overline{v_s'w_s'}+g_u^k\overline{v'w'}\right)$$

$$\times \frac{\partial \overline{u_s' w_s'}}{\partial z} \Bigg] \Bigg\} + \frac{\partial}{\partial z} \left\{ \frac{\alpha \tau_p}{3} \left[ \left( \overline{u_s'^2} + g_u^l \overline{u'^2} \right) \frac{\partial \overline{w_s'^2}}{\partial x} \right. \right.$$

$$+ \left( \overline{u_s' v_s'} + g_u^n \overline{u' v'} \right) \frac{\partial \overline{w_s'^2}}{\partial y} + \left( \overline{u_s' w_s'} + g_u^k \overline{u' w'} \right) \frac{\partial \overline{w_s'^2}}{\partial z}$$

$$\left. \left. + 2 \left( \overline{u_s' w_s'} + g_u^k \overline{u' w'} \right) \frac{\partial \overline{u_s' w_s'}}{\partial x} + 2 \left( \overline{v_s' w_s'} + g_u^n \overline{v' w'} \right) \frac{\partial \overline{u_s' w_s'}}{\partial y} \right] \right\}, \tag{9}$$

Equation of the $yz$ shear stress component of the Reynolds stress:

$$\frac{\partial}{\partial x} \alpha \left[ u_s \overline{v_s' w_s'} - \frac{\tau_p}{3} \left( \overline{u_s'^2} + g_u^l \overline{u'^2} \right) \frac{\partial \overline{v_s' w_s'}}{\partial x} \right]$$

$$+ \frac{\partial}{\partial y} \alpha \left[ v_s \overline{v_s' w_s'} - \frac{2\tau_p}{3} \left( \overline{v_s'^2} + g_u^n \overline{v'^2} \right) \frac{\partial \overline{v_s' w_s'}}{\partial y} \right]$$

$$+ \frac{\partial}{\partial z} \alpha \left[ w_s \overline{v_s' w_s'} - \frac{2\tau_p}{3} \left( \overline{w_s'^2} + g_u^k \overline{w'^2} \right) \frac{\partial \overline{v_s' w_s'}}{\partial z} \right]$$

$$= \frac{\partial}{\partial x} \left\{ \frac{\alpha \tau_p}{3} \left[ \left( \overline{u_s' v_s'} + g_u^l \overline{u' v'} \right) \frac{\partial \overline{u_s' w_s'}}{\partial x} + \left( \overline{v_s'^2} + g_u^n \overline{v'^2} \right) \right. \right.$$

$$\times \frac{\partial \overline{u_s' w_s'}}{\partial y} + \left( \overline{v_s' w_s'} + g_u^k \overline{v' w'} \right) \frac{\partial \overline{u_s' w_s'}}{\partial z} + \left( \overline{u_s' w_s'} + g_u^l \overline{u' w'} \right) \frac{\partial \overline{u_s' v_s'}}{\partial x}$$

$$+ \left( \overline{v_s' w_s'} + g_u^n \overline{v' w'} \right) \frac{\partial \overline{u_s' v_s'}}{\partial y} + \left( \overline{w_s'^2} + g_u^k \overline{w'^2} \right)$$

$$\left. \left. \times \frac{\partial \overline{u_s' v_s'}}{\partial z} + \left( \overline{u_s' v_s'} + g_u^n \overline{u' v'} \right) \frac{\partial \overline{v_s' w_s'}}{\partial y} + \left( \overline{u_s' w_s'} + g_u^k \overline{u' w'} \right) \frac{\partial \overline{v_s' w_s'}}{\partial z} \right] \right\}$$

$$+ \frac{\partial}{\partial y} \left\{ \frac{\alpha \tau_p}{3} \left[ 2 \left( \overline{u_s' v_s'} + g_u^l \overline{u' v'} \right) \frac{\partial \overline{v_s' w_s'}}{\partial x} \right. \right.$$

$$+2\left(\overline{v_s'w_s'}+g_u^k\overline{v'w'}\right)\frac{\partial\overline{v_s'w_s'}}{\partial z}+\left(\overline{u_s'w_s'}+g_u^l\overline{u'w'}\right)\frac{\partial\overline{v_s'^2}}{\partial x}$$

$$+\left(\overline{v_s'w_s'}+g_u^n\overline{v'w'}\right)\frac{\partial\overline{v_s'^2}}{\partial y}+\left(\overline{w_s'^2}+g_u^k\overline{w'^2}\right)\frac{\partial\overline{v_s'^2}}{\partial z}\Bigg]\Bigg\}$$

$$+\frac{\partial}{\partial z}\left\{\frac{\alpha\tau_p}{3}\left[\left(\overline{u_s'v_s'}+g_u^l\overline{u'v'}\right)\frac{\partial\overline{w_s'^2}}{\partial x}\right.\right.$$

$$+\left(\overline{v_s'^2}+g_u^n\overline{v'}\right)\frac{\partial\overline{w_s'^2}}{\partial y}+\left(\overline{v_s'w_s'}+g_u^k\overline{v'w'}\right)\frac{\partial\overline{w_s'^2}}{\partial z}$$

$$\left.\left.+2\left(\overline{u_s'w_s'}+g_u^k\overline{u'w'}\right)\frac{\partial\overline{v_s'w_s'}}{\partial x}+2\left(\overline{v_s'w_s'}+g_u^n\overline{v'w'}\right)\frac{\partial\overline{v_s'w_s'}}{\partial y}\right]\right\}, \tag{10}$$

where $g_u^l$, $g_u^n$, and $g_u^k$ are the coefficients characterizing the entrainment of particles into the fluctuating motion of the flow [9] for $x$, $y$, and $z$ directions, respectively.

### 2.2. Boundary conditions

The wall conditions are set for the gas at the side walls of the channel based on the control volume method by [27, 28] in a similar way as in the case of the coincidence of shear of the mean flow velocity and gravity.

The numerical simulation considers the turbulent dispersion of solid particles in horizontal channel uniform shear turbulent flow for two different cases: i) shear of the mean flow velocity is along the direction of gravity (**Figure 1a**) and ii) shear of the mean flow velocity is directed normally to gravity (**Figure 1b**). Therefore, two sets of the boundary conditions are used for the calculations.

The boundary conditions for the particulate phase are set at the flow axis as follows:

Case 1 for $z = 0$:

$$\frac{\partial u_s}{\partial z}=v_s=w_s=\frac{\partial\overline{u_s'^2}}{\partial z}=\frac{\partial\overline{v_s'^2}}{\partial z}=\frac{\partial\overline{w_s'^2}}{\partial z}=\overline{u_s'v_s'}=\overline{u_s'w_s'}=\overline{v_s'w_s'}=\frac{\partial\alpha}{\partial z}=0. \tag{11}$$

Case 2 for $y = 0$:

$$\frac{\partial u_s}{\partial y} = v_s = w_s = \frac{\partial \overline{u_s'^2}}{\partial y} = \frac{\partial \overline{v_s'^2}}{\partial y} = \frac{\partial \overline{w_s'^2}}{\partial y} = \overline{u_s' v_s'} = \overline{u_s' w_s'} = \overline{v_s' w_s'} = \frac{\partial \alpha}{\partial y} = 0 \tag{12}$$

The boundary conditions for the particulate phase are set at the channel walls according to [9]:

Case 1 for $y = 0.5h_y$:

$$\frac{\partial u_s}{\partial y} = 2\left(\frac{1-\chi e_x}{1+\chi e_x} - \frac{1-\chi}{1+\chi}\right)\left(\frac{2}{\pi \overline{v_s'^2}}\right)^{0.5} \frac{u_s}{\tau_p}, \tag{13}$$

$$v_s = w_s = \frac{\partial \alpha}{\partial y} = 0, \tag{14}$$

$$P_{uus} = -\overline{u_s' v_s'} \frac{\partial u_s}{\partial y} = P_{uus} = \eta_x \overline{v_s'^2} \frac{\partial u_s}{\partial y}, \tag{15}$$

and applying the expression $\overline{u'_s v'_s} = -\eta_x \overline{v'^2_s}$, where $\eta_x$ is the coefficient of friction between the particles and the wall,

$$P_{vvs} = P_{wws} = P_{uvs} = P_{uws} = P_{vws} = 0,$$

Case 2 for z = $0.5h_z$:

$$\frac{\partial u_s}{\partial y} = 2\left(\frac{1-\chi e_x}{1+\chi e_x} - \frac{1-\chi}{1+\chi}\right)\left(\frac{2}{\pi \overline{w_s'^2}}\right)^{0.5} \frac{u_s}{\tau_p} \tag{16}$$

$$v_s = w_s = \frac{\partial \alpha}{\partial z} = 0, \tag{17}$$

$$P_{uus} = -\overline{u_s' w_s'} \frac{\partial u_s}{\partial z} = \eta_x \overline{w_s'^2} \frac{\partial u_s}{\partial z}, \tag{18}$$

$$P_{vvs} = P_{wws} = P_{uvs} = P_{uws} = P_{vws} = 0. \tag{19}$$

$e_x$ is the coefficient of restitution in the axial direction, which is modeled as:

$$e_x = \begin{cases} 1-\xi_x, & 0 \le \xi_x \le \frac{2}{7} \\ \frac{5}{7}, & \xi_x > \frac{2}{7} \end{cases} \tag{20}$$

Here, the parameter $\xi_x = \eta_x (1 + e_r) tan\theta_x$, where $e_r$ is the coefficient of restitution of the particle velocity normal to the wall; $\theta_x = \tan^{-1}(v_s / u_s)$ is the angle of attack between the trajectory of the particle and the wall; $\chi$ is the reflection coefficient, which is the probability of the particles recoiling off the boundaries and back to the flow. The coefficient of restitution reflects the loss of the particle momentum as the particle hits the walls. In the given model, $\chi$= 1/3, $e_r$= 1 and $\eta_x$ = 0.39 [29].

The conditions for the transverse and spanwise components of the gas velocity are set at the channel walls in terms of impenetrability and no-slip.

The set of boundary conditions for gas and particulate phase at the exit of the channel is written, respectively, as follows:

$$\frac{\partial u_s}{\partial x} = \frac{\partial v_s}{\partial x} = \frac{\partial w_s}{\partial x} = \frac{\partial \alpha}{\partial x} = \frac{\partial \overline{u_s'^2}}{\partial x} = \frac{\partial \overline{v_s'^2}}{\partial x} = \frac{\partial \overline{w_s'^2}}{\partial x} = \frac{\partial \overline{u_s' v_s'}}{\partial x} = \frac{\partial \overline{u_s' w_s'}}{\partial x} = \frac{\partial \overline{v_s' w_s'}}{\partial x} = 0. \tag{21}$$

### 2.3. Computational method

The control volume method was applied to solve the 3D partial differential equations written for the unladen flow and the particulate phase (Eqs. (1)–(11)), taking into account the boundary conditions (Eqs. (12)–(21)). The governing equations were solved using the implicit lower and upper (ILU) matrix decomposition method with the flux-blending-differed correction and upwind-differencing schemes by [27]. This method is utilized for the calculations of the particulate turbulent flows in channels of the rectangular and square cross sections. The calculations were performed in the dimensional form for all the flow conditions. The number of the control volumes was 1120000.

## 3. Laboratory experiments

The obtained numerical results have been verified and validated in comparison with the data obtained by the experimental facility of Tallinn University of Technology.

The experimental method for the determination of the particle dispersion was based on recording the particle trajectories by means of a high-speed video camera on separate regions of a flow that locate at various distances from a point source of particles, and the subsequent processing of the frames [30].

The experimental setup for the investigations of particle dispersion (**Figure 2**) allowed to generate the shear flow similarly to [31] by means of flat plates installed with a varied pitch. The test section was 2 m long with 400 × 200 mm cross section.

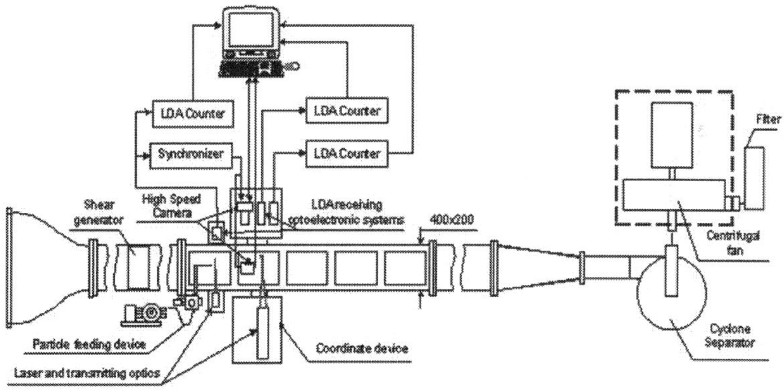


**Figure 2.** Experimental setup.

Two cases of spatial orientation of shear of the mean flow velocity were investigated. **Figure 2** shows the top view of the setup for the case when shear is along the direction of gravity (**Figure 1a**). For investigations of the particle dispersion when shear is directed normally to gravity (**Figure 1b**), the setup was turned sideways as a whole at an angle of *90°* around the axis of the flow.

The mean flow velocity was 5.1 m/s. Glass spherical particles (physical density of 2500 kg/m$^3$) with an average diameter of 55 μm were used in the experiment runs. The root-mean-square deviation of the diameter of particles did not exceed 0.1. The particles were entered into the flow through the source point which was the L-shaped tubule of 200 μm inner diameter.

All measurements and data processing were carried out at the flow location $x$ = 1212 mm.

The data processing technique [30] was applied to determine the particle spatial displacement along the $y$-axis, namely $D_y$, which characterizes quantitatively the particle turbulent dispersion. $D_y$ is calculated as the axial displacement of the maximum value of distribution of the particle mass concentration determined at the location $x$ = 1212 mm relative to the initial flow location that disposes near the exit of the source point.

## 4. Results and discussions

The numerical results presented below have been obtained at two locations of the flow: initial location signed "ini" and disposed at the exit of the particle source point and the location $2x/h_y = 12.63$ from the exit of the particle point source. The turbulent dispersion of 55-μm glass spherical particles was examined. The flow mass loading was about $10^{-6}$ kg dust/kg air.

**Figures 3–15** show the numerical data obtained by the presented model for two cases of spatial orientation of shear of the mean flow velocity: shear is along the direction of gravity (case 1), and shear is directed normally to gravity (case 2).

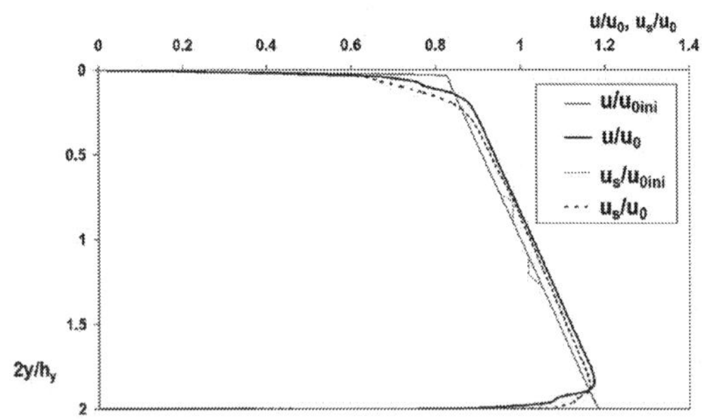


**Figure 3.** Transverse distributions of axial velocities of gas and particles, case 1. Here and below $u_0$ is the mean flow velocity; $u_0 = 5.1$ m/s.

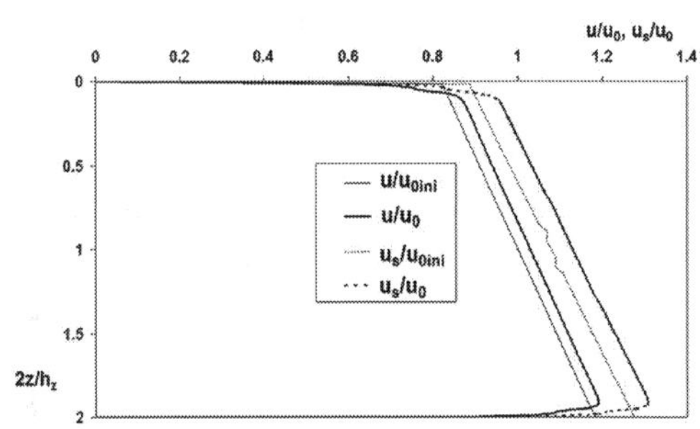


**Figure 4.** Spanwise distributions of axial velocities of gas and particles, case 2.

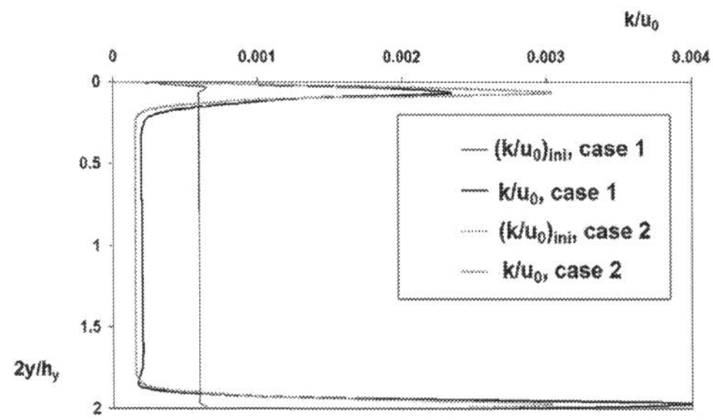


**Figure 5.** Transverse distributions of a turbulence kinetic energy; cases 1 and 2.

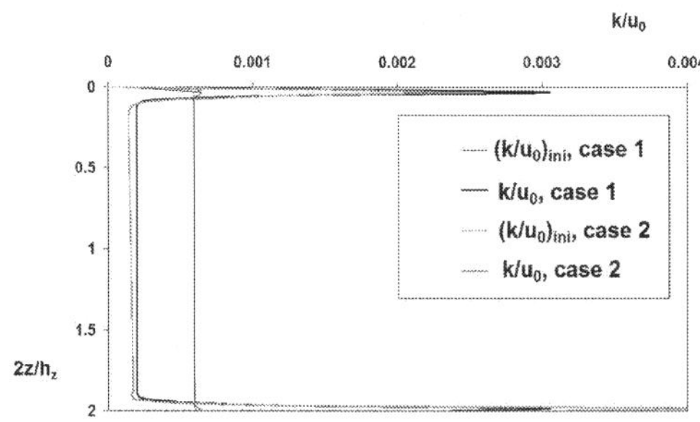


**Figure 6.** Spanwise distributions of a turbulence kinetic energy, cases 1 and 2.

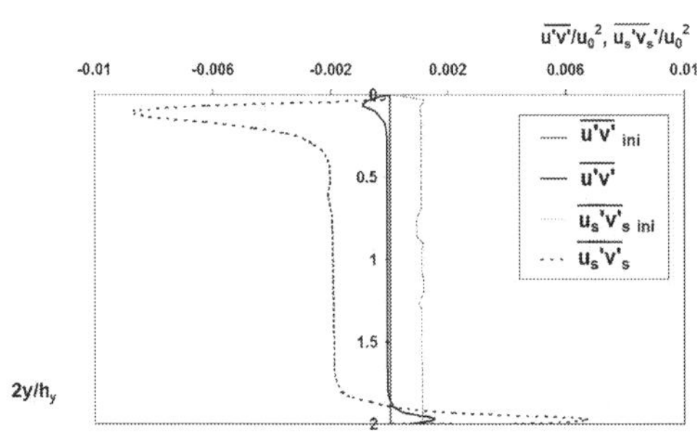


**Figure 7.** Transverse distributions of $xy$ shear stress component of the Reynolds stress of gas and particles, case 1. Here $\overline{u'v'} = \overline{u'v'}/u_0^2$.

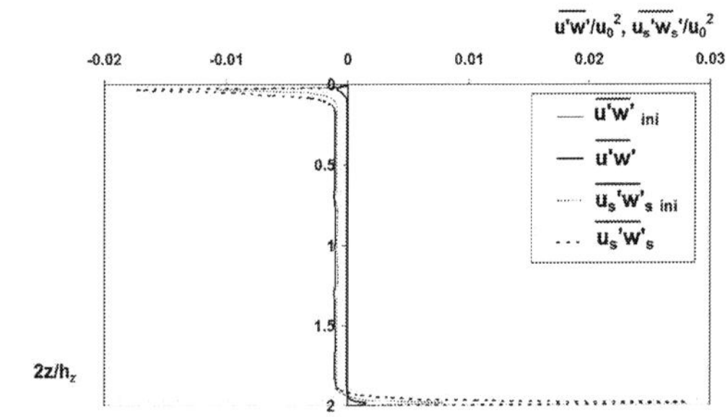


**Figure 8.** Spanwise distributions of *xz* shear stress component of the Reynolds stress of gas and particles, case 2. Here $\overline{u'w'}=\overline{u'w'}/u_0^2$.

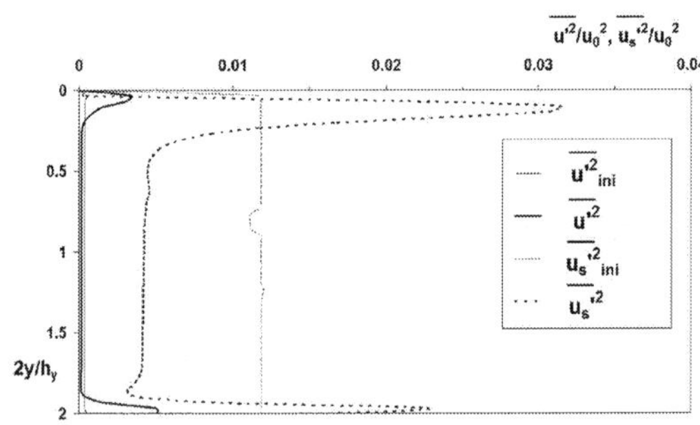


**Figure 9.** Transverse distributions of x-normal components of the Reynolds stress of gas and particles, case 1. Here $\overline{u'^2}=\overline{u'^2}/u_0^2$ and $\overline{u'^2_s}=\overline{u'^2_s}/u_0^2$.

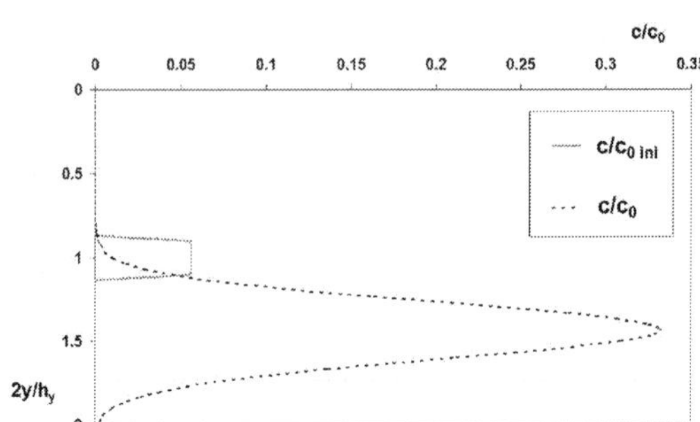


**Figure 10.** Transverse distributions of particles mass concentration, case 1.

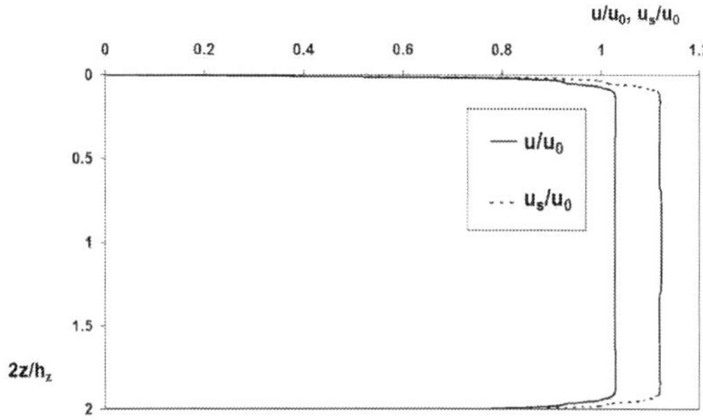


**Figure 11.** Spanwise distributions of axial velocities of gas and particles, case 1, location $2x/h_y$= 12.63.

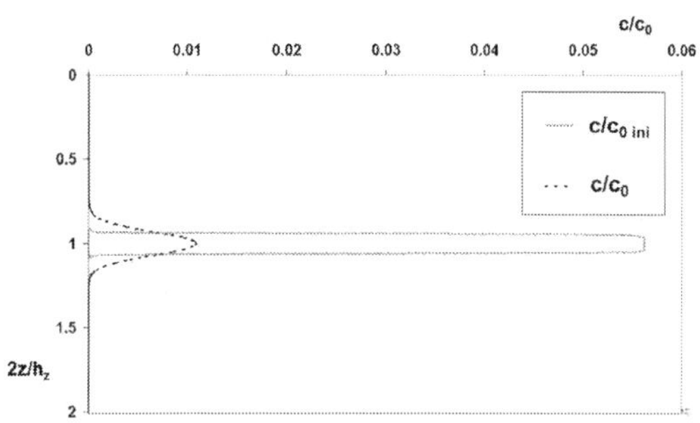


**Figure 12.** Spanwise distribution of particles mass concentration, case 1.

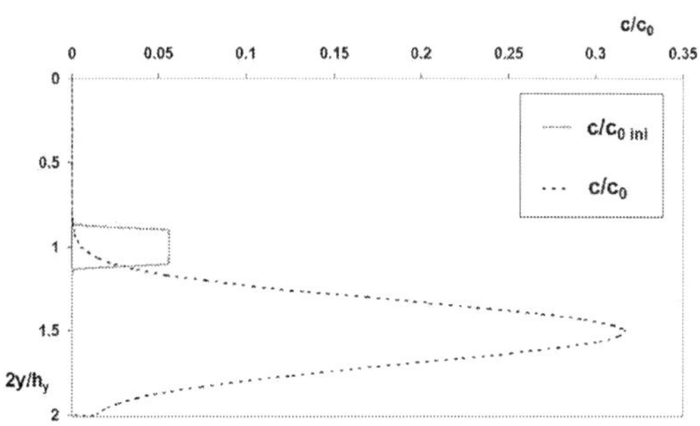


**Figure 13.** Transverse distribution of particles mass concentration, case 2.

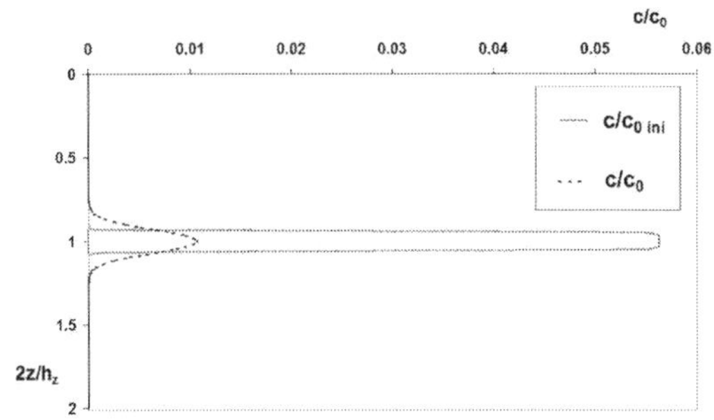


**Figure 14.** Spanwise distribution of particles mass concentration, case 2.

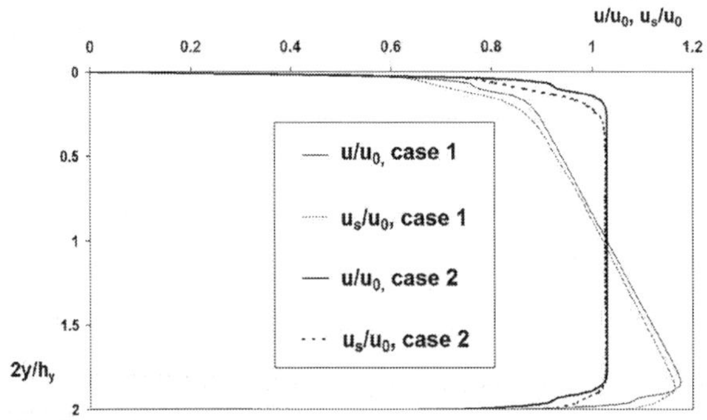


**Figure 15.** Transverse distributions of axial velocities of gas and particles, cases 1 and 2, location $2x/h_y$= 12.63.

**Figure 3** shows the transverse distributions of axial velocities of gas and particles for case 1. It is evident that the linear profiles of the averaged axial velocity components of gas and particulate phase across the flow are almost preserved starting from the initial cross section till the pipe exit. Besides, they occupy almost the whole turbulent core of the flow with slight increase of the values in the turbulent core and decrease near the walls due to the effect of a viscous dissipation. The similar profiles are observed with respect of distribution of the same averaged axial velocity components for gas and particulate phase along the spanwise direction (**Figure 4**).

Since the axial velocity increases toward the bottom wall, the profiles of a turbulence kinetic energy have their higher values near the bottom wall area (**Figure 5**). However, along the spanwise direction, the profiles of the turbulence kinetic energy are symmetrical, since there is no change of the axial velocity along this direction (**Figure 6**).

The profiles of the Reynolds shear stresses of gas and particulate phase are shown in **Figures 7** and **8**. Here it is evident that there is some kind of plateau in the turbulent core. This confirms that we deal with the shear flow; hence, it must be the constant value of the Reynolds shear stresses observed for cases 1 and 2, i.e., for the *xy*-plane (case 1) and *xz*-plane (case 2) Reynolds shear stress components. Here, the linear distributions of the averaged axial velocity components across the flow take place along the spanwise direction.

**Figure 9** show the transverse distributions of x-normal components of the Reynolds stress of gas and particulate phase obtained for case 1. It can be seen that unlike $\overline{u'^2}$, the maximum value of $\overline{u'^2_s}$ distribution located near the channel top wall is larger than the one near the bottom wall. This is due to the effect of particle inertia and their crosswise motion that cause different axial particle accelerations near the top and bottom walls (**Figure 3**).

**Figures 10–13** present the transverse and spanwise distributions of the particle mass concentration $c/c_0$ across the flow at the initial location and the location $2x/h_y = 12.63$ for both the cases of spatial orientation of shear of the mean flow velocity. Here $c_0$ is the value of the particle mass concentration at the initial location at the flow axis. These distributions reflect the character of the particle turbulent dispersion that occurs in the given channel shear flow. It is obvious that a) due to gravity the particles go down, and thus the mass concentration profile shifts toward the bottom wall (case 1) and b) the profiles become wider relative to their initial distributions due to the particle turbulent dispersion (**Figure 10**).

Since in case 1 there is symmetrical distribution of parameters along the spanwise direction (**Figures 6** and **11**), the symmetrical distribution of the mass concentration along this direction (**Figure 12**) can be observed, both at the initial and exit cross sections.

A similar situation is observed for case 2, when the linear change of the axial velocity takes place along the spanwise direction. Here the particles go down due to gravity (see **Figure 13**), and simultaneously there is no shift of the distribution of the mass concentration along the spanwise direction (**Figure 14**).

**Table 1** presents the values of the particle spatial displacement $D_y$ obtained experimentally and numerically for two cases of spatial orientation of shear of the mean flow velocity. This displacement characterized quantitatively the particle turbulent dispersion. It is evident that the numerical values of displacement fit satisfactory with the experimental ones that validate the reliability of the presented model.

| | Case 1 | | Case 2 | |
|---|---|---|---|---|
| | Experiment | Modeling | Experiment | Modeling |
| $D_y$, mm | 46.0 | 43.7 | 48.2 | 50.0 |

**Table 1.** Particle displacement.

**Table 1** shows that the particle dispersion in case 1 is smaller than in case 2. This fact can be explained by the particle axial velocity taking place in case 2 is smaller than the one for case 1 in the same y location (**Figures 10**, **13**, and **15**).

## 5. Conclusions

The 3D Reynolds stress turbulence model (RSTM) based on the 3D RANS and statistical PDF approaches has been elaborated for the turbulent dispersion of solid particles in particulate horizontal channel shear flow domain.

The main distinctive feature of the given model is in use of the same closure for both the carrier flow and particulate phase, namely the Reynolds differential equation.

The presented model has several important advantages over the Lagrangian approach:

1. direct simulation of the particle concentration;
2. direct simulation of the particles influence on a carrier flow;
3. there is no basic limit for the parameters of a particulate flow, namely the flow Reynolds number and value of the particle concentration.

Based on the given model, two cases of spatial orientation of shear of the mean flow velocity have been examined. It has been obtained that the effect of orientation of shear appears through decrease of the particle dispersion in case of directional coincidence between shear and gravity as compared with the case of their mutual perpendicularity.

The validity of the elaborated model has been confirmed by experimental investigations of effect of shear of the mean flow velocity on the turbulent particle dispersion.

## Acknowledgements

The authors are grateful for the technical support of Texas Advanced Computing Center (TACC) in Austin, USA. The authors are grateful for the fulfilled research to the Estonia-Norway project EMP230 support. This study is related to the activity of the European network action COST MP1106 "Smart and green interfaces—from single bubbles and drops to industrial, environmental, and biomedical applications."

## Author details

P. Lauk[1], A. Kartushinsky[2*], M. Hussainov[3], A. Polonsky[4], Ü. Rudi[3], I. Shcheglov[3], S. Tisler[2] and K.-E. Seegel[1]

*Address all correspondence to: aleksander.kartusinski@ttu.ee

1 Department of Aircraft Engineering, Estonian Aviation Academy, Ülenurme, Tartu County, Estonia

http://dx.doi.org/10.5772/63338

2 Chair of Fluid Mechanics, Faculty of Civil Engineering, Department of Mechanics, Tallinn University of Technology, Tallinn, Estonia

3 Research Laboratory of Multiphase Media Physics, Faculty of Science, Tallinn University of Technology, Tallinn, Estonia

4 Nordisc Sikkerhet, Lommedalsveien 182, 1353 Bærums Verk, Norway

## References

[1] Reeks, M. W. On the continuum equations for dispersed particles in nonuniform flows. Phys. Fluids A. 1992;4(6):1290–1303.

[2] Kartushinsky, A. I., Michaelides, E. E., Zaichik, L. I. Comparison of the RANS and PDF methods for air-particle flows. Int. J. Multiphase Flow. 2009;35:914–923.

[3] Gerolymos, G. A., Vallet, I. Contribution to single-point-closure Reynolds-stress modeling of inhomogeneous flow. In: Proceedings of the 4th ASME/JSME Joint Fluids Summer Engineering Conference (FEDSM 2003); July 6–10, 2003; Honolulu, Hawaii, USA. 2003. p. FEDSM2003-45346, CD-ROM.

[4] Kim, K.-Y., Cho, Ch.-H. Performance of Reynolds stress turbulence closures in the calculation of three-dimensional transonic flows. In: Proceedings of the ASME Fluids Engineering Division Summer Meeting (ASME FEDSM 2001); May 29–June 1, 2001; New Orleans, Louisiana, USA. 2001. p. FEDSM2001-18239, CD-ROM.

[5] Abouali, O., Ahmadi, G., Rabiee, A. Computational simulation of supersonic flow using Reynolds stress model. In: Proceedings of the ASME Fluids Engineering Division Summer Meeting (ASME FEDSM 2005); June 19–23, 2005; Houston, Texas, USA. 2005. p. FEDSM2005-77434, CD-ROM.

[6] Leighton, R., Walker, D. T., Stephens, T., Garwood, G. Reynolds stress modeling for drag reducing viscoelastic flows. In: Proceedings of the 4th ASME/JSME Joint Fluids Summer Engineering Conference (FEDSM 2003); July 6–10, 2003; Honolulu, Hawaii, USA. 2003. p. FEDSM2003-45655, CD-ROM.

[7] Taulbee, D. B., Mashayek, F., Barré, C. Simulation and Reynolds stress modeling of particle-laden turbulent shear flows. Int. J. Heat Fluid Flow. 1999;20:368–373.

[8] Kartushinsky A., Rudi Y., Hussainov M., Shcheglov I., Tisler S., Krupenski I., Stock D. RSTM numerical simulation of channel particulate flow with rough wall. In: Awrejcewicz J., editor. Computational and numerical simulations. Rijeka, Croatia: InTech; 2014. p. 41–63. DOI: http://dx.doi.org/10.5772/57035

[9] Zaichik L.I. A statistical model of particle transport and heat transfer in turbulent shear flows. Phys. Fluids. 1999;11(6):1521–1534.

[10] Mukin R. V., Zaichik L. I. Nonlinear algebraic Reynolds stress model for two-phase turbulent flows laden with small heavy particles. Int. J. Heat Fluid Flow. 2012;33:81–91.

[11] Reeks M.W. On the dispersion of small particles suspended in an isotropic turbulent fluid. J. Fluid Mech. 1977;83:529–546.

[12] Wells M.R., Stock D.E. The effects of crossing trajectories on the dispersion of particles in a turbulent flow. J. Fluid Mech. 1983;136:31–62.

[13] Yudine M.I. Physical consideration on heavy-particle dispersion. Advances in Geophysics. 1959;6:185–191.

[14] Csanady G.T. Turbulent diffusion of heavy-particles in the atmosphere. J. Atmos. Sci. 1963;20:201–208.

[15] Taylor G.I. Diffusion by continuous movements. Proc. London Math. Soc. 1921;20:196–211.

[16] Lumley J.L. An approach to the Eulerian–Lagrangian problem. J. Math. Phys. 1962;3(2): 309–312.

[17] Kraichnan R.H. Relation between the Lagrangian and Eulerian correlation times of a turbulent velocity field. Phys. Fluids. 1964;7(1):142–143.

[18] Gosman A.D., Ionnides I.E. Aspects of computer simulation of liquid fuelled combustors. AIAA Aerospace Sciences Meeting. 1981;81-0323.

[19] Squires K.D., Eaton J.K. Lagrangian and Eulerian statistics obtained from direct numerical simulations of homogeneous turbulence. Phys. Fluids A. 1991;3(1):130–143.

[20] Pozorski J., Minier J.-P. On the Lagrangian turbulent dispersion models based on the Langevin equation. Int. J. Multiphase Flow. 1998;24:913–945.

[21] Tanière A., Arcen B. Prediction of a particle-laden turbulent channel flow: Examination of two classes of stochastic dispersion models. Int. J. Multiphase Flow. 2014;60:1–10.

[22] Ahmed A.M., Elghobashi S. Direct numerical simulation of particle dispersion in homogeneous turbulent shear flows. Phys. Fluids. 2001;13(11):3346–3364.

[23] Zaichik L.I., Drobyshevsky N.I., Filippov A.S., Mukin R.V., Strizhov V.F.. A diffusion-inertia model for predicting dispersion and deposition of low-inertia particles in turbulent flows. Int. J. Heat Mass Transf. 2010;53:154–162.

[24] Kartushinsky A., Michaelides E.E. Gas-solid particle flow in horizontal channel: decomposition of the particle-phase flow and inter-particle collision effect. Trans. ASME J. Fluids Eng. 2007;129(6):702–712.

[25] Schiller L., Naumann A. Über die grundlegenden Berechnungen bei der Schwerkraftaufbereitung. (On the fundamental calculation of gravity preparation). Zeitschrift des Vereines deutscher Ingenieure (Union of German Engineers). 1933;77:318–320.

[26] Zaichik L. I., Alipchenkov V. M. Statistical models for predicting particle dispersion and preferential concentration in turbulent flows. Int. J. Heat Fluid Flow. 2005;26:416–430.

[27] Perić M., Scheuerer G. CAST: a finite volume method for predicting two-dimensional flow and heat transfer phenomena. GRS – Technische Notiz SRR–89–01, September 1989.

[28] Fertziger J.H., Perić M. Computational methods for fluid dynamics. 3rd ed. Berlin: Springer-Verlag; 2002. 426 p.

[29] Binder J.L., Hanratty T.J. A diffusion model for droplet deposition in gas/liquid annular flow. Int. J. Multiphase Flow. 1991;17:1–11.

[30] Kartushinsky A.I., Rudi Yu.A., Tisler S.V., Hussainov M.T., Shcheglov I.N. Application of particle tracking velocimetry for studying the dispersion of particles in a turbulent gas flow. High Temp. 2012;50(3):381–390.

[31] Phillips J.C., Thomas N.H., Perkins R.J., Miller P.C.H. Wind tunnel velocity profiles generated by differentially spaced flat plates. J. Wind Eng. Ind. Aerodyn. 1999;80:253–262.

Chapter 15

# Free Surface Flow Simulation Using VOF Method

Mohammad Javad Ketabdari

Additional information is available at the end of the chapter

http://dx.doi.org/10.5772/64161

**Abstract**

Viscous flow with moving free surface is an important phenomenon in nature which has broad applications in engineering. For these flows, temporal and spatial position of this moving free surface in unsteady or non-uniform conditions is very complicated. In this chapter, free surface simulation methods based on computational grid are presented. Volume of fluid (VOF) is a powerful and the most prevailing method for modeling two immiscible incompressible fluid-fluid interfaces. Herein, the governing equations of fluid flow including Navier-Stokes coupled with VOF equation are discussed and the most prominent VOF schemes hierarchically presented to the readers. Meanwhile, Compressive Interface Capturing Scheme for Arbitrary Meshes (CICSAM), Higher Resolution Artificial Compressive (HiRAC), High Resolution Interface Capturing (HRIC), Switching Technique for Advection and Capturing of Surfaces (STACS), and some other newly proposed methods are introduced, and the accuracy and time calculation of each method are evaluated. Moreover, surface tension modeling and its discretization as one of the most demanding phenomena in the nature are brought to the readers. Finally, two schemes of parametric study of interfaces are discussed.

**Keywords:** viscous flow, free surface modeling, Eulerian approach, volume of fluid, interface simulation

## 1. Introduction

Simulations of free surface flows have progressed rapidly over the last decade, and it is now possible to simulate the motion of complicated waves and their interactions with structures considering even deformable bubbles in turbulent flows. In the continuum mechanics, there are two methods to express the motion in the environment. The first description is the Eulerian approach. In this method, attention is paid to a special volume in the space. A mesh remains fixed in the Eulerian method and fluid regions change in shape and location on the mesh. It uses a fixed grid system which is not transformed during the solution procedure. The fluid is studied while passing this volume and continuously replaced in time. Therefore, this method is not appropriate for formulation of basic equations of fluid movement. The Eulerian method has some limitations. For example, when the portion of the perimeter to the area of a zone of fluid is large, the error of this method is increased. In the Eulerian method, it is not possible to decompose the equation on the boundaries with the same precision of inner region of fluid and accordingly, the finer mesh should be used near the boundaries. Therefore, when the free surface of a discontinuous region is modeled by this method, finer grid should be employed in order to achieve more precise results, specifically if this surface has large deflections. This is crucial when the portion of the area to the perimeter of a zone is low, for example on phase of a multiphase fluid. In this case, using finer mesh could increase the portion of the number of the inner elements to the boundary elements, which in turn, increases the precision of the numerical solution. The main superiority of the Eulerian description is the possibility of modeling of complicated surfaces. For example, the collapse of a column of a fluid could be modeled in the Eulerian grid which is shown in **Figure 1**.

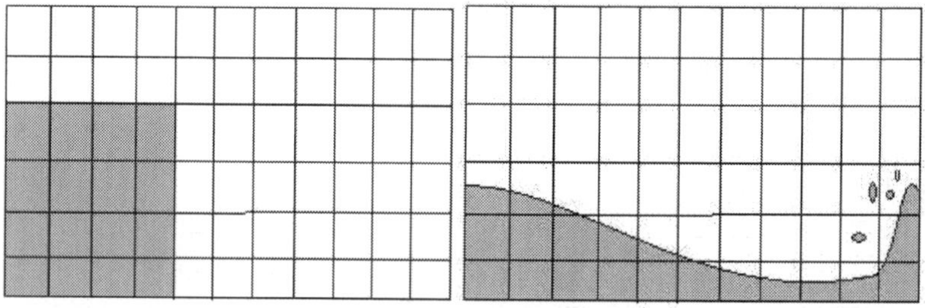

(a) (b)

**Figure 1.** Fluid column in Eulerian grid: (a) before collapse and (b) collapsing flow.

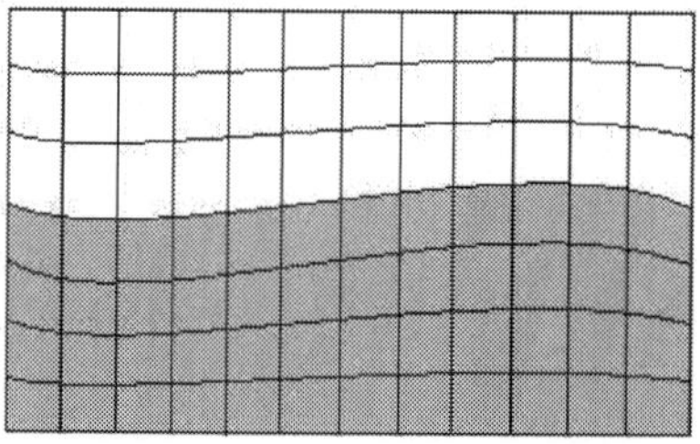

**Figure 2.** A sample of Lagrangian grid in vertical direction.

In Lagrangian method, the flow field of the considered fluid is covered by a mesh moving with the fluid. The fluid boundaries always coincide with the grid boundaries and the fluid inside each cell of the grid always remains in that computational cell. Although this method is not applicable to flows undergoing large distortions, where meshes can be twisted into unacceptable shapes, but its advantage is the ease with which it handles free surfaces and interfaces, which makes it applicable to a wide variety of problems. For example, the grid shown in **Figure 2** is Lagrangian in the vertical coordinate. For free surface problems, if the free surface movement or the tangential acceleration gradient in the perpendicular direction to its surface is not large, the Lagrangian method can be used to simulate free surfaces. The grid lines are located on the free surface and move with it. Therefore, there is no need for any special boundary condition in this location [1].

## 2. Governing equations

Governing equations for a compressible viscous fluid flow with no phase change are as follows:

$$\frac{\partial \rho}{\partial t} + \nabla \cdot (\rho \mathbf{u}) = 0 \tag{1}$$

$$\frac{\partial (\rho \mathbf{u})}{\partial t} + \nabla \cdot (\rho \mathbf{u}\mathbf{u}) + \nabla P = \rho \mathbf{g} + \mathbf{F}_s + \nabla \cdot \left[\mu \left(\nabla \mathbf{u} + \nabla \mathbf{u}^{\mathrm{T}}\right)\right] \tag{2}$$

In these equations, $\rho$, $\mathbf{u}$, $t$, $P$, $\mu$, $g=(g_x, g_y)$, and $\mathbf{F}_s$ are density, velocity vector, time, total pressure, kinematic viscosity, gravity acceleration, and body forces, respectively. Body forces include forces due to surface tension in the interface. Here, properties of a fluid such as density and viscosity are included in the equations. However, it should be kept in mind that the information changes from one fluid to another. Thus for mesh-based numerical methods, new properties based on fluid properties of both materials should be considered for Eq. (2) in the cell containing the free surface, and the governing equations should be rewritten in the following form:

$$\frac{\partial}{\partial t}(\alpha \rho_1) + \nabla \cdot (\alpha \rho_1 \mathbf{u}_1) = 0 \tag{3}$$

$$\frac{\partial}{\partial t}((1-\alpha)\rho_2) + \nabla \cdot ((1-\alpha)\rho_2 \mathbf{u}_2) = 0 \tag{4}$$

$$\frac{\partial (\alpha \rho_1 \mathbf{u}_1)}{\partial t} + \nabla \cdot (\alpha \rho_1 \mathbf{u}_1 \mathbf{u}_1) + \nabla P_1 = \alpha \rho_1 \mathbf{g} + \mathbf{F}_s + \nabla \cdot \left[\alpha \mu_1 \left(\nabla \mathbf{u}_1 + \nabla {\mathbf{u}_1}^{\mathrm{T}}\right)\right] \tag{5}$$

$$\frac{\partial\left((1-\alpha)\rho_2\mathbf{u}_2\right)}{\partial t}+\nabla\cdot\left((1-\alpha)\rho_2\mathbf{u}_2\mathbf{u}_2\right)+\nabla P_2=(1-\alpha)\rho_2\mathbf{g}+\mathbf{F}_s+ \nabla\cdot\left[(1-\alpha)\mu_2\left(\nabla\mathbf{u}_2+\nabla\mathbf{u}_2^{\mathrm{T}}\right)\right] \tag{6}$$

where indices 1 and 2 show first and second fluids properties, and $\alpha$ is a scalar phase indicator function which is defined as follows:

$$\alpha=\begin{cases}1 & \text{Control volume is filled only with phase 1}\\ 0 & \text{Control volume is filled only with phase 2}\\ 0<\alpha<1 & \text{Interface present}\end{cases} \tag{7}$$

This phase indicator function is the fluid property or volume fraction, which moves with it and can be derived as follows:

$$\frac{\partial\alpha}{\partial t}+\frac{\partial U_i\alpha}{\partial x_i}=0 \tag{8}$$

This function can be used to calculate the fluid properties in each phase as a weight function. In order to use a set of governing equations using the weight function, each fluid property should be calculated based on the volume occupied by this fluid in the surface cell as expressed in Eqs. (9) and (10) [2]:

$$\rho=\alpha\cdot\rho_1+(1-\alpha)\cdot\rho_2 \tag{9}$$

$$\mu=\alpha\cdot\mu_1+(1-\alpha)\cdot\mu_2 \tag{10}$$

Free surfaces considered here are those on which discontinuities exist in one or more variables. This has been the challenge for researchers to omit or reduce this problem as much as possible. The transient state as well as phenomena such as surface tension, changing of fluid phase and Kelvin-Helmholtz instability makes numerical simulation of such problems cumbersome. It is expected that methods used to simulate interface of fluids have a number of characteristics. These include mass conservation, simulating the interface as thin as possible, being able to reproduce complicated topologies, generalization of expansion to 3D problems, and being able to model surface phenomena and be computationally efficient.

## 3. Free surface modeling methods

There are different methods to simulate free surface flow, each of which has its own advantages and disadvantages:

### 3.1. Donor-acceptor method

The main idea of donor-acceptor approach is that the value of volume fraction in downwind cell, the acceptor cell, is used for anticipation of transferring fluid in each time step. The problem in this approach is that using downwind cell in calculations may lead to unreal situations which are values out of zero and unity domain in surface cells. **Figure 3a** shows this method with the first fluid with gray color and volume of fluid equals to unity. It could be seen that using donor-acceptor approach with downwind differencing scheme results in values greater than unity in donor cell. It is because the second fluid in the acceptor cell is greater than the value needed in the donor cell. Similarly in **Figure 3b**, using downwind differencing scheme leads to negative values for volume of fluid, which is because the needed fluid in acceptor cell is more than what is in the donor cell [3].

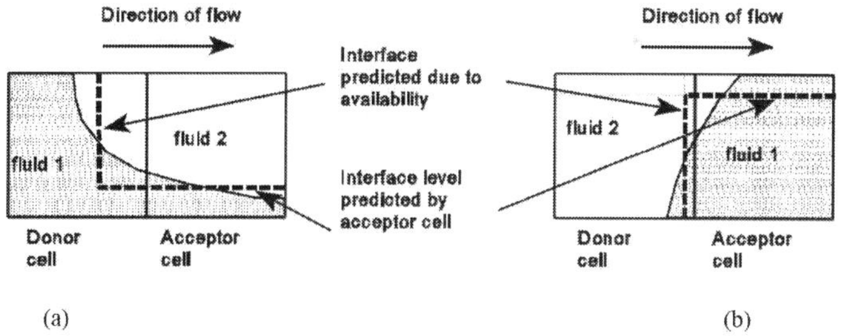


**Figure 3.** Schematic view of donor-acceptor approach [4].

In order to be assured that volume of fluid is between zero and one, the amount of fluid or volume of fluid in donor cell should be used to regulate the estimated fluid transferring between two adjacent cells [5].

One drawback of donor-acceptor method is that this method changes any finite gradient into step, and consequently increases the slope of the surface model in the direction of flow. This problem was alleviated by proposing a method to consider the slope of interface for flux transferring in adjacent cells by Hirt and Nichols [6]. For this purpose, a donor-acceptor equation was proposed so that it could detect the direction of the flow in interface and then define the upwind and downwind cells accordingly. Thereafter, this model was expanded for 3D domains by Torrey et al. [7]. The Surfer method is one version of volume of fluid which deals with merging and fragmenting of interfaces in multiphase flows [8].

The volume of fluid method is one of the most popular methods for anticipation of interfaces, and many researches have been conducted based on this method including dam break, Rayleigh-Taylor instability, wave generation and bubble movement [6, 9–12]. This method was modified in 2008 to get more accurate results by considering diagonal changes in fluxes of adjacent cells for structured grid domains [13, 14].

### 3.2. The Hirt-Nichols method

The volume of fluid (VOF) method was first proposed by Hirt and Nichols [6]. In this method, similar to the SLIC method, free surfaces can be reconstructed based on parallel lines with respect to one of the principal coordinates of the system. However, nine neighboring cells are considered for flux changes and defining the normal vector in a desired cell. Then, free surface is considered as either a horizontal or a vertical line in cell with respect to the relative normal vector components. **Figure 4** shows the actual free surface and what was simulated by Hirt-Nichols method.

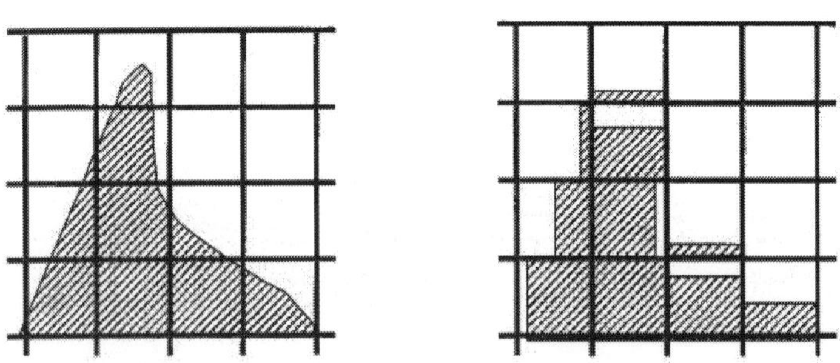

(a) (b)

**Figure 4.** Free surface (a) actual surface and (b) reconstructed surface based on Hirt-Nichols method [6].

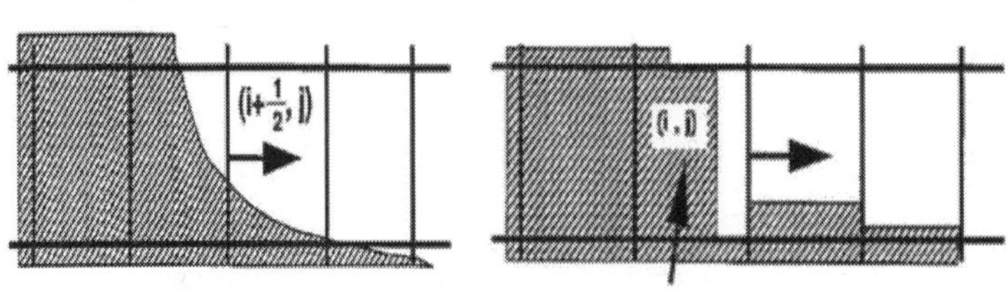

**(a)** **(b)**

**Figure 5.** Hirt-Nichols scheme (a) actual surface and (b) reconstructed surface.

Upwind fluxes are used for fluxes parallel to the reconstructed interface, while donor-acceptor fluxes are used for those fluxes normal to it. For instance according to **Figure 5a**, the interface in the cell $(i,\ j)$ is considered to have positive celerity direction with respect to $x$ coordinate in the face $i+{}^{1}\!/_{2}$ in donor-acceptor method. Therefore, the reconstructed surface in the $(i,\ j)$ cell is vertical (**Figure 5b**), and this cell is considered a downwind cell for the cell $(i+1,\ j)$, $(\alpha_{i,j}>\alpha_{i+1,j})$. According to donor-acceptor method, transferred flux from the face $\left(i+{}^{1}\!/_{2},\ j\right)$ can be calculated as follows:

$$F_{i+\frac{1}{2},j} = \delta y\left\{\min\left[\alpha_{i,j}\delta x, U_{i+\frac{1}{2},j}\alpha_{i+1,j}\delta t + \max\left(0, U_{i+\frac{1}{2},j}\left(1-\alpha_{i+1,j}\right)\delta t - \left(1-\alpha_{i,j}\right)\delta x\right)\right]\right\} \tag{11}$$

where $\alpha_{i,j}\delta x$ is the maximum fluid available for exiting the cell $(i,\ j)$; $U_{i+\frac{1}{2},j}\alpha_{i+1,j}\delta t$ is the estimation of downwind flux for the volume of the fluid, $\alpha$; $U_{i+\frac{1}{2},j}(1-\alpha_{i+1,j})\delta t$ is the estimation of downwind flux resulted from the convey of void portion of the cell $(i,\ j)$; and $(1-\alpha_{i,j})\delta x$ is the maximum void portion which can exit from the cell $(i,\ j)$.

The "min" operator has been designed to ensure the fluid leaving the cell $(i,\ j)$ is not more than the calculated available fluid in it from the previous time step. As the fluid in a cell transfers, so does the whole void space in the cell. Thus, the "max" operator has been designed in order to assure that amount of void exits the cell is bounded by what was in it calculated from the previous step. In this scheme, the combination of downwind and upwind fluxes has been considered in such a way that not only the solution stability is guaranteed, but also avoids the numerical diffusion.

### 3.3. Flux Corrected Transport (FCT) method

The FCT method is based on the idea to present a formulation which combines the upwind and downwind fluxes. This formulation aimed to leave out upwind numerical diffusion and instability of downwind scheme [15]. Idea of neighboring fluxes based on higher order translate scheme was first proposed by Boris and Book [16] and then developed by Zalesak [17] to multidimensional.

In this method calculations consist of some steps. First, an intermediate value of volume of fluid, $\alpha^*$, must be defined based on a first-order scheme. **Figure 6** shows schematically the solution for a 1D governing equation of fluid volume fraction for cell $i$ as:

$$\alpha_i^* = \alpha_i^n - \frac{1}{\delta x}\left(F_{i+\frac{1}{2}}^L - F_{i-\frac{1}{2}}^L\right) \tag{12}$$

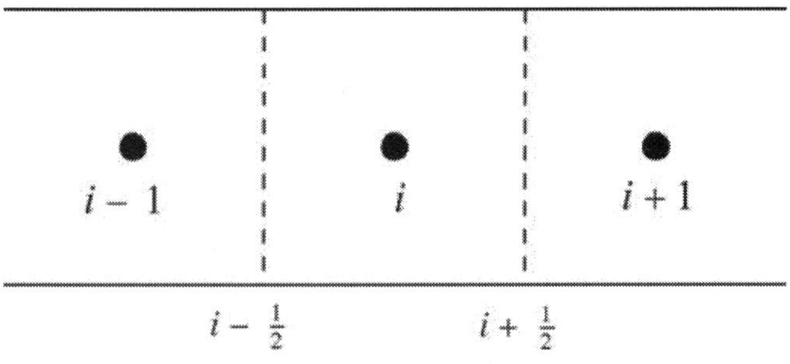


**Figure 6.** Three adjacent typical cells in FCT method.

where $F^L$ is the flux in the downwind cell, and $F_f$ is defined in the face $f$ as:

$$F_f = U_f \delta t \alpha_f \tag{13}$$

Thereafter, an anti-diffusive flux is needed to be defined ($F^L$) in order to correct the diffusion of the previous step. This is the difference between upwind and downwind fluxes as:

$$F^A_{i+\frac{1}{2}} = F^H_{i+\frac{1}{2}} - F^L_{i+\frac{1}{2}} \tag{14}$$

To make this stable, a correction factor, $q$, is needed to modify the fluxes values. Finally, a value for fluid fraction in next time step is defined as:

$$\alpha_i^{n+1} = \alpha_i^* - \frac{\left(q_{i+\frac{1}{2}} F^A_{i+\frac{1}{2}} - q_{i-\frac{1}{2}} F^A_{i-\frac{1}{2}}\right)}{\delta x} \tag{15}$$

### 3.4. Youngs' method

This method was first proposed by Youngs in 1982 [18]. It was then developed by Rudman [19] with more details. In this method, at first the slope of the interface position is estimated. Then, the free surface is defined as a straight line with the slope of $\beta$ in each cell of the numerical domain. The position of this line segment in each cell is defined such that the area reconstructed from the line and the perimeter of the cell is equal to the amount of volume of fluid, $\alpha$. The geometry of the polygon from this reconstruction is used to calculate the flux transferred from the cell faces.

Assuming that $\alpha_{i,j}$ is predefined in every cell, the first step is to calculate first-order upwind fluxes. Then, the Youngs exiting fluxes of every cell can be calculated by considering the values in each cell. To do so, the angle $\beta$, between free surface and x-coordinate, must be calculated. Different methods can be used for calculation of $\beta$. One of them is first using the gradient function of fluid volume fraction for defining unit normal vector of the free surface, and then calculating $\beta$ [20]. The method of defining the normal vector, however, can affect the accuracy of the final results. This formulation for uniform grid is as follows:

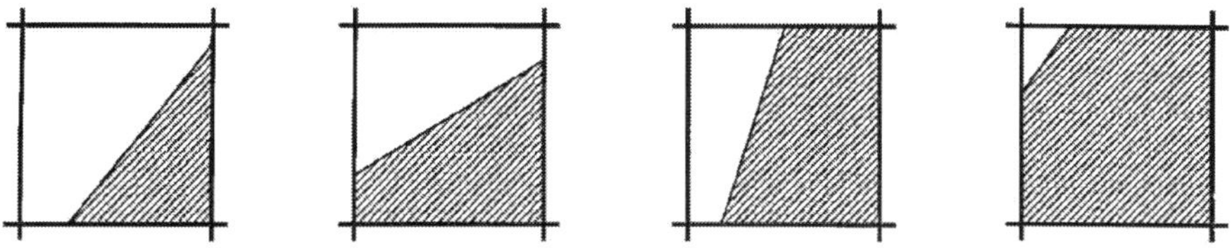


**Figure 7.** Four possible positions for free surface in Youngs' method [19].

$$n_{i,j}^{x} = \frac{\alpha_{i+1,j+1} + 2\alpha_{i+1,j} + \alpha_{i+1,j-1} - \alpha_{i-1,j+1} - 2\alpha_{i-1,j} - \alpha_{i-1,j-1}}{\delta x} \tag{16}$$

$$n_{i,j}^{y} = \frac{\alpha_{i+1,j+1} + 2\alpha_{i,j+1} + \alpha_{i-1,j+1} - \alpha_{i+1,j-1} - 2\alpha_{i,j-1} - \alpha_{i-1,j-1}}{\delta y} \tag{17}$$

Using components of the normal unit vector, the angle $\beta$ can be calculated as:

$$\beta = \tan^{-1}\left(\frac{-n_x}{n_y}\right) \quad (-\pi < \beta \leq \pi) \tag{18}$$

The angle $\gamma$ is also defined as:

$$\gamma = \tan^{-1}\left(\frac{\delta x}{\delta y}\tan\beta\right) \quad \left(0 \leq \gamma \leq \pi/2\right) \tag{19}$$

It is possible to set $0 \leq \gamma \leq 90$ by rotating the cell. Therefore, there are only four possible positions for the free surface, which are depicted in **Figure 7**.

What is behind this conclusion is as follows:

$$
\begin{array}{l}
\textit{if } \gamma < \pi/4 \\
\quad \textit{if } \alpha \le \tfrac{1}{2}\tan\gamma \\
\quad\quad \textit{Case I} \\
\quad \textit{elseif } \alpha \le \left(1-\tfrac{1}{2}\tan\gamma\right) \\
\quad\quad \textit{Case II} \\
\quad \textit{else} \\
\quad\quad \textit{Case IV} \\
\textit{else} \\
\quad \textit{if } \alpha \le \tfrac{1}{2}\cot\gamma \\
\quad\quad \textit{Case I} \\
\quad \textit{elseif } \alpha \le \left(1-\tfrac{1}{2}\cot\gamma\right) \\
\quad\quad \textit{Case III} \\
\quad \textit{else} \\
\quad\quad \textit{Case IV}
\end{array}
$$

| | Case I | Case II |
|---|---|---|
| $s_t$ | 0 | 0 |
| $s_r$ | $\sqrt{2\alpha\tan\gamma}$ | $\alpha + \frac{1}{2}\tan\gamma$ |
| $s_b$ | $\sqrt{2\alpha\cot\gamma}$ | 1 |
| $s_l$ | 0 | $\alpha - \frac{1}{2}\tan\gamma$ |
| *if* $U_t>0$ | *if* $U_t\delta t \le (1-s_r)\delta y$<br>$F_t=0$<br>*else*<br>$F_t=\frac{1}{2}[U_t\delta t-(1-s_r)\delta y]^2\cot\gamma$ | *if* $U_t\delta t \le (1-s_r)\delta y$<br>$F_t=0$<br>*elseif* $U_t\delta t \le (1-s_l)\delta y$<br>$F_t=\frac{1}{2}[U_t\delta t-(1-s_r)\delta y]^2\cot\gamma$<br>*else*<br>$F_t=U_t\delta t\delta x-(1-\alpha)\delta x\delta y$ |
| *if* $U_r>0$ | *if* $U_r\delta t \ge s_b\delta x$<br>$F_r=\alpha\delta x\delta y$<br>*else*<br>$F_r=\frac{1}{2}U_r\delta t\left(2-{U_r\delta t}/{s_b\delta x}\right)s_r\delta y$ | $F_r=U_r\delta t\left(s_r\delta y-\frac{1}{2}U_r\delta t\tan\gamma\right)$ |

| | Case I | Case II |
|---|---|---|
| *if* $U_b>0$ | *if* $U_b\delta t \ge s_r\delta y$<br>$F_b=\alpha\delta x\delta y$<br>*else*<br>$F_b=\frac{1}{2}U_b\delta t\left(2-{}^{U_b\delta t}/_{s_r\delta y}\right)s_b\delta x$ | *if* $U_b\delta t \le s_l\delta y$<br>$F_b=U_b\delta t\delta x$<br>*elseif* $U_b\delta t \le s_r\delta y$<br>$F_b=U_b\delta t\delta x-\frac{1}{2}(U_b\delta t-s_l\delta y)^2\cot\gamma$<br>*else*<br>$F_b=\alpha\delta x\delta y$ |
| *if* $U_l>0$ | *if* $U_l\delta t \le (1-s_b)\delta x$<br>$F_l=0$<br>*else*<br>$F_l=\frac{1}{2}[U_l\delta t-(1-s_b)\delta x]^2\tan\gamma$ | $F_l=U_l\delta t\left(s_l\delta y+\frac{1}{2}U_l\delta t\tan\gamma\right)$ |

| | Case III | Case IV |
|---|---|---|
| $s_t$ | $\alpha-\frac{1}{2}\cot\gamma$ | $1-\sqrt{2\alpha\cot\gamma}$ |
| $s_r$ | 1 | 1 |
| $s_b$ | $\alpha+\frac{1}{2}\cot\gamma$ | 1 |
| $s_l$ | 0 | $1-\sqrt{2\alpha\tan\gamma}$ |
| *if* $U_t>0$ | $F_t=U_t\delta t\left(s_t\delta x+\frac{1}{2}U_t\delta t\cot\gamma\right)$ | *if* $U_t\delta t \ge (1-s_l)\delta y$<br>$F_t=U_t\delta t\delta x-(1-\alpha)\delta x\delta y$<br>*else*<br>$F_t=U_t\delta t\left(s_t\delta x+\frac{1}{2}U_t\delta t\cot\gamma\right)$ |
| *if* $U_r>0$ | *if* $U_r\delta t \le s_t\delta x$<br>$F_r=U_r\delta t\delta y$<br>*elseif* $U_r\delta t \le s_b\delta x$<br>$F_r=U_r\delta t\delta y-\frac{1}{2}(U_r\delta t-s_t\delta x)^2\tan\gamma$<br>*else*<br>$F_r=\alpha\delta x\delta y$ | *if* $U_r\delta t \le s_t\delta x$<br>$F_r=U_r\delta t\delta y$<br>*else*<br>$F_r=U_r\delta t\delta y-\frac{1}{2}\tan\gamma(U_r\delta t-s_t\delta x)^2$ |
| *if* $U_b>0$ | $F_b=U_b\delta t\left(s_b\delta x-\frac{1}{2}U_b\delta t\cot\gamma\right)$ | *if* $U_b\delta t \le s_l\delta y$<br>$F_b=U_b\delta t\delta x$<br>*else*<br>$F_b=U_b\delta t\delta x-\frac{1}{2}(U_b\delta t-s_l\delta y)^2\cot\gamma$ |

| | Case III | Case IV |
|---|---|---|
| $if\ U_l>0$ | $if\ U_l\delta t\le s_b\delta x$ | $if\ U_l\delta t\ge(1-s_t)\delta x$ |
| | $F_l=0$ | $F_l=U_l\delta t\delta y-(1-\alpha)\delta x\delta y$ |
| | $elseif\ U_l\delta t\le s_t\delta x$ | $else$ |
| | $F_l=\frac{1}{2}[U_l\delta t-(1-s_b)\delta x]^2\tan\gamma$ | $F_l=U_l\delta t\left(s_l\delta y+\frac{1}{2}U_l\delta t\tan\gamma\right)$ |
| | $else$ | |
| | $F_l=U_l\delta t\delta y-(1-\alpha)\delta x\delta y$ | |

**Table 1.** Calculation of exiting flux in Youngs' method.

Four side fractions ($s_l$, $s_b$, $s_r$, $s_t$) for up, right, down, and left faces can be calculated with the selection of the free surface position in a cell. Thereafter, flow fluxes can be geometrically computed for each face ($F_l$, $F_b$, $F_r$, $F_t$) based on these side fractions. More details are presented in **Table 1**. In this table, positive value is set for velocities towards the outer edges of a cell, and there is no flux calculation for negative velocities into the cell.

### 3.5. Piecewise Linear Interface Calculation (PLIC) method

To solve fluid volume transfer equation with FDM or FVM, diffusion error in interface reconstruction occurs. This leads to poor modeling of free surfaces, specifically in the interface of two adjacent fluids with large density difference. PLIC is one of the methods to reconstruct the interface between fluids with second-order accuracy [20]. It can increase the accuracy of transferred flux estimation and geometric fluid distribution in each cell. In this method, unit normal vectors of the surface are calculated based on the volume fraction of fluid using Youngs' least square method as:

$$\vec{n}_{i,j}=-\left(\frac{\nabla\alpha_{i,j}}{\sqrt{\left(\nabla\alpha_{x,i,j}\right)^2+\left(\nabla\alpha_{y,i,j}\right)^2}}\right) \tag{20}$$

where $(\nabla\alpha)$ is defined as:

$$(\nabla\alpha)_{i,j}=\frac{1}{4}\left[(\nabla\alpha)_{i-\frac{1}{2},j-\frac{1}{2}}+(\nabla\alpha)_{i-\frac{1}{2},j+\frac{1}{2}}+(\nabla\alpha)_{i+\frac{1}{2},j+\frac{1}{2}}+(\nabla\alpha)_{i+\frac{1}{2},j-\frac{1}{2}}\right] \tag{21}$$

$$(\nabla\alpha)_{i+\frac{1}{2},j+\frac{1}{2}} = \frac{1}{2}\left(\frac{\alpha_{i+1,j}-\alpha_{i,j}}{x_{i+1,j}-x_{i,j}} + \frac{\alpha_{i+1,j+1}-\alpha_{i,j+1}}{x_{i+1,j+1}-x_{i,j+1}}\right)\vec{i} + \frac{1}{2}\left(\frac{\alpha_{i,j+1}-\alpha_{i,j}}{y_{i,j+1}-y_{i,j}} + \frac{\alpha_{i+1,j+1}-\alpha_{i+1,j}}{y_{i+1,j+1}-y_{i+1,j}}\right)\vec{j} \tag{22}$$

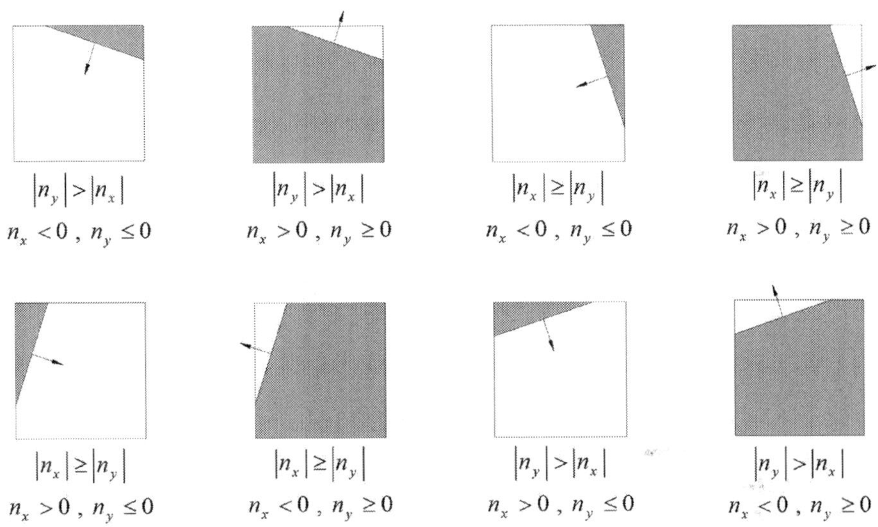


**Figure 8.** Different positioning of the interface for $(0 \leq \theta \leq \pi/4)$.

where $\theta$ is the angle between the normal vector and the horizontal coordinate varies between zero and $2\pi$. For $\theta$ in the first one-eighth space $(0 \leq \theta \leq \pi/4)$, eight different conditions are possible for the position of free surfaces as illustrated in **Figure 8** [21]. All other situations can be achieved with a mirror reflection of the first quarter with respect to the x and y axes and bisectors between them. The exact position of the free surface is determined defining surface unit normal vector using volume fraction of fluid in each cell. To do this, extreme values of $\alpha_{\lim,1}$ and $\alpha_{\lim,2}$ are determined as:

$$\alpha_{\lim,1} = \frac{n_{\min}}{2n_{\max}} \quad , \quad \alpha_{\lim,2} = 1 - \alpha_{\lim,1} \tag{23}$$

in which $v(i+1,\ j-\frac{1}{2})$ and $n_{\max}$ are calculated as:

$$n_{\min} = \min\left(|n_x|, |n_y|\right) \quad , \quad n_{\max} = \max\left(|n_x|, |n_y|\right) \tag{24}$$

$\alpha_{\lim,1}$ and $\alpha_{\lim,2}$ are shown in **Figure 9**.

When unit normal vector of a surface is defined, the true position of the interface can be easily determined using volume of fluid in each cell.

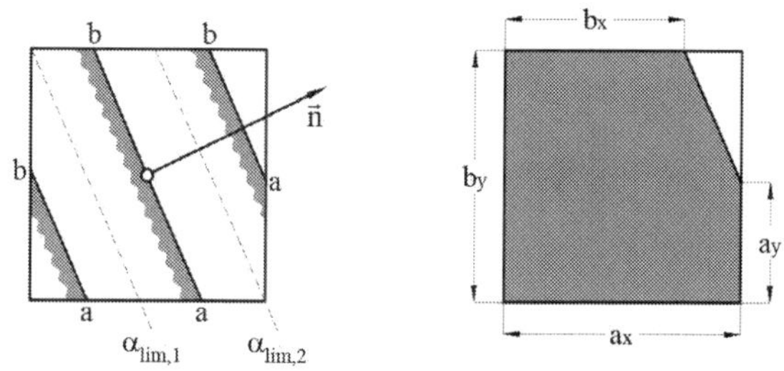


**Figure 9.** Various positions of an interface in a cell.

### 3.6. Higher order differencing schemes

Another method to reconstruct the interface between two fluids is to discretize the convection term using higher order differencing schemes or blended differencing scheme. The accuracy of less/non-diffusive schemes and compressive schemes was compared by Davis [22]. Less/non-diffusive schemes prevent the interface profile from being diffused. Compressive schemes not only prevent the interface from being diffused, but also omit any diffusion in the neighboring of the interface. Thus, they are considered as powerful tools for thin interface simulation.

Ghobadian [23] applied the higher order scheme proposed by Van Leer [24]. However, his results showed that this scheme has poor ability in terms of removing diffusion. Therefore, he proposed solutions for decreasing numerical diffusion. Other methods for omitting diffusion proposed by Pericleous and Chen [25] proved to be associated with interface diffusion. Although first-order upwind or downwind schemes lead to diffusion, higher order methods result in numerical fluctuations in the interface. There are other methods for reducing the interface as follows:

#### *3.6.1. Compressive Interface Capturing Scheme for Arbitrary Meshes (CICSAM) scheme*

The CICSAM scheme, presented by Ubbink, is a combined method to reduce the diffusion problem in interface modeling. This method imposes some limitations on the fluid fraction value. It is obvious that the value of a fluid in a cell should be constant in the absence of a source. The CICSAM approach presents an equation for free surface volume fraction as:

$$\tilde{\alpha}_f = \gamma_f \tilde{\alpha}_{f_{CBC}} + (1-\gamma_f)\tilde{\alpha}_{f_{UQ}} \tag{25}$$

where $\tilde{\alpha}_{f_{CBC}}$ is an index for transport bound which defines a bound as follows:

$$\tilde{\alpha}_{f_{CBC}} = \begin{cases} \min\left\{1, \dfrac{\tilde{\alpha}_D}{c_f}\right\} & when\ 0 \le \tilde{\alpha}_D \le 1 \\ \tilde{\alpha}_D & when\ \tilde{\alpha}_D \le 0,\ \tilde{\alpha}_D > 1 \end{cases} \tag{26}$$

where $\tilde{\alpha}_D$ is defined based on the following equation:

$$\tilde{\alpha}_D = \frac{\alpha_D - \alpha_U}{\alpha_A - \alpha_U} \tag{27}$$

$$\tilde{\alpha}_{f_{UQ}} = \begin{cases} \min\left\{\dfrac{8c_f\tilde{\alpha}_D + (1-c_f)(6\tilde{\alpha}_D + 3)}{8}, \tilde{\alpha}_{f_{CBC}}\right\} & when\ 0 \le \tilde{\alpha}_D \le 1 \\ \tilde{\alpha}_D & when\ \tilde{\alpha}_D < 0,\ \tilde{\alpha}_D > 1 \end{cases} \tag{28}$$

More details on determining $\tilde{\alpha}_f$ can be derived based on the combined schemes such as Normalized Variable Diagram (NVD) and discussed by Ubbink and Issa [26]. Accordingly, a local boundedness is defined for $\tilde{\alpha}_{f_{UQ}}$. In Eq. (25), $\gamma_f$ is a weight factor which is defined as:

$$\gamma_f = \min\left\{k_\gamma \frac{\cos(2\theta_f) + 1}{2}, 1\right\} \tag{29}$$

where $k_\gamma$ is a constant, usually set to unity, and $\theta_f$ is the angle between free surface normal vector, $(\nabla\alpha)_D$, and the vector $\vec{d}_f$ such that it connects the center of the adjacent cells based on **Figure 10**, and defined as:

$$\theta_f = \arccos\left|\frac{(\nabla\alpha)_D.\vec{d}_f}{|(\nabla\alpha)_D|\,|\vec{d}_f|}\right| \tag{30}$$

The CICSAM method well satisfies the bounds defined within it, and can be accurately reconstruct the free surface. The basis of the method, however, is on the 1D equations and linearization, which makes it less accurate for 3D modeling reconstructions.

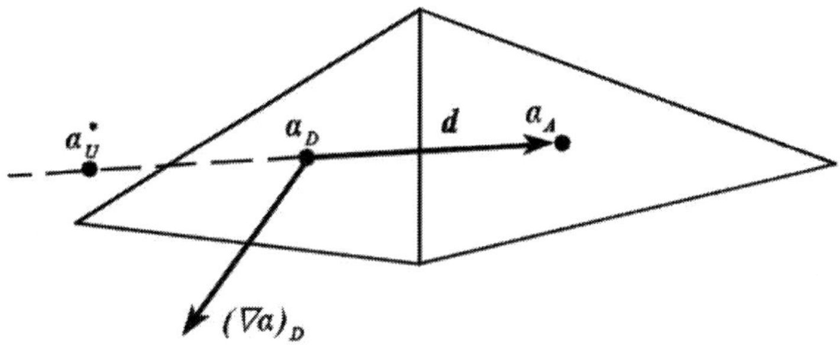


**Figure 10.** Calculation of the upwind value for an arbitrary mesh.

*3.6.2 THOR scheme*

This scheme is based on the CICSAM and switches smoothly between the upper bound of the universal limiter and ULTIMATE-QUICK, a combination of the universal limiter and QUICK, considering the angle between the interface and the direction of motion [27].

Analogous to CICSAM, this scheme is an algebraic advection scheme for the interface, which is designed for the implicit time advancing algorithm. In this method $\alpha_f$ is calculated using a weighting factor $\beta_f$ as follows:

$$\alpha_f = \left(1 - \beta_f\right)\alpha_D + \beta_f \alpha_A \tag{31}$$

where

$$\beta_f = \frac{\tilde{\alpha}_f - \tilde{\alpha}_D}{1 - \tilde{\alpha}_D} \tag{32}$$

$\tilde{\alpha}_f$ and $\tilde{\alpha}_D$ can be calculated by Eqs. (25) and (27), respectively.

*3.6.3. Higher Resolution Artificial Compressive (HiRAC) scheme*

HiRAC scheme is another modification of the CICSAM method [28]. This newly proposed method tries to improve the computational efficiency and maintain the accuracy. In this method, the weighing factor, $\gamma_f$, of Eq. (29) can be redefined as:

$$\gamma_f = min\left(\left(\theta_f\right)^m, 1\right) \tag{33}$$

where $\theta_f$ was previously defined in Eq. (30). For $m$=2, the new formulation reduces to the weighting function of Ubbink and Issa [26]. As $m$ increases, the interpolation becomes more biased towards the diffusive higher resolution scheme. It is shown that $m$=2 provides a good balance between the compressive and diffusive higher resolution schemes.

### *3.6.4. High Resolution Interface Capturing (HRIC) scheme*

This method is somehow similar to CICSAM, which benefits from a combined interpolation scheme. In HRIC method, the difference between two upwind schemes is calculated based on the normal vector angle of the free surface as [29]:

$$\tilde{\alpha}_f^{**} = \begin{cases} \tilde{\alpha}_D & \tilde{\alpha}_D < 0 \\ 2\tilde{\alpha}_D & 0 < \tilde{\alpha}_D < 0.5 \\ 1 & 0.5 < \tilde{\alpha}_D < 1 \\ \tilde{\alpha}_D & 1 < \tilde{\alpha}_D \end{cases} \tag{34}$$

$$\tilde{\alpha}_f^{*} = \begin{cases} \tilde{\alpha}_f^{**} & c_f < 0.3 \\ \tilde{\alpha}_D + \left(\tilde{\alpha}_f^{**} - \tilde{\alpha}_D\right)\dfrac{0.7 - c_f}{0.4} & 0.3 < c_f < 0.7 \\ \tilde{\alpha}_D & 0.7 < c_f \end{cases} \tag{35}$$

The portion of each of the two terms in the above equations can be defined as:

$$\tilde{\alpha}_f = \tilde{\alpha}_f^{*}\sqrt{\cos\theta} + \tilde{\alpha}_D(1 - \sqrt{\cos\theta}) \tag{36}$$

In this way, $\alpha_f$ is discretized based on the neighboring cells.

It should be noted that an improved scheme of HRIC, called Flux-Blending Interface-Capturing Scheme (FBICS), has been recently proposed. In this method, analogous to CICSAM and HRIC, the difference between two upwind schemes is calculated based on the normal vector angle of the free surface. Based on FBICS, Eq. (33) can be reformulated to obtain a more accurate scheme as:

$$\tilde{\alpha}^*_{f,FBICS} = \begin{cases} 3\tilde{\alpha}_D\tilde{\alpha}_D \leq 1/8 \\ \tilde{\alpha}_D + \frac{1}{4}\,1/8 < \tilde{\alpha}_D < 3/4 \\ 1\,3/4 < \tilde{\alpha}_D < 1 \\ \tilde{\alpha}_D\tilde{\alpha}_D \leq 0\, or\, \tilde{\alpha}_D \geq 1 \end{cases} \tag{37}$$

Some other modifications are also proposed by Tsui et al. [30].

*3.6.5. Switching Technique for Advection and Capturing of Surfaces (STACS) method*

One of the drawbacks of HRIC and CICSAM schemes is high Courant numbers. Both methods lack a proper switching strategy to accurately model the interface when Courant number increases. The Courant number, *Cn,* in HRIC method can be written as follows:

$$\tilde{\alpha}_f = \tilde{\alpha}^*_f + \left(\tilde{\alpha}^*_f - \tilde{\alpha}_D\right)\frac{0.7 - Cn}{0.7 - 0.3} \tag{38}$$

which is suitable for Courant numbers between 0.3 and 0.7. For a *Cn* below 0.3 the scheme is not modified, while for a Courant number above 0.7 the upwind scheme is used. This is true for CICSAM when the *Cn* is equal to unity.

STACS method has been proposed to improve the accuracy and stability of the results specifically in high Courant numbers by Darwish and Moukalled [31]. It uses an implicit transient discretization, i.e. no transient bounding is applied, and in order to minimize the stepping behavior of HRIC scheme, a modification is proposed. In this method, applying $\cos^4\theta$ term is designed instead of $\sqrt{\cos\theta}$ in Eq. (36) as follows:

$$\tilde{\alpha}_f = \tilde{\alpha}^*_{f,sup} cos^4\theta + \tilde{\alpha}^*_{f,stoic}\left(1 - cos^4\theta\right) \tag{39}$$

where $\tilde{\alpha}^*_{f,sup}$ and $\tilde{\alpha}^*_{f,stoic}$ are calculated as follows:

$$\tilde{\alpha}^*_{f,sup} = \begin{cases} \tilde{\alpha}_D \tilde{\alpha}_D \le 0 \\ 1 0 < \tilde{\alpha}_D < 1 \\ \tilde{\alpha}_D \tilde{\alpha}_D \ge 1 \end{cases} \qquad \tilde{\alpha}^*_{f,stoic} = \begin{cases} \tilde{\alpha}_D \tilde{\alpha}_D \le 0 \\ \frac{1}{2} + \frac{1}{2}\tilde{\alpha}_D 0 < \tilde{\alpha}_D < \frac{1}{2} \\ \frac{3}{8} + \frac{3}{4}\tilde{\alpha}_D \frac{1}{2} < \tilde{\alpha}_D < \frac{5}{6} \\ 1\frac{5}{6} < \tilde{\alpha}_D < 1 \\ \tilde{\alpha}_D \tilde{\alpha}_D \ge 1 \end{cases} \tag{40}$$

This enables a rapid but smooth switching strategy that works very well, especially where the normal to the free-surface face is not along the grid direction.

### 3.6.6. Inter-gamma scheme

In this method, presented by Jasak and Weller [32], free surface compression is modeled using additional compressive artificial terms.

$$\frac{\partial \gamma}{\partial t} + \nabla \cdot (\mathbf{U}\gamma) + \nabla \cdot \left(\mathbf{U}^r \gamma (1-\gamma)\right) = 0 \tag{41}$$

where $\mathbf{U}^r$ is a velocity field for compressing the free surface. This artificial term is activated only in the presence of free surface because of having the term $\gamma(1-\gamma)$. The solution to this equation is bounded from zero to unity with the inter-gamma scheme. Eq. (40) can be rewritten as:

$$\frac{\partial \gamma}{\partial t} + \nabla \cdot \left(\phi [\gamma]_{f(\phi,S)}\right) + \nabla \cdot \left(\phi_{r_b} [\gamma]_{f(\phi_{r_b},S)}\right) = 0 \tag{42}$$

where $\phi = \mathbf{S} \cdot \mathbf{U}_f$ is the volume flux and $\phi_{r_b} = (1-\gamma)_{f(-\phi^r,S)} \phi^r$. Eq. (43) is used to calculate $\varnothing^r$ as:

$$\phi^r = K_c n^* \max\left\{ \frac{|n^* \phi|}{|S|^2} \right\} \tag{43}$$

where $n^*$ is the free surface normal unit vector and $K_c$ is an adjustable coefficient, with an appropriate value of 1.5, which defines the compression rate of free surface. The inter-gamma scheme is also similar to CICSAM and is based on a donor-acceptor equation and normalized variable diagram, NVD. The formulation is as:

$$\tilde{\alpha}_f = \begin{cases} \tilde{\alpha}_D & \tilde{\alpha}_D < 0,\ \tilde{\alpha}_D > 1 \\ -2\tilde{\alpha}_D^2 + 3\tilde{\alpha}_D & 0 < \tilde{\alpha}_D < \frac{1}{2} \\ 1 & \frac{1}{2} < \tilde{\alpha}_D < 1 \end{cases} \tag{44}$$

**Figure 11** shows the NVD for inter-gamma scheme.

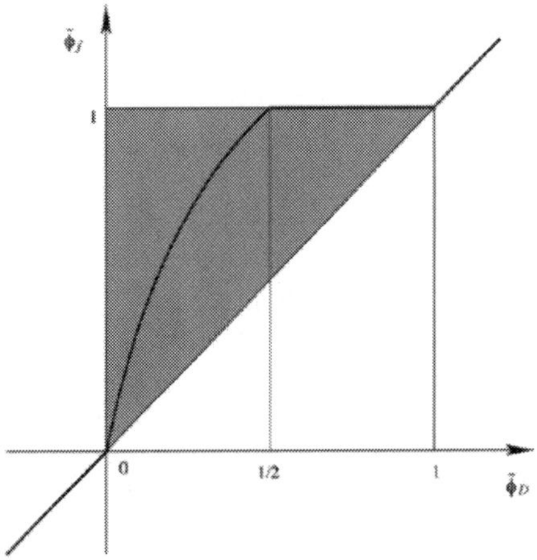


**Figure 11.** NVD for inter-gamma scheme.

### 3.7. Integrated methods

As mentioned before, volume of fluid is among the most popular methods in free surface modeling. Having in mind that this method is based on defining a discontinuous function, the color function, there is not a unique form for free surface. Therefore, it is required to reconstruct the free surface using volume of fraction function. In one hand, VOF method satisfies the conservation of mass while it is unable to calculate free surface parameters including curvature radius and normal unit vector directly. On the other hand, in level set methods as the distance function is smooth, the surface geometry can be easily calculated, while satisfying the conservation of mass is very demanding. In order to resolve the problems of level set methods, a number of different researches have been conducted. For example, higher order schemes were proposed to improve the conservation of continuity equation by Peng et al. [33]. Adaptive mesh refinement techniques were also proposed to increase the accuracy of the local mesh consistency. In 2009, an integrated method known as hybrid Particle Level Set (PLS) was proposed to improve the accuracy of the results. However, the problem still remained in relation with mass conservation.

In order to take the advantages of both methods and eliminate their disadvantages, integration of volume of fluid and level set methods was proposed in a new scheme known as coupled level set and volume-of-fluid (CLSVOF) method to model two-phase incompressible flows by Sussman and Pucket [34]. It should be noted that although accurate, this method cannot be easily employed, because these two methods, VOF and level set, should be individually solved and their effects need to be coupled based on the reconstructed interface.

## 4. Calculating surface tension

Defining the pressure difference inserted on the surface of two fluids with different densities and tension stresses is one of the most demanding problems in fluid mechanics. One method to do this is the Pressure Calculation based on the Interface Location (PCIL) method which is presented here. Surface tension, that changes the value of variables in momentum equations, imposes a discontinuity at the position of the interface between two fluids [21].

Stress from surface tension inserts a force upon the interface. The resultant force is perpendicular to the surface and its curvature is dependent on the geometry of the surface. Surface tension can be considered in two ways. In the first approach, it is considered as a boundary condition in the equations for the surface. This needs using an iterative method for true approximation of pressure, which in result, increases the time and cost of calculation and consequently makes it inefficient. In order to address this problem, some other methods have been proposed in which the precise calculation of interface position is not necessary. In these methods, the direct force of surface tension has been replaced with the body force in the momentum equation. The Continuum Surface Force (CSF) method is a base method for calculation of body forces of fluid surface tension [2]. The body forces can be considered to act smoothly on a narrow strip of cells in interface zone. In this method the surface stresses are replaced with the body forces which are calculated as:

$$\mathbf{F}_s = \sigma \int_S \kappa \mathbf{n} \delta(\mathbf{x} - \mathbf{x}_s) dS \tag{45}$$

where $\sigma$, $\kappa$, $\mathbf{n}$, $\delta(\mathbf{x}-\mathbf{x}_s)$ and $\mathbf{X}_s$ are surface tension force, curvature of the surface, normal unit vector, Dirac delta function, and the position of a given base point on the interface $S$, respectively. This equation has been discretized for numerical methods of two-phase fluids.

Another approach based on CSF method was proposed by Torrey et al. [7] called Continuum Surface Stress (CSS), in which body forces of CSF method were replaced by tension tensors of surface tension based on the following equation:

$$\mathbf{F}_s = \sigma \kappa \mathbf{n} \delta_s = -\nabla \cdot \mathbf{T}, \quad \mathbf{T} = -\sigma (\mathbf{I} - \mathbf{n} \otimes \mathbf{n}) \delta_s \tag{46}$$

where **I** and **T** are unit tensor and tangential tension tensor of the interface respectively.

It should be mentioned that employing CSF or CSS methods has some drawbacks. For instance, spurious velocities of the thinner fluid near the interface is one the reported problems.

A number of researches have been performed in order to resolve the problem of spurious velocities [35, 36]. In one approach, using virtual particles moving along with the surface could improve the results [37]. One of the latest methods presented in this field is PCIL. This method shows that having more precise border cells and calculating their associated pressure based on the momentum equation can lead to significant reduction of bothersome flows near this region. PCIL is a simple and efficient method of calculating free surfaces. The total pressure on the left side of the cell can be calculated as (see **Figure 12**):

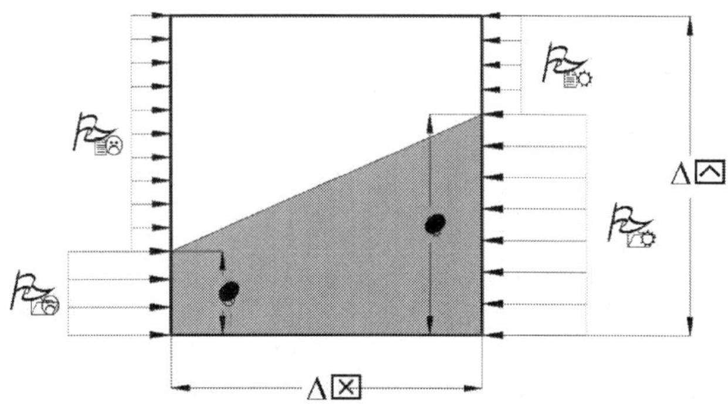

**Figure 12.** Cells on the interface in contact with left and right cells of the free surface [38].

$$P_L = P_{1L}\frac{l_L}{\Delta y} + P_{2L}\frac{\Delta y - l_L}{\Delta y} = P_{1L}H_L + P_{2L}(1 - H_L) = P_{2L} + H_L(P_{1L} - P_{2L}) \tag{47}$$

where $P_L$ is the mean pressure on the left side of the given cell. In the same way, mean pressure can be calculated for other faces of the cell as follows:

$$P_R = P_{2R} + H_R(P_{1R} - P_{2R}) \tag{48}$$

$$P_T = P_{2T} + H_T(P_{1T} - P_{2T}) \tag{49}$$

$$P_B = P_{2B} + H_B(P_{1B} - P_{2B}) \tag{50}$$

where $H$ is a dimensionless number which shows the position of free surface in different directions. For faces completely immersed in the main fluid, H is equal to 1, and for those completely in the secondary fluid, $H$ is zero. For other cases, $H$ varies between zero and unity. Note that for 3D models, it is just needed to replace edge faces with surfaces faces.

On the other hand, the change in pressure $P_s$ in every point of the interface is calculated as:

$$P_s = P_1 - P_2 = \sigma\kappa \tag{51}$$

Accordingly, the above equation can be reformulated for pressure in the $K$th face of every common cell as follows:

$$P_k = P_{2k} + H_k\sigma\kappa \tag{52}$$

where the second term introduces the normal force of the surface tension per unit area of the interface. This can be presented in the vector form as:

$$\mathbf{F}_s = H\sigma\kappa\mathbf{n} \tag{53}$$

where $\mathbf{F}_s$ is the surface tension force vector.

One of the most fundamental steps to perform surface tension calculations is defining the curvature of the interface. Defining this curvature is not so demanding as long as the precise position of the interface is known. However, using volumetric tracing methods and equivalent alternatives representing the interface position make the estimation of the curvature cumbersome.

The method of volume of fluid presented by Hirt and Nichols [6] is one of the earliest methods in this field. In this method, a curve $y(x)$ is fitted to the nine neighboring cells of the interface. In this way, summation of the volume of fluid of three cells located in a column creates a value for $y$. By fitting parabolic curve to the values of three neighboring columns and then two times differentiating of these values, one can define the curvature of the surface. This method, however, suffers from low accuracy and some limiting conditions. Another method is presented by Chorin [39] in which a circle is defined based on trial and error in order to satisfy the nine-cell set in the best possible way. Thereafter, curvature of the surface can be defined on the basis of the calculated circle. However the main problem of this method is its dependency on the several times of trials and errors in order to calculate the best way of estimating the circle, the thing that makes it practically inefficient. Ashgriz and Poo [40] proposed another method in which a parabolic curve is fitted to the 9 or 25 neighboring cells. This method is more accurate than the previous one; however, its applications are very limited to specific cases.

The value of the surface curvature can be defined based on the distance function as:

$$\kappa = -\nabla \cdot \mathbf{n} = -\nabla \cdot \frac{\nabla\phi}{|\nabla\phi|} \tag{54}$$

To discretize the above equation, it is required to first calculate the normal vector of the surface based on **Figure 13** and the following relations, and consequently estimate the curvature:

$$div_{x,i+\frac{1}{2},j} = 2\frac{\phi_{i+1,j} - \phi_{i,j}}{\Delta x_{i+1} + \Delta x_i}, \quad div_{y,i+\frac{1}{2},j} = \frac{\phi_{i+1,j} - \phi_{i,j-1} + \phi_{i+1,j+1} - \phi_{i+1,j-1}}{\Delta y_{j+1} + 2\Delta y_j + \Delta y_{j-1}} \tag{55}$$

$$n_{x,i+\frac{1}{2},j} = \frac{div_{x,i+\frac{1}{2},j}}{\left|\mathbf{n}_{i+\frac{1}{2},j}\right|}, \quad \left|\mathbf{n}_{i+\frac{1}{2},j}\right| = \sqrt{div^2_{x,i+\frac{1}{2},j} + div^2_{y,i+\frac{1}{2},j}} \tag{56}$$

$$\kappa_{i,j} = -\frac{n_{x,i+\frac{1}{2},j} - n_{x,i-\frac{1}{2},j}}{\Delta x_i} - \frac{n_{y,i,j+\frac{1}{2}} - n_{x,i,j-\frac{1}{2}}}{\Delta y_j} \tag{57}$$

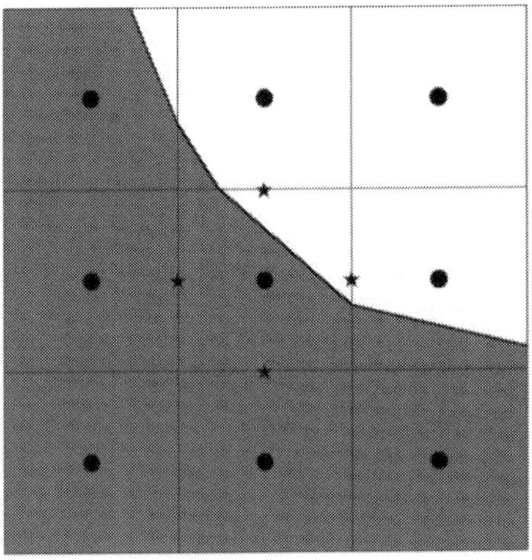

**Figure 13.** Position of the normal vectors of the surface in the cell faces.

One of the advantages of this approach, the level-set method, is using a distance function which is smooth and uniform, so that it increases the simplicity of the calculation and accuracy of the results.

The value of the body force from surface tension of the cell faces can be calculated in CSF method as:

$$\mathbf{F}_s = \sigma\kappa\mathbf{n}\delta_s = \sigma\kappa\mathbf{n}\frac{\left|\nabla\bar{\alpha}\right|}{[\alpha]} \tag{58}$$

where $\delta_s$ is the delta Dirac function which is infinite on the interface and zero otherwise, and its integration is equal to unity. The bar sign in Eq. (58) shows a smoothed (or filtered) value of volume fraction. The bracket sign shows the difference between maximum and minimum of volume of the fluid fraction. In CSF method, this function is estimated using $|\nabla \bar{\alpha}| / [\alpha]$. Some other references use the following equation to improve the results' accuracy [41]:

$$\mathbf{F}_s = \sigma\kappa\mathbf{n}\delta_s = \sigma\kappa\mathbf{n}\frac{|\nabla\bar{\alpha}|}{[\alpha]}\frac{\rho}{[\rho]} \tag{59}$$

in which the ratio of the densities is inserted in order to reduce spurious velocities of the thinner fluid. The discretized version of Eq. (58) can be obtained as follows:

$$F_{x,i+\frac{1}{2},j} = 2\sigma\kappa\frac{\bar{\alpha}_{i+1,j} - \bar{\alpha}_{i,j}}{\Delta x_{i+1} + \Delta x_i}\frac{\rho_{i+\frac{1}{2},j}}{\rho_{\max} - \rho_{\min}} \tag{60}$$

Based on what was discussed for PCIL method, the following relation is adopted to the present method:

$$F_{x,i+\frac{1}{2},j} = 2\sigma\kappa\frac{\bar{\alpha}_{i+1,j} - \bar{\alpha}_{i,j}}{\Delta x_{i+1} + \Delta x_i}H_{i+\frac{1}{2},j} \tag{61}$$

It can be seen that in this equation, the ratio of densities is replaced by the variable $H$.

## 5. Parametric method for calculation of curvature of free surfaces

This newly proposed method is based on two sub-models, the Four-Point Method (FPM) and the Three-Line Method (TLM). In the former sub-model, a curve is fitted to the intersection of the points of grid lines for central and two neighboring cells, while the latter fits a curve to the free surface so that the distance between the curve and its linear interface approximation is minimized [42].

### 5.1. The Four-Point Method (FPM)

In the four-point method, free surface (as illustrated in **Figure 14**) is approximated using a continuous function $f(\cdot) \in C^2(x_1, x_4)$ (a set of functions with continuous second derivation) so that the distance between the function and the points is minimized according to Eq. (62), and variations of curvature are bounded based on Eq. (63). In this case, the radius curvature can be calculated as in Eq. (64).

$$\inf_{f(\cdot)\in C^2(x_1,x_4)} I(f(\cdot)) = \sum_{i=1}^{4} |f(x_i) - y_i| \tag{62}$$

$$S.t.\begin{cases} |\kappa(x) - C_1| \le \varepsilon & x \in (x_1, x_2] \\ |\kappa(x) - C_2| \le \varepsilon & x \in (x_2, x_3] \\ |\kappa(x) - C_3| \le \varepsilon & x \in (x_3, x_4] \\ C_i \ge 0 & i = 1,2,3 \end{cases} \tag{63}$$

$$\kappa(x) = \frac{|\ddot{f}(x)|}{\sqrt{1 + \dot{f}^2(x)}} \tag{64}$$

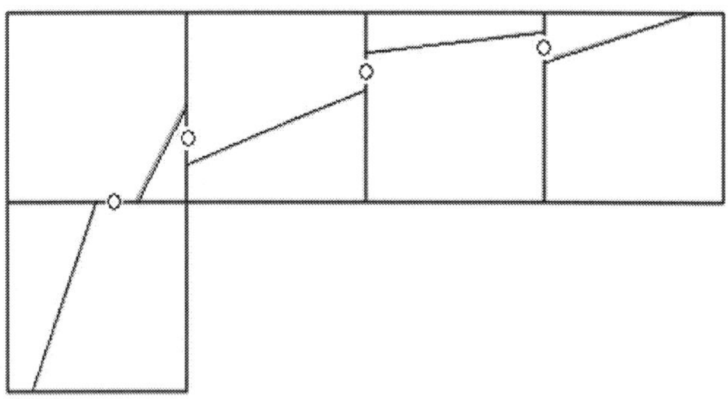

**Figure 14.** Free surface modeling in FPM.

where $\varepsilon$ is a small arbitrary given number.

In this method, the desired function is approximated using an n-degree polynomial function with unknown constant coefficients. Therefore, we have:

$$\inf I(P_n(\cdot)) = \sum_{i=1}^{4} |P_n(x_i) - y_i| \tag{65}$$

$$\kappa_n(x) = \frac{|\ddot{P}_n(x)|}{\sqrt{1 + \dot{P}_n^2(x)}} \tag{66}$$

where $\kappa$ is the curvature of the free surface.

It is supposed that Q is the set of $f(\cdot)\in C^2(x_1, x_4)$ such that Eq. (62) is feasible and Q(n) is the set of $P_n(.)$ such that Eq. (64) is feasible. Then, the following theorem proves that the sequence of solutions for Eqs. (65) and (66) converges to the solution of Eqs. (62) and (64) as $n$ goes towards infinity.

**Theorem 1**: if $\eta=inf_Q I(f(.))$ and $\eta(n)=inf_{Q_n} I(P_n(.))$ then $\eta=lim_{n\to\infty}\eta(n)$.

**Proof**. It is obvious that $Q(1)\subset Q(2)\subset\ldots\subset Q$, then $\eta(1)\geq\eta(2)\geq\ldots\geq\eta$. Therefore, $\{\eta(n)\}$ is a non-increasing and bounded sequence. Then it converges to a number called $\xi$. Set $W=\bigcup_{n=1}^{\infty} Q(n)$; therefore, $\inf_{Q_n} I(P_n(\cdot))=\xi$. Since $W\subset Q$, then $\xi\geq\eta$. By the properties of infimum, for every $\varepsilon>0$, there exists $f(\cdot)\in Q$ such that:

$$\eta < I\left(f(\cdot)\right) < \eta+\varepsilon \tag{67}$$

As we have $f(\cdot)\in C^2(x_1, x_4)$, there is a set of polynomials such that $\{P_n(\cdot)\}$, $\{\dot{P}_n(\cdot)\}$, $\{\ddot{P}_n(\cdot)\}$ are uniformly convergent. Therefore, there exists a natural number such that for every $n\geq N$ we have:

$$\left\|P_n(\cdot)-f_n(\cdot)\right\|_\infty < \delta \tag{68}$$

$$\left\|\dot{P}_n(\cdot)-\dot{f}_n(\cdot)\right\|_\infty < \delta \tag{69}$$

$$\left\|\ddot{P}_n(\cdot)-\ddot{f}_n(\cdot)\right\|_\infty < \delta \tag{70}$$

Now, it is claimed that there is an $N_1\geq N$ such that for $i=1, 2, 3, 4,$ the relation $|\kappa_n(x)-C_i|\leq\varepsilon;\ \forall x\in\left(x_i, x_{i+1}\right]$ is true. Since otherwise for every $n\geq N$, there is a $|\kappa_n(x)-C_i|\leq\varepsilon;\ \forall x\in\left(x_i, x_{i+1}\right]$. Therefore, $\lim_{n\to\infty}|\kappa_n(x)-C_i|>\varepsilon$ which contradicts the assumption of $f(\cdot)\in Q$. Thus, $P_N(\cdot)\in Q(N_1)\subset W\subset Q$. Based on what was mentioned, $|I(P_{N_1}(\cdot))-I(f(\cdot))|<\varepsilon$ or $I\left(P_{N_1}(\cdot)\right)<I(f(\cdot))+\varepsilon<\eta+2\varepsilon$ or $\eta\leq\xi+2\varepsilon$; therefore, $\xi=\eta$, or $\lim_{n\to\infty}\eta(n)=\eta$.

Thus, our aim is to solve Eqs. (63) and (64), and one can write them in the following forms:

$$\inf I\left(P_n(\cdot)\right)$$

$$S.t.\begin{cases}\int_{x_1}^{x_2}\left\|\kappa_n(x)-C_1\right|-\varepsilon+\left\|\kappa_n(x)-C_1\right|-\varepsilon\right\|dx=0\\ \int_{x_2}^{x_3}\left\|\kappa_n(x)-C_2\right|-\varepsilon+\left\|\kappa_n(x)-C_2\right|-\varepsilon\right\|dx=0\\ \int_{x_3}^{x_4}\left\|\kappa_n(x)-C_3\right|-\varepsilon+\left\|\kappa_n(x)-C_3\right|-\varepsilon\right\|dx=0\\ C_i\geq 0 \qquad\qquad i=1,2,3, n=1,2,\ldots\end{cases} \tag{71}$$

or

$$\inf I\left(P_n(\cdot)\right)$$

$$S.t=\begin{cases}\frac{h_1}{2}\left[E_{1n}(x_1)+E_{1n}(x_1+h)+\ldots+E_{1n}(x_1+m_1h)\right]=0\\ \frac{h_2}{2}\left[E_{2n}(x_2)+E_{2n}(x_2+h)+\ldots+E_{2n}(x_2+m_2h)\right]=0\\ \frac{h_3}{2}\left[E_{3n}(x_3)+E_{3n}(x_3+h)+\ldots+E_{3n}(x_3+m_3h)\right]=0\\ C_i\geq 0 \qquad\qquad i=1,2,3. \quad n=1,2,\ldots\end{cases} \tag{72}$$

such that $E_{in}(x)=\| \kappa_n(x)-C_i \mid -\varepsilon + \| \kappa_n(x)-C_i \mid -\varepsilon \|$.

Now, the intervals $[x_1, x_2]$, $[x_2, x_3]$ and $[x_3, x_4]$ are divided into three equal sections, $m_1$, $m_2$, $m_3$, respectively. This means that $h_1=\frac{x_2-x_1}{m_1}$, $h_2=\frac{x_3-x_2}{m_2}$ and $h_3=\frac{x_4-x_3}{m_3}$. Thus, using a numerical integration method such as trapezoidal rule, the problem above can be reformulated as:

$$\inf\sum_{i=1}^{4}\left|P_n(x_i)-y_i\right|$$

$$S.t=\begin{cases}\frac{h_1}{2}\left[E_{1n}(x_1)+E_{1n}(x_1+h)+\ldots+E_{1n}(x_1+m_1h)\right]=0\\ \frac{h_2}{2}\left[E_{2n}(x_2)+E_{2n}(x_2+h)+\ldots+E_{2n}(x_2+m_2h)\right]=0\\ \frac{h_3}{2}\left[E_{3n}(x_3)+E_{3n}(x_3+h)+\ldots+E_{3n}(x_3+m_3h)\right]=0\\ C_i\geq 0 \qquad\qquad i=1,2,3. \quad n=1,2,\ldots\end{cases} \tag{73}$$

This is a nonlinear set of equations and can be easily solved using Matlab or Lingo software.

### 5.2. The Three-Line Method (TLM)

In this method as illustrated in **Figure 15**, the main goal is to find a function as $f(\cdot) \in C^2(x_1, x_4)$ within $x \in [x_j, x_{j+1}]$ such that the distance between the function $f(x)$ and the line $L_i(x)$ which connects the given points $(x_i, y_i)$ and $(x_{i+1}, y_{i+1})$ is minimized for $i=1, 2, 3$. Thus, variation of curvature is bounded according to Eq. (74):

$$\inf I(f(\cdot)) = \sum_{i=1}^{3} \int_{x_i}^{x_{i+1}} \left| f(x) - L_i(x) \right| dx$$

$$S.t. \begin{cases} \left| \kappa(x) - C_1 \right| \le \varepsilon & x \in (x_1, x_2] \\ \left| \kappa(x) - C_2 \right| \le \varepsilon & x \in (x_2, x_3] \\ \left| \kappa(x) - C_3 \right| \le \varepsilon & x \in (x_3, x_4] \\ C_i \ge 0 & i = 1,2,3 \end{cases} \tag{74}$$

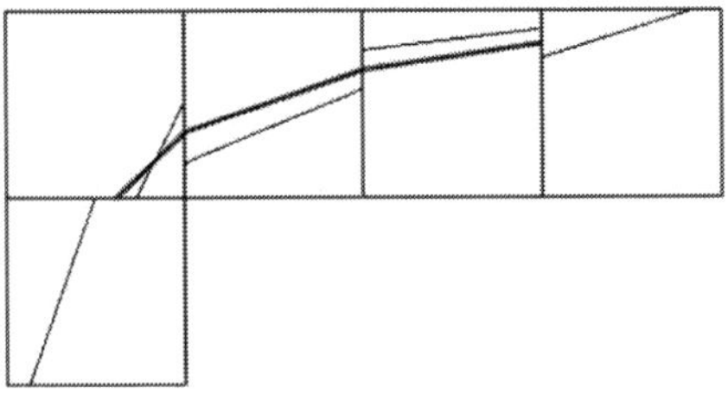

**Figure 15.** Free surface modeling by TLM.

Similar to what was discussed in the four-point method, in this method the function $f(\cdot)$ can be replaced with an n-degree polynomial, $P_n(\cdot)$ as below:

$$\inf I(P_n(\cdot)) = \sum_{i=1}^{3} \int_{x_i}^{x_{i+1}} \left| P_n(x) - L_i(x) \right| dx$$

$$S.t. \begin{cases} \left| \kappa_n(x) - C_1 \right| \le \varepsilon & x \in [x_1, x_2] \\ \left| \kappa_n(x) - C_2 \right| \le \varepsilon & x \in (x_2, x_3] \\ \left| \kappa_n(x) - C_3 \right| \le \varepsilon & x \in (x_3, x_4] \\ C_i \ge 0 & i = 1,2,3, \quad n = 1,2,\ldots \end{cases} \tag{75}$$

**Theorem 2**: Sequence of the solution of Eq. (75) converges to the solution of Eq. (74).

**Proof**: The method of proof of this theorem is similar to the previous theorem. In the same approach of FPM, the following problem is achieved:

$$\inf I\left(P_n(\cdot)\right)=\sum_{i=1}^{3}\frac{h_i}{2}\begin{pmatrix}\left|P_n(x_1)-L_i(x_1)\right|+2\left|P_n(x_1+h)-L_i(x_1+h)\right|+\dots\\ +2\left|P_n(x_1+(m_i-1)h)-L_i(x_1+(m_i-1)h)\right|+\\ \left|P_n(x_1+m_ih)-L_i(x_1+m_ih)\right|\end{pmatrix}$$

$$S.t=\begin{cases}\frac{h_1}{2}\left[E_{1n}(x_1)+E_{1n}(x_1+h)+\dots+E_{1n}(x_1+m_1h)\right]=0\\ \frac{h_2}{2}\left[E_{2n}(x_2)+E_{2n}(x_2+h)+\dots+E_{2n}(x_2+m_2h)\right]=0\\ \frac{h_3}{2}\left[E_{3n}(x_3)+E_{3n}(x_3+h)+\dots+E_{3n}(x_3+m_3h)\right]=0\\ C_i\geq 0 \qquad\qquad i=1,2,3. \quad n=1,2,\dots\end{cases}\tag{76}$$

The steps of using the above equations are as follows:

Step 1: Read $\varepsilon$, and set $n=1$.

Step 2: Solve Eq. (73) or (76) in the FPM or the TLM, respectively.

Step 3: If the previous step is infeasible, set $n=n+1$, and go to step 2, else set the value of target function in $I_n$.

Step 4: Set $n=n+1$, and solve Eq. (73) or (76) in the FPM or the TLM, respectively.

Then set the value of target function in $I_n$.

Step 5: If $|I_n-I_{n-1}|>\varepsilon_1$ then go to step 4, else $I_n$ is the final answer.

## 6. Conclusions

In this chapter volume of fluid (VOF) scheme was introduced. This is one of the most effective methods employed in the simulation of two fluid flows interfaces with dramatic changes in density and viscosity. . These interfaces are represented implicitly by the values of a color function which is the fluid volume fraction. The advantage of the method is its ability to deal with arbitrarily shaped interfaces and to cope with large deformations, as well as interface rupture and coalescence in a natural way. In VOF the mass is rigorously conserved, provided the discretization is conservative. However, advecting the interface without diffusing, dispersing, or wrinkling is a big issue. This can either be performed algebraically, in schemes such as CICSAM or geometrically, in schemes such as PLIC. Herein, the viscous fluid governing equations which are Navier-Stokes coupled with VOF equation were presented. Then the most popular VOF schemes such as donor-acceptor, Hirt-Nichols, FCT, Youngs, and PLIC were explained. CICSAM, HiRAC, HRIC, STACS, and some other up-to-date proposed methods were introduced and the accuracy and time calculation of each method were evaluated. Moreover, surface tension modeling and parametric study of interfaces were discussed. The author hopes this brief presentation of the VOF method will be beneficial for scientists and students in their further researches and will help them to massively and continuously expand this very challenging field of fluid mechanics.

## Author details

Mohammad Javad Ketabdari

Address all correspondence to: ketabdar@aut.ac.ir

Faculty of Marine Technology, Amirkabir University of Technology, Tehran, Iran

## References

[1] Noh WF. CEL: A Time-Dependent, Two Dimensional, Coupled Eulerian-Lagrangian Code. in Alder, B., Fernbach, S. and Rotenberg, M. (Eds.), Methods in Computational Physics, Volume 3, Fundamental Methods in Hydrodynamics, Academic Press, New York, NY 1964; 117–179.

[2] Brackbill JU, Kothe DB, Zemach C. A continuum method for modeling surface tension. Journal of Computational Physics 1992; 100: 335–354.

[3] Ketabdari MJ, Saghi H. A novel algorithm of advection procedure in volume of fluid method to model free surface flows. International Scholarly Research Network 2012; 10: 1–16.

[4] Ubbink O. Numerical prediction of two fluid systems with sharp interfaces. PhD Thesis, University of London 1997.

[5] Ramshaw JD, Trapp JA. A numerical technique for low-speed homogeneous two-phase flow with sharp interfaces. Journal of Computational Physics 1976; 21: 438–453.

[6] Hirt CW, Nichols, BD. Volume of Fluid (VOF) method for the dynamics of free boundaries. Journal of Computational Physics 1981; 39: 201–225.

[7] Torrey MD, Mjolsness RC, Stein LR. NASA-VOF3D: a three dimensional computer program for incompressible flows with free surfaces. Technical Report LA-11009-MS, Los Alamos National Laboratory 1987.

[8] Lafaurie B, Nardone C, Scardovelli R, Zaleski S. Zanetti G. Modelling merging and fragmentation in multiphase flows with SURFER. Journal of Computational Physics 1994; 113: 134–147.

[9] Heinrich P. Nonlinear numerical model of landslide-generated water waves. International Journal of Engineering Fluid Mechanics 1991; 4(4): 403–416.

[10] Tomiyama A, Zun I, Sou A, Sakaguchi T. Numerical analysis of bubble motion with the VOF method. Nuclear Engineering and Design 1993; 141: 69–82.

[11] Tomiyama A, Sou A, Hisato M, Sakaguchi T. Numerical analysis of a single bubble by VOF method. JSME International Journal Series B Fluids and Thermal Engineering 1993; 36(1): 51–56.

[12] Tomiyama A, Sou A, Sakaguchi T. Numerical simulation of a Taylor bubble in a stagnant liquid inside a vertical pipe. JSME International Journal Series B Fluids and Thermal Engineering 1996; 39(3): 517–524.

[13] Ketabdari MJ, Nobari MRH, Moradi Larmaei M. Simulation of waves group propagation and breaking in coastal zone using a Navier-Stokes solver with an improved VOF free surface treatment. Applied Ocean Research 2008; 30: 130–143.

[14] Nobari MRH, Ketabdari MJ, Moradi Larmaei M. A modified volume of fluid advection method for uniform Cartesian grids. Applied Mathematical Modelling 2009; 33(5): 2298–2310.

[15] Rezaei H, Ketabdari MJ. A modified flux corrected transport method for incompressible free surface flow. Canadian Journal on Computing in Mathematics, Natural Sciences, Engineering and Medicine 2012; 3(6): 213–219.

[16] Boris JP, Book DL. Flux-corrected transport. I. SHASTA, a fluid transport algorithm that works. Journal of Computational Physics 1973; 11: 38–69.

[17] Zalesak ST. Fully multidimensional flux-corrected transport algorithms for fluids. Journal of Computational Physics 1979; 31: 335–362.

[18] Youngs DL. Time-Dependent Multi-Material Flow with Large Fluid Distortion. in Morton, K.W. and Baines, M.J. (Eds.), Numerical Methods in Fluid Dynamics 1982; Academic Press, Reading, UK.

[19] Rudman M. Volume-tracking methods for interfacial flow calculations. International Journal for Numerical Methods in Fluids 1997; 24: 671–691.

[20] Rider WJ, Kothe DB. Reconstructing volume tracking. Journal of Computational Physics 1998; 141: 112–152.

[21] Shirani E, Ashgriz N, Mostaghimi J. Interface pressure calculation based on conservation of momentum for front capturing methods. Journal of Computational Physics 2005; 203: 154–175.

[22] Davis SF. Flux difference splittings and limiters for the resolution of contact discontinuities. Applied Mathematics and Computation 1994; 65: 3–18.

[23] Ghobadian A. Development of a method for numerical simulation of flows with moving interfaces. National Power Report 1991; TEC/L/0077/M91.

[24] Van Leer B. Towards the ultimate conservative difference scheme. IV. A new approach to numerical convection. Journal of Computational Physics 1977; 23: 276–299.

[25] Pericleous KA, Chan KS. The SEA Method for Free-Surface Problems with Heat Transfer and Change of Phase. in Crowe, C.T. (Ed.), Numerical Methods in Multiphase Flows 1994, presented at the ASME fluids engineering division summer meeting 1994; American Society of Mechanical Engineers, 227–236.

[26] Ubbink O, Issa RI. A method for capturing sharp fluid interfaces on arbitrary meshes. Journal of Computational Physics 1999; 153: 26–50.

[27] Hogg PW, Gu XJ, Emerson DR. An implicit algorithm for capturing sharp fluid interfaces in the volume of fluid advection method. European Conference on Computational Fluid Dynamics 2006; ECCOMAS CFD, TU Delft, The Netherlands.

[28] Heyns JA, Malan AG, Harms TM, Oxtoby OF. Development of a compressive surface capturing formulation for modelling free-surface flow by using the volume-of-fluid approach. International Journal for Numerical Methods in Fluids 2013; 71: 788–804.

[29] Muzaferija S, Perić M. Computation of Free Surface Flows Using Interface-Tracking and Interface-Capturing Methods. in Mahrenholtz, O. and Markiewicz, M. (Eds.), Nonlinear Water Wave Interaction, Computational Mechanics Publications, Southampton 1998; p. Chap. 3.

[30] Tsui YY, Lin SW, Cheng TT, Wu TC. Flux-blending schemes for interface capture in two-fluid flows. International Journal of Heat and Mass Transfer 2009; 52: 5547–5556.

[31] Darwish M., Moukalled F. Convective schemes for capturing interfaces of free-surface flows on unstructured grids. Numerical Heat Transfer, Part B: Fundamentals 2006; 49: 19–42

[32] Jasak H, Weller HG. Interface Tracking Capabilities of the Inter-Gamma Differencing Scheme. Imperial College, University of London, 1995; p. 9.

[33] Peng D, Merriman B, Osher S, Zhao H, Kang M. A PDE-based fast local level set method. Journal of Computational Physics 1999; 155: 410–438.

[34] Sussman M, Puckett EG. A coupled level set and volume-of-fluid method for computing 3d and axisymmetric incompressible two-phase flows. Journal of Computational Physics 2000; 162: 301–337.

[35] Renardy Y, Renardy M. PROST: a parabolic reconstruction of surface tension for the volume-of-fluid method. Journal of Computational Physics 2002; 183: 400–421.

[36] Jamet D, Torres D, Brackbill JU. On the theory and computation of surface tension: the elimination of parasitic currents through energy conservation in the second-gradient method. Journal of Computational Physics 2002; 182: 262–276.

[37] Popinet S, Zaleski S. A front-tracking algorithm for accurate representation of surface tension. International Journal for Numerical Methods in Fluids 1999; 30: 775–793.

[38] Bohluly A, Borghei SM, Saidi, MH. A new method in two phase flow modeling of a non-uniform grid. Scientia Iranica, Transaction B: Mechanical Engineering 2009; 16(5): 425–439.

[39] Chorin AJ. Curvature and solidification. Journal of Computational Physics 1985; 58:472–490.

[40] Ashgriz N, Poo JY. A computational method for determining curvatures. Journal of Computational Physics 1989; 84: 483–491.

[41] Kothe DB, Rider WJ, Mosso SJ, Brock JS, Hochstein JI. Volume Tracking of Interfaces Having Surface Tension in Two and Three Dimensions. AIAA 34th Aerospace Sciences Meeting and Exhibit 1996; AIAA 96-0859, Reno, NV, USA.

[42] Saghi H, Ketabdari MJ, Zamirian M. A novel algorithm based on parameterization method for calculation of curvature of the free surface flows. Applied Mathematical Modelling 2013; 37: 570–585.

Chapter 16

# Transport and Mixing in Liquid Phase Using Large Eddy Simulation: A Review

Juan M. Mejía, Amsini Sadiki, Farid Chejne and Alejandro Molina

Additional information is available at the end of the chapter

http://dx.doi.org/10.5772/63993

**Abstract**

Many mixing processes in engineering applications are turbulent. At high-Schmidt regime, the scalar scales are much lower than those of the velocity field, making difficult instantaneous measurements and direct numerical simulation for studying systems of practical interest. The use of large eddy simulation (LES) for analyzing transport and mixing of passive and reactive scalars at high-Schmidt (*Sc*) regime is addressed in this article. We present two different approaches for studying scalar transport and mixing in LES: the conventional approach is based on the modeling of the unclosed subgrid-scale scalar flux term in the filtered scalar equation by models commonly used for high-Sc flows. The second approach presented in this review for dealing with high-Sc flows is based on the use of a filtered mass density function (FDF) of the scalar field. Conclusions are presented about the relative merits of the two approaches.

**Keywords:** mixing, large eddy simulation, high Schmidt, filtered mass density function

## 1. Introduction

At molecular scale, the mixing of two or more fluids having different composition is driven by diffusion, a rather slow process. Turbulence increases the rate of mixing by the action of large-scale motions, making higher the contact surface area between adjacent unmixed fluid "elements." Turbulent mixing plays an important role in many engineering, biological, and environmental applications. In the case of reactive systems, chemical reactions can only take place after reactants are mixed at molecular level; in many of such systems, the availability of mixed reactants at the molecular scale limits the reaction rate; consequently, the mixing process can be a controlling rate.

In the chemical and pharmaceutical industries, an inadequate mixing can raise the production costs due to the reduction in selectivity, low yield, undesired product accumulation, and scale-up and process development problems. Some costs related to mixing are reported by Paul et al. [1]: in 1989, the cost of poor mixing in the U.S. chemical industry was estimated at $1 to $10 billion; yield losses of 5% due to poor mixing are typical. In the pharmaceutical industry, the costs due to lower yield and due to problems in scale-up and process development are on the order of $100 and $500 million, respectively. In the 1980s, the pulp and paper industry reported savings averaging 10–15% by introducing medium consistency mixer technology in their processes.

Numerous studies have dealt with transport and mixing of passive scalars in systems where the Schmidt number (*Sc*) is close to one, as it is the case for gas flows in which the smallest scalar scale (the Obukhov-Corrsin scale) is of the same order of magnitude or higher than the smallest flow scale, the Kolmogorov scale (see Refs. [2–5]). However, in many industrial and biological applications that take place in the liquid phase, the ratio of the fluid momentum diffusivity to molecular diffusivity of the scalar is much greater than 1; so, the scalar field holds finer structures than the velocity field (see Refs. [6–9]).The smallest scalar length-scale when the Schmidt number is greater than 1 is named the Batchelor scale ($\eta_B$) and is much smaller than the Obukhov-Corrsin scale, $\eta_{oc}$, and the smallest velocity length-scale,—the Kolmogorov scale ($\eta$). The small dimension of the Batchelor scale makes accurate measurement of the instantaneous concentration in turbulent liquid flows scarce and only possible with rather sophisticated systems [10].

To overcome many of the difficulties found in mixture-based processes, numerical simulation appears as an important tool for design and process improvement, as it can predict important information about the flow and scalar fields, which is hard to measure. When numerical simulations of industrial process are carried out, key requirements are the computational efficiency, algorithm robustness, and accurate representation of the process.

Models that correctly represent the mixing processes in turbulent flows are important for the design of various engineering and environmental applications where turbulence plays an important role. While the current understanding of turbulence allows a reasonable description of the flow field, a universal description of turbulent mixing processes remains a challenge [11, 12].

Direct numerical simulation (DNS) gives the most detailed information about the flow, as it resolves all the scalar length- and timescales by setting up the spatial resolution according to the smallest scalar/flow scale. No empirical closure or turbulence model assumptions are required. DNS has been useful for the study of transition and turbulent flows [13]. Because physics and chemistry are properly represented, DNS has also been used for the analysis of complex phenomena in combustion systems [14]. The use of DNS has been increasing as a complementary means of study of turbulent mixing process [15]. Sophisticated discretization schemes are used by DNS, imparting low flexibility when complex geometries are used

[13]. The full-scale resolution requirement makes very expensive the computational cost, and sometimes prohibitive, even for future computational capabilities. The computational cost rises as $Re^3$. Approximately 99% of calculations are used to solve the dissipation scales [16]. For these reasons, DNS is not a viable choice for systems of practical importance at high Reynolds and Schmidt numbers.

A more realistic alternative to DNS is the utilization of spatial filtering or temporal ensemble averages, such as large eddy simulation (LES) and unsteady Reynolds averaged Navier-Stokes equations (U-RANS) [17]. When LES and U-RANS formulations are used, additional terms appear in the transport equations. These terms need to be modeled. The information given by DNS has been useful to validate the unclosed terms of LES and RANS approaches [18].

RANS is based on the application of the Reynolds decomposition to any quantity $Q(x, t) = \overline{Q(x, t)} + Q'(x, t)$, where $\overline{Q(x, t)}$ is the mean of $Q$, and $Q'(x, t)$ is the deviation from the mean. The temporal average must be done for time intervals greater than any flow time-scales. Averaged equations contain additional unknown terms: Reynolds stresses, scalar fluxes, and averaged source terms. These terms are unclosed, and turbulence models must be provided in order to close the mathematical system. In RANS, the largest scales are solved, and the turbulent spectrum information is provided by turbulence models. By using RANS, a good balance between results and computational cost is obtained. RANS is useful in engineering, especially for industrial and environmental sectors [19]. It is possible to perform parametric studies, considering its low computational cost. The main limitation of RANS models is that they only give limited information about turbulence, because all turbulent scales are modeled. Although RANS has achieved reasonable good precision for simple flows, in the reproduction of large-scale organized and nonstationary turbulence structures, when strong streamline curvature or nongradient transport is present, RANS has achieved limited success [20]. Some inaccuracies arise from the turbulent viscosity hypothesis, the equation for $\varepsilon$ and the nonuniversality of the model's constants which have to be tuned in order to improve the simulation results [16]. Although RANS provides a reasonable computational cost-precision ratio, it does not always predict the concentration fluctuation distributions [21] in turbulent reacting liquid flows; in the case of stirred tank reactors (STR), the turbulent kinetic energy is unpredicted in the impeller region and discharge stream [22–25].

On the other hand, LES can be viewed as an intermediate approach between DNS and RANS, because in the former all turbulent structures are calculated, while in the latter they are modeled. The idea of LES is to solve the large, nonuniversal, anisotropic turbulent scales and to model the small turbulent scales, which contain less kinetic energy and are nearly universal and isotropic. These small scales are easier to model than the whole turbulent spectrum. The LES approach was proposed by Leonard [26]. A higher fidelity on the representation of the flow structure than RANS is expected, since the geometry-dependent, large turbulent scales are calculated.

The cut-off length must be proportional to the longitudinal integral length-scale [16], $L_{EI}$. Typically, 92% of the kinetic energy is resolved for a one-dimensional flow and 80% for a three-dimensional flow [16]. The proportionality constant depends on the filter specification. The uncertainty about residual motions is lowered by reducing the filter width; therefore, constitutive LES equations are grid-dependent, that is, LES is an incomplete model. References [27–29] review the LES literature.

Compared to DNS, LES saves the computational cost of solving the lower turbulent scales (99% of DNS calculations), and can be used for the simulation of systems of practical importance. However, it is more expensive than a $k$-$\varepsilon$ model for a given grid resolution.

In shear flows, LES prediction capabilities are diminished by the fact that in the viscous region, the energy-containing structures are of the same order of magnitude as the viscous length-scales ($\delta_v = v\sqrt{\rho / \tau_w}$), and LES cannot solve them. To face this issue, it is possible to refine the computational mesh in near-wall zones in order to consider the small coherent structures developed on those zones, but this refinement implies more computational effort. There are three additional possibilities: incorporating the fluid behavior in the wall region by wall models, simulating those zones with RANS (hybrid RANS-LES), or incorporating wall-adapted SGS closures.

Most research efforts in LES for reactive flows are concentrated on the SGS fluxes and Favre-filtered source terms [30]. In diffusion flames, chemical reactions take place after mixing of reactive species is achieved at the smallest scales of turbulence (unresolved in LES); so, in LES the combustion process must be modeled.

According to Ref. [31], the uncertainty initially contained in the nonresolved scales is propagated to the resolved ones; hence, it is said that SGS modeling is not a well-posed problem. LES results can be interpreted as a different realization of the flow. They could have the same statistical properties of the flow and may predict the same spatially organized structures but at a different location.

LES has been successfully applied to turbulent flows, in particular to complex geometries in liquid phase such as stirred tank reactors (see Refs. [10, 24, 32–34]). Because LES equations are unclosed, SGS models must be supplied in order to specify the SGS stresses, SGS scalar fluxes, and filtered reaction terms.

There are still unanswered questions about the behavior of high Schmidt turbulent flows. LES could be an alternative method for studying these flows, as long as the flow's physical behavior can be captured by the subgrid-scale models [15]. The LES equations are presented in the following section.

## 2. Large eddy simulation (LES)

Spatial scale separation is done by applying a low-pass filter to the governing balance equations. This set of filtered equations governs the dynamics of the large scales. Spatial fluctuations, lower than a defined filter cut-off length -Δ-, are smoothed or removed. The spatial filtering operation of a flow variable $Q$, being a function of time and space, is defined by the convolution integral:

http://dx.doi.org/10.5772/63993

$$\langle Q\rangle_L \equiv \frac{1}{\langle\rho\rangle_l}\int_D \rho G(x-x')Q(x)dx' = \frac{\langle\rho Q\rangle_l}{\langle\rho\rangle_l} \tag{1}$$

where $Q=\langle Q\rangle_L + Q''$. Favre filtering has been applied to Eqs. (1) and (2). $G$ is the filter kernel defined over the entire domain. The filter kernel depends on the filter width, $\Delta$, and must satisfy a set of conditions (see Ref. [16]). Favre-filtered mass, momentum, and scalars' balance equations are as follows:

$$\frac{\partial\langle\rho\rangle_l}{\partial t} + \frac{\partial}{\partial x_j}\left(\langle\rho\rangle_l\langle u_j\rangle_L\right) = 0 \tag{2}$$

$$\frac{\partial\langle\rho\rangle_l\langle u_i\rangle_L}{\partial t} + \frac{\partial}{\partial x_j}\left(\langle\rho\rangle_l\langle u_i\rangle_L\langle u_j\rangle_L\right) = -\frac{\partial}{\partial x_j}\left[\langle\rho\rangle_l\left(\langle\tau_{ij}\rangle_l + \tau_{ij}^{sgs}\right)\right] - \frac{\partial\langle p\rangle_l}{\partial x_i} + \langle\rho\rangle_l F_i \tag{3}$$

$$\frac{\partial\langle\rho\rangle_l\langle\phi_\alpha\rangle_L}{\partial t} + \frac{\partial}{\partial x_j}\left(\langle\rho\rangle_l\left(\langle\phi_\alpha\rangle_L\langle u_j\rangle_l + \langle J_{\alpha,j}\rangle_L + J_{\alpha,j}^{sgs}\right)\right) = \langle S_\phi\rangle_L \tag{4}$$

where the symbol $\partial$ denotes the partial differential operator, and the summation convention is used for repeated indices. Time ($t$) and spatial coordinates ($x_j$) are the independent variables; $\rho$ is the fluid mass density; $\phi_\alpha$ is the mass-weighted value of the scalar field (e.g., internal energy, mass fraction); $u_j$ is the mass-averaged velocity in the $j$-direction; $p$ denotes pressure; $\tau_{ij}$ is the shear stress tensor; and $J$ is the diffusive flux of the scalar.

New terms appear in LES equations, as it occurs in RANS. These terms account for resolved and subgrid scales' interactions. The SGS stresses $\left(\tau_{ij}^{SGS}\right)$ and SGS scalar fluxes $\left(j_{\alpha,j}^{SGS}\right)$ are defined by

$$\tau_{ij}^{sgs} = \langle u_i u_j\rangle_L - \langle u_i\rangle_L\langle u_j\rangle_L;\quad j_{\alpha,j}^{sgs} = \langle u_j\phi_\alpha\rangle_L - \langle u_j\rangle_L\langle\phi_\alpha\rangle_L \tag{5}$$

In addition, a model is needed for filtered source terms. Subgrid-scale (SGS) models must be supplied in order to specify the SGS stresses, SGS scalar fluxes, and filtered reaction terms.

The main task of SGS stress tensor model is to dissipate the energy transferred from turbulent large scales. The dynamics of the subgrid scales affect that of the resolved flow field through the subgrid-scale stress tensor.

There are several SGS stress tensor models (for review, see Refs. [17, 35]). The simplest models are based on the gradient assumption. More complex models are of first and second order. As the model complexity increases, so does the required number of equations. Those models based on eddy viscosity show good balance between accuracy and numerical computation and present good prediction abilities in turbulent combustion and other highly interacting processes. It is also possible to close the LES approximation by PDF methods, such as the velocity-filtered density function (VFDF) [36] and the velocity-scalar filtered mass density function (VSFMDF) [37], but this approach increases considerably the number of equations to be solved. This procedure increases the computational cost 15–30 times longer than the Smagorinsky [38] and dynamic Smagorinsky [39, 40] models, respectively.

### 2.1. The Smagorinsky model

The Smagorinsky model [38] is one of the pioneer SGS models in the development of LES. Its simple formulation and good performance have made it very popular, and it is used in this work. The Smagorinsky model is an eddy-viscosity based model, which assumes equilibrium between the turbulent kinetic energy dissipation and production rates to obtain a relation between the characteristic velocity and the resolved strain rate. A Boussinesq approximation is applied to the deviatoric part of the SGS stress.

$$\tau_{ij}^{sgs} - \frac{1}{3}\tau_{kk}^{sgs}\delta_{ij} \approx -\nu_T\left[2\langle S_{ij}\rangle_L - \frac{2}{3}\langle S_{kk}\rangle\delta_{ij}\right] \tag{6}$$

where $\nu_T$ is the subgrid eddy viscosity of residual motions and $\delta$ is the Dirac delta function. The filtered strain rate is given by

$$\langle S_{ij}\rangle_L = \frac{1}{2}\left(\frac{\partial\langle u_i\rangle_L}{\partial x_j} + \frac{\partial\langle u_j\rangle_L}{\partial x_i}\right) \tag{7}$$

The subgrid eddy viscosity is modeled in a similar way as the mixing length:

$$\nu_T = (C_s\Delta)^2|S|_L \quad , \quad |S|_L \equiv \left(2\langle S_{ij}\rangle_L\langle S_{ij}\rangle_L\right)^{1/2} \tag{8}$$

where $C_s$ is the Smagorinsky coefficient. This Model parameter is not universal and depends on the flow configurations. While for isotropic turbulence, the Smagorinsky coefficient is about 0.17 [41], for other configurations this value may not be correct; for a channel flow, the Smagorinsky coefficient is about 0.1 [42]. In addition, the spatial variation of this coefficient makes it difficult to find a proper value. This model parameter can be dynamically calculated by using the dynamic procedure [39, 40], in which, by assuming scale invariance, a test filter greater than the filter width, $\Delta$, can be used for calculating $C_s$ from the resolved flow field.

### 2.2. The dynamic Smagorinsky model

The major drawback of the Smagorinsky model is that a single universal constant cannot correctly represent different turbulent flows. Germano et al. [39] proposed a dynamic procedure for computing the Smagorinsky model coefficient, based on the instantaneous

http://dx.doi.org/10.5772/63993

information given by the filtered velocity field. The coefficient is locally recalculated during the simulations; so, it is no longer necessary to specify its value as an input parameter.

The dynamic procedure is based on the idea that the information given by the smallest resolved scales can be used to model the largest unresolved scales, as they have a similar behavior. The latter can be done by employing a test filter, with the test filter width larger than the filter width ($\Delta$), usually taken as $\hat{\Delta} = 2\Delta$.

A model for the SGS stress is

$$\tau_{ij}^{sgs} - \frac{1}{3}\tau_{kk}^{sgs}\delta_{ij} = -2C_{dyn}\Delta^2 \left|\left\langle S_{ij}\right\rangle_L\right| \left(\left\langle S_{ij}\right\rangle_L - \frac{1}{3}\left\langle S_{kk}\right\rangle_L \delta_{ij}\right) = -2C_{dyn}\alpha_{ij} \tag{9}$$

where $C_{dyn}$ is a Model parameter, and the term should be modeled. If the test filter is applied to the filtered momentum equation, the filter stress has the form:

$$T_{ij} = \left\langle u_i u_j \right\rangle_L - \left\langle u_i \right\rangle_L \left\langle u_j \right\rangle_L \tag{10}$$

As it was the case for the SGS stress, a model for the filter stress is

$$T_{ij} - \frac{1}{3}T_{kk}\delta_{ij} = -2C_{dyn}\hat{\Delta}^2 \left|\left\langle S_{ij}\right\rangle_L\right| \left(\left\langle S_{ij}\right\rangle_L - \frac{1}{3}\left\langle S_{kk}\right\rangle_L \delta_{ij}\right) = -2C_{dyn}\beta_{ij} \tag{11}$$

The coefficient has been assumed to be independent of the filtering process. By applying the test filter on the unresolved SGS scalar flux ($\tau_{ij}^{SGS}$) and subtracting it from the test filter stress ($T_{ij}$), the resolved part of the SGS stress tensor is obtained. This is the Germano identity [40]:

$$L_{ij} = T_{ij} - [illegible]_L \left\langle u_j \right\rangle_L - \left\langle u_i \right\rangle_L \left\langle u_j \right\rangle_L \tag{12}$$

The Germano identity can be partially satisfied by replacing model equations for the SGS and filter stresses [Eqs. (9) and (11), respectively] into Eq. (12), giving an approximation for the model coefficient ($C_{dyn}$):

$$L_{ij} - \frac{1}{3}L_{kk}\delta_{ij} = -2C_{dyn}\left(\beta_{ij} - \alpha_{ij}\right) = -2C_{dyn}M_{ij} \tag{13}$$

Equation (13) is overspecified, because there are five independent equations and one unknown value. There are different ways to calculate the coefficient. By applying a least-squares methodology, Lilly [40] minimized the error incurred in the calculation of the coefficient. The error is

$$E_{ij} = L_{ij} - T_{ij} + \tau_{ij} = L_{ij} - \frac{1}{3} L_{kk}\delta_{ij} + 2C_{dyn}M_{ij} \tag{14}$$

The minimum corresponds to

$$\frac{\partial\left(E_{ij}E_{ij}\right)}{\partial C_{dyn}} = 0 \tag{15}$$

leading to

$$C_{dyn} = -\frac{1}{2}\frac{L_{ij}E_{ij}}{M_{ij}M_{ij}} = 0 \tag{16}$$

The calculation of the parameter generates spatial and temporal fluctuations, as well as negative values [43]. Regions with a negative coefficient may be interpreted as regions where backscatter takes place. According to Carati et al. [44], the dynamic Smagorinsky model does not have information about the amount of energy that is available in the subgrid scales.

## 3. Subgrid-scale scalar flux models

In the context of mixing of scalars, the interaction between resolved and nonresolved scalar structures is accounted for by the unknown SGS scalar flux term, which must be provided via SGS scalar flux models. In the context of mixing, the aim of LES closures is to express the SGS scalar flux in terms of the known filtered values in order to close the numerical set or partial differential equations. Accounting for the nature of turbulent mixing, where various regimes are present in the scalar spectrum, modeling of the SGS scalar flux models is a complex task that is far from trivial [45].

Macromixing, mesomixing, and micromixing happen simultaneously as the mixing process is taking place. The spatial and temporal transport of large-scale structures describes the macromixing, and they can be solved in LES. Mesomixing is driven by turbulent fluctuations in the energy-containing range, and viscous convective deformations of fluid elements and molecular diffusion are responsible mechanisms for micromixing. Because the inertial range of the velocity spectrum is modeled in LES, mesomixing can be expressed by gradient correlations. On the other hand, characterization of micromixing can be based on the second statistical moment (variance) of the local concentration distribution [46–48]. A physical meaning of the concentration variance is that it provides a measure of the scalar distribution from small-scale homogeneity. The variance production, then, is dependent on the scalar flux.

There are many published works proposing SGS scalar flux models; most of them were developed for gas flow. For review of SGS scalar flux models in gas flows, see Refs. [27, 49]. Even though gas-based SGS scalar flux models have some limitations on the prediction of mixing where high Schmidt number effects are important [48], physically based models for the SGS scalar flux have been rarely proposed. One exception is the study of Jaberi and Colucci [50].

According to experimental data and DNS results, the assumption of isotropy at inertial and dissipation scales of the scalar field is no longer valid for structured functions and derivative skewness, when a mean scalar gradient is taking place [4, 8, 35]. Different models have been proposed in order to take into account the anisotropic behavior of micromixing, mainly focused on gas-phase (see Refs. [50–52]), but their application for fluids with high *Sc* numbers is scarce.

Few models have been developed or used for high Schmidt flows. The eddy diffusivity model [53] with constant and dynamically calculated turbulent Schmidt number [39, 54] has been widely used on the simulation of mixing at high Schmidt numbers [40, 55].

Other models used in the simulation of high Schmidt flows have been adapted from SGS stress tensors or extended from their RANS counterpart. These models include the following:

1. The dynamic mixed model, originally developed by Zang et al. [55] to represent the SGS stress tensor extended to the LES of scalar field by Na [56] in a turbulent channel ($Sc/Pr$ =1, 3, 10); The model was also used by Tkatchenko et al. [57] in the near-field of a coaxial jet mixer ($Sc = 1000$).
2. The dynamic structure model proposed by Chumakov et al. [58] and a priori tested using DNS data of a nonreacting mixing layer and decaying isotropic turbulence.
3. The multifractal SGS stress tensor model introduced by [59, 60] and extended to model the SGS scalar flux in a low Schmidt flow [61, 62] in a homogeneous isotropic turbulence at $Sc = 100$ [15] and a jet mixer [63].
4. The implicit method (non-SGS model), in which discretization methods are developed, so that the truncation error itself acts as an implicit SGS model. This approach was applied to a stirred tank reactor by Revstedt et al. [32] and isotropic turbulence and channel flow ($Sc = 1$, 3, 10, and 25) by Hickel et al. [45].

On the other hand, the anisotropy model [48] was proposed for the simulation of mixing of passive and active scalars. Simulation results of mixing at low and high Schmidt regime have shown its superior performance among other SGS scalar flux models. The anisotropy and the eddy diffusivity models are presented in the following subsections.

### 3.1. The eddy diffusivity model

In analogy to the Smagorinsky model, most of the SGS scalar flux models are based on the eddy diffusivity assumption. The eddy diffusivity model [53] can be viewed as a counterpart of the Smagorinsky model for the scalar field. The eddy diffusivity model relates the SGS flux to the local filtered scalar strain rate, and the transport is assumed to be aligned to the filtered scalar gradient [15]. The proportionality constant is called the turbulent Schmidt number, which appears as an adjustable parameter. However, the turbulent Schmidt number can be dynamically calculated by using the methodology proposed by Germano et al. [39] and further refined by Moin et al. [54].

$$J_{\alpha,j}^{sgs} = -C_{\phi}\Delta^2 \left|\langle S\rangle_L\right| \frac{\partial\langle\phi\rangle_L}{\partial x_j} = -\frac{\nu_T}{Sc_T}\frac{\partial\langle\phi\rangle_L}{\partial x_j} \tag{17}$$

where $Sc_T$ is the turbulent Schmidt number, which is given by the ratio of SGS viscosity to the SGS diffusivity ($Sc_T = \upsilon_T / D_T$).

The eddy diffusivity model has been often used due to its simplicity, and it shows good results for gas flows. The model has been widely used in simple and complex geometries, some involving reactive scalars.

The turbulent Schmidt number appears as an adjustable parameter that can be tuned in order to minimize the error with reference data. According to Durbin and Patterson [63], the value is dependent on the type of flow, and is in the range 0.1–1 [27]. Various authors (see **Table 1**) have proposed different values for the nondimensional parameter $Sc_T$ in high Schmidt flows.

| Configuration | $Sc_T$ | Reference |
|---|---|---|
| Stirred tank reactors | 0.8 | [23] |
| | 0.7 | [24] |
| | | [113], [114] |
| Channel | 0.25 | [110] |
| Inclined channel | 0.7 | [109] |
| Confined impinging jets | 0.4 | [108] |
| Coaxial jet | 0.7 | [107] |
| Jet in channel | 1.0 | [48] |
| Mixing layer | 1.0 | [48] |
| Co-flowing jet | 0.7 | [99] |

**Table 1.** Turbulent Schmidt number used in LES of high Schmidt flows.

In turbulent shear flows, different orientations of the mean scalar gradient yield different values for the turbulent Schmidt number [49]. A constant value of $Sc_T$ is, therefore, not adequate. The turbulent Schmidt number can be thought of as a parameter that characterizes the dissipative/diffusive cut-off scales of the velocity and scalar fields. The behavior of the scalar mixing spectrum, presented in Section 2.2, indicates that a universal distribution of an effective turbulent Schmidt number cannot exist [27].

### 3.2. The eddy diffusivity model with dynamic procedure

Similar to the dynamic Smagorinsky model, in the dynamic model, the $Sc_T$ in Eq. (17) can be dynamically calculated by using the methodology proposed by Germano et al. [39], which was further extended to scalar transport and compressible flow by Moin et al. [54]. By applying a test filter over the filtered velocity and scalar fields, the turbulent Schmidt number can be computed as follows [64].

The filter scalar flux is

$$\frac{1}{Sc_T} = \frac{1}{2C_{dyn}} \frac{F_i H_i}{H_i H_i} \tag{18}$$

where

$$F_i = Q_i - J_i^{sgs} = \langle u_i \rangle_L \langle \phi \rangle_L - \langle u_i \rangle_L \langle \phi \rangle_L, \quad H_i = \Delta^2 \left| \langle S \rangle_L \right| \frac{\partial \langle \phi \rangle_L}{\partial x_i} - \Delta^2 \left| \langle S \rangle_L \right| \frac{\partial \langle \phi \rangle_L}{\partial x_i} \tag{19}$$

| Configuration | *Sc* (*Pr*) | Reference |
|---|---|---|
| Channel | 0.1–200 | [105], [106] |
| | 1–100 | [104] |
| | 0.1–100 | [103], [104] |
| Mixing layer | 600 | [10] |
| | 600 | [34] |
| | 3300 | [48] |
| Coaxial jet | 1000 | [57] |
| Jet in channel | 3300 | [48] |
| Grid-generated turbulent flow | 600 | [102] |
| Co-flowing jet | 2000 | [98], [99]; [102] |

**Table 2.** Previous works of turbulent mixing of $Sc >> 1$ using the dynamic procedure.

On implementation of the dynamic procedure, negative values are clipped to zero, and a relaxation process is imposed to instantaneous values.

The dynamic procedure is one of the most popular SGS scalar flux models in LES of high Schmidt flows. **Table 2** summarizes the geometry and Schmidt numbers of previous works, using the dynamic eddy diffusivity model.

Theoretical considerations suggest that the dynamic procedure should be adequate for LES, where the scalar fluctuations are resolved but the velocity fluctuations are not, so that SGS kinetic energy transfer takes place [27]. This is the case of low Schmidt flows.

Since the eddy diffusivity model assumes the alignment of the scalar flux with the scalar gradient, this approach does not predict realistic values of the scalar flux components [45, 48]. In addition, errors are introduced, as the model does not account for the different dynamics of the velocity and scalar fields.

### 3.3. The dynamic anisotropy model

Another recent SGS scalar flux model is the anisotropy model [48]. Contrary to the eddy diffusivity and dynamic models, the anisotropic model [48] accounts for the nonlinear contributions of the SGS to the turbulent scalar flux. If it is assumed that the turbulent flow field (mean velocities and turbulence characteristics) is available from LES using the dynamic-based Smargorinsky SGS model [39], the anisotropy model is the simplest explicit anisotropic-resolving algebraic form, and consists of a cubic formulation in terms of the scalar gradients. This model is thermodynamically consistent as it agrees with the irreversibility requirement of the second law of thermodynamics [47, 65]. It combines the linear eddy diffusivity model with an additional term coupling the (deviatoric) SGS stress tensor and the gradient of the filtered scalar field. Pantangi et al. [65] present a detailed analysis:

$$J_{\alpha,i}^{sgs} = -D_T \frac{\partial \langle \phi \rangle_L}{\partial x_j} + D_{dev} T_{sgs} \tau_{ij}^{sgs(dev)} \frac{\partial \langle \phi \rangle_L}{\partial x_j} \tag{21}$$

where $D_{dev}$ is the anisotropy model coefficient. Both $D_T$ and $D_{dev}$ depend on the invariants of $\tau_{ij}^{SGS}$ and $\frac{\partial \langle \phi \rangle_L}{\partial x_j}$. The tensor diffusivity is defined by

$$D_{i,j}^{sgs} = -D_T \delta_{ij} + D_{dev} T_{sgs} \tau_{ij}^{sgs(dev)} \tag{22}$$

The anisotropy model may lead to other models proposed in the literature, according to the modeling level used for the deviatoric part of the SGS stress tensor. Note that the additional term is a measure of how local mixing, dependent on the molecular Schmidt number through the SGS timescale, is influenced by the nonresolved flow structures (see Eq. (9) in Ref. [65]).

If the turbulent flow field (mean velocities and turbulence characteristics) is available from the LES solver using the dynamic-based Smargorinsky SGS model, the anisotropy model is the simplest explicit algebraic model that solved accounts for the anisotropy found in turbulent flows. In the context defined by the Smagorinsky model, the anisotropy model can be developed by expressing the SGS timescale using the filter size and the subgrid viscosity. The anisotropy model reads:

http://dx.doi.org/10.5772/63993

$$J_{\alpha,i}^{sgs} = -\frac{\nu_T}{Sc_T}\frac{\partial \langle \phi \rangle_L}{\partial x_j} + D_{an}\Delta^2 \overline{S_{ij}^{sgs}} \frac{\partial \langle \phi \rangle_L}{\partial x_j} \tag{23}$$

The anisotropy coefficient, $D_{an}$, can be either specified or calculated by the dynamic procedure as well as the $Sc_T$. A preliminary evaluation of this procedure was reported in Ref. [47] for chemical liquid flows and for gases in Ref. [46]. In order to compute the anisotropy coefficient, the turbulent Schmidt number must be calculated using Eqs. (21)–(23). Then, the calculation of the anisotropy model coefficient is done as follows:

$$D_{an} = \left( F_i - \frac{C_s}{Sc_T} H_i \right) H_{2i} \; ; \; H_{2i} = \Delta^2 \left| \langle S \rangle_L \right| \frac{\partial \langle \phi \rangle_L}{\partial x_i} - \Delta^2 \langle S \rangle_L \frac{\partial \langle \phi \rangle_L}{\partial x_i} \tag{24}$$

## 4. The filtered density function (FDF) approach

A second approach in the LES mixing context is to solve the joint probability function of the SGS scalars [66], named filtered density function (FDF), in conjunction with the filtered momentum equations from LES. In this approach a filtered density function (FDF) is used to quantify the probability to find a filtered variable of the flow ($Y$) in the range ($Y^*-\Delta Y/2$, $Y^* +\Delta Y/2$). The fundamental property of the FDF method is to account, in a probabilistic way, for the effects of SGS fluctuations. The advantage of the FDF approach over other methods is that the chemical source term appears in a closed form, so that the turbulent/chemistry interaction can be correctly included. The counterpart of the FDF equation in the RANS context is named probability density function (PDF) equation. The main difference between PDF and FDF is that temporal fluctuations over different flow realizations are characterized by the use of PDF, while the instantaneous subgrid-scale fluctuations are characterized by the use of FDF [67]. The PDF is the expected value of the FDF in the limit of vanishing filter width [68].

The statistical information of the reactive scalar fields can be obtained explicitly from a transport equation. Pope [66] introduced the mathematical definition of the FDF transport equation. Pope [66] highlighted one of the major advantages of the FDF approach: the chemical reaction term in the FDF transport equation is closed; so, the modeling of this term is no longer required. Drozda et al. [69] present an overview of the state of progress in FDF.

The mass-filtered mass density function (FDF) is defined as

$$F_L(\psi;\boldsymbol{x},t) = \int_{-\infty}^{+\infty} G(\boldsymbol{x}-\boldsymbol{x}',t)\rho(\boldsymbol{x}',t) f'(\psi;\boldsymbol{x}',t) d\boldsymbol{x}' \tag{25}$$

where $\Psi$ is the sample space variable for each composition and $f'$ is the fine-grained joint FDF of compositions [16], defined as

$$f'(\psi;x,t) \equiv \prod_{\alpha=1}^{n_\phi} \delta(\phi_\phi[x,t]-\psi_\phi) = \delta(\phi[x,t]-\psi) \tag{26}$$

Based on the properties of Dirac delta functions and, after some manipulation, the FDF equation is [70]

$$\frac{\partial F_L}{\partial t} + \frac{\partial}{\partial x_j}\left[F_L \langle u_j|\psi\rangle_L\right] = -\frac{\partial}{\partial \psi_\alpha}\left[F_L\left\langle \frac{\mathrm{D}\phi_\alpha}{\mathrm{D}t}\middle|\psi\right\rangle_L\right] \tag{27}$$

The introduction of the scalar balance equation into Eq. (19) gives

$$\frac{\partial F_L}{\partial t} + \frac{\partial}{\partial x_j}\left[F_L \langle u_j|\psi\rangle_L\right] + \frac{\partial[F_L S_\alpha]}{\partial \psi_\alpha} = -\frac{\partial}{\partial \psi_\alpha}\left[F_L\left\langle -\frac{1}{\rho}\frac{\partial J_\alpha}{\partial x_j}\middle|\psi\right\rangle_L\right] \tag{28}$$

The zeroth, first, and second order moments of FDF are

$$\begin{aligned} &\int F_L(\psi;x,t)d\psi = \langle\rho\rangle_l \\ &\int \psi_\alpha F_L(\psi;x,t)d\psi = \langle\rho\phi_\alpha\rangle_l \equiv \langle\rho\rangle_l\langle\phi_\alpha\rangle_L \\ &\int \psi_\alpha\psi_\beta F_L(\psi;x,t)d\psi = \langle\rho\rangle_l\langle\phi_\alpha\phi_\beta\rangle_L \end{aligned} \tag{29}$$

.

Conditionally filtered terms of equations are unclosed. The conditional advection term can be modeled by the conventional gradient diffusion [70]:

$$\left(\langle u_j|\psi\rangle_l - \langle u_j\rangle_L\right)F_L = -\langle\rho\rangle_l D_T \frac{\partial}{\partial x_j}\left(\frac{F_L}{\langle\rho\rangle_l}\right) \tag{30}$$

where $D_T$ is the SGS diffusion coefficient. The conditional diffusion term in Eq. (30) accounts for transport in the physical space and mixing in the composition space. It has to be modeled by mixing models. The interaction by exchange with the mean model (IEM) or linear mean square estimation (LMSE) [71, 72] is described by Eq. (32) [70]:

$$\frac{\partial}{\partial \psi_\alpha}\left[\left\langle -\frac{1}{\rho}\frac{\partial J_\alpha}{\partial x_j}\middle|\psi\right\rangle_L F_L\right] = \frac{\partial}{\partial x_j}\left[\langle\rho\rangle_l\langle D\rangle_L \frac{\partial}{\partial x_j}\left(\frac{F_L}{\langle\rho\rangle_l}\right)\right] + \frac{\partial}{\partial \psi_\alpha}\left[\Omega_m(\psi_\alpha - \langle\phi_\alpha\rangle_L)F_L\right] \tag{31}$$

where $C_\Omega$ is the frequency of mixing within the subgrid, and it can be modeled as

http://dx.doi.org/10.5772/63993

$$\Omega_m = \frac{1}{\tau_m} = C_\Omega \left( \langle D \rangle_L + D_T \right) / \Delta_L^2 \quad (32)$$

where $C_\Omega$ is the SGS mixing time constant. The solution of the FDF equation by conventional difference schemes is intractable due to the high-dimensionality of the equation: the computational cost rises exponentially as the number of scalars increases [73]. To overcome this problem, stochastic methods have been used for the solution of the equation, because the computational cost rises linearly with the number of scalars [74].

The FDF approach also has a modeling requirement, because the conditional convective flux and conditional diffusion terms in the FDF transport equation are unknown. By deducing an equation for the conditional convective flux based on the velocity-scalar filtered density function formulation, Ref. [75] showed that a gradient transport hypothesis model performs well under many conditions. This model is usually implemented in FDF methods.

On the other hand, the conditional diffusion term accounts for transport of the FDF in the physical space and mixing in the composition space by the action of molecular diffusivity, and it has to be modeled by mixing models. From a theoretical point of view, McDermott and Pope [30] developed a set of desirable properties that an ideal FDF mixing model should fulfill. These properties differ from the corresponding PDF mixing models (see Ref. [16]). Most of the FDF mixing models have been adapted from their RANS counterpart.

A widely used mixing model is the interaction by exchange with the mean (IEM) model [71, 72]. The IEM model has a deterministic origin, initially formulated for PDF methods in RANS. The IEM states that the stochastic particle only interacts with itself, and the rate of change is proportional to the distance to the mean in the scalar space. Equivalently, the model relaxes the solution in the composition space toward the mean value; the relaxation is done over a subgrid-scale mixing time. The major drawback of the IEM model is that it preserves the shape of the PDF, avoiding the relaxation toward a Gaussian distribution [76], being an unphysical situation. However, as pointed by [77], large-scale mixing in inhomogeneous turbulent mixing problems also affects the shape of the distribution, and then limitation of the preservation of the distribution becomes less critical.

Numerical solution of the RANS/PDF equations has shown that the IEM model does not have good predictive capabilities (see Refs. [78, 79] for comparison of the accuracy of different PDF mixing models). On the contrary, the IEM model performs reasonably well in FDF/LES simulations. It has been used in most LES/FDF studies (see Refs. [70, 74, 78, 80–84] and others). There are few LES/FDF works in which other mixing models were used.

Mitarai et al. [78] and Olbricht et al. [74] implemented the modified Curl model—MCurl [85], which is a particle interaction model based on Curl's model [86]. In the Curl model, the PDF of the composition field is described by N stochastic particles. Mixing results from the movement of these particles in the composition space. According to the "simple" model, the mixing processes take place randomly between two stochastic particles, and the resulting composition of the new particle in the following time step is taken as the mean of the preceding particles. The Curl model produces a correct decay rate, but it relaxes the PDF to a bell-shaped curve instead of the Gaussian shape. This problem can be reduced by using improved models. In the modified Curl model of [85], the particle gradually mixes with the other one at a random mixing rate (for each pair of particles), instead of the originally instantaneous mixing assumption.

The Euclidean minimum spanning tree model (EMST) from Ref. [87] was evaluated by Mitarai et al. [78] and Shetty et al. [77]. The EMST is a sophisticated particle interaction model, where local mixing in composition space occurs between the selected group of particles, in contrast with the previous models (IEM, MCurl, etc.). Briefly, a Euclidean minimum spanning tree is constructed on the ensemble of particles which are selected based on a defined state variable. The Euclidean minimum spanning tree is formed by minimizing the length of the spanning tree. Mixing occurs between pairs of particles connected by a common branch of the tree. The EMST model has a superior performance over other PDF mixing models; however, it demands more computational time. In comparison to the IEM and MCurl, the implementation in the numerical solvers is more complicated.

Cleary et al. [88] implemented the multiple mapping conditioning (MMC) mixing model [89]. In the MMC model, a reference space is mapped to the physical space in order to attain local mixing in the composition space. This is done by choosing one or more reference variables (e.g., mixture fraction, sensible enthalpy, scalar dissipation, and others). Mixing occurs between particles that are close in both physical and reference spaces. The main difference of the MMC model with the EMST model is that local mixing in the former model is indirectly enforced in the composition space by assuring localness in the reference space, while it is directly enforced in composition space in the latter model [90]. Therefore, the principle of independence of scalars is assured in MMC. An advantage of the MMC model in FDF is that the averaged joint scalar distribution can be well predicted by using fewer particles in the computational domain than other models. However, the model has two unknown constants, and the reference space has to be solved in LES.

A recent PDF mixing model is the parameterized scalar profile (PSP), developed by Meyer and Jenny [91] and used by Shetty et al. [77] in LES/FDF. In this approach, it is assumed that one-dimensional effects dominate the dynamics of molecular diffusion at molecular interfaces. The PSP model is based on a parameterization of one-dimensional scalar profile in high Reynolds number flows. These scalar profiles are composed of scaled sinusoidal shaped sections, which move with the fluid within a reference frame. There are three parameters used by the scalar profiles; so, they become as additional properties of the particles. The latter makes the model very expensive, because three additional equations must be solved.

A mixing model developed in the LES framework is the fractal IEM (FIEM) [77]. The FIEM is a modified version of the IEM in which it is considered that the behavior of the system at the small scales is repeated at the large scales. It is done by splitting the control volume into many smaller control volumes, each one having the same size, allowing strong mixing in the smaller control volumes and further weak mixing in the larger control volume. The model uses two additional empirical parameters that account for the relative importance of the two mixing steps into the global mixing process. These constants are tuned by trial and error.

The performance of different mixing models was evaluated by Mitarai et al. [78]. These authors compared the numerical results of IEM, EMST, and MCurl in RANS/PDF and LES/FDF with DNS data of a gas diffusion flame with one-step reaction. The predicted filtered temperature was in an acceptable agreement with DNS results; the results from MCurl and IEM models were similar, while a better agreement was achieved with the EMST model. The mean and variance of the mixture fraction were accurately predicted by all mixing models. Their results also showed that LES/FDF approach provides much better results than the RANS/PDF in which marked differences between PDF mixing models were observed.

Shetty et al. [77] compared the predictions with IEM, EMST, PSP, and the FIEM mixing models in LES/FDF when modeling a low Schmidt three-stream turbulent jet. Comparisons with experimental data were done in the near-field of the configuration [max. downstream location = 7.2 jet diameters]. The simulation results of the mean and RMS of the radial scalar distribution obtained with all models followed the experimental observations. However, the FIEM results were in better agreement with the mean experimental observations at the largest downstream location. Results showed fast mixing of the scalar of the inner jet and slow mixing of the scalar of the annular jet, but, conversely, this did not happen when the FIEM was used. Large scale motions play an important role in mixing at the unstable shear layers formed between the inner, annular, and co-flowing streams, mainly due to entrainment processes. In the inner part of this jet, the scalar field may behave similar to the velocity field. Because the filtered velocity field is supposed to be the same for all tests [not showed in the chapter], little variations are expected in the performance of different mixing models, as was the case for the IEM, EMST, and PSP models. This suggests that the performance of the FIEM could be the result of artificial diffusion transport in the calculations.

Another aspect in the development of FDF is the fact that in LES there may be computational zones where the velocity field is locally fully resolved (the DNS limit). The mixing model has to take into account this aspect. McDermott and Pope [30] showed that the latter can be accomplished by using a mean drift term in the particle composition equation, rather than a random walk in physical space. The model developed by McDermott and Pope [30] correctly reduces to DNS in the limit of vanishing filter width and is able to deal with differential diffusion.

On a discrete representation of the FDF at a given time, the particles in the sample space correspond to particles in physical space, and distance between particles in the subgrid volume is small [67]. In a LES/FDF computational domain, the numerical solution of a FDF equation using a particle-based method may involve 106–108 stochastic particles. Therefore, the scalar resolution increases and may approximate to that of DNS, depending on the Schmidt number.

According to Klimenko [92], in the DNS limit, when the physical distance between particles becomes infinitesimally small (particle-based solutions of the FDF equation), many mixing models behave essentially the same. Furthermore, recalling the differences between PDF and FDF methods, the modeling requirements are different: in the RANS context, the PDF aims to solve mean scalar values, and fluctuations about the local mean value must be represented by the mixing models; contrarily, spatially filtered scalar values are sought in the LES approach, and the role of mixing models is to deal with SGS fluctuations about the local spatially filtered scalar. For these reasons, it is expected that simple mixing models used by the FDF method can provide a good approximation [68, 93]. In contrast, RANS has higher levels of sensitivity on the mixing model selection; so, the closure of the conditional diffusive term is the main difficulty in the application of PDF methods [88].

For review of the FDF method, see Haworth [93] who presents a comprehensive paper about theoretical aspects, physical models, numerical algorithms, and applications of PDF-FDF methods. Drozda et al. [69] present an overview of the state of progress of LES/FDF methods applied to the particular case of turbulent combustion.

The application of the FDF method to high Schmidt flows is scarce. Schwertfirm et al. [94–96] used the FDF approach to study high Schmidt number flows using the DNS of the flow field (a priori analysis). Schwertfirm et al. [94–96] showed for three different Schmidt numbers ($Sc$ = 3, 25), that if a correct definition of the SGS mixing frequency is done then the statistical and instantaneous behavior of the scalar field can be well predicted by using the IEM mixing model. One important finding is that the SGS scalar variance transport can be neglected in the SGS mixing frequency definition.

Van Vliet et al. [97] applied the LES/FDF approach to a tubular reactor with a moderated Reynolds number ($Re$ = 4000) and high Schmidt number ($Sc$ = 2000). They used IEM mixing model. They compared the mean and variance concentration distribution in the axial direction with a few experimental data, and without reaction (conserved scalar). From a qualitative point of view, simulation results are in agreement with experimental observations. However, the quantitative comparison of simulation results with experimental information shows that the simulated concentration (mean) decays faster. A similar behavior was exhibited by the scalar variance, showing a poor agreement with experiments. The discrepancy between experiments and simulations indicates that the mixing rate is overpredicted due to an inaccurate estimation of the subgrid-scale mixing time, rather than a feature of the IEM model. The performance of the reactor was studied by the LES/FDF approach by changing the Damköhler number over eight (8) orders of magnitude. A LES/FDF numerical study of a low-density polyethylene tubular reactor was done by Van Vliet et al. [81], at the vicinity of the initiator injection point. Multiple reactive scalars were solved (concentration and temperature), and a mechanism of six chemical reactions was used.

Experimental studies indicate that in gas flows, the subgrid mixing time constant is not universal, having values between 0.6 and 3.1 in the RANS context [76]. Different values of the SGS mixing time constant have been reported, mostly in the range 2–10 for gas flows. For liquid flows, Van Vliet et al. [97] used a value of 3. Mejía et al. [98] evaluated four values (between 4 and 10) in a turbulent round jet. They found that as the subgrid mixing time constant increases, the jet decay rate as well as the mixing rate decreases. The nonuniversality of this constant can affect the predictive capability of LES.

The works of Van Vliet et al. [81, 97] and Schwertfirm et al. [94–96] demonstrate the feasibility of performing (advanced) numerical simulations of systems of practical interest (e.g., industrial reactors), with minimum assumptions and complex chemistry. The numerical simulation is a valuable tool for designing, optimizing, and evaluating such processes. Their simulations showed that the calculation of the SGS mixing time, a common parameter in many mixing models, is an Achilles heel in their simulation of the high Schmidt flow, and it may be also the case for other high Schmidt systems.

## 5. Comparison between different SGS scalar flux models and the FDF method

In previous works [98, 99], we simulated a turbulent round jet ($Re$ = 10,000) discharging diluted rhodamine B in a co-flowing stream of water ($Sc$ = 2000), using large eddy simulation. The flow configuration is detailed by Antoine et al. [100]. Three different models for the unknown subgrid-scale (SGS) scalar flux term were used for closing the filtered scalar balance equation: eddy diffusivity model with both constant turbulent Schmidt number ($Sc_T$ = 0.7) and dynamically calculated turbulent Schmidt number, and the dynamic anisotropy model. In addition, the filtered density function (FDF) method was implemented. The interaction by exchange with the mean (IEM) mixing model was used for closing the conditional diffusion term in the transported FDF equation. The FDF transport equation was solved using a Monte Carlo method.

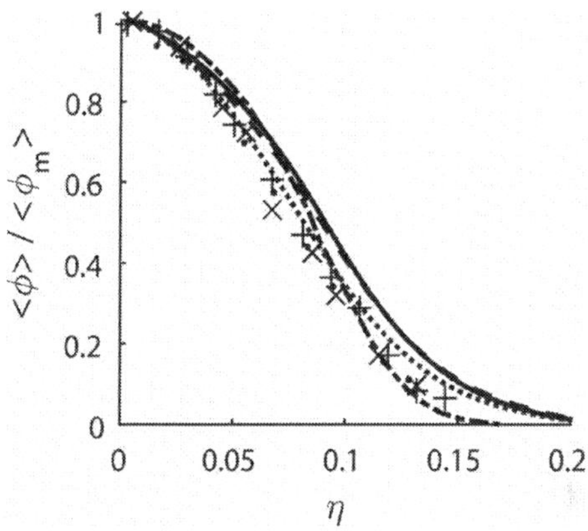


**Figure 1.** Radial mean concentration distribution across the jet. Experimental data (*symbols*) from Ref. [100]: + = 70; ● = 80; × = 90. Simulation results (*lines*) from Refs. [98, 99]: *Solid line*: eddy; *dashed line*: dynamic; *dotted line*: anisotropy; *dashed-dotted line*: FDF.

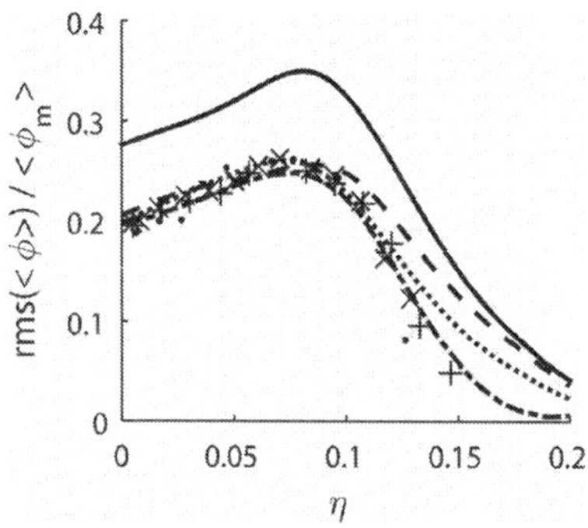


**Figure 2.** Radial mean (a) and fluctuation (b) concentration distribution across the jet. Experimental data (*symbols*) from Ref. [100]: + = 70; ● = 80; × = 90. Simulation results (*lines*) from Refs. [98, 99]: *Solid line*: eddy; *dashed line*: dynamic; *dotted line*: anisotropy; *dashed-dotted line*: FDF.

**Figures 1** and **2** compare the simulated radial mean and fluctuation distribution of the scalar concentration [98, 99], normalized by the centerline value ($\eta = r/x$, where $r$ is the radial coordinate and $x$ is the downstream distance from the nozzle exit), with the experimental data [101].

Having in mind the limitations of the eddy diffusivity model, it is noted in **Figure 1** that the mean concentration distribution is predicted reasonably well. On the other hand, **Figure 2** reveals that the three SGS scalar flux models fail to reproduce the concentration fluctuations at higher values of the nondimensional radial coordinate ($\eta$). Although the LES simulation results of the concentration distribution in radial direction are similar for the tested SGS scalar flux models in **Figures 1** and **2**, the dynamic anisotropy model provides a better performance. In LES, a mesh grid refinement would improve the simulation results. Mejía et al. [98] also showed that if the mesh grid is further refined, the dynamic eddy diffusivity improved its predictive capabilities.

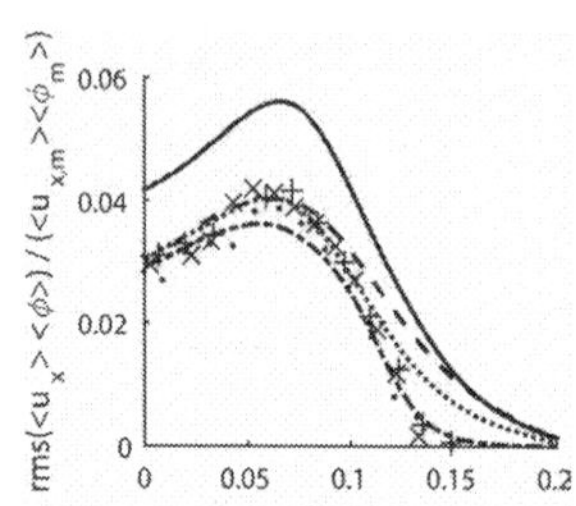


**Figure 3.** Streamwise velocity-concentration correlation across the jet. Experimental data (*symbols*) from Antoine et al. [100]: + = 70; ● = 80; × = 90. Simulation results (*lines*) from Refs. [98, 99]: *Solid line*: eddy; *dashed line*: dynamic; *dotted line*: anisotropy; *dashed-dotted line*: FDF.

http://dx.doi.org/10.5772/63993

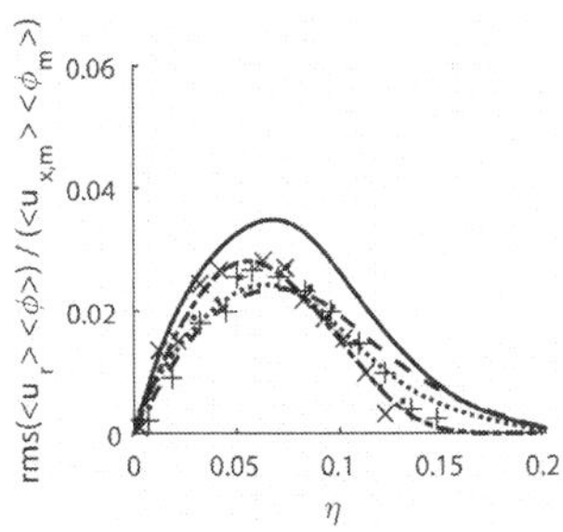


**Figure 4.** Radial velocity-concentration correlation across the jet. Experimental data (*symbols*) from Antoine et al. [100]: + = 70; ● = 80; × = 90. Simulation results (*lines*) from Refs. [98, 99]: *Solid line*: eddy; *dashed line*: dynamic; *dotted line*: anisotropy; *dashed-dotted line*: FDF.

The simulation results of the FDF approach are in good agreement with the mean and fluctuations concentration distribution for all regions of the jet. The radial distributions of the axial and radial scalar fluxes are presented, respectively, in **Figures 3** and **4**.

**Figures 3** and **4** show that the dynamic eddy diffusivity and anisotropy models reproduce the behavior of the scalar fluxes for low and intermediate values of the radial coordinates.

The agreement of the simulations of the FDF method (**Figures 3** and **4**) with the experimental data is good, and much better than that obtained with LES simulations using advanced SGS scalar flux models, such as the anisotropy model (see, e.g., **Figures 1** and **2** ). The LES/FDF can capture strong intermittency effects that take place on the surroundings of the superviscous layer formed between the jet and the co-flowing streams, leading toward anisotropy of the scalar field. Contrary to the SGS scalar flux models evaluated in [98, 99], the FDF equation does not spread the scalar away from the superviscous layer, as seen in the predicted *rms* and scalar fluxes distributions.

The computational costs of the dynamic and anisotropy models were 1.2 and 1.7 times that of the eddy diffusivity model, respectively. When a higher level model has to be considered, it is usual that more computational resource is required. From an engineering point of view, the dynamic model captures the most important mixing characteristics at a rather low computational cost. The computational time of the FDF, compared to the one required by using the eddy diffusivity model is approximately 1.9 times higher though [101].

## 6. Conclusions

Large eddy simulation of transport and mixing in high Schmidt flows remains a challenge, in particular for engineering applications. The appraisal of conventional and advanced SGS scalar flux models as well as the FDF method has to done based on the object of study. However, some of the merits of the approximations can be highlighted. The SGS scalar flux models have the advantage over FDF methods in that the simplest ones (e.g., eddy diffusivity model) are available in many CFD solvers. This closure strategy uses the same mesh grid of the flow solver as well as the numerical methods used for the numerical solution of the *N-S* equations. Therefore, one important consequence is that the programming of advanced SGS scalar flux models is straightforward. Having in mind the computational cost, simple SGS scalar flux models can reproduce important characteristics of the scalar field such as mean quantities on a moderate grid resolution. However, if the application requires a deeper understanding of mesomixing and micromixing (such as combustion and flow instability studies), the use of advanced SGS scalar flux models becomes mandatory. On the other hand, the main advantage of FDF method is that it allows for a detailed description and simulation of the scalar field. The FDF transport equation can be solved using particle-based methods, which are very simple to implement and to couple to LES solvers. The computational domain can be simpler than the one used by LES, since it only has to account for the spatial domain where the scalar field evolves.

## Acknowledgements

We thank Deutscher Akademischer Austausch Dienst (DAAD) and Departamento Administrativo de Ciencia, Tecnología e Innovación de Colombia (COLCIENCIAS) for logistic and financial support. The first author acknowledges the Institute of Energy and Power Plant Technology (EKT) at the Technische Universität Darmstadt (Germany) for its support during a 1-year academic stay. We thank the reviewers for their helpful comments on an earlier version of the manuscript.

## Author details

Juan M. Mejía[1*], Amsini Sadiki[2], Farid Chejne[1] and Alejandro Molina[1]

*Address all correspondence to: jmmejiaca@unal.edu.co

1 Departamento de Procesos y Energía, Universidad Nacional de Colombia, sede Medellín, Medellín, Colombia

2 Institute of Energy and Power Plant Technology, Technischen Universität Darmstadt, Darmstadt, Germany

## References

[1] Paul EL, Atiemo-Obeng VA, Kresta S. Handbook of insutrial mixing. Science and Practice. John Wiley & Sons; 2004.

[2] Sreenivasan K. The passive scalar spectrum and the Obukhov-Corrsin constant. Phys Fluids. 1996;8:189–7.

[3] Sreenivasan KR, Antonia RA. The phenomenology of small-scale turbulence. Annu Rev Fluid Mech. 29:435–72.

[4] Warhaft Z. Passive scalars in turbulent flows. Annu Rev Fluid Mech. 2000;32:203–40.

[5] Watanabe T, Gotoh T. Statistics of a passive scalar in homogeneous turbulence. New J Phys. 2004;6:1–36.

[6] Dahm WJA. Experiments on entrainment, mixing and chemical reactions in turbulent jets at large schmidt number. PhD Thesis. California Institute of Technology; 1985.

[7] Dahm WJA, Dimotakis PE. Mixing at large Schmidt number in the self-similar far field of turbulent jets. J Fluid Mech. 1990;217:299–330.

[8] Yeung PK, Xu S, Donzis DA, Sreenivasan KR. Simulations of three-dimensional turbulent mixing for schmidt numbers of the order 1000. Flow Turbul Combust. 2004;72(2-4 SPEC. ISS.):333–47.

[9] Donzis DA, Sreenivasan KR, Yeung PK. The batchelor spectrum for mixing of passive scalars in isotropic turbulence: submitted for the special issue dedicated to S. B. Pope. Flow Turbul Combust. 2010;85(3-4):549–66.

[10] Michioka T, Komori S. Large-eddy simulation of a turbulent reacting liquid flow. AIChE J. 2004;50(11):2705–20.

[11] Dimotakis PE. Some issues on turbulent mixing and turbulence. Turbulence Symposium in honor of W. C. Reynolds' 60th Birthday. Pasadena, California; 1993.

[12] Dimotakis PE. Turbulent mixing. Annu Rev Fluid Mech. 2005;37:329–56.

[13] Piomelli U. Large eddy and direct simulation of turbulent flows. In: 9e Conferencie anuelle de la Société Canadiené de CFD. 2001.

[14] Takeno T, Mizobuchi Y. Significance of DNS in combustion science. Comptes Rendus Mec. 2006;334:517–22.

[15] Burton G. Large-eddy simulation of passive-scalar mixing using multifractal subgrid-scale modeling. In: Annual Research Briefs. Center for Turbulence Research; 2005. pp 211–22.

[16] Pope SB. Turbulent Flows. Cambridge: Cambridge University Press; 2000.

[17] Janicka J, Sadiki A. Large eddy simulation of turbulent combustion systems. Proc Combust Inst. 2005;30:537–47.

[18] Chakraborty D, Paul P, Mukunda H. Evaluation of combustion models for high speed H2/Air confined mixing layer using DNS data. Combust Flame. 2000;121:195–209.

[19] Hanjalic K. Will RANS survive LES? A view of perspectives. J Fluids Eng. 2005;127(5): 831–9.

[20] Di Mare F, Jones WP, Menzies K. Large Eddy Simulation of a model gas turbine combustor. Combust Flame. 2004;137:453–80.

[21] Wang DM, Tarbell J. Closure models for turbulent reacting flows with a nonhomogeneous concentration field. Chem Eng Sci. 1993;48:3907–20.

[22] Yeoh SL, Papadakis G, Yianneskis M. Numerical simulation of turbulent flow characteristics in a stirred vessel using the LES and RANS approaches with the sliding/ deforming mesh methodology. Chem Eng Res Des. 2004;82(7):834–48.

[23] Yeoh SL, Papadakis G, Yianneskis M. Determination of mixing time and degree of homogeneity in stirred vessels with large eddy simulation. Chem Eng Sci. 2005;60(8-9 SPEC. ISS.):2293–302.

[24] Hartmann H, Derksen JJ, Montavon C, Pearson J, Hamill IS, van den Akker HEA. Assessment of large eddy and RANS stirred tank simulations by means of LDA. Chem Eng Sci. 2004;59(12):2419–32.

[25] Murthy BN, Joshi J. Assessment of standard k–ε, RSM and LES turbulence models in a baffled stirred vessel agitated by various impeller designs. Chem Eng Sci. 2008;63:5468–95.

[26] Leonard A. Energy cascade in Large–Eddy Simulations of turbulent fluid flows. In: Frankiel FN, Munn R, editors. Advances in Geophysics. New York: Academic Press; 1974.

[27] Sagaut P. Large Eddy Simulation for Incompressible Flows. An Introduction. Third Edition. Large Eddy Simulation for Incompressible Flows. New York: Springer; 2006. pp 449–493.

[28] Berselli LC, Iliescu T, Layton WJ. Mathematics of Large Eddy Simulation of Turbulent Flows. New York: Springer; 2006. pp 1–357.

[29] Lesieur M, Matais O, Comte P. Large–Eddy Simulations of Turbulence. Cambridge: Cambridge University Press; 2005.

[30] McDermott R, Pope SB. A particle formulation for treating differential diffusion in filtered density function methods. J Comput Phys. 2007;226(1):947–93.

[31] Lesieur M. Turbulence in Fluids. Dordrecht: Kluwer Academic Publisher; 1997.

[32] Revstedt J, Fuchs L, Kovács T, Trägårdh C. Influence of impeller type on the flow structure in a stirred reactor. AIChE J. 2000;46(12):2373–82.

[33] Roussinova V, Kresta SM, Weetman R. Low frequency macroinstabilities in a stirred tank: scale-up and prediction based on large eddy simulations. Chem Eng Sci. 2003;58(11):2297–311.

[34] Onishi R, Komori S. Thermally stratified liquid turbulence with a chemical reaction. AIChE J. 2006;52(2):456–68.

[35] Meneveau C, Katz J. Scale -invariance and turbulence models for large -eddy simulation. Annu Rev Fluid Mech. 2000;32:1–32.

[36] Gicquel LYM, Givi P, Jaberi F, Pope S. Velocity filtered density function for large eddy simulation of turbulent flows. Phys Fluids. 2002;14(3):1196–12.

[37] Sheikhi MRH, Drozda TG, Givi P, Pope SB. Velocity–scalar filtered density function for large eddy simulation of turbulent flows. Phys Fluids. 2003;15(8):2321–16.

[38] Smagorinsky J. General circulation experiments with the primitive equations I. Month Weather Rev. 1963;91(3):99–164.

[39] Germano M, Piomelli U, Moin P, Cabot WH. A dynamic subgrid–scale eddy viscosity model. Phys Fluids. 1991;A3(7):1760–5.

[40] Lilly D. A proposed modification of the Germano subgrid–scale closure method. Phys Fluids. 1992;4(3):633–2.

[41] Lilly D. The representation of small–scale turbulence in numerical simulation experiments. In: Proceedings of the IBM Scientific Computing Symposium on Environmental Sciences. IBM Data Process Div; 1967. pp 195–210.

[42] Deardorff J. A numerical study of three–dimensional turbulent channel flow at large reynolds numbers. J Fluid Mech. 1970;41:453–80.

[43] Wegner B. A Large–Eddy Simulation Technique for the Prediction of Flow, Mixing and Combustion in Gas Turbine Combustors. Darmstadt: Technische Universität Darmstadt; 2006.

[44] Carati D, Ghosal S, Moin P. On the representation of backscatter in dynamic localization models. Phys Fluids. 1995;7(3):606–10.

[45] Hickel S, Adams NA, Mansour NN. Implicit subgrid-scale modeling for the large-eddy simulation of passive-scalar mixing. In: Proceedings of Cent Turbul Res; 2008. pp 123–38.

[46] Löffler M, Pfadler S, Beyrau F, Leipertz A, Dinkelacker F, Huai Y, et al. Experimental determination of the sub-grid scale scalar flux in a non-reacting jet-flow. Flow Turbul Combust. 2008;81(1-2):205–19.

[47] Huai Y, Sadiki A. Large Eddy Simulation of mixing processes in turbulent liquid flows with chemical reactions. In: Proceedings of the 5th International Symposium on Turbulence and Shear Flow Phenomena. Munich, Germany; 2007. pp 1137–42.

[48] Huai Y. Large Eddy Simulation in the Scalar Field. Darmstadt: Technischen Universität Darmstadt; 2005.

[49] Montreuil E, Sagaut P, Labbé O, Cambon C. Assessment of non-Fickian subgrid-scale models for passive scalar in a channel flow. In: Volke RV, Sandham ND, Kleiser L,

editors. Direct and Large–Eddy Simulation III. Dordrecht: Kluwer Academic Publisher; 1999.

[50] Jaberi FA, Colucci PJ. Large eddy simulation of heat and mass transport in turbulent flows. Part 2: scalar field. Int J Heat Mass Transf. 2003;46(10):1827–40.

[51] Peng S-H, Davidson L. On a subgrid-scale heat flux model for large eddy simulation of turbulent thermal flow. Int J Heat Mass Transf. 2002;45(7):1393–405.

[52] Porté-Agel F. A scale -dependent dynamic model for scalar transort in les of the atmospheric boundary layer. Bound-Lay Meteorol. 2004;112(1):85–105.

[53] Eidson T. Numerical simulation of the turbulent Rayleigh–Bénard problem using subgrid modeling. J Fluid Mech. 1985;158:245–68.

[54] Moin P, Squires K, Cabot WLS. A dynamic subgrid–scale model for compressible turbulence and scalar transport. Phys Fluids. 1991;3:2746–11.

[55] Zang Y, Street RL, Koseff J. A dynamic mixed subgrid-scale model and its application to turbulent recirculating flow. Phys Fluids. 1993;A5:3186–10.

[56] Na Y. On the large eddy simulation of scalar transport with prandtl number up to 10 using dynamic mixed model. J Mech Sci Technol. 2005;19(3):913–23.

[57] Tkatchenko I, Kornev N, Jahnke S, Steffen G, Hassel E. Performances of les and RANS models for simulation of complex flows in a coaxial jet mixer. Flow Turbul Combust. 2007;78(2):111–27.

[58] Chumakov SG, Chumakov SG, Rutland CJ, Rutland CJ. Dynamic structure subgrid-scale models for large eddy simulation. Int J Numer Methods Fluids. 2005;47(December 2004):911–23.

[59] Burton G. Scalar-energy spectra in simulations of Sc>>1 mixing by turbulent jets using the nonlinear large-eddy simulation method. Phys Fluids. 2008;20(7):10–3.

[60] Burton G, Dahm WJA. Multifractal subgrid-scale modeling for large-eddy simulation. Part 2: backscatter limiting and a posteriori evaluation. Phys Fluids. 17:075112–9.

[61] Burton G. Large-eddy simulation of a free round jet using multifractal subgrid-scale model. In: Annual Research Briefs. Center for Turbulence Research; 2004. pp 157–67.

[62] Burton G. Large-eddy simulation of round turbulent jets using the Inertial LES method with multifractal subgrid-scale modeling. In: International Workshop on the Physics of Compressible Turbulent Mixing; 2006.

[63] Durbin PA, Patterson R. Statistical Theory and Modelling for Turbulent Flows. New York: Wiley; 2001.

[64] Cabot W, Moin P. Large eddy simulation of scalar transport with the dynamic subgid–scale model. In: Galperin B, Orzags S, editors. Large Eddy Simulation of Complex Engineering and Geophysical Flows. Cambridge: Cambridge University Press; 1993.

[65] Pantangi P, Huai Y, Sadiki A. Mixing analysis and optimization in jet mixer systems by means of large eddy simulation. In: Bockhorn H, Mewes D, Peukert W, Warnecke HJ, editors. Micro and Macro Mixing, Analysis, Simulation and Numerical Calculation. New York: Springer; 2010.

[66] Pope SB. Computations of turbulent combustion: progress and challenges. Proc Combust Inst. 1990;23:591–612.

[67] Wang L. On discrete representation of filtered density functions for turbulent combustion. In: Annual Research Briefs. Center for Turbulence Research; 2007.

[68] Haworth DC, Pope SB. Transported probability density function methods for Reynolds-averaged and Large-Eddy simulations. In: Echekki T, Mastorakos E, editors. Combustion Modeling: Advances, New Trends and Perspectives. New York: Springer; 2011.

[69] Drozda TG, Sheikhi MRH, Madnia CK, Givi P. Developments in formulation and application of the filtered density function. Flow Turbul Combust. 2007;78:35–67.

[70] Jaberi FA, Colucci PJ, James S, Givi P, Pope SB. Filtered mass density function for large eddy simulation of turbulent reacting flows. J Fluid Mech. 1999;401:85–121.

[71] Dopazo C, O'Brien EE. Statistical treatment of non–isothermal chemical reactions in turbulence. Combust Sci Technol. 1976;13:99–112.

[72] O'Brien E. The probability density function (PDF) approach to reacting turbulent flows. In: Libby PA, Williams F, editors. Turbulent Reacting Flows. San Diego: Academic Press; 1998.

[73] Jones WP, Navarro-Martinez S. Large eddy simulation of autoignition with a subgrid probability density function method. Combust Flame. 2007;150(3):170–87.

[74] Olbricht C, Hahn F, Sadiki A, Janicka J. Analysis of subgrid scale mixing using a hybrid LES-Monte-Carlo PDF method. Int J Heat Fluid Flow. 2007;28(6):1215–26.

[75] Heinz S. On Fokker–Planck equations for turbulent reacting flows . Part 2: filter density function for large eddy simulation. Flow Turbul Combust. 2003;153–81.

[76] Pope SB. PDF methods for turbulent reactive flow. Prog Energy Combust Sci. 1985;11:119–92.

[77] Shetty DA, Chandy AJ, Frankel SH. A new fractal interaction by exchange with the mean mixing model for large eddy simulation/filtered mass density function applied to a multiscalar three-stream turbulent jet. Phys Fluids. 2010;22(2):1–10.

[78] Mitarai S, Riley JJ, Kosály G. Testing of mixing models for Monte Carlo probability density function simulations. Phys Fluids. 2005;17(4):1–15.

[79] Meyer DW, Jenny P. Micromixing models for turbulent flows. J Comput Phys. 2009;228(4):1275–93.

[80] Colucci P, Jaberi F, Givi P, Pope SB. Filtered density function for large eddy simulation of turbulent reacting flows. Phys Fluids. 1998;10(2):499–16.

[81] Van Vliet E, Derksen JJ, van den Akker HEA, Fox RO. Numerical study on the turbulent reacting flow in the vicinity of the injector of an LDPE tubular reactor. Chem Eng Sci. 2007;62(9):2435–44.

[82] Mustata R, Valiño L, Jiménez C, Jones WP, Bondi S. A probability density function Eulerian Monte Carlo field method for large eddy simulations: application to a turbulent piloted methane/air diffusion flame. Combust Flame. 2006;145:88–104.

[83] Yaldizli M, Mehravaran K, Jaberi FA. Large-eddy simulations of turbulent methane jet flames with filtered mass density function. Int J Heat Mass Transf. 2010;53(11-12):2551–62.

[84] Zhao W, Zhang C, Chen C. Large eddy simulation of bluff-body stabilized flames using a multi-environment filtered density function model. Proc Combust Inst. 2011;33(1): 1347–53.

[85] Janicka J, Kolbe W, Kollmann W. Closure of the transport equation for the probability density function of turbulent scalar fields. J Non-Equilib Thermodyn. 1977;4:47–66.

[86] Curl R. Dispersed phase mixing: I. Theory and effects of simple reactors. AIChE J. 1963;9:175–81.

[87] Subramaniam S, Pope S. A mixing model for turbulent reactive flows based on euclidean minimum spanning trees. Combust Flame. 1998;115:487–514.

[88] Cleary MJ, Klimenko AY, Janicka J, Pfitzner M. A sparse-Lagrangian multiple mapping conditioning model for turbulent diffusion flames. Proc Combust Inst. 2009;32 I(1):1499–507.

[89] Klimenko AY, Pope S. The modeling of turbulent reactive flows based on multiple mapping conditioning. Phys Fluids. 2003;15(7):1907–18.

[90] Vogiatzaki K, Kronenburg A, Navarro-Martinez S, Jones W. Stochastic multiple mapping conditioning for a piloted, turbulent jet diffusion flame. Proc Combust Inst. 2011;33(11):1523–31.

[91] Meyer DW, Jenny P. A mixing model for turbulent flows based on parametrized scalar profiles. Phys Fluids. 2006;18:035105–15.

[92] Klimenko AY. On simulating scalar transport by mixing between Lagrangian particles. Phys Fluids. 2007;19(3):1–4.

[93] Haworth DC. Progress in probability density function methods for turbulent reacting flows. Prog Energy Combust Sci. 2010;36(2):168–259.

[94] Schwertfirm F, Manhart M. A-priori analysis of the LMSE micromixing model for filtered-density function simulation in high schmidt number flows. In: Wagner S,

Steinmetz M, Bode A, editors. High Performance Computing in Science and Engineering. Garching/Munich: Springer; 2009.

[95] Schwertfirm F, Manhart M. Development of a DNS-FDF approach to inhomogeneous non-equilibrium mixing for high schmidt number flows. In: Armenio V, Geurt B, Fröhlich J, editors. Direct and Large-Eddy Simulation VII Proceedings of the Seventh International ERCOFTAC Workshop on Direct and Large-Eddy Simulation. Springer; 2010.

[96] Schwertfirm F, Manhart M. A numerical approach for simulation of turbulent mixing and chemical reaction at high schmidt numbers. In: Bockhorn H, Mewes D, Peukert W, Warnecke H, editors. Micro and Macro Mixing Analysis, Simulation and Numerical Calculation. New York: Springer; 2010.

[97] Van Vliet E, Derksen JJ, Van Den Akker HEA. Turbulent mixing in a tubular reactor: assessment of an FDF/LES approach. AIChE J. 2005;51(3):725–39.

[98] Mejía J, Chejne F, Molina A, Sadiki A. Scalar mixing study at high-schmidt regime in a turbulent jet flow using large-eddy simulation/filtered density function approach. J Fluids Eng. 2016;138(2):021205–9.

[99] Mejía J, Sadiki A, Molina A, Chejne F. Large Eddy Simulation of the mixing of a passive scalar in a high-Schmidt turbulent jet. J Fluids Eng. 2015;137:031301–1.

[100] Antoine Y, Lemoine F, Lebouché M. Turbulent transport of a passive scalar in a round jet discharging into a co-flowing stream. Eur J Mech B/Fluids. 2001;20(2):275–301.

[101] Mejía JM. Large Eddy Simulation of Mixing in a Turbulent Round Jet. Colombia: National University of Colombia; 2011.

[102] Kurose R., Michioka T., Kohno N., Komori S, Baba Y. Application of flamelet model to Large-Eddy Simulation of turbulent reacting liquid flows. AIChE Journal, 2011; Vol.57, pp.911–917.

[103] Wang L., Lu XY. Large eddy simulation of stably stratified turbulent open channel flows with low-to high-Prandtl number. International Journal of Heat and Mass Transfer; 2005; 48: 1883–1897

[104] Wang L., Dong Y.H., Lu XY. An investigation of turbulent open channel flow with heat transfer by Large Eddy Simulation. Computers & Fluids; 2005; 34:23–47

[105] Dong YH., Lu XY. Zhuang LX. An investigation of the Prandtl number effect on turbulent heat transfer in channel flows by large eddy simulation. Acta Mechanica; 2002; 159:39–51.

[106] Dong YH., Lu XY., Zhuang LX. Large Eddy Simulation of turbulent channel flow with mass transfer at high-Schmidt numbers. International Journal of Heat and Mass Transfer; 2003; 46:1529–1539

[107] Walter, M., Kornev, N., Zhdanov, V., Hassel, E. Turbulent mixing with chemical reaction in a coaxial jet mixer. Turbulence Heat and Mass Transfer 6, Eds. Hanjalic K., Y. Nagano, S. Jacirlic, 14 – 18 September 2009, Rom, Italy, 2009; pp. 687 – 690.

[108] Marchisio DL. Large Eddy Simulation of mixing and reaction in a confined impinging jets reactor. Computers and Chemical Engineering; 2009; 33:408–420.

[109] Safrai AS., Tkachenko IV. Numerical modeling of gravity currents in inclined channels. Fluid Dynamics; 2009; 44(1):22–30.

[110] Gurniki F., Fukagata K., Zahrai S., Bark FH. LES of turbulent channel flow of a binary electrolyte. Journal of Applied Electrochemistry; 2000; 30: 1335–1343.

[111] Hartmann H., Derksen JJ., van den Akker HEA. Mixing times in a turbulent stirred tank by means of LES. AICHE Journal; 2006 a; 52(11):3696–3706.

[112] Hartmann H., Derksen JJ., van den Akker HEA. Numerical simulation of a dissolution process in a stirred tank reactor. Chemical Engineering Science; 2006 b; 61:3025–3032.

[113] Zadghaffari R., Moghaddas JS., Revstedtb J. A mixing study in a double–Rushton stirred tank. Computers and Chemical Engineering; 2009; 33:1240–1246.

[114] Zadghaffari R., Moghaddas J.S., Revstedtb J. Large–Eddy Simulation of turbulent flow in a stirred tank driven by a Rushton turbine. Computers & Fluids; 2010; 39:1183–1190.